D1356427

*The monasteries, magdalen asylums and reformatory schools of*

# OUR LADY OF CHARITY IN IRELAND

*1853-1973*

First published in 2017

by COLUMBA PRESS

23 Merrion Square North,

Dublin 2, Co. Dublin

www.columba.ie

ISBN: 978-1-78218-322-8


Set in Palatino 9.5/11

Cover design by Alba Esteban | Columba Press

Printed by Jellyfish Solutions

*The monasteries, magdalen asylums*
*and reformatory schools of*

# OUR LADY
# *of*
# CHARITY
# *in*
# IRELAND

*1853–1973*

JACINTA PRUNTY

the columba press

# OUR LADY of CHARITY in IRELAND

# Acknowledgements

Very many people have given their support and practical assistance over the twelve years or so since I first embarked on this research. My first debt of gratitude is to the archivists of the Sisters of Our Lady of Charity (OLC) in Dublin and in Caen; Sister Teresa Coughlan OLC was the first archivist for the Irish region and has been unfailingly generous in her encouragement and support since the outset, as has been Maryann O'Connor, the present archivist, who responded to countless requests with patience and great kindness. This research owes much to the professional expertise of these two remarkable women. In Caen, Delphine le Crom, the archivist for the Union of Notre Dame de Charité and for the French province, welcomed Sister Teresa and myself as researchers at an early point in this project and has responded with dispatch to countless queries ever since; I record my appreciation of the research she undertook on my behalf at long distance. Sisters who held leadership positions in OLC over the period of this research have granted access to records in Ireland, France and Rome without in any way interfering with the independence of the research; I extend thanks to Sisters Ann Marie Ryan, Sheila Murphy and Frances Robinson (Ireland), Marie Françoise de Brizaut and Anne Marie Klopstein (France) and Angela Fahy (Rome). Sister Angela also undertook some difficult translation work which was greatly appreciated. Sister Lucy Bruton helped in disentangling some of the Sean MacDermott Street records and Sisters Luke Keane and Gemma O'Connor helped with the graves research. Sister Angela Hanly assisted with queries on artefacts and donors. OLC employees whose support is also acknowledged are Kathleen Fahey (ministries desk), Vicki Perry (former contract archivist) and Mary O'Byrne (regional secretary).

While I intended to focus on the OLC congregation only, I quickly came to realise that the Good Shepherd congregation (GS) was always somewhere in the background and thus I needed to consult its records also. The decision to cover relations between OLC and GS has been validated by the 'reunification by merger' concluded in June 2014 between the two congregations, though it must be admitted that, at the time, the primary research was undertaken this could not have been foreseen, least of all by an outsider. Sister Ethna McDermott, the first provincial superior (Ireland) of the united Congregation of Our Lady of Charity of the Good Shepherd, and her team, supported the work as it was readied for publication, for which I am most grateful. I express thanks to Sisters Bernie McNally and Bríd Mullins who arranged for access to Good Shepherd records in Limerick and in Rome. I extend thanks to the international community of Bon Pasteur, Maison Mère, Angers and to all who facilitated my researches there: Sister Noreen O'Shea, co-ordinator of the Centre Spirituel, the archivists Sarah Elbisser and

Julie Hénault, also Sister Irma Valle del Galla and Sister Theresa Kim, and Soeur Magdalena Franciscus, the provincial superior. In Rome, access was granted to the records of both Notre Dame de Charité and Bon Pasteur; I express thanks to Sister Albertina Baćak and Sister Sharon Holland of the Sacred Congregation for Institutes of Consecrated Life and Societies of Apostolic Life who helped ensure the time spent in this repository was fruitful.

Archivists and researchers in a large number of other repositories also helped with this research; Marianne Cosgrave (Mercy Congregational Archives), Mary Coyle RSM (Mercy Archives, South Central Province), Teresa Delaney RSM (Mercy Archives, Western Province), Noelle Dowling (Dublin Diocesan Archives), Aideen Ireland, Elizabeth McEvoy and Mary Mackey (National Archives of Ireland), Paul Ferguson and Paul Mulligan (Glucksman Map Library, Trinity College Dublin), Alice Aylward CHF (Holy Faith congregational archives), Kate Kelly, Ronan Kelly (RCSI, Mercer's Library), Paul Maher , Brian Whelan, Gerry Kilgallon (An Garda Síochána), Tom Davitt CM and Karen de Lacey (Vincentian Archives), Martin Morris (Longford County Archives), George McCullough and Mervyn Colville (Glasnevin Cemetery Trust). Anne Matthews (independent scholar and NUIM graduate) generously shared her own knowledge of important sources, while Grace Neville, NUI Cork, brought travel and other French-language references to my attention. I acknowledge the assistance with Latin documents offered by †Peter Haughey OSA and that of his confrère David Kelly OSA who helped with points on the Augustinian rule. I am grateful to Fr Dermot Lane, former president of Mater Dei Institute of Education, for the invitation to contribute a chapter on the OLC sisters and Vatican II (as noted in the bibliography) which allowed me to explore material covered at greater length in chapter 13 of the present work.

Colleagues in Maynooth University and in a number of other institutes gave moral support and offered welcome advice; some also read sections and reviewed the work in a critical way, as did several anonymous readers. While in no wise responsible for its failings, these scholars must be given credit for improvements to early drafts and indeed for encouraging me to press on towards publication. Those whose names I do not know will, I hope, recognise where their good advice has been implemented and know that it was valued. I express thanks to Vincent Comerford, Marian Lyons, Jacqueline Hill, Colm Lennon and Thomas O'Connor of the History Department, Maynooth University, Maura Cronin (University of Limerick), Ethna Regan CHF (Mater Dei Institute of Education, Dublin City University), Thérèse McPhillips (St Patrick's College, Dublin City University), Joan Rahilly (Queen's University Belfast), Jo Newman (UCD), Margaret Mac Curtain (Dominican Sisters) and Phil Kilroy (Society of the Sacred Heart). Several other Maynooth colleagues also merit particular mention for support and practical assistance, most notably Ann Donoghue and Catherine Heslin of the History Department, Salvador Ryan (Theology, St Patrick's College), and Cathal McCauley, Hugh Murphy and Helen Fallon of the Library, Maynooth University. My fellow editors and other team members and researchers at the Irish Historic Towns Atlas, Royal Irish Academy, have given encouragement and wise advice throughout: Anngret Simms,

Howard Clarke, Raymond Gillespie, Sarah Gearty, Jennifer Moore, Angela Murphy, Frank Cullen and Anne Rosenbusch. The solidarity and kindness shown by Paul Walsh (Department of Arts, Heritage, Regional, Rural and Gaeltacht Affairs), co-author on the Galway fascicle, should also be acknowledged.

As this work stretched over so many years, a succession of Maynooth University students from both History and Archives programmes, but now graduates, must be named; some assisted as student interns in the cataloguing of OLC collections (Alan Kelly, Michael Keyes, Louise O'Reilly), another in checking references (†Caroline Gallagher), while others pointed me to literature and manuscript sources that I might never otherwise have encountered; these include Ann Bergin, Mary Eugenia Brennan (Sisters of St John of God), Ciarán Bryan, Alan Carthy, Neil Collins (Columban Missionaries), Carmel Connell, Terence Judge, Ciarán McCabe, Cora McDonagh, Martin McCarthy, Miriam Moffitt, Catherine Mullan, Brian O'Keeffe, Marion Rogan, Maeve Mullin and Marie Thérèse King (Presentation Sisters). Una Martin, a UCD postgraduate student, directed me to material on the history of social work and probation. I learned much about archives and their management from staff at Aberystwyth University; the excellent teaching and direction of Sarah Higgins and Jennie Hill is acknowledged in particular.

Within my own Holy Faith community, the Coombe, I have known genuine interest in the project and warm concern for my own well-being; I thank the sisters for putting up with my disappearances northside for long hours at a time and for allowing me the space to complete what turned out to be a far larger project than anyone, least of all myself, had envisaged. My own current local community is made up of Sisters Benignus McDonagh, Hilda Murphy, Jane Forde, Frances Barrett, Anna Bolger, Colette Mary O'Connor, Dympna O'Brien, Dorothea Glennon and Veronica Kirwan; to each of you I express the warmest thanks. Sisters in Holy Faith leadership roles have been continually supportive, including Evelyn Greene and Rosaleen Cunniffe (regional leaders) and Margo Delaney and Vivienne Keely (general leaders). †Sister Consolata Fitzpatrick undertook some proof reading; Sisters Una Collins, Siobhan Larkin and Eileen Houlahan, well schooled in the trials of academic writing, were always ready with sympathy and support. Sisters Barbara Perry and Miriam Anne Lucas provided a welcome refuge at Kilcoole. †Sister Euphrasia Bergin persevered over more than a decade as my French teacher; I am indebted to her for being able to bring school French up to a sufficient level to cope with this work and the travel to France that was involved. I was the privileged recipient of a summer scholarship from the Centre Culturel Irlandais at an early stage of this work and I thank Sheila Pratschke, director of the Centre, and my teacher Madame Razo of the Institut Catholique for that wonderful opportunity. The Eoin O'Mahony bursary from the Royal Irish Academy enabled the June/July 2014 research visit to Angers. A further note of thanks is due to a native speaker and former student, Greischa Raffin, for encouragement with the language and assistance with some difficult handwriting also. Long-standing and dear friends whose interest in this work – or at least, in seeing it completed – never flagged are Mary O'Byrne, Monica Delaney, Susan Jones CHF and Anna Byrne DC.

The interest taken by Garry O'Sullivan on becoming managing director at Columba Press brought this long-running project to what is, for me, a very happy conclusion and I thank him for the decision to publish the text as he had inherited it. The care taken by Kieron Wood, on behalf of Columba Press, in preparing the typescript for publication is also acknowledged and likewise the design skills of the team CPS, at Chennai Publishing Services, Chennai, India. Thanks are extended to Ellen Monnelly (marketing), Michael Brennan (sales), and to Patrick O'Donoghue who was my first contact at Columba Press. The National University of Ireland Publications Grant and Maynooth University Publications Scheme are also acknowledged with gratitude.

A final word of thanks must go, as always, to my parents Agnes and Joe Prunty, who have always believed in each of us children and given us the best of example, in their own love and devotion to each other and their unshakeable love for us. This book is certain to be given the warmest, unqualified welcome in one house at least and it will have nothing to do with its scope or contents. It will simply be because Mam and Dad will, as always, try to enter into what is important to each of us, regardless of the field.

# Contents

# List of Figures

# List of Abbreviations

| | |
|---|---|
| BP | Bon Pasteur |
| BP, Archives historiques | Maison Mère du Bon Pasteur, Angers, Archives historiques |
| CARE | Campaign for the care of deprived children |
| ch. | chapter |
| CICA | Commission to Inquire into Child Abuse |
| CIVCSVA | Archives of the Sacred Congregation for Religious and Secular Institutes, Rome |
| CJM | Congregation of Jesus and Mary (Eudist fathers) |
| CM | Congregation of the Missions (Vincentian fathers) |
| CPRSI | Catholic Protection and Rescue Society of Ireland |
| DARGS | Dublin Archives, Religious of the Good Shepherd |
| DDA | Dublin Diocesan Archives |
| GEC | General Electric Company |
| GRO | General Register Office |
| GS *Bulletin* | Bulletin of the Congregation of the Good Shepherd of Angers |
| GS | Sisters of the Good Shepherd of Angers/Sisters of Our Lady of Charity of the Good Shepherd |
| ISPCC | Irish Society for the Prevention of Cruelty to Children |
| NAI | National Archives of Ireland |
| NDC Caen | Union Notre Dame de Charité, Archives générales et provinciales de France, Caen |
| NDC | Notre Dame de Charité |
| NSPCC | National Society for the Prevention of Cruelty to Children |
| OLC | Sisters of Our Lady of Charity |
| OLCR | Our Lady of Charity of Refuge |
| OS | Ordnance Survey |
| RC | Roman Catholic |
| RGS | Religious of the Good Shepherd |
| RIRB | Residential Institutions Redress Board |
| SA | St Anne's School, Kilmacud |
| SCRSI | Sacred Congregation for Religious and Secular Institutes |
| SJ | Society of Jesus (Jesuits) |
| SJ | St Joseph's School, Whitehall (High Park) |
| TB | Tuberculosis |
| UISG | International Union of Superioresses General |
| VEC | Vocational Educational Committee |
| VO | Valuation Office |

# Introduction

This book is a multi-faceted history of the Sisters of Our Lady of Charity (OLC) in Ireland from their arrival from France in 1853 through to the modernisation of the 1960s and the massive upheavals that came in the wake of the Second Vatican Council.[1] The terms 'monasteries, magdalen asylums and reformatory schools' highlight the key concerns: this is a study of a religious institute with a rule of enclosure which had responsibility for magdalen refuges and a reformatory school in the mid- and later 19th century, the latter re-launched as an industrial school in 1927. These core works continued into the mid-20th century, in addition to the opening of girls' and women's hostels, teenage training centres, and the adoption of what was termed the 'small group system' of residential care across different settings. The monasteries themselves and the model of religious life which regulated daily life, to varying degrees, for all who lived under the banner of OLC, would also be subject to change from the 1950s onwards. The federal chapter of October 1973, which had the task of implementing at local level decisions around renewal and updating taken at the order's *aggiornamento* or renewal general chapter in Rome, itself called for by the Second Vatican Council, is a fitting point at which to conclude this story.

Though the number of OLC sisters in Ireland was always small and its geographical spread was limited to the archdiocese of Dublin (where there were four monasteries by 1956), there are several reasons why this institute merits scholarly attention. Foremost are its long involvement in residential care for vulnerable women and girls, the large numbers of residents over an unbroken period of time (spanning more than 160 years in Dublin at the time of writing) and the type of settings, namely, magdalen laundries and certified schools, both of which have been the subject of enormous public interest and official inquiry over two decades or so in Ireland. The institute is of interest in itself for its distinctive spirituality and world-view deeply rooted in 17th-century France and the teaching of its founder John Eudes, its apostolate carried out within the enclosure. The remaking by these sisters of their model of religious life, in response to demands in the 1960s by society and by the Catholic Church to engage more fully with the 'modern world', is a particularly striking case-study. The archival records created inside and outside the institute, by both secular and Church bodies, in terms of record

1   When the title of the institute is expressly meant capitals are used: the Sisters of Our Lady of Charity; Irish Federation of the Sisters of Our Lady of Charity. For consistency, capitals are used throughout the Introduction as it is the institute that is the subject of discussion. Lower case 'sisters' is employed otherwise, where the sense requires: the sisters of Our Lady of Charity, the Mercy sisters, the Good Shepherd sisters.

type, quality of information, range of creators and chronological span are remarkably full and have made possible this documents-based history. Most of the records employed in this study have not been used previously in academic research.

This book has been written with a rather mixed readership in mind, as reflected in its title. It is written first for the members of the institute, the Sisters of Our Lady of Charity (OLC) which since June 2014 has re-united with the Religious of the Good Shepherd (RGS), making a single congregation under a single generalate, the Sisters of Our Lady of Charity of the Good Shepherd. There have been Irish-born members of both OLC and RGS since well before either institute had a house in Ireland. Many of the communities internationally count Irish sisters among their founding mothers as well as their present membership, so that the Irish interest extends beyond Ireland alone. The Congregation of Jesus and Mary, also founded by John Eudes (1643), has played a significant role in the history of these two women's congregations so that Eudists will find points of intersection here with their own story. An important aspect of the training or formation of new members is reflection on how the institute operated in earlier times and in very different places that lessons might be learned from the struggles and mistakes, as well as the achievements of the past. This history of the Sisters of Our Lady of Charity in Ireland will, I trust, play a part in that educational process. For those who work alongside the newly-united congregation as associates, partners, employees, volunteers, co-workers and advisers, it will, I hope, play a similar role. Those who have known the sisters in former days as residents, neighbours, benefactors, relatives and friends or have other personal connections will find much to hold their attention. Those with Dublin connections are the most likely readership, but this book will be of interest to a wider public also.

From the outset, this book has been intended for historians, sociologists, social workers, journalists, legal professionals and others whose academic and professional interests touch on the areas in which the Sisters of Our Lady of Charity have been involved, namely, women's refuges – including magdalen laundries, the reformatory and industrial school systems of Britain and Ireland, childcare and adolescent care. As a case-study in the history of religious life in Ireland from the mid-19th century through to the early 1970s, it will assist researchers in the aforementioned fields to track developments in the applied social sciences alongside changes in Catholic Church teaching, and shifts in attitudes and practice in Irish society more generally. This book will also appeal to readers in the broader genres of religious biography, religious history and the history of spirituality. With its closeness to the documentary record and my own training in historical geography, there is certainly much of a local history interest here, across the four sites involved: High Park (1857), with extensive grounds, in the north city suburb of Drumcondra bordering on Whitehall; the tightly-confined complex of Gloucester Street (Sean MacDermott Street), (1887) in the north inner city; the gentleman's dwelling renamed St Anne's (1944) in the developing southside suburb of Kilmacud and, finally, The Grange (1956), Kill of the Grange, another southside location which, at the time of the sisters' arrival, was yet to be fully developed for suburban housing.

Though this is not a commissioned study, the Sisters of Our Lady of Charity (OLC) allowed me full access to the records they hold in Dublin and in Caen and, with their permission, I also had access to the records of the institute held in Rome. Similarly, the Good Shepherd sisters allowed access to their records in Angers and Rome. This access is noted, with thanks, in the acknowledgements, and the files utilised are listed in the bibliography. The study itself had its origins in a fortuitous meeting in 2003 with two members of the institute (Sisters Teresa Coughlan and Lucy Bruton), in what was the 250th year of the Dublin foundation. On realising the extent and quality of the records which had been brought together in a single provincial archives but were not yet described or arranged, my first idea, a booklet to mark the arrival in 1853 of the sisters to Dublin, was quickly discarded in favour of a larger history. On the understanding that this would be an independent, professional and academic study of the institute conducted within the parameters of university research (and the time-constraints of university and other commitments), I embarked on an uncharted journey, and one which took far longer than envisaged or intended. My varied background – in archives, historical geography, urban history, local history and the history of cartography – has been brought to bear on the task but may also account for the limitations that will be found by specialists. My own membership of a religious institute (Sisters of the Holy Faith) has also fuelled my interest in the history of religious life. It must be admitted that my first-hand experience of a rather modest community – which originated as a lay institute in mid-19th century Dublin for the boarding-out or family rearing of orphan children and which operated without formal constitutions for many decades – did not, in itself, equip me to engage with the history of these closely-regulated, autonomous monasteries where 'the rule' was central. What has, however, proved invaluable to the research process is the supervision of PhD and other projects in this and closely-related local history fields, while I had 'met before' several of the personalities who feature in this study, most notably successive archbishops of Dublin and prominent Catholic philanthropists.

My interest in the records of this particular religious congregation and the part the refuges played in the relief network of 19th and early 20th century Dublin city dates back to my doctoral research on the geography of poverty in 19th-century Dublin and the mission of Margaret Aylward (1810–89) and her co-workers. Margaret Aylward is foundress of what was to become the Congregation of the Sisters of the Holy Faith (1867), the institute to which I belong. This research resulted in a biography of Margaret Aylward and also the publication, *Dublin slums 1800–1925, a study in urban geography* (Dublin, 1998). In chapter 7 of *Dublin slums*, I analyse the response of Church organisations or charities to poverty, focusing especially on the options available to women and children and the role played by asylums for women, with the north inner city district of Gloucester Street (Sean MacDermott Street) as the case study (pp 263–72). In that study, I incorporated the women's refuges (of different types) into the larger story of how the poorest managed under pressure, placing the geography of poor relief alongside the geography of poverty. When I returned to the same theme in 2003, with a single institute but much longer timescale in mind, the challenges proved to be greater. First,

though in principle the OLC sisters were willing to allow access to their records (as they had allowed me before, as well as other university historians
and postgraduate students), I could not undertake serious, systematic work
without a substantial investment of time and effort in the description and
arrangement of the core collections. I have been involved in this over several years, alongside professional archivists, volunteer sisters and students on
work experience. In the interim, there had been intensive public interest in
the magdalen laundries or asylums in Ireland, both nationally and internationally, a concern which continues to the present day. Revelations about the
scandal of abuse of children in a number of residential institutions, during
the 1940s to 1960s in particular, also received extensive national and overseas
media attention while, at the time of writing, there is a major state inquiry
under-way into the mother-and-baby homes. All of this has affected me as a
researcher, making me more critical of different types of records and hesitant
to enter fields which have received extensive media coverage. However, it
has also made me conscious of the public service that is independent, academic research. While I am only too conscious of the many limitations of this
book, its unwieldy scope and great length, I nevertheless persevered with
the original ambition, of touching on all the works of this particular institute in the diocese of Dublin from the arrival of the sisters in 1853 until the
post-Vatican II period, stopping in 1973; the reasons behind this decision are
spelled out below.

## The Case for the Book's Design

The lengthy title, beginning with the terms 'monasteries, magdalen asylums
and reformatory schools', and the ambitious chronology of 1853 to 1973,
beg several questions. Why attempt to cover so much ground in a single
book when any one of these areas of operation would surely merit a study
in its own right? Why try to span both 19th and 20th centuries, when the
periods pre- and post-independence in 1922, at the very least, surely require separate treatment? Above, all, why include the convent history in the
history of the care facilities that these sisters ran? The case to be made for
this approach rests first on the interconnectedness of the primary sources
which reflects the very nature of the organisation under scrutiny. It is the
complex intertwining of the temporal and spiritual lives of these convents
with their associated refuges, residential schools, hostels and homes that
makes joint or overlapping histories necessary. Alongside the standard
three vows (poverty, chastity, obedience), the Sisters of Our Lady of Charity
took a fourth vow – the salvation of souls – which they sought to exercise
through providing a 'refuge' or home for women and girls in need of shelter.
Such a home was popularly known in the English-speaking world as a
magdalen asylum or (more recently) as a magdalen laundry. In all the upheavals of the post-Vatican II period, the sisters held to this fourth vow
as particular to their charism, though today it is named 'vow of apostolic
zeal' and carried out in a great variety of settings, as listed online (www.
buonpastoreint.org).

The magdalen refuge was not an 'accessory' work of the institute but
its founding purpose, *'sa fin propre et particulière'* which distinguished it from

other religious orders.[2] Along with the Sisters of the Good Shepherd of Angers (the congregation which originated with Our Lady of Charity of Refuge, operating under an independent generalate from 1835), the core work was the provision of 'refuges' or 'asylums' for women and girls who, in the words of its own constitutions, 'had fallen into the disorder or confusion of a dissolute life', and now, touched by the grace of God, wished to leave all that behind them and turn their lives around.[3] Thus, this study tries to understand how exactly the sisters saw their mission, the constraints within which they operated, and what life was like from day to day for those who lived in the refuges, whether for a few days or weeks, or for the rest of their lives. What was this model of care developed in 1640s Normandy under the founder John Eudes and his lay women co-workers? Why was it hailed as bold and innovative in its day, going as it did against contemporary social norms? How exactly was this same philosophy of care, along with a well-established and tightly regulated system, transposed, intact, to mid-19th-century Dublin, and preserved in its essentials into the 1950s? How did a Dublin convent come to be named in court as an address at which a girl would undertake to reside when on probation? And what were the philosophical and moral difficulties around acting as a place of remand, on behalf of the state, however short the stay?

The institute in Ireland very quickly extended its work to *'préservation'*, with the sisters agreeing in 1858 to set up a reformatory school for girls. As they explained to their sisters in France, the term *'Classe de Réformatory'* really meant the same work, preservation, that the order had undertaken for generations – namely, the protection of young girls who were at risk of ending up on the streets living by prostitution or crime.[4] This study looks at why the sisters in Ireland agreed to take charge of what was the first reformatory school in Ireland, where it fitted with what they saw as their mission in Dublin, and how they interacted with the authorities within this state-funded and state-regulated sector. Why did they have it certified anew as an industrial school in 1927 without giving up its reformatory licence? Why in 1944 did they set up another reformatory school, once more with dual classification as an industrial school? How was this school different to the other certified schools in receipt of state funding at the time?

The development of 'teenage groups', training centres and hostels which were quite distinct from the magdalen refuges from the mid-1950s onwards was in response to dissatisfaction expressed both within the order and among outside observers at the old-fashioned self-contained asylum model which was not serving at least the younger and more able of those who ended up there for want of alternative accommodation. Nor, its critics argued, did it serve those whose real need was for a safe and cheap (or free)

---

2  'Règles et constitutions pour les religieuses de Notre-Dame de Charité, édition entièrement conforme au texte original [1682] avec des introductions et des notes', *Oeuvres complètes de Bienheureux Jean Eudes*, x (Vannes, 1909), Constitution i, De la fin de cet institut, et des motifs qui doivent porter celles qui le professent à en faire de bon cœur les fonctions, p. 80. Hereafter, Constitutions.
3  Ibid.
4  High Park, *circulaire*, 30 décembre 1859 (DARGS, OLC1/3/1 no. 2). The circular letters composed in French are indicated thus, *circulaire*.

place to stay while they established themselves in the workforce. There was also the pressing issue of 'aftercare', not just for their own former schoolgirls but also for girls discharged from other institutions. The system of 'release under licence' or under supervision certificate, whereby an industrial school child was discharged just before his or her 16th birthday but remained legally under the supervision of the school for a further two years (or for a further three years if from a reformatory school) created a class of older teenagers who, in law, could neither be kept in the schools nor dismissed outright to fend for themselves.[5] Girls without family or other persons outside the institution prepared to take an interest in their welfare were thus caught between two worlds, neither schoolgirls nor independent adults. This study looks at the pressures exerted on the sisters to move into supporting this class of girl and other young women 'in transition' from the first separate teenage group in High Park, Drumcondra (Whitehall) through to similar developments at Gloucester Street/Sean MacDermott Street and the operation of hostels for girls in education, training or paid outside work at all four of the Dublin monasteries. The 'casual unit' at Sean MacDermott Street was a hostel of yet another type, this time to answer the need for city-centre emergency accommodation for those who, in all likelihood, would otherwise be sleeping rough, and to spare the women's home (the old refuge) the upheaval and disruption of managing one-night requests. The background and operation of what were distinct and independent operations attached to each monastery, albeit underpinned by a shared vision and common constitutions, is investigated here.

The 'small group system' of residential care applied to adult, teenage and children's services and was the mantra from the 1950s onwards to counter the impersonal, large-group system that was the standard way of operation in so many institutions, from industrial schools to homes for the aged. Kilkenny girls' school (run by the Religious Sisters of Charity), with 130 children, has been acknowledged as the first in Ireland to adopt the 'grouping system' in 1952, and a presentation by the sister-in-charge at a childcare course in Carysfort College, Blackrock, in August 1953 helped to popularise this system in social work circles.[6] A Catholic nun in England gave an account of her community's 'happy experience' with the break-up of large institutions into 'family group homes' to the Liverpool Congress of Religious in January 1956.[7] The Sisters of Our Lady of Charity in Ireland were early implementers, with St Anne's, Kilmacud, taking a lead in 1958.[8] The Sisters of Our Lady of Charity applied their understanding of the new thinking in remodelling the refuges at High Park and Sean MacDermott Street, in the development of the 'teenage group' and in the subdivision of St Joseph's school, Whitehall. It was to be most fully developed in the 'family group home' system of The Grange, Kill of the Grange (a developing

5   See for example, Department of Education, Reformatory and Industrial Schools Branch to the Manager, Whitehall Industrial School, 1930–31 (DARGS, SJ/4/1/1/no. 5).
6   *Final Report of the Commission to Inquire into Child Abuse dated 20th May 2009* (Dublin, 2009), vol. iv, p. 31. Hereafter, Ryan report. Online at www.childabusecommission.ie [27 Jan. 2017].
7   Sister Veronica, 'Social work in the light of the Curtis report', *Religious life today: papers read at the Liverpool Congress of Religious, January 2nd to 6th 1956* (Liverpool, 1956), pp 140–52.
8   St Anne's, Kilmacud, circular letter, Christmas 1958 (DARGS, OLC3/3/1 no. 7).

suburb to the south of the city), from 1967 where children from one to 18 years of age, both boys and girls, were reared together, and siblings were kept as a family unit.

Each of these approaches to residential care had its own internal dynamic and its own chronology. Even the refuge, which I argue here continued largely intact as a system of care into the 1950s, underwent change through refurbishments and extensions, the introduction of new technologies, changes in the numbers and profile of those seeking admission and those staying on or leaving, new superiors with new (or old) ideas and a lot of authority to implement them. Notwithstanding their self-sufficiency and regard for enclosure, none of these institutions operated in a vacuum; all were affected by wider political, legislative, social and economic changes, international as well as national. In this study, I explore the contexts in which they were first developed and the timing of their foundation, who was involved and why, the philosophies of care which prevailed, their funding and oversight, what was novel, borrowed or a continuation of existing practices, and the primary legislation, both internal and external, under which they operated. I try to identify points of departure, and to track decline, reform and innovation. I have undertaken analysis of the statistics pertaining to each refuge, school, hostel or other home, including full analysis of the registers (entrances, exits, length of stay, multiple stays, deaths, burials, where residents came from/where they went on leaving), insofar as the records allow, and for the period up to about 1971.

The closing date for each study varies a little but a decided and permanent shift to new systems or new models of care is under way by 1973 when the Irish OLC sisters held their federal chapter, which had as its task the implementation at local level of the decisions taken at the international 1969 *aggiornamento* or renewal chapter held in Rome. As a religious institute, there is a definite break on the threshold of the post-Vatican II era; to borrow from Margaret MacCurtain, whose own study of Catholic sisterhoods in the 20th century closes at this point, 'what happened next belongs to a new Ireland and a questioning catholicism'.[9] There are also compelling archival reasons to stop at this point. In St Mary's refuge, for example, there are very few admissions post-1971, therefore to continue the statistics for another decade or so would simply distort the analysis.[10] The study of the Kill of the Grange monastery ends in 1971 with the opening of the first architect-designed children's home; what happens from there on, though directly tied to the founding period, is beyond the scope of this work. The cut-off date prevents an exploration of some interesting OLC ventures which are a direct follow-on from the refuge work, such as the setting up of Ruhama in 1989 (jointly with the Good Shepherd sisters) to work with women affected by prostitution and other forms of commercial sexual exploitation.[11]

9  Margaret MacCurtain, 'Godly burden: Catholic sisterhoods in twentieth-century Ireland', reprinted in Margaret MacCurtain, *Ariadne's thread, writing women into Irish history* (Galway, 2008), p. 323.
10  From 1960 to 1969 inclusive, there were 382 admissions in total to St Mary's, an average of 38 per year; from 1972 to 1980 there was a total of eight admissions, fewer than one per year. St Mary's register (DARGS, OLC1/8/1 no. 8).
11  See Ruhama, www.ruhama.ie [27 Jan. 2017].

The coverage of different works across four convents and over a long time-span does bring some advantages. It allows the shifts to alternative models of care to be tracked, exploring the source of the inspiration – most often France, England and North America – the development of social science theory and practice, and the obstacles to change, both internal and external to the congregation. Clashes, conflicts and accommodations provide valuable insights into the internal workings of the congregation in Ireland and its approach to those women and girls in its care. The meeting of French and Irish devotional practices, domestic culture and religious life traditions and the experimentation and risk-taking inherent in adapting to new thinking in social science and religious life, set against the veneration of old and familiar ways, are examined. Geography matters throughout – though in different ways: to the north of the built-up city, the walled demesne of High Park, Drumcondra, promised 'rural' seclusion in the 1850s, though still within reach of the city customers it needed for a viable laundry business. Gloucester Street (Sean MacDermott Street), in the heart of the infamous north inner city red-light district of the later 19th century, acted as an immediate refuge to those who might be lured into the nearby brothels. Kilmacud and Kill of the Grange both catered for small numbers in highly respectable suburban addresses in the mid-20th century, with the latter working assiduously to keep itself free of any industrial school or reformatory stigma. Within the enclosure, each house had its own clearly-defined geography, no matter how small the premises or how few resided there. In this study, I make connections between internal or local changes and profound social and political changes nationally and internationally which had direct impacts on these monasteries and their associated homes and schools: from colonial status (and some government patronage) through to the independent (but cash-strapped) new Ireland; the anti-Catholic state campaigns in France (1902–10) which reverberated throughout all houses of the order; the shortages and rationing of the Emergency (1939–45); the austerity post-war when there was little heart and even less money for social welfare reforms; the cultural shifts of the 1950s that gathered pace in the 1960s; and the remaking of the Catholic Church, and within it of religious life, that came with Vatican II, at the same time as many other modern trends took hold.

## Public Concern in Ireland with Residential Institutions

While this is a historical, documents-based study covering the homes and schools run by one religious institute only, reference must be made to widespread public concern with the former treatment of women and children in residential institutions more generally in Ireland that has dominated public discourse over two decades or so. Notice must also be taken of the interdepartmental inquiry into the magdalen laundries, published in 2013, with which I was involved. The usefulness, or otherwise, of published reports to my research is noted under sources and methodologies below, but a brief summary is offered here for those readers who may not be aware of these debates and controversies. Public concern with the magdalen experience may be dated to Patricia Burke Brogan's play, *Eclipsed* (Galway, 1992), followed by a succession of TV dramas and cinema films which have generated outrage internationally, as well as in Ireland. The 2002 film by

Peter Mullan, *The Magdalene Sisters*, where the nuns are portrayed as sadists, punishing young girls with impunity and in the name of religion, has probably had the most enduring impact on the public mind. In addition, there has been Dáil, newspaper, radio and television coverage and formal statements by the Irish Human Rights Commission to the United Nations on the issue of reparation for former residents of these institutions.[12] There have been stage plays, poetry readings, art installations and commemorative public gatherings; these and other cultural representations of the magdalen have been dealt with comprehensively by James Smith in *Ireland's magdalen laundries and the nation's architecture of containment* (Notre Dame, Ind., 2007). There was also a sustained media investigation into the exhumation of bodies from the women's cemetery at High Park in 1993, and their re-interment in Glasnevin Cemetery, which led to investigations by the Department of the Environment and An Garda Síochána, a full account of which has been published.[13] In July 2011, an 'Inter-Departmental Committee set up to establish the facts of State involvement with the Magdalen Laundries', under the chairmanship of Senator Martin McAleese, began its work; its remit encompassed all four religious congregations which ran 'magdalen laundries' in Ireland, not just the Sisters of Our Lady of Charity and their two refuges of High Park and Sean MacDermott Street. Dr McAleese issued a progress report in October 2011 and published the final and very lengthy report in February 2013.[14] The report and its reception, including Dáil debates and a statement of apology by An Taoiseach, Enda Kenny, was covered extensively by media outlets in Ireland and internationally. This was followed by a three-month review, chaired by Mr Justice John Quirke, on the setting up of what became the 'Restorative Justice Scheme' administered by the Department of Justice and Equality (June 2013), and involving, among other types of assistance, the *ex gratia* payment of a lump sum to any former resident of the ten magdalen laundries covered by the McAleese inquiry and the other two institutes to which the scheme was extended.[15] The setting up of that scheme generated further media coverage and, at the time of writing, its work is still under way.

The McAleese report has laid to rest some of the wildest accusations about the magdalen laundries. There are, however, some who strongly dispute its findings, very many who have not read it (the printout, including appendices, runs to more than 1,000 pages) and many more who continue

---

12　A submission was made by Justice for Magdalenes to the UN Committee Against Torture, co-authored by James M. Smith and Maeve O'Rourke, May 2011, including an oral presentation in Geneva, see www.magdalenelaundries.com/about.htm [27 Jan. 2017].

13　'Death registration, burial and exhumation', *Final report of the Inter-Departmental Committee set up to establish the facts of State involvement with the Magdalen Laundries* (Dublin, 2013), part 3, ch. 16.

14　*Final report of the Inter-Departmental Committee set up to establish the facts of State involvement with the Magdalen Laundries* (Dublin, 2013). Hereafter, McAleese report. Online at www.justice.ie.

15　The *ex gratia* payment consisted of €11,500 for less than three months' residence up to a maximum of €100,000 for ten years and more. The additional institutions included under the scheme are St Mary's Training Centre, Stanhope Street, and House of Mercy Training School, Summerhill, Wexford.

to regard what is portrayed in cinema and TV drama as history. A 22-page analysis of the McAleese report by Bill Donohue, president of a US group, the Catholic League for Religious and Civil Rights, is intended to dispel what it titles 'the myths of the magdalene laundries'; its strident tone and failure to reference the McAleese report line-by-line means it is unlikely to be accepted by academic scholars or indeed by those whose mind is already made up on the issue, though for the most part Donohue is simply re-stating findings from the report that he has selected as most likely to be news to the general public and for which there is evidence.[16] The problem, though not unique to this issue, is that, once errors of fact are taken up by academic historians, they become difficult if not impossible to displace. One misconception is that the magdalen asylums were for pregnant girls, though this was expressly forbidden in the homes run by the Sisters of Our Lady of Charity, either of the Refuge or of the Good Shepherd, and is corroborated by the archival record.[17] As Dr McAleese himself noted in the introduction to his lengthy report, fuelled by the absence of access to records, over the years 'stories grew to fill these gaps' in public knowledge, with even the basic facts of numbers and length of stay unknown.[18] I am one of several university academics who assisted the interdepartmental committee – my contribution included making available the fruits of extensive research that I – with others – had undertaken in relation to women buried at High Park and at Glasnevin. The efforts made by the chairman and his research team to be compassionate, objective, just and fearless impressed me greatly, as did the breadth, depth and quality of the research undertaken by the committee (summarised in chapter 4 of the report) with the full collaboration of the very large number of bodies involved, a point which is acknowledged repeatedly in the report. These included the four religious orders, advocacy groups and 16 government departments or agencies.

My hope is that this book will contribute to deepening the knowledge and understanding of the complex issue of magdalen refuges or laundries, thereby advancing the process that was set in train by the McAleese report, bringing into the public domain a wealth of historical facts previously unknown and now explored as part of a larger, and longer, story. The focus on a single congregation and the homes that it operated, all in Dublin, will, I trust, bring the discussion back from sensationalist portrayals to real-world, specific settings. The understandable but nevertheless unhelpful – and ahistorical – tendency to sweep all under a generalised 'magdalen laundry' heading may be checked to some degree by this study, and change over time, given due recognition.

The other controversial area in this study is the residential care of children and teenagers in reformatories and industrial schools, most of which were

16    Bill Donohue, *Myths of the Magdalene laundries,* Catholic League for Religious and Civil Rights (New York, 2013).
17    A *Sunday Tribune* report dated 24 Mar. 2002 is given as the source for the claim in Diarmaid Ferriter, *The transformation of Ireland 1900–1970* (London, 2004), p. 538 that, in the 1960s, pregnant girls were committed to magdalen laundries run by Catholic nuns for their 'crimes'. Several of the other claims made here have been disproved by the McAleese inquiry which postdates this publication and was based on documentary and oral evidence not previously available.
18    'Introduction by the Independent Chair', McAleese report, para. 6.

run by Catholic religious congregations, though subject to state regulation and inspection, and many of which were closed by (or shortly after) 1970. Throughout the 1990s, historic abuse in many of these institutions became the subject of investigation by the journalist Mary Raftery (d. 2012) and others, and received extensive coverage on radio and television, as well as in film and drama, in newspapers, journals and other publications. Memoirs of childhood provided shocking and moving accounts of what it felt like to be rejected and cruelly treated.[19] The Taoiseach of the day, Bertie Ahern, in the name of the state, issued a formal apology in May 1999 to victims of child abuse in residential institutions and announced the establishment of what was to become an independent statutory body, the Commission to Inquire into Child Abuse (CICA). The Congregation of Religious of Ireland (CORI) issued a formal apology on behalf of its members in January 2002.[20] The Department of Education expressed its 'deep regret' for its 'significant failings' in relation to children in care in these institutions in June 2006.[21] The Commission (CICA) published its five-volume report in May 2009 having received evidence from more than 1,500 witnesses covering the period 1936–99.[22] First chaired by Ms Justice Mary Laffoy, the report is known by the name of its second chairperson, Mr Justice Sean Ryan.

The Commission to Inquire into Child Abuse (Ryan) makes separate and detailed reports on 21 named institutions (vols 1–2), including transcripts of the shocking and incontrovertible evidence presented of serious abuse by religious and/or lay staff. None of these 21 schools was run by the Sisters of Our Lady of Charity, nor do the congregation's schools feature elsewhere in the report in a way that can be identified.[23] Most of the complaints about girls' industrial schools related to one particular school (Goldenbridge, in the west city suburbs of Dublin, run by the Mercy Sisters), 'the other 21 schools were each the subject of a small number of complaints. They were small schools run by religious orders of nuns and were generally in rural locations throughout Ireland'.[24] While not at all intending to downplay the truth of individual experiences, Ryan notes that, of the 493 witnesses who gave evidence to the Investigation Committee's legal team, more than 150 institutions featured but some were cited by one or two witnesses only. He says the evidence consists of 'uncorroborated allegations that were unchallenged and unproven and therefore did not have probative value in yielding conclusions about any institution or event'.[25] This makes it difficult

19   For a list of memoirs see Dáire Keogh, 'Peter Tyrrell, Letterfrack and the Ryan Report' in Tony Flannery (ed.), *Responding to the Ryan report* (Dublin, 2009), pp 55–7. Most noteworthy is Peter Tyrrell's, *Founded on fear: Letterfrack Industrial School, war and exile*, edited by Diarmuid Whelan (Dublin, 2006) which was written in the 1960s but not published for another 40 years.
20   Ryan report, i, p. 15.
21   Ibid., i, p. 1.
22   Ibid., i, preface; xv, p. 15.
23   Chapter 18 of the Ryan report covers residential settings outside the main remit of the Commission to Inquire into Child Abuse and the detailed complaints of seven witnesses from four different laundries are recorded; because the information is anonymised there is no way of knowing whether any of the OLC refuges are intended.
24   Ryan report, iv, p. 434.
25   Ibid., iv, p. 431.

for researchers to use the CICA in relation to individual institutions, other than those actually named. Of those who gave evidence of abuse to either the Investigation Committee or to the Confidential Committee, there is no way of knowing if any was a past-pupil of St Joseph's, Whitehall (High Park) or of St Anne's, Kilmacud, or of any other care facility run by the OLC sisters. Evidence was given to the Commission that the OLC sisters were aware at the time of five complaints.[26] What can be said with certainty is that the CICA was not presented with complaints of such a number and gravity concerning the childcare ventures of the Sisters of Our Lady of Charity that it needed to name the institute in the published report and to devote a section to it. The Ryan report did suceed in bringing the issue of child abuse and neglect in residential settings to public notice with a force and authority that could not be challenged. It also enabled some persons at least who had suffered grievous abuse to have their story heard and believed and for redress to be made, insofar as that is ever possible. The report is a major resource for the writing of the history of residential care in Ireland, bringing into the light much documentation that was previously closed to researchers. It gives glimpses into what was happening – or indeed, not happening – in the government department that had a statutory duty to inspect and monitor the schools.

While the significance of the Ryan report is beyond question, it has for this research project the drawback of suppressing the names of institutions in its transcripts of evidence, other than those which were the subject of individual reports, so that it is impossible to identify data specific to any of the OLC schools or homes. Chapter 18 of volume III deals with residential settings outside the main remit of the CICA, and the detailed complaints of seven witnesses from four different laundries are recorded but, because the information is anonymised, there is no way of knowing whether any of this evidence relates to an OLC refuge. The Ryan report is a deeply distressing catalogue of wrongdoing and pain; it is also overwhelming in its emotional impact. The danger is that researchers, anxious to ward off any accusation of minimising the evil of child abuse, will make the presumption that what happened in one or even many schools happened universally and across all decades. As with McAleese, the Ryan report is important to this study but the redacted nature of its evidence does not allow it to be used in the detailed way one might expect.

The Ryan report led directly to the establishment of the Redress Board, an independent body (chaired by Mr Justice Esmond Smyth) charged with making awards to persons who, as children, had been abused while resident in these schools; 18 religious orders that had been involved in childcare contributed to the redress fund.[27] In practice, the definition of abuse in the Residential Institutions Redress Act 2002 was sufficiently broad that any person who could prove residency as a child (up to 18 years of age) in any of the institutions named in the schedule to the Act could apply for redress.[28] The applicant was not required to produce to the Board

---

26   Ibid., i, p. 6.
27   Ibid., i, p. 15; Residential Institutions Redress Board, www.rirb.ie.
28   Residential Institutions Redress Act, 2002, section 1.1 a–d.

any evidence of negligence.[29] The award of a payment did not constitute 'a finding of fact relating to fault or negligence'.[30] In accepting a redress payment, the person was precluded from starting civil proceedings against the institution.[31] It was this indemnity against future claims that was the chief advantage to those congregations which contributed to the redress fund. The published list of 128 institutions included not just reformatory and industrial schools but also orphanages, training centres, teenage hostels, children's homes, special schools (for children with intellectual disability), schools for the hearing impaired, for the visually impaired and schools attached to orthopaedic and children's hospitals, that is, every institution in Ireland in operation since the foundation of the state in 1922, Catholic and Protestant alike, 'in which children were placed and resident and in respect of which a public body had a regulatory or inspection function'.[32] The great majority were Catholic-run, with An Grianán Training Centre, Martanna House Hostel and St Joseph's Industrial School, Whitehall (all part of the High Park complex) and St Anne's Reformatory School (Kilmacud) included in the published schedule. The statistics returned by the Redress Board hint at the scale of its operations: by the end of 2011 the Redress Board had received 15,404 valid applications.[33] The conflation in the public mind of the Redress Board with the earlier Ryan Commission is understandable but from the research perspective, there is the danger that a single harsh judgement will be applied to all institutions across all dates by virtue of being listed under the redress scheme.

The setting up by the Irish government of an independent inquiry into mother-and-baby homes has placed yet another type of residential insti-tution run by religious but funded by the state under scrutiny; its report was expected in February 2018.[34] The research of a local historian, Catherine Corless, into infant deaths at a home in Tuam, County Galway, between 1925 and 1961 led to demands in the Dáil and in the press for a full commission of investigation into the operation of all such homes for unmarried mothers in the state, most of which had closed by the early 1970s.[35] The names of a small number of women who gave birth in mother-and-baby homes (or the local authority healthcare facilities associated with them) are entered in the registers of the refuges run by the Sisters of Our Lady of Charity. So too the McAleese inquiry noted the role of magdalen laundries in receiving un-married mothers from these homes. On leaving the mother-and-baby homes,

29  Ibid., section 7.5.
30  Ibid., section 5.3.
31  Ibid., section 13.12.
32  Ibid., section 4.1.
33  As of 31 Dec. 2011, the Redress Board had made awards totalling €875.25 million; the average award was €62,895, the largest, €300,500. The legal costs of the scheme up to 31 Dec. 2011 were €159,533,868.16, that is, €159 million for the 13,327 finalised applications (other costs were still outstanding). The average cost and expenses paid to solicitors, including payments made for medical reports, amounted to €11,592 per applicant or 18.4% of the award. There were 555 lawyers involved. Report online at www.rirb.ie/annual report.
34  *Irish Times*, 30 Dec. 2016.
35  Report of the Inter-Departmental Group on Mother and Baby Homes, Department of Children and Youth Affairs, 16 July 2014, p. 2, online at www.dcya.gov.ie.

what number or percentage of women resorted to or were sent to magdalen asylums? The geographical location, established network of contacts and range of local alternatives will be, I suspect, relevant factors but, in the absence of full data, that is merely speculation. The OLC refuges record only a handful of girls entering from or going to mother-and-baby homes, which I discuss insofar as the sources allow (chapters 11–13). Mother-and-baby homes have been equated with magdalen laundries by at least some commentators, a confusion that is understandable but not especially helpful. This point was noted also in the McAleese inquiry which found that, despite the two types of institution being 'perhaps closely associated in the public consciousness', mother-and-baby homes accounted for only 3.9% of known routes of entry to all ten magdalen laundries.[36] This finding is in line with the OLC register evidence but, as discussed below (under methodology), as there is very little recorded about most of the girls and women entering High Park or Gloucester Street/Sean MacDermott Street, or indeed entering some of the other institutions covered by McAleese, numbers and percentages must be treated with caution. A comprehensive and independent state investigation into the operation of all mother-and-baby homes will be a complex and sensitive undertaking; the three-person commission entrusted with the powers necessary for the investigation is Judge Yvonne Murphy (chair), Professor Mary Daly (historian) and Dr William Duncan (legal expert on child protection and adoption).[37] In common with other state inquiries to date, it is certain to highlight once more the stigma that attached to an unmarried woman who found herself pregnant in independent Ireland, the obstacles in her way should she try to rear the child on her own, and the especially precarious position of the illegitimate infant prior to the 1952 Adoption Act.[38] The 1964 newspaper series by Michael Viney titled 'No birthright' stands as a succinct but heart-rending study of public attitudes to the Irish unmarried mother and her child while also exploring in some detail the operation of the Adoption Act in its first decade.[39] Viney's overall judgement was that, by the early 1960s, 'the legal machinery for good child care' was in place but implementation and practice of it fell woefully behind due primarily to collective social taboo, where 'What will the neighbours say?' held sway, and allowed many cruel things to be done in its name.[40]

## Sources and Methodologies

Locating the key archival collections, managing access and deciding on research methodologies were the first steps; the ethical challenges were also uppermost from the outset. Will the study be independent, fair and historically sound? Is there a sensitivity to what the writing of this history may

---

36    McAleese report, part 3, ch. 11, para. 184.
37    Minister Reilly, Announcement on the setting up of the Commission of inquiry into Mother and Baby Homes and certain related matters', 19 Feb. 2015, online at www.dcya.gov.ie.
38    Moira Maguire, *Precarious childhood in post-independence Ireland* (Manchester, 2009), pp 48–112, 133–142.
39    Michael Viney, *No birthright, a study of the Irish unmarried mother and her children, the Irish Times articles*, Sept. 1964.
40    Ibid., p. 56.

mean for persons formerly resident in these institutions or connected in other ways? To paraphrase Keith Jenkins, am I as author sufficiently aware of my epistemological, methodological, ideological and practical positioning?[41] Self-awareness is probably what matters most, and I am certainly conscious of my limitations as a researcher, and how one's stance is always coloured by cultural conditioning and previous experience, including academic opportunities. This book is a contribution to scholarship in which every effort has been made to deal critically and fairly with the available sources, drawing on historical, geographical and theological understandings that have developed over several decades of research, writing and teaching.

Record-keeping was part of the culture of Notre Dame de Charité from its foundation. Realising that the documentary records relating to the sisters in Ireland were remarkably complete and, for the most part, had not previously been used by researchers, led me to decide at an early stage of this research to make the fullest possible use of them. This decision was also driven by a realisation that there is much evidence within OLC records that simply does not exist elsewhere. For example, meetings, assemblies and chapters at local (community), federation and general (international) level were pivotal in setting direction for the works or ministries of the sisters, as well as regulating their own internal life. Important questions (as well as much that was routine or insignificant) were decided at council meetings and by elected delegates in chapter, and carefully written up for their own successors. There is no proxy for these records which, though difficult to handle (the canon law and constitutional contexts need to be appreciated), repay close attention. In addition to what has been centralised in the Dublin Archives of the Religious of the Good Shepherd (DARGS) at Beechlawn (High Park, Drumcondra), I had access to the records held at the French provincial and Union archives of Notre Dame de Charité at Cormelles-le-Royal, Caen and found matching correspondence and newsletter or *bulletin* information in the archives of the Good Shepherd (GS) mother house in Angers. I had access to papers relating to both OLC and GS in the Sacred Congregation for Religious and Secular Institutes, Rome, and in the Dublin Diocesan Archives, Clonliffe College. I also found material of significance in the files of the Department of Justice held in the National Archives of Ireland. Chapter 4 of the McAleese report gives a good summary of the difficulties inherent in accessing departmental files, even with the active co-operation it had of a large number of well-placed and experienced departmental officials and archivists, difficulties with which I can certainly concur. Previous to my research, there had been some examination of the registers of entry to the refuges of High Park and Gloucester Street by other university researchers, while the annals of both houses had been used in the compilation of jubilee histories (1903, 1953 for High Park; 1937 for Gloucester Street) but, as far as I could judge, nothing else of the records, either inside or outside Ireland, has previously been subjected to academic scrutiny. Until the register material was in electronic format, a full exploration was not feasible, and neither physical nor intellectual access was possible to the great body of records

---

41   Keith Jenkins, *Rethinking history* (London, 1991, reprinted 2008), p. 31.

(90 archival boxes for High Park alone) until they were described and arranged. Nor could much be made of the documents held in other archives until the principal collections at Beechlawn were in order. The repository code DARGS, followed by OLC (Our Lady of Charity), SJ (St Joseph) or SA (St Anne) refer to items held in the archive at Beechlawn. The individual collections, with their abbreviations, are listed in the bibliography. While most catalogue entries are at item level, some are at file level, which may explain some repeated numbers. At the time of writing, catalogue numbers had yet to be assigned to items in the OLC4 (The Grange) collection.

What John Scott calls the 'quality control criteria' of authenticity, credibility, representativeness and meaning, understood as interdependent, may be applied to the principal collections utilised in this research.[42] The OLC and GS collections held in Dublin, Caen, Angers and Rome, meet the criterion of authenticity. These comprise manuscript originals, along with authenticated copies of outgoing correspondence, where the authorship can be established, and the role played by a secretary or scribe identified, especially relevant in group correspondence (on behalf of the community) and in communications with state bodies. There is ample internal evidence of the soundness of the documents. That they have been held continuously within the congregation up to the present day, without being split, places provenance beyond question.

Assessing the credibility of a document involves, as Scott sets out, an appraisal of how 'distorted' its contents are likely to be, allowing that 'there is always an element of selective accentuation in the attempt to describe social reality'.[43] In questioning the 'sincerity' of a document, the researcher always asks what individual or collective interest may have been felt by the author(s) of the document under scrutiny, what was the author's situation at the time of its creation and the degree of proximity to the events in question. In the case of OLC, the sisters created, signed and dated records in the discharge of their duties in the knowledge that they could be moved without notice to another post, while the cycle of elections meant that the superior and her councillors 'laid down their charge' at three-yearly intervals, even if they were re-elected. The sisters created records safe in the knowledge that, outside of the business purposes for which they were created (such as dismissing a novice or admitting a sister to profession of vows), they would be kept confidential in perpetuity which enhances the credibility of the records and their usefulness to historical research.

The representativeness of the records is more difficult to address. The long delay in putting the OLC collections at Beechlawn (DARGS) on a professional footing, and the good judgement of the first person appointed to the task (Sister Teresa Coughlan OLC), spared many records from being culled before they were even examined, so that what has been catalogued may be taken as what has indeed survived. My involvement in the arrangement and description of the High Park papers (OLC1) allows me to vouch for that with unusual authority. There have been some sad losses due

42   John Scott, *A matter of record, documentary sources in social research* (Cambridge, 1990), pp 19–35.
43   Ibid., p. 22.

to carelessness or a misguided zeal for tidying, while the issue of deliberate destruction – what was not kept at all for posterity, and why – is something that the historian has always to ponder.[44] But what can be said in the case of the OLC collections is that very, very much was held, as the various catalogues demonstrate. The prescriptions of the rule and constitutions, and the self-governing or autonomous character of each house, did make for meticulous record-making and record-keeping well beyond anything that I have encountered for other apostolic communities operating in Ireland over the same period.

The bombardment of Caen in June 1944 destroyed the archives and library of the founding house of the order; the loss included an unbroken series of letters from High Park which had faithfully maintained the link with the 'old cradle'. But correspondence from Ireland was found among the collections of other OLC houses in France, most usefully *circulaires*, election letters and obituaries of which no file copy had been kept by the Dublin side. Minutes and annals from other houses confirmed visits from Irish sisters, with notes on fluency in French giving an inkling of how useful the visit might have been. The material held in Rome was of the utmost importance in revealing what was happening behind the scenes to persuade OLC monasteries to agree to a union of some sort, and the very real basis there was for apprehension about a forced incorporation into the Good Shepherd congregation. It is the access to opinions offered in confidence in blunt form that make these records so useful, and similarly with the McQuaid papers in the Dublin Diocesan Archives. Where incoming letters were annotated – terse comments, question marks, heavy, red underlining – the real matters at stake stand out. The Department of Justice files (National Archives of Ireland) from the 1950s complete a triangle with the McQuaid and OLC papers, a three-sided conversation with interesting offshoots. Access to relevant papers from several government departments (Education, Justice, Health, Finance) can also be made via the Ryan report by way of its extensive quotations from internal departmental records.

The ultimate purpose of documentary research, arriving at an understanding of the meaning and significance of what the document contains,[45] is the historian's greatest challenge. There is first the literal understanding, requiring language skills and palaeography. Interpretative understanding requires much more but, at its simplest, according to Scott, 'interpretation requires an understanding of the particular definitions and recording practices adopted and of the genre and stylisation employed in the text', and how these might have changed over time and from place to place.[46] The criterion of 'meaning' cannot be applied without simultaneously balancing what the researcher has decided in respect of the other criteria (authenticity, credibility, representativeness); all are interdependent. [47] The founding correspondence for High Park, for example, is extensive, frank and very detailed, involving multiple parties and different perspectives, in both French and English, while

44   Ibid., p. 25.
45   Ibid., p. 28.
46   Ibid., p. 30.
47   Ibid., p. 30.

the official McQuaid correspondence can be cross-checked and augmented from draft letters, copy letters, private memos, manuscript annotations and entries in the federation council minute books. There are other records which, though complete, contain far less detail than one new to the field might expect, especially the registers of admission to the women's refuges (for reasons that are explored in chapter 2). Some areas lend themselves to meticulous record-making, as in building, engineering and repairs where the records are very full. Benefactors are always remembered. Accounts of religious ceremonies can be lengthy and finely detailed where they are meant to recreate the liturgy for those who did not have the privilege of being present. Architectural and landscape word-pictures can be so vivid as to transport the reader imaginatively to the place being described, their express intention. Accounts of religious art were in themselves meditations on divine mysteries; in the case of OLC, references to Church art and furnishings presume, not just a shared Catholicism, but also a shared spiritual heritage through the founder, John Eudes. Reformatory and industrial school records employ the language and structure of the state regulating body which issued pre-printed forms and registers along with instructions on the information to be kept.

The temptation is to write up what the records allow, rather than to sift out what is truly significant. I admit to erring on the side of including rather than stripping back, but this is done with future researchers in mind and the varied threads that they might wish to follow up. While there is an abundance of evidence to support some lines of inquiry, others are more difficult to follow through satisfactorily as there are traces or hints only in the documentary record. In so many areas, life carried on without needing written records at all, as in the friendships forged, the games played, the meals served, the prayers memorised. Most internal records were created by sisters in leadership positions, as superior, secretary, bursar, mistress, principal, manager or director, making it difficult to hear the voice of the 'ordinary' sisters or women residents, let alone that of the teenagers and children in care. Some records are missing, such as the annals from Gloucester Street which were certainly extant in 1937 when a booklet was published to mark its golden jubilee.[48] Because of the lack of local council minutes for Sean MacDermott Street in the 1950s and 1960s (minutes may not have been kept), its modernisation process cannot be covered in the same detail that was possible for High Park. Where state funds and state regulation were involved, as in the reformatory schools, the paper record is much fuller compared with, for example, the hostels – though, in all cases, it is not just what was created that matters but what was preserved. Uneven sources have meant uneven treatment in this study, though none of the houses or works was without a body of records. Overall, the range of record types within OLC is very broad – correspondence, constitutions, annals, minutes, visitation reports, registers of admissions and departures, sodality lists, obituaries, title deeds, receipts, feast-day greetings and more. These are found in a variety of archival formats, including bound volumes, folded bundles of accounts, ornate liturgical books, music scores, postcards, scrapbooks, building plans, relics, audio tapes and 16mm film.

48   *Souvenir of Golden Jubilee of Monastery of Our Lady of Charity of Refuge, Gloucester Street* (Dublin, 1937), p. 21.

My initial plans for this study included oral histories, architectural surveys, examination of art and artefacts, and more besides. Set against this was the lengthy chronology, the complex intertwining of several histories in one book, and the wealth, volume and detail of the archival sources which had come to light in Dublin, Caen, Angers and Rome. As the research progressed, I decided to concentrate on documentary records. At the time of writing, there is a major oral history project under way at University College Dublin, funded by the Irish Research Council (directed by Dr Katherine O'Donnell of the Magdalenes for Justice group). This, it is expected, will be making available to researchers interviews with women who formerly spent some time in magdalen laundries and other residential institutions in Ireland. There are transcripts of oral evidence, as well as of documentary evidence, throughout the McAleese report, while chapter 19 of that report records memories of the living and working conditions of the magdalen laundries shared with the committee by former residents, sisters and others with direct, first-hand knowledge, including medical practitioners and probation officers. There are several other memoir projects currently under way (or completed), including interviews with past and current residents of OLC homes and with sisters who worked in these settings by Kathleen Fahey, a former director of Ruhama, who from 2010 led what was called the OLC Ministries Desk.[49] Through the supervision of doctoral and post-doctoral work in oral history, I am cognisant of its importance in the writing of social history from the mid-20th century onwards but this involvement has also brought a greater awareness of its ethical demands as a research methodology, and the time, preparation and professional expertise required. My decision not to try replicating the work of others with the resources to undertake it properly was a conscious one. In the meantime, it is hoped that this documents-based history will be found useful to those working on oral projects and vice versa.

The decision to make the most extensive use possible of archival sources has had repercussions in terms of the range of secondary literature that it was possible to review in the text or to consider in any depth. This deficiency is acknowledged. The historiography in the two core areas, magdalen laundries and reformatory/industrial schools, is considered below, albeit briefly. But first, notice must be taken of at least some of the literature in the fields of childcare and social work more generally. E. Fahy's 1942 paper in the Trinity College journal *Hermathena* is a well-informed critique of the certified school systems post-independence north and south, an early but rare study of how childcare provision in the Free State compared with the UK.[50] Journal articles more generally on 'the deprived child' can be identified in numbers from the early 1950s, led (it appears) by *Christus Rex, an Irish Quarterly Journal of Sociology*. The 'small group system of residential care' features

49   According to an internal OLC memo dated June 2010, the vision behind the setting up of the OLC Ministries Desk and its purpose was 'that OLC embraces its past and uses it constructively to inform present and future direction and mission' and that the Ministries Desk 'facilitate the achievement of this vision by initiating a process of exploration, discussion and analysis of former OLC ministries and to ensure that the learning gained from this process is brought to bear on the development of present and future ministries' (OLC regional office).
50   E. Fahy, 'Reformatory schools in Ireland', *Hermathena*, lx (1942), pp 54–73.

in reports on childcare provision, such as *Children deprived, the CARE memorandum on deprived children and children's services in Ireland* (June 1972). The progress made in residential childcare and protection services between 1970 and 1995 is the subject of *Focus on residential care in Ireland, 25 years since the Kennedy report* (Patricia McCarthy, Stanislaus Kennedy, Caroline Matthews, Dublin, 1996). Noreen Kearney's work on the setting up of the social studies course in Trinity College Dublin in 1934,[51] and Maria Luddy's on the developing professionalism of social work in Ireland[52] help illuminate the larger contexts in which the changes in work practices by the OLC sisters can be set, for they were among the first religious communities in Ireland to send professed sisters to train in the specific fields of childcare and social work. Mel Cousins in *The birth of social welfare in Ireland, 1922–1952* (Dublin, 2003), tracks the changes in legislation that had the greatest impact on poor women trying to keep themselves and their families together, but also what was happening behind the scenes under successive governments to mould policy. The history of probation in Ireland and the 1907 legislation which allowed it has been summarised by Gerry McNally (2007); both paid and voluntary officers were involved, with a strengthening of the role of voluntary denominational organisations in the 1940s. McNally's study highlights the political preference for voluntarism over state intervention that continued into the 1960s, paralleling what was happening in other sectors.[53]

There is a wealth of scholarship and commentary in the fields of women's studies, childhood, Roman Catholicism, religious life, sexuality and (rather broadly defined) Irish society in independent Ireland of relevance to this study. Prominent among the contributors is Diarmaid Ferriter of UCD, whose *Occasions of sin: sex and society in the modern Ireland* (London, 2009) can be read with profit in association with the McAleese report, as indeed can Clíona Rhattigan's work on single motherhood in Ireland.[54] Myrtle Hill's *Women in Ireland, a century of change* (Belfast, 2003) traces the major shifts and developments in women's experience over the course of a century of turbulent economic, social and political change; running throughout this highly-readable academic study is the diversity of female experience and the significance of the local. Philip Howell's work on the proposed regulation of prostitution in the Irish Free State throws light on the difficulties the government of the day had in facing up to the more contentious areas of social life and how, so often, decisions were postponed or sidestepped.[55] Cousins (2003) is excellent on the differential treatment of mothers (unmarried with one child, unmarried with more than one child, married, widowed, deserted) in the 1929 Commission on Relief of the Poor and on

51    Noreen Kearney, 'The historical background', in *Social work and social work training in Ireland, yesterday and tomorrow* (Dublin, 1987), pp 5–15.
52    Maria Luddy, *Women, philanthropy and the emergence of social work in Ireland*, TCD pamphlet (2005).
53    Gerry McNally, 'Probation in Ireland, a brief history of the early years', *Irish Probation Journal*, vol. 4 no. 1 (2007), pp 5–24.
54    Clíona Rhattigan, *"What else could I do?" Single mothers and infanticide in Ireland 1900–1950* (Dublin, 2012).
55    Philip Howell, 'Venereal disease and the politics of prostitution in the Irish Free State', *Irish Historical Studies*, 33:131 (2003), pp 320–41.

the formulation of policy in subsequent decades against a backdrop of very straitened public finances and a view of woman's role that presumed the family home was her proper sphere, that should she be employed she would receive lower rates of pay than a man and correspondingly lower benefits in terms of sickness or unemployment assistance, and that she would leave the labour market on marriage, relying thereafter on the husband's income.[56] Cousins also treats of the impact of the Beveridge report on the patchwork that was social welfare policy in Ireland 1942–52.[57] The research of Jennifer Redmond on the position of unmarried Irish women in Britain, and the role of religious welfare societies in assisting them through repatriation and other schemes, is refreshingly original in its exposition of the great variety of personal experiences to be found under this single category and in its insistence on how analysis of documentary evidence can offer only 'a piece of the story', leaving the historian with even more questions.[58]

On the transformation of the Catholic Church in 20th-century Ireland, Louise Fuller's, *Irish Catholicism since 1950: the undoing of a culture* (Dublin, 2002) stands in a class of its own, while useful work on institutions has been completed by Catherine Cox.[59] Maryanne Confoy's work on religious life in the era of Vatican II era is a succinct but well-informed account of the major debates.[60] Literature in this field has been augmented by new scholarship marking 50 years since the closing of the Council; in the collection of essays edited by Dermot Lane (2015), I use the case study of the Irish Federation of the Sisters of Our Lady of Charity to explore how communities in Ireland received the call of Vatican II for the renewal of religious life.[61] An introduction to the historical literature on religious life in Britain and in Ireland is provided by Susan O'Brien in the context of a larger Europe-wide survey, pointing out how the tradition of national, independent, single-institute studies badly needs to give way to intertwined, cross-channel and comparative studies, as the experience of religious life in the two islands has so many points of connection.[62] The same argument could be made in relation to Ireland and France, as my study shows in respect of the OLC sisters and their colleagues in the Good Shepherd. Carmen M. Mangion, *Contested identities: Catholic women religious in nineteenth-century England*

56   Mel Cousins, *Social welfare in Ireland, 1922–1952* (Dublin, 2003), pp 53–5, 193.
57   Cousins, *Social welfare in Ireland, 1922–1952*, chs 6 and 7.
58   Jennifer Redmond, 'In the family way and away from the family: examining the evidence for Irish unmarried mothers in Britain' in Elaine Farrell (ed.), *"She said she was in the family way": Pregnancy and infancy in modern Ireland* (London, 2012), p. 185.
59   Catherine Cox, 'Institutionalisation in Irish history and society, 1650–2000' in Leeann Lane, Katherine O'Donnell & Mary McAuliffe (eds), *Palgrave advances in Irish history* (Hampshire, 2009), pp 169–190.
60   Maryanne Confoy, 'Religious life in the Vatican II era: "State of perfection" or living charism?', *Theological Studies*, 74 (2013), pp 321–45.
61   Jacinta Prunty, 'Reception of the call of Vatican II for renewal of religious life: case study of the Irish Federation of the Sisters of Our Lady of Charity' in Dermot Lane (ed.), *Vatican II in Ireland, fifty years on, essays in honour of Pádraic Conway* (Bern, 2015), pp 121–50.
62   Susan O'Brien, 'A survey of research and writing about Roman Catholic women's congregations in Great Britain and Ireland (1800–1950)' in Jan de Maeyer, Sophie Leplae & Joachim Schmiedl (eds), *Religious institutes in Western Europe in the 19th and 20th centuries, historiography, research and legal position* (Leuven, 2004), p. 115.

*and Wales* (Manchester, 2008) is a thoughtful and painstaking examination of what attracted women to religious life, how their training shaped identity, the links between their work, missionary fervour and professional identity, and the development of an institute's corporate identity. All of these issues have applicability to the project in hand, and my only regret is that Mangion's study did not extend to the OLC and Good Shepherd sisters, both of whom had houses in Britain over the period of my work. Mangion's historiography is more than a succinct introduction to the key literature on religion and women, and on religious life across Britain, Ireland, France and the new worlds of Australia and America in the 19th century; it stands as an authoritative guide to the field. Phil Kilroy's *The Society of the Sacred Heart in nineteenth-century France, 1800–1865* (Cork, 2012), is an exemplar of how Catholic institutional history, in this case involving schools for girls, needs to be studied in relation to the internal life of the religious community for whom the work was an expression of their vocation. Deirdre Raftery's work on a sample of Irish nuns who worked in education in the 19th century sets out to determine how they reconciled their individuality with the demands of religious life; her analysis of how the vow of obedience was lived out and the theology behind it could be usefully extended well beyond the three institutes that were her chief focus.[63] Margaret MacCurtain sees the nuns' story as integral to the history of women in the 20th century as she demonstrates in several of the papers gathered in the aptly-named *Ariadne's thread, writing women into Irish history* (Galway, 2008). MacCurtain pushes beyond institutional histories and religious biography to ask difficult questions, such as what attracted Irish women to enter convents in extraordinary numbers up to the 1960s, how the demands of professionalisation from the 1950s could possibly sit with the obligations of conventual living set in a 19th-century mould, and how it came about that women's congregations, 'powerful as negotiating tools in the state's educational and welfare plans' in the independent state and in Northern Ireland post-1922, 'became in reality pawns in the struggle for control between church and state, between bishops and departments of government'.[64] The present book does not offer answers but, it is hoped, makes possible a better-informed exploration of these and other serious questions about the role of religious sisters in Irish life in the 20th century especially.

The published literature dealing with the magdalen laundries or asylums is of varied quality. Historian Maria Luddy's work remains the most comprehensive and scholarly dealing with this and allied issues published to date. Her paper 'Magdalen asylums in Ireland 1765–1922', based on her previously published work, was the principal source for chapter 3 of the McAleese report and provides the historical background and context for the committee's work. As Luddy has noted in print, and taken up by McAleese, the perception of the Magdalen laundries in 20th-century Ireland is extremely negative and, without access to the written records of these institutions,

---

63    Deirdre Raftery, 'Rebels with a cause: obedience, resistance and convent life, 1800–1940', *History of Education*, vol. 42, no. 6 (2013), pp 729–44.
64    Margaret Mac Curtain, 'Late in the field: Catholic sisters in twentieth-century Ireland and the new religious history', reprinted in MacCurtain, *Ariadne's thread*, p. 276.

only oral histories provide a standard by which to consider them.[65] Luddy has repeatedly highlighted the need for a comprehensive study based on full access to the records across all institutes, most especially for the 20th century. In contrast, Frances Finnegan's *Do penance or perish, a study of magdalen asylums in Ireland* (Piltown, Co. Kilkenny, 2001) is sensationalist and burdened with errors of interpretation; its misleading use of register evidence from the Good Shepherd laundries was pointed out in the McAleese report.[66] Despite its shortcomings, this text has been taken as authoritative. For example, the Irish material in Rebecca Lea McCarthy's *Origins of the Magdalene laundries: an analytical history* (Jefferson, N.C., 2010) is derived largely from Finnegan, while James Smith also relies heavily on Finnegan's text. What is original in Smith's landmark work, *Ireland's magdalen laundries and the nation's architecture of containment* (2007) is the focus on the architectural fabric of the asylums, analysis of the cultural representations of the magdalen laundries from the 1990s onwards, and the connections he makes between the asylums and the post-1922 nation-state's 'nativist' policies. Describing himself as a non-historian and advisor to the Justice for Magdalenes advocacy group, Smith expresses the book's aim in activist terms: 'It challenges the nation to acknowledge its complicity in Ireland's Magdalen scandal and to respond by providing redress for victims and survivors alike'.[67] As Smith correctly points out, the magdalen laundry exists in the public mind chiefly at the level of *story* (cultural representation and survivor testimony) rather than *history* (archival records and documentation).[68] My hope is that this academic history with its heavy reliance on contemporary documentation will go some way to fulfil the need identified by Luddy, Smith and others for new research based on the records of these institutions.

The classic study of childcare in Ireland remains Joseph Robins, *The lost children* (Dublin, 1980), though it is strongest on the 19th century. A more recent text based on unrivalled access to the records of the Irish Society for the Prevention of Cruelty to Children (ISPCC) and to a range of departmental files, is Moira Maguire's *Precarious childhood in post-independence Ireland* (Manchester, 2010). Sarah Anne Buckley's *The cruelty man, child welfare, the NSPCC and the State in Ireland, 1889–1956* (Manchester, 2013), a moving study of the operation of the NSPCC, bears out many of Maguire's findings and indeed much of what I too found via other documentary routes. The mother's perspective is to the fore in Lindsey Earner-Byrne, *Mother and child, maternity and child welfare in Dublin, 1922–60* (Manchester, 2013); though focused on Dublin, this meticulous research is important to the wider national story.

The Ryan report includes a number of essays and shorter reports that provide context and background to reformatory and industrial schools and children's homes from 1936 (Cussen report) through to 1970 (Kennedy report). There is an historical overview of the functions, structures and relationships of the various government departments which had responsibility

---

65  McAleese report, part 1, ch. 3, para. 115.
66  Ibid., part 1, ch. 3, paras 100–2.
67  James Smith, *Ireland's magdalen laundries and the nation's architecture of containment* (Notre Dame, Ind., 2007), Acknowledgements, xi, Preface, xiii.
68  Smith, *Ireland's magdalen laundries*, Preface, xvi.

for children in care, namely Education (which had overall responsibility), Justice and Health, and of the differences in policy between them. Relationships between the departments, and with the different congregations running the schools, are covered by Ryan, as are the recommendations made – and largely ignored – up to 1970. The inspection system in place, how complaints were handled, the innovations and improvements in the 1960s and the extraordinarily large number of files which went missing from the Department of Education are also dealt with by Ryan. Overall, this had a direct impact on the work of the commission of inquiry. This historical overview enables the departmental correspondence held in the OLC archives to be placed in context. A closely-referenced essay by David Gwynn Morgan titled 'Society and the Schools', is a succinct but expert commentary on the social, economic and family background of industrial school children and (up to 1965) the attention given to the schools by outside monitors, including the Oireachtas and the press, among other issues.[69] The sociologist Eoin O'Sullivan covers policy, legislation and practice in residential child welfare from 1965 to 2008 inclusive, the follow-through to the work by Gwynn Morgan.[70] While the two schools run by the Sisters of Our Lady of Charity made up a very small part of a large and complex national picture, the changes which occurred in High Park and Kilmacud can be seen as local manifestations of larger trends, such as the irreversible fall in the numbers committed to industrial schools after the peak of the 1940s.[71] The section titled '1965–1976 – residential childcare in transition' is especially valuable to this study, as it explores the arguments offered in public and in private around models of care, management, funding and implementation through reports, policy documents, discussion papers, pamphlets and newspaper articles. Parties to the debate included study groups, social workers, Church bodies, local authority officials, probation officers and civil servants, as well as concerned private individuals, when public opinion turned strongly against the industrial schools. Commissions and committees of enquiry as well as interdepartmental committees produced papers; O'Sullivan is able to throw light on who was, or was not, appointed to these committees and the background politics involved through his access to files of the government departments involved, namely, Education, Finance, Justice and Health.[72] This also allowed him to explore the immediate and often confidential responses to these reports and the positions that various parties took. O'Sullivan's sequential study allows the work of the OLC sisters to be positioned, and their involvement in the debate to be assessed, for example, as members of the Association of Residential Managers of Reformatory and Industrial Schools and, more provocatively, through the 'Group for the Advancement of Child Care' (established 1970, relaunched as CARE, Campaign for the care of deprived children). Diarmaid Ferriter's paper on the social context provides a

69   David Gwynn Morgan, 'Society and the schools', Ryan report, iv, pp 201–244.
70   Eoin O'Sullivan, 'Residential child welfare in Ireland, 1965–2008: an outline of policy, legislation and practice, a paper prepared for the Commission to Inquire into Child Abuse', Ryan, iv, pp 245–423.
71   O'Sullivan, 'Residential child welfare in Ireland, 1965–2008', p. 285.
72   Ibid., pp 285–363.

broader but no less valuable overview of the real world within which these institutions operated and within which reform was brought about, while also drawing attention to the cursory and formulaic nature of many of the records produced by institutions and on which research such as his (and by extension, my own), must rely.[73]

O'Sullivan notes how the difference between the industrial and reformatory school experience of boys and girls in the 1960s was closely observed. Sent by the Minister for Education, George Colley, to investigate every aspect of the schools in 1966 and report back privately, a Dr C.E. Lysaght was struck by the 'marked difference' between those for girls, run by nuns, and those for boys, under the care of brothers:

> The former [the girls' schools] are without exception much superior in every way and beyond explanation by way of smaller numbers. The vast majority of girls' schools are most satisfactory and in many cases can compare favourably in regard to care and comfort with not only the ordinary run of boarding schools for girls but with the most exclusive ones.[74]

The senior boys' schools he condemned, in the main, as 'rough and ready' and badly needing a woman's hand.[75] One of the key findings of the Commission to Inquire into Child Abuse was how much worse boys fared in the industrial schools under practically all headings when compared with girls, a finding which was not in any way to undermine complaints made by girls, but reflected what was reported in the 1960s by a number of outside, independent observers.

The final multi-volume report of the 'Inter-Departmental Committee set up to establish the facts of State involvement with the Magdalen Laundries' (February 2013), under the independent chairmanship of Senator Martin McAleese and hence known as the 'McAleese report', is the other landmark inquiry of significance to this study. Included is a scrupulous account of its identification, examination and archiving of the fullest possible range of records (chapters 4, 6 & 7). It also gives a very useful review of existing historical analyses of the magdalen laundries prior to 1922 (chapter 3). Under routes of entry to the magdalen laundries, it deals with the criminal justice system (chapter 9), industrial and reformatory schools (chapter 10) and health authorities and social services (chapter 11), in each case including the legislative basis for placements in these institutes and the policies and practices of the many bodies involved. Lengthy extracts from documentary and witness testimony is included in all cases. On publication, the McAleese report was applauded for the pre-eminence it gave to the personal testimony of former residents whom it praises for their courage in speaking up after many years

73   'Report by Dr Diarmaid Ferriter, St Patrick's College, DCU, June 2006', Ryan report, v, pp 1–37 after p. 353.
74   Dr C.E. Lysaght, Report on industrial schools and Reformatories, submitted to the Minister for Education, 11 Nov. 1966, quoted in Ryan report, iv, p. 290.
75   Ibid.

of feeling forgotten and not believed. Its note that most of the former residents who shared their experiences with the committee had previously been in an industrial school adds to the poignancy of their personal accounts.[76]

But while the McAleese report must be hailed as a landmark in its own right and an invaluable resource for the history of magdalen laundries in Ireland, some restrictions around how I have used it in this history of the Sisters of Our Lady of Charity in Ireland need to be stated. These arise out of its particular mandate – 'to establish the facts of State involvement with the Magdalen Laundries' – and its inclusiveness, covering all ten institutions of this type, run by four different religious congregations, with varying levels of completeness in terms of records.[77] First is the issue of admissions. The finding that 26.5% of all admissions were 'referrals made or facilitated by the state' is widely quoted without Dr McAleese's important caveat that this figure is based on the cases 'for which routes of entry are known'. In High Park, something about how a person came to be there can be gleaned from the register for 11% of all admissions between 1922 and 1971. Out of every 100 women, therefore, there is nothing whatsoever known of the background story for 89. This was in accord with the community's policy of giving accommodation to any woman who sought shelter (once a bed could be found); no questions were asked and the absolute minimum information was kept. The dangers in extrapolating from the minimum data held in the register are self-evident. The register for Sean MacDermott Street is a little fuller in that something of the 'route of entry' can be deduced for 45 out of every 100 entrances between 1922 and 1966, but that still leaves a large number of women about whom nothing can ever be known from the documentary record on why they sought admission. These were the women who were not 'brought by' or 'sent by' any person or institute according to the register. Some may – or may not – have been 'self-referrals'; judgement must be left completely open as it is simply not possible to know what circumstances were behind each case (as the evidence currently stands). Register information for the other institutes that were part of the McAleese inquiry appears to have been fuller in terms of detail, though there was one institute where no registers were extant and another where some years were missing.[78] It would be methodologically unsound, therefore, to 'retrofit' the general findings of the McAleese report, based on cases 'for which routes of entry are known', to the refuges run by the Sisters of Our Lady of Charity in Dublin.

The second issue with the McAleese report is the protection of the identities of the women involved and the treatment of the magdalen laundries as a collective, so that there is simply no way of matching certain statistical findings or personal testimony with either of the refuges under study here, namely,

---

76   'The majority of the small number of women who engaged with the Committee had been admitted to the Laundries either by a non-state route of referral or, most common of all, following time in an industrial school'; 53 former residents 'as members of representative and advocacy groups'; seven former residents who 'did so directly in their own right as individuals', and a further 58 women currently resident in nursing homes under the care of the religious congregations. McAleese report, Introduction, paras 7, 18, 23.

77   McAleese report, part 1, ch. 3, para. 7.

78   Ibid., part 1, ch. 4, paras 13–16.

High Park and Sean MacDermott Street, or indeed with any other institution. The protection of sensitive personal data was paramount and rightly so, and special legislation was passed to permit full disclosure to the committee. The committee also decided that 'with regard to broader principles of privacy and confidentiality' no woman who was admitted to any of the laundries would be named or otherwise identified by the report, regardless of whether she was living or deceased.[79] The formal, individual names were used whenever the report refers to that particular institution, but the term 'magdalen laundries' was used when referring collectively to the ten institutions, and statistical analysis was based on one massive database of residents created from all extant records covering all ten institutions.[80] The McAleese inquiry was set up 'to establish the facts of State involvement with the Magdalen Laundries' and the OLC story is subsumed into this. The McAleese report is crucial to this study but not exactly in the particular, detailed way that one might expect.

## Autonomy, the Role of Caen and the Good Shepherd Congregation

The structure and internal government of the Sisters of Our Lady of Charity in Ireland needs to be grasped at the outset as it affected every aspect of its mission, lies behind the making of its records and their archival arrangement, and has influenced the design of this book. In brief, each house was autonomous, that is, self-governing with control over its own finances and property, record-making and preservation, recruitment of members, election of superiors, deployment of personnel and everything about its work. Each new monastery was founded by sisters sent from another house (in the case of the first monastery of Dublin, the 1853 founding sisters were from Paris and Rennes) but either immediately or shortly after the foundation, the parent house held no authority whatsoever. Its role in the foundation would always be honoured but it had no further responsibility and the links between the houses would be spiritual rather than practical. The completeness of the cut-off is nicely illustrated in what was called the second monastery of Dublin, Gloucester Street which, though founded from High Park in 1887, was completely autonomous from the outset, the only real link for many years being an agreement brokered by the archbishop that the nuns from Gloucester Street, a confined city-centre complex, might be buried in the nuns' burial ground in High Park.[81] The third monastery of Dublin, Kilmacud 1944, was founded directly from High Park. The Grange, 1956, was founded with sisters jointly from High Park and Sean MacDermott Street; it sought and achieved autonomy (within the federation) in 1969. The federation of the monasteries in Ireland in 1948, though it imposed a mother general with rights of visitation and the responsibility (with her council) of appointing the local superior, as well as establishing a common novitiate at High Park, did not otherwise impinge on their independence each of the

---

79   'Data protection and confidentiality', McAleese report, part 1, ch. 4, paras 47–57.
80   McAleese report, part 1, ch. 1, para. 14.
81   Memo, 'Document in reference to the sepulture of the sisters from our monastery of Gloucester Street'. 11 June 1901 (DARGS, OLC1/2/2 no. 10).

other.[82] It was only in 1969 with the setting up of the apostolate committee as a communications mechanism that there was any real interchange across the federation.[83] The replacement of autonomy-within-federation by more centralised and democratic structures for what was at all times in Ireland numerically a very small religious institute, post-dates this study, with the Irish houses becoming a province when they joined the Union of Our Lady of Charity in 1995.

What held these autonomous houses together was the adherence to a common constitution and common rule as handed on by the founder John Eudes. In addition, the 'old cradle' of Caen exercised the role of guardian of the tradition; it set itself up as a working model of how the wishes of the founder might be lived out and the place where the early customs and practices were most perfectly preserved. It became a touchstone against which all houses might measure themselves. The autonomy of individual OLC monasteries must be set against the enormous moral authority wielded by Caen right up to June 1944. The institute's rule, constitutions, customs and practices, and the spiritual heritage of John Eudes, are explored in this study, and Caen is ever-present, at least until the original quayside premises was levelled in the bombardment of 1944. Chevilly, its successor in terms of leadership in the post-war reconstruction of the OLC network in France, would never carry the same weight.

The autonomy of OLC houses gave the local bishop a greater role (and greater trouble) than he had with convents under a strong, central authority, such as the Good Shepherd sisters, the Religious Sisters of Charity or the Holy Faith Sisters. The ambitions of bishops for their own diocese could also be at odds with the plans and self-understanding of local monasteries. In the case of Our Lady of Charity of Refuge in Dublin, the influence of successive archbishops is noted in this study, for example, with Archbishop Byrne overruling the sisters' decision to join in a loose type of union with their French houses in 1932. The heaviest shadow by far is cast by the long-reigning and extraordinarily active Archbishop John Charles McQuaid (1940–72). It was Dr McQuaid who effected, with great speed, an Irish federation of the three monasteries (High Park, Sean MacDermott Street, St Anne's, Kilmacud) in 1948 to thwart moves towards amalgamation of the Dublin houses with others overseas. He was founder of the third (Kilmacud) and fourth (The Grange) monasteries and, while he did not have a free hand in what they undertook or how they ran it – the constitutions were the sisters' principal protection – he certainly tried to exercise authority over their affairs.

When the OLC house at Angers, under Soeur Marie Euphrasie Pelletier, was granted permission by Rome to establish a generalate or central government in 1835, it marked the start of a new congregation, Notre Dame de Charité du Bon Pasteur d'Angers or the Good Shepherd sisters. Though this new congregation had little to do with the arrival in Dublin of the OLC sisters in 1853, it needs to be mentioned as in the course of this research I found it to be ever-present in the background. The fear of being overtaken by a far more

82   Declaration signed by J.C. McQuaid, 3 Nov. 1951, relating to decree of the Sacred Congregation of Religious, 28 June 1948 (DARGS, OLC1/5/1 no. 20).
83   'Report on the work of the Apostolate Committee, appointed August 1969', 1972 (DARGS, OLC5/5/7 no. 1).

dynamic institute (in terms of new foundations and numbers) was soundly based in that several OLC houses did shift allegiance to the generalate of Angers over the timespan of this study (as discussed in chapter 7). There was no denying that Rome favoured centralised government, which the Good Shepherd epitomised. However, every threat to OLC autonomy was met with an increasingly trenchant attachment to the 'primitive observance' and the most 'faithful', and narrow, interpretation of the institute's rule of life. Caen and Paris/Chevilly, the French houses with which Dublin had the closest historic ties, were implacably opposed to any sort of centralised government that might undermine the traditional autonomy of the houses, making for an ever more political and (to my mind) senseless campaign. The recent 'reunification by merger' can be seen as a final resolution of this division. By happy coincidence, I was present in Angers working in the archives on 28 June 2014 when the liturgy to mark this historic union took place and can testify to the excellent relations that were in evidence on that occasion.

## Terminology and Language

There are numerous difficulties with language and terminology in this study which need to be addressed along the lines of what is envisaged by Scott in the assessing of documentary sources.[84] The language employed in the internal documents of Our Lady of Charity is generally invested with religious and moral weight and, while I have tried to maintain a professional, critical distance from the sources, it is simply not possible to write history without employing some at least of the language and concepts used at the time. The reader needs to be alert to this challenge, and to bring his or her own judgement to bear on the records used in what is an academic study, and on the language and tone in which they are written. An election letter will communicate the strong points of the new superior and note the merits of her predecessor; a jubilee booklet will burnish the achievements of the institute, an account of a school play will make much of the talents of the young actors and the rapt attention of the audience; these are not necessarily false or biased in the literal sense but the reader needs to be alert to the type of source upon which the narrative is based at any particular point and the audience that the record-creator had in mind.

There are particular problems with translation, while there are shifts in meaning over time. What is now rightly taken as offensive may not have caused offence at the time and vice versa. The 'disposal' of children was the legalistic term used by the state departments responsible for reformatory and industrial schools where something like 'destination on leaving school' would be employed today. What is now termed 'special needs' or 'learning needs' is a field that is especially difficult to deal with, with 'mentally deficient', 'subnormal' and 'retarded' just some of the many now-derogatory terms in common use across the period of this study. The term 'sexual immorality' is another contentious concept and is employed in numerous instances where 'sexual abuse' would be more correctly used today. The shocking term 'depraved' was used of children, as well as of adults. There is always

84   Scott, *A matter of record*, pp 30–1.

the question of context; language is culturally embedded, institutionally and socially, and where there is no understanding of the culture, the language – even if in the vernacular – may be misread. In any closely-knit organisation, terms and phrases are used that have a resonance that may not be picked up by the outsider; where a distance of decades and even centuries intervenes, there is an increasing likelihood that this will be lost. What might be termed 'insider jargon' is one problem; another is inconsistency in use and spelling so that one is not sure if the same thing is meant again in the same way. A few examples might underscore the challenges that were inherent in this re-search, while the issue is also dealt with in the chapters as the problem arises.

Across the records of Notre Dame de Charité du Refuge, there is the use of French terms in English and English terms in French; the culture of the organ-isation, with its shared constitutions and customs, meant that not everything was – or needed to be – translated. A literal translation may not at all convey the meaning that term carried to those who used it. A devotion that was *sensible* car-ried great feeling or emotion, such as undertaking the Way of the Cross or plac-ing oneself imaginatively before the newborn Jesus of Bethlehem ready to ren-der him some spiritual service. The common English understanding of foyer, a waiting area in an office block or hotel, does not do justice to the French term *le foyer*, the hearth of the home, a warm and welcoming place where one shares with family and close friends. The OLC 'foyer project' in Dublin carried this latter meaning which was probably lost on anyone outside the order. Similarly the term *surveillant(e)* does not carry as negative a force in French, where it gen-erally means supervisor, superintendent, guardian, caretaker, the person who watches over or looks after; the schoolmaster on duty is termed the *surveillant* while the term *surveillante de salle* is employed for a ward sister or head nurse.[85] The term 'a relaxed monastery' was one of real contempt; a 'regular' monas-tery, that is, one which followed *le règle* to the letter, was truly edifying. *Tourière*, meaning outdoor or extern sister, is used as if *tourière* was a common and uni-versally understood English term, as are many other inhouse or archaic terms such as clothing, *la prise d'habit* or reception of the religious habit.

Misreadings are possible with Latin terms used in English, and even more so when the Latin term comes to English via French. Capitulants, as every-body knew, were the delegates at a chapter with voting rights. The term 'cell' refers to the bedroom of an individual sister; the same term, *leurs cellules*, is used in reference to the women retiring to their bedrooms after night prayers.[86] The term 'penitent' itself is particularly problematic; taken as part of the spir-itual culture of the 19th-century Catholic Church, it was the term used for all who sought to break with their past and embark on a new life of virtue. Thus every person who frequented the Sacrament of Penance (confession) was a penitent, and as all Catholics were obliged to do so at least once yearly, and exhorted to do so more frequently, there are countless sermons addressed to

---

85  *Concise Oxford French-English dictionary* (Oxford, 1974); *Dictionnaire Cambridge Klett Concise* (Cambridge, 2002); F.E.A. Gasc, *A concise dictionary of the French and English languages* (London, 1892).

86  'Règlement pour les filles et femmes pénitentes', *Oeuvres complètes de Bienheureux Jean Eudes*, x (Vannes, 1909), chapitre I, de leur réception, p. 176. The term *dortoir*, dormitory, is also used.

penitents and on the subject of penitence, and innumerable pious tracts with the term in the title which have nothing to do with magdalen asylums *per se*, as any search of the contemporary literature will reveal. In the use of the term 'penitent', the emphasis was not on the past sinfulness of the person but on his or her 'firm purpose of amendment', on the making of the new man, or indeed the new woman, who has been forgiven and is starting out afresh. The use of the term 'penitent' therefore in the 19th and early 20th-century records needs to be considered within the larger and more general discourse around sinfulness and penitence, which were by no means reserved to the class of women most usually associated with magdalen asylums. And well into the 1960s, the Catholic Church did not tire of warning its members of all grades and stations of their inherent sinfulness and their need for penitence.

The terms *'enfants'* and 'children', in relation both to sisters (whether novices or professed) and to women residents, were widely used within the congregation of Our Lady of Charity over much of the time period covered by this study, and feature repeatedly in direct quotations. Soeur Marie de St Stanislas Brunel, the superior of the Paris house from which the first sisters were recruited for Dublin, solicited help for these 'children' about to travel so far away from her.[87] While use of that term in relation to adults would rightly cause outrage today inside or outside religious life, the term did not carry the same weight of offence in the pre-Vatican II era with its culture of obedience, patriarchy and spiritual motherhood. For a novice to be judged 'docile and submissive' augured well for her future in the convent, but it meant she was teachable and willing, not merely (one would hope) a doormat. The term 'girls' was used in general conversation and correspondence in OLC into the 1950s without too much regard for the age of the women concerned.[88] It is not likely at the time that women in their late teens, twenties or even thirties took grave offence at this, while the term 'our older girls' probably did not unduly upset the ladies concerned either, but this is merely presumption and the issue of language is not really addressed in OLC until the 1960s.

Allowance needs to made for the style of address and the vocabulary employed in some records, modelled as they were on traditional forms brought from France and composed for specific ends. The *circulaires* were produced, as the title suggests, to be read aloud in the other houses, to inform the sisters of the graces received and the sufferings endured since the date of the previous circular letter that the spiritual ties that bound the houses might be strengthened and all encouraged in their common vocation. The overwrought language that characterises the circular letters is surpassed only in the obituaries of both women residents and sisters, where much is made of the holy dispositions of the person at the point of departure to edify the reader and cause him or her to reflect on his or her own impending death.[89] The text of a sermon or lecture delivered before a live audience for fundraising purposes, where hyperbole may well be used for dramatic effect, can

---

87  Soeur M. de St Stanislas Brunel, Paris, to Mgr l'Archevêque de Dublin, 31 Aug. 1853 (DDA, Cullen, 325/8 nuns no. 208).
88  This was the position in other refuges also, see McAleese report, part 1, ch. 1, para. 8.
89  See, for example, High Park, draft circular letter, 6 Jan. 1878, pp 9–13 (DARGS, OLC1/3/1/ no. 12).

seem wildly exaggerated when published; nor did the sisters themselves have the power to restrain an overly zealous preacher once he got into the pulpit or, even worse, when he undertook to deliver a radio appeal.[90]

Personal names have given rise to difficulties throughout this study. The form of the name to use, the spelling to adopt and whether or not to abbreviate the name are not easily decided. The French form of the founder's name, Jean Eudes, is frequently found in English-language documents but for the sake of consistency the English form, John Eudes, is used except when quoting directly. All sisters of Our Lady of Charity (whether of the Refuge or of Angers) had their family names and then their religious names, with both French and English versions used interchangeably in the early years. Thus the founding superior in Dublin was Mère Marie de Coeur de Jésus Kelly or Mother Mary of the Sacred Heart Kelly (Evelina Marie) referred to by lay people and in outside correspondence simply as Mrs Kelly; her successor was Soeur Marie des S.S. Cinq Plaies O'Callaghan/Sister Mary of the Five Wounds O'Callaghan (Mrs O'Callaghan) and the first novice admitted to profession in Dublin was Soeur Marie de Coeur de Marie Tobin/Sister Mary of the Heart of Mary Tobin. For legal purposes, it was always the family name that was used: 'to Mrs Mary Tobin, superioress for the time being at High Park Convent'.[91] The title 'Mother' was substituted for 'Sister' on election as superior but was still used by the community when she was no longer in office as a term of honour (though she would sign herself Sister, to add to the confusion). Soeur Marie de St Ambroise Desaunais, Caen, also used the English spelling Ambrose, and she was not the only person to have more than one signature. The name of the Good Shepherd foundress, Soeur Marie de Ste Euphrasie Pelletier, is spelt Euphrasia in English; similarly the name of one of her successors, Soeur Marie de Ste Domitille Arose is spelt Domitilla in English but in these and many other cases, there is no consistency of use in the records. The use of surnames only for second and subsequent references in the same section, as is usual in academic writing, cannot be adopted where, for example, there are four O'Callaghan sisters involved in the story (and there are very many instances of siblings in this study). And as the sisters did not use their surnames in their usual daily exchanges among themselves and were rarely known by their surname alone (unlike, for example, their male contemporaries), it would be odd to refer in writing to Tobin or Goss or Staunton (unless the full name has already been used in the same paragraph). No claim to consistency is made for this writing. In most places the full version of the English form of the name is used except where the woman is French and/or that is the form of the name used in the document then under discussion.

The register entries for the women residents in the refuges or asylums also pose problems as every woman will have more than one name, at least. First, there is her own family name, then the house name assigned on

---

90   For an example of an overwrought appeal, see text delivered by R. J. Tyndall, SJ on 10 Jan. 1937, Gardiner Street church, 'Victims of the slums, moving appeal for penitents', *Irish Catholic*, 21 Jan. 1937. The first radio appeal appears to date from 1938 on behalf of Gloucester Street and is in the same style (DARGS, OLC2/2/2).

91   Grant of right of burial in Prospect Cemetery, no. 12627, issued 6 Jan. 1878 (DARGS, OLC1/8/2 no. 19).

admission and by which she was known during her stay, to afford anonymity. Some of the women left and re-entered several times and so had several house names. In addition, a small percentage of the women opted to stay as 'consecrates' and took what was a religious or consecrate name, for example, Julia Byrne entered aged 40 years 13 October 1914, given name Cyril; entered again 5 June 1918, given name Rachel; consecrate name 'Magdalen of St John', died 22 November 1927.[92] Surnames also create problems, as some women used first their single and then their married names, while others appeared in the register first under their married names and subsequently gave their single names. The way in which databases have been constructed from the registers of entry is discussed as it arises in the text, but for the most part the house names of the women and girls are used, as they afforded anonymity at the time – and continue to do so. The full family names of women or girls who entered any of the homes post-1911 are not used, in accordance with data protection legislation and for ethical reasons (to honour the commitment to absolute confidentiality given to each woman at the time of her entrance); 1911 is taken as the cut-off date due to the publication online of the census of that year while it also gives a full 'closure period' of 100 years.[93] Similarly, post-1911 photographs in which women residents, teenagers or children might be identifiable are used only when previously published, as in jubilee or centenary booklets or in the newspapers.

The placename that causes most difficulty in this study is Gloucester Street North or Lower/Sean MacDermott Street Lower.[94] The second OLC monastery of Dublin, founded 1887 from High Park, was the Mercy convent and magdalen asylum at Gloucester Street in the north inner city, which was itself the successor to the Mecklenburgh Street lay asylum, which backed onto Gloucester Street and became incorporated into it. The placename 'Gloucester Street' (without reference to 'Lower') was still used in OLC circulars and other records long after the city corporation renamed the street in 1933 (after one of the signatories to the 1916 Proclamation of Independence). As all property leases were in the name 'Gloucester Street' this is understandable from a legal perspective, but there was also force of habit and (it appears) widespread continued popular use of the old, familiar name. Both names were used for the same street in the 1930s, 1940s and 1950s. The entry in Thom's street directory for these decades reads 'Sean MacDermott Street Lower (formerly Lower Gloucester Street)'. Only in the 1960s does 'Lower Sean MacDermott Street' or simply 'Sean MacDermott Street' become the standard form of the street name used in OLC circles. 'Gloucester Street' is therefore employed in this study, qualified when necessary with the name 'Sean MacDermott Street' until the 1960s, when only the later name is used. The elements 'North' or 'Lower' are not generally used in this study except

92  Register of penitents, St Mary's Asylum, High Park (DARGS, OLC1/8/2 no. 6). Hereafter, Register, St Mary's.
93  An exception is made of the case of Julia Byrne for the purposes of illustrating this point, and because her date of death is more than 80 years ago.
94  Spelling of Sean MacDermott Street confirmed on www.logainm.ie. This is also the spelling in *Thom's directory* and in most official documents but the variants 'Sean McDermott Street' and 'Sean MacDermot Street' are also to be found.

when they occur as part of a quotation or help to situate a particular plot or premises geographically. One further placename that may give rise to confusion is Whitehall, the correct address of St Joseph's school adjoining the convent of High Park, Drumcondra. In this study, 'Whitehall' is used from 1927 when St Joseph's is certified as an industrial school and the Department of Education uses this official address only, in both Irish and English forms.

Whether to use the popular understanding or the canon law interpretation of ecclesiastical terms is another issue that had to be resolved. As Margaret MacCurtain explains, the terms 'nun' and 'sister' are widely employed interchangeably despite their distinct meanings in canon law.[95] The French term *religieuse* never really took hold in its English form in Ireland at least. Strictly speaking, as the Religious of Our Lady of Charity did not have papal or full enclosure and did not make solemn vows, they were sisters not nuns and their institute was a religious congregation, not a religious order.[96] This at least was Rome's early 20th-century ruling in which religious women taking simple perpetual (not solemn) vows and without papal enclosure were recognised as 'real' religious and their apostolic activity as a legitimate exercise of a convent's mission (*Conditae a Christo*, 1900), points which were further developed in the document titled *Perpensis* (1902), and confirmed in the revised code of canon law promulgated in 1917.[97] In an effort to allay concern around the status of the vows taken by the Sisters of Our Lady of Charity, the Eudist priest Gabriel Mallet in 1911 explained that the vows taken by the founding mothers in 1666 and approved by Alexander VII were indeed 'solemn vows' but this category was suppressed in the early 1800s by Pius VII for all French monasteries. The 'simple perpetual' vows which replaced them were no different in meaning or status, except that they did not carry the exterior sign of papal enclosure.[98] Despite this clarification, the sisters of Our Lady of Charity, the Presentation sisters and numerous other members of 'active orders' with simple vows continued to be referred to by clergy and laity alike as nuns. In media coverage, they were practically always nuns, not sisters. The term *religieuse*, which features strongly in the documents held in Rome, in the early records of the Dublin houses and in correspondence from Caen and other French houses, is translated here by the term 'sister'. 'Sisters' is used most often in this narrative, but there are occasions when 'nuns' is used, as that was the term employed in the document or debate under discussion at that point. As both terms were used interchangeably, even by the sisters themselves, it would be straining a point to make an absolute ruling. A decision had also to be made on whether to use the term 'order', which was used by the sisters right up to Vatican II; it is used throughout this study in its general, popular sense, as it was employed by the sisters themselves and as it was used by the general public. The term 'enclosure' also gives rise to difficulties, as the sisters did not have 'strict enclosure' in the canonical sense, which is confined to religious

95   MacCurtain, 'Godly burden', p. 310.
96   Caen, *circulaire*, 1 avril 1911, refers to the terms 'simple perpetual' and 'solemn' vows, and the implications these have for enclosure (DARGS, OLC1/2/3 no. 7).
97   Louise O'Reilly, *The impact of Vatican II on women religious: case study of the Union of Irish Presentation Sisters* (Newcastle Upon Tyne, 2013), pp 15–16.
98   Gabriel Mallet, à la très Révérende Mère Supérieure du Vénérable Monastère de Notre Dame de Charité de Caen, Rome, avril 1911, copie (DDA, Walsh papers, EV6).

who take solemn (not perpetual) vows. What matters for this historical study is that, as far as the sisters understood their rule and the prescriptions of the 1917 revised code of canon law, any breach of the enclosure – such as admission to hospital or study at college – required a special written permission from the archbishop, or his deputy in these matters, the vicar for religious, and was most carefully recorded in the register of profession.[99] Well into the 1960s, exit beyond the cloister was only for the most exceptional reasons and most of the sisters had never crossed outside since the day they had professed their vows. That the sisters used only the term 'monastery' for houses of the order, not the more usual term 'convent', reflects this self-conscious sense of being a community set apart from 'the world' by the rule of enclosure. The term 'monastery' is employed most usually in this study as reflecting this self-understanding and to avoid confusion, as this is the term found in practically all the source materials. However, it is acknowledged that a strong case could be made for its replacement in the discourse by 'convent' and that is certainly the more appropriate term when the reforms of Vatican II take hold.

Another layer of difficulty arises from the replacement in the public discourse (since the 1990s) of the terms 'magdalen refuge' and 'magdalen asylum' with the generic term 'magdalen laundry', a shift that has now probably been made permanent by its use in the title of the interdepartmental committee to establish the facts of state involvement in these institutions and throughout the resulting report. The OLC sisters who ran refuges in Dublin take offence at the term 'laundries' as at no time did they run laundries but rather refuges (or asylums), homes and hostels for women, nor did the women ever 'live' in the laundries which were always quite separate from the residential quarters, a point which others also made and which is taken up in the McAleese report.[100] One instance only of the term 'magdalen laundry' has been found in the course of research in the OLC records and that is on a rubber stamp used in the laundry at Gloucester Street on an unknown but early date bearing those words. Another rubber stamp, probably from the 1950s, carries the text 'Gloucester Laundry and O.L.C. Home'.[101] Laundries were simply the means of generating an income adopted by practically all 19th-century charitable enterprises in Ireland trying to help women or girls. They were not particular to magdalen refuges, though these were the institutes that relied on them the longest.[102] The laundry business was already in place in each of the two asylums the sisters came to manage, while washing was the principal means of livelihood for hundreds – and perhaps thousands – of women in the city.[103] Women's

99   High Park register of profession; sisters resident outside the monastery (date, name, reason, return) pp 151–5 (DARGS, OLC1/6/1 no. 1).

100  'Terminology', McAleese report, part 1, ch. 1, paras 5, 6.

101  Laundry stamps (DARGS, OLC2/12/1 no. 1).

102  Jacinta Prunty, *Dublin slums, a study in urban geography* (Dublin, 1998), p. 267; McAleese report, Introduction, para. 18.

103  The occupations with significant numbers of women in Dublin, 1841 were: boot and shoemakers 1,408; washerwomen 1,529; dealers (unspecified) 1,756; servants (domestic) 18,274. Semptresses, dressmakers, milliners, staymakers, hatters, bonnetmakers, hatmakers and glovers (numbers combined) 8,661. Census of Ireland for the year 1841, City of Dublin, vi, 'Table of Occupations of persons above and under 15 years', General report, p. 23.

charities invariably fell back on laundry work, as did individual poor women too; had some other enterprise been capable of generating a regular weekly income, no doubt that would have been adopted instead, but the women at the time, laywomen or sisters, did not see other openings in Dublin.

The term *le refuge* is used in the French tradition on which the Dublin monasteries are based. The first monastery of Caen on maps of the 1700s is simply labelled *'Le Refuge'* and the sisters were generally known as Notre Dame de Charité du Refuge, that is, the Religious of Our Lady of Charity who followed the tradition of Caen, to distinguish them from Notre Dame de Charité du Bon Pasteur d'Angers, the Religious of the Good Shepherd under the Angers generalate. However, 'asylum' was the term in general use throughout Britain and Ireland. The title 'St Mary's Asylum' had been given by Fr Smith to his Drumcondra Road institution long before the sisters arrived to take charge, and that is the term that travels to High Park where it is used in correspondence and advertising well into the 1880s and intermittently afterwards. 'Magdalene Asylum' labels the premises on the 1838 six-inch Ordnance Survey map that was to form the core of the extensive Gloucester Street/Sean MacDermott Street complex. The term 'refuge' has always had positive connotations, implying safety, respite and care. The term 'asylum' had similarly positive connotations in the 19th century, as in orphan asylum, blind asylum, widows' asylum, asylum harbour.[104] It was applied in particular to proper facilities for the mentally ill to convey a place of safety and refuge, where specialised care and humane treatment would prevail, as opposed to the punishment of prison, the harshness of the workhouse or the notorious cruelty of the private and profitable 'madhouses'.[105] As a shorthand for 'lunatic asylum' it became associated in Ireland with the county or district facilities for patients with mental illness, overtaking the wider and more general understandings. Both 'refuge' and 'asylum' are found throughout the sources for this study; the term 'refuge' is generally preferred in the writing, as historically the more accurate term and the one used most often within the order itself, considering that these homes or shelters were modelled, albeit at many removes, on *le refuge* of Caen. However, where contemporary fundraising literature and correspondence refers to the 'asylum' – the title carried from Drumcondra Road to High Park in 1857, and already in place when a small group of OLC sisters took charge of Gloucester Street in 1887 – then that term is employed in the discussion, as it would make no sense to do otherwise. Both terms should be considered as interchangeable in the text which follows and the concepts of safety and shelter which they embodied when first employed in 19th-century Dublin kept in mind.

The issue of terminology was a sensitive one for the McAleese inquiry which had to contend with the sensationalist language of popular commentary, as well as archaic and offensive historic terminology, and everything in between. Moreover, there were four separate religious congregations involved, each with its own 'inhouse' language, operating ten 'laundries' in

104  'Asylum', *The Oxford companion to the mind*, ed. Richard L. Gregory (Oxford, 1987).
105  *Report from the select committee appointed to inquire into the expediency of making provision for the relief of the lunatic poor in Ireland*, 1817, H.C. 1817 (430) viii.

different circumstances and in different parts of the country, most of which had been inherited from a lay body to start with and so carried with them the terminology of their foundation and early years. The chronological span of McAleese's study, from 1922 to 1996, made for an additional layer of complexity, as terms that were in widespread use across different types of institutions, such as 'inmate', were replaced in time by more respectful terms. The inter-departmental committee chaired by Dr McAleese sought 'to avoid language which might in any way label, stigmatise or demonise those concerned', while it was also determined 'to avoid any terminology which might prejudge its findings or suggest a bias in any particular direction'. After extensive consultation with former residents. some of whom objected strongly to the use of labels such as 'victim' or 'survivor', the committee decided to keep to the non-emotive and factually accurate term, 'women admitted to the Magdalene Laundries' and 'the women of the Magdalene Laundries' as required by the context.[106] Similarly, the McAleese report steers clear of emotive terms such as 'incarceration', 'torture' and 'slavery', all of which have been widely and unquestioningly used in public discourse and indeed in some academic writing. Keeping to the evidence it gathered, and to the fair analysis of that evidence, its findings are all the more compelling by being expressed in careful and unambiguous language. In my use of language in this study, I have tried to follow the practice employed by Dr McAleese, 'to avoid distress to any party and to avoid labelling those women against their wishes'.[107]

## Notre Dame de Charité, Historical Records and the Writing of History

In this history of the Sisters of Our Lady of Charity in Ireland, I have drawn on the full range of records produced by the institute, including records self-consciously made for the writing up of its own internal history. These are annals, obituaries and *circulaires*, created in accordance with established patterns and using standard formulae, and extensively mined for the compilation of promotional house, jubilee and centenary histories. An appreciation of the spiritual as well as practical purposes for which these classes of records were created is necessary, as is the institute's understanding of history which is as much theological as chronological and narrative.

Annals in Notre Dame de Charité were to trace in the events of history the wondrous working out of God's providence. Just as the order itself, at Caen, had been founded against all odds, where a 'hidden and wonderful providence, in spite of all the efforts of hell, at a time when all seemed ruined, and against all human probability',[108] the troubled monastery of Dublin was 'destined from all Eternity by the Providence of our Celestial Father' to be

---

106 'This terminology is not intended to obscure historically used terms, to convey a sense of voluntary residence to all cases, or indeed to convey any particular meaning other than to identify in a respectful way the women to whom this Report refers.' McAleese report, part 1, ch. 1, para. 10.

107 Ibid., part 1, ch. 1, para. 10.

108 'Souhaits particuliers', *Oeuvres complètes de Bienheureux Jean Eudes*, x (Vannes, 1909), p. 76.

the 17th house of the institute.[109] Obituaries or 'virtuous lives' of sisters and women residents were composed and copied out to honour the memory of the dead and to edify the living with particular emphasis placed on the holy dispositions of the dear departed at the time of her death and the many spiritual comforts that were extended to her. As with the annals, the obituary was intended to demonstrate how God was active in that person's life, through storms and tears, working out her salvation right up to the ultimate encounter with him that is death and eternal life. Models of this type of writing were to hand, with other monasteries providing Dublin with suitable examples.[110] There are few problems with the factual content of the obituaries – parentage, dates of reception and profession, offices held, and final illness – but the genre of writing must be understood by the historian and corroboration of, for example, the virtues listed, sought in other records, insofar as that is possible.

Notifying other houses of the death of a sister, to ensure that she received the suffrages or prayers she was entitled to, and following this up with an obituary or 'death letter', collectively called '*Les fleurs de Notre Dame de Charité*', was one part of a rather formal correspondence between autonomous houses best expressed in the circular letters. The *circulaire* tradition dates from the foundation by John Eudes who wrote frequently and with fervour on the unity and bonds of charity he wished to be found among the sisters.[111] The novice mistress was to tell the novice news of other houses, 'in order to enlarge her sympathies and stir up their zeal and affection for everything that concerns our Sisters'.[112] Though heavily stylised, the community circulars are important historical records. All letters were headed with the aspiration, '*Vive Jésus et Marie*' and opened with a pious wish or appropriate line from sacred scripture. The salutation, opening spiritual reflection and offering of respect to the recipients followed an expected pattern.[113] The concluding assurances of affection and spiritual unity were similarly formulaic though no less sincere. In between, the circular letter carries, as per instructions, 'an account of the spiritual and temporal state of the house', the superior's two fields of responsibility. Religious highlights of the year (feast-days, processions, preached retreats) are dealt with, followed by an account of professions, jubilees, illnesses and deaths among the sisters, before turning to the mission of the house, the refuge, where a similar pattern is followed (religious high-

109    'Donations and bequests received from the foundation of this convent in the year 1853' (DARGS, OLC1/9/4 no. 2).
110    For example, 'Abrégée de la vie et des vertus de notre très honorée Mère Marie de la Ste Trinité Heurteaut, décédée en notre Monastère de Vannes, le 25 février 1709'. Note at end, 'copié en février 1857 pour notre M[onastè]re de Dublin' (DARGS, OLC1/7/3 no. 5).
111    Constitution XL, de la directrice, p. 147.
112    Explanation of the rules, constitutions and customs of the Religious of Our Lady of Charity, taken from the replies of the Blessed Mother de Chantal, and from the Venerable John Eudes, founder of this congregation, collected by the first Religious of the Order and the original revised by the superiors and deputies who assisted at the general council held at our monastery of Caen in the year 1734'. Transl. of 1734 edn (DARGS, OLC1/5/1 no. 1). Explanation of constitution XXXIX, p. 286.
113    *Customs and usages of the Congregation of Our Lady of Charity, order of St Augustine, with the formulary of the clothing and the profession of the religious*, text of 1738 edn, trans. Peter Lewis (Aberdeen, 1888), article XXII, Style of letter-writing, pp 241–3.

lights, retreats, jubilees of the 'consecrates', and obituaries of the women), an update on the laundry and other means of generating an income, the life or progress of the 'class' (which was invariably positive or gave grounds for hope) and an account of building projects completed or in hand. A figure for the total household was always given, broken down into professed sisters and novices of each class (choir sisters, *converses* or lay sisters, and *tourières* or outdoor sisters), penitents, boarders (*pensionnaires*) and schoolchildren, and finally the chaplain and various workmen (vanman, gardener, carpenter, engineer, errand boy).[114] The earliest surviving *circulaire* from Gloucester Street is handwritten and in French. Once the sisters here resort to print (1892), far more content can be carried, following the example set by High Park and Caen, but without departing from the traditional formula.[115] The circular letters and annals are inter-related in that one provided material for the other, and the moral obligation to produce a lengthy, informative missive at no more than three-year intervals ensured that the writing-up of the annals was not neglected for too long.[116] In both circular letters and annals, the factual content – places, dates, names, events – causes few problems where they are produced, as the term suggests, during or at the end of the year to which they relate. Where they are copies, summaries, extracts or translations – all of which feature in the Dublin monasteries of OLC as well as original circular letters and annals – things are a little more problematic, while the lapse of years before annals are continued introduces difficulties. In this research, drafts of circular letters, where they have been retained, are preferred over the final version as more frank in style and fuller in content; this is the case regardless of whether the draft was composed in French or in English. Letters, minutes and accounts are generally preferred over annals, especially where there is a conflict of dates but, in some cases, there is no source other than the annals. Obituaries of the sisters and of the women residents feature in both the annals and the circular letters and there are also accounts of the jubilee celebrations of both, but in neither class of record is there full coverage. To convey a sense of how God had been active in the community – against a timeline that stretched to eternity – neither annals nor circular letters needed to be comprehensive and complete, nor was it intended that they be treated as such. House histories which are derived large from the annals need to be recognised for what they are and the genre of historical writing that they continue.

## Summary of the Structure of this Study

Chapters 1–3 track the introduction of the Sisters of Our Lady of Charity to Dublin and the trials undergone while trying to identify what made this first monastery a distinctive addition to the diocese and city. The particular Eudist tradition of *le refuge* is examined *vis à vis* the established British and

---

114 Acknowledgement is made of notes by Delphine Le Crom, titled 'La correspondance entre les monastères', 27 août 2010.
115 Les soeurs de la communauté de Notre D. de Charité de Dublin, 104 Gloucester Street, to Très honorées et chères Sœurs, 24 avril 1890 (NDC Caen, Archives Versailles).
116 The missing Gloucester Street annals may be reconstructed, in part at least, through the circular letters, copies of which have been provided by NDC Caen to DARGS.

Irish 'magdalen rescue and reform' movement. Why the sisters chose to participate in the state system of reformatory schools, with the certification of St Joseph's at High Park in 1858, is the key question posed in chapter 4. The re-classification of St Joseph's as an industrial school in 1927 is dealt with in chapter 5, as is the Children Act of 1908 (and later amendments) under which all certified schools operated.

Attention is then directed to the establishment of the second monastery of Dublin, in Gloucester Street (Sean MacDermott Street) in 1887, formerly under the Mercy sisters and earlier still a small, lay-run asylum. The physical reconstruction is only the most visible aspect of the takeover – the extension of the standard OLC regime, with its particular devotions, work and recreations are tracked across both monastery and asylum. The presence of former prisoners and women on probation among its general intake is examined. The house jubilee of 1937 allows for an assessment of its first 50 years, with the analysis brought up to *c.*1949.

The focus then moves to upheavals internationally which impinged on the monasteries in Ireland and the fears that were entertained across the order of a forced union with the effectively-organised and more numerous Good Shepherd sisters. Landmark events are the beatification of the founder John Eudes in 1909 and his canonisation in 1925. Chapter 7 concludes the international debate with the decision by John Charles McQuaid to impose a federation on the Irish houses.

Chapters 8–10 inclusive deal with the 'new' approaches to the welfare of children and teenagers in residential care undertaken by the sisters in the post-war era. The third OLC monastery in the diocese, St Anne's, Kilmacud, opened in 1944, in many ways exemplified this willingness to innovate, despite its reformatory school label. The development of hostels and teenage units 1950–72 attached to all three monasteries (High Park, Sean MacDermott Street, St Anne's, Kilmacud) are then disentangled and the principles on which they tried to operate, despite many constraints and contradictions, are set out. The opening of the fourth monastery of the order, The Grange, Kill of the Grange, in 1956, first dealing with older teenage girls but very quickly embracing the philosophy of 'family group homes' for both boys and girls, including toddlers, is treated in its own right. Chapters 11 to 13 trace the incremental changes that gathered pace following federation in 1948 and need to be read as a unit. The modernisation of the asylums attached to the two larger monasteries of High Park and Sean MacDermott Street, starting in the 1950s, are dealt with in turn. Overlapping and underpinning these changes was the fundamental remaking of religious life and the self-conscious realignment of ministries brought about by the Second Vatican Council and given momentum by profound social change in the 1960s and 1970s. The engagement of the Sisters of Our Lady of Charity in Ireland with the conciliar teaching is the subject of the final chapter. In the conclusion some key findings are sketched out, insofar as that has been judged feasible across what is a wide-ranging and lengthy study. A fuller interpretation, based on greater engagement with other published studies and a broader range of sources, will be the work of a successor.

# Chapter 1

## 'Notre Monastère de Dublin': Founders, Friends and Vicissitudes, 1853–57

In 1853 a group of four professed sisters and one novice arrived to take charge of a small magdalen asylum in Drumcondra, Dublin.[1] Their journey had taken several days – from Paris via Norhoust and on to London, then by train to Holyhead where they took the ferry to Dublin, arriving at cockcrow on 4 September.[2] They were brought to the Presentation convent in George's Hill, in the north inner city, where they changed from their secular travelling clothes into their religious habits, heard Mass and were given breakfast by their kindly hostesses, some of whom had a few words of French.[3] At 4pm, their sponsor, Fr John Smith, who had travelled with them from Paris, arrived with two carriages to take them on the last stage of the journey.[4] The vehicles drew up outside a small nondescript two-storey house (*une médiocre maison bourgeoise*) and their hearts sank; none could hold back the tears. Fr Smith pointed out the unfurnished room they were to use as a dormitory, then showed the tiny garden, and finally in the chapel, he gave benediction and the sisters responded with *laudate* and *alleluia* – though, as the first annalist recorded, the chanting was far from tuneful.[5] The sisters were then introduced to the 40 or so women residents of the house who had gathered to greet them; some were delighted with their arrival, others not so. The three *matrones* in charge were openly hostile; the names of Miss Nolan and Miss Moore are recorded in the annals.[6] The women, *les pénitentes*, had prepared them a supper of mutton and boiled turnip. Fr Smith withdrew to his own house next door, keeping to his bed

---

1 'Annals of this monastery of Our Lady of Charity of Refuge, at High Park, Drumcondra, Dublin, since the arrival of the Religious the 27th September 1853'. The 'first book' concludes with the transfer to High Park in 1858. Volume one ('books first and second') covers 1853–10 Mar. 1939 and volume two ('continuing book the second') 14 June 1939–25 Sept. 1974 (DARGS, OLC1/5/3 nos. 5 & 6). Hereafter, Annals.
2 High Park, draft *circulaire*, 15 novembre 1853 (DARGS, OLC1/3/1 no. 1).
3 Another version states that they stopped first at a vestment and book depository held by Fr Smith where they changed into their habits before proceeding to the Presentation convent. This was probably 23 Essex Quay. 'Abridgement of the life and the virtues of our dear Mother Mary of the Sacred Heart Kelly, deceased in this Convent of Our Lady of Charity, High Park, Dublin, 29 June 1863', typescript, p. 8 (DARGS, OLC1/6/4 no. 64). Hereafter, Abridged life of Mother M. Sacred Heart Kelly.
4 Paul Cullen to Madame la Supérieure, [Paris], 20 d'août 1853 (DARGS, OLC1/1/1 no. 7).
5 High Park, draft *circulaire*, 15 novembre 1853.
6 The annals say two matrons but the contemporary *circulaire* says three; Annals 1853, p. 27; 1854, p. 65.

for several days to recover from a severe fall he had suffered in London. The earliest account of the foundation describes this moment as the beginning of many crosses, when the sisters, *exilées de leur Patrie*, found themselves shunned as strangers, begging their daily bread from the women in charge, forbidden to do anything at all, even to ring the bells to announce the office.[7] The delay in having the formal installation, what would be recorded as the foundation day, until 14 September, the feast of the Holy Cross, was read by the new arrivals as a portent of things to come.[8]

The work for which Fr John Smith (or Smyth) of the parish of St Michael's and St John's, Lower Exchange Street, had secured the services of the sisters had been defined in crystal-clear terms in the exchange of letters that preceded their arrival. Soeur Marie de St Stanislas Brunel, superior of Saint Michel, the Paris house of Notre Dame de Charité du Refuge, spelled out for the benefit of the archbishop of Dublin her understanding of the venture. After the usual courtesies, she outlines the plan, using the language of the *coutumier* or customs book: the sisters in Dublin will, in conformity with their institute, receive 'voluntary penitents', will say and chant the Divine Office, and will live according to the rules, regulations and customs of the monastery of Caen.[9] The same formula is used by the archbishop of Paris, Monsignor Sibour, a few weeks later when he names the five sisters who are to travel to Dublin.[10] The founder was providing a furnished house 'sufficiently commodious to make a beginning', with gardens and the necessary enclosure, and guaranteeing all costs 'until Providence shall have provided the religious with means of subsistence from other sources'.[11] The apostolic purpose of the project is underlined again and again, with the sisters setting out to labour for 'the conquest of souls' and the glory of God,[12] 'the object of the institute being to receive female penitents'.[13] The model of religious life they will follow, in all respects, is that of Caen. But where they now find themselves falls far short of what they had been led to expect.

## The Heritage of St John Eudes and the Role of Caen

The founding story of Notre Dame de Charité – preserved in the letters of the founder, St John Eudes (1601–80), retold in early biographies and histories, and kept alive through countless sermons and the oral tradition – was very much an active understanding among the sisters travelling to Dublin. The 'penitents' were to be an integral part of the household, the reason for which the institute was founded; they were given a rule of life which closely

7   High Park, draft *circulaire*, 15 novembre 1853.
8   Ibid.
9   Soeur M. de St Stanislas Brunel, Paris, to Mgr l'Archevêque de Dublin, 9 July 1853 (DDA, Cullen, 325/8 nuns, no. 208).
10   Auguste Sibour, Archevêque de Paris, to La supérieure et les religieuses de Notre Dame de Charité du Refuge établis à Paris, 27 juillet 1853 (DDA, Cullen, 325/1 foreign bishops, no. 149).
11   Article II, Foundations, *Customs and usages of the Congregation of Our Lady of Charity, order of St Augustine, with the formulary of the clothing and the profession of the religious*, iii, p. 165, text of 1738, trans. Peter Lewis (Aberdeen, 1888) (DARGS, OLC1/5/1 no. 12). Hereafter, *Customs and usages*.
12   Soeur M. de St Stanislas Brunel, Paris, to Mgr l'Archevêque de Dublin, 31 Aug. 1853 (DDA, Cullen, 325/8 nuns, no. 211).
13   Standard questionnaire on religious houses in Dublin diocese, 20 Sept. 1854 (DARGS, OLC1/1/1 no. 12). Hereafter, Standard questionnaire.

mirrored that of the sisters, was underwritten by the same spirituality and shot through with the same regard for the common life, the virtue of obedience and the centrality of prayer. Agreeing to take over an existing refuge that had been described to them as a place where poor women sheltered from misery and from sin might do penance and serve God, was indeed in the spirit of Notre Dame de Charité but, not unreasonably, the sisters expected to be in charge.[14] The terms 'voluntary' and 'refuge' were significant; the monastery was to be a safe place to which women would be admitted at their own request, and for whatever length of time was necessary, be it overnight, longer or for their remaining years.

Founded in 1641 in Caen, Normandy, by John Eudes (beatified 1909, canonised 1925) the first monastery developed after several unsuccessful attempts by Eudes at providing for women involved in prostitution whom he encountered in the course of giving parish missions in this neglected region. Moved by the preaching of the missioners and determined to make a new start in life, they were, however, trapped by their poverty and shunned by respectable society. They urgently needed a refuge or home in which they might be lodged and supported in their resolve. Several charitable lay women, most notably Madeleine Lamy, from about 1634 agreed to take a number of these distressed women into their homes where they would teach them how to work and pray, and help them to re-enter society.[15] With a steady stream of this class of women looking for the chance to turn their lives around, it was Madeleine Lamy, according to the first biographer of Eudes, who challenged what she saw as the hypocrisy of the missioners: going off to spend hours on their knees in the church, it would suit them better to establish a house for these poor souls who were lost because they did not have material means.[16] This precipitated the opening by Eudes of a house for 'repentant' women, to which, to give them sisterly support, 'good' women would also withdraw. Several houses for women in this type of need had already been founded in France with which Eudes must have been familiar.[17] After some experimentation with lay management and in rented premises, John Eudes managed to engage the services of the Visitation sisters, most significantly the capable and devoted Mère Françoise Marguerite Patin, to train the first generation of OLC novices, while he also adapted the Visitation rule of life to the purposes of his new institute.[18] But notwithstanding these borrowings, what was developed by Eudes was distinctive as well as enduring: a refuge for repentant women under the care of a religious order created expressly for the purpose, the whole enterprise to be driven by a spirituality that centred on the compassionate heart of Jesus. He is represented in the iconography of the institutes he founded holding either a crucifix or a heart in one hand, symbols of the love of Jesus for sinners, and in the other a scroll representing the rules he bequeathed to the Congregation of Jesus and Mary (priests) and to Notre Dame de Charité (sisters) (figure 1.1).

14   High Park, draft *circulaire*, 15 novembre 1853.
15   Paul Milcent, *Un artisan du renouveau Chrétien au XVII^e siècle, Saint Jean Eudes* (Paris, 1985), p. 55.
16   Ibid., p. 103.
17   Ibid., pp 166–7.
18   Françoise Marguerite Patin spent, in all, 20 years as novice mistress and superior in Caen where she died in 1668, Milcent, *Un artisan du renouveau Chrétien au XVII^e siècle*, pp 172, 176, 292–3.

**Figure 1.1** St John Eudes giving the constitutions to the first sister of Our Lady of Charity of Refuge. *Order of Our Lady of Charity of Refuge, spirit, aim and work* (Dublin, 1954), p. 9.

The immediate circumstances of 1640s Normandy dictated the cloistered character of the first house, its autonomous status and the type of care it offered to destitute women. All women religious were bound strictly by rules of enclosure. The 'English ladies' of Mary Ward who dared to 'wander about freely not restricted by the laws of enclosure and under the guise of helping souls' were suppressed by papal edict in 1631.[19] The Visitation sisters, founded in 1610 by St Jane de Chantal and St Francis de Sales as a new form of religious life among the needy outside the cloister walls, were forced to become enclosed.[20] Autonomy under the bishop of the diocese was the sole model of government allowed to women religious; the centralised system of, for example, the Jesuit order or the Congregation of Jesus and Mary (Eudist fathers), where the houses give obedience to a superior general under direct papal jurisdiction, was judged unsuitable for mere women, who needed a male figure at the helm. The Daughters of Charity of St Vincent de Paul, founded in 1633, avoided the restraint of enclosure by constructing themselves as a lay community without solemn or perpetual vows taken in public.[21] Their success as an institute hinged on avoiding the label of 'nuns', while having the superior general of the Congregation of the Mission

---

19   Mary Wright, *Mary Ward's institute: the struggle for identity* (Sydney, 1997), p. 29.
20   Ibid., p. 2.
21   *Règles des Filles de la Charité, servants des pauvres maladies*, Paris, 5 Aug. 1672; translated as *Common rules of the Daughters of Charity*, trans. approved Paris, 14 May 1892, ch. 1, no. 2 (DC archives, Irish Province).

(Vincentians) at the head protected them from being reduced to a diocesan body subject entirely to the bishop.

John Eudes established a single monastery in Caen in 1641; before his death in 1680 Caen had assisted a house in Rennes that became the second monastery of the order. By 1683, it in turn had sponsored three more houses. The pattern of new foundations was simple enough: each was founded with sisters sent from one or more parent houses and quickly, if not immediately, achieved autonomy. While its historic role in the foundation was ever to be cherished, the parent house had no authority whatsoever over its 'daughter'. By the outbreak of the French Revolution in 1789, there were seven autonomous OLC monasteries, mostly in north-west France (figure 1.2). The sisters were expelled from Caen on 19 August 1792 and, in common with countless other communities, could not know what to expect next. The re-founding that followed the Revolution, starting with the legal recognition of the Paris house in 1807 and of the other OLC houses in 1811, resulted in a wave of expansion throughout France, although some of the earlier houses failed to re-open in the same place. By 1853, when the Dublin monastery opened, sponsored by Paris and Rennes, there were 16 houses in France. The first foundation outside France was that of Dublin, but was quickly followed by the first North American house, at Buffalo 1855 (from Rennes), and new foundations in Italy, Spain, England and Canada.

Over all houses, Caen held a particular place of honour as the cradle of the congregation, *le vieux berceau*. As the superior of the Paris monastery made clear when sponsoring the new Dublin foundation, Caen was for all, *le dépôt de la Règle*, the repository of wisdom and tradition, the monastery which models how the rule is to be lived and to whom all the houses have recourse in their doubts and difficulties.[22] Some weeks before the sisters named for Dublin (from Rennes and Paris) undertook the long journey overseas, they spent time in Caen imbibing its spirit and taking instruction. Sister Mary of the Sacred Heart (Eveline Mary Kelly) who was to lead the pioneer group was well employed 'in examining and considering all the manuscripts and the different points of the rule and observance, treasuring in her mind and memory all that might be useful to her foundation'.[23] The basis for the considerable moral authority of Caen is set out in the customs book, which records the founder's desire for 'the closest union of charity, a complete conformity and a constant intercommunion' between the first monastery of Caen and all the other houses. On the sisters of Caen was placed the responsibility of zealously preserving its traditions 'without change or innovation' so that the other houses might find 'everything pertaining to their institute practised therein in all its pristine vigour and perfection'. As Caen was founded and organised by John Eudes himself, it was to be the model or template for all OLC monasteries, 'the chief depository of the spirit and of the meaning of the rules and of the statutes'. Should the other houses need advice they were to ask Caen which would reply in a spirit of humility and charity; in addition, the other houses were to make known to Caen 'all the blessings they have received'. Conformity to the practice of Caen and continued communication with it were the principal means by which unity was maintained among far-flung autonomous houses. The houses were also

22   Soeur M. de St Stanislas Brunel to Cullen, 9 July 1853.
23   Annals, 1853, p. 15.

**Figure 1.2** Our Lady of Charity of Refuge, house foundations
1641–1891

| France | | |
|---|---|---|
| Caen | 1641 | |
| Rennes | 1673 | from Caen |
| Hennebont | 1676 | from Rennes, to 1687 |
| Guingamp | 1676 | from Rennes, to 1792 |
| Vannes | 1683 | from Rennes, to 1792 |
| Tours | 1714 | from Guingamp |
| La Rochelle | 1715 | from Vannes |
| Paris (rue St Jacques) | 1724 | from Guingamp; transferred to Chevilly 1907 |
| Saint-Brieuc | 1783 | from Guingamp |
| Versailles | 1804 | from Paris |
| Nantes | 1809 | from Paris |
| Lyon | 1811 | from Paris; to Good Shepherd 1935 |
| Valence | 1819 | from Paris; to Good Shepherd 1935 |
| Toulouse | 1822 | from Caen |
| **Angers** | 1829 | from Tours; **Good Shepherd motherhouse 1835** |
| Le Mans | 1833 | founded by Good Shepherd Angers |
| Blois | 1836 | from Tours |
| Montauban | 1836 | from Caen |
| Marseilles 1st monastery | 1838 | from Tours; to Good Shepherd 1935 |
| Besançon | 1839 | from Tours |
| Valognes | 1868 | from Caen; to Good Shepherd 1935 |
| Marseilles 2nd monastery, Le Cabot | 1864 | from Marseilles 1st monastery; to Good Shepherd 1935 |

**Figure 1.2** Our Lady of Charity of Refuge, house foundations
1641–1891 (*Continued*)

| Ireland | | |
|---|---|---|
| Dublin 1st monastery High Park | 1853 | from Paris |
| Dublin 2nd monastery Gloucester Street/ Sean MacDermott Street | 1887 | from High Park |
| **North America: United States** | | |
| Buffalo, 1st monastery | 1855 | from Rennes |
| Allegheny | 1872 | from Buffalo |
| Green Bay | 1882 | from Toronto |
| **North America: Canada** | | |
| Ottawa | 1866 | from Buffalo; to Good Shepherd 1938 |
| Toronto | 1875 | from Ottawa |
| New Westminster | 1890 | from Ottawa |
| **Italy** | | |
| Loreto | 1856 | from Le Mans |
| **Spain** | | |
| Bilbao | 1857 | from Toulouse |
| **England** | | |
| Bartestree | 1863 | from Caen |
| Waterlooville | 1885 | from Bartestree; re-established 1900 from High Park |
| **Austria** | | |
| Salzburg | 1888 | from Caen; to Good Shepherd 1934 |

Compiled from Joseph-Marie Ory, *Les origines de Notre-dame de Charité ou son histoire depuis sa fondation jusqu'à la Révolution* (Abbeville, 1891), pp 60–8; 'Liste des Monastères de l'Ordre de Notre Dame de Charité, dates de fondation et adresses'; 'État actuel des Monastères de l'Ordre de Notre-Dame de Charité, 1909' (CIVSCVA B79/2).

instructed to address themselves in their needs to the other houses, 'with great candour and affection', in case of real necessity asking for 'some talented and useful sister of another monastery', admonishing where decline or laxity was known to have set in, the well-off houses ready to offer modest financial assistance to houses in dire need, 'everywhere a holy and universal charity'. Above all, the houses were to promptly offer spiritual succour to each other, to pray for their sisters in time of trial, to remember the recently-deceased and to intercede for their intentions, which depended to large degree on the faithful discharge of the duty to correspond with the other houses once or twice a year.[24]

This 'union of charity', a network of autonomous houses but with strong bonds of affection and sharing a common spiritual heritage, was especially significant in the foundation of the *petite colonie* of Dublin. The means through which the ties were strengthened were long established: triennial *circulaires* to all the houses covering the spiritual and temporal life of the house (including the affairs of the refuge); letters announcing elections of superiors and conveying Christmas greetings; death letters (claiming the suffrages of all the houses for the dear departed); and special appeals for funds, prayers or other support. In terms of personnel, individual monasteries offered hospitality on the rare but memorable visits of sisters from other houses; sisters were 'lent' to other houses in cases of urgent need; novices could be sent to be 'properly' trained elsewhere before return; and promising applicants could be directed to other houses of the order which were in greater need of postulants. Individual sisters and especially superiors exchanged personal letters and, whenever the opportunity of travel arose, they knew they were welcome to avail of the hospitality of as many monasteries en route as could conceivably be fitted in. Many favours were reciprocated, with a 'daughter house' feeling specially bound to assist its 'mother house' in times of crisis. The level of interaction and mutuality varied between houses and over time, but means of communication and practical examples of support were already well established when the Dublin foundation was proposed. About eight weeks after arriving in Dublin, the first lengthy *circulaire* was prepared for all the houses in France, drawing on their compassion, interest and affection for the poor exiles in Dublin and cementing the union between all the members of *'notre sainte et vénérable institution'*.[25] The flow of gifts of all sorts – embroidered altar falls and a processional cross from Paris, 30 pairs of *sabots* and a relic of St Victoire from Rennes – shows this network of affection and support in action; the impact on morale can well be imagined.[26]

## Notre Dame de Charité du Bon Pasteur d'Angers

The sisters of the new foundation in Dublin were under no doubt as to where on the Eudist tree they might be placed: all could be traced back to the old trunk of Caen. But an added complication had arisen from the creation of a second branch of Notre-dame de Charité, this time giving allegiance to Angers,

24   Article V, Union between the monasteries, *Customs and usages*, iii, p. 173.
25   High Park, draft *circulaire*, 15 novembre 1853.
26   'Livre V, registre des fondateurs et bienfaiteurs du Monastère de Notre Dame de Charité de Dublin, établie le 14 Septembre 1853', pp 2–4 (DARGS, OLC1/9/4 no. 1). Hereafter, Register of benefactors.

and far better known internationally. Faithful adherence to the rule composed by John Eudes and the founding sisters coupled with a desire for a new style of centralised government, namely a generalate directly under Rome, led to the *scission* of 1835 when the OLC house at Angers, under Soeur Marie Euphrasie Pelletier (venerable 1868, beatified 1933, canonised 1940), became the mother house of a new congregation, Notre Dame de Charité du Bon Pasteur d'Angers. Its creation was greeted with outright hostility by a number of the 'old' houses, namely, Tours, Nantes and Caen ('let us pray for them ... they believe that we deceived them'); the other OLC houses, according to a well-placed source, 'have no candidates and remain quiet'.[27] The politics behind the break are well known: the monastery of Tours received an appeal from the Bishop of Angers, Charles Montault, to open a refuge in his town; the desire of the superior, Euphrasie Pelletier, to accede to the request was opposed by the Tours community but eventually, in 1829, the undoubtedly gifted young sister was allowed to undertake an exploratory visit.[28] This led to the opening of a new house on 31 July 1829, named 'Good Shepherd' in memory of a previous but long defunct establishment with that patronym. Caught between the two communities of Tours and Angers, in 1831 Pelletier was elected superior of the new house and was able to devote herself wholeheartedly to its development, supported by wealthy local patrons. Almost immediately, sisters were sent from Angers to open refuges elsewhere, with houses in Le Mans, Poitiers, Grenoble and Metz all in operation by August 1834 in response to the requests of their respective bishops. But appeals to other OLC houses to release professed sisters to help out were repeatedly refused.[29] With first-hand experience of the impossibility of extending the mission of the order by relying solely on the charity of autonomous houses, Pelletier decided that a new type of government which would unite all the houses was required. In this, she was supported by Count de Neuville, the major patron of the Angers refuge.[30]

Zeal for the extension of the mission of Our Lady of Charity is given in all the early documentation as the overriding reason for the innovation of a generalate. The small group in Grenoble petitioned in 1834 for a *bref* that would allow the establishment of houses under Angers; their house was making 'great progress' but needed further help from its parent, while Angers was besieged with requests for new foundations. The desire to extend overseas is stated explicitly, with the sisters wishing to divide between them the four corners of the world in the manner of a new Francis Xavier or Ignatius Loyola, that the greatest possible number of souls might be won for Christ.[31] Euphrasie Pelletier's unflagging missionary zeal is communicated

27 The informant was a sister of whom it was reported she 'suffered much' on her transfer from Nantes to Angers, 'they even took off her chemise, her silver heart, her habit, her shoes', refusing to allow her to leave in the habit of the order. A fourth house identified as M. was also 'dead set' against Angers; this may be Montauban. M. Euphrasie Pelletier to Sister M. of St John of the Cross David, Nancy, 8 Aug 1836, *Letters, Mary Euphrasia Pelletier*, trans. (Angers, 1996), ii, 343, pp 303–4, hereafter, Letters.
28 P.A. Pinas, *Venerable Père Eudes and his works 1601–1901*, trans. (Edinburgh, 1903), pp 220–2.
29 See reports and comments from M. Euphrasie Pelletier 1825–34, Letters, i.
30 Noreen O'Shea, *Brief sketch of the life of Mary Euphrasia* (Waterford, n.d.), pp 11–12.
31 Soeur M. St Louise Royne, St Robert près Grenoble, à Mgr, le Cardinal Odellcalchi [Odescalchi], 9 octobre 1834 (CIVCSVA, A.7–1 (1), no. 23).

in letters to sisters she has already sent out from Angers, as in the correspondence with the German-born Sister Mary of St John of the Cross David who was to lead the community in Munich:

> Found, my daughter, found, spread the work, the time has come, follow the lights that God gives you, and which I see clearly. Let us pray that the ancient houses and our enemies will finally recognise this work.[32]

The arguments in favour of a generalate which Euphrasie Pelletier made in the 1830s were to be rehearsed in OLC circles exactly a century later (Chapter 7). The common novitiate was to strengthen the bond of unity by ensuring that the same spirit would permeate all the communities, 'enabling the needs of all to be met more effectively'. A central 'higher authority' would constitute 'a means of continuity and strength for the institute' and would facilitate its development and extension. The appointment, rather than election, of superiors, 'wisely undertaken so as to prevent abuse and provide due safeguards and assurances for their charges', was to ensure 'continuity to valuable projects' and 'stability to new foundations'.[33] The concept of a *mère maison* was central to this vision, a place from which virtuous, well-trained and zealous young sisters drawn from all nationalities and language groups could be sent to any part of the world.[34]

The approval of Pope Gregory XVI came surprisingly quickly, in January 1835, thanks largely to the interest taken in the Angers project by its promoter in Rome, Cardinal Odescalchi and despite the opposition of at least 13 bishops.[35] Following on the granting of the decree, the number of vocations increased greatly and requests for new foundations multiplied, all of which was taken by Pelletier as evidence that the new arrangement was indeed the will of God. Foundations would multiply even more rapidly after 1855 when the congregation was divided into provinces, by which date there were Good Shepherd houses as far away as Mysore (India), North and South America, Algiers and Cairo, Glasgow and Limerick and across most of Europe.[36] Pelletier would continue at the helm for 33 years, overseeing

---

32   M. Euphrasie Pelletier to Sister M. of St John of the Cross David, Nancy, 7 Dec. 1836, Letters, ii, 361, pp 336–8.

33   Sister M. of St Euphrasia Pelletier (superior), Sister M. of St Philip Neri Mercier (councillor), Sister M. of St John of the Cross David (councillor), Sister M. of the Good Shepherd Potherie (councillor), Sister M. Chantal of Jesus, Vve [widow] de la Roche (assistant), approved and signatures certified by Charles Montault, Bishop of Angers, to Gregory XVI, Rome, 30 Dec. 1834, Letters, i, 195, pp 429–31.

34   Pinas, *Venerable Père Eudes and his works 1601–1901*, pp 220–2.

35   Paul Milcent, 'Notre-Dame de Charité, relations entre maisons', unpublished typescript, Nov. 1998, p. 11 (NDC Caen). According to Euphrasie Pelletier, Cardinal Odescalchi, who from Apr. 1835 was to act as cardinal-protector of the new congregation, 'drew the attention of the Pope to the relentlessness with which the bishops of France pursued the new institute, and the number of contradictions and calumnies in their letters', M. Euphrasie Pelletier to Sister M. of St Louis Royne, Grenoble, 3 May 1835, Letters, ii, 237, pp 102–3.

36   Superior general and the sisters of the council to the Sisters of the communities of the Good Shepherd, 15 Oct. 1855, Letters, vii, 1492, pp 358–9.

110 foundations with *c*.3,000 religious, divided into 16 provinces, at her death on 24 April 1868.[37]

At the time of the Dublin OLC foundation (from Paris), the rift made by Angers was a live issue, not least because the first question any outsider posed was whether or not the new arrivals were Good Shepherd sisters.[38] No-one could deny that the two institutes had the same rule, the same founder and undertook the same work with the same end in view, described as 'the salvation of souls'. The instrument setting up the generalate at Angers had 'fixed and decreed' that the new congregation 'will observe the rules established by Father Eudes and approved by the Holy See'.[39] Referring to the transfer of a young OLC Nantes sister to Angers, Euphrasie Pelletier herself had noted, 'There is nothing to fear. The Rule here is of such vigour, that all the institute could come here'.[40] The judgement that the observance of the founding rule had been in no way diminished by the new governance structures was important to the identity of the new institute, which continued to hold fast to this belief. So, too, was the fact that Rome allowed the new institute into the future 'all the privileges and graces accorded by the Holy See to the monasteries called Refuge' that there might be nothing second-rank about it.[41] Most obvious of all to outsiders, both institutes had the same white habit; only the cincture or cord worn under the scapular was different – white for OLC, blue for Good Shepherd – and the emblem, with a figure of the Good Shepherd engraved onto the silver heart that all OLC sisters had worn since the order's foundation.[42] It is no surprise that the visitor Fanny Taylor described the nuns of High Park as Sisters of the Good Shepherd in her 1867 review of Irish convents, though she at least was sufficiently well informed to be able to explain that there are two distinct branches of this French order in Ireland, 'differing only in their form of government'. High Park sisters 'are independent of any other house, receive and train their own novices, and are entirely under the bishop of the diocese'.[43] Seeing Good Shepherd as the founding institute and others as independent houses of the same institute was a common misconception and made more intractable by appearing in print.

But the problem with Angers was more than just a matter of confusion in the public mind. The permission granted by Rome in 1835 could be construed as an open invitation to any OLC sister or house which wished for the advantages of a generalate to give obedience to Angers. A few individual sisters did transfer to Angers, and the language used by Pelletier about an early arrival does give grounds for believing that she did harbour hopes for a single congregation incorporating all OLC houses: 'This sister is sincere and, we believe, begins the

37 O'Shea, *Brief sketch of the life of Mary Euphrasia*, p. 15.
38 Lady Tichborne, Tichborne Park, Alresford, Hants, to Mrs O'Callaghan, High Park, 24 June 1862 (DARGS, OLC1/1/1 no. 17).
39 Decree approved by Gregory XVI on 16 Jan. 1835, reprinted in Letters, ii, pp 13–15.
40 M. Euphrasie Pelletier to Sister M. of St Stanislaus Bedouet, Poitiers, 17 July 1836, Letters, ii, 336, pp 293–4.
41 Decree approved 16 Jan. 1835.
42 Ibid.
43 Fanny Taylor, *Irish homes and Irish hearts* (London, 1867), pp 88, 91.

accomplishment of God's designs'.[44] Three of the four houses founded before 1835 from Angers – namely, Poitiers, Grenoble and Metz – asked to give allegiance to their mother house; Le Mans stayed outside, having voted to become an autonomous house in the tradition of OLC shortly after its foundation.[45] From the outset there were instances of Good Shepherd communities taking over works that OLC communities could not manage, though more usually Good Shepherd expanded by taking on existing lay refuges or similar ventures when requested. A refuge at Lille was taken over in 1836 at the request of the elderly founder who joined the community and was appointed assistant;[46] the foundation at Limerick in 1848 would follow the same general pattern.[47]

That Mère Pelletier wished to open a house of the Good Shepherd in the city of Dublin is evident from her initial reaction to the news that the Sisters of Our Lady of Charity in Paris had already been asked, and had agreed. A much-desired but precarious new Good Shepherd foundation in London was, in March 1841, 'without a house, without friends, abandoned by all', and

> To crown our misfortunes, St Michael's in Paris has been asked to open a house in Dublin. They have accepted and it is really our fault. Fiat! This news will cause a lot of harm![48]

A passing reference to a request by a Sulpician father in Paris for a Good Shepherd house in Dublin, in July 1842, may refer to the same project or to an entirely new venture but, whichever the case, nothing happened on the ground.[49] In October 1842, Mother Euphrasie Pelletier set out on the first of two journeys to visit the sisters in Hammersmith, London, writing en route to 'To the cherished little Mother, foundress of Dublin', a project which she would soon learn, in person, was not among the immediate plans of the local superior and community and certainly not among those of their bishop, the redoubtable Cardinal Wiseman. At the same time there were multiple demands closer to home, with a Bishop Regnier of Angoulême, who was to be visited en route to London, pressing for a house in his diocese:

> ... but I carry in my heart the divine work of Dublin. Having considered everything I think the latter equals a hundred houses in Angoulême ... I dearly love my cherished daughters

44    Pelletier to Bedouet, 17 July 1836.
45    Introduction to correspondence, Apr. 1833–30 Dec. 1834, Letters, i, pp 93–5.
46    M. Euphrasie Pelletier to Sister M. of St Sophie Lavoye, Metz, 2 Sept. 1836, Letters, ii, 346, pp 308–9.
47    Madame Reddeau [Reddan] is named as founder of this house for penitents. There were 50 women in residence at the time that the house was organised along Good Shepherd lines, with three sisters sent from London to assist the newly-professed Madame Reddan. Fondation du Monastère de Limerick (Irlande), 18 fèvrier 1848 (BP archives, HC–444b, Irlande, Limerick).
48    M. Euphrasie Pelletier to Sister M. of St John of the Cross David, Munich, 21 Mar. 1841, Letters, iv, 713, p. 261.
49    Same to Sister M. of St Joseph Regaudiat, London, 18 July 1841, making reference to a letter dated 13 July 1841 from M. of St Louis Royne in Paris, Letters, v, 737, p. 17.

of London, who have fought together with us! This work of
your tears, my dear children, is becoming the joy of all Isra-
el! It is the sacred door, introducing us to Dublin. My God,
what a work, who could be insensitive to it! Our chapters, our
prayer, our communions, all are now focused on Dublin. Write
to me, my very dear daughter, as soon as you get to know
anything.[50]

That Pelletier did not give up easily on hopes for a Dublin house is evident
from a formal letter to Rome dated November 1842. At the time, the local
bishop of Angers was attempting to exert authority over the fledgling institute well beyond what the constitutions allowed and what was acceptable
in civil law overseas, causing the foundress endless worry.[51] To strengthen
their case for protection against a bishop accused of being Gallican rather than Roman, the superior general and council claimed that their own
attachment to and dependence on Rome made them, Good Shepherd
sisters, the preferred institute of all those devoted to the same end for
the work which they had not yet established in Ireland. And moreover,
the Irish bishops concurred in the view that a house of refuge ought to
be opened in the great city of Dublin to serve Ireland and even perhaps
England also.[52] Later in the same month, Pelletier looked forward to the
clothing ceremony of 20 postulants, 'among them 2 charming Irish girls,
who will one day be founding the magnificent establishment of Dublin'.[53]
Throughout 1843, continued reference is made to Dublin; with two more
Irish postulants received in Angers,[54] with a cryptic note about continuing negotiations and 'great hopes for an establishment in Dublin which is
preferable to the first'.[55] Multiple difficulties with the London foundation,
and the well-documented and very real danger of separation entirely from
Angers which persuaded Pelletier to undertake a second visit to London
in June 1844, are probably behind the closing down of the Dublin discussion from then onwards. The first Irish house of the Good Shepherd
was to be opened in Limerick in 1848, to be followed by houses in Waterford (1858), New Ross (1860), Belfast (1867) and Cork (1870). The failure to open a Good Shepherd house in Dublin had probably more to do
with timing than any lack of ambition on the part of Mère Pelletier as she

50   Same to same, London, Monday, before dawn! [28 Oct. 1842], Letters, v, 831, p. 130.
51   'My heart is weary from negotiating with Monseigneur of Angers! I know of nothing to
equal it. He has really plunged my understanding and my heart into utter darkness. This is the
sword [that wounds me] and certainly, my poor child, M. Robson [ecclesiastical superior of the
London house] is yours. I join you in your sufferings, you whom I tenderly love....' Pelletier to
Regaudiat [28 Oct. 1842].
52   Les religieuses du Conseil de la Maison Générale de la Congrégation de Notre Dame de
Charité du Bon Pasteur à Son Eminence le Cardinal Futrici, Vicaire de sa Sainteté, Protecteur
de la Congrégation du Bon Pasteur d'Angers, 11 novembre 1842 (CIVCSVA, A.7–1 (1) 23).
53   M. Euphrasie Pelletier to Sister M. of St John of the Cross David, Munich, 20 Nov. 1842,
Letters, vi, 843, p. 147.
54   Same to Sister M. of St Joseph Regaudiat, London, 6 Jan. 1843, Letters, vi, 855, p. 162.
55   Same to same, 12 Apr. 1843, Letters, vi, 869, p. 180.

juggled multiple overseas demands during the 1840s, as well as facing down powerful ecclesiastical opposition.[56]

The 'original' OLC monasteries increasingly used the suffix '*du Refuge*' to distinguish themselves from the 'breakaway' Good Shepherd sisters. Resentful of the public success of the younger institute, Notre Dame de Charité du Refuge placed great emphasis on its strict adherence to the 'primitive observance', and its status as the faithful carrier, through many vicissitudes, of the traditions established by John Eudes, including monastic autonomy. The ties of the new Dublin foundation were to Caen, to Paris and to Rennes, all pre-Revolution houses who, on being allowed to function once more were, not surprisingly, convinced that fidelity consisted in returning to what was done before. The commitment of the first monastery of Dublin would therefore be to the most faithful, exact – and narrow – interpretation of the rule of John Eudes. And there was no danger that the sisters would voluntarily enter into communication with the Good Shepherd sisters in Ireland or anywhere else, despite all they had in common, at least insofar as outsiders could judge.

## Fr Smith's Asylum and the Introduction of New Management

The magdalen asylum into which the five OLC sisters were dropped in the first week of September 1853 had been founded in 1829 in a rented house by the diocesan priest Fr John Smith.[57] In 1832, he had purchased, in his own name and with his own funds, a private house, 2 Drumcondra Road (west side), which he named 'St Mary's'.[58] Soon he was advertising that the women were under the careful instruction of Mercy sisters from Baggot Street, which probably meant a weekly visit by two nuns for moral instruction, prayers and catechism.[59] From 1839 or 1840 onwards, Smith was trying to recruit a religious order from continental Europe to live in and take charge of the asylum. There is a report in the convent annals that he sought to place it under the Good Shepherd but baulked at the requirement of Angers that half of each dowry would be forwarded to the mother house.[60] The insistence that property be registered in the name of the sisters, and thus belong to Angers, may well have been another obstacle to co-operation.[61] Smith then turned to the Sisters of Our Lady of Charity and was undoubtedly persistent in his demands. Eventually, on the feast of St Mary Magdalen, 22 July 1842, he sent four young women to Paris to be trained as Sisters of Our Lady of

---

56   See for example, 'Extrait d'une lettre de S. Em. Mgr. Le Cardinal de Bonald, archevêque de Lyon, en date du 31 janvier 1844' in which he calls for the deposition of Euphrasie Pelletier as superior general, adding that 'j'ai eu moi-même bien des discussions désagréables avec la Supérieure Générale qui est une tête forte exalté' (CIVCSVA, A.7–1 (1) 28).

57   'The Magdalene, a fragment, by a Catholic priest' (Patritius), *Catholic Penny Magazine*, 21:1 (12 July 1834), 237–40. While the text gives the founding date as 1831, a contemporary hand has corrected this to 1829 in the copy held at Beechlawn (DARGS, OLC1/1/1 no. 1).

58   High Park, draft *circulaire*, 15 novembre 1853; also named 2 Drumcondra Hill, *Freeman's Journal*, 17 Apr. 1838; Drumcondra Hill, *Dublin almanack* (Dublin, 1846).

59   *Freeman's Journal*, 5 May 1838.

60   Annals, preface to first volume, p. 6.

61   M. Euphrasie Pelletier to Sister M of St Louis Royne, Grenoble, 22 Dec 1834, Letters, i, 189, pp 416–7.

Charity.[62] These are named in the annals as Miss O'Callaghan, Miss Carroll and Miss O'Hara, the fourth being Jane O'Callaghan who died in 1849 in Rennes.[63] His plan was that they would return to Dublin after profession, equipped and willing to take charge of his asylum. In the meantime, he continued to advertise that the women were under the instruction of Mercy sisters from Baggot Street and supervised by a matron, Miss Nolan.[64] At all stages, he kept full personal control of the enterprise and the arrival of the OLC sisters was at his request.

The background negotiations to the foundation are easily disentangled. Approaches were made, repeatedly, by John Smith to 'Notre Dame de Charité, dit S. Michel', at rue St Jacques 193, Paris. Dr Murray, as archbishop of Dublin, opposed the project consistently but, on his death in February 1852, Smith immediately approached his successor, this time with better results.[65] A letter from Dr Cullen permitting the Dublin foundation arrived on the desk of the archbishop of Paris, Monseigneur Sibour, who was somewhat taken aback by the speed with which things were being forced through.[66] Not having sufficient sisters in Paris free to undertake the task, and under no obligation to send back Irish-born sisters who had made vows in her house, the Paris superior made application to Rennes, its founding house (via Guingamp), for reinforcements. With the approbation, eventually, of the bishop of Rennes two sisters were duly sent on to Paris in readiness for the day of departure.[67] Fr Smith personally carried some of the letters between Cullen and Sibour on his visits to and from Paris, and Cullen himself called to the Paris house in October 1853, a few weeks after the sisters' arrival in Dublin.[68] It is certain that Smith gave additional pledges in person and presented the Dublin project in a far more positive light than was fair or prudent.[69] The sisters named for the new foundation by Sibour in July 1853 were Soeur Marie du Coeur de Jésus Kelly, *irlandaise de naissance* (Paris) as superior, Soeur Marie de Saint Ignace Pavot (Rennes) as assistant, and also Soeurs Marie de St Stanislas Poterlet (Rennes), Marie de Ste Madeleine Gageary (Gagey or Gogin, Paris) lay sister, and Marie de St François Xavier O'Neill ('Armeille'), *novice irlandaise* (Paris).[70] The party therefore was made up of three choir sisters, one lay sister and one choir novice, with Paris sending three persons and Rennes

62 Margaret O'Callaghan, Paris, to Thomas O'Callaghan, 5 May 1844 (DARGS, OLC1/1/4 no. 2); Jane O'Callaghan, Versailles to Thomas O'Callaghan, 13 May 1845 (DARGS, OLC1/1/4 no. 3).
63 Annals, preface, pp 6–7.
64 *Freeman's Journal*, 5 May 1838; Advertisements, St Mary's Asylum Drumcondra Road, *Thom's Irish Almanac and Official Directory* (Dublin, 1847, 1850, 1852). Hereafter, *Thom's*.
65 Abridged life of Mother M. Sacred Heart Kelly, p. 5.
66 Auguste Sibour, Archevêque de Paris, to Monseigneur [Cullen], 15 juin 1853 (DARGS, OLC1/1/1/no. 3).
67 Evêque de Rennes to the Sisters going to Dublin, 22 July 1853 (DARGS, OLC1/1/1/ no. 6).
68 Sister Five Wounds O'Callaghan, Paris, to Thomas O'Callaghan, 17 Oct. 1853 (DARGS, OLC1/1/4 no. 33).
69 Cullen to Madame la Supérieure, 22 juillet 1853.
70 Sibour to Notre Dame de Charité du Refuge, 1853; High Park, draft *circulaire*, 15 novembre 1853.

two. This was the absolute minimum allowed for a new foundation, according to the customs book.[71] Three of the five spoke no English. None of the
first group were women sent by Fr Smith to France, to his great vexation.[72]

The very first postulant, Anastasia Mary (Maria) Finlay, aged 38 years,
was admitted with some fanfare on the foundation day, 14 September 1853,
the earliest report from Dublin declaring that she was sent from heaven
at the beginning of the troubles of the foundation to assist and advise the
superior, having an unrivalled knowledge of all the business of the asylum
and of the persons involved with it, including Fr Smith, and having long
desired to be a religious sister.[73] She had indeed worked closely over the
preceding 19 years with Smith in both paid and unpaid capacities, as cartress for the laundry, as co-worker and personal nurse, and for some time
had charge of the religious goods shop that he operated at 23 Essex Quay to
raise funds for the asylum.[74] It was at his insistence that she was admitted
as a choir postulant immediately the sisters arrived.[75] On her clothing, she
took the religious name Soeur M. du Coeur de Marie, a title drawn from
the devotional teaching of John Eudes and particularly appropriate in the
circumstances. Regrettably, far from being an asset to the community and
the first stone in the new edifice,[76] she was to be a menace, carrying false
testimony to outsiders both secular and religious, including to the Presentation Convent, George's Hill.[77] She was dismissed on the basis of having
dealt deceitfully and treacherously with the community, repeating private
conversations to Fr Smith and 'adding fuel to the fire of prejudice and animosity that consumed the old man'.[78] The register records her departure
with the note 'left not having a vocation for our order', but the first book of
the annals devotes lengthy sections to recounting the grief she caused the
community and the damage that could not be undone, with references also
in contemporary correspondence and obituaries.

The first novice to be admitted to profession of vows was Helen O'Callaghan (Sister Mary of St Joseph), the first of three siblings who were to
prove the mainstay of the fledgling community. But there were disappoint-
ments also. A succession of postulants came and went, which was not good
for the reputation of the convent, already trying to cope with being misrepresented by the matrons and by Fr Smith. One or two had little sense and
spoke of what went on in the convent to all and sundry but, even where
no mischief was intended, such stories 'passing from mouth to mouth (as
is always the case) were much exaggerated and were believed all the more
readily as they came from a source not to be doubted'.[79] One of the stories
doing the rounds was that 'when the penitents of St Mary's transgressed

71    Article II, Union between the monasteries, *Customs and usages*, iii, p. 166.
72    Abridged life of Mother M. Sacred Heart Kelly, p. 5.
73    High Park, draft *circulaire*, 15 novembre 1853.
74    See association of Miss Finley (*sic*) with the Depository, 24 Lower Exchange Street and
23 Essex Quay, *Dublin almanack* (Dublin, 1843), p. 337, *Thom's*, 1850, p. 659.
75    Annals, 1853, pp 30–1; 1854, p. 76.
76    High Park, draft *circulaire*, 15 novembre 1853.
77    Annals, 1854, p. 48.
78    Abridged life of Mother M. Sacred Heart Kelly, p. 8.
79    Annals, 1853, pp 40, 46; 1854, p. 68.

their rule, the manner of correction adopted by the religious was to throw knives at them'; though preposterous, once out in the public domain, there was no recalling it.[80] This was the very last thing a newly-arrived foreign order relying on public good will needed.

The mixture of Irish and French surnames gives some hint of the complicated going and coming that marked the early years of the foundation. Appeals were made by Mother Mary of the Sacred Heart Kelly, herself in poor health, to Paris, Rennes and Caen for further help, or at least, to replace those sisters that were returning to France for whatever reason. The Irish-born novice, Sister Mary of St Francis Xavier O'Neill, asked to make her vows for Paris so that she might have the right of return; she made her vows in Drumcondra Road on 23 May 1854 and was recalled to Paris the following year.[81] The sending of Soeur Marie des Cinq Plaies (Margaret) O'Callaghan from Paris in May 1855, one of Fr Smith's candidates but also a noviceship companion and loyal friend of the ill superior, Mother Sacred Heart Kelly, and a sister to the novice Helen O'Callaghan (Sister Mary of St Joseph), was to prove significant. She was accompanied by Sister Mary of St Anne Carroll, another protégée of Fr Smith, who stayed in Dublin for a year and five months, and by a young French choir sister, Soeur Marie de St Vincent de Paul Besançon, who was left in Dublin for two years.[82] Another early recruit was Mary Brennan (Sister Mary of St Stanislaus) for whom Mother Sacred Heart Kelly in 1855 arranged a one-year novitiate in Paris, 'in order that she might have the opportunity of being well-trained in religious observances', a formation which the struggling Dublin community could not yet provide.[83] Her sister was Mrs Sims who, with her husband, was to be ranked among the chief benefactors of the house. Another early recruit was Bridget Langan (Sister Mary of the Holy Angels), aged 22 years and a native of Westmeath who knew the O'Callaghans, having lived several years in their home. When she was admitted as a lay postulant she seemed to have all the qualities that were requisite, 'and the community never had any reason to regret their choice'.[84] From Caen, following heart-rending appeals, the highly capable former superior (*déposée*) Soeur Marie de St Jerome (Letitia Hanrahan) was dispatched in March 1857, along with a very young sister, Soeur Marie de St Ignace de Loyola (Clémentine Lemonnier), who returned shortly afterwards to Caen.[85]

80   Annals, 1854, p. 78.
81   Annals, 1853, p. 15; 1855, pp 86–8.
82   Soeur M. des Cinq Plaies O'Callaghan first made vows in Paris in 1847 and renewed vows in Dublin 21 Nov. 1855; Sister M. of St Anne Carroll first made vows in Paris 19 May 1845 and renewed vows in Dublin, 21 Nov. 1855 (once only). See 'Livre dans lequel les Soeurs de La Congrégation de Notre Dame de Charité ecrivent les ans et les jours de leur voeux et des annuelles confirmations qu'elles font en ce Monastère de Dublin, lequel a été établi le 14 de septembre de l'année 1853' (DARGS, OLC1/6/1 no. 1); see also annals, 1855, pp 85, 88; 1857, p. 90; 1858, p. 96.
83   Death letter, Sister M. of St Stanislaus Brennan (Mary), d. 22 July 1896 (DARGS, OLC1/4/4); annals, 1858, p. 97.
84   Annals, 1854, p. 69.
85   Letter of authorisation, signed Charles [Didiot], Archevêque de Bayeux et Lisieux, and Marie Duclos, Chan. Secretaire, 17 mars 1857 (DARGS, OLC1/1/1 no. 13).

Recalled to Caen at her own request after about eight months, Sister Jerome Hanrahan would later go on the foundation to Bartestree, the first OLC house in England (1863).[86] On the arrival of the two sisters from Caen, Soeur Vincent de Paul Besançon left Dublin for Paris (April 1858); she had come with the two Irish sisters in May 1855.[87]

The founding sisters – taken as all those who came from France between 1853 and 1858 – consisted of Irish-born Sisters of Our Lady of Charity who had trained in France and native French sisters. Some were sent to help out for a short while only; others were recalled when their home superior decided it was too much for them or she had need of them, and all had the right to return to the house of their profession. At least some of the French-born sisters had great difficulty with English, another factor in the decision to stay or not. There was a significant number of Irish-born sisters in the Paris house of Notre Dame de Charité but, having made vows for life in an order that prided itself on its strict rule of enclosure, stability and perfect conformity with rule and customary usage, few would be suitable candidates for the upheavals of an Irish mission, even if they were willing and the community decided to ask that sacrifice of them. Some were incorporated to such a degree that one woman confided 'I as well as those other Irish sisters lose daily the facility of speaking in our native tongue'.[88] The critical importance of the superior in any new foundation must also be acknowledged as the rule concentrated significant power in her hands. The person named as the founding superior, Soeur Marie du Coeur de Jésus (Mother Mary of the Sacred Heart Kelly) was not one of the young women sent by Fr Smith, but came to Paris through her own family connection, a first cousin Dr Matthew Kelly of the Irish College. The garden of the convent of 193 rue Jacques faced the Irish College and it was he who made arrangements for her to try her vocation there in 1841.[89] A young woman of much promise (*une sujet de grande espérance*), she made her profession in St Michael's in 1845, despite being frequently in the infirmary. She subsequently served as counsellor, mistress of penitents, mistress of novices and assistant to the community, the last-named charge given as the principal reason why she was selected to be superior of the new foundation.[90] In addition, it was thought that her poor health – she had a 'violent and alarming haemorrhage of the lungs' before ever she left Paris – might be improved by being 'restored to her native air'.[91] Regrettably, that was not to prove the case, though she did live for almost ten years more (d. 29 June 1863). Her obituary refers to 'the contradictions, insults and

86    Death letter, Sister M. of St Jerome Hanrahan (Letitia), d. 20 July 1880 (DARGS, OLC1/6/4, no. 51); annals, 1857, p. 93.
87    Letter of authorisation, unsigned copy, from Archbishop Cardinal Cullen, 1 Apr. 1858 (DARGS, OLC1/1/1 no. 14); annals, 1855, p. 85.
88    Sister M. of the Five Wounds O'Callaghan, Paris, to My dearest brother [Thomas O'Callaghan], 7 Apr. 1850 (DARGS, OLC1/1/4 no. 27).
89    Dr Matthew Kelly d. 30 Oct. 1858 and is buried in Maynooth; see Edmund W. Kelly, Bella Vista, Tramore, to Mother Cecelia (DARGS, OLC1/6/3 no. 20).
90    Death letter, Soeur M. du Coeur de Jésus [Kelly], d. 29 June 1863, signed by Soeur M. du St Sauveur Billetout, Paris (DARGS, OLC1/6/4 no. 64).
91    Abridged life of Mother M. Sacred Heart Kelly, p. 6.

persecutions' she suffered over the first two years and three months in Dublin, when sorrows crowded 'from within and from without', the most insupportable of all perhaps 'having no kindred spirit with whom she could divide her pain, no second half to whom she could unburden her heart'.[92] Her misplaced confidence in the postulant Maria Finlay was excused on the grounds of isolation, 'as much a stranger to the affairs of the institute as she was to the people who surrounded her'.[93]

The assistant might have been expected to be the superior's confidante and support, but the annals imply that the 'blunt and determined' Soeur Marie de St Ignace Pavot had little sympathy for the physical frailty and indecision of her superior. She herself had discharged the office of superior in Rennes where she had been considered 'one of the most efficient women in her convent' – though typhoid fever, the annalist claims rather cryptically, weakened her mind, 'and led to that want of soundness of judgement from which others had to suffer so much'.[94] Another rather enigmatic statement is that Pavot found it hard to accept her inability to learn to understand even a word of English, though there are many other achievements to her credit, including putting the sacristy to rights, setting up the convent books and keeping the annals for the first two years and six months. Along with the great difference in personality – the annalist places them at opposite extremes – what came between the superior and her assistant was that one was trained in Paris and the other in Rennes and, despite all the claims to the contrary, local practices did differ. As the foundation was from Paris, the superior, Mother Sacred Heart Kelly, expected the practices of that house to take precedence, but Soeur Marie de St Ignace, 'who had followed the usages of her own convent for 30 years', felt otherwise – and strongly – on this and on so many other points, leading to the reflection that, 'Never perhaps did Divine Providence place two characters more opposed to work out His designs.'[95]

When the first group of five sisters (four professed and one novice) destined for Dublin was assembled for departure, the archbishop of Paris gave them a lengthy teaching on the qualities they were to exemplify in their pious and laudable enterprise. Their prudence, piety, humility and the entire submission with which they had accepted the mission confided to them were extolled, and they were exhorted to be shining examples of modesty, virtue and edification, spreading everywhere they went *la bonne odeur de Jésus Christ*.[96] With instruction such as this, and armed with their rule (one manuscript copy, newly translated into English), they were more than adequately armed with ideals for the venture. From the OLC houses they had known in France, they had models of how the community might live out its apostolic mission and religious life in this new setting. Each one had her individual store of experience, resilience and good health and the group as a whole left France on a tide of good will. But outside of this, they had little practical preparation for what they were to meet in Dublin and (for some time) they had few wise advisers and real friends.

92   Ibid., p. 10.
93   Annals, 1854, p. 55.
94   Ibid., p. 51.
95   Ibid., p. 50.
96   Sibour to Notre Dame de Charité du Refuge, 1853.

## The Role of the Extended O'Callaghan Family in the Dublin Foundation

It was the O'Callaghan sisters who effectively established the Dublin monastery, helped to a considerable degree by generous brothers and a formidable network of friends and relations. A tightly-bound family of 12 children from Julianstown, County Meath, the mother a convert from Protestantism, four of the seven girls were eventually to become sisters of Notre Dame de Charité, three of them in High Park. Two of the brothers, Thomas and Richard, on the death of the parents, provided for their sisters as best they could, paying their noviceship fees and other expenses in France and continuing a close and affectionate relationship with them all their lives. A substantial bequest came to High Park on the death of Richard O'Callaghan in 1874, his generosity continuing to the end.[97] The peregrinations in France of two of the girls, Margaret and Jane, is an adventure story in its own right. Their experiences of several OLC convents, as recounted in private family letters,[98] provide valuable insights into their own spiritual journeying, the devotional traditions which were promoted, the experience of Irish women in French convents, the impact of political upheaval on individual convents and, above all, the model of religious life and women's refuge which would be transplanted, with great zeal and exactitude, to Ireland.

The arrival of Soeur Marie des Cinq Plaies O'Callaghan marked a turning point in the fortunes of the Dublin monastery. Though one of Fr Smith's protégées, Margaret O'Callaghan was a sharp judge of character and, as early as 1844, criticised the way in which the priest had pocketed all £8 of her young sister's travelling funds, leaving her with nothing but a receipt.[99] In her extensive correspondence with and about her brothers and sisters before her return to Ireland, Margaret shows herself to be a spirited woman who knows something of the business of the world, offering an opinion on whether or not to take on a farm ('a good situation would be more lucrative perhaps than to risk taking land these bad times'),[100] and watching the changing price of flour ('the baker trade I suppose rises and falls with the market').[101] She follows politics in Ireland and the dreadful spread of the 1845 potato blight, comparing it with what she can learn of its impact on France.[102]

As noted already, Margaret O'Callaghan was one of the four young women whom Fr Smith tried to get trained as OLC sisters in France; her sister Jane was another.[103] Unlike Margaret, Jane always had difficulty with the French language which must have gone against her prospects of success

---

97    Richard W. O'Callaghan left the convent £950 on his death in 1874, Register of benefactors, p. 34.

98    See O'Callaghan correspondence (DARGS, OLC1/1/4).

99    Margaret O'Callaghan to Thomas O'Callaghan, 5 May 1844.

100    Sister M. of the Five Wounds O'Callaghan, Paris, to Thomas O'Callaghan, 28 Jan. 1850 (DARGS, OLC1/1/4 no. 26).

101    Same to same, 16 Jan. 1852 (DARGS, OLC1/1/4 no. 30).

102    Soeur M. du Bon Pasteur O'Callaghan, Versailles, to Thomas O'Callaghan, 21 Nov. 1845 (DARGS, OLC1/1/4 no. 5).

103    Soeur M. de Saint Pierre, Rennes, death notice of Sister M. of St Magdalene [Magdeleine] O'Callaghan, d. 21 June 1849 (DARGS, OLC1/1/4 no. 22).

in any OLC house.[104] After a short stay in St Michael's in Paris, Margaret and Jane reluctantly agreed to go to Versailles which had such immediate need of recruits that it was, it appears, willing to accept promising young women without a dowry.[105] The time in Versailles was not happy; Margaret was accepted into the novitiate and took the religious name Soeur Marie du Bon Pasteur, but Jane was refused her votes and both left together, arriving on the doorstep of rue St Jacques seeking re-admission. According to Jane, they left Versailles only after much prayer and receiving good advice, their principal reason being 'the order nor the rules were not there observed, without that there is no happiness for a religious'.[106] Margaret was welcomed back to St Michael's 'with joy' and received the habit, this time taking the religious name Soeur Marie des Cinq Plaies. Jane was boarded outside the monastery until the community decided her fate.[107] Refused permission to stay in Paris –which she blamed on the vindictiveness of the superior of Versailles – Jane was accepted by the community of Rennes into their novitiate where she took the religious name Soeur Marie de Ste Madeleine and had all her expenses paid, once again, by her brother Thomas in Dublin. She was diagnosed with tuberculosis soon after arriving in Rennes and made profession on her death bed, 21 June 1849. Regarded locally as a saint, miracles were attributed to her intercession in 1862; her sister Margaret (des Cinq Plaies or Five Wounds) preserved relics and correspondence with a view to promoting her cause for canonisation at some future date.[108]

By all reports, Soeur Marie des Cinq Plaies O'Callaghan settled down in the well-regulated monastery of Paris, ready to return to Ireland when providence decreed but otherwise quite satisfied to stay put. Before leaving for Rennes, her sister prophesied that 'you will see her yet a holy religious in her own country with the blessing of God', that 'she is every day improving in virtue and in piety, her health is excellent, she never knows what it is to be a day sick'.[109] When the day of her vows was settled (20 July 1847), she wrote with real feeling of the 'five years of combat and struggling with the waves of adversity', and now to see ahead the 'port of rest'. Her appreciation of her OLC vocation was perhaps all the deeper for having come through so much: she was about 'to become the spouse of Jesus Christ, united to Him by the bonds of the most sacred, consecrated to Him by the four

104  Jane O'Callaghan, Paris, to Thomas O'Callaghan, 23 Oct. 1846 (DARGS, OLC1/1/4 no. 7).

105  Soeur M. du Bon Pasteur O'Callaghan to Thomas and Charlotte O'Callaghan, 21 Nov. 1845.

106  Jane O'Callaghan, Paris, to Thomas James O'Callaghan, 17 Sept. 1846 (DARGS, OLC1/1/4 no. 6).

107  Ibid.

108  For example, see 'Literal translation', letters from Rennes to High Park convent with details of miracles attributed to the intercession of Jane O'Callaghan (Sister M. of St Magdeleine) 1862–75 (DARGS, OLC1/1/4 no. 37); Soeur M. de St Ignace, Rennes, to superior, High Park, account of miraculous cure at Rennes, 2 Mar. 1862 (DARGS, OLC1/1/4 nos. 38, 39); Rennes, *circulaire*, with note of miraculous cures attributed to Soeur M. de Ste Magdeleine O'Callaghan.3, 20 Oct. 1861 (DARGS, OLC1/3/3 no. 14). Wooden box, marked 'Relics of Sister M. of St Magdalane (*sic*) of Rennes', including envelope marked 'Aunt Jane's hair, died at Rennes in the odour of sanctity' (DARGS, OLC1/12/1 no. 1).

109  Jane O'Callaghan to Thomas James O'Callaghan, 17 Sept. 1846.

vows that will be either my crown of glory or my reprobation in the next world.'[110] Surprised not to be among those chosen for Ireland in the summer of 1853, she nevertheless took it in her stride: 'I am perfectly happy here but notwithstanding am ready to part at the first notice when He wills I should go'.[111] Her business skills were being employed in Paris, where she kept the house accounts and learned first-hand of the precarious financial basis on which OLC convents generally subsisted.[112] While she was certainly imbued with the spirit of her vocation and devoted to the founder, John Eudes, there was a streak of independence that would prove useful in Dublin. For example, she did not co-operate with the visit of a Colonel Latouche from Rathmines, Dublin who, 'young and pious', called to the convent at rue St Jacques and asked to see all his compatriots. She refused to join the others, giving as her reason her difficulty with English and 'I hate to be parloir (*sic*) above all to strangers'.[113] She was not a woman to be patronised, least of all by some young tourist who wanted to satisfy his curiosity.

The other O'Callaghan siblings who became OLC sisters joined the community directly in Dublin. The first was Helen O'Callaghan (Sister Mary of St Joseph), whom Mother Kelly managed to accept as a choir postulant (18 November 1853) only by ignoring the objections of Fr Smith and applying directly to the archbishop, Dr Cullen. As the young woman had no fortune, 'having nothing except herself to offer', the superior needed the archbishop's permission to dispense with the dowry requirement, which he freely gave.[114] Fr Smith was set against the admission of any subjects not of his own choosing,[115] and the speed with which Helen took on positions of responsibility in the asylum probably fuelled his animosity towards her and all whom he viewed as taking the side of the mother superior in outright opposition to him. Aged 36 years on reception of the habit (2 June 1856), she was the first to make vows explicitly for the Dublin house.[116] The choice of religious name was not random: weeks after Helen O'Callaghan's admission as a postulant, the superior had made a solemn vow, in the name of the community and inscribed in the annals, to honour the blessed foster father St Joseph, placing in his hands 'this little community so besieged with difficulties since its commencement'.[117]

The next O'Callaghan sister arrived in 1857 in what were described as '*des circonstances particuliers*'. Cecilia O'Callaghan came as a lay woman, at the request of Mother Sacred Heart Kelly, to take charge of the girls' reformatory at High Park and only later, aged 43, did she enter the novitiate,

110    Soeur M. des Cinq Plaies to Thomas O'Callaghan, 7 July 1847 (DARGS, OLC1/1/4 no. 10).
111    Sister Five Wounds O'Callaghan, Paris, to Thomas O'Callaghan, 17 Oct. 1853.
112    Same to same, 16 Jan. 1852 (DARGS, OLC1/1/4 no. 29). Same to same, 19 Sept. 1849 (DARGS, OLC1/1/4 no. 24)
113    Same to same, 7 Apr. 1850.
114    Annals, 1853, p. 40.
115    Ibid., p. 41.
116    Abstract of clothings and professions, 3rd book (DARGS, OLC1/6/1 no. 3).
117    Annals, 1854, p. 49.

taking the name Sister Mary of St Magdalen.[118] Together, these three sisters – Five Wounds, Joseph and Magdalen – were a formidable trio and well able to strike out anew, their relatives, friends and acquaintances quickly finding themselves drawn into supporting this new project in one way or another. The brothers Richard and John O'Callaghan are named as committee members in the reformatory's first published report and the oldest brother, Thomas, as its first treasurer.[119]

## Struggles Around the Management of 2/4 Drumcondra Road

Difficulties in reconstructing exactly what happened between the sisters and Fr Smith over the Drumcondra Road asylum are compounded by the anxiety of the founding sisters to leave for posterity a charitable version of the falling-out. The register of benefactors, and the first register of profession, are both prefaced with sanitised accounts of the roles played by Fr Smith and by Archbishop Cullen in the foundation of the Dublin house, the 17th in the institute. The last, spiteful act of the dismissed novice Maria Finlay was to withhold and presumably destroy a valuable manuscript 'with many details and circumstances regarding the commencement of St Mary's'.[120] The sister writing the obituary of Mother Sacred Heart Kelly wanted to put on record the trials suffered by the deceased but, out of respect for the 'sacerdotal character' of Fr Smith, decides 'to bring oblivion on the words and deeds of one who whilst binding himself to be her protector became her most cruel persecutor'.[121] In saying nothing she still manages to convey something of the trauma of the first two years and the reason why the community history glosses over the details of the time in Drumcondra Road:

> However, as this trial like all others was willed and ordained
> by an all wise Providence, the good work to which they had
> so generously devoted themselves, let the cloak of charity be
> thrown over the events of these two years, which if revealed
> might be questioned as a reality hard to understand by our
> dear readers.[122]

From the extant correspondence and from the annals (the early period was reconstructed from documents and from living memory in 1875),[123] it is clear that, for the first few months, the community felt utterly abandoned and ill-used. Fr Smith had already established a laundry in the asylum, spelled out as the sole and ordinary means by which charitable establishments could generate an income in Ireland, but Smith's claim that it was properly equipped was but

---

118   Death letter of Sister M. of St Magdalen O'Callaghan (Cecile/Cecilia), d. 22 Apr. 1889, signed Soeur M. du Sacre Coeur de Marie Tobin (DARGS, OLC1/6/4 no. 86).
119   *General and first annual report of St Joseph's Reformatory School for Catholic girls, High Park, Drumcondra, established under the Act 21st and 22nd Vic. cap 103* (Dublin, 1862), p. 2.
120   Annals, 1855, p. 82.
121   Abridged life of Mother M. Sacred Heart Kelly, p. 8.
122   Ibid.
123   Annals, 1854, p. 65.

one of too many exaggerations.[124] The sisters found the women residents badly clad, in dirty wrappers (*mauvaises chemises*) and with one sheet or blanket each, if even that. There was no chance of imposing discipline or giving instruction because they were constantly moving from room to room, between about nine rooms in all. The only chance to talk with them was on Saturday afternoon and Sunday.[125] As far as the care of the women was concerned, the accommodation, resources, revenues and the housekeeping – everything, in the sisters' eyes – fell far below the minimum standard. The bedding of the women was so poor that they made use of the blankets sent to be washed in the laundry to keep themselves warm; they had 'neither towels, basins nor other requirements still more necessary'.[126] There was torn paper in the chapel, a soiled humeral veil and old wooden forms. They could not have believed the Blessed Sacrament would be housed in such poverty and dirt. The toilet or 'necessary' was beyond belief. Everything betrayed 'neglect, dirt and disorder'.[127] Perhaps the worst accommodation was that assigned as the sisters' refectory, an underground basement 8 feet by 4 feet with a damp clay floor and one window about 18 inches square. The water closet in the area above overspilled into the room in wet weather, while the coal pit, stone stairs and enormous boiler where the women's food was prepared all added to the unfitness of the room for any sort of civilised purpose.[128]

But the most serious problem was Fr Smith's treatment of the sisters. Trying hard not to injure charity, the first sister to recount the story of their arrival states that he kept total control over the government and management of the household, sustained in this by his *première matrone*, she and the second matron being entirely under his control and impossible to dismiss. He could not, or would not, accept what his proper position was *vis à vis* the sisters, and moreover turned against them.[129] Until mid-October 1853, he continued to live next door at 4 Drumcondra Road, the six-room house which he had promised would be the sisters' accommodation pending the building of a proper convent and chapel. After the humiliation of six weeks' pleading, they were allowed to sleep there but, as nothing with Fr Smith was ever straightforward, they then had to put aside a few rooms in the asylum (the house at number 2) to accommodate his elderly sister who had been living with him. He had a door opened in the wall of the asylum to communicate with the garden of number 4, enabling him to keep the closest possible watch on all that happened and to enter at will, six or seven times a day, which continued even for the short time the sisters were in occupation of number 4.[130] The opening, blocking and re-opening of this door was to be a bone of contention for the rest of the time the sisters were in Drumcondra Road. According to the obituary of Mother Sacred Heart Kelly, Fr Smith displayed unbridled animosity towards her, viewing her

---

124 High Park, draft *circulaire*, 15 novembre 1853.
125 Ibid.
126 Annals, 1853, p. 38.
127 Ibid., p. 29.
128 Abridged life of Mother M. Sacred Heart Kelly, p. 9.
129 High Park, draft *circulaire*, 15 novembre 1853.
130 Annals, 1853, pp 29, 32, 39, 40, 46.

as usurping his authority and infringing his rights: 'He opposed her in all her views, disapproved of all her plans', to such a point that he begged her to return to Paris, 'for I never knew peace of mind since you came to Ireland'. She was allowed nothing to do with the house and would not be given the keys. The books were held by the first matron who received all monies and issued the provisions, and the sisters were expected to keep to their sitting room – 'at least, they were given to understand as much from the comportment towards them'. They were handed their meals, cooked by the women residents, in the aforementioned refectory below ground, and 'in fine were merely as visitors and suspected visitors in their own house'.[131] Without any forewarning, Fr Smith disappeared to distant parts on 1 October, leaving the sisters without a penny, despite the obvious and multiple needs in the house.[132] That was merely a foretaste of his way of managing the house finances, where agreements to pay for 'indispensables' such as the purchase of refectory tables, were reneged on, leaving the superior to face irate tradesmen and suppliers.[133] The one consolation, according to the annalist, was that the women were good by nature and the sisters held out great hopes of their becoming 'truly good'.[134] A later summing-up described Fr Smith as having no idea of what the religious life is or should be, 'he neither understood its rules or its disciplines nor did he deem it necessary at least as far as his foundation was concerned' and, right until the sisters set foot in Dublin, 'he wisely kept his mind to himself'.[135] He hugely objected to the sisters' recitation of the office in choir, though it was for them woven into the fabric of religious life. He is reported as denigrating it to outsiders with the remark 'they would be better employed at riddling the cinders'.[136]

The matrons seem to have had their own difficulties with Fr Smith, and the new dispensation must have compounded their problems. A Miss Teresa Nolan, of a 'most respectable' family, her disposition 'noble and generous', 'a gentle, kind-hearted girl who knew how to sympathise with and share the sorrows and joys of others', is recorded in the convent annals as having taken care of the penitents for more than 20 years.[137] This Miss Nolan continues as matron even when Mrs Evelina Kelly is named superioress, a joint authority that never worked, at least, from what the annalist set out as the real story.[138] Miss Nolan was employed by Fr Smith as senior matron at a salary of £21 per year 'but the salary was never received except occasionally a few pounds to buy clothes and after long demands and supplications', a fact the annalist states she has from Miss Nolan herself, 'nor was this a solitary case amongst those who were employed in the asylum'.[139] That Fr Smith allowed only the barest necessities to be supplied to the asylum is amply documented; 'nothing more was to

131  Abridged life of Mother M. Sacred Heart Kelly, p. 9.
132  High Park, draft *circulaire*, 15 novembre 1853.
133  Annals, 1854, pp 54–5.
134  High Park, draft *circulaire*, 15 novembre 1853.
135  Abridged life of Mother M. Sacred Heart Kelly, p. 5.
136  Annals, 1853, p. 42.
137  Annals, Preface, p. 4.
138  *Thom's* 1854, p. 811.
139  Annals, Preface, p. 4.

be asked for or to be required', so that the matron as well as those employed in the depository were obliged to resort to 'many subterfuges' in order to secure 'necessities and little comforts' for themselves and the women. The sufferings of Miss Nolan, who had her faults but was withal 'an upright woman and in every way adapted for the post she held' under the capriciousness of her employer are dwelt on at length by the annalist, perhaps to prepare the reader to accept what will be said of his relations with the sisters.[140] She was dismissed after about two months of doing everything she could to drive the sisters out: 'the 21st November 1853 saw the door close on this good Matron and the only grief of the religious was that all the followers of the Revd Father did not take the same route.'[141]

The women themselves, notwithstanding the exhortations of Dr James Taylor at the blessing and installation of Mother Sacred Heart Kelly as superior, were discommoded by the arrival of the French – or French-trained – sisters. They had been used to running the house on their own terms with full stewardship of the kitchen and the provisions, the most important function in the house; 'they had charge of the chapel and the altar, in a word, they looked on the house as their own and were met at every turn by the religious whom they regarded as intruders on their rights'.[142] Not all took kindly to being taught new and more orderly ways of conducting the laundry, dismissing the sisters as 'taskmasters', 'fortified in their repugnance by conduct of the matrons towards our mothers'.[143] Several of the older women 'who possessed great influence with the founder' carried stories and exaggerations to him, which strengthened the bad impressions already formed in his mind by the matrons'.[144] Among themselves, they were forever telling stories of robbers and ghosts and hobgoblins, according to the annalist, 'so that a ghost was to be found in every quarter', which the sisters found unnerving.[145] A dog managing to get himself locked in – or out – of the yard was sufficient to set in train a night of frenzied armed stalking. If any rumour went around the house – for example, that one of their number was being prevented from entering or leaving the house or was in some sort of fix – they would rise up in a body with such a clamour that the sisters could not calm them down, but had to turn to Fr Smith 'who alone was capable of bringing them to the usage of their sound reason'.[146] The annalist complained of the 'state of fermentation in which the minds of the penitents were kept' due to the tension in the house, and it is not difficult to imagine that the petty conflicts of authority which the women witnessed made for a fraught daily life and an uncertain future.[147]

Placing Soeur Marie de St Stanislas Portelet as the mistress of penitents – there was no other sister for the office – should have made for more trouble, but it was reported that she charmed them 'with her kindness of

140    Ibid., p. 5.
141    Annals, 1853, p. 41.
142    Ibid., p. 33.
143    Ibid., p. 37.
144    Ibid., p. 33.
145    Ibid., p. 44.
146    Annals, 1854, p. 53.
147    Annals, 1853, p. 43.

manner and her charity towards them'. Before long, the women were joining together in prayers and novenas 'that the little French mother might
soon learn the English language'.[148] She was young, affectionate and gay
in manner; according to the annalist, she 'loved Ireland, its people and its
usages and would willingly have remained forever had her choice been
consulted'.[149] While most of the women warmed, in time, to the sisters,
and appreciated the improvements they brought, they had real and understandable grievances. In advance of the sisters' arrival, Fr Smith had
met every demand with the reply that, once they arrived, they would supply every want. The women felt cheated when it became obvious that the
purses of the French ladies were as light as their own. Feeling that in this
the women had indeed been treated unfairly, the superior decided that the
£40 which had been brought from Paris as 'private resource' or emergency
money should be expended on a set of aprons, chemises, petticoats, wrappers and shawls, the only disappointment being that the women expected
each to keep control of her own set, while the sisters had come with a strong
tradition of communal living whereby there was a common wash and a
common mending.[150]

In February 1854, the superior at Paris, Soeur Marie de St Stanislas
Brunel, in receipt of too many troubling reports, could hold out no longer
and addressed herself directly to Fr Smith:

> At your arrival at Paris last August you *seemed* to consent to all
> the conditions and settlements necessary for the foundation
> of our holy order at Drumcondra, and in verity you made me
> so many promises and in appearance with so much sincerity
> and good skill, that I did not for a moment hesitate to believe
> them. Can you blame me now if I ask what may be your rea-
> sons for not complying with what you at that time so heartily
> promised?[151]

Five months had elapsed since the sisters' arrival and, despite great patience and forbearance, there appeared no remedy for the difficulties they
faced, so that Soeur Brunel proposed abandoning the project:

> Allow me to say Revd dear Sir, that if at present you regret the
> step which you have taken, it is not as yet too late to remedy
> it. St Michael's is ever ready to receive our dear Sisters, and it
> is needless to add that as far as I am concerned my arms will
> be ever open to them.[152]

---

148  Ibid., p. 37.
149  Annals, 1854, p. 52.
150  Annals, 1853, p. 43.
151  Soeur M. de St Stanislas Brunel, Paris, to Revd. Dear Father [Smith], 9 Feb. 1854 (DDA,
Cullen 332/4, file II nuns, no. 13). Emphasis as in the original.
152  Ibid.

Fr Smith appealed to multiple parties in Paris, including Mrs O'Neill, the older sister of the novice still in Dublin, giving his version of how he was treated under Mrs Kelly, 'deprived of all power as connected with the asylum, except to collect funds', useless except when they had to call on him 'to settle down a storm amongst the penitents' and how, at every turn 'rule, rule, thrown up at me so frequently that I am now silent'.[153]

The re-appropriation of house number 4 by Fr Smith on 1 May 1854 crowded the sisters once more into the asylum house and, though by no means their only problem, this became the issue on which the continuation or abandonment of the project rested.[154] Advised by the archbishop through Dr Taylor not to yield to him, the superior's refusal 'added fuel to the fire of his discontent which had already reached the highest point'.[155] Forced to allow Fr Smith to re-occupy the house under the pretext of getting a boundary wall erected, the one month agreed turned into an open-ended occupation, over a hot summer. So sure were the sisters of returning quickly that they left filled trunks and bookcases in a locked room which he broke into; his appropriation of furniture, fittings and church requisites from the asylum, including gifts sent from France, is enumerated item by item in the annals.[156]

Although matters went quickly from bad to worse, a succession of clerical friends had tried to take up the sisters' cause since their arrival, including Vincentian priests at Castleknock.[157] Probably the best placed to help would be the priest appointed as 'spiritual father'. This well-defined role was limited to that of adviser, visitor and confidant, a support to the community but with no juridical authority and no right to alter the rule of life.[158] But it did place him under an obligation to visit in person, at least yearly, to find out for himself exactly how the women and the sisters were treated.[159] A good spiritual father, therefore, had an unrivalled insider view of all that pertained to St Mary's and might be expected to advocate in times of difficulty, as was indeed to be the case. The other key role was that of confessor. Before the sisters left for Dublin, the Paris superior had tried to get the Vincentian provincial, Fr Philip Dowley (Dean Duly or Dooley in the annals) appointed to this role, and to have some French-speaking priest as confessor, 'requested with all the solicitude of a mother for her children so far away'.[160]

The first priest appointed by Cullen to the role of spiritual father (15 October 1853) was his own secretary, Dr James Taylor, who was also a Vincentian or Lazarist. Not surprisingly, he quickly learned the true state of affairs, helping out insofar as his personal resources would allow (he supplied carpets for the parlour and the sanctuary) and is named as one of the chief

---

153    John Smith to Mrs O'Neill, Paris, 13 Feb. 1854, transcript in annals, 1854, p. 57.
154    Annals, 1854, p. 62.
155    Ibid., p. 55.
156    Ibid., pp 47, 58, 64.
157    The clergymen of St Vincent's college were among those named as willing to accept donations on behalf of St Mary's, *Freeman's Journal*, 5 May 1838.
158    Explanation of constitution XXXIV, the spiritual father, in 'Explanation of the rules, constitutions and customs of the Religious of Our Lady of Charity ....', trans. of 1734 edn, p. 230 (DARGS, OLC1/5/1 no. 1). Hereafter, Explanation of [chapter or constitution or rule no.].
159    Ibid.
160    Soeur M. de St Stanislas Brunel to Mgr l'Archevêque de Dublin, 31 Aug. 1853.

benefactors and friends of the early days.[161] But his involvement was short-lived as, early in 1854, he was appointed to a parish in County Carlow.[162] The Vincentian provincial did not shirk responsibility for the little French community adrift in Dublin, reporting in March 1854 to Dr Cullen that 'the French nuns at Drumcondra are protesting loudly against the threatened betrayal of them and of the best hopes built up for them by Fr Smith before they moved a foot from Paris'.[163] Sometime in 1855, Dr Cullen appointed the newly-ordained Fr Murray, aged twenty-four years and also his secretary, as spiritual father to the community. The annalist recalls how from the outset he was disposed 'to help and assist' the mother superior in every way and able, from his closeness to Cullen, to refute the wild accusations being made about the sisters.[164] Murray was to play a pivotal role in rescuing the community from an insufferable situation.

Over the first two years Cullen undoubtedly tried to keep from getting drawn into the troubles of Fr Smith's project. He did visit the community twice, encouraging the superior to 'bear her cross with patience' which her companions at least thought she was already doing to a heroic degree.[165] On his first short visit, he allowed for Dr Moriarty of All Hallows College to be the confessor, and authorised Dr Taylor to conduct the formal installation – delayed until the 14 September 1853, when Mother Kelly would make her profession of faith and be confirmed as superior. On that occasion, Taylor said all that could possibly be said to bring the women along: in their fidelity and their zeal to observe their rule, they had drawn down on themselves the mercy of the Lord; God in his goodness had sent to them these religious; what a wonderful grace was before them – before finishing up with an outline of their duties towards these good religious.[166] No preacher could have done more. However, the impact of this solemn exhortation must have been undermined by the fact that it all happened in the absence of Fr Smith who could not be present due to illness and took grave offence at the ceremony going ahead without him.[167]

For her part, Mother Sacred Heart Kelly let pass the very few opportunities she had to make her troubles with the reverend founder known directly to Dr Cullen. She said nothing at their first brief meeting, a few days after arriving and, on the second occasion, was too reserved and embarrassed, even though Cullen had come expressly to find out what was wrong.[168] She naively believed that the slightest concession by Fr Smith was a sign that the tide was turning, 'saying to herself that what was not given today might perhaps be given the next'.[169] Above all, she kept the wrongs to herself 'out of deference to the sacred character of him who was the cause of all

161 Annals, 1854, p. 64.
162 John Kingston, 'Rev. John Smyth, C.C., 1791–1858', *Reportorium Novum, Dublin Diocesan Historical Record*, 4: 1 (1971), p. 28.
163 Philip Dowley, St Vincent's, Castleknock, to Dr Cullen, 25 Mar. 1854 (DDA, Cullen, 332/2 priests regular and secular, no. 16).
164 Annals, 1855, p. 83–4.
165 Annals, 1854, p. 60.
166 High Park, draft *circulaire*, 15 novembre 1853.
167 Annals, 1853, p. 36.
168 Annals, 1853, p. 33; 1854, p. 67.
169 Annals 1853, p. 39.

her troubles'.[170] To complain about a priest, any priest, to his bishop was a step too far for Mother Sacred Heart Kelly. Cullen intervened only when the superior 'foreseeing no possibility of a right understanding taking place between herself and the Rev. Fr Smith' sought permission to return to France.[171] Dr Cullen was forced to take action by his own well-informed secretary, Fr Murray, and by the arrival of an outsider, the French Eudist Fr Vaubret.

As 'vicissitude followed vicissitude and all hopes of redressing so many vexations was found only in prayer', it was the providential visit of Revd F. Vaubret CJM from Redou in Rennes – described as 'a saviour and friend' in the annals – that broke the impasse.[172] He arrived in the parlour of St Mary's on 20 September 1854 where Mother Sacred Heart Kelly told him freely of all her trials and crosses. He listened carefully, 'thoroughly taking notes of all he saw and making himself master of all that concerned the difficulties the religious family had to contend with'. A room was then prepared for him in house number 4, and he was invited to dinner by Fr Smith – who in turn proceeded to tell of his trials and crosses. Having promised Mother Sacred Heart Kelly that he would do all to arrange things 'one way or another', he then proceeded to force a call on the archbishop, Dr Cullen, who, 'too much occupied to see him', eventually, on the sixth day, gave him a few minutes of his time. Cullen declared that his only desire was 'that matters would be set to rights' and was as good as his word. Three days later, on the feast of St Michael, 29 September 1854, Dr Cullen led an inspection of numbers 2 and 4 Drumcondra Road, accompanied by his two vicars general, also by Dr Dowley CM and Fr Smith. The superior, fortunately, realising that this visit would decide the fate of the foundation, 'spoke with much liberty to His Grace telling him all they had to suffer from want of air and space and the utter impossibility of their remaining as they were'. The vicars general were ordered to examine all, that they might be 'convinced by their own eyes'. It was obvious that the inspection party had the full story from Fr Vaubret, including the stinking basement refectory, and how the sisters had to sleep in whatever space they could find at night – one on a table in the inner parlour, another on a shelf in the pantry, another on the landing lobby and five in one tiny room.[173] The French priest was told by Cullen to withdraw while the inspection was under way but he made sure, by follow-up calls and by letter, that what he had set out to do was indeed achieved.[174]

The outcome of the inspection was immediate and decisive. There and then Fr Smith was told by Dr Cullen to yield the house to the sisters and find lodgings in the neighbourhood; he and Fr Vaubret were to vacate the house by the following day.[175] Cullen had already ordered that he be shown the deeds of the house.[176] Although unable to withstand such a direct command, Fr Smith did take some small revenge by insisting on another few days during which he removed all the furniture, books, pictures, everything

170   Annals 1854, p. 75.
171   Abridged life of Mother M. Sacred Heart Kelly, p. 9.
172   Annals, 1854, pp 69–70.
173   Ibid., p. 66.
174   Ibid., pp 71, 78–9.
175   Ibid., p. 72.
176   Standard questionnaire, 20 Sept. 1854.

belonging to the sisters, 'all was gone, from the top to the bottom', excepting only the two refectory tables. Nevertheless, the annalist records that Mother Sacred Heart Kelly and her sisters 'blessed God for having given them the means of breathing a little more freely'. Fr Vaubret blessed the house, room by room, and the sisters took free possession for the first time, cooking and taking their meals in the convent house, one year and one month from the date of their arrival.[177]

The free possession of house number 4 was the first and most obvious outcome, but there were other positive results. The sisters got control of the annual charity sermon in support of the asylum and, despite the refusal of Fr Smith to aid them in any way, the collection far surpassed that of the previous year which they found most encouraging.[178] The appointment of Dr Bartholomew Woodlock as spiritual father was inspired; he was to prove a wise adviser and defender of their interests. The esteem in which he was held among (for example) the people of Wicklow was to work in the community's favour when it came to fundraising.[179] He played a major role in enabling the move to High Park, within easy reach of the All Hallows seminary (where he was president 1854–79). There was a perceptible shift in public opinion due probably to the interest taken by Drs Cullen, Woodlock, Murray and other persons of standing – but credited at the time to the counter-reports ('the true state of affairs') spread by a young French governess, Miss Paslique, and the removal of scandalmongers from the house.[180] Fr Vaubret urged Mother Kelly to dismiss a number of people which she had shirked up to this, fearing a backlash from Fr Smith. The novice Maria Finlay was dismissed.[181] The carter William, and the cartress, Margaret Doran, who had greatly disturbed the peace through carrying messages to and from Fr Smith, were let go; they had sought to secure wage rises by threatening to leave and were greatly displeased at seeing themselves 'so coolly dealt with and so easily replaced'.[182] Up to this, according to the annalist, the only story in circulation was that of Fr Smith, 'the rehearsal of his wrongs, his persecutions, all he had to suffer from the Reverend Mother of St Mary's was the topic of conversation in every family with whom he was acquainted – communities – priests – from the opulent to the tradesmen, all were in possession of his imaginary wrongs'.[183] By mid-January 1855, the house was freed of the 'evil reports' of Fr Smith's followers and the sisters, for the first time, 'felt they were at home and could act freely without fear of having their actions and intentions ill-judged and misrepresented'.[184] Many families withdrew their washing when the two carters went, but others took their place, which was interpreted by the annalist as the kind working out of providence, marking the end of two and a half years of hard work and still harder trials and seen as a suitable place to conclude the

177  Annals, 1854, p. 73.
178  The charity sermon was held 28 Jan. 1855 and raised over £100; annals, 1855, p. 82.
179  Hugh Gaffney, Newtown Mount Kennedy, to Mrs O'Callaghan, High Park, 19 May 1862 (DARGS, OLC1/1/1 no. 16).
180  Annals, 1854, pp 64–5.
181  Ibid., pp 78–9.
182  Annals, 1855, p. 80–1.
183  Annals, 1854, p. 75.
184  Annals, 1855, p. 81.

first volume of annals.[185] A line was drawn under this fraught period; in whatever was to happen next, the sisters, not Fr Smith, would be the active agents.

## Taking Control of 2/4 Drumcondra Road and the Move to High Park

Once in possession of the convent house (October 1854), the sisters tried to manage the business for which they had come to Dublin and in accord with the conditions they had agreed with the diocese, even as relations with the reverend founder continued to be fraught. But it was obvious to anybody who cared that they would never be able to run Fr Smith's asylum on the pattern or to the standards they had known in France and on the scale that made such ventures sustainable. In December 1853, the community numbered three professed choir sisters, one novice and two postulants (choir), also one lay sister (*converse*), and a lay postulant; there were 41 women (penitents), making a total household of 49 persons.[186] 'The locality does not allow us to receive more' was the verdict after one year's experience – by which time the number of women residents ranged between 47 and 50.[187] There were four servants employed, and the community numbers were much the same (four choir sisters, one lay sister, two novices and one postulant), giving a total household of 62 persons.[188] There was no space to extend, let alone to build anew and there was nowhere to put novices. No comparison could be made between Drumcondra Road and either of the households from which the founding sisters were drawn, namely Paris (total number 302 in 1848) and Rennes (total number 265), which occupied capacious premises. The women and girls were subdivided into 'classes', managed with the greatest attention to regularity and good order, according to long-established rules, and where each person's role and place in the community – whether choir sister, lay sister, *tourière* or extern sister, penitent, schoolchild, *dame pensionnaire*, servant or workman – was clearly defined.[189] The impossibility of effecting a proper separation between the 'first' and 'second' class (unsettled newcomers and tested, trustworthy women), between the women residents and the sisters' community, and between the asylum/convent complex and the public (*le monde*), due to the 'position' and internal layout of the house, is the subject of an early appeal to Caen. Although undated, it most likely refers to the Drumcondra Road premises in 1855.[190] The superior of Caen responds in some alarm, noting especially that the links with *le monde* are not alone dangerous, but even pernicious and destructive of the good that has been achieved to date towards the conversion or perseverance of the women. While allowing that the great inconveniences currently endured by the Dublin monastery were

185   Ibid.
186   High Park, draft *circulaire*, 15 novembre 1853.
187   Standard questionnaire, 20 Sept. 1854.
188   Ibid.
189   Paris, *circulaires*, 1836–61 (DARGS, OLC1/3/3 nos. 3–13); Rennes, *circulaires*, 1861, 1862 (DARGS, OLC1/3/3 nos. 14, 15); Rennes, *circulaire*, 28 janvier 1848 (NDC Caen, Archives Besançon).
190   Undated memo in envelope marked 'Letters from Caen on different points' (DARGS, OLC1/3/2 no. 3).

not easily rectified, the tenor of the reply from Caen makes clear that nothing that might threaten or undermine enclosure could be tolerated. Sympathy for the difficulties faced by other monasteries did not in any way dilute the advice offered from Caen.

Faced with the insuperable difficulties of making a proper monastery out of numbers 2 and 4 Drumcondra Road and the association of the houses with the tyranny of Fr Smith, it is not surprising that starting afresh in an entirely new place had its attractions. All the sisters suffered from the lack of space, bad air, damp and want of exercise but Mother Sacred Heart Kelly's health degenerated into pleurisy, making a change imperative.[191] It was news of her grave illness in April 1855 – penned by a rather hysterical assistant – that precipitated the speedy dispatch of the two sisters from Paris, Sister M. of the Five Wounds O'Callaghan, a close friend of the superior, and Sister M. of St Anne Carroll. However, when news of the state of poverty and privation in Dublin reached the superior of Rennes (through Fr Vaubret), she immediately recalled her two sisters and could be persuaded only to leave them a few months until replacements arrived.[192] With Paris already stretched, two sisters were sent on short-term loan by Caen, a kindness which was regarded at the time as placing the community eternally in its debt. The Irish-born former superior of Caen, Sister M. of St Jerome Hanrahan, would serve for eight months as a prudent director of the novices in Dublin, a service that was crucial to the future well-being of the community.[193] It was these new sisters, in union with the superior Mother Sacred Heart Kelly, who had the energy and even the audacity to consider a move to somewhere new, with all the risks and trouble that would certainly entail.

Active negotiations were in hand by 1856 to acquire the house and grounds of High Park.[194] The 'original assignment', in the names of Dr Cullen, archbishop of Dublin, and the sisters, is dated 25 February 1857.[195] The account circulated to other houses of the order explains that the sisters petitioned the Blessed Virgin to find a place suitable to their needs and more conducive to health.[196] An advance party, consisting of the ill superior (Sacred Heart Kelly), the newly-arrived novice mistress (Jerome Hanrahan) and her little band of novices, moved to High Park on 1 April 1857. The other sisters, led by the assistant superior (Cinq Plaies O'Callaghan) had to stay in the old premises with the women residents for almost another year until there was sufficient accommodation for all. On their departure, Fr Smith took over house number 4 once more as his residence and stayed there until his death.[197]

191   High Park, *circulaire*, 30 décembre 1859 (DARGS, OLC1/3/1 no. 2).
192   Annals, 1855, p. 80.
193   The High Park *circulaire* dated 30 décembre 1859 states eight months but, in her death letter, it is 18 months and in the annals six months. Eight months is more than likely correct. Death letter of Sister M. of St Jerome Hanrahan (Letitia), d. 20 July 1880 (DARGS, OLC1/6/4, no. 51).
194   The year 1856 is erroneously given in some published histories as the date of transfer to High Park, for example, see title page, *Report and statistical sketch of the magdalen asylum, High Park, Drumcondra, June 1881* (Dublin, 1881).
195   Schedule of deeds relating to High Park, 4 July 1907 (DARGS, OLC1/9/1 no. 12).
196   High Park, *circulaire*, 30 décembre 1859.
197   Annals, 1857, p. 93. 'St Mary's asylum of Drumcondra is removed to High Park, Drumcondra', *Freeman's Journal*, 5 Apr. 1858.

The gentleman's residence of High Park was not large and a new building was necessary, but there was ample space and all the fresh air that could be desired. During this time of separation, the sisters in Drumcondra Road went, in turn, to High Park to spend a day with the superior, who continued to lead the community in every respect and did somewhat recover her health under the influence, it was reported, of the pure air and the greater calmness of their new home. Finally, on 1 March 1858, the day of unification arrived, and the houses at Drumcondra Road were vacated, with every detail of the transfer written up at the time. Two ominibuses had been hired to bring the 52 asylum residents and the four remaining sisters to High Park. Strangers who noticed the crowd of women in the omnibuses in the late evening presumed they were on their way to a dance and would be back that night! The sisters were anxious about the move – after all, they were vacating a city premises facing onto one of the principal thoroughfares, which had been home to at least four of the women (and perhaps more) for many years, into a thoroughly rural setting, albeit only a mile or so further north. Fears of an uprising proved unfounded – the women were reportedly charmed with the new accommodation and facilities (spread between two buildings not yet joined) and endured the hardships attendant on the upheaval with great good humour.[198]

Problems with Fr Smith followed the sisters to High Park. These were handled robustly on behalf of the sisters by Soeur Marie des Cinq Plaies O'Callaghan, with the full backing of Bartholomew Woodlock of All Hallows in his role as 'spiritual father' to the community. The Sisters of Our Lady of Charity, with the approbation of the archbishop of Dublin, were effectively continuing Fr Smith's asylum, under its original name, in the High Park premises and under their sole management. Within days of the move, they discovered that Fr Smith was doing all he could to undermine the new project. While he had lost 'his' penitents to High Park, the Drumcondra Road premises, with its equipment and furniture, was still held in his own name.[199] The first attack was on the laundry business and goodwill which 'his' asylum had built up and which had moved, with the women, to High Park. Soeur Marie des Cinq Plaies (writing on behalf of the ill superior) reported that 'it is now certain that Fr Smith is sending round to our customers soliciting their washing', both through his carters and in person. Some of the customers yielded and transferred their business; others took offence and reported the outrage to High Park. In several cases, where he could not persuade the woman of the house to transfer her business, he appealed to the father or husband 'arguing his claim as being the priest to whom he had given his support'. Further enquiries by Soeur Marie des Cinq Plaies with her own carters enabled her to draw up a list of names and addresses, which she duly forwarded to Dr Woodlock, who sent it on to the archbishop, who in turn sent it on to Fr Smith with a demand that he explain himself.[200] Fr Smith's boast that the archbishop 'could not prevent him' running a new asylum in competition with High Park, 'that he had already seven penitents, five that left our own

198    High Park, *circulaire*, 30 décembre 1859.
199    Annals, 1858, p. 94.
200    Soeur M. des Cinq Plaies to Revd. Father [Woodlock], 23 Mar. 1858 (DDA, Cullen, 319/4 nuns, no. 8).

asylum back to him (and that he expected more to leave) and two other poor creatures that he took in' could not be left unchallenged.[201] In addition to these well-founded reports, there was the physical evidence of 'scaffolding poles outside the old asylum, as if Fr Smith was about to get the home plastered, and the front renewed', as noted by Fr Woodlock who underlined the points he wished to emphasise:

> Under the circumstances I deem it my duty to say to your Grace, that I think it absolutely necessary for the welfare of the Institution, with which you have been pleased to charge me, that Father Smyth should publicly declare the object to which he intends to apply the old Asylum – otherwise mistakes must occur, especially as he has published his intentions of establishing another Magdalen Asylum there. Moreover, since, as he stated, he has no money, except the contributions of the faithful, it is due to St Mary's Asylum that the charitable to whom he may apply should know, that is it not for a magdalen asylum, but for some other work of charity, ex. q. for a Chapel, for an Asylum, for the blind etc. they are contributing.[202]

Fr Smith was ordered by the archbishop to keep well away from projects for penitents – 'It will be better to turn the house at Drumcondra into an Asylum for the Blind or to make some other similar use of it, rather than do anything that would be injurious to the sisters, whom you were instrumental in bringing into this country, and whom, if you assist them, will certainly profit and succeed'.[203] His protracted rebuttal of the charges – 'if any reason to complain let them come to me, and not to be annoying your Grace with messengers fabrications and lies' – is unconvincing, and his complaint that it was a personal vendetta by Dr Woodlock is unlikely to have impressed the diocesan leadership, where Dr Woodlock was greatly esteemed: 'it is not the first time my Rev. friend has hurted my feelings, indeed unjustly, by similar allusions'.[204] The postscript he appends to his reply to the archbishop could be taken as evidence of an extraordinary self-assurance and buoyancy: 'PS I expect to have a sketch of a chapel for Drumcondra Road ready in a few days to lay before your Grace'.[205] In any case, he features little in the story of High Park from thence, though the annals note that, just before his death, 23 or 25 August 1858, he was reconciled with the community, leaving £100 to them in his will, and that the sisters derived much comfort from this fact.[206]

201    Ibid.
202    Bartholomew Woodlock, All Hallows College, to My dear Lord Archbishop [Dr Cullen], 31 Mar. 1858 (DDA, Cullen, 319/4 nuns, no. 8).
203    Paul Cullen, archbishop, to Fr Smith, Easter Saturday 1858 (DDA, Cullen, 319/4 nuns, no. 8).
204    Fr Smith, Exchange Street, to My Lord Archbishop [Dr Cullen], Easter Monday 1858 (DDA, Cullen, 319/4 nuns, no. 8).
205    Ibid.
206    Annals, 1858, p. 96.

# Chapter 2

# The 'Magdalen Rescue and Reform' Movement and the Tradition of Notre Dame de Charité du Refuge

When the Sisters of Our Lady of Charity of Refuge (OLC) arrived in early September 1853 to St Mary's, Drumcondra Road, they found they were in charge – or rather, not in charge – of an institution that had been operating since 1829. It in turn was but one of the many small, lay-run asylums or refuges that were to be found in urban centres throughout Britain and Ireland, with dates of foundation from the 1760s to the 1840s and with varying life-spans and modes of governance but all part of a larger 'magdalen rescue and reform' movement. Dublin had been a leader in the field with the founding of the Protestant Leeson Street asylum in 1765, though most of the small asylums, under both Protestant and Roman Catholic management, date from the early decades of the 19th century. Fr Smith's asylum, first in rented premises, then in 2 Drumcondra Road, is a fairly typical Catholic example. The asylum in Gloucester Street (present-day Sean MacDermott Street) is another of the type; it started out in 1822 as a lay asylum.

But the sisters who left Paris for Dublin were coming from a much older, well-tested tradition and had a rather different type of institution in mind. Notre Dame de Charité was a conventual system, where sisters, 'penitents' and other residents alike observed enclosure.[1] Its philosophy and practices of care had been worked out in 1640s Caen. By the time the carriages with the first group of sisters drew up outside the overrated two-storey house that was St Mary's, the refuge system in which they had been trained had been in operation for more than two hundred years, its founding character preserved in most details. The spirituality which underpinned it was that of 17th century rural France, the urgent need which propelled it into existence the difficulties faced by outcast women of the villages and small towns of Normandy, and the internal structures those which were grudgingly allowed at the time, by Rome, after much delay and compromise. The example and teachings of its founder, John Eudes (1601–80), centred on the compassionate heart of Jesus and of his mother Mary, was so thoroughly documented and built into the daily life of the institute that he was made actively present in the monasteries in a real and vibrant way.

---

1   John Eudes to Mother Margaret Frances Patin, 10 Sept. 1661, 'that only those are received who, being called by God, voluntarily enter the house to do penance there; that during the time they spend there, they remain perfectly cloistered'. *Letters and shorter works by Saint John Eudes*, trans. Ruth Hauser (New York, 1948), p. 165. Hereafter, *Letters of John Eudes*.

Attachment to its heritage was further enlivened by the order's more recent history of persecution. Forcibly closed in France in 1791, most (but not all) OLC communities re-established themselves legally in 1811 and struggled for the next few decades to become viable once more. The stories of the persecution of the Paris community between 1789 and 1807 – hostile state inspections and control of house elections, the martyrdom of their confessor with other priests at Les Carmes, the confiscation of their convent, the sacrilege of the chapel, the dispersal of the community, the expulsion from Paris of the superior who was of noble birth, and the efforts made by a core group to stay together secretly and penniless in a succession of rented rooms – were real, and recent.[2] During the 1848 revolution, when the O'Callaghan sisters and other young Irish women were training in France, the convent at rue St Jacques found itself at the very centre of the action, being used as a field hospital, with fugitives from both sides hiding in the enclosure.[3] The tumult of 1848 revived memories of all that had been suffered by their foremothers. Acknowledging the hand of providence in bringing them through all these storms, the sisters clung ever more tenaciously to the founding model of the community. Its rule of life at least could be viewed as immutable, the one sure guide in a stormy, uncertain world. The sisters who travelled to Dublin carried with them the same remarkable attachment to their rule and to the model of care that originated in the first monastery of Caen under John Eudes and the founding mothers.

With the arrival of the sisters in 1853 there was certainly a clash of cultures: the French Eudist tradition meeting the home-grown and much looser local tradition, religious management replacing lay management, rule by written constitutions and written customs replacing the autocratic rule of Fr Smith. French standards of housekeeping, food preparation, personal cleanliness and general domestic comfort among the poorer classes were higher than what was common in mid-19th century Ireland, as numerous travellers testified.[4] The small, lay-run asylums, in the poorest backstreet locations, reliant on intermittent charity and for a class of persons that few wanted anything to do with, had little to boast of in terms of facilities. But what the French Eudist tradition did have in common with the 'rescue and reform' magdalen movement in Britain and Ireland was its concern for outcast women and its strong scriptural basis. This chapter, therefore, first considers the origins of the British and Irish rescue and reform movement of which Drumcondra Road and the dozen or so other asylums that can be identified as operational in 1850s Dublin and environs were a part. The arguments used to awaken sympathy in the 1750s and 1760s for this despised class of persons are then discussed, with the gospel figure of Mary Magdalen proving to be instrumental in winning the public's favour. Some comments are then made on the origins, numbers,

2   Joseph-Marie Ory, *Les origines de Notre-Dame de Charité ou son histoire depuis sa fondation jusqu'à la Révolution* (Abbeville, 1891), pp 596–604.
3   Paris, *circulaire*, 25 août 1848 (NDC Caen, Tours).
4   See for example, St Germain Leduc, *L'Angleterre, l'Écosse, l'Irlande, relation d'un voyage dans les trois royaumes* (Strasbourg, 1838); Edouard Déchy, *Voyage, Irlande en 1846 et 1847* (Paris, 1847); Napoleon Roussel, *Trois mois en Irlande* (Paris, 1853).

organisation and management of magdalen asylums in Dublin city into the 1850s, insofar as the records allow. Threads in the larger rescue and reform debate are identified that appear to have direct applicability to Dublin in the two or three decades prior to the arrival of the Sisters of Our Lady of Charity.

The distinctive asylum model brought to Drumcondra Road by the Sisters of Our Lady of Charity and given full expression in High Park from 1858 onwards is then explored and the principles and rules which underpinned it. The early history of the Gloucester Street asylum (incorporating Mecklenburgh Street) is referred to only in passing, but all of the principles applicable to High Park were applicable to Gloucester Street – as they were to Caen, Rennes, Paris, Buffalo, Bartestree or wherever an autonomous monastery of OLC was to be found.

## Origins of the 'Magdalen Rescue and Reform' Movement in Britain and Ireland

The modern 'magdalen rescue and reform' movement in Britain and Ireland can be dated to the mid-18th century when there was extensive public debate about the plight of young women drawn into prostitution and for whom no refuge existed should they wish to abandon that path. The establishment of state lock hospitals, for the treatment of venereal diseases, in London in 1746 and in Dublin in 1755 exposed the wretchedness of women who, on their discharge, had little choice but to return to the situation and lifestyle that had rendered them diseased. 'Shall the humble and earnest voice of penitence, that voice which never fails to reach Heaven, be heard in our streets and none attend to it?'[5] was the appeal made on behalf of the first London asylum, opened in 1758 and reiterated on behalf of a similar asylum proposed for Dublin. Lady Arabella Denny's Leeson Street asylum admitted its first residents on 17 August 1767. By 1834, when a public appeal (figure 2.1) was launched to support Fr Smith's asylum at 2 Drumcondra Road, there were several small Catholic asylums in operation, with addresses at Bow Street, Chancery Lane, Mecklenburgh Street and Townsend Street.[6] The arguments promoting the new Drumcondra Road asylum are essentially those of the mid-18th century, appealing on behalf of 'those who might be the purest of mortals' now reduced to the foulest depths.[7]

The initial energy behind the magdalen movement in Britain and Ireland may be credited to a Revd Mr Dingley 'who rose superior to mean and popular prejudices' and appealed, with passion and eloquence, for an

---

5  Quoting Dr Dobbs, preaching on behalf of the governors of the Lock Hospital, London, who agitated for the setting up of the London magdalen asylum. *A letter to the public on an important subject* (Dublin, 1767), pp 4, 22. Hereafter, *A letter to the public.*
6  The Magdalene, a fragment, by a Catholic priest' (Patritius), *Catholic Penny Magazine*, 21:1 (12 July 1834), pp 237–40. (DARGS, OLC 1/1/1 no. 1). See also under Topographical information: 22 Residence, Almshouses, asylums and orphanages, in Rob Goodbody, *Dublin part III, 1756–1847*, Irish Historic Towns Atlas no. 26 (Dublin, 2014), pp 100–101.
7  'The Magdalene, a fragment', p. 239.

**Figure 2.1**  Popular nineteenth-century image of Mary Magdalen washing the feet of Jesus at Bethany. 'The Magdalene, a fragment, by a Catholic priest' (*Patritius*), *Catholic Penny Magazine*, 21:1 (12 July 1834), p. 237.

asylum for those women who wished to put prostitution behind them.[8] While yielding to the fact that 'in the present disordered state of things, there will always be brothels and prostitutes', the promoters of the asylum movement nevertheless argued that this of itself did not necessitate that 'the wretched instruments of passion, the unhappy women assigned to this base service, should endure all the extremities of misery, and perish in troops, un-pitied, and unregarded, as if they were not fellow-creatures, and fellow-heirs of eternity'.[9] An appeal to Christian solidarity was bolstered by presenting asylums as a means of controlling vagrancy – 'suppressing Lewdness and Cleansing our streets of those foul disgraces of this City'.[10] To those who objected that these women were 'the very dregs of the people, and therefore unworthy of so much attention and expence', and moreover were certain to relapse 'into their former courses', asylum promoters repeatedly brought forward the example of Jesus as the 'great physician of souls', the one to whom even the most loathsome sinner could turn and know forgiveness.[11]

The arguments surrounding the 'rescue' of women and girls from the trade of prostitution were varied and often contradictory. Much of the public discourse of the 18th and early 19th century emphasised the youth of these women, 'so young and unsuspecting when they forfeited their innocence,

---

8    William Dodd, *An account of the rise, progress, and present state of the Magdalen Hospital, for the reception of penitent prostitutes* (5th edn, London, 1776), p. 1.
9    Ibid.
10   *A letter to the public*, p. 10.
11   Ibid., p. 14.

that they plunged into ruin almost before they apprehended their danger'.[12] While allowing that many were in truth the victims of seduction ('by artful and execrable traders in youthful innocence') and that many men set out purposely 'to delude unexperienced innocence, or encourage perseverance in vice', the betrayed woman nevertheless shouldered practically all the blame for her fall from virtue.[13] Even when presented as the unfortunate victims 'of these incarnate villains who glory in vices, not fit to be named among Christians', it was solely the females who were expected to carry the burden of penitence. The double moral standards that applied were accepted as a regrettable fact of life: 'one false step' ruins a woman and consigns her to contempt and disgrace', while at the same time the author of her distress 'may triumph in his villainy' and escape without reproach.[14]

Genuine sympathy for the plight of women forced into prostitution and an active concern for their eternal salvation – rescuing them 'from the grasp of a hell that is ready to receive them'[15] – were behind the asylum movement. This was allied with some understanding of the reasons young girls were drawn into this trade and the difficulty of breaking with it in the absence of a viable alternative. Larger and more politically subversive questions, even when recognised, were not tackled, as in the double moral standards that applied to men and to women, the protection that class afforded to even the most dissolute of men (regarded indulgently as 'rakes'), the sexual licence that was allowed to members of the army and navy (and largely unchallenged until the internal reforms of the 1850s),[16] the social structure that left poor young women without a protective father, husband or other male relative perilously exposed and the huge number of vagrants, beggars and the 'idle poor' who subsisted from day to day and into whose ranks those fractionally above were always liable to fall. The magdalen asylum movement of the 18th and early 19th century limited itself, on the whole, to those women currently seeking an alternative (temporary or permanent) to work on the streets and to those young women on the threshold of this disastrous way of life. Awakening the conscience of the public to the point where people would support asylums for such women, however grudgingly, was in itself a landmark achievement.

The wealth of publications from the 1750s to 1770s which established the lineaments of the magdalen movement in Great Britain and Ireland vary between emotive rallying calls for the establishment of asylums, those papers which propose exactly how such might be established (mixing statements of principle and sweeping generalities with intricate regulations), early house rules for the first projects in London and Dublin, and revisions and reflections on those rules as a result of some years' experience of operation. Numerous sermons were preached in support, presenting to the public the most

---

12    Ibid., p. 7.
13    Ibid., p. 4.
14    Dodd, *An account of the rise, progress, and present state of the Magdalen Hospital*, p. 83.
15    'The Magdalene, a fragment', p. 240.
16    Jacinta Prunty, 'Military barracks and mapping in the nineteenth century: sources and issues for Irish urban history', in Jacinta Prunty, Howard Clarke & Mark Hennessy (eds), *Surveying Ireland's past* (Dublin, 2003), pp 503–4.

melodramatic aspects of the movement, with pitiable case studies and inspiring stories of redemption. As the 'success' of such sermons was measured in the size of the collection taken up, it is best to treat the content with some care. In a solemn church setting, the religious and moral aspects were most brightly burnished; the day-to-day realities were usually more mundane.

Detailed plans were published in 1758 for a 'charity house for penitent prostitutes' (Joseph Massie) and 'reformatory for penitent prostitutes' (John Fielding).[17] Plans for and reports on 'magdalen asylums' in London and Dublin in the 1760s and 1770s also provide insights into the arguments surrounding the establishment of such refuges and how matters might be best organised internally to achieve their ends. The approach taken in the literature depended on the author's social standing, sympathies and religious convictions; the research methodology (if any) behind the propositions, whether he (and the early pamphleteers were all male) had held genuine first-hand inquiries with women working in prostitution or had experience of rescue work with women on the streets, or whether they relied entirely on religious ideals, received information and well-rehearsed prejudices, recycling ideas drawn from other papers. The tone of addresses to the women themselves, usually in the form of sermons, differs from appeals to the benevolence of the public. Indeed what was understood as 'prostitution' and hence 'rescue work' varied enormously, with most of the leading thinkers in the founding decades emphasising the youth and vulnerability of those drawn into the trade, an approach that was most likely to win the support of a tight-fisted and judgemental public.

To generate financial and moral support for the early asylums, each promoter drew stark contrasts between the situation of the targeted women before and after admission. In Leeson Street:

> Instead of loathsome disease they will enjoy the blessings of health. They will exchange gross ignorance for useful knowledge, the pangs of guilt for peace of mind, the base drudgery of Prostitution for profitable employment and innocent recreations. Instead of the extremens of night-walking and starving at one time, and madly rioting and surfeiting at another, they will have warm houses, comfortable and temperate meals. Instead of lewd and blasphemous discourses they will enjoy the sweets of virtuous conversation and pious exercises. Instead of being the detested pests of society they will be useful and well regarded members of it. In short, instead of being Devils, they will become Christians.[18]

The sharpest distinctions were drawn between a 'former' life and the 'reformed' life, with the wild excesses of the former compared with the sober,

17   Joseph Massie, *A plan for the establishment of charity-houses for exposed or deserted women and girls and for penitent prostitutes* (London, 1758); John Fielding, *A plan for a preservatory and reformatory, for the benefit of deserted girls, and penitent prostitutes* (London, 1758).
18   *A letter to the public*, p. 8.

temperate, measured management of the latter. Central to such a total reorientation was a realisation of the sinfulness and folly of the former ways, marked by true repentance, in effect, a profound religious conversion. The core emphasis, in all asylums, was therefore on the moral reform and religious training of those 'once deluded wanderers, but now reclaimed and afflicted Penitents'.[19] The term 'penitent' was widely employed to denote the break that had been made with a sinful past, with the woman now contrite or sorrowful on account of transgressions and newly embarked on a virtuous road. Acknowledging a sinful past was but the first step; support in the new resolutions was crucial. In Leeson Street, above all else the penitents were to be 'carefully and conscientiously instructed on the principles of true religion, and powerfully assisted in their virtuous resolutions'.[20] In the various small city asylums which opened from the 1760s onwards, it was the denominational background of the promoters and managers – Anglican, Methodist, Catholic or other – which determined what Christian doctrine would be taught and to which church credit for reform might be ascribed.

## Use of the Figure of St Mary Magdalen in Promoting the Asylum Movement

Most individuals and groups who got involved in the late 18th and early 19th century 'rescue and reform' of women working in prostitution or in danger of resorting to it, were irresistibly drawn to the gospel figure of Mary Magdalen. In the process, the figure gained layer upon layer of allusions that went far beyond the gospel evidence. In the hands of even the least skilled orator or preacher, this heart-rending image of helpless ruin and abject penitence was guaranteed to appeal. As the woman 'from whom seven demons had gone out',[21] Mary Magdalen is also named as one of the select group of disciples who followed Jesus throughout Galilee,[22] stayed loyally with him at the foot of the cross,[23] was the first witness to the resurrection,[24] and carried the news that he was risen to the other disciples.[25] However, by conflating the unnamed 'sinful woman' who anointed Jesus at the house of the Pharisee (Luke 7:36–50), with the Mary Magdalen who was among the group of women 'healed of evil spirits and infirmities' (Luke 8:2–3), and further identifying as the Magdalene the woman who anointed Jesus in Bethany at the house of Simon (Matthew 26:6–13; Mark 14:3–9; John 12:1–8), there was boundless potential for dramatic moralising, which had long been exploited by preachers.

Other gospel personalities and scenes were frequently employed by asylum promoters, managers and clergy, including the woman caught in adultery and forgiven by Jesus (John 8:1–11), the outcast Samaritan woman whom Jesus engaged in conversation at the well (John 4:5–29) and

19  Ibid., p. 14.
20  Ibid.
21  Lk 8:2, also Mk 16: 9.
22  Lk 8:1–3.
23  Mt 27:56; Mk. 15:40; Jn 19:25. Also unnamed woman, Lk 23:55.
24  Mt 28:1; Mk. 16: 9–11; Lk 24:10; Jn 20:1–2, 11–18.
25  Mk 16: 9–11; Jn 20:1–2, 11–18.

the lost sheep which the Good Shepherd rejoices in finding once more (Luke 15:1–7).[26] However, the pre-eminent figure was St Mary Magdalen. When stretched to include all possible allusions, this character provided the asylum movement with the ideal of the reformed prostitute. The decoration of an altar to the saint sufficed to mark her feast-day in Dublin where there is no evidence of any overwrought devotion within either High Park or Gloucester Street asylums. In these houses the spiritual focus was always on the loving hearts of Jesus and Mary and the promoter of this devotion, John Eudes himself. But so compelling was the figure of the Magdalene and so useful in the loosening of purse-strings, that clergy of all denominations, preaching on behalf of different asylums, could rarely resist drawing on it, even where they must have known that they were travelling ever further from the scriptural evidence and from the real situation of the women to be assisted.

The promotional literature for Fr Smith's Drumcondra Road asylum (established 1829) can be taken as an early published example of how the Magdalen story was reconstructed for maximum dramatic effect. The accompanying line drawing (Fig. 2.1) is an undistinguished but typical artist's impression. The various accounts of the woman who anointed the feet of Jesus at Bethany or in the house of the Pharisee, and separate references to Mary of Magdala, are combined as one, along with elements of the Song of Songs, the prophecies of Isaiah and miscellaneous other Old Testament and New Testament references, into an elaborate and lengthy melodrama. The 'beauteous maid' of Bethany, bright, fragrant and lovely, is seduced by 'the spoiler', stealing her lustre, colour and peace of mind. In darkness and despair arises the thought of 'one who will stretch forth an arm of mercy to save and to heal her' and, with the grace of repentance ('a tear drop of sorrow melts her stony heart'), she seeks 'the beloved of her soul'. The news that Jesus will visit Bethany causes her to run with joy, bursting through the opposing crowd, her soul on fire with love and her heart melted with sorrow, where she sits at his feet, anointing them with spices and wiping his feet with her 'dishevelled and golden tresses'. The restoration to beauty, to health, to virtue and to inner peace is effected in an instant and could not be more complete: '"Mary's sins are forgiven her because she loves much". O moment of happiness and joy!'[27]

The appeal to the popular imagination of such reconstructions cannot be doubted. Their effectiveness in fundraising is evident from how frequently they were recycled well into the 20th century.[28] No matter how fanciful the interpretations, the case for the support of society's poorest and most despised women had the backing of sacred scripture. All women, no matter how dire their circumstances, could find in Mary Magdalen the comforting example of someone who had been lifted from the depths of sin and

26  *A letter to the public*, p. 14. For example, see the scripture references in Richard Durnford, *A sermon preached in St Paul's Church, Knightsbridge, for the Church Penitentiary Association, on Thursday, May 4, 1871* (London, 1871), pp 3–9.
27  'The Magdalene, a fragment', p. 239.
28  Scrapbook of newspaper cuttings, notices and texts of charity sermons, Gloucester Street, from 1890 (DARGS, OLC2/12/4/ no. 13).

despair to stand erect once more, secure in the personal and infinite love of Jesus. The stereotyping of the 'penitent magdalen' was reinforced by those preaching most enthusiastically on behalf of the asylums and both audience and author were undoubtedly familiar with the rhetorical conventions employed, and the gulf between oratory and local realities. Nevertheless, the repeated recourse to the magdalen figure and the constant use of the term 'penitent' hints at the thinking which informed the rescue and reform movement in the first half of the 19th century: the absolute renunciation of a sinful past; the restoration to a state of once-perfect innocence; the utter reliance on Jesus as Saviour.

The preaching undertaken on behalf of the Mecklenburgh Street penitents' asylum – formally established as a charity, with trustees, in 1833 (and later incorporated into the Gloucester Street asylum, Chapter 6) – is another early example. The 'poor, degraded, abandoned, fallen penitent' is described as the only one beyond the embrace of family, friendship or pity.[29]

> Industry refuses her capacity, service spurns her labour, charity will not commiserate nor aid her – even those who know her sorrow will not approach the contagion of her shame.[30]

According to this effusive preacher, the old and infirm are struck by want, their days cut short, 'but even in their misery there is a sympathy winds itself round them', which affords them some comfort.[31] For the poor, friendless penitent, there is not even this. There is also a rather dark warning of the repercussions should those listening be hard-hearted enough to ignore her appeal: she will turn on society and wreak havoc, until she is carried to the grave by four men, 'to the dark black pit of hell, invoking curses upon those she has left behind, her own destiny, a curse forever more.'[32]

Many of the arguments advanced in the 1760s on behalf of women 'imploring refuge from shame, temptations, insults and want' as they tried to escape prostitution, are rehearsed again in the 1840s when a number of highly motivated evangelical preachers took a lead against this 'great social evil'. William Logan's ground-breaking exposé of female prostitution in cities across Britain and Ireland was based on his own first-hand experience as a city missionary and the access this gave him to the opinions of other authorities. First published in 1843, Logan's study ran into three editions before being reworked and reissued as *The great social evil: its causes, extents, results and remedies* (London, 1871).[33] When appointed in 1841 by the directors of the City Mission to visit one of the 'lowest' districts in Glasgow, Logan extended his weekly visiting schedule to include all the local organisations

---

29  *Sermon preached by the Reverend Dr O'Brien of Limerick on behalf of the Female Penitents' Retreat, Mecklenburgh Street, on Sunday 15th October 1848* (Dublin, 1849), p. 6.
30  Ibid., p. 6–7.
31  Ibid.
32  Ibid., p. 7.
33  William Logan, *An exposure from personal observation of female prostitution in London, Leeds and Rochdale, and especially in the city of Glasgow, with remarks on the cause, extent, results and remedy of the evil* (3rd edn, Glasgow, 1845).

associated with poor women, including the lock hospital, female house of refuge and police office. Thorough research into the 'fearful system' of prostitution in Glasgow, following on his earlier missionary experiences (including St Giles, London) and a number of study visits elsewhere (including to Ireland), convinced him that 'the *rules* which regulate the accursed system in London are essentially the same in Leeds, Manchester, Liverpool and Dublin'.[34] Through questionnaire surveys, field visits, participant interviews or 'testimony', 'expert' interviews as well as inviting submissions on the topic and reviewing studies conducted overseas – what would later be standard social science research methodologies – he put together the first major body of data on why so many women ended up in prostitution throughout Britain and Ireland.

Throughout Logan's study there are flashes of insight into what might truly be behind the evil, starting with the impossibility of doing anything to reduce the demand for prostitution when 'the wealthy and influential and respectable portion of the male community' see nothing wrong with it.[35] There is sympathy for the women who end up in this way: 'the terror of meeting a demon mistress, without money, is the reason why many turn out, and *not a real desire* to follow the hopeless course.'[36] The remedies Logan proposes range widely: to punish procuresses by law, indict houses of known ill-fame, promote abstinence from intoxicating liquor, make juvenile begging a crime, prosecute those who let premises as brothels, withdraw the licences of pubs 'supported by harlots', publish the names of men found in prostitution ('why not shun the seducer as well as the seduced? Why show less sympathy to the weaker vessel than the stronger vessel?'), authorise the police to prevent women in prostitution from parading the streets, and greatly extend both primary schooling and city missions, 'where the knowledge might be acquired and the restraining influence begin to be felt of those principles of religion which are the best safeguards of all virtue'.[37] The more he learned of the 'monster evil', the more convinced Logan became of the need for legislation which would criminalise any man found seducing a young girl and setting her on the path to ruin.[38] Recognising that asylums would never strike at the root of the evil, he nevertheless saw as the most immediate response an increase in the number of 'probationary penitentiaries, homes and Magdalene asylums' so that no woman in need might have to cry 'Good God, there is no door open to us but hell's.'[39]

Logan's work goes well beyond the stereotyping of the magdalen figure and the moralising that accompanied it. Avoiding melodrama, it was his shocking honesty that was lauded at the time: 'The public needed such an exposure to let them know what atrocities as well as debaucheries are being practised in our city'.[40] The reality was much, much worse and more complicated than the

---

34   Ibid., p. 11. Emphasis as in the original.
35   Ibid., p. 17.
36   Ibid. p. 39. Emphasis as in the original.
37   Ibid., pp 34–40.
38   Logan, *The great social evil*, pp 49–50.
39   Ibid., p. 199.
40   William Anderson, Preface to William Logan, *An exposure*.

public was willing to accept and, while individual women were not all blameless, society carried some culpability for turning a blind eye to all that drew girls into this destructive way of making a living. Another frank inquiry, titled 'The great sin of great cities' by William Rathborne Greg,[41] drew expressly on the Paris researches of Alexandre Parent Duchâtelet[42] to arrive at much the same shocking conclusion for Britain: that there was an enormous trade in forced sex, including children, with men of all classes frequenting brothels, that most women working as prostitutes were involved in larceny also and that syphilis – then untreatable – was rampant but ignored.[43] Some women in London, as in Paris, were driven to prostitution to save from hunger their dependants – young children, aged and infirm parents.[44] Countless obstacles stood in the way of reducing an evil that was 'so sanctioned by custom as to have become a thing of course', including marriages impeded by scantiness of means, urgent poverty overruling the will, the prevalence of idleness among the rich and of widespread ignorance among all classes.[45] There is a scientific exactitude to these mid-century exposés – taking the lead from French studies with an impressive basis in statistics and field surveys – and a refreshing openness to new ideas.[46] While measures could be taken to mitigate the evil and reduce the numbers involved, real, longterm change depended on a change in 'social ethics'.[47] Until men who boasted of using brothels found themselves branded for seduction and desertion 'with the same kind of reprobation with which society now visits the coward and the cheat', there would be no real shift.[48] The harshness of public opinion, whereby a single act of unchastity was held to be 'unpardonable and irreparable' in the woman, but held 'trivial and venal' in the man, would have to soften.[49] But while advocating changes in attitude and the kind of structural reforms that would see no woman or girl having to choose between starvation and prostitution, an expansion of the magdalen asylum provision was urged 'for those poor girls who wish either to escape from a life of prostitution, or to avoid having recourse to it'.[50] Logan continues the argument made by his 18th-century predecessors in the rescue and reform movement in presenting the asylum as the principal and urgent practical means of serving women in dire need. He and others who shared his concern were all the time meeting girls 'with a strong desire to lead a different life, but where can they go or what can they do?'[51]

41   William Rathborne Greg. *The great sin of great cities, being a reprint, by request, of an article entitle 'Prostitution' from the Westminster and Foreign Quarterly Review for July 1851* (London, 1853).
42   Alexandre Parent Duchâtelet, *De la prostitution dans la ville de Paris, considerée sous le rapport de l'hygiène publique, de la morale et de l'administration, ouvrage appuyé de documents statistiques puisés dans les archives de la Préfecture de police*, 2 vols (Paris, 1836).
43   Greg. *The great sin of great cities*, pp 24–5.
44   Ibid., pp 14, 19.
45   Ibid., pp 24–5.
46   As well as the extensive work of Duchâtelet, see for example A. Potton, *De la prostitution et de la syphilis dans les grandes villes: dans la ville de Lyon en particulier, de leurs causes, de leur influence sur la santé* (Paris, 1843).
47   Greg. *The great sin of great cities*, p. 49.
48   Ibid., pp 50–51.
49   Ibid., pp 23.
50   Ibid., pp 48.
51   William Anderson, Preface to William Logan, *An exposure*, p. 46.

## The Magdalen Rescue and Reform Movement in Dublin City to *c*.1853

When the Sisters of Our Lady of Charity of Refuge arrived in 1853 to take charge of Fr Smith's Drumcondra Road asylum, there was already a number of small asylums operating in Dublin, under both Protestant and Roman Catholic management, along with the well-known Leeson Street refuge founded by Lady Denny in 1765 (first admissions 1767). As elsewhere in Britain and Ireland, there were as many different visions of the magdalen asylum in Dublin as there were advocates and as many different versions on the ground as local circumstances, resources and individual patronage and personalities allowed. Extracts from the British press covering the reality of prostitution and efforts made to address it were reprinted in Irish newspapers, so there was certainly an awareness that the problem extended across these islands, though the term 'the social evil in our streets', as coined by William Logan, was not taken up as a euphemim for prostitution by commentators in Dublin until perhaps 1862.[52] Whatever the different opinions held on the extent of prostitution, causes and solutions, there was general agreement that additional 'rescue' accommodation was required. It is impossible to be certain of the exact number of asylums or refuges in operation on a given date, as not all are covered by advertisements or other contemporary references. Some for which funds were solicited may not have operated at all, or only briefly, while temporary closures, amalgamations, relocations and 'relaunches' under new management further confuse the record. Some have left summaries of their founding philosophy, admission regulations, governance and other important facts. For others, the approximate location and one year of operation – possibly – is about all that is known. Nevertheless, it is possible to learn something of the rescue and reform movement in Dublin just before the arrival of the Sisters of Our Lady of Charity.

In terms of numbers of asylums, the superintendent of the Dublin City Mission, William Robertson, advised William Logan on a visit to Dublin in the 1840s that there were 12 or 14 magdalen asylums operating in Dublin city. When pressed to estimate the number of 'unfortunate females' in the city, Robertson suggested about 1,700 prostitutes and 'showed me a back street near the Barracks where there were 200 girls. I observed over a door 'Old Hell' regularly painted as a direction'.[53] And there appeared to be no end in sight to recruitment to the unhappy trade, with claims that procuresses lured girls reared in the union workhouse as they turned 15 and were assigned to the female able-bodied ward where no sort of classification or separation was practised. The South Dublin Union workhouse (opened 1840) in particular was condemned as 'a nursery for replenishing the streets of the Metropolis with numbers of unhappy beings, who it must be admitted received their initiation into vice within its walls'.[54]

---

52    See for example, reports in *Freeman's Journal*, 11 Mar., 8, 21 July 1858; address by the Lord Lieutenant to the inaugural meeting of the Dublin Statistical Society, *Freeman's Journal*, 27 Nov. 1862.

53    Logan, *An exposure*, p. 10.

54    Printed extract from parliamentary inquiry into workhouses in Ireland, 'Corruption and profligacy have been promoted by the mixture of the most degraded characters from the streets with young and innocent females' , 1854 (DDA, Cullen, 332/3, laity, no. 2).

The oldest of the Protestant asylums still in operation in the 1850s and by far the best known was Lady Denny's project, 8 Leeson Street, founded 1765. It was intended only 'for young women who have for the first time fallen into vice', as later advertisements made clear.[55] Other Protestant homes were the Dublin Female Penitentiary, Berkeley Place, with a foundation date of 1812 or 1813, Brown Street asylum (1830), and Baggot Street (1835), while there was also a shelter for discharged female prisoners at 5 Harcourt Street (1821).[56] All were under the control of ladies' committees and had a modest capacity, with Baggot Street, at 40 places, probably the largest.[57]

The earliest of all asylums – at least, of those listed in 1850 – was the Catholic Olivemount Institute, Dundrum, founded 1742 by the Revd B. Kirby. It had a larger remit than just 'penitent women' and was connected with the Richmond Female Penitentiary, Grangegorman. There was a Catholic magdalen asylum operating at 28 Dominick Street (formerly Bow Street asylum, founded 1780) and a 'Female Penitents' Retreat' at Marlborough Street (formerly at Little James's Street and before that Chancery Lane). Two other early asylums were by 1850 under the care of religious sisters: the Donnybrook asylum (formerly Townsend Street 'General Magdalene Asylum' founded 1798, under the care of the Sisters of Charity 1832, moved to Donnybrook by 1837) and St Patrick's Refuge, Crofton Road, Kingstown (Dun Laoghaire), also founded 1798 and later placed under the care of the Sisters of Mercy.[58] The other Catholic-run asylums in Dublin city are the two which will be managed by the Sisters of Our Lady of Charity: the refuge at 2 Drumcondra Road (at this address from 1832, moved to High Park in 1858) and the female penitents' retreat at 76 Mecklenburgh Street (under the Mercy sisters 1873, under OLC 1887).

Some, if not all, of the Catholic asylums owed their existence to the efforts of individual priests: Revd John Vincent Holmes and Revd William Young were credited as priest founders, as was the Revd B. Kirby (Olivemount), James Laphen (Mecklenburgh Street) and John Smith (Drumcondra Road).[59] A committee of laymen met weekly at the old library rooms of SS Michael and John's church, Essex Street West, in support of Mecklenburgh Street asylum.[60] The priest about to be appointed as chaplain to the Westmoreland Lock Hospital for venereal diseases in Townsend Street in 1855 saw his role as 'keeping myself in constant communication with the several magdalen asylums in and about the city' so that he could ensure, as opportunity arose, that girls leaving the Lock were 'fittingly placed'.[61] All of the religious-run asylums in Dublin originated as small Catholic lay asylums, a pattern which was replicated elsewhere – for example, an

---

55   *Thom's Irish Almanac and Official Directory* (Dublin, 1882), p. 1318.

56   *Thom's* 1851, p. 731; the latter's earlier address of 4 Harcourt Row refers to the same establishment.

57   Ibid.

58   *Thom's* 1851, pp 729–31; 1882, p. 1317.

59   'The Magdalene, a fragment', p. 240. The immediate lessor of the 'Female Penitentiary' at 76 Mecklenburgh Street Lower is named as the Revd James Laphan in the tenement (Griffith's) valuation of 1854, while the premises is also listed in the first valuation of 1830. B. Kirby is named as founder of Olivemount, *Thom's* 1851, p. 729.

60   *Thom's* 1851, p. 731.

61   T. O'Malley to Mgr Meghan, 31 Oct. 1855 (DDA, Cullen, 332/7 file I secular priests, no. 125).

asylum founded 1812 in an old lace factory in Clare Street, Limerick, was later managed by the Good Shepherd Sisters[62] while the Gibraltar Lane (Lombard Street) asylum in Galway, founded 1824 in an old malt house, was later under the auspices of the Mercy sisters.[63]

The work of all asylums was clothed in similar language: the 'rescue' and 'reform' of poor 'penitent females' who were trying to support themselves by their own labour and needed every encouragement to persevere, including practical support from a charitable public. At Berkeley Place, the committee of ladies in charge directed their exertions to 'the religious and moral improvement of the women and their advancement in habits of order and industry'. At Brown Street 'industrious habits are strictly enforced'; there was daily scripture reading and religious instruction was held twice weekly.[64] In all cases, the public was assured that the moral restoration of the women would be zealously attended to and that they would be surrounded with every support that religion could offer.

All of the asylums were maintained in large part, if not entirely, by the work of the residents. The employment of the women was never merely a matter of keeping them occupied; a weekly income had to be generated or the house would close, while the moral imperative, to support oneself by honest labour, was always present. The difficulty of finding suitable and remunerative work was probably the principal obstacle faced by all promoters and managers; a 'small but certain income' was preferred, but this was always a lot easier to argue for than to procure.[65] Some of the earliest advocates of the asylum expected the institution to be practically self-sufficient, looking after its own clothing needs, shoemaking and washing.[66] But that was far removed from the reality on the ground. All of the asylums in Dublin, without exception, relied on washing and needlework, confirming what the OLC sisters discovered on arrival from France, that this was indeed the only way an income could be generated.[67] Seeking the favour of orders from the public and advertising that work would be done 'on the most moderate terms' underlines the competition that existed between countless deserving charities all seeking a share of a limited market. The earliest published call to support Fr Smith's Drumcondra Road asylum is prefaced by a standard appeal 'for the asylums generally' in the form of subscriptions ('any sums, from one penny a week upwards') and 'work for the penitents', which was listed as 'laundry-work, bleaching, washing, mangling and fancy needle-work', with the additional note that such work was always 'executed during the hours not employed at spiritual exercises'.[68] Public chapels attached to the

---

62   Topographical information: 22 Residence, in Eamon O'Flaherty, *Limerick*, Irish Historic Towns Atlas no. 21 (Dublin, 2010), p. 53.

63   Deed of conveyance of a house and premises in Gibralter Lane, Galway, 23 Oct. 1824 (Mercy Archives, Western Province, GY6/1/69a). Other documents give the spelling Gibraltar Lane.

64   *Thom's* 1851, p. 731; 1882, p. 1318.

65   Massie, *A plan for the establishment of charity houses*, p. 8.

66   Fielding, *A plan for a preservatory and reformatory*, p. 23.

67   'Un seul ouvrage lucratif et ordinaire aux établissements en ce pays', High Park, draft *circulaire*, 15 novembre 1853.

68   'The Magdalene, a fragment', p. 240.

refuge were a particular feature of Protestant refuges (Leeson Street, Berkeley Place and Baggot Street); the collections taken up at the Sunday and other occasional services were an important income stream.[69] The physical separation of an asylum from the temptations of the city was advocated by some promoters. Joseph Massie was insistent that it should be in an isolated, healthful rural setting, accessible by a main road but secure from 'ill-designing or inquisitive people' who might well be expected to haunt a reformatory, such as 'wealthy rakes', men with 'felonious intentions' and street robbers looking for female associates.[70] For Massie, the rural environment itself could bring healing; 'the constant prospect of a pleasant country would gradually dispel their gloom of mind', the food would be more nourishing and a 'general appearance of decency, good order, sobriety, industry' could be imposed.[71] Of the early Dublin asylums, the Olivemount Institution at Dundrum best fulfilled the rural criterion, as it was well beyond the city bounds to the south and there was ample space for more building. However, overriding the claims of a rural retreat was the need to be close to where the girls and women seeking refuge were to be found, so most of the Dublin asylums were to located in densely built-up and very poor parts of the city or (in the case of Leeson Street in the 1760s) adjoining an area renowned for prostitution. None had anything like the space required to be models of good order. The advertising for Fr Smith's Drumcondra Road refuge lauded its ideal location, its 'air, room and convenience'.[72] But on all these counts it fell far short and its transfer by the OLC sisters to the aptly-named High Park (1858), a rural idyll, reflected the earlier move of the Townsend Street asylum to Donnybrook (1837).

Proponents of the asylum or refuge had to guard against accusations of maintaining the women in comfort and idleness and glossing over the sinfulness of prostitution. Outsiders were given assurances that the inmates were desperately in need and sincerely wished to turn their lives around, and that all worked towards their maintenance. Fr Smith's 'twenty destitute creatures' were described as 'comfortably sheltered from vice and want'.[73] At Gloucester Street 'the inmates come and remain as long as they wish, to avoid temptation; they are free to leave when they desire'.[74] The discharged prisoners' refuge at Harcourt Road sheltered only women 'who may appear desirous of reforming and are willing to put up with hard fare, continued labour and strict discipline'.[75] All denominations were welcome at Donnybrook, provided only that an assurance was given by the candidate 'that she is in earnest in wishing to reform'.[76] While discipline had to be maintained, proponents constantly pointed out how kindliness and sympathy were most effective 'in promoting instruction, reformation and obedience'. Punishments, such as withdrawing the privilege of walking in the fields or making the woman eat alone, 'all of which may be done

69   *Thom's* 1882, p. 1318.
70   Massie, *A plan for the establishment of charity houses*, p. 35.
71   Ibid., pp 35, 40.
72   'The Magdalene, a fragment', p. 240.
73   Ibid.
74   Rosa M. Barrett, *Guide to Dublin charities* (Dublin, 1884), p. 6.
75   *Thom's* 1851. p. 731.
76   Barrett, *Guide to Dublin charities*, p. 5.

without passion', were recommended by Massie.[77] The single most effective tool of course was that an incorrigible woman could be required to leave, and all knew that.

All of the small magdalen asylums provided accommodation for women in immediate need and advertised the moral and religious support they offered. None were training centres or employment agencies, although hopes were always entertained that, through the kind interest of lady patrons and friends of the institute, 'reclaimed' women and girls might be found positions where their previous character was not known or would not be held against them.[78] At the Catholic asylum at Little James's Street (later of Marlborough Street), in between the washing and mangling, 'no opportunity is lost to refit them to fill, with credit, at some future date, their proper station in life'.[79] Emigration to the British colonies offered the hope of a truly new start and some women did seek the means to emigrate, 'so that they might avoid the fatal necessity of returning to vice through mere want of sustenance'.[80] But emigration was an expensive option and (its promoters argued) suited only to women who could be relied on.[81] Emigration was offered to select female ex-prisoners through the well-designed scheme run by Sister Magdalen Kirwan of the Sisters of Mercy at Goldenbridge in the 1860s, while the Discharged Female Roman Catholic Prisoners' Aid Society, finding it impossible to place the girls in its charge, was also in the 1880s very keen on them emigrating to America, as it met all their hopes – immediate employment, complete change from old associations, good wages and kind employers ('up to this' at least).[82] But the principal end of all the magdalen asylums was to make it possible, by providing accommodation, food and other necessities and by kindly interest and moral support, for a woman to leave work on the streets. To paraphrase the mission of the Little James's Street asylum, it was to bring the woman to know – perhaps for the first time – the value of her immortal soul and to weep over her past sins, to bring her from being 'the disgrace and scourge of society' to be ranked among its 'useful and edifying members'.[83] And in this mission, all who supported the 'rescue and reform' of 'magdalen women' were carried along by the assurance given in scripture that success would not be measured in numbers. In Fielding's proposed reformatory, 'the smallest success more than rewards the greatest difficulties; for we are told that *There is more joy in heaven over one sinner that repententh than over ninety and nine just persons that need no repentance.*'[84]

77    Massie, *A plan for the establishment of charity houses*, p. 42.
78    Ibid., pp 36, 42.
79    Advertising leaflet, Female Penitent Asylum, Little James's Street, n.d. (DDA, Murray, 33/1 no. 17).
80    Dodd, *An account of the rise, progress, and present state of the Magdalen Hospital*, p. 9.
81    Massie, *A plan for the establishment of charity houses*, p. 44.
82    Sister Mary Magdalen Kirwan, Goldenbridge, to Revd Mother, High Park, 27 Nov. 1860 (DARGS, OLC1/2/6 no. 1); *Third Annual Report of the Dublin Discharged Female Roman Catholic Prisoners' Aid Society* (Dublin, 1884), p. 4.
83    Advertising leaflet, Female Penitent Asylum, Little James's Street.
84    Fielding, *A plan for a preservatory and reformatory*, p. 15.

## The Refuge Tradition of Notre Dame de Charité and its Basis in the Rule, Constitutions and Customs of 1641, 1666 and 1734

While sharing many of the same characteristics of the 'rescue and reform' magdalen movement of Britain and Ireland discussed above, the tradition which the sisters of Notre Dame de Charité du Refuge brought to Dublin in 1853 was different in several important respects. Central to the OLC system was adherence to a written rule and to customs long established and also preserved in writing. Care for the common life is one of the key threads holding this rule together, as is the pre-eminence given to the love of God and of neighbour, transcending all other commandments.[85] A commentary on the constitutions and practices of the institute, published in 1734 'for the sake then of perfect conformity of opinion and decision' among all the houses, concludes with a section titled 'Explanation of the Rule of the Penitents'.[86] These texts are key to understanding the origins and cultural context of the OLC refuge. However, day-to-day practices in the monastery of Dublin, even in its first decades, did not follow Caen in every detail, nor would it have been possible to do so. Some articles were of historical interest only, even in the 1850s, such as the instructions on evacuating the monastery due to plague.[87] Allowance must also be made for the quiet abandonment of archaic and unnecessary practices over time and the impossibility, or downright foolishness, of implementing in Dublin what was clearly meant for a warmer, continental climate and locally-specific conditions. The penitents' rule was obsolete in High Park by the 1930s — and possibly earlier — but nevertheless its influence can be read into the daily routine and general spirit of the refuge into the 1950s when 'modernisation' began to take hold.[88] Some of the early differences between the practices in Ireland and in France can be deduced from the succession of queries and appeals, mostly undated, made by Dublin to the first house of Caen as *le dépôt de la Règle* to which 'all houses of the order have recourse in their doubts and difficulties'.[89] Specific points were clarified in a question-and-answer format. That the advice given was implemented exactly as Caen suggested cannot be assumed, as it was never a ruling, but merely a sharing of experience.

The parallels between the rule of *les Soeurs Pénitentes* and the constitutions of *les Religieuses de Notre Dame de Charité* – bound as a single volume – are

---

85   Introduction, *Oeuvres complètes de Bienheureux Jean Eudes*, x (Vannes, 1909). pp 37–9. Hereafter, Introduction.

86   'Explanation of the rules, constitutions and customs of the Religious of Our Lady of Charity ...', trans. of 1734 edn (DARGS, OLC1/5/1 no. 1). Hereafter, Explanation of [chapter or constitution or rule no.], Explanation of the rule of the penitents.

87   Explanation of constitution xxxv, The mother superior, p. 255.

88   The 1939 printing of the constitutions, directory and rule omits the penitents' rule entirely (DARGS, OLC1/5/1 no. 18), and no written penitents' rule was known to exist by sisters who entered the community in the 1930s. Personal communication, Sister Teresa Coughlan OLC, 6 June 2013.

89   Soeur M. de St Stanislas Brunel, Paris to Mgr l'Archevêque de Dublin, 9 July 1853 (DDA, Cullen, 325/8 no. 208).

striking.[90] In the language employed, the practices advocated and the virtues extolled, one rule mirrors the other. The spirituality of self-abnegation and penance promoted in the refuge dominates the convent with equal vigour. In many places, the *Rituale* or directions concerning the administration of the sacraments noted 'the same as for the religious' and the ceremonial was followed exactly for the women as for the sisters. The women kept the times of silence observed by the sisters, most especially the night-time 'grand silence' from the first stroke of the bell.[91] The reader of the penitents' rule is repeatedly directed back to the appropriate article in the main part of the text, that is, the sisters' rule, while the greater part of what was imposed on or recommended to the women matches that which was imposed on or recommended to the sisters. Differences are often in degree rather than in essence – for example, while the mortifications demanded of sisters were specified, those expected of the women were left to their own preference.[92] Should a woman become ill, she was to be brought to the infirmary and – like the sisters – expected to co-operate obediently with whatever the infirmarian and doctor prescribed for her health. Should recovery fail and death approach, she was to be given every spiritual assistance, neither more nor less than the sisters (*ni plus ni moins que les Religieuses*).[93] The position held by the mistress of the penitents in the refuge matched in importance that held by the mistress of the novices in the convent, with the newly-elected superior urged to make a right selection (*un bon choix*) for these two key posts. Only sisters known to be very spiritual, prudent and virtuous were to be considered, and full of zeal for the final end of the institute, the salvation of souls.[94] The language used in relation to the novices parallels that used in reference to the penitents; in both cases, obedience and docility are the preferred virtues and are to be assiduously cultivated from the time of arrival in the enclosure.[95]

Just as the sisters were repeatedly urged to submit to the rule wholeheartedly, as the surest path to sanctity, so too new women residents were to be won over to embrace willingly 'their' rule. And lest they be ignorant of its contents, Caen prescribed that it be read aloud once a month in the women's refectory, exactly paralleling the way in which the sisters' constitutions were kept always before their eyes.[96] As the rule was there to protect individual sisters (a 'private' sister or 'inferior' was not obliged to follow a direction contrary to conscience or outside the rule,[97] while the superior could not act unilaterally outside the rule[98]), so too the penitents' rule afforded them some

90  'Les constitutions des religieuses du Monastère de Notre-Dame de Charité de Caen', pp 79–174; 'Règlement pour les filles et femmes pénitentes', pp 175–87, in *Oeuvres complètes de Bienheureux Jean Eudes*, x (Vannes, 1909). Hereafter, *Constitutions* and *Règlement* respectively. The term 'les Sœurs Pénitentes' is used in the heading to *Règlement*, vii, p. 184.
91  *Règlement iv, Du silence qu'elles garderont*, p. 181.
92  Explanation of the rule of the penitents, ch. 5, Penance, p. 364.
93  *Règlement vii, Autres règles générales que toutes les Sœurs Pénitentes doivent observer*, p. 187.
94  *Constitution lii, De l'élection de la supérieure et autres officières*, p. 170.
95  *Constitution xl, De la directrice*, pp 145–8; *Règlement, i, De leur réception*, p. 177.
96  *Règlement vii, Autres règles générales que toutes les Sœurs Pénitentes doivent observer*, p. 187.
97  *Constitution lii, Brève déclaration de l'obligation des Soeurs à l'observation de la règle et des constitutions*, p. 171.
98  *Constitution xxxviii, De la manière que la supérieure doit tenir pour les affaires*, p. 140.

protection from the whims and caprices of individual sisters. The women, for example, could not be kept up late out of the ordinary, other than on Spy Wednesday and Holy Thursday during Holy Week when the liturgical ceremonies continue into the late evening.[99] The annual inspection by the 'spiritual father' was to protect all residents against unreasonable hardships; he was expected to taste the food and drink provided so that he might see for himself how the sisters were treated 'and the same in regard to the Penitents'. His obligation on this annual visitation to admonish faults and to encourage renewed efforts applied to both groups; the observation that 'wherever the visitor expresses satisfaction with the sisters' good behaviour it gives them more courage and good will to advance in perfection than all the reproofs he could give' was applied also to the women and girls, who were invariably spurred on more by encouragement than chastisement.[100]

The 'Explanation of the Rules, Constitutions and Customs of the Religious of Our Lady of Charity' brought to Dublin in the 1850s was a faithful handwritten copy of the version approved in 1734, which itself made much of its exact fidelity to the rule drawn up by John Eudes in 1641 and approved in 1666 after much uneasiness on the part of Rome about religious sisters working so closely with girls and women 'of low morals'.[101] The first rule relied heavily on the constitutions of the Visitation sisters. Similarly, the customs book or *Coutumier et directoire* was based on the customs and directory of the Sisters of the Visitation, as was the directory of the office, the ceremonial of the choir and directories for each of the offices in the house. All were compiled at the first monastery of Caen in its role of ensuring fidelity to the spirit and practice of the founding days.

Some of the inconsistencies and harshness to be found in the constitutions can be traced to the efforts made to have the new congregation approved in the 1660s, in the face of concerted opposition and misrepresentation at Rome. As noted already, John Eudes relied heavily on the constitutions of the Visitation sisters (founded by Francis de Sales and Jane Frances de Chantal), who trained the first recruits to Notre Dame de Charité and provided a local superior to Caen until the sisters elected one from among their own number.[102] This first rule was substantially extended in 1661 with respect to the penitents and their government, with further modifications before approval in 1666. Contemporary correspondence between John Eudes, Mother Margaret Francis Patin (the superior in Caen) and representatives, advisers and ecclesiastical authorities in Rome reveals some of the obstacles which were placed in the path of its approval, the ways in which these were overcome or deflected and the changes made to the 1641 constitutions in the process.

The new institute was viewed with great scepticism as 'an innovation' and its first application for formal approval, in 1647, refused. The core objection was to the fourth vow, 'instructing and harbouring those poor souls

99    Explanation of the rule of the penitents, ch 3, The order of the day, pp 346, 355.
100   Explanation of constitution xxxi, The spiritual father, p. 230.
101   John Eudes to Mother Margaret Frances Patin, n.d. but early 1662, *Letters of John Eudes*, p. 188.
102   The first superior from among the OLC sisters was elected in 1668, to succeed Mother Margaret Frances Patin; see M. Ch. de Montzey, *Life of the venerable John Eudes, with a sketch of the history of his foundations from A.D. 1601 to 1874* (London, 1883), pp 195–6.

who have been wounded by sin', on the basis that Rome held 'it is impossible for virtuous women to associate with these others without real danger to their own morals'.[103] But this was 'the divine and only work' which defined the order; this was its reason for being. As John Eudes reminded the sisters, 'this is the object for which you have been founded, that the town [of Caen] has received you on this condition, and that at the hour of death God will require of you an account of the manner in which you have fulfilled this obligation'.[104] Each sister, whether working directly with 'our sister penitents' or not, was 'absolutely bound to do all that care, diligence and the example of a holy life can do' to win for Christ 'the souls which He has redeemed with His blood'.[105] The order had no existence outside this fourth vow, so that there could be no question of compromise on this point.

A special envoy, Fr Francis Louis Boniface, was contracted by John Eudes and the sisters in 1661 to advance the process of approval by Rome after years of deadlock.[106] His dispatches confirmed that there had been no shift in Rome's position, despite the lengthy, and successful, trial period. As before, 'they are raising formidable objections over the danger which they believe results from having religious govern penitents'.[107] Similar ventures had been refused permission, always based on a fear that nuns would somehow be 'defiled' by working with 'fallen women', no matter how penitent or reformed.[108] In response, affidavits were submitted to show how, for example, the Daughters of Charity of St Vincent de Paul of the Hôtel Dieu in Paris 'are constantly in the midst of numerous sick persons, convalescents, doctors, surgeons, apothecaries, hospital attendants, and even fallen women who come there to be confined' without any ill effect on the sisters. Religious life was indeed compatible with apostolic service; 'both employments exist without giving rise to any disorder'.[109] One concession penned by Fr Boniface, to answer Rome's difficulty with the overlap of convent and refuge, was to state the impossibility of accepting former penitents as nuns ('but if they desire to be such they are sent to the monasteries of other convents in other cities, if they wish to go there').[110] Another compromise was that OLC sisters working at this dangerous interface would be not less than 20 years of age on profession, although the age at which women could make religious vows was set at 17 by the Council of Trent. When the revised rule was eventually approved in January 1666, the diocesan bishop was authorised to add to the regulations if necessary.[111] The resulting text was an uneven amalgam of petty regulations, broad ideals and spiritual

103   John Eudes to Mother Margaret Frances Patin, n.d. but early 1662, *Letters of John Eudes*, pp 187–90; see de Montzey, *Life of the venerable John Eudes*, p. 186.
104   Sermon delivered at the first profession of vows after the approval of the institute, Caen, feast of the Ascension, 1666, quoted in de Montzey, *Life of the venerable John Eudes*, p. 195.
105   John Eudes to Sister M. of the Nativity Herson, early 1672; John Eudes to the Community of Our Lady of Charity at Caen, 15 Aug. [n.d. but before 1656], *Letters of John Eudes*, pp 220, 93.
106   John Eudes to Mother Margaret Frances Patin, 21 Sept. 1660, *Letters of John Eudes*, p. 153
107   Same to same, summer 1661, *Letters of John Eudes*, p. 163.
108   Ibid.
109   Ibid.
110   Ibid., p. 164.
111   De Montzey, *Life of the venerable John Eudes*, p. 194.

exhortations. The accretion of customs and practices sanctified by their adoption in the holy cradle of Caen, and the extensive commentary appended in the edition of 1734, further obscures the early constitutions while the loss of the archive of Caen on the night of the Allied bombing (D-Day), 6 June 1944, makes it impossible to unravel the various stages authoritatively. Wherever a 'large-minded' and generous commentary interrupts[112] – and contradicts – some of the more inflexible and harsh passages, it is usually drawn directly from the teachings of John Eudes, Francis de Sales or Jane Frances de Chantal, connecting to the founding spirit and early decades. How exactly the rule that was brought to Dublin in 1853 matched the founder's intentions must be open to question, but there can be no doubt that the sisters who formed this first overseas community were convinced of its sacred origins and absolute inviolability. The image of John Eudes 'giving the constitutions to the first sister of the Order', Mère Marie de la Nativité Herson, first superior of Caen (see Figure 1.1) was reinforced in the iconography of the institute, as was John Eudes' wish that Divine Love might engrave on the heart of the novice 'the Rules, Constitutions and Customs of the Order'.[113]

## Enclosure

Enclosure, or separation from the world, was the defining characteristic of the asylum model offered by Notre Dame de Charité du Refuge and the basis on which religious life in this institute (as in most other women's institutes of the 17th century) was constructed. The terms 'refuge' – flee to – and 'asylum' – a place of sanctuary or safety – were understood literally.[114] Sisters and penitents alike fled voluntarily to a place where they could work out their salvation separated from 'the world', and where 'success' might be measured in terms of spiritual progress. While the rule spelled out that 'the penitents shall not be kept in the convent all their lives' (and the vast majority of the women in High Park were short-term residents),[115] 'during the time they spend there, they remain perfectly cloistered'.[116] In the case of the sisters, the rule stated simply that no religious after her profession was allowed to leave the monastery, no matter what the pretext.[117] Dire warnings were issued against any relaxation on this point – for example, sending infirm sisters elsewhere for a change of air: 'if once the door were opened, says St Francis de Sales, we would often see nuns going about'.[118] One of the core responsibilities of the superior was to maintain the integrity of the

112   'Let us walk in the path of simplicity and large-mindedness, without being held back by mere trifles and exaggerated politeness', Explanation of constitution xxxi (xxvii), Cells and beds, p. 227.
113   For example, see the centenary booklet, *Order of Our Lady of Charity of Refuge, spirit, aim and work* (Dublin, 1954), pp 9, 11.
114   *Refugio* (verb): I run away, flee to, shrink back, recoil from; asylum (noun): place of refuge, sanctuary, *Electronic pocket Oxford Latin dictionary* (Oxford, 2002).
115   See analysis of High Park register data in chapters 3 and 12 of this book.
116   John Eudes to Mother Margaret Frances Patin, 10 Sept. 1661, *Letters of John Eudes*, p. 165.
117   *Constitution xvii, De la clôture*, p. 103. For a legitimate reason, approval might be sought from the bishop but constitution xviii makes it clear that this would be in exceptional or extraordinary circumstances.
118   Explanation of constitution xvii (xxix), Enclosure, p. 146.

enclosure.[119] Visits to the parlour by any sister or other resident were to be discouraged, though they were not banned. In the case of the penitents, 'such interviews usually only serve to make them long after liberty, and awaken curiosity to hear news, in a word, to unfit them for their duty'. Even those older women 'who desire to remain in the house all their lives may be allowed to see their near relatives when these latter are above suspicion, but only seldom, and in presence of the mistress or in her absence of some other religious'.[120] The reception of fee-paying residents, such as 'pious ladies and secular persons desirous of confirming themselves in a devout life', or of school girls received as boarders, did not infringe the 'complete enclosure' which was the pride of the monastery, as their parlour visits were also to be closely regulated, their exits and entrances to the enclosure marked by the ringing of bells.[121]

Sundering – or at least disrupting – the connections with a former life which was demanded of all residents of the monastery of Our Lady of Charity was symbolised by the grille which the rule specified for the parlour. The 'wicket gate' in the grille was opened only as necessary, such as 'to allow the Professors to show the pupils how to draw or to Paint', or a seamstress to fit a boarder with a new costume.[122] The practical obstacles to involvement with 'the world' were reinforced by the stress on silence, regarded in all religious institutes as essential to the maintenance of a 'spirit of regularity' or fidelity to the rule:[123]

> Let us be very zealous for the silence and not talk even at other times of recollection without necessity. It will be a means of retrenching many sins and of overcoming the chief obstacles which oppose our perfection.[124]

The times of silence enjoined on the women could be filled with singing hymns and canticles according to the time of the Church's year, or saying aloud the rosary and other prayers, 'to keep up their fervour and to drive away temptations and weariness'.[125] The ban on talking about their previous life was probably the sharpest tool of all those designed to effect a complete break with the 'outside world'; allotting a 'house name' to each woman on arrival made at least nominal compliance possible:

> From the first day they should be warned that they are not to speak to any of their companions of the disorders of their life, nor anything concerning the past lives of their others (*sic*), supposing they know of them; this being a fault which is

119   *Constitution xvii, De la clôture*, pp 104–5.
120   Explanation of the rule of the penitents, ch. 4, Silence, p. 362.
121   Explanation of constitution xvi (xxix), Enclosure, p. 148; of constitution xliii, The portress, p. 296.
122   Explanation of constitution xvi (xxix), Enclosure, p. 150.
123   *Constitution xxviii, De silence*, p. 125.
124   Explanation of constitution xxviii (xxii), Silence, p. 213.
125   Explanation of the rule of the penitents, ch. 4, Silence, p. 362.

severely punished. In order to avoid allowing them to become acquainted with each other's family, they are given a name on their entrance, and must not be called by any other.[126]

Entering the enclosure had to be a voluntary act. A novice prior to taking vows was examined by a priest to ensure that she was taking vows of her own free will.[127] Women penitents were similarly regarded by John Eudes as specially called by God and freely seeking the shelter of the house.[128] In the language and legal realities of 17th-century France, however, jurisdiction over a woman could be held by a father or husband or guardian who could place her in the house, and was answerable 'for any trouble or annoyance which might be brought on the monastery by the detention of so and so, placed among the Penitents'.[129] Should a woman whom the sisters judged to be insufficiently instructed or not yet grounded in the fear of God insist on leaving, they might remonstrate with her and advise against it, but if she insisted, she had to be allowed leave; no-one was to be held against her will. However, the phrase that she might be placed in the care of parents, guardians or other interested friends (*on la remettra entre les mains de ses parents ou de ceux qui l'ont amenée*) again reflects the position of females in 17th-century France.[130] A kindly reception and some special consideration was advocated towards all newcomers, whether novice or penitent. While the novices were not to be spared public humiliations, the novice mistress 'should also now and again give them marks of kindness when they endeavour to do their duty well, and acknowledge their frailties. Such signs of affection win their confidence, give fresh courage, and besides they are more ready to profit by the advice given them'.[131] The rule emphasised the difference 'some kindliness and compassion' meant to a woman on arrival at the monastery; 'this plan finds the way to their heart, awakens their confidence, and shows them that they are not so badly off as they believed'.[132] The 'general plan of conduct in dealing with these poor girls is to strive to win them to God by gentleness and kindly reasoning', so that they might embrace 'their rule' willingly.[133] Correspondence with Caen confirms that the Dublin house tried to adopt this practice from the outset; 'we [Caen] act absolutely as you do with our Penitents newly entered; we try to gain them [win them] to God by kindness [sweetness], as they are seldom corrected by rigour'.[134]

---

126  Explanation of the rule of the penitents, ch. 1, Their reception, p. 337.
127  See canonical examination before profession in 'Livre dans lequel les Soeurs de La Congrégation de Notre Dame de Charité écrivent les ans et les jours de leur voeux et des annuelles confirmations qu'elles font en ce Monastère de Dublin, lequel a été établi le 14 de septembre de l'année 1853' (DARGS, OLC1/6/1 no. 1).
128  Eudes to Patin, 10 Sept. 1661, 'that only those are received who, being called by God, voluntarily enter the house to do penance there; that during the time they spend there, they remain perfectly cloistered'. *Letters of John Eudes*, p. 165. See also Explanation of the rule of the penitents, ch. 2, Their departure, p. 340.
129  Explanation of the rule of the penitents, ch. 1, Their reception, pp 336–7, 339.
130  *Règlement, ii, De leur sortie*, p. 178.
131  Explanation of constitution xxxix, The mistress of novices, p. 284.
132  Explanation of the rule of the penitents, ch. 5, Penance, p. 364.
133  Explanation of the rule of the penitents, ch. 2, Their departure, p. 343.
134  MS notes on the customs and practices of Our Lady of Charity of Refuge; n.d. (DARGS, OLC1/5/1 no. 14).

## Obedience

Obedience was recommended as the foundation of the rule for all members of the household of Notre Dame de Charité, sisters and women alike. It was primarily through obedience that *'leurs ennemis spirituels'* would be overcome.[135] These spiritual enemies were listed in the sisters' constitutions as

> The first of our enimies (*sic*) is the wicked Spirit, then our own will, our own judgement, the world, our Passions, and our evil inclinations. These are so many spiritual foes, whom we overcome by obedience; by it we carry the Victory over them all.[136]

The 'dispositions which should accompany our obedience' were listed as obeying faithfully (to the letter), promptly (without delaying for a single instant), simply (without comment or reflection), frankly (without uneasiness or restraint) and cordially (with a good heart and cheerfully). This spirit of ready, cheerful obedience was to be extended to all superiors equally, 'whether they are old or young, more or less perfect',[137] and manifested itself in countless minor ways, such as seeking permission to cut one's hair.[138]

The women were expected to embrace the same understanding – or at least practice – of obedience as the sisters. In their case, 'the greatest respect and obedience' was due directly to their mistress; 'this point well observed will help in the practice of all the others, and will maintain good order among these poor girls'.[139] Deliberately thwarting the mistress or taking 'a malicious delight' in trying her patience could result in 'strong measures or punishment'; obedience played such a central role in the life of the monastery that undermining it could not be ignored.[140] However, elevating the mistress in this manner placed a huge responsibility on her shoulders; she therefore 'should strive to render it easy for them to pay the honour and respect' due to her as superior by carefully reflecting in advance of speaking. Where a mistress issued orders which had to be revoked, or was otherwise hasty, she would be brought into contempt, attributable solely to her own imprudence. Just as obedience was urged on all subjects, humility was to be the defining character of the mistress or superior; the women 'are as much edified by Sisters whom they see acting with humility as they are scandalised by those whom they see puffed up by their own merits'. Any hypocrisy on this account was likely to be swiftly exposed; 'such girls are usually very keen observers whose ears and eyes are constantly open and on the watch on their mistress'.[141]

The superior was obliged, by her position, to govern with firmness and charity 'as the occasion may arise' and to the extent of imposing penances on

---

135   *Constitution xv, de l'obéissance*, p. 100.
136   Explanation of constitution xv (vii), Obedience, p. 139.
137   Ibid., p. 141.
138   Explanation of constitution ix (xxvi), The two obediences, pp 121–2.
139   Explanation of the rule of the penitents, ch. 1, Their reception, p. 335.
140   Explanation of the rule of the penitents, ch. 2, Their departure, p. 343.
141   Explanation of the rule of the penitents, ch. 1, Their reception, pp 335–6.

the sisters, for the correction of their faults and for their spiritual growth.[142] The examination of conscience (*examen*), the confessing of faults (*coulpe*), asking pardon, seeking penances, practising 'mortifications' (such as kissing the floor) and asking for a spiritual challenge (*défi*) were specified briefly in the rule and spelled out in great detail in the guide to the customs of the first monastery of Caen. There was no limit to the minor and perceived faults which a sister might work on or a superior might point out to her; an example of a 'grievous fault' which might be found among the sisters was named as eavesdropping outside the superior's room, or 'taking and stealthily abstracting things from among the cells and offices'.[143] A parallel system operated within the women's quarters – examples of faults requiring correction were similarly those 'against obedience', those which upset the well-regulated routine established in the house or those which caused others to fall from virtue: 'to defy the mistresses, to swear, to use impious expressions, to turn others from good, to urge them to do wrong by evil advice, to break the night's rest maliciously, without cause, to give way to a fit of anger, to reproach others with their past bad conduct, and so forth'.[144]

While the superior's responsibility extended to all persons in the community, 'the poor Penitents, above all, ought to feel the effects of her benevolent charity'.[145] This concern was exercised by being in attendance when each woman was admitted, insofar as that was possible, and through private interviews or conversations with each woman at least twice yearly.[146] In a large refuge such as High Park, with constant comings and goings, the superior could not be present for every admission nor could she hold individual meetings with all residents but the principle was set down by Caen. The superior was bound to visit the class periodically to deliver short exhortations and 'to reprove those who may deserve it', but the main purpose of her visit should be to encourage and uplift, leaving the women 'filled with a holy joy and fresh courage to labour for their salvation'.[147] The close of the penitents' annual retreat was an occasion on which the superior might speak individually with each girl or woman, 'to encourage them to profit of the graces they have received during the retreat', and to receive her blessing.[148] Where there were schoolchildren or 'young boarders' under the monastery's care, she played a similar role.[149]

## Humility

Humility, a 'heartfelt love of our own lowliness' – when found together with obedience, 'an entire and utter submission to the Will of God, and that of our Superiors' – was idealised as the virtue which best befitted those

---

142 Explanation of constitution xv (vii), Obedience, p. 142.
143 Explanation of constitution xxvii (xxiv), Correction, penances and punishment, p. 209.
144 Explanation of the rule of the penitents, ch. 2, Their departure, p. 344.
145 Explanation of constitution xxxv, The mother superior, p. 260.
146 Ibid.
147 Ibid., p. 261.
148 Explanation of the rule of the penitents, ch. 3, The order of the day, p. 359.
149 Explanation of constitution xxxv, The mother superior, p. 261.

who were part of the community of Notre Dame de Charité.[150] The spiritual starting point for novices, penitents and sisters alike, humility could be fostered by frequent 'serious reflection' on one's nothingness and by taking care 'to remain hidden beneath the shadow of our own abjection and lowliness'.[151] The subjects of meditation regarded as most suitable for postulants and novices were 'those which incline to the knowledge and contempt of self and the love of Our Lord Jesus Christ'.[152] The novice mistress was directed:

> let her strip them entirely of self, and render them pliable under every hand, let her go against their inclinations, their opinions, their self-love; these are the best mortifications in which she can exercise them. Let her teach them to preserve calm and peace of mind in the midst of humiliations and contempt; evenness of temper amidst the conflicts of opinions, of business, of events; a prompt, simple, thorough obedience despite dislike, weariness and difficulties.[153]

Similarly the penitents were

> to practise humility at every opportunity, obedience to their mistress, gentleness towards their companions, mortification of the tongue, to bear uncomplainingly what vexes or annoys them, and the like little acts which gradually lead them to the habit of virtue.[154]

Modesty in dress, language and demeanour was expected of all who resided in the enclosure of Our Lady of Charity. On admission, the penitents were to 'lay aside all trappings of their vanity', namely, 'garments of too worldly a style or gaudy in colour' and jewellery. The fashions of 1640s Normandy are no doubt invoked in the outright ban on 'hooped skirts' and trains, the toleration of powder 'for the purpose of drying pomade from their hair', and the introduction of a 'square neckerchief' or modest cover-up where necklines were low. There was a general ban on 'ribbons, laces, curled hair, bracelets, diamond crosses or necklaces'.[155] The postulants, on admission, retained their ordinary secular clothing, 'but if they have several outfits they shall be made wear the simplest, and the same remark holds good concerning their head dress'. The ban on ribbons, hooped skirts and hair-curling applied as strictly to them as to the penitents and they too wore 'a handkerchief', along with 'a black coif in the Choir, the guest room, and the chapter of the Novitiate'.[156] There was no requirement

---

150  Explanation of constitution xxi (xix), Humility, p. 176
151  Ibid., p. 173.
152  Explanation of constitution l, The clothing of novices, p. 318.
153  Explanation of constitution xxxix, The mistress of novices, p. 283.
154  Explanation of the rule of the penitents, ch. 7, Other regulations, p. 369.
155  Explanation of the rule of the penitents, ch. 1, Their reception, pp 337–8.
156  Explanation of constitution l, The clothing of novices, p. 317.

in the OLC rules to have the hair of the women residents cut short, though the fact that this was done in jails and asylums generally can be deduced from William Logan's condemnation of the practice as demeaning in 1843.[157] There is a recommendation in an 1866 edition of the Mercy rule that the haircutting rule 'so generally established in asylums' be continued,[158] but haircutting as penance was not part of OLC rule or policy.[159]

The principle that the women penitents 'shall all be clothed simply and modestly' had immediate resource implications as the sisters had to provide underwear and dresses to all who needed them.[160] The constant supply of clothing required great ingenuity; in Caen the *robière* (the sister in charge of the wardrobe) left old clothes at the door of the guest room or parlour which a sister might unravel during her visit, 'and the sister in charge of our poor penitents' clothes takes them away from time to time, to help in weaving into dress material'.[161] The dress provided was to be fairly standard, 'so that there may be no difference and no jealousy between them on this point'.[162]

The culture of modesty extolled in the monastery prevented the least discussion of sexual matters. The section of the rule dealing with the vow of celibacy was brief and idealistic: 'the sisters should live, breathe and sigh for their heavenly spouse alone', and were to guard against all the 'frivolities we had formerly seen and heard in the world'. Great reserve was to be exercised with the women: 'we should use extreme caution never to speak to the Penitents of the sin against this Virtue, and we must abide strictly by the letter of it, never violating it under pretext of charity or zeal for their salvation'.[163] The sanction against prying into their personal histories by the sisters afforded the women some privacy and reserved the role of confessor to the appointed priest. The general ban on worldly frivolities, such as dancing,[164] fencing,[165] playing dice or cards or keeping 'useless' pets (*bêtes d'amusement inutiles*)[166] did not extend

---

157   Logan, *An exposure*, p. 24.
158   Extract from *Guide for the Religious called Sisters of Mercy* (London, 1866) reprinted as document 20 in Maria Luddy, *Women in Ireland 1800–1918, a documentary history* (Cork, 1995), p. 59. Note, *Rule and constitutions of the Religious called Sisters of Mercy* published by James Duffy (Dublin, 1863) lists the congregation's works as 'the most assiduous application to the education of poor girls' (chapter II), the visitation of the sick (chapter III) and the protection of poor women of good character, admitted to the House of Mercy (chapter IV); there is no mention anywhere in this edition of penitents or of a penitents' rule.
159   There is a description of local practice in Caen in 1734 where haircutting is listed along with washing and cleaning of articles of clothing on reception, but this was not written into the rule of the penitents. There is, for the 20th century at least, ample photographic and documentary evidence for the Irish OLC houses that the women residents did not have their hair cut short as a matter of policy (see chapters 11, 12, 13 of this book); this was also one of the explicit findings of the McAleese inquiry across all institutions. 'Explanation of the rules, constitutions and customs', p. 337; *Final report of the Inter-Departmental Committee set up to establish the facts of State involvement with the Magdalen Laundries* (Dublin, 2013), part 4, ch. 19, p. 940.
160   Explanation of the rule of the penitents, ch. 1, Their reception, p. 338.
161   Explanation of constitution xxiii (xxix), Manner of speaking with strangers, p. 191.
162   Explanation of the rule of the penitents, ch. 1, Their reception, p. 338.
163   Explanation of constitution xvi (viii), Chastity, pp 145, 150.
164   Explanation of constitution xvii (xxix), Enclosure, p. 150.
165   Explanation of constitution xxiv (xxiii), Recreation and conversation, p. 199.
166   *Constitution xxiv, des récreations et conversations*, p. 120

to 'the representation of some sacred drama' or 'plays on sacred subjects', once they did not deviate from 'strict modesty and religious propriety', a loophole that was to be interpreted in Dublin in a very generous sense.[167]

## Poverty, Work and Recreation

The vow of poverty taken by the sisters was understood first as not possessing 'private and particular' property, but 'all that shall be given or brought to the Convent shall be held absolutely in common'.[168] The property of each newcomer, whether as postulant or penitent, was inventoried on arrival that it might be restored to her on leaving,[169] and the property of each resident, whether in the refuge or convent, was open to inspection on occasion.[170] There was no separation of accounts; whatever was needed by the women was listed by the sister in charge and given to the *économe*, the sister bursar, 'who charitably makes up the excess of the expenditure according to the orders of the Mother Superior'.[171] Anything that went against submitting readily and cheerfully to whatever deprivations and difficulties might be encountered in daily life was understood as going against the spirit of this virtue. The sisters' rule dealt severely, and at length, with those 'who fill the monastery with tears, complaints and melancholy countenances, who persuade themselves that every slight difficulty is an insurmountable obstacle, and everything which does not fit in with their own inclinations is unbearable'.[172] Similarly, dissatisfied women residents were to be exhorted by their mistress 'to accept in a spirit of penance, all the disagreeable things that may happen to them from morning to night, either in their food, their clothing, their sleeping accommodation, and the like things'.[173] Gratitude was urged on all members of the household, as the favourite virtue of the founder John Eudes, embracing the least to the greatest favour bestowed by friends and benefactors.[174]

The work ethic of the monastery included every resident, whatever the daily tasks appointed to her. The duties and responsibilities attaching to each sister's role are outlined at great length in the rule: as superior, assistant, mistress of novices, *économe* (bursar), portress, sacristan, infirmarian, *robière* and *lingère* (who had charge of the sisters' clothing), refectorian and dispenser. Whatever her rank – choir sister, lay sister or extern sister (*tourière*) – each was expected to apply herself assiduously and without complaint to her assigned tasks and to employ whatever 'free' time she might have in a profitable manner. Handiwork was expected to be undertaken during parlour visits and recreation, lest idleness creep in.[175] Similarly the penitents

---

167  Explanation of constitution xxiv (xxiii), Recreation and conversation, p. 198.
168  Explanation of constitution xviii (ix), Poverty, p. 157.
169  *Règlement, i, De leur reception*, p. 177.
170  Explanation of the rule of the penitents, ch, 2, Their departure, p. 343.
171  Explanation of the rule of the penitents, ch. 1, Their reception, p. 340.
172  Explanation of constitution xlix (iii), The first reception of novices, p. 316.
173  Explanation of the rule of the penitents, ch. 5, Penance, p. 365.
174  *Constitution xx, de la gratitude ou reconnaissance*, p. 111.
175  *Constitution xxiii, De la manière de parler avec les étrangers*, p. 117; *Constitution xxiv, Des récréations et conversations*, p. 119.

were expected to work generously and without complaint, according to each woman's capacity, and side-by-side with the sisters assigned to work in the refuge. There is nothing in the rule specifying the type of work to be undertaken, but household chores loomed large, as did needlework, handicrafts and laundry work for both the institution and for outside customers. The latter provided a constant, if small, stream of income to the first refuge at Caen, and to the majority of subsequent foundations, including the first Dublin monastery of 1853. Public laundries, run on the basis of the inmates' unpaid labour, were attached to the vast majority of charity asylums in Britain and Ireland throughout the 19th century, as evidenced in handbills and advertisements in commercial directories and in the 1834 appeal for Fr Smith's new asylum at Drumcondra Road.[176] Entrusting one's household's washing to such an asylum was regarded as a praiseworthy and practical way of supporting the project. But as the operation of a laundry – whether for the sole use of the institution or as a commercial enterprise – was not intrinsic to the founding ethos of the monasteries of Our Lady of Charity, there is no mention of its role in either the sisters' or penitents' rules. What was presumed was that all the residents, sisters, novices and penitents alike worked for the general upkeep of the monastery, into which each one's individual support was subsumed. The issue of wages did not arise for any of the workers, whether professed sisters, novices or women residents, but small discretionary awards were made to the women residents annually; this 'customary practice' was spelled out by Caen as small sums given 'in proportion to the amount of work they have done for the house'. This 'little attention' was viewed as an encouragement, rather than as a right and contributed to 'keeping them in peace'.[177] It had its parallel in the treatment of novices who could be occasionally 'indulged'.[178]

A system of 'spiritual monitoring' or 'surveillance', both explicit and implicit, was in place in the enclosure of Our Lady of Charity to observe, support and correct each resident in her own personal striving towards virtue and the beating down of 'spiritual foes'. On election, the new superior appoints a 'spiritual monitor' with the office of admonishing the superior, so that she 'who has to help and correct the sisters' should know 'the happiness which there is in being also helped and corrected, since being of the same nature she may fall just as well as others'.[179] While it was preferable that sisters would confront the superior directly with the faults they observed in her, they could also report to the superior's spiritual monitor.[180] 'Surveillantes' were appointed to monitor the behaviour of all those holding high office in the monastery and specifically to ensure that the rule was observed with great fidelity and exactitude.[181] 'Surveillance' extended down the ranks to the least member, where the superior 'gives to each one a Spiritual Aid to be our visible angel, to point out to us our failings and encourage

176  'The Magdalene, a fragment', p. 240.
177  Explanation of the rule of the penitents, ch. 2, Their departure, p. 341.
178  Explanation of constitution xxxix, The mistress of novices, p. 284.
179  *Constitution xli, des surveillantes*, p. 149.
180  Explanation of constitution xli, The monitor of the superior, p. 294.
181  Explanation of constitution xl, The surveillantes, p. 291.

us to correct them'. No one was excluded from this system, where juniors could admonish seniors and the latter were instructed to accept the admonition with humility and gratitude.[182] The novices, as trainees, were subjected to the intense but discreet observation of their mistress ('even their slightest actions should be watched').[183] The women penitents were similarly under near-constant supervision, at work and during recreation, at least in principle.[184]

Rather than interrupting the interior life of the monastery, periods of recreation were viewed as further opportunities to advance spiritually. The regulations governing recreation and conversation for all residents reiterate the core values of modesty, humility, hard work and constant recourse to God. Recreation was carried out, in convent, novitiate and refuge, under the observation or supervision of a sister, whether the superior, deputy, *surveillante* or mistress. When the sisters came together for their daily recreation, they were instructed 'to often turn their minds to God, work steadily, because we are recommended to do so, and find pleasure in mingling a few good words with our recreation' to enkindle fervour among their companions.[185] The conversation was always to be general and inclusive, 'Those who are round the fire should talk loud enough to be heard by those near them, and the same remark applies to those who are engaged on any work, a little away from the community'.[186] The topics of conversation which might be introduced were somewhat limited, as they had to be on 'some agreeable and pleasant (but not too profane) subject'.[187] Above all, 'in willingly imparting our little griefs and our little joys, our fervour and our consolation, our good thoughts, the holy things we have learned, and even talking of our work and little incidents of our daily life', the sisters were to keep in mind the injunction of St Francis de Sales to speak freely 'and with that holy spirit of liberty without which it is impossible to take one's recreation'.[188] On 'recreation days' or holidays, such as the feast-day of the superior, the usual restraints applied; should the sisters forget themselves and indulge in worldly pleasures, such as fencing or dancing, 'we should run the risk of losing in one day what we had gathered together with much toil during many years'.[189] Matching regulations governed the conduct of the women during their daily recreation, with exhortations to be edifying in their conversation and inclusive of all present, never to speak uncharitably of each other or to mock or tease or quarrel, but to act towards each other as sisters, as indeed they are.[190] Singing was welcome once limited to

182  Explanation of constitution xxvii (xxiv), Corrections, penances and punishments, pp 204, 207.
183  Explanation of constitution xxxix, The mistress of novices, p. 284.
184  *Règlement iii, Exercice de la journée*, p. 180; vii, *Autres règles générales que toutes les Sœurs Pénitentes doivent observer*, p. 186.
185  Explanation of constitution xxlv (xxiii), Recreation and conversation, p. 194.
186  Ibid., p. 196.
187  Ibid., p. 194.
188  Ibid., p. 197.
189  Ibid., p. 199.
190  *Règlement, vii, Autres règles générales que toutes les Sœurs Pénitentes doivent observer*, p. 185.

such canticles 'as may inspire them with profound reverence for our holy mysteries'. The ban on 'any kind of worldly song' was extended to hymns 'which treat of Divine Love in too sensible a style' and, as such, were open to misinterpretation.[191]

## The Order of Day and the Church's Year

The order of the day was highly regulated for all within the enclosure. From early rising (5am summer weekdays, 6.30am feast-days and winter, according to the 1734 edition of the rule)[192] through to the great silence at night, the day was punctuated with prayer and devotional exercises, and the devil was kept at bay by employing every moment in a pre-determined way. All was intended to assist the soul in its striving to the summit of Christian perfection, no less, women and sisters alike.[193] Attendance at daily Mass was expected of all. The choir sisters chanted the Divine Office in Latin at set intervals during the day, the lay sisters had their lighter load, in the vernacular, while the penitents had their own compendium of devotions to mark the progress of the day, including recitation of the rosary, the singing of hymns and the reading of some pious book or listening to an extract read aloud. Many of the rituals and devotional exercises were identical. Sisters and penitents asked pardon of one's companions through the superior or mistress; practised the *examen* of conscience; processed in silence to separate refectories; and could request a *défi* or spiritual challenge to mark a special feast.[194] All residents were soon familiar with a large repertoire of prayers and antiphons for private or communal use, including several composed by the founder.[195] Though the titles are in Latin, prayers that were not part of the Church's liturgy would have been said in the vernacular.[196] Three days after receiving Communion, each woman was required to give 'an account of the benefit they have drawn from this holy action, and the acts of virtue they have practised in consequence', just like the sisters.[197] (This practice was limited to the period before frequent Communion was encouraged by the Church). Similarly, women were expected to reflect on the spiritual reading they had been set or had heard read, as were the sisters.[198] Time was carefully measured: a short pause might be the length of an *Ave* or *Pater*. The signal to rise, proceed to Mass, morning prayers

191  Explanation of the rule of the penitents, ch. 3, The order of the day, p. 347.
192  Ibid., p. 346.
193  Introduction, p. 36.
194  Explanation of the rule of the penitents, ch. 3, The order of the day, p. 351.
195  'Prières journalières qui se disent aux pénitentes', *Oeuvres complètes de Bienheureux Jean Eudes*, x (Vannes, 1909), pp 188–90.
196  The following prayers are mentioned either in this list or elsewhere but were not necessarily the only prayers employed: Angelus, Memorare, Magnificat, Veni Sancte Spiritus, Veni Creator, Ave Maria, Ave Maris Stella, Maria Mater Gratiae, Stabat Mater, Salve Regina, O Passio Magno Anima Christi, De Profundis, Confiteor, Litany of the Holy Name of Jesus, Litany of the Holy Angels, Litany of Divine Providence, Litany of the Infant Jesus (Christmas Day and Christmastide only), rosary, Chaplet of the Divine Love, Ante Thronum, Jesus Tibi, Fidelium, Crown of Our Lord. Among the best known of the prayers composed by John Eudes were: Ave Cor Sanctissimum, Ave Maria Filia Dei Patris and Chaplet of the Holy Heart of Mary.
197  Explanation of the rule of the penitents, ch. 3, The order of the day, p. 369.
198  Introduction, p. 35.

or other exercise was marked by the ringing of the 'little bell'. Periods of silence were kept before work and throughout the day – though in the refuge
some, at least, of these times could be occupied in the singing of hymns and
the recitation of the rosary or other prayers, 'to keep up their fervour, and
drive away temptations and weariness'.[199] They could also take time apart
in the evening to pray in private (*'celles qui en auront le talent'*). Part of the
morning was allotted to teaching newly-arrived women the standard prayers
and 'little catechism', while an explanation each day was given of the epistle
and gospel by the penitents' mistress. The commandments were frequently
explained, and short pious instructions given daily, as well as more formal
catechesis.[200] Reading lessons were to be given to those who were illiterate
and 'whom the superior judges well to be taught'; when formulated in 1640s
Normandy, this injunction was probably more generous than it sounded by
the 1850s when the first Dublin house was opened.[201]

The cycle of the Church's year was the calendar followed within the
enclosure: the feasts of Our Lord and of key saints, Advent, Christmas, Lent,
Holy Week, the Easter festival and Pentecost. Para-liturgies, or additional devotions specified in the rule, included exposition of the Blessed Sacrament,
the recitation of the 'acts of reparation' by all on the last day of the year and,
occasionally, 'the exercise of preparation for death'.[202] The approach of a feast-
day was to be grasped by the mistress as an opportunity to explain to the
women 'the mysteries and ceremonies of the Church'.[203]

A number of homely French religious customs, long practised in Caen,
were also introduced to Dublin, for all residents, while there were also
specified days of retreat. Parallel liturgies were held in refuge and convent;
there were also liturgies in common, in the chapel, with each group – sisters,
women, children – seated in its own section. On Palm Sunday, which opens
Holy Week, the women had their own procession with palms, the recitation
of the seven penitential psalms and the veneration of the cross. Just as the
superior washed the feet of the sisters at the *Mandatum* on Holy Thursday,
the symbolic re-enactment of Jesus' washing of his disciples' feet at the Last
Supper, the mistress washed the penitents' feet. That night, the women kept
vigil before the tabernacle (after 'a good dinner' to ensure they were fit to
stay up 'to nightfall'). All inside the enclosure kept the customary silence on
Good Friday, while the women made their own stations of the cross around
the garden.[204]

Some of the traditional religious customs which travelled from France
involved drawing cards with mottos or pictures from a set, and attaching
oneself to the virtue or image indicated. On Christmas Day, the women (and
sisters) 'draw offices in the Court of the King Jesus', the 'offices' included
that of the straw, the manger, the ox, the star – points of meditation to assist
in imagining oneself actually present in Bethlehem and to stir the heart to

199   Explanation of the rule of the penitents, ch. 4, Silence, pp 361–2.
200   *Règlement, iii, Exercice de la journée,* p. 181.
201   Explanation of the rule of the penitents, ch. 4, Silence, p. 360.
202   Explanation of the rule of the penitents, ch. 3, The order of the day, pp 352, 349.
203   Explanation of the rule of the penitents, ch. 4, Silence, p. 361.
204   Explanation of the rule of the penitents, ch. 3, The order of the day, pp 354–7.

an appropriate spiritual response, such as to be more humble, more welcoming, more loving.[205] On the feast of Pentecost, 'they draw the gifts of the Holy Ghost after High Mass'.[206] On the feast of All Saints, 'the mistress makes them draw the beatitudes in turns after High Mass'.[207] There was some welcome gaiety on the feast of the Epiphany: 'after grace the Mistress makes them draw the cake for the bean; she who is queen is put at a little table in the middle of the refectory and some little extra are given her to enjoy herself with her companions'.[208]

The feast of St Mary Magdalen, 21 July, was marked in a special way, though the Dublin celebrations appear low-key when compared with reports of the melodramatic scenes played out at Caen. All the sisters of the community joined the women for recreation to mark what was a religious festival and welcome holiday from all work.[209] The evening prayer of St Mary Magdalen was to be celebrated with the fullest honours the house could muster (*'pour faire l'office majesteusement'*) and St Magdalen's altar lavishly decorated with flowers. The feast was preceded by the spiritual preparation of the women, an annual retreat for which a priest was engaged 'in order to instruct them thoroughly in the truths of salvation and prepare them to make a good confession'.[210]

## Entrances and Exits

Entrances to both convent and to refuge were carefully recorded in bound registers. The convent registers recorded clothing or admission to the noviceship, profession of vows and the canonical examination of candidates before making vows. In the case of the refuge, a large bound book was prescribed 'for registering the entrances and departures of Penitents, with the day of the month and the year, together with the names of those who presented them, and of those to whose care they were committed on leaving'.[211] For all its timeless structures, it was intended that the women would seek refuge or asylum under the mantle of Our Lady of Charity for a short period only. The second chapter of the penitents' rule is titled 'their departure' (*'De leur sortie'*) and opens with the blunt statement, quoting the founder John Eudes, that the penitents shall not be kept in the convent all their lives. As soon as each is sufficiently instructed and solidly grounded in the fear of God, she shall be returned to her parents or relatives, placed in some honest employment or (should God send the opportunity) marry and thus, it is implied, be the responsibility of her husband for the rest of her life.[212]

The Dublin register notes only the barest minimum in line with the practice of 1600s Caen: the name of the girl or woman, age (usually), whether parents were alive or dead, home town or county of birth, date of admission and

205  Ibid., p. 352.
206  Ibid., p. 357.
207  Ibid., p. 359.
208  Ibid., p. 353.
209  Ibid., p. 359.
210  Ibid., pp 357–9.
211  Customs and usages, article XXIII, Books to be kept for entering the affairs of the monastery, p. 253.
212  *Règlement, ii, De leur sortie*, p. 178.

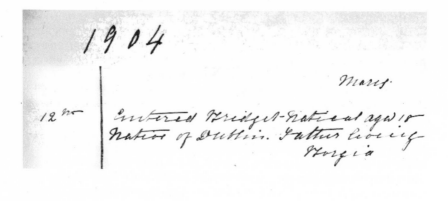

**Figure 2.2**   Sample extract from register of admissions to St Mary's Refuge, High Park, dated 1904 (DARGS, OLC1/8/1 no. 2).

date of departure (figure 2.2). A 'house name' is recorded for each woman by which she was known during her time in the refuge and, for a small proportion of entrants (as explained below), there is also a magdalen or consecrate name. Though complete, in that it appears all entrances were faithfully noted, practically nothing can be gleaned from the register of the woman's story before, or after, her time in the care of Our Lady of Charity. This is in line with the institute's long-established policy of not prying and allowing the slate (whatever it might hold) to be wiped clean.

Once a girl's moral reformation had been effected and her character had been bolstered by sufficient catechesis (in the judgement of the mistress), there was no reason why she would not return to 'the world' and blend, unnoticed, back into society, supporting herself by honest labour and living an exemplary, upright life. But even in its founding decades, it was clear that few of those who had recourse to the refuge had a welcoming home to which they could safely return, or means to support themselves independently. All the resources of the monastery – personnel, funds and spiritual ethos – were centred on providing a safe retreat for 'wounded souls' within the enclosure; there was no follow-up service beyond spiritual support and the promise of a place to return, should a former resident be once more in need. The pattern of entrances and departures is analysed in later chapters but, from the short stays of most and the multiple entrances and exits of some women, from its foundation, the Dublin monastery was certainly a place of frequent comings and goings. The occasional practice ('rare exceptions') of the monastery of Caen of holding several women 'even though they should testify to no desire of remaining' for the reason that 'we noticed in them a character and disposition anxious to return to their former evil ways and to drag others after them' was condemned as clearly in breach of the rule and of the spirit behind it, no matter what defence was offered.[213]

The general rule that 'penitents who have passed a sufficient time in

213   Explanation of the rule of the penitents, ch. 2, Their departure, p. 341–2.

the house ought to give place to others' was all very well when individual women had a safe and acceptable alternative to the refuge.[214] However, it went entirely against the founding spirit of the institute simply to dismiss women from the house without any care for how they might manage. At any point therefore, alongside the short-term residents, there were numbers of women who continued in the refuge for the want of any alternative. But a different case was presented by those women who requested to remain and to make the refuge their permanent home. As with aspirants to the religious life, they needed to display the qualities of humility, docility and obedience and to have already proved themselves; above all, they needed to have an appreciation of what was deemed to be a very special vocation, loving and cherishing it above all others as the means which God had given them to work out their salvation.[215] A note on the practical aspects of this vocation advised that a 'mutual agreement' be drawn up. 'The girl ought to sign it as one of the parties most interested in the deed, so that should she grow discontented later on, she will have nothing to reproach us with.'[216] Paralleling the procedures which accompanied the admission of sisters to full membership through the profession of vows, the request was also brought formally before the superior and the sisters assembled in chapter, 'for this engagement constitutes a perpetual charge on the house'.[217] This charge continued to death, when these women could be buried within the enclosure, with the suffrages or prayers set out for them as they were for the sisters, their holy deaths recorded in the annals of the order and communicated to the other monasteries through the *circulaires*, in the same way as were the deaths of the sisters.[218] 'Life sojourners' were always part of the refuge community, not the convent – and, lest there be any misunderstanding on this point, the mistress was warned against showing them familiarity, 'which however, need not prevent these sisters from bestowing kindness and satisfaction when the girls discharge their duty well, and are faithful to their rule'.[219]

## Conclusion

Many of the themes that recur in the British and Irish 'magdalen rescue and reform' movement of the mid-18th century to the mid-19th century, of which the Drumcondra Road, Mecklenburgh Street and Gloucester Street refuges formed part, are found again in the model of asylum proposed by the Sisters of Our Lady of Charity for High Park. Whether the sisters realised it or not, pre-existing understandings and prejudices would bear heavily on their work, both in their inability to go along with what they found at Drumcondra Road and in the language that would be used to promote their ambitions for accommodation on a scale not yet seen in the city. When they

---

214  Ibid., p. 342.
215  *Règlement, ii, De leur sortie*, p. 178.
216  Explanation of the rule of the penitents, ch. 2, Their departure, p. 342.
217  Ibid., p. 342.
218  *Règlement vii, autres règles générales que toutes les Sœurs Pénitentes doivent observer*, pp 186–7.
219  Explanation of the rule of the penitents, ch. 2, Their departure, p. 342.

sought funds to erect a 200-bed refuge at High Park in 1868, the language employed could have been lifted from any of the English-language appeals drawn up a century earlier; it was to be erected for the 'despised daughter of frailty, outcast of outcasts, poor wayward lamb, ill-fated victim, towards whom the softest heart of tenderness beats not often with pity'.[220] The figure of the penitent Mary Magdalen – compounding several scripture passages into one much-embellished and irresistible image – was also utilised in connection with the OLC refuges at High Park and later at Gloucester Street, though without overwhelming the traditional Eudist devotion to the loving hearts of Jesus and Mary which always took precedence.

The redevelopment or refounding of small lay asylums as OLC refuges at High Park and Gloucester Street has to be seen as building on an existing local 'rescue and reform' movement. Though denominational in management and ethos, all asylums used much the same arguments in advertising and fundraising. The challenge for the early asylums was to change attitudes, to persuade the public to support what too many saw as the least deserving of all charity cases. Women sponsors – in the case of Leeson Street and Mecklenburgh Street, at least – got asylums up and running. Zealous clerical promoters employed every rhetorical device and flourish they could muster, including hyperbole and antithesis, in support of what was never to be a popular cause. That so many did survive for several decades under lay or parish committees, albeit on rather precarious financial grounds, is testimony to the efforts made by lay and clerical supporters to keep them afloat. Their continuation is above all due to the women residents and lay managers whose hard work enabled the institutes to subsist from week to week and provide what was rightly termed a retreat or refuge for at least some women in dire need. While the opening of the union workhouses post-1838 provided poor women everywhere in Ireland with the guarantee of shelter and food, however basic, the asylum accommodation available in the city in the 1850s fell far short of demand.

Many of the ideas which were promoted in plans, reports and commentaries published from the 1750s onwards relating to Britain and Ireland feature independently in the model brought to Dublin from 1640s Caen (via Paris and Rennes). This is no great surprise, as many are fairly obvious: the asylum as a retreat from the world, a place of healing and recovery both spiritual and physical; keeping young, innocent or deluded girls from those who were regarded as experienced in vice; the need for the women to work towards the upkeep of the institute and their own support; the overriding importance of religious and moral instruction; close supervision and the discipline of set times for rising, prayers, meals, work and retiring to bed. All of these are common across the board. But at a deeper level, Notre Dame de Charité in Dublin was different to its lay predecessors. The refuge was attached to the convent – and moreover a convent with a proper, monastic enclosure and an approved rule of life, which the sisters treated as sacrosanct. There was no contradiction between the institute's conventual character

---

220    Advertising leaflet, 'A remedy for the "Social Evil", wanted, 250,000 pennies for the management of Magdalen Asylum, High Park, Drumcondra', 22 July 1868 (DARGS, OLC1/1/1 no. 18).

and apostolic purpose; they were seen as inextricably bound together. With reference to 2/4 Drumcondra Road, it was stated 'The object of the institute being to receive female penitents there are from 47 to 50 instructed and supported, principally by their own labour'.[221] The same applied, at a later date and with much larger numbers, at High Park and later still at Gloucester Street (Sean MacDermott Street). The rule of life, daily schedules, annual cycle and overall atmosphere of the refuge were all derived from – and closely tied into – that of the convent proper. The strengths of the enclosed convent lifestyle – its security, good order, regularity, predictability and regard for the common life – would also be its weaknesses in relation to both convent and refuge – for example, favouring traits such as obedience and docility over initiative and self-direction. But in mid-19th century Dublin, let alone in 17th-century Normandy, few would have had any problem with the Eudist model of care.

221 Standard questionnaire on religious houses in Dublin diocese, 20 Sept. 1854 (DARGS, OLC1/1/1 no. 12).

# Chapter 3

# From Drumcondra Road to High Park 1857–1903, the Making of a Model Monastery and Refuge in the Tradition of John Eudes

Once the sisters at Drumcondra Road decided to move the entire project of St Mary's – the asylum, laundry business and convent – to a more healthy, spacious location, there was no looking back. The reason given publicly for the move was the serious illness of the founding superior, Mother Mary of the Sacred Heart Kelly, whose very life was believed to be in danger from the small, damp and miserable house into which she and her sisters were packed. The women's quarters were also overcrowded and there was no space to extend.[1] The chance to get out from under the overbearing control of the founder, Fr John Smith, was undoubtedly another good reason for leaving Drumcondra Road behind (Chapter 1). In a new house, held in their own name, they could do all they had formally agreed with the archdiocese, namely, to receive 'voluntary penitents', to say and chant the Divine Office, and to live according to the rules, regulations and customs of the monastery of Caen.[2] The move would allow, in time, the making of a model monastery and refuge, with enclosure, as set out by the founder John Eudes. Benefactors could be called on when the sisters had oversight of the finances. In a new location, they could have stability, continuity and good order – and, they hoped, calm. The advantages of the move therefore were as much psychological and spiritual as environmental, economic and political.

The house and grounds of High Park were acquired with so little trouble and delay that the entire move was regarded at the time as a sign of God's care of the enterprise, with this particular house 'destined from all eternity by Divine Providence as a refuge and shelter for the lost sheep of his fold'.[3] The Blessed Virgin was credited with responding speedily to the prayers of the community; within days of commencing special pleading, news of the availability of High Park had reached the ears of Dr Woodlock, president of All Hallows, who met the owner, Mr Baker; the sale was agreed

---

1  High Park, *circulaire*, 30 décembre 1859 (DARGS, OLC1/3/1 no. 2).
2  Soeur M. de St Stanislas Brunel, Paris, to Mgr l'Archevêque de Dublin, 9 July 1853 (DDA, Cullen, 325/8, no. 208).
3  'Annals of this monastery of Our Lady of Charity of Refuge, at High Park, Drumcondra, Dublin, since the arrival of the Religious the 27th September 1853', vol. 1, 1857, p. 90 (DARGS, OLC1/5/3 no. 5). Hereafter, Annals.

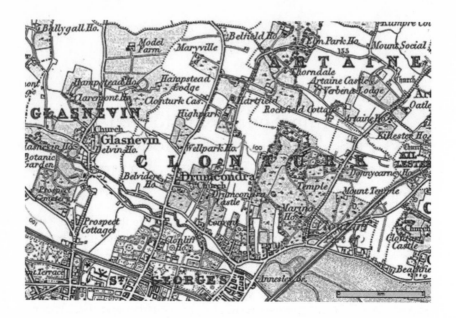

**Figure 3.1**   Location of High Park monastery (OS one inch (Dublin) sheet 112, 1863).

and the papers drawn up.[4] The site itself was perfect. It had a water supply, which was essential to the laundry business – other houses had been turned down on that score alone.[5] There was a dwelling house, 15 acres, a garden, a small lodge and some kitchen outhouses.[6] An early visitor described how the convent 'stands in the midst of a small but exceedingly pretty park'.[7] The place had all the rural quiet, fresh air and separation from *le monde* that an enclosed religious community could desire.

The location (figure 3.1) was also ideal: off Grace Park Road in the northern suburbs and within walking distance of the city proper. The name given by Fr Smith to his asylum, St Mary's, was brought to High Park and the address was still Drumcondra, which helped to smooth the transfer of allegiance of laundry customers and other supporters to the new venture. Proximity to the missionary college of All Hallows, in Drumcondra House, was another bonus. One of the earliest acts of Dr Woodlock, appointed 'spiritual father' to the sisters in 1854, was to transfer the college washing contract, for more than 150 students and also staff, to High Park, providing the asylum with an immediate weekly stream of income that was crucial to its survival in the first few years.[8]

4   Annals, 1856, p. 89; High Park, *circulaire*, 30 décembre 1859. Schedule of deeds received by Cartan O'Meara, solicitors, 24 July 1907, in relation to High Park, 12 documents dated 5 Feb. 1851 to 28 Sept. 1894 (DARGS, OLC1/9/1 no. 12).
5   Annals, 1855, p. 89.
6   Annals, 1856, p. 89; 1857, pp 90–1; 1859, p. 98. Beardwood and Son, accounts, 21 Apr. 1857–11 Apr. 1859 (DARGS, OLC1/9/2 no. 3).
7   Fanny Taylor, *Irish homes and Irish hearts* (London, 1867), p. 88.
8   Annals, 1858, p. 97.

**Figure 3.2** Superiors and assistants, monastery of Our Lady of Charity of Refuge, High Park, 1853–1930

| | | Superior | | Assistant | |
|---|---|---|---|---|---|
| Order | Date of election | Name | | Name | |
| 1 | 8 Sept. 1853, confirmed 14 Sept.1853 | Mother Mary of the Sacred Heart Kelly | d. 30 June 1863 | Soeur Marie de St Ignace de Loyola Pavot | returned to France |
| 2 | 24 May 1860 | Mother Mary of the Five Wounds O'Callaghan | d. 12 Jan. 1895 | Sister Mary of St Joseph O'Callaghan | |
| 3 | 17 May 1866 | Mother Mary of St Joseph O'Callaghan | d. 26 June 1885 | Sister Mary of St Stanislaus Brennan | d. 22 July 1896 |
| 4 | 16 May 1872 | Mother Mary of St Bartholomew McDonnell | d. 22 June 1898 | Sister Mary of the Five Wounds O'Callaghan | |
| 5 | 6 June 1878 | Mother Mary of the Holy Heart of Mary Tobin | | Sister Mary of the Five Wounds O'Callaghan | |
| 6 | 29 May 1884 | Mother Mary of St Peter Pilkington | d. 22 Feb. 1889 | Sister Mary of the Five Wounds O'Callaghan | |
| 7 | 7 Mar. 1889 | Mother Mary of the Holy Heart of Mary Tobin | d. 14 Nov. 1898 | Sister Mary of the Five Wounds O'Callaghan | d. 12 Jan. 1895 |
| 8 | 30 May 1895 | Mother Mary of St Aloysius Morris | | Sister Mary of the Nativity Plunkett | |
| 9 | 24 May 1901 | Mother Mary of St Genevieve Byrne | d. 23 Mar. 1930 | Sister Mary of the Nativity Plunkett | d. 18 Aug. 1905 |
| 10 | 16 May 1907 | Mother Mary of St Aloysius Morris | d. 21 April 1917 | Sister Mary of St Ignatius Ryan (died in office, replaced by Sister Mary of St Cecilia McVeagh, 21 Mar. 1909) | d. 19 Feb. 1909 |

*(Continued)*

**Figure 3.2** (Continued)

| Order | Date of election | Superior Name | | Assistant Name | |
|---|---|---|---|---|---|
| 11 | 23 Mar. 1914 | Mother Mary of St Genevieve Byrne | | Sister Mary of the Sacred Heart Pilkington | |
| 12 | 20 May 1920 | Mother Mary of St Cecilia McVeagh | | Sister Mary of the Sacred Heart Pilkington | d. 25 Mar. 1929 |
| 13 | 20 May 1926 | Mother Mary of St Genevieve Byrne | d. 23 Mar. 1930 | Sister Mary of St Cecilia McVeagh | d. 29 April 1945 |

*Source:* Table de Noms des Soeurs qui ont été Supérieurs en ce Monastère, Livre de Chapître (DARGS, OLC1/5/1 no. 2).

The establishment of a model monastery of the order of Notre Dame de Charité du Refuge at High Park from the arrival of the superior, novice mistress and novices on 1 March 1857, followed by the women residents and the other sisters exactly a year later, can be marked out in phases. It began with what is termed the *superiorité* of the foundress and first reverend mother, Mother Mary of the Sacred Heart Kelly, who held office until May 1860. Thereafter the phases can be associated with successive superiors, but with the proviso that only death marks a real break, otherwise the same four women managed the affairs of the monastery between them in the key roles of superior and assistant, at three-yearly intervals, from 1860 to 1884 (Figure 3.2). The period between 1884 and 1903 might be described as one of consolidation and self-assurance, culminating in the jubilee celebrations of 1903 when High Park was lauded in the *Freeman's Journal* as 'one of the noblest works of charity to which the last half-century has given birth'.[9] This chapter opens with a brief consideration of the centrality of 'the rule' to the institute before tracking how the spiritual and temporal affairs of the monastery were advanced under successive superiors with lay support, selecting one or two aspects in each case. The golden jubilee of 1903, when the sisters reflected on all that had happened since the move to High Park, is a fitting point at which to close this chapter.

## Introduction to the Rule and Constitutions of Our Lady of Charity and the 'Wishes of the Founder'

As noted previously, it was adherence to the rule of Caen that held together the autonomous monasteries of Notre Dame de Charité du Refuge. John Eudes relied primarily on the rule of St Augustine as interpreted in the rule

9   High Park, circular letter, May 1906, pp 9–11 (DARGS, OLC1/3/1 no. 22).

produced by St Francis de Sales for the Visitation sisters and developed in the exhortations of St Jane de Chantal, because it was from this community that he managed to engage the services of sisters to train the first OLC novices.[10] Worked out in collaboration with the founding mothers at Caen, it received the approval of Rome in 1666 and was taken as marking out with certainty a path to perfection.[11] Throughout the difficult early years in Dublin, the hope was held out 'that all affaires would be peaceably arranged and settled according to the order stated by our holy rules'.[12] The rule was the basis on which the sisters could put down roots, the only yardstick by which they would, or could, measure progress.

The opening statement of the OLC constitutions (as with the Visitation rule) is taken directly from the Rule of St Augustine:

> Before all things, my dear sisters, let God be loved, and after Him your neighbour; for these, above all other commandments, have been given to us.[13]

The very name of the order, John Eudes maintained, should act as a continual incitement to the love of neighbour, the sister thinking often of the charity that burns in the loving hearts of Jesus and Mary and resisting with all her strength 'those little animosities, jealousies, coldnesses and envies which are utterly opposed to the perfect charity that should reign in the heart of a true Daughter of Our Lady of Charity'.[14] Community life is spelled out as the practice of love, a love which is manifest in countless small acts of kindness and thoughtfulness. The purpose of coming together in community was to live the gospel precept to love God and neighbour in harmony or unity of spirit; the desire 'that you may have but one heart and one soul in God' was spelled out in terms of the wholehearted observance of the rule by all members without exception.[15]

According to the Rule of St Augustine, the good of all is to be preferred to the interests of the individual. This care for the common life runs strongly through the OLC rule (and that of the Visitation Sisters) in terms of property ownership, food, and work. All employments within the enclosure – among sisters and women alike – were to be understood in the communal sense also: 'Let all work for the common benefit, and do so with far greater zeal and

---

10   Paul Milcent, *Un artisan du renouveau Chrétien au XVIIᵉ siècle, Saint Jean Eudes* (Paris, 1985), pp 172, 176, 292–3.
11   'Règles et constitutions pour les religieuses de Notre-Dame de Charité, édition entièrement conformé au texte original [1682] avec des introductions et des notes', *Oeuvres complètes de Bienheureux Jean Eudes*, x (Vannes, 1909), Constitution LIII, briève déclaration de l'obligation des Soeurs a l'observation de la Règle et des Constitutions, p. 172. Hereafter, Constitutions.
12   Soeur M. de St Stanislas Brunel, Paris, to Revd Father [Smith], 9 Feb. 1854 (DDA, Cullen 332/4, file II, nuns, no. 13).
13   'Explanation of the rules, constitutions and customs of the Religious of Our Lady of Charity ...', trans. of 1734 edn (DARGS, OLC1/5/1 no. 1). Hereafter, Explanation of [chapter or constitution or rule no.].
14   Explanation of chapter 1, p. 10; of chapter 2, p. 10.
15   Ibid., pp 10–11.

alacrity than if each one worked for herself'.[16] In attempting to place the interests and advantages of the community over her own personal comfort and pleasure, the sister was urged to practise charity in countless small things, such as not staying too long at the fire when others were cold, 'to choose always the worst and the most difficult to do when the choice rests with us'.[17]

Union between rich and poor and an equality of treatment across the community was another distinctive feature of the rule of St Augustine, and indeed of those later rules that were derived from it. In Notre Dame de Charité, those coming from aristocratic families were not to retain their titles or be allowed to lord it over the others, 'the poor and those of humble condition must be cherished as much as the rich and noble'.[18] All were to be respected, 'all are the temples of God' and, where this was grasped, 'we shall pay each other mutual honour and respect, not in word nor in mere outwards seeming but in truth and in deed'.[19] Equality did not mean uniformity, and some might rightly carry a heavier load than, for example, those who were weighed down with illness. Those of good health and strong constitutions were urged to set about their work 'cheerfully, and with a hearty good will, looking on it as a special privilege to be able to serve the house without requiring any singularities'.[20]

St Augustine's rule is noted for the kindliness and humanity that runs through it. For all its emphasis on the common life, service in the community is to be undertaken in a way that is sisterly and personal, with consideration for human weaknesses and frailty. In cases of sickness in mind or body, 'the superior should always lean to the side of charity and forbearance', noting also that the sister herself ought to co-operate with medical advice and be obedient to the infirmarian.[21] In the requirement to 'subdue the flesh' by fasting, the sister is warned not to make herself ill by misplaced abstinence, and that mortification can be found 'in taking without choice and indifferently whatever is set before us'.[22]

The obligation to pray is incumbent on all the sisters for all of their lives; in the Rule of St Augustine, each sister is enjoined not to neglect prayer at the appointed time, not to dispense herself from prayer. Nor would it be in the spirit of the rule, with its focus on the common life, to make of prayer an entirely private affair.[23] Allowing that many women, even if literate, will not be able to understand the Latin text of the liturgy, each should nevertheless try to keep herself in the presence of God, according to the grace given her, raising her heart to God and desiring to praise Him: 'when you pray to God in psalms or in hymn let the heart feel what the voice uttereth'.[24] The cultivation of an awareness of the presence of God in daily life was characteristic of the teaching of St Augustine. This was supported by a set timetable of

16  Explanation of chapter 16, p. 35.
17  Ibid., p. 37.
18  Explanation of chapter 5, p. 18.
19  Ibid., p. 20.
20  Explanation of chapter 8, p. 22.
21  Explanation of chapter 17, pp 40–1.
22  Explanation of chapter 7, p. 21.
23  Explanation of chapter 6, p. 20.
24  Ibid.

hours of prayer in common. It was encouraged also by numerous homely customs and by the environment itself, with statues and holy pictures, silence and hymn-singing all intended to bring to mind the things of God in the course of the ordinary day.[25]

In the tradition of St Augustine, the superior held an honoured role, and obedience to her was expected. OLC sisters were taught 'to see God commanding and directing us through means of her, and obey in her the person of God', taking as example Christ himself who became obedient unto death, death on a cross.[26] Her authority was not to be overbearing, but she was to govern with 'gravity and sweetness', a model of virtue to her sisters, holding herself in the least estimation.[27] To the superior belonged the duty of seeing that all that the rule prescribed was indeed carried out, and that 'no transgression be passed over heedlessly'.[28] She was to admonish sisters, but 'in a spirit of charity and unfeigned humility', more severe on herself than on them.[29] On the sisters was laid the obligation 'of receiving with great deference all that is said, to correct them of their faults and, with great humility, turning to their advantage'.[30] They were to be prompt to ask for pardon when offence was given; indeed, a heartfelt willingness to seek forgiveness of each other was held up as vital to community life.[31] The obligation of reading the rule once a week — that is, hearing it read aloud in the refectory or chapter room — was that it might act as a mirror in which the sister might see her defects and endeavour to correct them by means of 'exact observance' of all the rule contained.[32]

One further core document, and bound with the Rule of St Augustine and the constitutions, was the *Souhaits particuliers* or 'Wishes of the founder'. In this short letter St John Eudes expounds on the privileges of the members of the new institute who, as daughters of the Holy Heart of Mary, are called to labour for the salvation of fallen souls, a vocation which has its source in a special manner in the all-charitable Heart of Jesus on fire with the love of souls.[33] Eudes expressed his hope in the words which were to become the motto of the institute: that none may write her vows except those with a true vocation to the order and who come to it with a large heart and an ardent will, *Corde magno et animo volenti*.[34] He urges the sisters to abide in the motherly heart of Mary, Queen of Heaven,

> That its grace may sanctify you, that its charity may enkindle you, that its love may set you ablaze, and above all that you may be devoured by its zeal for the salvation of souls.[35]

25   Explanation of chapter 12, p. 28.
26   Explanation of chapter 23, p. 51.
27   Explanation of chapter 25, pp 56–7.
28   Explanation of chapter 24, p. 54.
29   Explanation of chapter 25, p. 57.
30   Explanation of chapter 21, p. 49.
31   Explanation of chapter 20, p. 47.
32   Explanation of chapter 27, pp 61–2.
33   'Souhaits particuliers', *Oeuvres complètes de Bienheureux Jean Eudes*, x (Vannes, 1909), p. 71.
34   Eudes,'Souhaits particuliers', p. 74.
35   Ibid., p. 75. Trans. by J. Prunty.

Eudes enjoins on the sisters the importance of keeping with exactness the rules and constitutions and, above all, never to deviate from the holy work that is proper to the institute, 'which associates you in a wonderful manner with the Saviour of the world and with his most beloved Mother', and for which they have made their fourth vow, to occupy themselves in the conversion and instruction of erring souls, *des âmes dévoyées*.[36] The 'Wishes of the founder' is therefore a succinct exposition of the core spirituality of the order. It was transcribed into the first profession book of Dublin, where the sisters signed their vows.[37] It was reprinted as a preface to successive editions of the rule and constitutions with the intention – as Eudes himself stated – that these core texts be understood in the light of his wishes for them: that living in the motherly heart of Mary, which is 'one with the Divine Heart of her Son Jesus', and imbued with all the virtues to be found therein – pure love, ardent charity, deep humility, invincible patience and more besides – they might be unwaveringly faithful to their vocation to labour for the salvation of erring souls.[38] It was this last or fourth vow, and the spiritual tradition from which it came – that of the Holy Heart of Mary at one with the heart of her divine Son, all burning with love – that distinguished Notre Dame de Charité from other religious institutes. Whatever their personal weaknesses and the appropriateness of the Eudist refuge model to 1850s Dublin, the sisters who moved to High Park had certainty around what their mission was to be, a well-tested and – within the context of the 19th century – a generally sound rule of life upon which to build, and a deep reservoir of spirituality, from scripture and from tradition, on which to draw. They would need it all.

## Acquisition and Establishment of High Park under the *superiorité* of Mother Mary of the Sacred Heart Kelly, September 1853 to May 1860

The momentous decision to strike out anew and acquire High Park in 1857 was taken by Mother Mary of the Sacred Heart Kelly after almost four years of unbroken strain and serious ill-health, and without funds. The move was made possible by a small circle of friends and relatives, all of whom knew first-hand at least something of what the sisters had endured under Fr Smith's despotic rule and must have seen sufficient of the sisters' capabilities to hold out hopes of their success in their particular work if given a fair chance. Dr Murray, the archbishop's secretary and, prior to the appointment of Dr Woodlock, 'spiritual father' or visitor to the OLC sisters, also acted as guardian to the orphanage of the Carmelite convent, Lakelands, Sandymount. He managed to persuade the Carmelite nuns to give a loan of £2,000 'on condition of a mortgage on the property of some friend for the security of their convent'.[39] This friend was found in Mr Michael Murphy of Hebron

---

36  Eudes, 'Souhaits particuliers', p. 76.
37  'Livre dans lequel les Soeurs de La Congrégation de Notre Dame de Charité écrivent les ans et les jours de leur voeux et des annuelles confirmations qu'elles font en ce Monastère de Dublin, lequel a été établi le 14 de septembre de l'année 1853', pp 12–14 (DARGS, OLC1/6/1 no. 1). Hereafter, High Park profession register.
38  Eudes, 'Souhaits particuliers', p. 76.
39  Annals, 1857, p. 92.

House, Kilkenny, brother-in-law to the first superior, Mother Sacred Heart Kelly, who allowed a deed of mortgage to be drawn up on his property. Of the total loan, £300 was in the name of the orphanage and given 'on the joint security of Dr Murray and Dr Woodlock'.[40] An architect was engaged, Mr William Fry (or Fox), 'at 12/- per week and 3 tons of coal per year'.[41] The site for the first asylum building was blessed on 3 May 1857; there was a procession, led by Dr Murray, Dr Woodlock and some students from All Hallows college, followed by friends of the institute. Into the first stone were placed medals of the Immaculate Conception, St Joseph 'and other saints'. At the close of the ceremony, £100 from a Mr Richard Devereux of Wexford was handed over to Mother Sacred Heart Kelly, while other principal benefactors at this early stage of the project were relatives of the sisters (Thomas Kelly, the O'Callaghan brothers) and a Miss Frances (Fanny) Farrell.[42]

The detailed accounts for the builder, Beardwood and Son, from 1857 to 1860, divided between 'contracts' and 'extra works', reveal how several projects were under way simultaneously. With costs totalling £3,602 in the first phase, none of this work came cheap.[43] There was the erection of a new asylum or accommodation block, the remodelling of what was headed 'old house' to be the convent, and the renovation and equipping of outbuildings as a laundry. Shortly after the work commenced, an additional project was added: the remodelling of kitchen outbuildings to be a girls' reformatory (chapter 4). Workmen employed on the site included slater and slater's boy, labourer, carpenter, bricklayer, pumpmaker and plumber. The tasks undertaken included chimney repairs, hanging old doors, fitting gate, forming window openings, breaking out doors, putting up shelving, mangles, troughs and copper bleach boiler in the laundry, putting up Communion rail and confessional boxes in the chapel, also work at the bleach pound and on the lodge.[44] All that belonged to the old laundry at Drumcondra Road had to be left there; they were effectively starting from scratch.[45] 'Taking down figures over hall door' refers to the removal of what the annalist calls three 'heathen goddesses'; a later remodelling of the entrance saw a statue of Mary take up this space (Figure 3.3).[46] The 'ancient lions' that guarded the pillars of the entrance gates, however, were left *in situ* for some decades more.[47] The overall scale and complexity of the development is hinted at in the number of windows – '36 windows in back of houses', distinguishing ground floor, reformatory and asylum. Dormitory accommodation was a priority, and one

40  Annals, 1866, p. 126.
41  The 'original assignment' is dated 25 Feb. 1857, and is in the name of Dr Cullen, archbishop of Dublin and the sisters of High Park. Item 4, schedule of deeds received by Cartan O'Meara, 24 July 1907.
42  'Livre V, registre des fondateurs et bienfaiteurs du Monastère de Notre Dame de Charité de Dublin, établi le 14 septembre 1853', p. 7 (DARGS, OLC1/9/4 no.1). Hereafter, Register of benefactors.
43  MS notes re building contract, 24 Feb. 1857–30 Dec. 1861 (DARGS, OLC1/9/2 no. 2).
44  Beardwood and Son, accounts, 21 Apr. 1857–11 Apr. 1859; 17 July 1861–7 Sept. 1861 (DARGS, OLC1/9/2 nos. 3, 4).
45  Annals, 1858, p. 94.
46  Beardwood and Son, accounts, 21 Apr. 1857–11 Apr. 1859; High Park, English draft of *circulaire* dated 30 mai 1865, p. 57 (DARGS, OLC1/3/1 no. 1).
47  High Park, circular letter, 26 July 1898, p. 8 (DARGS, OLC1/3/1 no. 19).

**Figure 3.3**   High Park 1877 and 1953, illustrating the extent of the remodelling of the original house (DARGS, OLC1).

of the earliest orders was for 'strong bedsteads' ('such as they made for the nuns of Waterford and Arva's Court').[48]

The 52 women who transferred from Drumcondra Road had few comforts at first beyond the new iron bedsteads. They did not yet have a refectory in their own building but had to cross the yard to take their meals in the main house.[49] A later report refers to 'a large barn' with a clay floor being used as a refectory and how this would have to suffice 'until such time as Divine Providence would send means to build one'. An old boiler house adjoining the refectory served as kitchen. There was no proper chapel, though there were

48    MS notes re building contract, 24 Feb. 1857–30 Dec. 1861
(DARGS, OLC1/9/2 no. 2).
49    High Park, *circulaire*, 30 décembre 1859.

some furnishings, namely an altar and choir stalls purchased for £30 from the Presentation Sisters at nearby Richmond Convent. The altar was set up at the end of the corridor in the old house, the women 'arranged along its length', the sisters using as choir a room off the corridor.[50] The women had to travel outside to get to the chapel and the plan to join the two premises was put on hold.[51]

Compared to the old house at 2 Drumcondra Road, the women found the new stone asylum 'very cold and damp', and the snow that fell for their first month as they traversed the yard three times a day no doubt added to the hardship. Nor did they relish the 'system and regularity' of the new asylum, which the older women in particular found irksome, used as they were to the nooks and crannies of the old house and the many chances it afforded for a private chat. The new system, with its emphasis on having everything in common, did away with what the annalist termed 'the little satisfactions of *mine* and *thine*, in the way of food and clothing'.[52] The founder, Fr Smith, according to the same source, continued to cause 'restlessness and independence' among the women, some of whom still espoused his cause even where they did not approve of his 'open opposition' to all that involved the sisters from France. Two of the women abandoned the bracing heights of the new St Mary's and its strict regime for Fr Smith's re-opened Drumcondra Road premises and its old way of working.[53] Not until after Smith's death in August 1858 did these women return and, with the others, settle down and exhibit the docility and 'good spirit' that the sisters had hoped for.[54]

The move to High Park of the superior, the novices, the sisters and the women residents, and the associated building and refurbishment works, were the most visible and public aspects of the new beginning. But this was merely the start of the High Park project. What was more necessary still in terms of the tradition of Our Lady of Charity was 'to give to that foundation the proper spirit'.[55] This required the organisation of the life of the house around the rule and constitutions in which the sisters had already been trained, what was referred to repeatedly as establishing the house canonically. Under the ill but still indefatigable Mother Sacred Heart Kelly (superior to May 1860), the essentials were soon in place.

The first was separation from 'the world' and the imposition of enclosure, according to the decree of the Council of Trent. The sisters saw their ministry as exercised entirely within the enclosure, and by their profession undertook never to leave the enclosure, except for a grave and lawful reason and with the express permission of the local bishop.[56] Only the *tourière* sisters lived outside it, their role being to carry out the necessary exchange with 'the world'. The burial of the sisters would be within the enclosure, a privilege that was extended to the small number of women residents who promised perseverance unto death and made vows to that effect, namely,

50   Annals, 1858, p. 94.
51   High Park, *circulaire*, 30 décembre 1859.
52   Annals, 1858, pp 94–5. Emphasis as in the original.
53   Ibid., pp 93, 95–6.
54   High Park, *circulaire*, 30 décembre 1859.
55   High Park, English draft of *circulaire* dated 30 mai 1865, p. 44.
56   Constitution XVIII, de la clôture, p. 103.

the consecrates.[57] The bishop was charged with protecting the enclosure and none could enter without his written permission. Not even sisters from other orders could be brought within the enclosure, the only exception being the Sisters of the Visitation on account of the honoured role of Mère Patin in the foundation of the order, or where the OLC community needed to reciprocate the hospitality already afforded their own sisters by some other convent.[58] In practice, all lived within the enclosure, sisters, women penitents, pension boarders and children, though only the choir and lay sisters were bound to keep enclosure for life.[59] Being within the one enclosure did not mean that all lived as a single undifferentiated community; each group had its own rooms or buildings, its own recreation spaces and its own daily timetable. Where 'pious ladies and secular persons desirous of confirming themselves in a devout life' sought admission to the monastery for a time, they could be facilitated but would be expected to abide by enclosure also.[60] Short visits merely out of curiosity were not to be allowed.[61] Where there were schoolchildren to be taught by outside professors, all sorts of contrivances were suggested by France – such as a wicket gate in the grille in the parlour, which could be opened for the duration of the lesson – to keep the boarders inside the enclosure and the professors outside.[62] A grille or grating was erected in the parlour in High Park on arrival and in accordance with the first constitutions, but Dr Cullen disapproved entirely and did not allow it to be used.[63]

But it was not by grilles and high walls that the enclosure was kept; a spiritual and psychological separation from *le monde* was what the rule sought to promote. To make the separation from the world more explicit there were rituals around the necessary entrance and exits of workmen, confessor or doctor, whereby a bell was rung to accompany the opening or closing of the door, alerting the sisters to a temporary breach of the enclosure and warning them to keep out of sight.[64] When a visit to the parlour was necessary, the sister was to 'cut short all worldly and idle discourse' insofar as that was practicable, to retire promptly when the bell rang and, above all, never to show herself eager for 'news of the world', but to place all her delight in conversing with God.[65] Similarly, the women at recreation time were urged to speak of spiritually and morally uplifting matters, rather than wordly fashions, vanities and curiosities.[66] All were urged to keep the

---

57  Permission to bury lay people within the enclosure was allowed under the general heading, 'desquels la dévotion singulière méritera exception', Constitution LIV, De l'enterrement des Soeurs, p. 172.

58  Explanation of constitution XXIX (XVII), Enclosure, p. 148.

59  Pendant qu'elles seront dans le Monastère, elles garderont parfaitement la clôture, 'Règlement pour les filles et femmes pénitentes', *Oeuvres complètes de Bienheureux Jean Eudes*, x (Vannes, 1909), p. 176. Hereafter, 'Règlement'.

60  Explanation of constitution XXIX (XVII), Enclosure, p. 148.

61  Ibid., p. 150.

62  Ibid.

63  Constitution XVIII, de la Clôture, p. 105; annals, 1869, p. 131.

64  Constitution XVIII, de la Clôture, p. 105; Explanation of constitution XLIII, The portress, p. 296.

65  Explanation of constitution XXIX (XXIII), Manner of speaking with strangers, p. 189.

66  Chapitre III, Exercice de la journée, 'Règlement', p. 180.

business of the house within the house, keeping guard over what they said and even more so what they wrote to outsiders, lest they damage its good reputation or honour.[67] The admonition to avoid retelling 'all the gossip of the town' was part of this effort to honour the spirit of religious enclosure, embracing all residents and making of every OLC monastery a place apart.[68]

The proper setting up of the books 'for entering the affairs of the monastery' was another essential first step in the making of an autonomous OLC monastery.[69] Alongside this might be placed the copying, by hand, of the core texts of the institute brought from France. The mission to Dublin marked the first occasion on which the constitutions were translated into English.[70] The first assistant, Soeur Marie de Saint Ignace Pavot from Rennes, though she never managed to grasp any English, was credited in her obituary with establishing proper book-keeping, in the canonical sense, in the first monastery of Dublin, and for keeping the annals for the first two and a half years.[71] The various convent books – the profession book, register of penitents, register of benefactors, accounts book, register of title deeds and contracts, annals, *circulaires* and obituaries – that were set up on or soon after the founding date of 14 September 1853 – testify to the efforts made to be faithful to the rule and constitutions, customs and directives brought from France. The book-keeping system was logical and well-tested; not alone did it make of Dublin a true daughter of Caen, but it gave the community control over its self-understanding and its internal history, the story that would be handed on to the other houses over successive generations.

Each community of Our Lady of Charity governed itself through a chapter, as indeed was the general pattern among apostolic religious institutes whose rule of life can be traced back to that of the Visitation sisters and St Francis de Sales. For Our Lady of Charity, the weekly chapter, usually held on Thursdays, was a gathering of all the sisters, lay and choir, called to listen to an extract from the constitutions or from some pious book, followed by a spiritual exhortation from the superior and the public confession of faults by at least some of the sisters.[72] Announcements of general interest – such as donations received and prayers sought – were made by the superior. It was also a forum for raising matters that impinged on the entire community, such as the purchase or alienation of property; questions were invited, opinions sought and some discussion ensued. The real tool of government was the chapter of vocals at which the professed choir sisters of four or more years' standing had a voice. The election of a superior, the admission of a postulant

---

67 Explanation of constitution VII (XV), Obedience, pp 143–4.
68 Explanation of constitution XXIX (XVII), Enclosure, p. 153.
69 *Customs and usages of the Congregation of Our Lady of Charity, order of St Augustine, with the formulary of the clothing and the profession of the religious*, text of 1738 edn, trans. Peter Lewis (Aberdeen, 1888), article XXIII, Books to be kept for entering the affairs of the monastery, pp 245–56 (DARGS, OLC1/5/1 no. 12). Hereafter, Customs and usages.
70 'Abridgement of the life and the virtues of our dear Mother Mary of the Sacred Heart Kelly, deceased in this Convent of Our Lady of Charity, High Park, Dublin, 29 June 1863', typescript, p. 5 (DARGS, OLC1/6/4 no. 64). Hereafter, Abridged life of Mother M. Sacred Heart Kelly.
71 Annals, 1854, p. 51.
72 Constitution XXIX, du Chapître, p. 127.

to clothing and the admission of a novice to profession of vows all required the deliberative vote of the chapter, while other matters of importance would also be put to a vote.[73] Thus one of the first books to be set up by the newly-arrived sisters in 1853 was *Livre de Chapître de ce Monastère de Notre Dame de Charité de Dublin*.[74] Not having a dedicated chapter room for many years, they assembled in the choir of the tiny chapel in Drumcondra Road, and later in the makeshift choir looking onto the chapel corridor of High Park. Entries to 1856 were in French only. As well as lectures from the superior, the sisters were called to chapter for the annual visit of the father superior, but written records of these routine gatherings were not usually kept. The chapter book occasionally includes obituaries of sisters and women residents while, in the early 20th century it was also used to keep a record for posterity of both international and local events, such as the canonisation of St John Eudes in Rome (31 May 1925), the holding of a sodality, unveiling of a statue and travel to or from another monastery.[75] But its primary purpose was to ensure a record of all votes, properly taken, on the election of superiors and the admission of candidates.

The holding of elections for a superior, her deposition after three years and her possible re-election for a further term of three years (the usual outcome) was a much-cherished aspect of the autonomy of an OLC monastery. Only in the case of a brand new foundation or some exceptional crisis would there be outside involvement.[76] The recording of elections merited a separate book.[77] At the end of each *triennium*, on the Saturday after the feast of the Ascension, the chapter being assembled in the choir and the bishop or his delegate being present, the superior resigned her charge. The new election was held five days later, in accordance with the protocols set out in the constitutions, the new superior proposing for election the names of those to be her assistant and councillors.[78] The admission of candidates to vows was also intrinsic to the autonomy of an OLC monastery. Only when new sisters made vows tying them to Dublin would the future of the foundation be secure. The title page of the High Park profession register is followed by an account of the foundation of the house by sisters from Paris and from Rennes and the role played by Fr Smith and other named ecclesiastics – the version of the history that the founding sisters wanted to perpetuate. The register recounts the confirmation on 14 September 1853 of Mother Mary of the Sacred Heart Kelly as first superior, with Sister Mary of St Ignatius of Loyola Pavot as assistant, and lists all High Park superiors from Mother Sacred Heart Kelly onwards, with the dates of each mandate. It also reproduces the wishes of the founder, John Eudes, *Souhaits de notre digne Instituteur*. The signed entries testify to the membership

73  Ibid., p. 128.
74  'Livre de Chapître de ce Monastère de Notre Dame de Charité de Dublin, commencé et établi le 14 du mois de septembre de l'année 1853' (DARGS, OLC1/5/1 no. 2). Hereafter, Chapter book.
75  Chapter book.
76  The rule allowed for a sister from another house to be elected as superior, though it was expected that this would be rare and for 'very strong reasons' only. Explanation of constitution LI, The election of the superior, p. 325.
77  'Livre des élections de ce Monastère de Notre Dame de Charité de Dublin commencé et établi le 14 du mois de Septembre de l'année 1853' (DARGS, OLC1/5/2).
78  Constitution LII, de l'élection de la supérieure et autres officières, pp 166–70.

of the founding community and the houses from which they were drawn. The first entry is the canonical examination before profession of Sister Frances Xavier O'Neill, the young Irish-born choir novice from Paris who was later recalled by that monastery. She made profession of vows for Paris in Drumcondra Road on 21 November 1854, the feast of the Presentation of Our Lady and the usual day for profession and renewal of vows. The year following, on the same feast-day, Sister Mary of St Anne Carroll signs her name with the note that she has previously confirmed vows 'in our convent of Paris'; Sister Mary of the Five Wounds O'Callaghan makes a similar declaration. The annual confirmation of vows is closed in each case with a short obituary of the sister, bringing her life in religion full circle.[79]

In the move from Drumcondra Road, the hope was expressed that the better set-up at High Park would attract postulants.[80] There was indeed a stream of candidates during the period of Mother Sacred Heart Kelly's *superiorité*, but few stayed and so there are few entries in the chapter book and even fewer in the register of profession. The names of those who came and went, also of some who were sent home because of ill-health, are recorded by the annalist.[81] She also notes that some, though 'rich in the good things of this world', were turned down after a trial, judged not to be blessed with the treasure of a religious vocation.[82] Few of those who were eventually received as novices were possessed of other dowry 'than that of their own sterling worth and virtue'.[83] In December 1859, when Mother Sacred Heart Kelly was still superior, there were six novices and five postulants in High Park.[84] The noviceship was even smaller in May 1865 when the sisters in France were told, by way of explanation, that 'vocations to our work are very rare in this country. Still we feel confident that our Divine Lord will send us subjects in his own time'.[85] Even allowing that most did not persevere, sufficient numbers were coming through to allow the annalist to claim by March 1867 that 'our little community began gradually to increase, gaining subjects and becoming more known'.[86]

The first entry to the register of penitents was made by the sisters at Drumcondra Road on 12 September 1853, preceded by the names of four women who had entered the asylum 1839–40 and were to finish out their days in High Park.[87] Some other long-resident women may have transferred to High Park but subsequently returned to 'the world', as indeed was the expectation.[88] Numbers and approximate lengths of stay can be deduced

79    Sister M. of St Anne Carroll made her profession of vows in Paris 19 May 1845; Sister M. of the Five Wounds O'Callaghan made her profession in Paris also, 20 July 1847. The custom of examining candidates before profession ceased in Nov. 1967, High Park profession register.
80    High Park, *circulaire*, 30 décembre 1859.
81    Annals, 1856, p. 89; 1858 p. 97; 1861, p. 102; 1862, p. 103; 1866, p. 127.
82    Annals, 1861, p. 102.
83    Ibid.
84    High Park, *circulaire*, 30 décembre 1859.
85    High Park, English draft of *circulaire* dated 30 mai 1865, p. 62.
86    Annals, 1867, p. 130.
87    'Livre quinzième de l'entrée et sortie des pénitentes commencé le 14 jour septembre de l'année 1853, jour de l'établissement de ce Monastère de Notre Dame de Charité de Dublin' (DARGS, OLC1/8/1 no. 2). Hereafter, Register of penitents.
88    Chapître II, de leur sortie, 'Réglement pour les filles et femmes pénitents', p. 178.

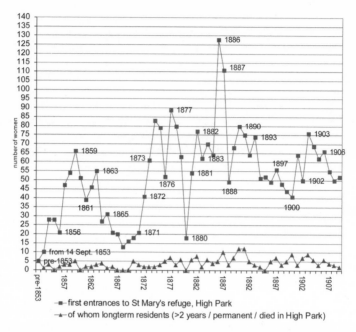

**Figure 3.4**    Admission of women to St Mary's refuge, High Park, 1853–1906.

from the register of admissions and bear out statements made elsewhere (and not always approvingly) that few of those who resorted to High Park in its founding decades made it their permanent home. After many is simply entered 'left' with no further note or comment; 'entered before' hints at repeated short-term stays. Those who are known from the register entries, sodality notebooks, obituaries and other internal records, and from information gleaned from the General Register Office and the censuses of 1901 and 1911 to have stayed at least two years, or to have died in St Mary's (or, where they died in hospital, to have been recorded as a resident of St Mary's) have been classed as 'long-term residents' (Figure 3.4). These calculations found that an average of four women out of each year's intake up to 1906 stayed long-term, that is, 7.6% of all first-time admissions. Exact numbers cannot be known, but the general trend – a very small percentage of all entrants staying long-term – is true to the documentary record.

A number of entrants can be identified as coming directly to High Park on discharge from prison. In the early decades, several women who had spent time in Grangegorman prison were sent along by a chaplain named Fr Murphy, most of whom left High Park after a few days. Between 1859 and 1895 there were 46 such cases: three in the 1850s, 13 in the 1860s, 15 in the 1870s, and 11 between 1880 and 1886. One woman entered on 30 October 1885 and has the term 'convict prisoner' after her name; seven more women, all entered on 7 November 1885, are similarly noted; none of these eight women stayed on in High Park, but the dates of departure are not given. The High Park 'sent from prison' cases decreased sharply in line with positive

developments elsewhere, namely, the certification and state funding of prisoners' aid societies under the General Prisons (Ireland) Act 1877. The role of
these societies was to aid prisoners after their discharge by providing suitable
lodgings, furnishing temporary maintenance and subsequently exercising a
'friendly supervision' over them or, as one promoter summarised it at the
time, 'getting them swallowed up in the tide of life'.[89] A grant not exceeding
£2 per person was allowed, to be applied by the society for the benefit of
the discharged prisoner.[90] Our Lady's Home, 10 Henrietta Street, the project of the Dublin Discharged Female Roman Catholic Prisoners' Aid Society,
founded 1881, and from 6 April 1899 under the day-to-day management of
the Daughters of Charity of St Vincent de Paul, would supersede High Park
as the place of first resort for women on leaving prison in Dublin at least.[91]
But even when it did serve that purpose, there is only the briefest, fleeting
reference to this fact. Whatever the circumstances, practically nothing can be
gleaned of the individual stories before, or after, time spent in the refuge.
Notes such as 'left', 'left own request', 'sent away' and (occasionally) date
of death give little scope for further inquiry. There are some case studies or
exemplary tales in the obituaries of women who died in the institute and
which have survived as they were written into the annals or circular letters.
However, for most women, the information is minimal, and relates almost exclusively to their time in High Park, their spiritual trials and other sufferings
bravely borne, and their crossing over into what in each case is confidently
hoped to be the possession of eternal bliss.

Control over the income and expenditure of the house, or at the very
least, knowledge of to whom the community owed thanks and to whom
they owed money, was another important factor in the establishment of an
autonomous OLC monastery. There was also a spiritual reason, with much
made of how gratitude was the 'favourite virtue' of the founder and ought
to be the special devotion of the Daughters of Our Lady of Charity.[92] Within
weeks if not days after arriving in Dublin a sturdy, leather-bound register of
benefactors was started, containing names, sums donated, donations in kind,
and other services rendered. As with the register of profession, it is prefaced
by an account in French and in English of the opening of this the 17th house
of the institute and the reasons for recording the names of benefactors in this
book, 'that their liberalities may be of eternal memory'. Fr Smith and Cardinal Cullen head the list of founders and benefactors; nothing is to be allowed
to erase the fact that it was Smith who brought them to Dublin even if relations with him were far from amicable. The same donations are recorded in a
second volume but alphabetically from 1853 to 1898 and at shorter intervals
thereafter, distinguishing 'larger amounts' of more than £5 from bequests

---

89   James G. Alcorn, 'Discharged Prisoners' Aid Societies', *Irish Quarterly Review* (Dec. 1881),
vol. viii, part lviii, p. 222.
90   General Prisons (Ireland) Act 1877, 40 & 41 Vic., c. 49, sec. 44.
91   Jacinta Prunty, Bríd O'Neill, and Eileen Devlin, 'Our Lady's', Henrietta Street, accommodation for discharged female prisoners', in Jacinta Prunty and Louise Sullivan (eds), *The
Daughters of Charity of St Vincent de Paul in Ireland, the early years* (Dublin, 2014), pp 181–99.
92   Explanation of constitution XX (XVIII), Gratitude, p. 167; Constitution XX, de la gratitude
ou reconaissance, pp 111–2.

and other donations. This was to facilitate the formal recalling of their generosity as prescribed by the constitutions, at the first chapter in March and
in September, when the names of those to whom the house was under an
obligation to remember in perpetuity would be recited, both those who had
assisted in a small way and the 'great benefactors'.[93]

Similarly, the earliest bound account book is dated from 14 September
1853, 'jour d'arrivée de notre Très Honorée Mère Marie de Coeur de Jésus
Kelly et des Soeurs de la Fondation'.[94] The accounts are first signed off on 31
December 1854, covering a most unhappy phase when everything concerning
the funds of the asylum was a matter of contention between Fr Smith and
the unfortunate superior, Mère Kelly. That the accounts to December 1854
are so full reflects very well on her administrative and leadership skills, but
there is no way of knowing what was still under the control of Fr Smith and
so does not feature here. The accounts are more trustworthy from January
1855, when the sisters got charge of the annual charity sermon in support of
the asylum and managed it most successfully.[95] The vast bulk of the income,
for example in 1855, came from washing and needlework; there were also
'benefactions', 'divers sales', and small sums 'on the entrance of penitents'.
The *rôles* or categories under which expenditure was made included (for example, 1855), bread, meal and flour; wine, porter and vinegar; meat, fish and
eggs; butter and milk; fruit and vegetables; sugar, tea and coco (*sic*); gas, oil
and candles; coal; household; *robière* (clothing); ironware and delph; infirmary;
church; *jardin* (*sic*), postage; reparations (repairs); presents and alms; work
(soap, wages to carter, horse hire, etc.); stable yard; extra (included insurance and rent). The constitutions required that the *économe* or bursar keep a
carefully-dated and well-arranged account of all the money given her for expenditure, as well as all income from 'the work' (mainly from the laundry)
and donations, submitting her accounts monthly to the superior and her
council.[96] The exemplary way in which the High Park accounts were set up,
with receipts signed and dated and bound into packages each month, must
be credited to Mother Sacred Heart Kelly and her immediate successors.
The system was to continue with virtually no change into the mid-20th
century. The account was closed annually 'in presence of the principal officials
of the house' – superioress, assistant, councillors and surveillants – who sign,
while the spiritual superior (in 1855 Fr Bartholomew Woodlock) also signs.[97]

The same type of care was extended to property ownership and the making of contracts, with title deeds, receipts and all associated papers signed
and dated and also summarised periodically in schedule form (instrument,
parties and dates),[98] all to be kept safely 'in a vaulted chamber or in some

93   Constitution XX, de la gratitude ou reconaissance, pp 111–2.
94   'Comptes des derniers reçus et employés chaque année en ce Monastère de Notre Dame
de Charité de Dublin, commencé le 14 de septembre de l'année 1853 jour d'arrivée de notre
Très Honorée Mère Marie de Coeur de Jesus Kelly, et des Soeurs de la Fondation' (DARGS,
OLC1/9/3 no. 2). Hereafter, Comptes des derniers reçus et employés.
95   The charity sermon was held 28 Jan. 1855 and raised over £100. Annals, 1855, p. 82.
96   Constitution XLIII, de l'économe, p. 152.
97   Comptes des deniers reçus et employés.
98   Schedule of deeds received by Cartan O'Meara, solicitors, 24 July 1907, in relation to High
Park (DARGS, OLC1/9/1 no. 12).

other place under lock and key'.[99] Before ever they left Drumcondra Road, a standard questionnaire from the diocesan authorities concluded with the note 'The Archbishop will require to see and inspect all deeds by which houses, lands or funded property are held'.[100] Though they as yet owned nothing in their own name, Mother Sacred Heart Kelly was very quickly brought to understand the importance the Catholic Church placed on having legal proof of rights of ownership and occupation, an area that was particularly vexed in Ireland where penal restrictions on the endowment of Catholic charities were not lifted until 1861.[101]

The construction of a community history in the form of annals was as much a foundation task as setting out the register of vows and ruling up the accounts book. The High Park annals were started within a fortnight of the sisters' arrival from France, with the first part written up in French by Soeur Marie de St Ignace de Pavot according to a long-established OLC formula.[102] Translations of the early annals of Caen and other pre-Revolution houses, and of 'the virtuous lives' of several French mothers, were also made in the founding years and for the same purpose, 'to the greater honour and glory of God, and the edification of the Sisters of the Institute'.[103] All too soon, the High Park sisters had to honour the memory of their own dead, sisters and women residents, through the construction of obituaries and the setting aside of a burial ground in the enclosure. It might well be expected that the ailing Mother Sacred Heart Kelly would be the first interred, but that was not to be, as the move to High Park brought her some respite.[104] According to the annalist, between 1859 and 1860 'provision was made for a cemetery at the extremity of the High Park grounds for the Religious and Penitents'.[105]

The first religious to take possession of this 'city of the dead' was Sister Mary of St Xavier O'Reilly, described as 'the first flower that the Divine Master was pleased to cull from the little garden of the foundation thus to form a second house of the order in heaven (if we may be allowed the happy thought)'.[106] The brief account of her death has all the standard elements of an OLC obituary – family background, seeds of vocation, virtues, sufferings in her final illness – but it also prefigures the death from tuberculosis of a

99   Customs and usages, article XXIII, Books to be kept for entering the affairs of the monastery, p. 253.
100   Questionnaire on religious houses in Dublin diocese, 20 Sept. 1854 (DARGS, OLC1/1/1 no. 12).
101   Jacinta Prunty, 'Religion' in H. B. Clarke and Sarah Gearty (eds), *Maps and texts, exploring the Irish Historic Towns Atlas* (Dublin, 2013), p. 165.
102   Annals, 1854, p. 65.
103   'The Annals of the Order of Our Lady of Charity, instituted by the Revd John Eudes, under the rule of St Augustine, where are recorded the most remarkable events that have happened in the Monastery of Caen, as well as in the other monasteries of the same Order, with the character of several of the Religious who have been distinguished for their virtues, compiled by order of the Council of the Monastery of Caen, to the greater honour and glory of God, and the edification of the Sisters of the Institute. By a religious of the same Order. 1st vol. Caen, 1723', MS trans., in notebook stamped Browne and Nolan, Dublin (DARGS, OLC1/5/3 no. 3).
104   High Park, *circulaire*, 30 décembre 1859.
105   Annals, 1861, p. 101.
106   Ibid., pp 100–1.

succession of sisters, mostly in their mid-20s, in the early decades of the foundation. Sister Mary of St Xavier O'Reilly, born in India, the daughter of a sea
captain, died in June 1861, less than a year after making vows; though not
strong 'there was no indication of the disease that that was to carry her to an
early grave'. The community held out great hopes that she would be 'most
useful' but, having unwisely thrown off her flannels, she suffered 'haemorrhage of the lungs' and was dead within weeks.[107] The same cause of death
was given for the tall and strongly-built Sister Mary of St Agnes Power, who
died one year and six days after professing her vows. Just as Mother Sacred
Heart Kelly was growing weaker, a further two young sisters died ahead of
her, Sister Mary of St Teresa Hayes, 'from hysterical affection that ended in
consumption' and Sister Mary of St Francis de Sales Duffy 'from internal in-
flammation which made her suffer a martyrdom'.[108] The catalogue of early
deaths continued throughout the 1870s and 1880s.[109]

Tuberculosis is highly infectious and Mother Mary of the Sacred Heart
Kelly was in an advanced stage of the disease before ever she left Paris in 1853;
her active role in the nursing of all the sick up to her own death, keeping vigil
on numerous occasions, would not have helped to control its spread.[110] But
some at least of the women had symptoms of TB when received as novices,
with notes such as 'never robust' and others admitted to profession despite
their fragile health. 'Our young people cannot boast of strong constitutions'
may be said of the first 30 years or so of the foundation.[111] Illness was always
accepted as the will of God, a sacrifice that the Lord was asking of the community, a sharing in His chalice of suffering. What was said on the death of
Sister Mary of St John the Evangelist O'Connor in 1874 was said of many:
'she expired calmly and happily and with perfect consciousness, yielding her
soul lovingly into the hands of her Lord and spouse', giving an example of
how to die as an OLC sister.[112]

Among the women residents, the first deaths to be recorded for High
Park, in 1859, were of two elderly ladies who had come from Drumcondra
Road. They were buried in the cemetery *au fond du Park*, described later
as 'their little cemetery beside that of the sisters'.[113] Mary Ann Molloy was
described by the obituarist as 'always most respectful and submissive to the
religious when others gave them much trouble and was greatly attached to
them'; as a resident of 30 years' standing in the asylum, she was probably

107    Annals, 1860–61, pp 99–100. See also death letter, in French, in which it is stated she died
2 June 1861, aged 27 years, 9 months in religion (copy from NDC Caen in OLC1/6/4).
108    Annals, 1861, p. 123; High Park, English draft of *circulaire* dated 30 mai 1865, pp 45–6.
109    For example, Sister Patrick Bisset, professed 1861, died 1867 of 'rapid consumption',
Annals, 1867, p. 130; Sister M. of the Sacred Heart Byrne, novice, died of 'an internal ulceration';
Sister Ignatius Loyola Kelly, one year professed, died probably of TB; Sister M. of St Bridget
Connor, 'never strong' but managed 12 years of religious life, died of disease of the lungs, all
died 1870, High Park, draft circular letter 1871 (DARGS, OLC1/3/1 no. 7), also Annals 1870,
pp 133, 135, 136; Sister M. of St Agnes Galvin, died 1878 and Sister Seven Dolours Nolan, died
1881, Annals, 1878, p. 144; 1881, p. 150.
110    High Park, English draft of *circulaire* dated 30 mai 1865, pp 46–49.
111    High Park, draft circular letter, 1868 (DARGS, OLC 1/3/1 no. 6).
112    Annals, 1874, p. 141.
113    High Park, *circulaire*, 30 décembre 1859; Annals, 1866, p. 128. OS 1:2,500 Dublin sheet
14–16 (1867).

the senior among those who transferred to High Park. Her companion Anne Doyle, who died shortly after, was described as 'a very superior woman, endowed with much good sense and judgement' who, under the earlier management, had 'entire charge of the packing room and the laundry accounts'. She too had taken the side of the sisters in the struggle with Fr Smith, a stance which probably mattered much at the time as she was credited with having 'great influence among the women'.[114] On transfer to High Park, more deaths were expected among the women, as so many were in poor health.[115] Several of the women who started out in Drumcondra Road were to live to a great old age at High Park, such as Mary Peter and Jane Bell, described as 'great companions and full of affection for each other' who died almost at the same time, in 1882.[116]

The holy, happy deaths of individual women are recalled at intervals in the annals and the circular letters.[117] As with the obituaries of the sisters, efforts made to overcome faults, and the crosses carried in life were highlighted. Emily who entered in 1854 and died eight years later, succeeded by fidelity to the grace of God and long perseverance in overcoming an angry, violent nature.[118] Similarly, Catherine, who had 'many combats with nature', expired after a long residence in the asylum with the words 'Jesus, Mary and Joseph I give you my heart and soul' on her lips.[119] Only occasionally is the obituary expanded sufficiently to give an inkling of the woman's life before her entrance to High Park or of how she conducted herself as a resident. One such study is of that of Mary Anne, 'a noted character and much dreaded even by the police on account of her violent temper'. Strong-willed but with a real desire to be converted (according to the obituarist), her admission to High Park was 'a great triumph of grace' and, once she overcame her 'natural inclinations', she became a model to all – hardworking, respectful to the sisters, greatly beloved by her companions 'being most kindly and bright and quaint in her sayings and always ready to assist others' – all in all, a 'truly good consecrated penitent'. Although she died suddenly in 1877, her death 'was not an unprovided one' and the obituarist had every confidence in the happy repose of her soul.[120]

The arrival of women in time to die at High Park was taken in a positive way. If the core purpose of the house was to work for the salvation of errant souls, what more satisfactory work was there than to help such women prepare for death? Watching the death-bed gave the sisters the absolute assurance that the woman had not returned to her 'old life', where that was feared to be one of sin. While giving her the physical comforts of the infirmary – the cleanliness, quiet and good order, nourishment, medicines, nursing care and companionship – the greatest stress was laid on ensuring the patient had the opportunity of confession and of receiving the last rites, and keeping vigil as she entered her last agony. In 1872, there were three deaths, of whom

---

114 Annals, 1866, p. 128.
115 Ibid.
116 Annals,1882, p. 153.
117 For example, see the death of 'Julia', High Park, *circulaire*, 1862, p. 40 (DARGS, OLC1/3/1 no. 1).
118 Ibid., p. 41.
119 High Park, English draft of *circulaire* dated 30 mai 1865, p. 60.
120 Annals, 1877, p. 143.

two were recent arrivals, 'all died holy, peaceful deaths, resigned and happy to go to the dear Master, who had worked such wonders in their regard'.[121] Similarly in 1876, two of those who died 'had entered only in time to prepare for death, being but a few weeks in the house'.[122] Of the 12 who died between 1878 and 1884, several were young and newly-arrived: of Christina and Charlotte, both brought to the infirmary on their entrance, it was said 'they turned with their whole hearts to their loving Master' in the short time left to them, 'and died full of hope that He would receive them with mercy'.[123]

The wholehearted commitment of the first superior Mother Sacred Heart Kelly to establishing the cordial relationships with other OLC houses that John Eudes had urged is evident in successive drafts of circular letters, annual Christmas greetings and notices of elections.[124] Dublin sent out its first full *circulaire*, via Paris, in November 1853, just two months after the sisters' arrival, while it received letters and some welcome material support from houses and their lay supporters in France from the outset. The circular letter for 1859, in French, has as heading the quotation from scripture, 'Those who have sown in tears shall reap in joy'. The foundation was truly marked with the sign of the cross, the other houses were told, a precious treasure and the solid basis on which all divine works are founded.[125] The *circulaires* show how the injunction to reflect on events from a spiritual perspective was taken up, as also the invitation to include 'any diverting news however trifling it may be'.[126] Through the *circulaires*, Kelly and her successors tapped into the network of support that kept autonomous OLC houses connected and interested in each other, and made for Dublin a position on the Eudist tree well-rooted in Caen.

The liturgical and devotional life of the house was also established under the *superiorité* of Mother Sacred Heart Kelly, who reported on progress towards the ideal she had known in France in the Christmas and other community letters. The chanting of the praises of God in the Divine Office was held up as one of the sisters' holiest occupations, shared with the angels, the saints, with the Blessed Virgin Mary and with their divine spouse, Jesus. But as their first and principal employment was to labour for the salvation of souls, the choir sisters were bound not to the full monastic hours of the orders with solemn vows, but to the Little Office of Our Lady, in Latin.[127] The lay sisters had the option of either reciting at intervals and a set number of times, the *Pater* and *Ave*, or (where they were literate) taking on the Little Office in the vernacular. All were present in choir at the same time but the lay sisters could slip in and out during the office if their duties required.[128] The small number of choir sisters and choir novices during the first decade of the foundation, with much illness and cramped chapel arrangements, meant

---

121   Annals, 1872, p. 138.
122   Annals, 1876, p. 142.
123   Annals, 1882, p. 152.
124   Draft circular letters with dates are as follows: Nov. 1853, Nov. 1854, Nov. 1856, 18 June 1857, 18 Dec. 1859, 20 Dec. 1859, 30 Dec. 1859, 27 May 1860, 1862, 30 May 1865; most are in French (DARGS, OLC1/3/1).
125   High Park, *circulaire*, 30 décembre 1859.
126   *Customs and usages*, article XXII, Style of letter-writing, p. 244.
127   Constitution III, de l'Office divin, p. 84.
128   Ibid., p. 87.

that the standard of singing and associated ceremonial was nowhere near that of Paris or Rennes or Caen, the monasteries from where the first sisters were drawn, but they could at least take on the injunction to bring to the holy exercise all the recollection and interior devotion they could muster.[129]

As superior, Mother Sacred Heart Kelly had some responsibility for the spiritual progress of all her children, professed sisters, novices, women penitents and reformatory children. The 'spiritual helps', though less abundant than she was used to in France, were not altogether lacking in Dublin. Daily Mass, opportunities for confession, Eucharistic and Marian devotions, sermons, retreats and sodalities were all set in train at High Park. There were, she reported, few priests in Ireland relative to the large Catholic population. The association with All Hallows was thus a real advantage, with priests 'lent' as occasion required from the college. In the absence of a good preacher, Kelly herself filled the gap with her own lectures.[130] She quickly organised confessors for the women and established their week-long preached retreat preceding the feast of St Mary Magdalen. The care of the terminally-ill and the writing up of obituaries (death letters, *les petit fleurs*), with heavy emphasis always on the holy dispositions at the time of death, were also part of her spiritual duties as superior. Under her leadership, religious pictures and statues began to multiply both inside and outside. A little oratory to St Joseph was erected at the bottom of the garden by December 1859 and Kelly, a keen devotee, was reported as awaiting with impatience the day of its inauguration.[131] She also introduced into the house a sincere devotion to their founder, John Eudes, a saint (pronounced venerable 1874, beatified 1909, canonised 1925) practically – if not completely – unknown in the diocese at the time.[132]

Before the end of Mother Sacred Heart Kelly's second triennial in 1860, she reported the statistics of the house as six choir sisters, one lay sister, six novices (three choir, three lay), one *tourière* sister, two postulants for the choir and three for the kitchen, 68 penitents, 22 schoolchildren in the *classe de Réformation*, two gardeners, one van man, three workmen and two lady boarders (*séculiares*) – in all, 119 persons.[133] The numbers on the campus of High Park, after less than two years of operation, and with very limited accommodation, is quite remarkable. The register shows that, once the transfer was completed, large numbers came – and left – as had been the pattern in Drumcondra Road (figure 3.4). But the greater numbers facilitated was only part of the story, and not perhaps the most significant over the longterm. By the time Mother Sacred Heart Kelly had completed two terms of office, all the principal elements of an autonomous monastery of Notre Dame de Charité were in place. The remodelling and building, begun by Kelly, would be greatly advanced under her successors, but she had led them safely out of Drumcondra Road and to a site with huge potential. Setting up a modest reformatory project and then abandoning that to be part of an untested government scheme, opening the first reformatory school in Ireland (Chapter 4), was a

129    Ibid., p. 85.
130    High Park, draft *circulaire*, 1862, p. 36.
131    High Park, *circulaire*, 30 décembre 1859.
132    Annals, 1877, p. 143.
133    High Park, *circulaire*, 30 décembre 1859. Note: the error in the arithmetic is in the original.

bold decision. Her great ambition had been to organise the house canonically and that was certainly well under way: separation from the world, setting up the various convent books and establishing the liturgical and devotional life of the house are well documented.

## *Superiorité* of Sister Mary of the Five Wounds O'Callaghan, 1860–66

The election of Soeur Marie des S.S. Cinq Plaies O'Callaghan as superior in May 1860 was announced to the other houses in France in gushing language; a true *fille de Notre Dame de Charité*, she had come to the community in 1855 from Paris, where she had trained. She had since been assistant, *économe* and infirmarian and the right hand of the previous superior (*chère déposée*), with whom she had a perfect union and for whom she had already deputised due to frequent illness. All would know that the new superior and *déposée* had been noviceship companions together in rue de Jacques, Paris, their friendship cemented by the trials shared in Dublin. The election letter was also a paean of praise for Mother Mary of the Sacred Heart Kelly's time at the head of the new foundation, for her magnanimity, gentleness and wisdom in directing the interior and exterior affairs of the little family.[134]

During the first two years of the *superiorité* of Mother Mary of the Five Wounds O'Callaghan, 'nothing of note occurred to be recorded'.[135] The first round of reconstruction and new building was still under way, according to the accounts, and there was now a household of more than 100 persons (figure 3.5), so there was certainly plenty of activity on site.[136] But what the annalist wanted to highlight was the absence of tyranny and trouble as the community settled down in High Park and, for the first time, enjoyed the autonomy that was after all written into their rule:

> The tempest of persecution that for so many years swept over the work of God, and which seemed so often to crush its every effort to maintain its ground, was abated, and although still a few of the old Revd. Fr Smith's old supporters circulated their wrong ideas and prejudices against the nuns, the majority saw things in their right light and each year brought new friends to the Convent who helped the Institution by their liberal donations as well as by the services they rendered it.[137]

The erection of a chapel was prioritised by O'Callaghan, to replace the corridor setup where the Lord was housed 'in a mean manner and all crowded', the women and children 'assisting as best they could on the stairs and elsewhere'.[138] In a rather poignant turn of events, the temporary chapel, to hold 100 persons, was completed in time for the funeral service of the foundress, Mother

---

134    High Park, election letter, 27 May 1860 (in French), pp 33–4 (DARGS, OLC1/3/1 no. 1).
135    MS notes re building contract, 24 Feb. 1857–30 Dec. 1861 (DARGS, OLC1/9/2 no. 2); annals, 1861, p. 102.
136    High Park, *circulaire*, 30 décembre 1859.
137    Annals, 1861, p. 102.
138    High Park, *circulaire*, 1862, p. 38; Annals, 1861, p. 101.

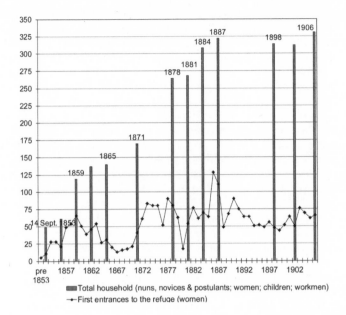

Figure 3.5 Total household and entrances to St Mary's refuge, High Park, 1853–1906.

**Figure 3.5** Total household and entrances to St Mary's refuge, High Park, 1853–1906.

Sacred Heart Kelly, 'the first ceremony performed in this little sanctuary'.[139] Ensuring that the memory of Mother Kelly was as fully written up as possible on her death (29 June 1863, aged 43 years), fell to her successor as superior, Mother Mary of the Five Wounds O'Callaghan – though the death letter or announcement, with obituary, was composed in Paris, the house of her profession, and circulated from there.[140] The 'abridged life' by O'Callaghan runs to 25 pages.[141] A lengthy obituary was also inserted in the annals, opening with the dramatic statement: 'Her death fell like a thunderbolt on her Community, who revered her as a Mother, loved her as a sister and friend, and regarded her as the foundress, the staff and the firm support of the foundation'.[142] The recounting of the virtues of the first superior and all she had done and suffered before her holy death, and its careful recording in the annals, as well as in the form of an 'exemplary life', was to edify the sisters who would come after and to demonstrate to posterity how providence had never failed the institute, despite trials and tribulations. It put in train what can be called the cult of the foundress, which came into its own on the centenary of the Dublin foundation when a version of the story was told publicly, in print, for the first time.[143] The circular letter which followed Kelly's death spoke of the real affection

139   Annals 1861 p. 101; High Park, English draft of *circulaire* dated 30 mai 1865, p. 47.
140   Death letter for Soeur M. du Coeur de Jésus, d. 29 June 1863, signed by Soeur M. du St Sauveur Billetout, Paris (DARGS, OLC1/6/4 no. 64)
141   Abridged life of Mother M. Sacred Heart Kelly.
142   Annals, 1863, pp 104–123.
143   *The Order of Our Lady of Charity of Refuge, 1853–1953, a centenary record of High Park Convent, Drumcondra, Dublin* (Dublin, 1953), pp 30–60. Hereafter, *Centenary record*.

Dr Woodlock had for his friend of many troubles, how he 'wept like a child' at her interment and now 'he hovers around our community like one whose sole occupation is our welfare'. Dr Murray, still 'co-labourer with him in our little vineyard', stayed steadfast also, ever ready to assist, 'from the commands of the archbishop to the least little service'.[144] The friends she had made for the community would prove to be an important part of Kelly's legacy – above all to the superiors who held office over the following two decades.[145]

Regrettably for Mother Five Wounds O'Callaghan, and despite the many pledges of support, the 'heavy cross' of the death of the founding superior and her close friend would become (in the words of the annalist) the harbinger of the many other crosses it would please Divine Providence to send her during her second triennial.[146] A fire in the chapel on the feast of the Ascension 1864 consumed 'everything rich and beautiful in the way of laces, silks, velvet, vases and flowers'.[147] Later that year, a sister contracted typhus which was reported to France as a huge embarrassment to the community, as well as a real threat to the health of all. O'Callaghan took on the patient's sole care, in isolation, for three months, to save the house from contagion. (The sister survived).[148] These crises occurred as the numbers for whom the superior had overall responsibility increased steadily, with a household of 140 persons by 1865 (figure 3.5).[149] Though five of the sisters 'can translate a little', O'Callaghan was reportedly the only one who could write fluently in French; 'the burden of the circular letters therefore falls on her'.[150] She had to follow up contacts who had previously communicated with the house and had the trial of explaining repeatedly that, no, they were not the Good Shepherd sisters but, yes, they did the same work and had the same founder and also came from France.[151]

The debts due to building, including the cost of the temporary chapel, loomed large throughout the *superiorité* of Five Wounds O'Callaghan.[152] Rent had to be paid on the leases, and land agents were never a moment behind in pressing their clients' demands.[153] The good name of their two most important clerical friends, Dr Murray and Dr Woodlock, helped fundraising efforts, but nevertheless, as reported by one supporter, collecting door-to-door among the better-off was fatiguing and difficult work, with little to show for it.[154] The appointment of Dr Murray as bishop of Maitland, Australia, in 1866 precipitated a crisis in that the £300 lent 'on the joint security of Dr Murray and Dr Woodlock' needed to be refunded to the Dublin diocese before his departure. A raffle or 'drawing of prizes' was determined to be the most

144    High Park, English draft of *circulaire* dated 30 mai 1865, p. 55.
145    Ibid., p. 47.
146    Annals, 1863, p. 123.
147    High Park, English draft of *circulaire* dated 30 mai 1865, pp 47–8.
148    Ibid., p. 49.
149    Ibid., p. 63.
150    Ibid., p. 62.
151    Lady Tichborne, Tichborne Park, Alresford, Hants, to Mrs O'Callaghan, High Park, 24 June 1862 (DARGS, OLC1/1/1 no. 17).
152    Annals 1861 p. 101
153    See correspondence, 20 items, concerning payment of rents due on High Park lands, 1864–69 (DARGS, OLC1/9/1 no. 2).
154    Hugh Gaffney, Newtown Mount Kennedy, to Mrs O'Callaghan, High Park, 19 May 1862 (DARGS, OLC1/1/1 no. 16).

speedy and effective plan by 'three of the commercial men of the city', raising the handsome sum of £360, so that debt at least was cleared.[155]

## *Supériorité* of Sister Mary of St Joseph O'Callaghan, 1866–72

The election of Sister Mary of St Joseph O'Callaghan as superior in May 1866 was celebrated for the continuity it epitomised. As the first to make profession of vows for the Dublin monastery, she was the 'first daughter of our foundation' having had as 'her guide and instructress in the duties and obligations of the religious life' none other than the dearly-departed Mother Mary of the Sacred Heart Kelly.[156] What is not mentioned, perhaps as too obvious to need stating, is that she was the younger sister of the outgoing superior, Mother Mary of the Five Wounds O'Callaghan. She had been received into the order only ten years earlier (when she was aged 36 years), and had already served as assistant to the superior (her sister). That she was leadership material must have been evident from the day of her reception, judging from the offices she had already held, in stormy times. The two triennials of her *supériorité* (1866–72) were marked by building projects on a scale not yet attempted. She set these enterprises in train without neglecting her first responsibility as superior, namely, to exhort the sisters, by advice and instruction, 'but more especially, by her own example' to the 'fervent accomplishment of all points of rule', at least according to the annalist.[157]

The turning away of women at the door of the asylum for the want of space was the recurrent complaint from the arrival in High Park; the numbers turned away were given as from six to eight weekly in 1865, each a poor soul 'come to seek refuge from the sin and misery of the world'.[158] There was a larger context also, with increasing public concern over prostitution.[159] The sisters' version of the story was that a group of 'good and well-intentioned men' became determined 'to procure homes for these poor wanderers by enlarging the houses of refuge (or asylums as they are called) in the city or by building new ones'.[160] St Mary's was spoken of 'as best suited to the purpose' and the co-operation of Mother Joseph O'Callaghan was immediately forthcoming.[161] The decision to extend St Mary's was announced to the public in January 1867 and subscriptions sought.[162] A letter of approbation from the archbishop was printed in the newspapers in July 1867.[163] Fundraising quickly moved beyond the usual charity sermons to the distribution of leaflets, boldly headed: 'A remedy for the "Social Evil", wanted, 250,000 pennies for the management of Magdalen Asylum, High Park, Drumcondra'.[164] The headline is

---

155 Annals, 1866, p. 126.
156 Ibid., p. 127.
157 Ibid.
158 High Park, English draft of *circulaire* dated 30 mai 1865, p. 58.
159 'The social evil in Dublin', *Freeman's Journal*, 29 Mar. 1865.
160 High Park, draft circular letter 1871.
161 Ibid.
162 'Magdalen asylum, Drumcondra', *Freeman's Journal*, 26 Jan. 1867.
163 'The social evil', *Freeman's Journal*, 10 July 1867.
164 The leaflets were printed by Browne and Nolan Ltd, 24 Nassau Street, dated 22 July 1868 (DARGS, OLC1/1/1 no. 18).

taken from the term popularised by William Logan in his exposure of the shocking reality across Britain and Ireland of desperately poor women unable to leave prostitution for the want of a place where they might find shelter and safety.[165] The Dublin Statistical Society, at its inaugural meeting in November 1862, was urged to include, among its research concerns, 'the social evil in our streets'.[166] The same phrase appears in letters to the newspapers throughout the 1860s and 1870s.[167] The headline, 'A remedy for the "Social Evil"' therefore had a modern ring to it. The appeal itself was couched in the overwrought language of the rescue and reform movement that had been in use for decades and draws on the figure of the penitent Mary Magdalen. The plan, however, was simply stated: £1,000 was sought towards the costs of erecting a building with room for 200 women (the present St Mary's could house 70). The list of those who would receive subscriptions is headed by Dr John McVeagh, 24 Frederick Street North, a physician and one of the community's earliest friends.[168] Another familiar name is that of Mrs Sims, 51 Dawson Street, who had a sister in the community (Sister Mary of St Stanislaus Brennan, assistant to the superior at the time) and who would prove an indefatigable friend to her death. But most of the 16 names were not already benefactors or otherwise connected with the community, so that it does appear to be a stand-alone lay committee set up for the express purpose of this public appeal.

The project began in earnest with the commissioning of the renowned architect J.J. McCarthy sometime before September 1867, and was brought to a close in April 1872 when Mother Mary of St Joseph O'Callaghan demanded that all outstanding bills be submitted for payment before she relinquished office (in May 1872). McCarthy undertook a research visit to the OLC convent in Marseilles as part of his planning, and confidently predicted that he and Mother Joseph O'Callaghan, together, would be able 'to devise (on paper at least), a complete establishment'.[169] This could be read as a recognition of expertise on her side; the sisters themselves maintained that their current reverend mother 'is a regular architect'.[170] Draft letters dating to this period were composed by a sister who was surely both architect and engineer, such is the understanding and obvious delight in complex technologies and innovative building processes.[171]

165    William Logan, *An exposure from personal observation of female prostitution in London, Leeds and Rochdale, and especially in the city of Glasgow, with remarks on the cause, extent, results and remedy of the evil* (3rd edn, Glasgow, 1845); various editions and reprints, including William Logan, *The great social evil, its causes, extent, results and remedies* (London, 1871). The person quoted here is Samuel Warren.
166    Address by the Lord Lieutenant to the inaugural meeting of the Dublin Statistical Society, *Freeman's Journal*, 27 Nov. 1862.
167    For example, letter to the editor, *Freeman's Journal*, 29 Mar. 1865.
168    'A remedy for the "Social Evil"', wanted, 250,000 pennies for the management of Magdalen Asylum, High Park, Drumcondra' (DARGS, OLC1/1/1 no. l8). His daughter, Agnes (Sister Cecilia) was to enter High Park and was elected superior 1920–26.
169    J. J. McCarthy, Marseilles, to Revd. Mother [M. of St Joseph O'Callaghan], 7 Sept. 1867 (DARGS, OLC1/1/5 no. 1).
170    High Park, draft circular letter, 1871.
171    For a full account of the new technologies to be adopted, see High Park, draft circular letter, n.d. but *c.*1871 (DARGS, OLC1/3/1 no. 8). Note: this is not the same item as draft circular letter dated 1871.

The initial enthusiasm of McCarthy for the project is not in doubt. However, from cancelled meetings, mislaid plans and failure to communicate instructions to the builder, it is hard to avoid the judgement that he was seriously overstretched, with commissions the length and breadth of Ireland, and could not give the High Park work the attention it needed.[172] The sisters themselves gave the greater share of the credit to a disinterested friend and benefactor, Patrick Kennedy, of whom they certainly saw much more. The extensive correspondence O'Callaghan had with the parties involved – architect (J.J. McCarthy), building contractor (Matthew Gahan) and onsite volunteer supervisor (Patrick Kennedy) – are testimony to skills in mediation, as there were countless disputes between these parties and with the community itself. Yet Sister Joseph managed to maintain amicable relations with all, the builder himself declaring in the heat of a lengthy tirade against those giving him contradictory orders that 'as suppose we never do another job in High Park we have always met the very greatest of kindness from the Revd Mother and all the community'.[173]

The public appeal resulted in about £400 which, though welcome, was nothing like what was needed to extend capacity.[174] A low-interest loan of £500 from a Mrs Michael Murphy was accepted with thanks – but that, of course, was not the same as money in the bank.[175] In 1874, an extra storey was added over the ground floor (which had been roofed temporarily)[176] giving two large, well-ventilated dormitories, each holding 36 beds; 'all the beds are covered with white quilts and look very nice although their only costly ornament is cleanliness'.[177] There was a bedroom at the end of each dormitory for the mistress. As reported to France, 'This addition enabled us to accomplish the ardent desire of our hearts, that of adding thirty to the number of our Penitents (and, we sincerely hope, to the number of the Saints)'.[178] There was also, on the top floor, a small infirmary (with a lavatory) for the sick and ailing women, 'a luxury we never before possessed'. Architecturally, there was one feature of note, 'a splendid staircase of granite which will last forever', wide enough to take three abreast.[179]

Fulsome credit for seeing the project through to a satisfactory conclusion was heaped on the head of Patrick Kennedy, who lived locally in Clonliffe. Though not a man of exceptional personal wealth, the grateful community reported that he was 'gifted with wonderful talents of mind and heart'[180] and, jointly with his wife, was to be ranked first of all their benefactors and friends.[181] His wife had already taken an interest in the work and, according to the annals, towards the end of 1870 managed to induce her husband to visit, from which date he promised to render whatever services were in his

172   See, for example, Mr McCarthy to Madam, 21 Nov. 1871 (DARGS, OLC1/1/5 no. 8).
173   Matthew Gahan to J.J. McCarthy, 16 Jan. 1872 (DARGS, OLC1/1/5 no. 10).
174   High Park, draft circular letter, 1871.
175   Register of benefactors, p. 22.
176   Mother M. of St Joseph O'Callaghan to Mr McCarthy, 12 Feb. 1872 (DARGS, OLC1/1/5 no. 11); Annals, 1870, p. 132.
177   High Park, circular letter, 20 Oct. 1874, pp 5, 21 (DARGS, OLC1/3/1 no. 9)
178   Ibid., p. 21.
179   Ibid., pp 5, 21.
180   High Park, circular letter, 20 Oct. 1874, p. 5.
181   Register of benefactors, pp 25–6.

power, asking only that he and his young family might be remembered in prayer. The annalist added that 'surely never was promise so faithfully kept or friends more truly to be relied on'.[182] From the date of his first involvement, practically every circular letter includes a paean of praise, right up to 1902, when his death is lamented.[183] His importance to the community is amply documented in the benefactors' books, accounts and correspondence.

Patrick Kennedy was credited first with the 'self-imposed mission' of collecting money throughout the city, resulting in £1,324, most of which was made up of small sums, as enumerated in the register of benefactors.[184] The improvements to the various departments of the laundry were to his design, demonstrating a real understanding of the processes involved and an ability to adapt new technologies to this very specific setting in a way that made business sense.[185] The creation, for the first time, of a boiler house was his project; this large room held a steam engine ('fire engine') and six metal tubs for boiling the clothes, and a copper one for boiling starch.[186] The person who most appreciated this advance was the lay sister in charge, probably Sister Mary of the Holy Angels Langan – herself 'quite an expert in the art of Engineering' after 20 years' experience, and rightly proud of her capabilities.[187] Also credited to the initiative of Kennedy was a long, bright ironing room and a packing room lined with shelves of oak, each square compartment labelled with the name of the customer.[188] The hot air drying closets were regarded as a work of genius: wooden horses, bars of six feet long, hidden behind '28 panels of polished wood, like so many doors, which can be drawn out at pleasure' to the full width of the room.[189] Later advertisements made much of the high standards and efficiency of the laundry (Figure 3.6). While the introduction of modern machinery in the 1870s was significant, it was the water infrastructure, on which the viability of the enterprise ultimately depended, that would prove to be Kennedy's most important long-term contribution.[190] He is credited with the construction of 'two monster cold water cisterns' into which water gathered at all times and built over the new coal vault, a remarkable piece of engineering which obviated the danger of heat building up within the coal store.[191] Getting the city corporation to extend the piped Vartry water supply to High Park, giving year-round certainty of an excellent supply, was another singular achievement:

> Armed with the shield of faith and relying not on the power
> of men but on God alone, and against the opinion of every-
> one consulted who had long before abandoned the enterprise,
> he went to the Committee and pleaded our cause so well

---

182   Annals, 1871, pp 137–8.
183   High Park, circular letter, 22 May 1902 (DARGS, OLC1/3/1 no. 21).
184   Register of benefactors, pp 26–7.
185   For the fullest account of the various processes, see High Park, draft circular letter, n.d. but c.1871 (DARGS, OLC1/3/1 no. 8). Note: this is not the same item as draft circular letter dated 1871.
186   High Park, circular letter, 20 Oct. 1874, p. 5.
187   Ibid., p. 21.
188   High Park, draft circular letter, c.1871.
189   High Park, draft circular letter, 1871.
190   High Park, English draft of *circulaire* dated 30 mai 1865, p. 57.
191   Annals, 1870 p. 132; 1871 p. 137; High Park, circular letter, 20 Oct. 1874, p. 21.

**Figure 3.6**   Laundry technology and premises, St Mary's refuge, High Park, *c*.1925.

(telling them that they were obliged to co-operate in encouraging and supporting an institution such as ours, and one so useful to the city at large) that wonderful to relate all at once they consented, not only to give the water, but also to lay the pipes to our convent gates.[192]

192   Ibid., p. 22.

Around the same time but attributed to the miraculous intercession of St Joseph ('guardian of the community and its protector against all dangers'), the Dublin Gas Company was induced to bring gas (initially for light) to All Hallows and from there on to High Park.[193]

The canonical visitation of all convents in the archdiocese of Dublin ordered by Dr Cullen in 1869 in advance of his journey to attend the Vatican Council in Rome, provides insights into the state of the monastery at the midpoint of Sister Mary of St Joseph O'Callaghan's *superiorité*. There were four professions that year (two choir sisters, two lay sisters), a most encouraging sign.[194] Expressing himself with 'perfect frankness', the visitor, Fr Walsh P.P., could not understand the need for strict enclosure and gratings. He wished to see Holy Communion dispensed every day, and urged that the 'manifestation of conscience' by subjects to the superior be altogether abolished, a practice which many priests feared was rather too close to the sacrament of confession.[195] While the sisters wrote of the 'dear solitude' of High Park, it is clear that the diocesan authorities were not at all keen on the enclosed, monastic character of the institute, which was becoming more apparent as the new campus developed.[196] As the sisters explained to their colleagues in France, the only communities that observed strict enclosure in Ireland were the Carmelites, the Poor Clares and the Redemptoristines. 'The gates or strict enclosures is abolished in all the other communities or active orders – being a missionary country *all* have poor schools attached to their convents'.[197] They thus found themselves an apostolic order offering refuge, 'preservatory' and reformatory services with strict enclosure, something of an anomaly in Ireland.

## *Superiorité* of Mother Mary of St Bartholomew McDonnell, 1872–78

The election of a young superior in 1872 was presented in the annals in terms of continuity, rather than change. Received as a novice in High Park 12 years earlier, Mother Mary of St Bartholomew McDonnell, now aged 26 years, had indeed been formed to all the duties of the religious life 'by our first mothers' and – the standard formula of approval for all superiors – 'was full of zeal for the observance of the rule'.[198] The good Patrick Kennedy 'continued his labour of devotedness' so that, under McDonnell's *superiorité*, the asylum accommodation was further expanded and the infrastructure upgraded.[199] There were 83 new or first-time entrances during 1873, the highest recorded to date, and the average number in residence at any point in the year

---

193 High Park, draft circular letter, 1871; annals 1870, p. 132
194 High Park profession register, pp 117, 121, 125, 129.
195 High Park, draft circular letter, 1871.
196 The sisters protested that gratings had been done away for nearly a decade as forbidden by the archbishop, but a grating must still have been visible on the premises in Sept. 1869, annals, 1869, p. 131.
197 High Park, draft circular letter, 1871. Emphasis as in the original.
198 Annals 1872, p. 138.
199 Ibid.

was given as 75 women.[200] Further laundry improvements were a matter of particular pride, allowing a higher standard of work and greater quantities to be processed, but also a lessening of the heavy labour on all the parties involved, choir sisters, lay sisters and women alike.[201] The largest and most ambitious of the projects promoted by Kennedy was the construction of a private sewer, three miles in length, to carry off the laundry water directly into the sea at Clontarf.[202] Another major project, commenced under Mother Bartholomew McDonnell and completed in her second triennial, was a proper reformatory school building (Chapter 4). By December 1874, the building was finished and in use, thanks to a most successful fundraising campaign masterminded by the indomitable Kennedy, his friends and relations.[203]

The decision by Mother Bartholomew McDonnell to visit Paris in 1874, the house from which Dublin was founded, and to include Rennes and Caen en route, from which sisters had also been drawn, was regarded as quite exceptional by the community, but no-one could challenge the reason she gave: 'to have personal experience of a well-regulated community where primitive rule and pristine vigour was upheld'.[204] There were copies of the rule, constitutions, customs and the 'explanation of the rule' in High Park, but that was not the same as seeing how these were worked out on the ground. Having been at High Park since she was aged 14 or 15 years, the now 28-year-old superior had no experience of France, nor did she have more than, at best, a very few words of French, but her companion was to be Mother Mary of the Five Wounds O'Callaghan (aged 62 years). She had made her profession of vows in the Paris house two decades earlier and was now in the roles of assistant to the superior and novice mistress, having formerly been superior herself.[205] With the support of Monsignor Woodlock and the permission of Archbishop Cullen, the sisters set out on 7 April 1874, accompanied by a brother of one of the sisters, Revd P. O'Connor. In their absence, charge of the house was placed in the able hands of *chère déposée*, Sister Joseph O'Callaghan.

On the positive side, the local superior, Mère Marie de St Sauveur Billetant, and her community welcomed them with cordiality and affection. At the first evening recreation, 'a feast of the heart', Mother Five Wounds O'Callaghan found among those assembled 'many dear familiar faces' from happier days, including Soeur Marie de St Stanislas Brunel, who had sent out the pioneers more than 20 years earlier.[206] The Dublin superior had the 'deep satisfaction and contentment' of knowing that the rules and observances which were followed in her house, with few exceptions, matched those of Paris.[207]

---

200  Calculations based on Register of penitents, also High Park, circular letter, 1 Dec. 1873 (DARGS, OLC1/3/1 no. 3).
201  High Park, circular letter, 1 Dec. 1873; draft circular letter, *c*.1871.
202  Annals 1873, p. 139. High Park, circular letter, 20 Oct. 1874, p. 7; Thomas and Charles Martin, North Wall, Saw Mills, bills for construction materials including pipes, sewers, timber, moulding, sink traps, cement, laths, cess post, 1 June–24 Sept. 1874 (DARGS, OLC1/9/2 no. 22).
203  Annals 1873–4, p. 139.
204  High Park, circular letter, 20 Oct. 1874, p. 14.
205  Death letter for Sister M. of the Five Wounds O'Callaghan, d. 2 Jan. 1895, signed by Sister M. of the Heart of Mary Tobin (DARGS, OLC1/6/4 no. 87).
206  High Park, circular letter, 20 Oct. 1874, p. 15; annals 1874, pp 139–40.
207  High Park, circular letter, 20 Oct. 1874, p. 15.

The down side was that the experienced Mother Five Wounds O'Callaghan was ill for practically all of the six-week visit, even during the stop-over in Rennes. The visit to Caen was abandoned, as was the last leg of the journey, a call to Bartestree, the newly-founded OLC house in England.[208] Though little can be deduced about what they learned in Paris and in Rennes – beyond that Dublin was following its dear mothers in all essentials – the visit did serve to strengthen the bonds of affection and loyalty between the houses.[209] Fundraising for a badly-needed proper chapel for High Park was perhaps given fresh impetus by what the sisters saw on the continent.[210] Above all, the visit reinforced High Park's commitment to 'the *integrity* of the Rules and Observances of our holy Institute', as articulated in response to a query from Caen that arrived shortly after the two sisters had returned from France: 'the security and beauty of religious communities consists in their uniformity and conformity of each monastery in the faithful observance of the primitive Rules and Customs'.[211]

## *Superiorité* of Mother Mary of the Holy Heart of Mary Tobin, 1878–84

In the election of Mother Mary of the Holy Heart of Mary Tobin as superior in 1878, the High Park community was invited to see once more the unerring hand of providence at work. There were certainly tangible links with the difficult founding days. She had been clothed with the habit in Drumcondra Road and was one of two novices (the other left) to be instructed by Sister Mary of St Jerome Hanrahan, sent by Caen to help out as novice mistress for a limited period only.[212] Mother Tobin made her profession of vows in the corridor chapel of High Park, the first such ceremony in the new monastery, and meriting special mention in the annals as the date on which this foundation on Irish soil took root.[213] The principal project for which her *superiorité* was lauded was the new chapel – a pressing necessity, since the extra dormitories had greatly increased the household numbers.[214] St Mary's refuge also took on its final and much-improved form under her leadership with the addition of a new wing; both chapel and refuge building projects were under way simultaneously.

When Mother Tobin took over, funds towards the new chapel were already in the bank, thanks in particular to the unflagging efforts of a liberal and frequent benefactor, Mrs Sims.[215] The foundation stone of the

---

208   Sister Bartholomew McDonnell, Dublin, to Ma chère soeur [Rennes], 19 June 1874 (DARGS, OLC1/3/1 no. 3). High Park, circular letter, 20 Oct. 1874, p. 14.
209   High Park, circular letter, 20 Oct. 1874, p. 15.
210   A major bazaar was held in 1877, but the labour for it filled 1876, see Annals 1875–6, pp 141–2.
211   'Copy of the letter written to Caen on the subject of the General Assembly', 28 Oct. 1874 (DARGS, OLC1/3/1 no. 10). Emphasis as in the original.
212   Letter of authorisation, signed Charles [Didiot], Archevêque de Bayeux et Lisieux, and Marie Duclos, Chan. Secrétaire (DARGS, OLC1/1/1 no. 13).
213   The note refers also to the profession of Sister M. of St Bridget Connor which was in Sept. 1859, annals 1859, p. 98.
214   Annals 1878, p. 145
215   High Park, circular letter, Feast of the Patronage of St Joseph, 1884 (DARGS, OLC1/3/1 no. 14); Register of benefactors, p. 34–5.

new chapel was blessed with due ceremony by Monsignor Woodlock on 19 March 1879, the feast of St Joseph.[216] The patronym chosen for the dedication, held on 29 August 1880, was the Sacred Heart of Jesus, connecting with the spirituality taught by John Eudes but also recalling the religious name of the Dublin foundress, Mother Kelly. An architectural description, in French, was circulated to all the houses overseas shortly after, though the chapel was still to be furnished and ornamented. It was cruciform in shape, that is, a nave and two aisles, one for the women and one for the schoolchildren; the choir was in the nave. The roof was vaulted, with pillars; the walls were of brick with a façade of stone; on the gable to the west was a belfry. On the back wall was a stained glass window to the Sacred Heart, with the two hearts, the badge of the order, in the centre.[217] Behind the main altar were two lancette windows, and above that again a rose window. Over each of the side altars, to the Blessed Virgin and to St Joseph, was a rose window.[218] The dedication was conducted by the new archbishop of Dublin, Edward McCabe, with Bishop Woodlock of Ardagh and Clonmacnoise and Bishop Murray of Maitland both present, the community's oldest and truest clerical friends. A Dominican priest (Monsignor Daly) spoke of the privilege of being able to freely enter the church at any time, to enter the presence of God Himself, 'who remains always your father, your protector, your friend'.[219] The consecration of the high altar and the two side altars was held on 7 May 1884, just before Mother Tobin left office, by which date the interior of the church was completed:

> The church looked, and still looks, lovely, the pure white marble showing out against the pale uniform grey of the walls, with no other colouring save the tinted sunlight through the windows, the oaken stalls and roof, with the handsome tiled floor.[220]

Over the next two decades, the chapel decoration would be completed. The widow of Judge O'Hagan, a long-standing friend of one of the sisters (Sister Mary of the Good Shepherd Stevelly), before entering the Franciscan Convent of the Perpetual Adoration, Drumshambo, commissioned the sculptor John Hogan to produce a large-sized marble statue of the Sacred Heart, which was duly erected in the chapel in the niche on the gospel side of the main altar. Smaller donations together funded a counterpart for the other niche, a marble statue of the Immaculate Heart of Mary, by another Irish artist named Smith.[221] The devotional ambience was further enhanced by new stained glass windows.[222]

---

216   High Park, *circulaire*, 8 février 1881, p. 2 (DARGS, OLC1/3/1 no. 13); High Park, circular letter, 6 Dec. 1879 (DARGS, OLC 1/3/1 no. 3). Dr Woodlock was succeeded as 'spiritual father' by Archdeacon MacMahon. High Park, *circulaire*, 8 février 1881, pp 12–13.
217   Annals, 1879, p. 149
218   High Park, *circulaire*, 8 février 1881, p. 16.
219   Ibid., p. 17.
220   Annals, 1884, p. 157.
221   Ibid. Possibly the sculptor George Smith who had a business at 193 Great Brunswick Street at this date.
222   The Good Shepherd, St Anthony with the Holy Infant, the Agony of Our Lord in the Garden of Olives, High Park, circular letter, May 1906, p. 7.

The project of extending the refuge was architecturally more challenging than the chapel and, once more, lay fundraisers were key. A new and influential benefactor, the Lord Mayor Mr Hugh Tarpey, came forward just as Mother Tobin took office. He is reported as calling a public meeting of the well-to-do to see what might be done to increase the provision for those seeking to leave prostitution, pleading the cause of the women in a touching manner, and setting collections afoot.[223] His commitment extended beyond his term as Lord Mayor (1877-9) and the new asylum was credited as a monument to his energy.[224] Mrs Sims was also, as so often before, 'unwearied in her exertions'.[225]

What was decided on jointly by the superior with the architect (Mr Byrne) and builder (Mr Toole) was much more than an extension to the first building, erected at the lowest possible cost in 1857 and admitted by all to have a gloomy look about it.[226] There was also the portion raised in 1871, that is, the two storeys added above the refectory and kitchen. The jumble of buildings, the dark limestone walls and the blank gable that was the first view did nothing to lift the spirits. The challenge was to hide the dismal side and to make out of all a single building whereby the new would not disgrace the old. This was achieved by having two wings at right angles so that the space between the oldest portion and the newest became a courtyard, as illustrated in the ground plan of 1909 (Figure 3.7). A new kitchen and its out-offices on the ground floor (west), joined the gable ends of the old (south) and new (north and east) wings. The result was an entirely new orientation, a three-storey, symmetrical building, its façade and external walls plastered and whitewashed, and described as '*un bâtiment simple, solide et substantiel*'.[227] The new portion was higher than the old, but steps allowed the corridors to connect and the arches created a convent-like atmosphere which was intended to aid recollection. It was a building without architectural pretensions, but hailed as one which had shed its miserable frontage and presented now to the world as a peaceful, holy place of penitence and solitude.[228] This work effectively completed the building of the refuge started 22 years earlier.

The ceremony of laying the first stone was held on 1 June 1879, the first public engagement of Archbishop McCabe, with whom relations were decidedly more cordial than with his predecessor.[229] McCabe set the example with a donation of £60 (1,200 francs). The new wing was ready for habitation in May 1881 when the archbishop came back to bless it, room by room, with no less ceremony and generosity.[230] A 43-page booklet to mark the occasion was produced, to give to the 'numerous kind benefactors and subscribers' a report, with statistics, 'on the end and working of the Institution' which was, after all, still little known to most people in Dublin.[231] The description

223   High Park, *circulaire*, 8 février 1881, p. 5; Register of benefactors, pp 39–40.
224   High Park, *circulaire*, 8 février 1881, pp 3–4.
225   Annals, 1880, p. 150.
226   Taylor, *Irish homes and Irish hearts*, p. 88.
227   High Park, *circulaire*, 8 février 1881, p. 6.
228   Ibid.
229   High Park, *circulaire*, 8 février 1881, p. 18; circular letter, Feast of the Patronage of St Joseph, 1884, p. 3.
230   High Park, circular letter, Feast of the Patronage of St Joseph, 1884, p. 3.
231   *Abstract report and statistical sketch of the magdalen asylum, High Park, Drumcondra, June 1881* (Dublin, 1881), p. 3. Hereafter, *Abstract report*.

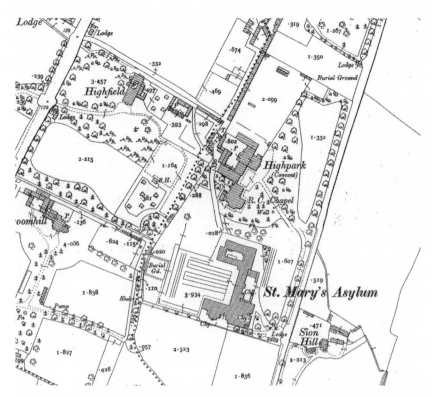

**Figure 3.7**  St Mary's refuge and High Park monastery, Drumcondra, 1909 (OS
1:2,500, Dublin sheets 18–4, 14–16, revised 1907, published 1909).

of the new wing is an abridgement of the update, in French, sent earlier that
year to the other OLC houses. Among the internal features pointed out as
especially noteworthy were the crucifixion scene on the ground floor corridor where time might be spent in private prayer, the large new refectory
(incorporating the old packing room) which allowed all the women to eat at
the same time, the long recreation room with an altar to Mary at the top, and
the central heating pipes throughout the ground floor. The kitchen was the
special attraction – or, at least, would be when fully equipped. On the top
floor, the infirmary with its high ceiling and seven windows was the boast
of the house, described as a place of calm and tranquillity for convalescents
and where those on their last journey might close their eyes in peace and
comfort, surrounded by all the consolations of religion. There was a doctor's consulting room, for privacy, also a food lift operated by a suction
pump leading down to the kitchen. The view from the attic windows, over
the city, was unparalleled.[232] There were few new entrants in 1880, due to the
building work that was under way. At the start of 1881, the capacity of the
asylum was announced as 170 women, with 130 already in residence.[233]

232  High Park, *circulaire*, 8 février 1881, p. 7.
233  Ibid., pp 8, 18.

Over the seven years 1881–87 inclusive, the total new admissions (first entrances only, not returns) comes to 566 women (Figure 3.4) making it appear that there was indeed unmet demand in the city for refuge accommodation, as those who had invested so much – in planning, fundraising and building work – believed at the time.

The enlargement of the asylum, that the sisters might be enabled to receive and support all who sought admission, became the driving concern after the turmoil of getting established had settled down.[234] But the new building which was opened in May 1881 did more than provide extra bed spaces and upgrade the standard of accommodation for all. As explained to the other OLC houses, 'whilst providing them most amply with all temporal conveniences, it in no slight degree facilitates the maintenance of good order, silence, the spirit of recollection, and prayer'.[235] It was this 'good spirit' that the sisters sought to create in the refuge, as in the convent, among the sisters, the novices and the women alike. This was a spirit of docility and obedience, a willingness to submit to routine and timetable, and a readiness to work for the common good, not just one's individual needs. It put great store on unity and harmony among themselves, and a patient carrying of human frailty, both physical and moral.

With the salvation of souls – all souls – the overriding purpose of the monastery, whatever might promote a spirit of prayer or help lift the mind to the things of God, was incorporated into the new asylum building and adopted into the daily routine. The rule that a sister was always to be with the women, in the different work departments and during recreation, was easier to implement in the new setup, with the 1881 report assuring benefactors that two or three were always present in the recreation room to keep order, 'but also to amuse the penitents by reading entertaining books, telling stories, and endeavouring to make their recreation pass as innocently and gaily as possible'. With a ratio of more than 100 women to two or three sisters, it was hardly close supervision, but the more 'steady' and longest-resident of the women could usually be relied on to maintain the spirit of peace, charity and harmony that was urged so much on all.[236] By the end of the Tobin period, it was reported that there was a core of 33 'consecrated penitents', all permanent residents, and nearly double that number enrolled as 'Children of Mary' so that the majority of the women, 'are in a special manner, though voluntarily, devoted to piety and the service of God'.[237] It might also be added that, all through the Tobin period (and beyond), Patrick Kennedy was present, working closely with the bursar, seeing to the machinery room and all attached to the laundry work, attending the market on the community's behalf to buy and sell cows, horses and pigs, and looking after the men and the vans, 'in fact everything connected with the outdoor work', with no reward for his time and trouble, other than the promised prayers.[238]

---

234   Annals, 1879, p. 147.
235   High Park, circular letter, Feast of the Patronage of St Joseph, 1884, p. 7.
236   *Abstract report*, p. 24.
237   Ibid., p. 27.
238   Annals, 1883, p. 155.

One further small-scale project from the Tobin period, the Lourdes grotto, merits mention as it would become iconic for High Park, featuring in post-cards and publications (Figure 11.3). The blessing conducted by Dr Woodlock on 25 March 1879 – feast of the Annunciation – at which the women and chil-dren carried banners, the sisters wore their choir cloaks, all singing litanies and hymns in procession, prefigured many more colourful outdoor displays of devotion.[239] Constructed in imitation of its French original, alongside water (over a well), it was sited to the left of the avenue approaching the convent, with kneelers – *deux rustique prie Dieux* – in front, the whole designed to draw passers-by to turn quietly to the Blessed Mother with fervent prayers and aspirations.[240] The grotto itself was planned by Mr P. Kirwan, brother to Sister Mary of St Paul. The landscaping was the work of the bursar (and former superior), Sister Joseph O'Callaghan: 'she planned the walks and curves with much care and saw all carried out by our man, she chose all the shrubs and flowers, directed the planting and position of each with minute attention to their ultimate effect when grown'. The costs were met by the ever-generous Mrs Sims, who also presented the statues which were unveiled with dramatic timing on the occasion of the blessing, 'disclosing the graceful figure of Our Lady and the pretty kneeling figure of Bernadette'.[241]

## Golden Jubilee of the Foundation, Celebrated 20 October 1903

The standard story of the founding of High Park, taken from the annals and retold whenever the early days were to be commemorated, is how 'God sent us kind friends to help to build it' under a succession of valiant superiors.[242] This was the thrust of the 1881 booklet, published to mark the opening of the new wing that year. In the years up to and including the jubilee of 1903, the same themes are played out in the circular letters: 'the Fatherly Providence of God has been carefully and tenderly watching over us', evident in the continued custom for the laundry ('the mainstay of the institution'); the goodness of the priests of All Hallows and other named clergy; protection from storm and fire; the kindness of benefactors and their loyalty over many years.[243] The strain of a lawsuit with Clontarf Urban Council around sewerage and drainage issues was lifted, providentially, by the passing of the legislation that brought Drumcondra and Clontarf within the city boundary for the first time.[244] The erection in January 1900 of a Celtic cross in the convent cemetery was presented as a much-delayed and well-merited monument to the founding mother, Sister Mary of the Sacred Heart Kelly.[245]

The superior elected 1901 was the young but very capable Mother of St Genevieve Byrne who, as with her predecessors, was commended in the official record for her 'unwearying industry' in carrying out improvements,

---

239   High Park, *circulaire*, 8 février 1881, p. 3.
240   Ibid.
241   Work on the grotto commenced 24 Sept. 1878 and it was blessed 25 Mar. 1879; Annals, 1879, p. 146.
242   *Centenary record*, p. 67.
243   High Park, circular letter, May 1906, pp 3, 5, 8, 9 (DARGS, OLC1/2/3 no. 22).
244   High Park, circular letter, May 1902, p. 4 (DARGS, OLC1/2/3 no. 21).
245   Ibid., p. 5.

and for her 'vigilant rule' under which 'The course of our lives runs on tranquilly and there is great peace and good observance'.[246] During her first *superiorité* (1901–7), she had the machine room of the laundry enlarged, ventilation and lighting improved and some very expensive but sophisticated machinery installed, so that the laundry, 'multiplied in its power and utility, is fitted to compete with the best in the city'.[247] The brave new technologies are described in intricate detail (the Majestic ironing machine had 'steam heated rollers and steam heated bed', the collar and cuff machines 'are all belted and coupled up to the steam service by which they are worked'). The postcard collection created in 1925 (the year of the canonisation of the founder, John Eudes) includes photographs of the engine room, hand ironing room, principal linen machine room, second machine room, packing room and outdoor drying ground, most of which dates from this period of investment (figure 3.6). In the middle of all this wondrous speed and efficiency, the spacious workrooms were still seen as places of recollection and prayer, with statues of the Sacred Heart, the Immaculate Conception and St Joseph presiding over the washing room, and St Anthony set as guardian of the counting and marking room.[248] Among the workers, the 'consecrates' can be identified from their linen headdresses, taken directly from the fashions of Caen of a much earlier date.

By 1893, High Park had become quite a visitor attraction, according to the community scribe.[249] The 'concourse of distinguished visitors' continued each summer so that, by 1898, it was claimed the opinion 'so repeatedly expressed by the sight-seers themselves' is that 'our Institution is the finest of its kind in the Kingdom'.[250] Prelates, visiting clergy and missionaries from Britain, Canada, US, Australia, Trinidad, China, Rome and elsewhere are named, most of whom would have signed the visiting celebrants' book in the sacristy, hence the authoritative list. The proximity of All Hallows Missionary College drew some clergy (including past students) to High Park, while it was also within easy reach of the North Docks terminal for the steam packet to Britain. Titled lay visitors are named, for example, Dr Klein (from Alsace), the daughter of the Marquis of Townsend and Lady Talbot, but there were, the reader is assured, 'many other persons of note too numerous to mention'.[251]

Not surprisingly, some of the visits led to requests for foundations overseas; openings in Australia – in Perth and in the diocese of Sandhurst – were turned down in the 1890s, as were requests from England and Scotland.[252] The sole exception was Waterlooville in the diocese of Portsmouth which, in 1892, was the object of an emergency rescue mission – the local superior had abandoned her community 'for the world' and taken herself and a novice off to London, the house was mired in debts and without friends, the rule badly neglected and the public scandal – in a Protestant country! – such

---

246   High Park, circular letter, May 1906, p. 15.
247   Ibid.
248   Ibid., p. 5.
249   High Park, circular letter, 8 Dec. 1893, p. 12 (DARGS, OLC1/3/1 no. 16).
250   High Park, circular letter, 26 July 1898, p. 5 (DARGS, OLC1/3/1 no. 19).
251   High Park, circular letter, 8 Dec. 1893, p. 12.
252   High Park, circular letter, 8 Dec. 1893, p. 12; circular letter, 26 July 1898, p. 9.

**Figure 3.8**   High Park as seen from the air, 21 June 1980 (Tom Cox, DARGS, OLC1).

that the archbishop of Portsmouth contacted other houses of the order to see what might be done.[253] Caen helped out temporarily but it was High Park, perceived as a model house with the advantage of English-speaking sisters also, that would take on the role of mentor and 'refound' Waterlooville. With the agreement of the archbishop of Dublin, a band of six sisters and one postulant set out on 1 April 1900.[254] The increase in size of the High Park community by the early 1900s made possible the sending forth of this group on what was a one-way ticket. The number of women living in the refuge in May 1902 (figure 3.5), on the eve of the jubilee, is given as 200 (of whom 47 were 'consecrated Magdalens'); the sisters (including postulants and novices) numbered 64, and when the schoolchildren (33) and various workmen (15) are added, the total High Park community of 1902 came to 312 persons.[255] The total number for May 1906 is slightly higher at 331, accounted for mainly by additional women in the refuge (211).[256]

At the day-long jubilee celebrations in October 1903, there was public praise for 'The priceless good this institution has conferred on our city and our country'.[257] The sung Mass, presided over by the archbishop and attended by friends and benefactors, including many clergymen, was, according to all accounts, impressive and memorable. A decorated banner hung from

253   Soeur M. de St Ambroise Desaunais to Ma très honorée et très chère Sœur, 10 octobre 1892 (DARGS, OLC1/3/2 no. 114).
254   High Park, election letter, 18 Apr. 1900 (DARGS, OLC1/3/1 no. 18).
255   High Park, circular letter, May 1902, p. 24.
256   High Park, circular letter, May 1906, p. 24.
257   Ibid., p. 11.

the tribune: 'the Sacred Hearts of Jesus and Mary, artistically painted on a white satin ground surrounded by rays of light, with the motto "Vive Jesus et Maria" under which roses and passion flowers entwined' with the words 'Golden Jubilee 1903' at the top.[258] An open party was held on the Sunday following for the children of the workmen and 'for those children of humble parentage who live in the neighbourhood of the convent', along with the schoolchildren.[259]

The newspaper account has nothing of the early founding story, except to quote from the preacher who simply stated that the nuns took charge of a home in Drumcondra begun by Fr John Smith and soon obtained their present site, to which they quickly moved. The account circulated, in print, to the other houses of the order noted that, at one end of the refectory, 'a handsome scroll in Irish' had been placed around the picture of the founder in Caen, the Venerable John Eudes. At the other end of the room, there were matching portraits of the founders in Dublin, Fr John Smith and Mother Mary of the Sacred Heart Kelly. Fr Smith was necessary to the founding story, but nothing more needed to be said. The announcement a year earlier that John Eudes was to be beatified had generated interest in the spirituality and teaching of the founder, and energy went in that direction, rather than settling on the figure of John Smith.[260] The monastery of High Park, in its life, work and spirituality, was very much the foundation of the sisters that came from Paris, Rennes and Caen, and those they trained. Here the sisters managed to do what they had agreed with the diocese – to receive 'voluntary penitents', to say and chant the Divine Office, to live according to the rules, regulations and customs of Caen.[261] But this was worked out in an Irish context, with local support. The great majority of the sisters, women and children for whom High Park was home, no matter how briefly, during its first 50 years, were natives of the city and district of Dublin. That John Eudes was wreathed in an Irish-language scroll, presiding over the dining room of this Dublin institution in 1903, was entirely fitting.

258   Ibid., p. 10.
259   High Park, circular letter, May 1906, pp 12–13.
260   Caen, circular letter, 30 Aug. 1908 (DARGS, OLC1/3/2 no. 14)
261   Soeur M. de St Stanislas Brunel, Paris, to Mgr l'Archevêque de Dublin, 9 juillet 1853 (DDA, Cullen, 325/8).

# Chapter 4

# The Juvenile Reform Movement and the Establishment of St Joseph's Reformatory School, High Park, 1859–1927

Both branches of the order of Notre Dame de Charité – that of Caen, of the Refuge, and that of Angers, of the Good Shepherd – were well known in 19th-century France for their work of *préservation*, the protection of young girls at risk of ending up in prostitution or crime. According to its own account, the Catholic Reformatory Committee of Dublin approached High Park as soon as it learned that these sisters had had many years' experience in the management, in Paris, 'of precisely the same class of girls likely to be sent to a Dublin reformatory'.[1]

The proper business or particular end of the institute was set out by the founder John Eudes; a literal translation of the first constitution is to work wholeheartedly with girls and women who had fallen into the disorder or confusion of a dissolute life and who, touched by the grace of God, wished to turn around their lives. The means that were to be harnessed to this end, according to Eudes, were the example of the sisters' lives, the fervour of their prayers and the effectiveness of their instruction, while the spirit which was to inform all was the burning love of the hearts of Jesus and Mary, enkindled in the souls created in God's image and likeness, and already purchased or ransomed by Christ when He poured out His precious blood on the cross.[2] *Préservation*, the work of protection, was understood within this larger scheme for the salvation of souls, for why should help be withheld until the person was driven by poverty, ignorance and desperation into a life of crime and sin? Why not focus on prevention, rather than simply on cure? The protection of souls, each of infinite value, applied across all ages, classes and levels of ability. 'Prevention' work could therefore be with females of any age or background, though giving priority to those perceived as most vulnerable, including the unprotected orphan, the friendless and

---

1 *General and first annual report of St Joseph's Reformatory School for Catholic girls, High Park, Drumcondra, established under the Act 21st and 22nd Vic. cap 103* (Dublin, 1862), p. 3. Hereafter, *First annual report of St Joseph's Reformatory School.*
2 'Règles et constitutions pour les religieuses de Notre-Dame de Charité, édition entièrement conforme au texte original [1682] avec des introductions et des notes', *Oeuvres complètes de Bienheureux Jean Eudes*, x (Vannes, 1909), Constitution i, De la fin de cet institut, et des motifs qui doivent porter celles qui le professent à en faire de bon cœur les fonctions, p. 80. Hereafter, *Constitutions.*

destitute girl, the woman liable to be taken advantage of due to what would today be termed 'special needs'. Similarly, the work of conversion, the reform of those already putting their eternal life in jeopardy, at least insofar as external signs might be read, was not tied to age. Young girls, as well as older women, could stand in need of that radical turning around of their lives and encouragement to persevere in virtue, prayer and penance. Though the brightest hopes might be pinned on the younger person, conversion could come about right up to the moment of death. The salvation of one's soul was the work of a lifetime and not until the last breath was drawn could it be said to be at a close; *persévération*, therefore, as understood in OLC, applied across all ages and unto death.

While the constitutions of Our Lady of Charity did not refer explicitly to children, the education and training of female children within the enclosure dates back to the first monastery of Caen which had a 'junior novitiate' or boarding school from 1654.[3] As every subsequent OLC foundation was to model itself on Caen, taking on its constitutions, customs and practices with as much fidelity and exactitude as possible, these autonomous monasteries were always free to involve themselves in schools in accordance with local circumstances and local needs. Rennes, which had long catered for women prisoners, had a 'preservation' section for girls as early as 1840, and gradually other houses in France followed suit.[4] Also involved in childcare were the increasingly numerous houses of the Good Shepherd congregation, Notre Dame de Charité du Bon Pasteur d'Angers, with which High Park was so often confused. To the forefront of the movement in France (and indeed in Canada also) for the protection and re-education of young female offenders,[5] the Good Shepherd founder's response to the possibility of providing the same service in England was unequivocal: 'Oh, it is a lovely work, and entirely in the spirit of our vocation!'[6] It was the law of 5 August 1850, recognising the right of young prisoners to receive instruction, that opened up the possibility of 'agricultural colonies' (or training schools) authorised by the Ministry of the Interior and funded by the French state. The Good Shepherd was especially prompt in reply, with a farm it owned in Angers renamed 'Nazareth' and authorised in June 1852 to instruct and educate girls aged 16 years and older 'according to the terms of the law, trying also to make these young people happy'.[7] In March 1853, 30 girls were transferred from prison to the Good Shepherd in Rennes and, over the following

3   *Dans la charité du Christ: Vie de la Très Honorée Mère Marie de Saint Ambroise Desaunais* (Caen, 1939), p. 81. Hereafter, *Vie, Mère Marie de Saint Ambroise Desaunais*.
4   MS retreat notes, n.d., titled 'Our Lady of Charity, the challenge of mercy', provided by Sister Teresa Couglan OLC.
5   Véronique Strimelle, 'La gestion de la déviance des filles à Montréal au XIXe siècle: les institutions du Bon-Pasteur d'Angers (1869–1912), *Revue d'Histoire de l'Enfance Irréguliere*, no. 5 (2003), p. 64.
6   'The Good Shepherd sisters in Vienna had recently taken on this work also', M. Euphrasie Pelletier to Sister M. of St Aloysia Gillet, provincial superior, London, 7 Apr. 1856, *Letters, M. Euphrasie Pelletier*, trans. (Angers, 1996), viii, 1522, p. 21. Hereafter, Letters.
7   The farm was first called 'Mary-Joseph' and was obtained by the community in 1846. The colony at Nazareth was authorised 21 Apr. 1852 and the first young prisoner arrived 26 June 1852. Letters, Introduction, vii, p. 8.

months, further groups were transferred to newly-established places of detention and training.[8] The largest and most ambitious venture in terms of scale, grand architecture and public visibility, was probably St Nicholas Abbey (replacing 'Nazareth') at Angers, on an impressive and entirely separate site to the convent and refuge complex but linked by a tunnel underneath the public road, as the enclosure had still to be maintained. On 9 May 1855, it was to open as a school for 100 underage prisoners, all girls.[9]

Whether under the heading of colony, reform school, preservatory, orphanage, *pensionnat* or boarding school, and even where the intake included girls from better-off families who sought a convent education for their daughters, the two branches of Our Lady of Charity were in agreement that work with young girls could be understood as *préservation*. As the earliest French houses had demonstrated, this good work could, and should, be done without prejudice to the founding mission of Notre Dame de Charité, the welfare of girls and women desirous of leaving a life of 'disorder' for the path of virtue.

Some insights into the practical operation of the École de Préservation at Caen can be gleaned from an account of how the government decree demanding its closure in 1905 was received. The redoubtable superior at the time, Mère Marie de Saint Ambroise Desaunais, protested that the children they were looking after were poor, orphaned or abandoned, were reared by the sisters without any private fees or state support, and had no homes to which they could be sent. Twenty-four of them were aged under 13 years.[10] The other monasteries from which the first sisters in Dublin were drawn also had small 'preservation classes' from an early date, namely, St Michel in the rue St Jacques in Paris and St Cyr in Rennes. The Dublin sisters would also have been well aware, through the *circulaire* system of regular communication, of OLC school ventures in Marseilles and elsewhere in France. They would surely have known something of the Good Shepherd initiatives also, as they were so numerous and public money was involved. The obituary of the first director of the High Park school, Miss Cecilia O'Callaghan (Sister Mary of St Magdalen), states that she first 'visited similar institutions elsewhere to gather information on how they should be directed' and, as there was nothing yet to investigate in Ireland, this must refer to France where she and her siblings had many connections and the reformatory or 'agricultural colony' movement was well advanced.[11] Whatever the differences in local circumstances, all OLC monasteries implemented the strict separation of

8   M. Euphrasie Pelletier to Sister M. of St Celestine Husson, Lauretana, Rome, 29 Mar. 1854, Letters, 1432, vii, p. 220.
9   By May 1854 St Nicholas Abbey had more than 200 young prisoners, of whom 40 were working on plots of land and on the dairy farm. The government grant was up to 20,000 francs. 'The majority of our little ones are good; they love their Mothers, their land, their garden, and they think of it all as belonging to them. Our lay sisters sacrifice themselves there, and show them how to do everything: the laundry, the bakery, the kitchen, you will find them everywhere in their little linen bodices and aprons'. M. Euphrasie Pelletier to Sister M. of St John of the Cross David, Munich, 10 May 1854, Letters, vii, 1436, p. 224.
10   *Vie, Mère Marie de Saint Ambroise Desaunais*, p. 82.
11   Death letter of Sister M. of St Magdalen O'Callaghan (Cecile/Cecilia), died 22 Apr. 1889 (DARGS, OLC1/4/1 no. 86).

classes. Whether as *préservées*, orphans or fee-paying boarders, in all cases, schoolchildren were to be kept quite separate from the women residents. The children were to have their own distinct quarters, including dormitory, schoolroom, refectory and recreation spaces, as well as their own mistress who was to preside over a daily programme encompassing religious, moral, literary and vocational instruction at a level judged suited to the children's ages and prospects, and in line with the order's overall spiritual focus on the infinitely loving hearts of Jesus and of His mother Mary.

That the protection of younger girls was considered by the foundress and first superior, Mother Mary of the Sacred Heart Kelly, and her companions to be intrinsic to the new Dublin mission is evident from the early start-up date of 'preservatory' work at High Park. Shortly after the women and the last of the sisters had moved from Drumcondra Road to High Park, steps were taken to start a *classe de préservation* in outhouses attached to the gentleman's residence that now served as the convent. This was mid-to-late 1858, and only two girls were involved.[12] This tentative OLC scheme was abandoned in December 1858 when it was overtaken by larger events: pressure from the archbishop and from a number of leading politicians, government officials and businessmen to co-operate immediately, amid fears of under-supply of Roman Catholic places, with the state-funded reformatory project in Britain newly extended to Ireland.[13] Although the terminology was new to the sisters, they explained to their sisters in France that by the term '*Classe de Réformatory*' was really meant the same work, *préservation*, that the order had undertaken for generations.[14] Central to the negotiations was the zealous and energetic layman Patrick Joseph Murray (also spelled Murry), inspector of reformatory schools in Ireland until January 1868, and a man with whom the sisters were to have serious difficulties. He had, it was reported, a particular devotion to St Joseph and presented the new institution with a stone statue of the saint, for outdoor display.[15] As noted already, the committee which had been given the task of enlisting a religious community to manage a reformatory for Catholic girls, gave the experience of the High Park sisters in Paris as the reason for approaching them.[16] As the sisters in Dublin explained to their colleagues in France, they abandoned their own scheme in favour of the government scheme, which was to receive girls below 14 years of age who had been brought before a magistrate for stealing, sentenced to a term of detention which could never be more than five years, and for whom the sisters would receive a fitting payment (*une retribution convenable*) of 8F 20 centimes weekly for each child.[17]

Not having a sister to staff the school, and because the need was urgent ('and would be for the glory of God and the salvation of souls'), Mother Mary of the Sacred Heart Kelly 'solicited the assistance of

12   High Park, *circulaire*, 30 décembre 1859 (DARGS, OLC1/3/1 no. 2).
13   21 and 22 Vic., 'An Act to promote and regulate Reformatory Schools for Juvenile Offenders in Ireland', 1858.
14   High Park, *circulaire*, 30 décembre 1859.
15   High Park, English draft of *circulaire* dated 30 mai 1865, p. 56 (DARGS, OLC1/3/1 no. 1).
16   *First annual report of St Joseph's Reformatory School*, p. 3.
17   High Park, *circulaire*, 30 décembre 1859.

Miss O'Callaghan' who, as noted already, visited similar institutions over-seas so that she might better plan this new venture.[18] Cecilia O'Callaghan, who later entered the novitiate aged 43 years, was the fourth in her family (see Chapter 1) to take vows as an OLC sister and the third O'Callaghan sister in High Park (Five Wounds, Joseph and Magdalen). A small local committee was formed to support the new project, with a treasurer and honorary secretary.[19] There were two priests, Dr Bartholomew Woodlock of All Hallows and 'spiritual father' to the community, and Dr James Murray, their chaplain and secretary to the archbishop, along with seven other gentlemen, all of whom appear to have been already much entangled in the affairs of High Park through family and professional ties and are list-ed among the earliest benefactors. These were Richard, John and Thomas O'Callaghan, brothers to the aforementioned OLC sisters, also Dr John F. McVeagh, physician to the establishment (whose daughter Agnes was later to enter the community) and two others whose names alone are known, namely, J.J. Byrne Esq. and John O'Dwyer Esq.[20] P. J. Murray, introduced already as the first inspector of reformatory schools in Ireland, was named honorary secretary to the committee. The school was formally approved as 'useful and efficient for the purpose of a Reformatory School, for the better training of Juvenile Offenders in Ireland' on 15 December 1858, the first accredited reformatory, Catholic or Protestant, in the country.[21] The first girls were admitted on 14 February 1859 and, by the end of the year, it was reported that there were 22 children enrolled.[22]

## Background to the Reformatory Movement in Britain and Ireland

The reformatory movement of Britain and Ireland into which the new Dublin monastery of Notre Dame de Charité was so speedily and unexpectedly thrown arose from public concern with the extent of child criminality among both boys and girls, the further corruption caused by the imprisonment of young offenders with adults in the common gaol and the outrageous and long-term expense of all this to the nation. The advocate for the reformatory movement best known in Ireland was Miss Mary Carpenter. Her insistence that society had a responsibility towards children – and, if it knowingly left them in a state of degradation, it owed them reparation – profoundly altered the way in which juvenile delinquency was viewed by many in public life. The Red Lodge refor-matory for Protestant girls founded by Mary Carpenter in Bristol and certified in December 1854, was cited as the model for the regime at St Joseph's. But Car-penter was not the sole authority; others whose arguments were much quoted in the High Park context included the prison chaplain Alexander Thomson as well as Alfred and Micaiah Hill and Joseph Kingsmill.[23]

---

18  Death letter of Sister M. of St Magdalen O'Callaghan.
19  *First annual report of St Joseph's Reformatory School* , p. 2.
20  High Park, circular letter, 8 Dec. 1893, p. 14 (DARGS, OLC1/3/1 no. 16).
21  *Dublin Gazette*, 21 Dec. 1858.
22  High Park, *circulaire*, 30 décembre 1859.
23  See Mary Carpenter, *Juvenile delinquents, their condition and treatment* (London, 1853); 'Reformatory and Ragged schools, article v, *Irish Quarterly Review*, iv (June 1854), pp 361–429.

As hinted at already, inspiration was drawn most especially from France, which was several years – if not decades – ahead of the United Kingdom in terms of juvenile penal reform. Under the Napoleonic code of 1810, the judge could decide on the level of discernment of a child brought before him accused of a crime. He could acquit on the basis of insufficient power of discretion, but place the child in the care of the state and order that he or she be placed in a house of correction. The French state, therefore, possessed a greater capacity to intervene than its UK counterpart, where acquittal of a child meant that he or she was set at liberty.[24] The additional powers of the French judicial system also gave more scope for philanthropic experiments. One such was the reformatory school at Mettray, an agricultural colony outside Paris, without walls, created in 1839 by Fréderic Auguste Demetz. Here delinquent boys were taught agriculture and industrial occupations intended to serve them in later life, and their moral and religious education was also given close attention.[25] Concern with child delinquency reached its peak in France during the 1840s, the decade when Mettray became a *cause célèbre* inside and outside the country. The loss of parental control, manifested by the child's delinquent act, offended both Calvinist and Catholic morality which placed great store on the authority of the father and the submission of children. Mettray, with its division into brigades and close discipline and regularity, was to be a substitute family, giving the child a sense of belonging within the hierarchy.[26] The task of socialising and forming the child, that inept parents could not – or would not – manage, could therefore be taken on by others out of real loving concern for the child and with due regard for religious and moral dimensions, as well as practical training. Christian charity had to be the motivation, not material profit. The generally greater readiness to intervene in France was also prompted by shifts in the perception of childhood that can be tied to the theories of Johann Pestallozi and of Philip von Fellenberg; childhood was not merely governed by age but was a privileged point in the formation of the new man.[27] 'Lock him up' public protection arguments therefore competed with arguments in favour of the placement of the child in an environment where he or she might blossom, and of not allowing the precious opportunity of childhood to be squandered.

The French law of 5 August 1850 allowed for the moral, religious and professional or industrial training of young offenders and allowed state funds to be spent on such children in suitable institutions. It encouraged initiatives already under way and enlarged the field of operations for those religious orders, in particular, who saw their mission in terms of the protection, reform and education of the class of children most likely to come to the attention of the judicial system.[28] Other European countries were also passing legislation

---

24   Jean-Marie Facteau, 'Note sur les enjeux de la prise en charge de l'enfance délinquante et en danger au XIXe siècle', *Lien Social et Politiques*, no. 40 (1998), p. 136, footnote 12.
25   'Reformatory and industrial schools', *Dublin University Magazine* (Nov. 1858), vol. lii, pp 554–8.
26   Facteau, 'Note sur les enjeux', p. 130.
27   Ibid.
28   Jean-Claude Caron, Review of Marie-Sylvie Dupont-Bouchat and Eric Pierre (eds), *Enfance et justice au XIXe siècle* (Paris, 2001), *Revue d'Histoire Moderne et Contemporaine*, no. 1 (2003), p. 185.

that facilitated the removal of children from the prison system. Indeed, the advance of the reformatory movement internationally was quite remarkable, with France – but also Germany, Belgium and the Netherlands – leading in the first half of the 19th century, and progress throughout Europe, as well as in India, Canada and the US, all the subject of discussion in 1865.[29]

The child-centred philosophies advocated by Mary Carpenter and other reformers, and their practical application, required a major shift in official policy, as was evident at a conference held in Birmingham in December 1851.[30] The issue of child delinquency was quickly taken up by political, social and religious commentators of all sorts, using the meetings of learned societies, Church groups and charitable associations to air their views, and generating a massive amount of pamphlet and journal literature, as well as coverage in the newspapers and in the House of Commons. Some of the reportage was based on field visits to continental institutions but more often was a distillation of their published reports, with some reworking and personal observations suited to a local audience. P. J. Murray, through his report-writing, elaborate statistical analyses and published commentaries on the legislation and its revisions, might be given special credit for advancing the reformatory debate in Ireland. He was certainly in command of the overseas literature, commenting on the efforts and ideas of others and placing his own projects – most notably, St Joseph's, High Park – within larger philosophical and international frameworks.[31] His successor, John Lentaigne, who held the position of inspector of reformatory and industrial schools 1869–86, was another who advocated in person and in print for the separation of child offenders from adults, as well as bringing in closer regulation of the education and health of the children in these new state-funded institutions.[32] Perhaps the best informed of all those who spoke publicly on the issue was Mrs Hélène Woodlock (née Mahony). She was sister-in-law of Bartholomew Woodlock, at that time president of All Hallows College (1854–79), loyal friend to the High Park sisters and their 'spiritual father' (also 1854–79). As a widow, she had tried her vocation with the Sisters of St Louis in Juilly, France.[33] Not alone had she some first-hand knowledge of what might be called enlightened French methods, but she had practical experience with girls of this class in Cork and in Dublin. With Sarah Atkinson

---

29  'Extracts from Proceedings of the Council', *The Reformatory and Refuge Journal*, no. xxvi – xxxiii (1865–6), p. 82. See also, Marie-Sylvie Dupont-Bouchat and Éric Pierre (eds), *Enfance et justice au XIXe siècle, essai d'histoire comparée de la protection de l'enfance, 1820–1914, France, Belgique, Pays-Bas, Canada* (Paris, 2001).

30  'Reformatory and industrial schools', *Dublin University Magazine*, vol. lii (Nov. 1858), pp 554–8.

31  Patrick Joseph Murray, *An Act to promote and regulate Reformatory Schools for Juvenile Offenders in Ireland, 21st & 22nd Vic. Cap. 103, with commentary and forms of procedure, and hints on the formation and management of reformatory institutions* (Dublin, 1858). Hereafter, *An Act to promote and regulate Reformatory Schools, with commentary*.

32  John Lentaigne, 'The treatment and punishment of young offenders', *Journal of the Statistical and Social Inquiry Society of Ireland*, vol. viii, part lxiii (1881), appendix 3; Jane Barnes, *Irish industrial schools 1868–1908* (Dublin, 1989), p. 53.

33  Sister Mary Pauline, *God wills it! Centenary story* [of the Sisters of St Louis, Monaghan] (Dublin, 1959), pp 39–41, 65–7, 78–9.

and encouraged by John Lentaigne, she founded St Joseph's Industrial Institute, 14 Richmond Avenue, Fairview (March 1856) where girls on leaving
the South Dublin Union workhouse might be trained in skills that would fit
them for employment. She played a major role in the opening of the Spark's
Lake girls' reformatory by the St Louis Sisters in County Monaghan in 1859,
and also addressed conferences on the topic.[34]

The moral principle on which the reformatory movement was to rest
was taken up by an inquiry into the state of juvenile crime in the English
cities of Newcastle and Gateshead held in 1852, and reiterated in countless
reports, commentaries and newspaper articles over the following decade.[35]
It was, according to its promoters, a principle long recognised on the
Continent and more recently adopted in the US and elsewhere:

> That young persons who have broken the laws of the land
> ought not to be held responsible for acts which clearly indi-
> cate they have had neither the guardianship nor the education
> which every child ought to receive in a Christian country; that
> for the benefit of society as well as an act of justice to each
> individual, the erring child should be put in such a position as
> to be able to discharge his duty to God and to man instead of
> being punished and hopelessly branded in gaol.[36]

Put more succinctly, this principle states 'that a child, even when criminal,
should be treated as a child, and sent to a reformatory school, and not to a
gaol'.[37]

The passing of the Youthful Offenders Act of 1854, which authorised
the establishment of reformatory schools in Britain by voluntary bodies
certified by the state and partly funded by the Treasury, immediately led
to calls for its extension to Ireland.[38] There were also arguments in support of extending the ragged school network, an initiative of evangelical
missionaries targeted at the very poorest class of children, from which the
reformatory movement in Britain had sprung.[39] That Dublin needed reformatory schools more than most other places was argued on the strength of
the police statistics, which were truly shocking. According to the Dublin
police, 8,619 offences were committed in 1853 by persons under 20 years
of age. Almost 1,000 of the offences were committed by children under

---

34  Mrs Woodlock, 'The relief of pauper children', to the Social Science Association, 22 Aug.
1861; 'Woodlock, Ellen'; 'Atkinson, Sarah', in *Dictionary of Irish biography*, online at http://dib.
cambridge.org [1 Feb. 2017].
35  'Reformatory and ragged schools', article v, *Irish Quarterly Review*, iv (June 1854), p. 399.
36  Mary Carpenter, 'Reformatory schools for girls', *The Reformatory and Refuge Journal*,
xxxiv – xlv (1867–9), p. 273.
37  *First annual report of St Joseph's Reformatory School*, preamble.
38  'Reformatory and Ragged schools', *Irish Quarterly Review*, iv (June 1854), pp 361–429.
39  'A Ragged School is one into which children, too poor or too vicious to be received into
ordinary schools, may enter as a matter of right'; some provide instruction only, others provide
food, instruction and clothing and (in some cases) lodging or dormitory accommodation also.
'Reformatory and Ragged schools', article v, *Irish Quarterly Review*, iv (June 1854), p. 375.

ten years, divided nearly equally between girls and boys, and mostly for vagrancy or being of 'suspicious character'. Of the 2,611 offences committed by children aged between ten and 15 (of which 29% were committed by girls), the crimes of unlawful possession of goods and 'disorderly character' were recorded, while the offences committed by the oldest group, teenagers aged between 15 and 20 (of which 39% were committed by girls), included assaults, common assaults, drunkenness and prostitution, in addition to the offences listed for the younger cohorts. There were 725 convictions for prostitution, of which just over a third were of girls. There were more convictions for drunkenness among older girls than older boys, while convictions for disorderly conduct and assault were more likely among the older boys, offences where drink may also have been involved.[40] The number of children who appeared before the Dublin magistrates in 1853 and were sent to gaol is much smaller than the number of recorded offences: there were four children under ten years sent to gaol; 74 children aged ten to 15 (56 males and 18 females); and 353 teenagers between 15 and 20 (266 males and 87 females), making a grand total of 431 young people jailed, of whom about one third were girls.[41] Analysis of the police statistics undertaken at the time revealed that most of these children were illiterate and most had parents living. These findings were used to justify the new role proposed for the state, as the children were clearly neglected and it would be hypocrisy to deny them their right to an education on the basis of 'the liberty of parents to bring up their children'.[42]

The most compelling argument in favour of the reformatory movement was that of finance, with one commentator calculating that child criminals, the 'city Arabs' or 'home heathens' could be secured from future crime and enabled to support themselves by a trade, at a cost of £3 15s per annum in the reformatory and industrial schools, a fraction of what it cost in the poor house (£10), gaol (£20) or convict settlement (£143 including cost of prosecution).[43] Even where calculated at a somewhat higher rate, the cost to the Treasury of an inmate of a reformatory was still less than the cost of an inmate of a gaol, and 'the former is saved, the latter is happy if she comes out not worse than when she entered'.[44] Indeed, it was difficult to argue against the general claim that there were 'vast savings to be derived by society and by the ratepayers in all points, from the adoption of schools for destitute or criminal juveniles'.[45]

The reformatory system in Britain was strongly Protestant in origin, with the London City Mission the sponsor of what was described as the first such institution.[46] The 1852–3 committee inquiring into juveniles and crime had one Roman Catholic member only, and of the 51 witnesses who

---

40  *Irish Quarterly Review*, iv (June 1854), p. 418.

41  Ibid., p. 417.

42  Ibid.

43  'Reformatory and Ragged schools, article v, *Irish Quarterly Review*, iv (June 1854), p. 363, see also p. 429.

44  *First annual report of St Joseph's Reformatory School*, p. 13.

45  *Irish Quarterly Review*, iv (June 1854), p. 410.

46  Ibid., p. 383.

gave evidence, none was Catholic.[47] An impetus towards the introduction of reformatories was the 1851 census of England and Wales which included, for the first time, a question on religious affiliation. The Established Church – the Anglican Church of England and Church in Wales – was exposed as having lost millions of adherents, and there was every sign that the downward spiral would continue. Commentators correlated high levels of criminality with widespread irreligion, a cause of sadness for those good persons who cared to take notice of 'the uneasy heaving of the black sea of ignorance and crime that hourly casts up its poor human weeds'.[48] As heathenism was blamed for the frightening statistics of juvenile crime, 'the sanctions and influences of religion' were held up as the most needful element in the education of those likely to feature in these statistics, namely children from the lowest social class.[49] At the Red Lodge Girls' Reformatory in Bristol, Mary Carpenter urged that the will of the child be enlisted to work with the teacher so that conscience might be gradually awakened:

> It is evident that in the whole of this, religion must have a real part, constantly influencing the institution, and that special attention must be paid to bring every child to that knowledge of the Scriptures and love for them, which may make them influential in life. The Reformatory will thus not be regarded by the young girl as a place of punishment, but as one mercifully provided to prepare her to lead a good life.[50]

There were advocates for the reformatories who argued for Protestant scriptural teaching only, on the basis that, where Roman Catholics had neglected the rearing of their children, a Protestant state was entitled to educate, 'and as a Protestant people we dare not educate them by any other means but the use of the Word of God'.[51] Such provocative statements set alarm bells ringing for the Catholic authorities first in Scotland and England and Wales, but also in Ireland. Both the first Bill that aimed to extend the system to Ireland, and an amended version, were defeated in parliament.[52] It was, after all, the decade when the missionary methods of certain English evangelical organisations among the Irish poor were being laid open to public scrutiny, most skilfully by the Catholic activist Margaret Aylward and her co-workers in St Brigid's boarding-out orphanage.[53] Under the 1858 Act, a child had to be sent to an institution under the exclusive management of persons professing the same religious denomination. Fear that this protection might be

---

47  Report of select committee on criminal and destitute juveniles, June 1852, H.C. 1852 (515) vii. *Idem*, H.C.1852–3 (674) xxiii, q. 4190. I am indebted to Terence Judge for this observation.
48  *Irish Quarterly Review*, iv (June 1854), p. 410.
49  Ibid., p. 414.
50  Carpenter, 'Reformatory schools for girls', p. 275.
51  *Irish Quarterly Review*, iv (June 1854), p. 414.
52  Joseph Robins, *The lost children, a survey of charity children in Ireland 1700–1900* (Dublin 1980), p. 297.
53  Jacinta Prunty, *Margaret Aylward 1810–1889, lady of charity, sister of faith* (Dublin, 1998, 2011), pp 40–55.

revoked if there were insufficient places for Catholics was easily stoked, with P. J. Murray warning darkly that 'judges are pressing the Government to allow a change in the Act, by which, as in England, a child may be sent to any school the judge or magistrate pleases'.[54]

The strongly Protestant ethos of the movement was further promoted by the Reformatory and Refuge Union established in 1856 for the dissemination of information between reformatories and similar institutes and their mutual support. It articulated its aims as:

> Promoting the religious, intellectual and industrial education of the inmates of such institutions, and encouraging those who conduct them in every effort to elevate and reclaim the neglected and criminal class, by educating them in the fear of God, and the knowledge of the Holy Scriptures.[55]

In addition, it was intended to be a means 'of concerted action with reference to the Government, the Legislature and the Public', holding annual conferences and field visits and publishing its own journal.[56] The Catholic reformatories in Ireland had little, if any, involvement with this important body, though published reports of Catholic institutes were occasionally reviewed in its journal and reports carried of activities in Ireland. At least some of the Protestant ragged schools, homes and training institutes in Ireland did engage with the Reformatory and Refuge Union and received grants in support of their work.[57]

There were some parallels with the 'rescue and reform' debate surrounding 'penitent women' (Chapter 2), including a heavy reliance on memorable gospel passages and iconic images. In this case, it is the picture of Jesus calling the little children to Himself, assuring that 'Anyone who welcomes a little child in my name welcomes me', and issuing dire warnings to the adults against placing any obstacle in their way.[58] Pioneers of the reformatory movement testified that 'It was the Christian love within us which impelled us to the work, and which must ever guide us'. The rescue of 'these poor young immortal beings' made in the image and likeness of Jesus Christ was thus placed before the public as a work that Christians could not shirk 'if we would truly follow Him who came to seek and to save the lost, and who said, "Inasmuch as ye have done it unto one of these little ones, you have done it unto me".'[59]

There were numerous points of overlap between the Protestant, British reformatory movement, the Catholic, Eudist *préservation* tradition of Notre Dame de Charité and the French state's view of its responsibilities towards its youngest and most vulnerable citizens. All believed in the protection

54  P. J. Murray to Dr Cullen, 6 Apr. 1863 (DARGS, OLC1/8/2 no. 4).
55  *Thirteenth Annual Report of the Reformatory and Refuge Union* (London, 1869) p. 6.
56  Ibid.
57  Ibid., p. 48.
58  Mt 18:1–7; see also Mk 10:15 and Lk 18:17.
59  Carpenter, 'Reformatory schools for girls', p. 279.

of young girls who – through vagrancy, begging and generally being left to fend for themselves in the town – were at real risk of being enticed into prostitution or crime. All believed in early intervention, and that true reform took time. Practical skills were to be inculcated with a view to enabling the child to support herself in adulthood, and every attention was to be given to moral and religious instruction, as indeed was promised by the advocates of practically every philanthropic project at the time. That the state should actively intervene where parenting, for whatever reason, had failed was long accepted in France. So was the notion that convents might actively co-operate with the state in caring for such children, to the extent of accepting them on the orders of a magistrate and receiving public funds towards their maintenance. Indeed, one of the things that amazed the OLC sisters on arrival in Dublin was the lack of any state support for charities such as refuges for women and girls.[60] St Joseph's, High Park, was the working out of these larger philosophical, political and religious movements on a local scale and in a very concrete way.

## The Reformatory System in Ireland and St Joseph's High Park, 1859

The reformatory system that was introduced into Ireland in 1858 was in essence the system already tested in Britain, where 40 reformatories were certified and opened between 1854 and 1857; the Irish system however had additional protections against proselytism.[61] The reform schools were to be set up by voluntary bodies, who would carry the costs of whatever construction, refurbishment and fitting-out was involved, and submit the premises to inspection, so that it might be licensed by the Office of the Chief Secretary as 'fit and proper' for the reception of a set number of children. All the premises, therefore, were provided at no cost to the state which merely approved them. The local grand jury or town council was required to pay a maintenance grant for each child sent to a reformatory via the courts, out of monies raised locally (so that the schools were in fact funded in the same way as the prisons). There was also to be a maintenance grant from central government funds, namely, from the Treasury on representation from the Chief Secretary.[62] However, charitable funds would still be necessary towards running costs. This was recognised by the superior of High Park who sought to hasten the date of the first inspection as 'there are peculiar circumstances which render this a favourable time for announcing the fact to our friends and subscribers of our having been certified'.[63] The financial basis of each school was set out plainly for the archbishop of Dublin, Dr Cullen, in 1863 by P. J. Murray in his role as inspector:

> The schools must be got up by voluntary subscription, and when certified as fit for the purpose, the school is a legal one,

---

60    High Park, *circulaire*, 30 octobre 1862 (DARGS, OLC1/3/1 no. 4).
61    Murray, *An Act to promote and regulate Reformatory Schools, with commentary*, Introduction, xxxvii
62    Ibid., viii, xvi.
63    Draft of letter, n.d., addressed to the Chief Secretary, Upper Castle Yard (DARGS, SJ/1).

and for each child sent to it the Treasury pays (quarterly) 6/-
per week. Grand Juries, and Corporations, may pay any sum,
not exceeding 5/- per head per week, for children sent from
their districts. Nearly all the Grand Juries pay 2/- per head
per week, so that the schools receive 8s per head per week for
the children. To teach parents that by neglect or mis-rearing
of their children they cannot escape their responsibility, they
are compelled to pay any sum not exceeding 5/- per week
towards the support of each child in a reformatory school.[64]

The pursuit of the funds to which the school was entitled was always to prove
hugely complicated and time-consuming but, in its first decade, St Joseph's
was fortunate in having a true friend in one of the places where it mattered
most, in the treasurer's office, City Hall. It was a borough official, Denis Costigan, who ensured that claims to this office were processed as speedily as the
system allowed,[65] while the same man was also, in his private capacity, a generous contributor to St Joseph's.[66] The same scrupulosity was not shown by
P.J. Murray who intercepted large payments intended for St Joseph's – £172-
15-11d or 'two gales of the Corporation money' – putting the sisters to the
trouble and embarrassment of pursuing him over several years for monies
that (it appears) were never recovered.[67] But whatever the paperwork, delays and deferrals across the different funding bodies, and trusting that no
official would abuse his position of trust (P.J. Murray was an exception), the
maintenance grants were underpinned by legislation and the sisters could
rely on their coming through, eventually. The contributions of parents, covered in principle in the legislation, were of course a different matter entirely,
as the class of parent whose child was detained was the least likely to have
anything to contribute.[68] It was the legal security of the public money that was
so important in the late 1850s and 1860s and gave the sisters a guarantee that
the work they had started with these younger girls could be carried through.

The system placed huge emphasis on accurate and legalistic record
keeping; each child came with a copy of the warrant of committal but also
a signed memorandum stating she was the same person as named on the
warrant. This was the legal instrument that gave authority to the school to
detain the child for the length of time set out by the judge.[69] The records of

64   Murray to Cullen, 6 Apr. 1863.
65   Denis Costigan, 28 Rathmines Road, to the Superior, High Park Reformatory, 27 and
28 Jan. 1868, 30 Jan. and 19 July 1869, 7 June 1870, 22 Jan. 1871, 13 Feb. 1872; to Dr Woodlock,
3 June 1870 (DARGS, OLC1/8/2 no. 12).
66   Denis Costigan to the Superior, High Park Reformatory, 22 Jan. and 24 Mar. 1871; to
Dr Woodlock, 3 June 1870 (DARGS, OLC1/8/2 no. 12).
67   P.J. Murry to Mrs O'Callaghan, 5 Sept. 1866; Sister M. of St Joseph O'Callaghan to
Mr Murry, 15 Aug. 1866; draft letter, unsigned but to Mr Murry, 11 Sept. 1866; 'Copy of letter
written to P.J. Murry posted 7 Aug. 1871'; P.J. Murry to Sister Magdalen, 7 Jan. 1868, same to
Mrs O'Callaghan, 28 Dec. 1869, same to Mgr Woodlock, 10 Oct. 1871 (DARGS, OLC1/8/2 nos.
8–11); Dr Woodlock to Revd Mother, High Park enclosing letter from Mr Power dated
15 Jan. 1872 (DARGS, OLC1/1/3 no. 4).
68   Murray *An Act to promote and regulate Reformatory Schools, with commentary*, xxiii, also lii–liii
69   Ibid., xv.

conviction and sentence and the orders of detention were all to be kept safely and, from the passing of the Act, there were minute instructions on how to lay out the register book and why so much information was needed.[70] The administrative burden was significant at the passing of the Act, but would increase decade on decade.

The voluntary body or religious order had some control over admissions, in that the school manager reserved the right to refuse admission to a child, for what he or she put forward as good reason. The management was also free to develop its own plans, subject only to inspection. It was the sisters in High Park who decided on the daily timetable, diet, school curriculum and type of vocational training or 'work' to be offered, though the heavy influence of P.J. Murray in the founding decade can be deduced from the first school report of 1862 which he composed. St Joseph's features in the annual reports of the inspector of reformatory schools (appointed by the Lord Lieutenant) which were to be laid before parliament each year, along with the accounts of receipts and expenditures, and an up-to-date list of the certificates granted and withdrawn.[71]

One aspect of the new Irish reformatory system that its proponents saw as most useful was the control that could be exercised over children by allowing early, supervised release:

> after half the time for which a young offender has been sent to the school has elapsed, the Manager may allow him, or her, out on licence to live with anyone the Manager may select. If the child does not act well he can be at once taken back to the school. This is a most excellent point as it enables the Manager to test the child's reformation.[72]

The High Park management spelled out how the child may be given a licence 'to reside with any approved person who may employ her, or she may be tested by being sent on errands beyond the precincts of the school'.[73] That early supervised release was the exception, not the rule, in St Joseph's in its first decades is evident from the school records, but nevertheless the legal provision was there where a suitable place, under suitable supervision, could be arranged.

For all the fine principles that underpinned the 1858 Act and the autonomy it allowed the sisters in the management of the school, and despite their own conviction that this was indeed a noble work in the spirit of the order, the work on the ground in the first few years was truly difficult. The early annals, *circulaires* and reports all refer to the unimaginable trouble and labour involved, aggravated by the unsuitable buildings where 'nothing was in keeping or tended to regularity in connexion with a class of children who required a never-ending surveillance both night and day'.[74] They

---

70  Ibid., xv; xxix, xxv.
71  Ibid., Introduction vi.
72  P. J. Murray to Dr Cullen, 6 Apr. 1863.
73  *First annual report of St Joseph's Reformatory School* , p. 8.
74  'Annals of this monastery of Our Lady of Charity of Refuge, at High Park, Drumcondra, Dublin, since the arrival of the Religious the 27th September 1853', vol. 1, 1859, p. 98; 1861 p. 102 (DARGS, OLC1/5/3 no. 5). Hereafter, Annals.

were far too poor to build and, up to 1874, had to make do with the out-houses of the kitchen yard for schoolroom, refectory and dormitory.[75] This accommodation was probably no worse than that of reformatories in Britain, where 'simplicity, plainness and practical utility' were the terms used to describe the unplastered, unpaved and unheated facilities that were typical, but that was little comfort to those who had to endure the inadequacies of converted sheds.[76] The 'vice and audacity' of the first children to arrive, according to the annalist, was beyond belief, as was their complete ignorance of religion and prayers.[77] Practically all were illiterate and found it difficult to learn 'having, from their past lives, imbibed unsettled, volatile habits and a great dislike for study'.[78] All entered the reformatory 'entirely ignorant of even the lowest knowledge of needlework', a deficiency that women trained in France, where standards of domestic life among the peasantry were so much higher, could not pass over without comment.[79] These young children 'gave us much to do and much to suffer' for a number of years, and the sisters confessed to being close to despair 'so audacious and refractory were they'.[80] One poor child of ten or 12 years 'was worn to a shadow from smoking'.[81] A visitor to High Park in 1867, the well-travelled Fanny Taylor (later foundress of the Poor Servants of the Mother of God) was taken aback by what she termed 'the bold glance and the hardened manner' of the children, 40 in number, who at the time of her visit were in the playground and evidently difficult to manage.[82] The nun she interviewed (whom she referred to as a Good Shepherd sister) admitted that the work with the children was far, far more arduous and discouraging than that with the women:

> She told us sad histories of some of the Reformatory children. One of them had come from a family of thieves – father, mother, brother, sisters and even grand-parents, having followed the train. She told us of others whose parents drove them out to steal – of parents waiting like harpies for the day on which their child's sentence expires, to drag it into fresh crime, utterly ignoring and defeating the efforts of the sisters to provide honest employment for it in the future.[83]

Despite the undoubtedly rough start and all the drawbacks of the ramshackle out-offices, some success did accompany the first few years. The sisters also become more definite about the school, for whom it was intended and who ought to be refused admission or transferred elsewhere. An update of October 1862 reported with satisfaction that, of the current number of 38 *jeune filles de Réformatory*, 21 had recently made their First Communion and received the sacrament of confirmation, a great number of whom knew

75　Annals, 1859, p. 98.
76　Murray, *An Act to promote and regulate Reformatory Schools, with commentary*, xli.
77　Annals, 1859, p. 98.
78　*First annual report of St Joseph's Reformatory School*, p. 10.
79　Ibid.
80　High Park, draft circular letter, n.d. but 1868 (DARGS, OLC1/3/1 no. 6).
81　Annals, 1859, p. 99.
82　Fanny Taylor, *Irish homes and Irish hearts* (London, 1867), p. 89.
83　Ibid.

nothing more than that there is a God when they arrived into St Joseph's.[84] The sacrament of confirmation was administered again by Dr Paul Cullen in 1870, this time to a number of women as well as children [85] At the end of ten full years of operation, the sisters could report to their houses in France how 'time and patience on our side, and *grace* on the other, have worked wonders amongst these juvenile offenders, and from being *little demons* they have become *little lambs*'.[86] A more sober assessment was offered by the outsider Fanny Taylor – some were improved by their time in detention due to the kindness they were shown, and for those others, on whom time and anxiety had apparently been wasted, the hope was held out that the good seed now lying dormant might some day bear fruit:

> They have at all events been taught what is right, their detention has been a time for learning good, not of increasing evil, and those to whose charge they have been committed can feel they have done what they could.[87]

Throughout 1868, the average number was between 45 and 50 children, all reported (to the sisters in France) to be 'full of good will and even piety', so much so that a stranger would guess nothing of their pickpocketing and refractory backgrounds.[88] The second inspector of reformatory schools, John Lentaigne, appears to have thought well of St Joseph's from the outset. He is listed among the principal benefactors for 1858 and, in April 1868, he sought to arrange for an English clergyman friend of the Lord Lieutenant with an interest in asylums, probably John W. Gregg, with some other officials, to visit High Park with the note 'For many reasons I am anxious that they should see your good works'.[89] In February 1878, he brought along the Duchess of Marlborough to see, first hand, the manner in which the school was run, a visit which merits recounting for the style of her arrival alone (*dans un equipage superb avec une suite d'attendants et accompagnée de son aide de camp*). After the minutest inspection (which included the women's asylum), she declared herself greatly impressed with all, especially the good order that reigned throughout.[90] It was Lentaigne also who arranged for a group of 'scientific men' attending a congress in Dublin in 1883 to inspect the reformatory school and women's asylum at High Park.[91] Lentaigne's involvement with St Joseph's spanned three decades and included the transfer from the converted sheds of the convent yard to the exemplary new school house, making the pride he took in its development all the more understandable.

The evidence is that the first cohort of children received was the most difficult, but that the later intakes were 'less depraved and more docile', 'more amenable to rule, and more submissive and obedient to their

---

84   High Park, *circulaire*, 30 octobre 1862. Spelling as in original.
85   High Park, draft circular letter, n.d. but 1871 (DARGS, OLC1/3/1 no. 7).
86   High Park, circular letter, n.d. but 1868. Emphasis as in the original.
87   Taylor, *Irish homes and Irish hearts*, p. 90.
88   High Park, circular letter, n.d. but 1868.
89   John Lentaigne, Dublin Castle, to Mrs O'Callaghan, 22 Apr. 1868 (DARGS, OLC1/1/5 no. 2).
90   High Park, *circulaire*, 8 février 1881, p. 12 (DARGS, OLC1/3/1 no. 13).
91   High Park, circular letter, 15 Apr. 1884 , p. 5 (DARGS, OLC1/3/1 no. 14).

mistresses'.[92] By 1881, the children were reported to be hardworking, obedient and respectful under their mistress, who never ceased in her efforts to make of them good Christians. This was the energetic Sister Mary of St Bartholomew McDonnell, who as superior (1872–78) had pushed forward the erection of the new schoolhouse and, at the end of her term of office, took over its day-to-day charge.[93] She employed the structure of the Children of Mary sodality to encourage the reformatory children on the path of virtue, as was done in St Mary's refuge and indeed in schools throughout the country, especially those run by religious.[94] The reason given for the introduction later of the devotional practice of 'the Guard of Honour of the Sacred Heart' was that 'The practices will train the minds of the children to habits of prayer from the beginning'.[95] Drama and music were also encouraged – and not just for religious instruction; the report of an entertainment titled 'Babes in the wood' was that all the children did their parts very well.[96] Much was made of the difference proper nourishment and fresh air could achieve in a few months, from 'pinched faces and sunken eyes' to 'merry little lassies, with altered appearance, abounding with joyousness'.[97]

As the first reformatory in operation, St Joseph's initially served the entire country and had to take older girls. Goldenbridge, also in Dublin, operated briefly as a juvenile reformatory under the Mercy sisters but, in 1863, its director sought permission to use the space instead for 'a decent class' of adult female convicts who would otherwise have to languish in Mountjoy prison.[98] With the opening of the Good Shepherd school in Clare Street, Limerick (also called St Joseph's, 25 January 1859) and the St Louis school at Spark's Lake, Monaghan town (14 October 1859),[99] the lay committee behind the High Park reformatory could return to its 'original resolution' of taking girls from the city and county of Dublin aged 14 years or younger, and protecting them from the influence of older, hardened offenders:

> By this separation, the peculiar training which that most difficult class, criminal children of tender years require, can be fully developed, whilst they are saved from the contamination too often springing from association with those older in years, though less troublesome and irksome to control.[100]

That St Joseph's reformatory was indeed a thoroughly Dublin institution is evident from analysis of the county of origin over the full period of its operation: of the 624 children admitted from 1859 to 1926, 454 (or 73%) have Dublin as the county of origin (Figure 4.1). The only other county

92  Annals 1859, p. 99; 1866, p. 130.
93  High Park, *circulaire*, 8 février 1881, p. 12.
94  High Park, circular letter, 15 Apr. 1884, p. 11.
95  High Park, circular letter, 22 May 1902, p. 17 (DARGS, OLC1/3/1 no. 21).
96  Ibid.
97  High Park, circular letter, 26 July 1898, p. 18 (DARGS, OLC1/3/1 no. 19).
98  Sister Mary Magdalen Kirwan to My dear Archbishop [Cullen], 26 Feb. 1863 (DDA, Cullen papers, 340/9 nuns, no. 26).
99  Limerick date from *Fifty-seventh report of the Inspector appointed to visit the reformatory and industrial schools of Ireland* (Dublin, 1920), appendix 1, p. 19; Monaghan date from *God wills it!*, p. 163.
100  *First annual report of St Joseph's Reformatory School*, p. 4.

**Figure 4.1**  County of origin, children admitted to St Joseph's
Reformatory School, High Park, 1859 –1926

| No. | County of origin: alphabetical order | Numbers admitted | County of origin: in order of significance | Numbers admitted | Percentage admissions |
|---|---|---|---|---|---|
| 1 | Antrim | 11 | Dublin | 454 | 72.8 |
| 2 | Armagh | 4 | Kildare | 27 | 4.3 |
| 3 | Cavan | 4 | Wicklow | 17 | 2.7 |
| 4 | Cork | 2 | Wexford | 16 | 2.6 |
| 5 | Donegal | 5 | Antrim | 11 | 1.8 |
| 6 | Down | 3 | Mayo | 9 | 1.4 |
| 7 | Dublin | 454 | Queen's County (Laois) | 9 | 1.4 |
| 8 | Fermanagh | 3 | Galway | 7 | 1.1 |
| 9 | Galway | 7 | King's County (Offaly) | 7 | 1.1 |
| 10 | Kildare | 27 | Louth | 7 | 1.1 |
| 11 | Kilkenny | 5 | Meath | 7 | 1.1 |
| 12 | King's County (Offaly) | 7 | Monaghan | 7 | 1.1 |
| 13 | Leitrim | 1 | Donegal | 5 | 0.8 |
| 14 | Limerick | 2 | Kilkenny | 5 | 0.8 |
| 15 | Londonderry | 1 | Armagh | 4 | 0.6 |
| 16 | Longford | 3 | Cavan | 4 | 0.6 |
| 17 | Louth | 7 | Down | 3 | 0.5 |
| 18 | Mayo | 9 | Fermanagh | 3 | 0.5 |
| 19 | Meath | 7 | Longford | 3 | 0.5 |
| 20 | Monaghan | 7 | Sligo | 3 | 0.5 |
| 21 | Queen's County (Laois) | 9 | Westmeath | 3 | 0.5 |
| 22 | Roscommon | 2 | Cork | 2 | 0.3 |
| 23 | Sligo | 3 | Limerick | 2 | 0.3 |
| 24 | Tipperary | 1 | Roscommon | 2 | 0.3 |
| 25 | Tyrone | 2 | Tyrone | 2 | 0.3 |
| 26 | Westmeath | 3 | Leitrim | 1 | 0.2 |
| 27 | Wexford | 16 | Londonderry | 1 | 0.2 |

| No. | County of origin: alphabetical order | Numbers admitted | County of origin: in order of significance | Numbers admitted | Percentage admissions |
|-----|------|------|------|------|------|
| 28 | Wicklow | 17 | Tipperary | 1 | 0.2 |
|    | No information | 2 | No information | 2 | 0.3 |
|    |         | 624 |       | 624 | 100 |

*None from:*

| 29 | Carlow |
|----|--------|
| 30 | Clare |
| 31 | Kerry |
| 32 | Waterford |

*Source:* St Joseph's Reformatory, books of admission and discharge of juvenile offenders 1859–1926 (DARGS, SJ/8/1 nos. 3–8).

that is well represented is the adjoining county of Kildare, with 27 children (or 4% of the admissions), with the remainder, 141 children, drawn from 26 different counties (with no children at all from Waterford, Kerry, Carlow or Clare). The facility for redirecting children to 'other reformatories' was rarely used but, when it was, the most likely transfer was an older and 'incorrigible' girl to the reformatory in Monaghan, the home town of the chief inspector, Mr Lentaigne.[101]

Separation was regarded as one essential element, time another, for 'reformation is slow in progress if it is certain in result'.[102] Long-term detention was the whole point of the reformatory school system which was set up in opposition to short but frequent terms in prison which, it was generally agreed, served to steep the child further in crime.[103] The minimum term of detention under the Act of 1858 was one year, the maximum five; the High Park management maintained that 'there are none of whose reformation we should despair had the full period of confinement named in the Act been given in all circumstances'.[104]

Within a few years of opening, the reformatories practically cleared the common gaols in Ireland of young offenders. This is amply documented, while the detention of children for the full five years allowed by the 1858 Act very quickly broke up the gangs of 'young trained criminals' for which Dublin had become notorious.[105] High Park, as the first reformatory in operation, was centrally involved in all the difficulties of these first years. Where once a child, on conviction for some minor offence, was given perhaps

101   *God wills it!*, p. 165.
102   *First annual report of St Joseph's Reformatory School*, p. 8.
103   *Fifteenth annual report of the Reformatory and Refuge Union* (1871), p. 18.
104   *First annual report of St Joseph's Reformatory School*, p. 8.
105   *The Reformatory and Refuge Journal*, no. xxvii, Apr. 1865, p. 37. Annals, 1859, p. 98;
*First annual report of St Joseph's Reformatory School*, p. 10.

14 days' imprisonment and was then free to resume 'thieving', now the same child found herself, after a compulsory prison stay of 14 days, transported to a secure and remote location – as High Park was to any child – with no right to leave before the expiration of the term specified by the magistrate, which in Dublin, as a 'general rule', was five years.[106] Absconders faced sanctions, as did those who assisted them, making the reformatory as secure as any gaol.[107] The cycle of repeat offending was broken (or at least suspended) for those years. The training of entrants to the 'craft' of pick-pocketing was interrupted, as 'the less criminal, open to reformation' were removed from the control of older thieves.[108] Multiple short terms in prison ended for very many.[109] St Joseph's played its part in bringing about this transformation, but it was at great cost to the first unfortunate sisters who did not expect to find the work of *préservation* so difficult. The first young inmates, plucked from the city streets, must have found the 'healthy and retired' location of High Park, with no other houses nearby, its 15 acres bounded by ditches and hedges, frighteningly rural, and the closely-supervised daily programme a most sudden extinction of all the freedoms they were used to.[110]

One other result of the sisters' involvement in this new state-funded and much publicised work was that they themselves became better known, no small consideration for a group of outsiders with a French rule who had, to say the least, a shaky start in the Dublin diocese. The school brought them to public notice and into contact with persons of influence, some of whom were to become benefactors and protectors of the institute, as gratefully acknowledged in the *circulaire* that marked the school's first anniversary.[111]

## New School Building 1873–4 and Developments to 1927

While the conversion of several outhouses to reformatory use in 1859 was accomplished with great ingenuity, it was acknowledged both inside and outside High Park that a proper building was needed: 'neither air not space are sufficiently allowed in the present one, besides which, room for additional children is very much required'.[112] An outbreak of illness among the children in 1873 was attributed to the unsuitable accommodation, and the authorities insisted on a new building.[113] There was however no money to build. It was the lay benefactor, Mr Kennedy, who was credited with advising them to turn to Divine Providence, as the need was so obvious, and to trust in 'our powerful protector' St Joseph, to whom the new building was to be dedicated and who had not been found wanting thus far.[114] Kennedy worked hand-in-hand with the new and very capable superior, Sister Mary of St Bartholomew McDonnell. He drew on his family and social connections,

106    *First annual report of St Joseph's Reformatory School*, p. 8.
107    Murray, *An Act to promote and regulate Reformatory Schools, with commentary*, xvi
108    *The Reformatory and Refuge Journal*, no. xxvii, Apr. 1865, p. 37.
109    *Fifteenth annual report of the Reformatory and Refuge Union* (1871), p. 18.
110    *First annual report of St Joseph's Reformatory School*, p. 4.
111    High Park, *circulaire*, 30 décembre 1859.
112    Taylor, *Irish homes and Irish hearts*, p. 90.
113    Annals 1873 p. 139.
114    Ibid.

with his brothers and other family members first to come forward with contributions to the school fund.[115] It was for this project that Kennedy's niece, Mrs Palles (wife of the Chief Justice), worked jointly with Lady O'Hagan (wife of the Lord Chancellor) to raise funds. They organised a concert in the private home of the Lord Chancellor and, to the funds raised on the occasion, they added a joint contribution of £50.[116]

The first stone was laid on 7 January 1873 and construction took 12 months; 100 feet in length and 33 feet in width, the ground floor contained 'a spacious hall and two large classrooms', the first floor a dormitory the length of the building, with 60 beds, and the top floor was divided into three departments, including an infirmary for the children. 'Simple and modest', its only architectural ornament was a niche prepared for the statue of St Joseph and two wrought iron crosses, 'signs of salvation', to decorate the gable ends.[117] It was joined to the chapel by a corridor on the ground floor so that the children did not have to go out of doors in all weathers. The construction costs came to £3,285, higher than had been anticipated, but there were few complaints:

> The light, ventilation and drainage are perfect. New iron bed-steads and bedding have been provided for all the children. Desks of the most approved design have been placed in the class hall and suitable benches, work tables &c. are being made for the Recreation Room. Six Irish acres of grassland immediately adjoining have been added to the farm.[118]

The new building greatly increased the capacity of the school, allowing it to be certified for 80 children.[119] One year later, the new building was reported as giving every satisfaction and in addition,

> water, gas and sewerage have been provided throughout and the arrangement may be considered complete. The cost was £1,200 but the accommodation provided even at so large an outlay will it is considered be of very considerable advantage in impressing on the minds of the children who are to have the sole care of the building's order and cleanliness.[120]

From the outset, St Joseph's had tried to offer the kind of programme expected by the proponents of the reformatory system on the Continent, as well as in Britain and Ireland, namely religious, moral, literary and vocational instruction within a tight horarium that left little space for indolence or mischief. In

---

115   'Livre V, registre des fondateurs et bienfaiteurs du Monastère de Notre Dame de Charité de Dublin, établie le 14 Septembre 1853', p. 29 (DARGS, OLC1/9/4 no.1).
116   High Park, circular letter, 20 Oct. 1874, p. 9 (DARGS, OLC1/03/1 no. 9)
117   Ibid., p. 10.
118   Draft note for circular letter, n.d. but 1874 (DARGS, SJ/9/2).
119   Annals, 1877, p. 144.
120   Memo, 'State of premises 1874' (DARGS, SJ/9/2).

the British reformatories, 'managers generally look upon labour and industrial exertion as more powerful Reformatory instruments than school instruction' and the day was organised accordingly, with the children at their work
by 6am, the boys in the fields, the girls indoor, and putting in about 8 hours
labour per day with a further 3 hours in school for 'mental instruction.[121] The
programme published for High Park in 1862 was similar in structure to that
published in the same year for Spark's Lake: early rising, 9pm bedtime, and
every hour of the day assigned to a particular aspect of the child's formation,
but the greatest time taken up with manual labour.[122] The 'general education'
at High Park, reading, writing and ciphering, took up three hours each morning (in Spark's Lake, the schoolwork was in the evenings, 5pm to 8pm). What
was termed 'general work' or vocational training, timetabled for six hours a
day, consisted of needlework, knitting, darning and repairing. In addition,
there was a small laundry attached to the school (not the laundry attached
to the women's asylum, which was a separate institute in every respect), in
which the girls were taught 'making up and smoothing shirts', with 'particular attention being paid to advance those whose sentences are nearest to
expiration'.[123] The rest of the day was divided between prayers, rosary and
religious instruction (2 hours), meals (1½ hours) and recreation (3 hours), a
packed programme made possible only by having a very early start (5am
weekdays, 6am Sundays). The St Louis regime at Spark's Lake was similarly
heavily slanted towards needlework, laundry work and 'household duties',
with the addition of gardening 'when the weather permits'.[124]

The new building allowed for the implementation of a disciplined regime and closer oversight of the children. Proper classrooms and a large
workroom-cum-recreation hall allowed for better school work and instruction in handicrafts, such as glove-making, while the different 'departments'
could be used for training in domestic skills.[125] Laundry work, ironing, bak-
ing and the care of the pigs were listed as skills to be learned alongside the
lay sisters who had charge of these areas, in the circular letter celebrating
the opening of the new premises.[126] These departments were subject to inspection also and the state authorities expected to see improvements on
each visit. The schoolhouse was no sooner completed than the community
had to replace old sheds with a proper 'farmhouse' where the children were
given some sort of instruction. The rebuild included a bake-house which
was declared to be a wonderful advantage as it could supply bread for the
entire community (the refuge, convent and school), implying that it was a
thoroughly professional, mass-production facility.[127] The additional play
space, screened from the women's area and facing onto fields, gave more
scope for outside activities and nature study. The gathering of sticks from
under the trees in the summer, one of many examples, was commended as
simultaneously teaching the children thriftiness and improving their health

121    Murray, *An Act to promote and regulate Reformatory Schools, with commentary,* xlii and xlvi.
122    *Spark's Lake Reformatory, Monaghan, report for 1861* (Dublin, 1862)
123    *First annual report of St Joseph's Reformatory School,* p. 10.
124    *Spark's Lake Reformatory, Monaghan, report for 1861.*
125    High Park, circular letter, 15 Apr. 1884, p. 2.
126    High Park, circular letter, 20 Oct. 1874, p. 12.
127    High Park, draft circular letter, 6 Jan. 1878, p. 6 (DARGS, OLC1/3/1 no. 12).

through fresh air and exercise.[128] More bedroom space meant that the school was ready and willing to cater for 80 to 100 children, and fully expected to operate at that capacity within a short period of time. New account books were started in 1874 to keep track of the grants from grand juries and town councils, sums which the local authorities were bound to provide but which nevertheless needed the closest monitoring.[129]

That the new premises was rather a showpiece is evident from the reports of 'a concourse of distinguished visitors' in the 1880s and 1890s. Some came purposely to see for themselves the much-acclaimed, modern women's asylum.[130] The visit to the women's section was generally rounded off with a visit to the school, where the charm of the children never failed to delight. Such was the visit from conference participants gathered in Dublin in 1883 'with the view of testing the progress of science, literature and civilisation' who, though they managed only a short visit to High Park, 'Nonetheless they had their eye to business, particularly in the school, where they instituted strict inquiries into the training of the juvenile offenders'.[131] There were also more formal and serious inspections by state officials and Church authorities, including the statutory visits by the 'government inspector' and the catechetical examinations undertaken by the diocesan priest appointed to that task.[132] One of the best-documented inquiries was that of the Aberdare commission. This was set up in 1883 in response to great unease about the effectiveness, appropriateness and value for money of the training provided in reformatories and industrial schools in Ireland, and the involvement of so many religious orders. Almost overlapping in time was the Samuelson commission, which had a much wider brief, a review of all technical instruction throughout Britain and Ireland.

The internal record of the February 1883 visit notes how all anxiety about the inspection was dispelled on the arrival of the seven commissioners led by Lord Aberdare, Lord Norton and the Chief Secretary of State:

> These gentlemen at once proceeded to the school, and so exceedingly affable and courteous were they in their behaviour, that they put our Sisters quite at ease with them. Dressed in holiday attire, the children were ranged around the room, engaged at various types of needlework, particularly at glove and shirt-making. As they rose to greet the visitors with a smile, their bright happy voices told no tale of hard or cruel treatment, and even at first sight helped not a little to make a favourable impression on and remove the prejudices of these gentlemen.[133]

At one point in the tour of inspection, the children sang the melody by Moore 'I saw from the beach'. Lord Aberdare expressed delight that they

---

128    High Park, circular letter, 26 July 1898 , p. 18.
129    Murray, *An Act to promote and regulate Reformatory Schools, with commentary*, viii.
130    High Park, circular letter, 26 July 1898, p. 5.
131    High Park, circular letter, 15 Apr. 1884, p. 5.
132    High Park, circular letter, 26 July 1898, p. 18.
133    High Park, circular letter, 15 Apr. 1884, p. 5.

were taught vocal music because it had 'an elevating moral influence on the character'.[134] Accompanied by a medical doctor whose task was to inspect the sanitary condition of the premises, the commissioners entered every nook and cranny of the building, asking questions as they went:

> No better examiners could the Government have appointed for it might be said that these gentlemen fulfilled their duty with scrupulous fidelity, and did not leave till they had seen the entire establishment, and thoroughly informed themselves of the statistics of the school. They inquired into the moral and religious training of the children; they asked what was their diet and how they were treated in general. The discipline of the school, the faults and the punishments – all was gone into, nothing was omitted.[135]

That St Joseph's received a glowing report under all headings is not surprising, as it was already a much-examined institute in a new purpose-built premises with small numbers. It had a permanent core staff of sisters who, whatever their own personal limitations, were selected for the work on the basis of aptitude, there being many other less demanding occupations in High Park across its different departments. The readiness of the superior and school staff to allow all and sundry to visit St Joseph's that they might see for themselves what was going on is also noteworthy. This was calculated to interest the wider public in the work, that it might be supported financially and politically, and can be read as a vote of confidence in their own efforts and pride in the progress of the children under their care. What is rather more worrying is that the commissioners took what they saw at High Park in February 1883 as an exemplar of practice more generally:

> They visited likewise all the institutions in Dublin, and were so satisfied with the result of their examination, that they proceeded no further, taking the Dublin schools as a specimen of those in other parts of Ireland. They gave, later on, a most favourable report to the Government, and pronounced the highest eulogium on the Irish schools, saying that the Irish possessed the happy knack of knowing how to train and educate their children.[136]

No official inspection appears to have been undertaken in person again until 1893, and then at irregular intervals up to 1915. But from 1916 through to 1926, two officials, Mr MacCormack and Miss McNeill, were scrupulous about the twice-annual inspection, so that the total number of recorded and signed inspections over 33 years (from 1893 to 1926) comes to 34.[137]

---

134    Ibid.
135    Ibid.
136    Ibid.
137    'St Joseph's Reformatory, book of admissions of juvenile offenders no. 2', 1907–55 (DARGS, SJ/8/1 no. 6).

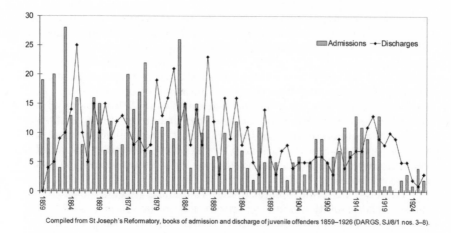

Compiled from St Joseph's Reformatory, books of admission and discharge of juvenile offenders 1859–1926 (DARGS, SJ/8/1 nos. 3–8).

**Figure 4.2** St Joseph's Reformatory School, High Park, admissions and discharges, 1859–1926

The question put by the Aberdare commission, and which most exercised the public, was how these juveniles fared afterwards. Was there evidence that the money expended on their training and education fitted them 'to be honest and useful members of the great family of mankind'? The gentlemen commissioners were 'much gratified' on being told that the greater number of those discharged from High Park were known to be conducting themselves well.[138] But the issue of follow-up and aftercare could not be so easily answered. The early annals and circular letters of High Park reported on girls being able to support themselves 'respectably' on discharge. The sisters pinned their hopes on the employability of the girl, that the domestic skills she had developed would help her to keep a family together and that the care taken with her moral and religious instruction would keep her safe from harm.[139] They did find that some of those most rebellious under detention, 'to the astonishment of all pursue quite a different course of life outside, and thus exemplify that the seeds of virtue, sown even in the hardest heart, can by the grace of God be made to bear fruit and yield a hundred fold for one'.[140] Frequent return visits to St Joseph's were expressly encouraged from the outset.[141] One former resident, after several years' exemplary conduct outside as a domestic servant, was accepted back into her old place ('out of charity') when she could no longer work due to the ravages of TB.[142] She was not the only girl to turn to St Joseph's when faced with no door other than the workhouse or worse.[143] There was

138  High Park, circular letter, 15 Apr. 1884, p. 5.
139  Annals, 1877 p. 144.
140  High Park, circular letter, 15 Apr. 1884, p. 11.
141  Annals, 1877, p. 144.
142  High Park, *circulaire*, 8 février 1881, p. 12.
143  See also, High Park, circular letter, Feast of the Patronage of St Joseph, 1884, p. 11
(DARGS, OLC1/3/1 no. 14).

provision in the Act of 1858 for early discharge on licence, which would, in theory at least, give the child a chance to settle into outside life while still under the superintendence of the school. This was used in only 11 cases in High Park between 1859 and 1926, so it was very much the exception.[144] But on the final discharge of the child, the 1858 legislation was silent, a problem that was recognised from the outset but never resolved.[145] Some of the families to whom the girls would have to return were far from being able or willing to support them, while the new start that emigration would make possible was closed to most for lack of funds.[146] The problem of 'final destination' or aftercare was one shared by all bodies involved in institutional childcare, a problem which was on hold for the duration of the child's stay, but did not go away.

Whatever the philosophical underpinning and religious justification, the financial viability of the enterprise rested on the numbers sent by the courts. Advocates of the reform school could do no more than press its advantages over prison and, even where the 'government inspector' was 'favourably disposed' towards the school, it counted for nothing.[147] The decision to add a term of detention in a reformatory school to the given prison sentence was entirely up to the magistrate or judge. The numbers admitted each year to High Park fluctuated greatly, as did the numbers discharged (Figure 4.2), but the general trend in the numbers under detention was steadily downwards from the late 1870s, and there was nothing the sisters could do about it.[148] Over its first three years of operation, 1859–61 inclusive, 48 children were received, with nine discharges. The capacity of the school, in the converted outhouses, was extended from 30 to 40 girls, and every bed must have been occupied most nights. By 1871, there were 50 children resident and, though below the official capacity of 60, it must have been densely packed.[149] The new building, opened in 1874, had immediate and admirable facilities for 80 girls, which could be extended to 100 should the demand be there, as the sisters hoped. But at no point was it to be used to its full capacity. In the five years before 1874 and the opening of the new building, a total of 49 children under detention were admitted; in the five years after, including 1874, 80 children were admitted. Admissions must always be balanced against discharges, and a peak in admissions (of girls about the same age) leads invariably to

---

144   P. J. Murray to Dr Cullen, 6 Apr. 1863.

145   Murray, *An Act to promote and regulate Reformatory Schools* , li.

146   Ibid., l.

147   High Park, circular letter, 26 July 1898, p. 18.

148   The incidental school register for St Joseph's starts in 1887 and gives the total number under detention on 31 Dec. of each year from there on; for the period 1859 to 1886, the total number under detention for each year has been calculated by the author directly from the register of admissions and discharges. Total enrolment and the number of non-court or 'free children' have been taken from the High Park circular letters (DARGS, OLC1/3/1). Only minor discrepancies have been found between these two sources and may be accounted for by the constant moving in and out of children and the date on which the calculation is based, which is not always clear in the convent sources.

149   High Park, circular of 1862 says capacity is 60, but 38 children in residence; High Park, draft circular letter, n.d. but 1871 (DARGS, OLC1/3/1 no. 7).

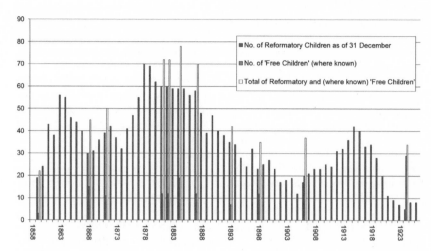

**Figure 4.3** St Joseph's Reformatory School, High Park, total numbers, 1859–1926

a peak in discharges four or five years later. The consistently high numbers admitted in the 1870s, practically all for the maximum period of five years, set the school up for another decade. The total number of children under detention probably reached its highest-ever in 1876, when there were about 70 children in the school. The highest number to arrive in a single year was in 1863, when 28 girls were admitted under detention, of whom seven came on 13 June 'on the breaking up' of Goldenbridge, to join another girl who had previously absconded from Goldenbridge and was under court order in St Joseph's from April of that year.[150] The next most noteworthy year was 1883 when 26 children were admitted (with the predictable peak in discharges in 1888). It may be that the public focus on the reformatory question that year and the publicity given to High Park made magistrates more inclined to commit girls to St Joseph's. But this was a spike, not a trend. The number of new admissions was in single digits most years from 1889 onwards, a slight increase from 1914 to 1918, immediately ending with the close of the war and the upheavals to the justice system that came with the Sinn Féin electoral success of 1918. One child only was admitted under detention in 1919, but the viability of St Joseph's as a reformatory school was over long before then. The total number under detention was 12 in 1905, the lowest number up to then, but predictable given the excess of discharges over admissions practically every year since 1888. No more than 13 children were admitted under detention over the eight years from 1919 to 1926 inclusive, with a collapse in total numbers between 1920, when there were 20 children under detention, and 1926, when there were eight.

But the number under detention was only part of the story of St Joseph's. From the outset, the school also provided for a small number of destitute

150   Entry no. 58, 1 Apr. 1953, 'St Joseph's Reformatory, book of admissions of juvenile offenders', 1859–1907 (DARGS, SJ/8/1 no. 3).

children or orphans, who were termed 'free children' or voluntary cases – that is, not under court orders (Figure 4.3). Though the statistics cannot be given for each year, the internal circular letters give a sense of the balance of numbers over time. At the end of the first year of operations, 1859, there were 22 *'enfants de notre classe de Réformation'*, of whom three were not under detention.[151] These may have included the two girls who started in 1858 and were deemed to be in urgent need of protection, but whose names are not in the state-issued register book. The *circulaire* for 1881 reports on 72 *'enfants de la Classe de Réforme'*, of whom 12 appear to be 'free children'.[152] That of 1887 gives the number of schoolchildren as 58 'under detention' and 12 orphans, 'all of whom claim our vigilance and care'.[153] By 1898, there were 23 under detention and 12 free children, a total of 35 children in 'a fine building upon which we have expended much money' and capable of accommodating 100.[154] That June, four 'little waifs' had been admitted to the school by reverend mother 'for different intentions' and in the knowledge that there was a huge demand in the city for Catholic school places for desperately poor girls at risk of being targeted by zealous evangelical missionaries:

> The Catholic poor about Dublin have a dread of the proselytisers who are like birds of evil, ever ready to take their little ones from them, and in pursuance of this object stop not at stratagem and force when they cannot succeed by wily tempting them through their poverty.[155]

The space was there to take in additional 'little waifs', and it could certainly be justified as work proper to the institute, fitting in with its overall mission to work for the glory of God and the salvation of souls. However, there was no public funding to support such children, other than through the reformatory or industrial school systems, and – unlike the women residents – children could contribute nothing towards their keep. The 'small remittances' that came with some of these children, though most welcome, were nowhere near sufficient or dependable. The school building had been erected through public charity and private funds (largely the income derived from the sisters' dowries), but these could not be relied on fully to fund the day-to-day running costs of a residential school should there be no state grants and no school fees. By the end of 1902 the writing was on the wall:

> Our school is growing less year by year. At present we have only 20 girls who were sent to us by committal, and 13 free children, for some of whom a small remittance is paid annually.[156]

151  High Park, *circulaire*, 30 décembre 1859.
152  High Park, *circulaire*, 8 février. 1881.
153  High Park, circular letter, 24 Mar. 1887, p. 9 (DARGS, OLC1/3/1 no. 15).
154  High Park, circular letter, 26 July 1898, p. 17.
155  Ibid.
156  High Park, circular letter, 22 May 1902, p. 17 (DARGS, OLC1/3/1 no. 21).

By 1906, the balance between state-funded and charity cases had tipped: there were 37 children in the school, '17 are reformatory cases, 20 are free children towards whose maintenance little or nothing is paid'.[157] Convictions were few and in almost every year of the previous decade had been surpassed by the numbers discharged as their term of detention was up.[158] An additional inspection by a three-man team on 7 May 1906 was probably in response to the sisters' request that the facilities on offer be fully appreciated and better utilised.[159] By then, the total strength of the school had been supplemented by the arrival of five women, 'whose services are of use, while they themselves are provided with a safe home which shields them from the temptations and danger to which they were hitherto exposed'. These were women of no doubt respectable and 'virtuous' backgrounds who, in return for accommodation in the school – which had ample spare apartments – worked mainly at sewing; a small pension was paid for one of them.[160] The census of 1911 includes four women under the reformatory returns (dressmaker, sewing, two milliners).[161] A later reference to what might be termed lady boarders refers to three women in the school who did needlework, 'and in return are provided with a home and their needs supplied for which they are grateful as a preventive against their weakness for stimulants which otherwise they might be unable to overcome'. The implication is that these women are recovering from addiction to alcohol and that the school is a place of safety and shelter for them, and more suited to their class or circumstances than St Mary's refuge, from which the school was entirely separate.[162]

One further development that brought down the number and age of girls sent to St Joseph's arose from the Children Act 1908 and its provision (section 108) for remanding a child accused of a crime to a place other than prison. Managers of industrial schools and reformatories could now apply to have their premises recognised as a place of detention and would receive a capitation grant for each child remanded to their care. Within a few years, there were 19 places of detention named for Roman Catholic female children (under 14 years) across the country, while the three existing RC girls' reformatories, in Dublin (High Park reformatory), Belfast (Abbeyville industrial school) and Limerick (St Joseph's reformatory), were recognised as places of detention for RC female 'young persons' only, that is, girls aged between 14 and 17.[163] Younger girls, therefore, were no longer sent to St Joseph's, the very

---

157    High Park, circular letter, May 1906, p. 23 (DARGS, OLC1/3/1 no. 22). The census number for 1901 was 37 pupils rising to 40 schoolgirls in the census of 1911, Household census returns for 1911, City of Dublin, Parliamentary division of North Dublin, Poor Law Union of North Dublin, District Electoral Division of Drumcondra, Constabulary district of Drumcondra, Townland of Goosegreen, Ward of Drumcondra, Parish of Clonturk, Street Grace Park Road (NAI).
158    High Park, circular letter, May 1906, p. 23.
159    Messrs Fagan, Dunlop and Burns visited on 7 May 1906 and the usual annual inspection was undertaken on 7 Aug. 1906 by Mr Graham; High Park circular letter, May 1906, p. 23.
160    High Park, circular letter, May 1906 , p. 23.
161    Household census returns for 1911.
162    High Park, circular letter, Feast of the Sacred Heart, 1924, p. 12 (DARGS, OLC1/3/1 no. 26).
163    *Fifty-seventh report of the Inspector appointed to visit the reformatory and industrial schools of Ireland*, p. 17.

type of children the sisters were always anxious to receive as they felt, with good reason, that they could do most with them.

In the last internal report for St Joseph's as a reform school, circulated in 1924, the number of 'reformatory cases' is given as 7, with 29 'orphans or free children' and three women accommodated in the school in return for needlework services, with mention yet again of the potential accommodation for 100 children.[164] The school has effectively ended as a reformatory maintained by public funds. The future of St Joseph's, High Park, the first of all the reformatory schools in the country, was tied to whatever would be decided about the childcare and social service infrastructure of the new state. This, it must be admitted, was not high on the political agenda of the time, nor would it be for several decades more.

---

164    High Park, circular letter, Feast of the Sacred Heart, 1924, p. 12.

# Chapter 5

# The Industrial School System, the Children Act 1908, and the Post-independence Regulation of Certified Schools: St Joseph's School, Whitehall, 1927–52

The very small numbers of children committed to St Joseph's High Park from the mid-1880s onwards made it clear that, barring some extraordinary happening, it had no future as a reformatory school alone.[1] The archbishop's advice of 1899, 'to remain passive in the hope that Providence will bring about a change for the better' did not resolve matters.[2] Numbers continued to fall. Yet the sisters felt strongly that there was scope for the work of *préservation* or protection of destitute young girls, and not just those who had gone through the criminal process. They could justify the work of St Joseph's – which kept vulnerable young girls safe from sin and crime – as a reflection of the order's zeal 'for the glory of God and the salvation of souls'.[3] But how could it continue? The answer came with its re-certification as an industrial school without losing its reformatory school licence.

On 8 February 1927, the assistant secretary in the Department of Education certified that St Joseph's Industrial School for Roman Catholic Girls, situated at Whitehall, Drumcondra, Dublin, was 'fit for the reception of female children to be sent there under the Children Act, 1908'.[4] The person named in the application was Mrs Elizabeth Byrne (Mother Mary of St Genevieve) for the Community of the Sisters of Our Lady of Charity of Refuge, Whitehall, Drumcondra, and an inspection had been carried out previously by Charles J. McCormack, the inspector of reformatory and industrial schools in the Saorstát.[5] The announcement was duly published in *Iris Oifigiúil*. A new register was started, beginning with entry number 1 on 18 March 1927.[6]

1 Sister M. of St Aloysius Morris to Dr Walsh, 30 May 1899 (DDA, Walsh papers, Religious, 1899); High Park, circular letter, 22 May 1902, p. 17 (DARGS, OLC1/3/1 no. 21).
2 Sister M. of St Aloysius Morris to Dr Walsh, 1 June 1899 (DDA, Walsh papers, Religious, 1899).
3 Death letter of Sister M. of St Magdalen O'Callaghan (Cecile/Cecilia), d. 22 Apr. 1889 (DARGS, OLC1/6/4 no. 86).
4 Copy of *Iris Oifigiúil*, 18 Feb. 1927 (DARGS, SJ/1/2 no. 2). 'Whitehall' is the correct, registered address of the school and is used in state correspondence from 1927 onwards. 'High Park' continues in more general use.
5 *Iris Oifigiúil*, 18 Feb. 1927
6 Register for St Joseph's Industrial School, 1927–73 (DARGS, SJ/8/1 no. 10). The remand register continued without a break, as did the incidental register or daily log, Entry register for St Joseph's School, children on remand, 1910–70 (DARGS, SJ/8/1 no. 7); Incidental school register, St Joseph's Industrial School, 1889–1966 (DARGS, SJ/8/1 no. 5).

There was no obstacle in the order to shifting from reformatory work to industrial school work, nor does it appear that the government departments with an involvement (Education, Justice, Local Government and Public Health) made difficulties. The legislation governing both was essentially the same. Under section 44 of the Children Act 1908, an industrial school is specified as 'a school for the industrial training of children, in which children are lodged, clothed and fed, as well as taught'.[7] The identical definition is given for a reformatory school, except that the term 'youthful offenders' replaces the term 'children'. The age limits that applied in industrial schools matched those that applied in reformatories: at first under the age of 14 (under the Children Act 1908), but later revised upwards to 17 (under the Children Act 1941). The transfer of a child from reformatory to industrial school and vice versa was possible once duly authorised.[8] The intention of the sisters 'to resign the certificate for the Reformatory School' was communicated to the inspector on 3 January 1927, but the department evidently saw no reason why it could not continue as both so that, for several decades, it was in the unusual position of having the legal status of both a reformatory and an industrial school.[9] It continued as a place of remand, under the Children Act 1908, for girls whose cases were before the courts, and the same register is used without comment or break in numbering from 1910 through to 1970.[10]

That it was a new chapter, rather than a new story, is evident from the seamless transfer of the eight remaining St Joseph's reformatory children to St Joseph's industrial school and the continued use of the same premises under the same holy patron with the same personnel. The school principal, Sister Mary of St Finbarr Dowling, continued in her post. There was a medical doctor among the community who took responsibility for the health of the reformatory children, Sister Mary of St Paul Cooke. She continued with the industrial school children, examining and prescribing for the first 80 or so admissions without any real change to her work, other than the increase in numbers.[11] The chief inspector who advised on its change of status in 1927, Mr MacCormack, had signed reports on five previous occasions.[12] Another official, Miss Margaret McNeill, who had first inspected the reformatory school in 1912 and was a frequent signatory up to 1926, was sent to inspect the industrial school yearly from 1927 through to her retirement in 1937.[13] Whitehall, the registered address, was used in official correspondence with the state, but the more familiar name of 'High Park' continued to be used both internally and among the general public.

7   Children Act 1908 (8 Edw. 7, ch. 67), 'An Act to consolidate and amend the Law relating to the Protection of Children and Young Persons, Reformatory and Industrial Schools, and Juvenile Offenders, and otherwise to amend the Law with respect to Children and Young Persons'.
8   Children Act 1908, sections 66(3), 69(2), 72(2).
9   Incidental school register, St Joseph's Industrial School, 1889–1966; High Park, circular letter, 15 Aug. 1935, p. 18 (DARGS, OLC1/3/1 no. 27).
10  Entry register for St Joseph's School, children on remand, 1910–70.
11  Death letter of Sister M. of St Paul Cooke (Agnes Elizabeth), died of leukaemia, 18 July 1928, aged 38 (DARGS, OLC 1/6/4).
12  MacCormack is used in signature but McCormack in official documentation.
13  Entry register for St Joseph's School, children on remand, 1910–70.

Both reformatory and industrial schools arose out of concern for the neglected child who, it was argued, was destined to end up in prison unless someone intervened. In the absence of a 'capable' parent, that intervention would have to be made by the state. Both types of school were founded on the principle that the state, in *loco parentis* to the child, gave the school the power of legal detention in place of the 'neglectful' or absent parent, and paid a weekly sum towards the child's maintenance. Those sent to reformatory schools had already been before the courts and suffered imprisonment of at least 14 days; those sent to the industrial schools were 'under legal detention without having incurred the stain of the gaol'.[14] As explained to a Belfast audience in 1865, the reformatory schools were intended to cut off 'the supply of adult criminals', while the industrial schools, 'by applying a similar treatment to slighter offences, and still younger offenders', were intended 'to diminish the stream still nearer its source'.[15] The court order accompanying each child had to be transcribed verbatim into the school register, whether reformatory or industrial school. In terms of philosophy of education, there was little difference between them, and both types of school were 'under the same general management'.[16] The Industrial Schools (Ireland) Act 1868 was largely an extension of the English Act of 1866, and the system it created was very quickly taken up, and to a much greater extent than the reformatory schools which, after all, dealt with only that small portion of the juvenile population that had been found guilty in court of a crime and who were first given a prison sentence of 14 or more days. In Ireland, the industrial schools quickly filled up with destitute children, rather than the 'waifs and potential criminals' the Act intended, a widespread abuse of the legislation as established by an 1898 investigation.[17] This chapter looks first at the 1908 legislation on which St Joseph's Industrial School, Whitehall, was founded, before exploring the register evidence for admissions and transfers under court order to the school, 1927–52, followed by placement and employment under supervision of this cohort of children and what is termed 'final discharge'. The register of girls on remand from the courts is examined separately. The discussion then turns to the daily regime of the industrial school, as laid down in the Department of Education's rules and regulations 1933 and as implemented in St Joseph's, Whitehall, insofar as can be gleaned from the documentary record. The commission of inquiry into the reformatory and industrial school system 1934–36, under the chairmanship of District Court Justice Cussen, raised concerns and made recommendations, some of which are then explored in relation to the case study – namely, standard of schooling, home leave and family contact, dietary, safety, medical care, rates of funding and the first building grants. The chapter concludes with a study of the sodality of the Children of Mary, the chief instrument through which the sisters maintained contact with past-pupils on 'licence' or supervision certificate. While

14   *The Reformatory and Refuge Journal*, no. xxxiv – xlv (1867–9), pp 273–4.
15   'Extracts from Proceedings of the Council', *The Reformatory and Refuge Journal*, no. xxvi – xxxiii (1865–6), p. 82.
16   *The Reformatory and Refuge Journal*, no. xxxiv – xlv (1867–9), p. 273.
17   *Thirty-sixth report of the inspector appointed to visit the reformatory and industrial schools of Ireland, 1898*, HC 1898 [C.9042].

**Figure 5.1** St Joseph's Industrial School, Whitehall, admissions, detentions, detentions, discharges numbers 'chargeable', 'in excess', on licence or supervision certificate, under 6 years, and 'voluntary', 1927–57

| Year | Admissions in this year | Total no. under detention on 31 Dec.* | Chargeable | Number of discharges in this year | Number 'in excess'[1] | No. on licence/ supervision certificate* | Number under 6 years | Number 'voluntary'[1] |
|---|---|---|---|---|---|---|---|---|
| 1927 | 62 | 60 | 42 | 2 | | | | |
| 1928 | 12 | 69 | 50 | 3 | 6 | | 13 | |
| 1929 | 8 | 75 | 50 | 2 | 12 | | 13 | |
| 1930 | 9 | 78 | 50 | 6 | 22 | | 6 | |
| 1931 | 3 | 70 | 50 | 10 | 17 | 2 | 3 | |
| 1932 | 11 | 75 | 50 | 7 | 18 | 1 | 7 | 1 |
| 1933 | 2 | 63 | 50 | 12 | 13 | 3 | 2 | 5 |
| 1934 | 10 | 69 | 49 | 5 | 16 | 3 | 4 | 1 |
| 1935 | 19 | 78 | 50 | 9 | 19 | 4 | 9 | 2 |
| 1936 | 15 | 82 | 50 | 13 | 18 | 5 | 14 | 2 |
| 1937 | 8 | 77 | 50 | 13 | 15 | 4 | 12 | |
| 1938 | 10 | 76 | 50 | 11 | 15 | 1 | 11 | |
| 1939 | 10 | 77 | 50 | 9 | 18 | 3 | 9 | |
| 1940 | 10 | 69 | 60 | 18 | 4 | 2 | 5 | |
| 1941 | 10 | 72 | 60 | 7 | 4 | 1 | 8 | |
| 1942 | 4 | 68 | 60 | 9 | 4 | 3 | 4 | |

| Year | Admissions in this year | Total no. under detention on 31 Dec.* | Chargeable | Number of discharges in this year | Number 'in excess'[1] | No. on licence/supervision certificate* | Number under 6 years | Number 'voluntary'[1] |
|---|---|---|---|---|---|---|---|---|
| 1943 | 17 | 75 | 70 | 10 | 1 | 5 | 4 | 3 |
| 1944 | 13 | 78 | | 11 | | 3 | | 1 |
| 1945 | 9 | 78 | | 9 | | 3 | 6 | 1 |
| 1946 | 17 | 78 | | 17 | | 5 | 8 | 1 |
| 1947 | 9 | 79 | | 8 | | 4 | 6 | |
| 1948 | 7 | 71 | | 17 | 1 | 5 | 5 | 3 |
| 1949 | 10 | 74 | | 6 | 1 | 4 | 9 | |
| 1950 | 7 | 65 | | 16 | 4 | | 5 | |
| 1951 | 12 | 60 | | 15 | | 9 | 9 | 5 |
| 1952 | 11 | 57 | | 14 | | 8 | 10 | 4 |
| 1953 | 16 | 64 | | 10 | | 6 | 15 | 5 |
| 1954 | 11 | 65 | | 9 | | 6 | 16 | 4 |
| 1955 | 9 | 65 | | 8 | | 5 | 17 | 2 |
| 1956 | 7 | 56 | | 12 | | 5 | 16 | |
| 1957 | 14 | 52 | | 16 | | 7 | 14 | 1 |

[1] not always given * date is not always 31 December.

Compiled from St Joseph's register data (DARGS, SJ/7, SJ/14, SJ/25).

the statistics for admissions and discharges are given up to 1957 (figure 5.1), the discussion in this chapter halts in 1952 when legal adoption was possible for the first time and when other major shifts in the philosophies and practices of childcare were under way.[18]

## The Children Act 1908 and Certified Schools Post-independence

Post-independence, the primary legislation which governed industrial schools and reformatory schools was still the Children Act 1908. On its passing, it superseded or amended separate pieces of child welfare legislation under a broad range of headings and made for a more streamlined, uniform system across the United Kingdom. This was the Act which introduced juvenile courts, allowed for proceedings involving a child witness to be heard *in camera*, abolished penal servitude and the death sentence for children and tried to enforce the attendance of parents in court.[19] It also ended the requirement that a youthful offender undergo a term in prison before he or she began their reformatory school sentence.[20] With regard to industrial and reformatory schools, the 1908 Act reiterated most of what was already in place since their creation: the state undertook to inspect and certify a school as fit for the reception of children, published its decision in the *Dublin Gazette* and, at least once a year thereafter, inspected the school, all of which was the responsibility of the Chief Secretary's office.[21] It also recommended the level of funding to be provided and the conditions to be attached, subject always to the approval of the Treasury.[22] The certificate could be withdrawn if the Chief Secretary was dissatisfied 'with the condition, rules, management or superintendence of any certified school' or, alternatively, he could simply prohibit the admission of youthful offenders or children to any named school.[23] The school could make rules 'for the management and discipline of the school' as the managers wished or as required by the Chief Secretary, but in all cases subject to his approval.[24] The Act gave the Chief Secretary considerable powers over the children sent to certified schools and over the schools themselves. He could at any time order the discharge of a child or their transfer to another school in Ireland or elsewhere in the UK.[25] He could revoke the licence under which a child was discharged from a school or vary the conditions under which he or she was held.[26]

Under the Ministers and Secretaries Act 1924, certification and inspection of reformatory and industrial schools, the approval of school rules and ultimate authority over the continued detention, discharge and transfer of

---

18 See 'Report of a Special Committee of the National Conference of Catholic Charities, 1944' [US], excerpts reprinted under the heading 'Standards in the placement of Catholic children for adoption', *Christus Rex*, viii, no. 2 (1954), pp 138–44.
19 Children Act 1908, sections 98, 102, 103, 111, 114.
20 Ibid., section 57.
21 Ibid., sections 45, 46, 88.
22 Ibid., section 73.
23 Ibid., section 47.
24 Ibid., section 54.
25 Ibid., section 69.
26 Ibid., section 105.

children was vested in the Department of Education (replacing the Chief Secretary) with the Department of Finance now acting in the role of the Treasury – though with nothing like the same resources.[27] *Iris Oifigiúil* replaced the *Dublin Gazette* as the means by which official decisions were announced. The address of the office dealing with the four reformatory and 53 industrial schools now in Saorstát Éireann was still Dublin Castle.[28] The sequence of published reports shows how, pre- and post-independence, the structures for oversight were essentially the same; the report for 1923 is titled the *Sixty-second report of the inspector appointed to visit the reformatory and industrial schools for the year ended 31st December 1923* (Dublin, 1924). The printed form titled 'Rules and Regulations for the Certified Industrial Schools in Ireland' that Elizabeth Byrne (Sister Mary of St Genevieve) signed on 14 February 1927 on behalf of the sisters had the terms 'Chief Secretary' struck though and replaced by 'Minister for Education', 'magistrate' replaced by 'district justice', and 'constabulary' by 'Garda Síochána'. Everything else stood.[29]

Under the 1908 Act, the school manager had first to be willing to receive the child but, once admitted, he or she undertook to teach, train, lodge, clothe and feed that child during the whole period set out by the court for his or her detention.[30] Under the legislation, both the state and the local authority were obliged to provide funding towards the costs of a child maintained in a certified school. Each local authority (county council, borough council) was required to provide for the 'reception and maintenance' of those children resident within its bounds who were sent to a certified school 'suitable to the case'.[31] In its role as the local education authority, each county council and borough council also had responsibilities connected with school attendance. It could report a child for non-attendance at school to the court (under the Irish Education Act 1892). If found guilty, the child would be sent to an industrial school, with the local authority bound to contribute to the cost.[32] Treasury contributions per child in 1909 were slightly higher for reformatory school 'ordinary cases' (6s per week) than for industrial school 'ordinary cases' (5s per week), with school attendance and 'incorrigible' cases attracting the lowest rate (at 2s per week).[33]

27  Ibid., sections 57, 58 (3), 67 (1), 68. For a summary of the functions of the Minister for Education, see *Report of the Commission of Inquiry into the Reformatory and Industrial School System, 1934–1936*, para. 39. Hereafter, Cussen report.
28  Cussen report, paras 8, 15, 16. By 1934, the office was at 9 Upper Mount Street and later was moved to Teach Thalbóid, Talbot Street in Dublin.
29  'Rules and Regulations for the Certified Industrial Schools in Ireland, approved by the Minister for Education under the 54th Section of the Act 8 Edw. VII, Ch. 67', signed by Elizabeth Byrne and J. M. O'Sullivan, 14 Feb. 1927 (DARGS, SJ/4/1/1/ no. 3). Hereafter, Rules and regulations signed 14 Feb. 1927.
30  Children Act 1908, sections 52, 62.
31  The county councils were obliged under the Local Government (Ireland) Act 1898 and the borough councils under the Public Health (Ireland) Acts, 1878–1907; Children Act 1908, sections 74, 133 (19).
32  Children Act 1908, sections 133 (20), 58 (6).
33  As defined by Children Act 1908, sections 57, 58 (1–4), and 133 (20); 'Scale of Treasury contributions to Reformatory, Industrial and Day Industrial schools', n.d. but May 1909 (DARGS, SJ/4/1/2 no. 1).

The 1908 Act greatly extended across the UK the reasons for which a child aged under 14 years could be brought before the Court of Petty Sessions and sentenced to detention in a certified school. Any concerned person could bring a case; they did not have to have any direct interest in or responsibility towards the child, and there was no lower age limit. The reasons included begging, 'wandering and not having any home or settled place of abode, or visible means of subsistence', where the parent or guardian failed to exercise 'proper guardianship' or where the child was found destitute, its parents (or, in the case of an illegitimate child, the mother) being in prison. Other reasons for being called before the judge were where a child was found 'under the care of a parent or guardian who, by reason of criminal or drunken habits, is unfit to have the care of the child', where the child was frequenting the company of a reputed thief or reputed prostitute or found in any circumstances 'calculated to cause, encourage or favour the seduction or prostitution of the child'. The sentence for any of the above reasons would generally be to an industrial school, but a child charged with an offence punishable (in the case of an adult) by penal servitude, could also be ordered to an industrial school, rather than to a reformatory, once the court was assured that the 'character and antecedents' of the child were such that he or she would not exercise an 'evil influence' over the innocent – though poor and neglected – children of that institution.[34]

Under the Act, members of the local police force were expected to take court proceedings against any child within their district who appeared to meet these conditions (begging, wandering, unsupervised) unless the policeman was satisfied 'that the taking of proceedings is undesirable in the interests of the child'.[35] A parent or parents could request the district justice to send the child to an industrial school on the grounds that they were unable to control him or her.[36] Poor Law guardians could similarly apply to have a child resident in their union workhouse or union school whom they deemed 'refractory', or whose parent had been 'convicted of an offence punishable with penal servitude or imprisonment', sent to an industrial school. The guardians could also request a term of imprisonment in the case of a child 'who had no settled place of abode and who habitually wandered from place to place through the districts of various local education authorities'. The child did not have to be a resident of that union.[37] And as if these UK-wide reasons were not sufficiently inclusive, an additional clause stated that the provisions of the Act whereby a child might be sent to an industrial school, were extended in Ireland to apply to 'any child found destitute, being an orphan'.[38] That each child was under a sentence of detention, not merely placed in the school, is underlined by the clause in the Act that states that should a child abscond, he or she could be apprehended without warrant and anyone assisting the child could be tried in court, with the expenses incurred in returning him or her to be met by the school.[39]

34    Children Act 1908, section 58 (3).
35    Ibid., section 58 (8).
36    Ibid., section 73.
37    Ibid.
38    Ibid., section 133 (17).
39    Ibid., section 72.

## Admissions and Transfers Under Court Orders, St Joseph's Industrial School, 1927 to 1952

The new register of admissions and discharges started for St Joseph's on 18 March 1927 shows the Children Act 1908 in practice.[40] From 1927 to 1952 inclusive, of the 315 children admitted under detention orders (figure 5.1) practically all were sentenced via the Dublin Metropolitan District Court (285) or District Courts in the suburbs or county of Dublin (12), making a 94% Dublin intake. A small number were sentenced by District Courts sitting in the adjoining counties of Meath, Kildare and Wicklow (14), and a yet smaller number from a little further afield (4).[41] The transfer of a child from another industrial school to St Joseph's happened rarely, with three orders issued by the Dublin Metropolitan District Court between 1927 and 1952 (two girls from Loughrea, one from Summerhill). On a separate note, there are two cases of children convicted for absconding from an industrial school (Booterstown) who were now to be detained in St Joseph's. One of these girls had a history of absconding which, not surprisingly, she continued at Whitehall; she soon found herself before the justice once more, to be next sent to St Vincent's school in Limerick.

In practically all of the court orders issued from 1927–52 detaining children in St Joseph's, Whitehall, the charge was one of the reasons listed in section 58 of the Children Act and the proceedings were taken under that Act, as amended in 1929 and 1941.[42] It is not possible to offer an exact statistical analysis, as more than one reason was listed under section 58 in some cases, and changes in the legislation meant that a single catch-all term came to be used more often than a more specific charge. Almost all the detention orders for 1927–9 are for 'receiving alms', and begging accounts for about a quarter of all convictions across the period (74 entries). This was a clear-cut offence, it appears, as it was never conflated with another charge but always stands alone in the register. But by far the most frequently used charge, made under the Children Act 1929, is also the most generic: 'has been found destitute not being an orphan, her surviving parent (or in the case of an illegitimate child, her mother) is unable to support her and consents to her being sent to a certified industrial school' (118 entries, or more than a third).[43] This finding is very much in line with Moira Maguire's close analysis of the system in post-independence Ireland, where she found that, from the 1920s to the 1950s, endemic poverty was the prevailing reason for industrial school committals. Trapped in a cycle of poverty and homelessness, such was the scarcity of

40 The Children Act 1908 came into force on 1 Apr. 1908. John Fagan, HM Inspector, Reformatory and Industrial Schools Office, Apr. 1908 (DARGS, SJ/4/1/1 no. 3).
41 From 1927 to 1952 inclusive, children were sentenced to be detained at St Joseph's by the following District Courts: 297 Dublin Metropolitan, 4 Dundrum, 3 Kilmainham, 2 Swords, 2 Balbriggan, 1 Drumcondra (all city and county of Dublin); 2 Trim, 1 Ballivor (Co Meath); 4 Wicklow, 4 Newtownmountkennedy, 1 Bray (Co Wicklow); 2 Naas (Co Kildare); 2 Edenderry (Co Offaly), 1 Muinebeag (Co Carlow), 1 Granard (Co Longford), Register for St Joseph's Industrial School, 1927–73.
42 The legislation under which proceedings were brought is entered in the register as '8 Edw. 7, ch. 67' or later '58-1908 as amended by Sec. 10-1941'. There are also cases taken under the School Attendance Act, entered as 'School Attendance Act 1926, section 17'.
43 Margaret McNeill, inspector, Department of Education, to Whitehall Industrial School, 16 Aug. 1929 (DARGS, SJ/4/1/1 no. 4).

resources that parents simply could not afford to rear their own children.[44] Home assistance was experienced as random and grossly insufficient and the assessment made by the court (and indeed by society at large) was according to their parents' failures rather than the children's needs.[45]

There is one entry only under the 1941 section 10 amendment which allows the court to dispense with the consent of the parent, and this relates to a child aged ten years who was adopted at birth but whose foster mother was now (1943) seriously ill. The other reasons given (in order of frequency) are 'having a parent who does not exercise proper guardianship' (34), 'not having any home' (30), 'has been found destitute and being an orphan' (13), 'has been found wandering and not having any settled place of abode or visible means of subsistence' (11). Larceny is the charge against ten girls, all 12 or older. There are two cases of conviction due to being 'found under the care of parents who by reason of their criminal habits are unfit to have the care of the child'. In one of these cases, the father of the ten-year-old girl was serving a sentence of 15 months in Mountjoy Prison for cruelty to her and she carried the scars of multiple assaults. There are two cases of 12-year-old girls committed by the courts because of being 'in circumstances calculated to cause, encourage, or favour seduction or prostitution'. One of them was taken from an 'evil house' on Eden Quay, another from a house in Bridge Street. One mother whose child was sentenced for receiving alms had a house where she 'keeps undesirable girls', evidence which the judge no doubt took into consideration when sentencing the child.

The vast majority of the children (240 or 77%) admitted over the period 1927–52 under court orders were entered as of 'legitimate birth'. Most still had one or both parents living at the time of their court appearance. In the absence of any lower age limit, infants could be admitted as readily as children aged 14 years. The same language was used of toddlers as of juveniles, most usually, 'has been found destitute not being an orphan, her surviving parent is unable to support her and consents to her being sent to a certified industrial school'. That St Joseph's was principally for young children is evident from the breakdown of ages on admission (figure 5.2): 64% of all children from 1927–52 inclusive were aged under nine years on admission; a further 20% were between nine and 12 years, and 16% were aged 12 and older on admission. There was a financial disincentive in accepting very young children, as no state payment could be made for a child under six years. Where an infant or toddler was sent by the court under a detention order, she would become 'chargeable to the state grant' only on her sixth birthday.[46]

The primary reason behind the vast majority of the court orders was destitution having led already to neglect or likely to lead to neglect. The crisis which precipitated the child's court appearance was very often the illness, hospitalisation or death of a parent. Unemployment, overcrowding, vagrancy and homelessness also featured in the record. Criminality, assault and placing the child on the road to prostitution might also be reasons, but these were always in the context of severe want and neglect. Outside events had their own

44    Moira Maguire, *Precarious childhood in post-independence Ireland* (Manchester, 2010), pp 18–19.
45    Ibid., pp 30–7.
46    Section 17, Rules and regulations signed 14 Feb. 1927.

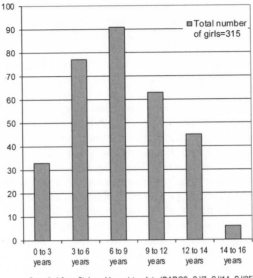

Compiled from St Joseph's register data (DARGS, SJ/7, SJ/14, SJ/25).

**Figure 5.2**  St Joseph's Industrial School, Whitehall, age on admission, 1927–52

immediate and very real impact: 'Family badly affected by the builders' strike, 1938'. Whatever the reasons for the family crisis, the break-up of the home was the most usual outcome – if it had not already happened. The brothers of girls detained in St Joseph's were frequently to be found among the boys detained in Artane or Carriglea industrial schools and noted in the Whitehall register.

Housing unfit for human habitation is recorded for city, suburbs and countryside alike. In one case, the family was living in 'a dark cellar' at 5 Henrietta Street (and running a book stall at 2 Aston Place) but, when circumstances improved, they moved to 'more healthy surroundings' in Gloucester Street and the two girls returned to live with the mother. An example from Ballybough is typical of the overcrowding that characterised the Dublin tenements into the 1950s:

> Five brothers and one sister at home, all living in one room. Family in great want, living on relief received from the St Vincent de Paul Society. Some of the boys were in the British Army but are now without any occupation.

Rural conditions could be every bit as miserable, as evidenced by a comment on the Roundwood, County Wicklow, home of a child detained by the court for non-attendance at school: 'House in a dilapidated condition, unfurnished, sleeping accommodation wretched. Father unable to obtain employment. One girl in a situation [domestic service]. 2 boys and 3 girls at home'. Unemployment or underemployment was widespread: 'father idle, mother does an occasional day's washing'. Where there was alcoholism also, the child was all too likely to suffer neglect: 'father drinks the few shillings he gets, leaves the mother nothing'.

That the housing crisis led directly to children being taken into institutional care is evident in the case of sisters committed by the court in February 1949 for the 'crime' of 'not having any home'. The register gave the parents' address as a condemned tenement house on North Great George's Street: 'The home was reported to be clean and tidy. The father is a skilled labourer, a fine type, but is idle at present. If he had been employed the children would not have been admitted to an industrial school'. This family was re-housed in Keogh Square, Inchicore, a few months later, and the children were discharged by ministerial order, but it was not an isolated case. Another entry stated rather poignantly that 'The mother not having a home of her own was unable to look after the children, she really is very fond of them and visits them frequently.' Where a mother had the child discharged into her care and the note 'very comfortable home' was added, it takes on a special warmth among so many distressing accounts. A family could be made homeless 'due to change of landlords' or where the home was tied to the job of the father and was lost on his incapacity or death. In at least one case, where children were found sleeping out of doors with no apparent parental supervision, 'members of the Society of St Vincent de Paul asked us to take them pending their committal', which was duly processed by the District Court.

The hospitalisation or death of a parent could leave children in dire want. The crisis could be summed up in very few words: 'No one to look after them since the mother's death'. One child was admitted whose father was a pensioner, 'sings sometimes on the streets', mother 'in the union hospital', the Richmond, formerly attached to the North Dublin Union workhouse. By far the most significant health reason, and closely linked with overcrowding, was TB, with several parents inmates of the Pigeon House hospital at the time of their child's court appearance. In one typical case, 'The mother died of TB. A neighbour took Alice, but as her husband developed TB she could not keep her'. Of the children admitted from 1927–52, seven had been diagnosed with, or were suspected to have contracted, TB themselves. Children could be, and were, removed by the local authorities from foster homes where TB had been diagnosed, despite the affection and care of the foster parents acknowledged in the register. One child had 'shared the same bed with the tubercular mother' up to the week she died and was to die of the same disease, aged 7 years, less than a year after admission to St Joseph's. Mental illness, in some cases ascribed to the stress of making ends meet, was also a cause of parental incapacity and could result in the child being subject to a detention order.

Children born to unmarried mothers were more likely than others to have already been boarded out, whether as an informal, private arrangement, through the local authority or under the auspices of a charitable association. Where both mother and foster mother were dead, the child's welfare was very much in the hands of the state. The collapse or termination of foster care arrangements was the reason for a significant number of court orders, as was found also by Maguire in her work on childcare post-independence.[47] Often there were several parties involved. In one case, a domestic servant (a fellow worker of the mother) 'adopted the child when she was a year old is now in

47  Maguire, *Precarious childhood*, p. 42.

very poor circumstances and no longer able to support her'. The mother was not to be found (according to the court record) and the justice issued the detention order. In another, the 'child [was] removed from the nurse with whom she was placed as she was not being properly cared for, Catholic [Protection and] Rescue Society, when told, took the case in hand'. A local authority brought a case 'owing to the dirty condition of the home and the neglect with which she was treated', though the foster mother was very fond of the child. In another similar case, 'the foster parents are tubercular' and the child was removed forthwith. The preference of local authorities for the industrial school system, which cost less and relieved them of the trouble of finding and supervising foster families, is well established.[48] There is a case dated 1934 of four girls aged between 4 and 9 years, not siblings, at the same District Court sitting directed to St Joseph's, all charged with 'receiving alms' and all previously nursed, under St Brigid's boarding-out orphanage, in Sandyford. No other reason is given, but it certainly appears to be the intention of St Brigid's Orphanage to transfer the care of these children to St Joseph's and to have the state pay for their maintenance, though these children did return to their foster families for summer holidays in subsequent years.[49] An earlier St Brigid's case, dated 1929, is of an older child found wandering after the death of her nurse in Celbridge and sent by court order to St Joseph's. This fits the general pattern of local authorities and other organisations not even attempting to get new foster placements for teenagers, but letting the industrial schools fill the role instead.

A typical case of a child admitted aged six years in 1941 explains why the school held little or no information on the parentage of so many of the children entered as illegitimate. Born in the Coombe hospital, 'whereabouts of mother unknown', sent to be nursed, then a second foster-care placement, from there to St Kevin's Institution (what was formerly the union workhouse), and then by court order to St Joseph's, aged ten years. Only three of the children admitted from 1927–52 came directly from a mother-and-baby home (one from the Sacred Heart Home, County Cork, two from Pelletstown, Dublin), but there were a number of children in the charge of the local authority who spent periods in hospital before sent on by the court to St Joseph's who might be grouped with them. There are also two cases of 'extra marital' children; in each case, the mother's husband refused to support the child that was not his (or that he swore in court was not his) and the child became the subject of an order detaining her in St Joseph's.

The condition on admission reflected the previous varied experiences of the children, which ranged from very well cared for to criminally abused and neglected. About 70% of the children were entered as in good health or this box was left blank, as there was nothing noteworthy on admission. About 30%, however, were variously entered as delicate, undernourished, suffering from tuberculosis, rickets, anaemia and bronchial complaints, 'teeth decayed', 'septic spots, 'sore eyes and head'. One child was so severely malnourished that her hair had fallen out. Another was entered as

48   Ibid., p. 59.
49   Incidental school register, St Joseph's Industrial School, 1889–1966. No further information has been gleaned from the register of St Brigid's Orphanage (Holy Faith Generalate Archives, Glasnevin).

'marked emaciation'. One nine-year-old was entered as 'backward in character and intellect, apparently the result of absolute neglect'. That so many children recovered their health was credited to the skill of Sister Mary of St Paul Cooke, who oversaw the first 80 or so admissions (died 1928), and after 1934 to Sister Mary of St Joseph Carton (died 1989). Both were qualified doctors (Carton had trained also as a nurse) before joining the community, placing St Joseph's in rather a different rank in terms of health care from any other certified school (or refuge) in the country, as far as this research could establish.[50] Among a significant percentage of the intake, about 25%, the terms 'no apparent disease but greatly undernourished and neglected', or 'delicate from want of sufficient food' would apply on admission. The average national school population over the same timeframe would also have a number of children in this 'badly in need of nourishment and care' category. The register records evidence of serious neglect, for whatever reason, among at least 90 of the 315 children admitted to St Joseph's over the period.

There are ten cases, out of a total of 315 admissions under court orders, of St Joseph's management requesting the Minister for Education to transfer children to other industrial schools; four of these cases are of siblings and two others are of single children. At just 3% of the total admissions, transfer must be seen as exceptional. One case, to Benada Abbey, Sligo, was at the request of the mother. Two others, aged 14 years on admission, were quickly transferred to the newly-opened St Anne's, Kilmacud (chapter 8), the school which the sisters at least envisaged as the more suitable setting for older entrants. Of the remaining seven transfers, the records state (or imply) that it was to remove them as far as possible from the influence of their parents, who had the right to visit their children (at set times) unless the school manager deemed the parents were interfering in 'the discipline of the school'.[51] One child was transferred to Birr in 1928 to remove her 'from the influence of her mother and associates'. She was the child who was found, aged 12 years, living in a brothel and committed by the courts for that express reason. Two young sisters, committed for begging, were transferred to the Clonakilty industrial school, County Cork, in 1931, following frequent and troublesome visits by the mother; the reason was entered as 'mother's influence feared would be harmful'. Another transfer of siblings to Clonakilty happened in 1944 after a very brief stay in St Joseph's and was also 'on account of parental interference'; the father was serving a sentence in Mountjoy Prison (for housebreaking) and the mother's very poor circumstances were detailed. Two sisters were transferred to the industrial school in Dundalk in 1940; the father had assaulted one of the girls and later served a prison term, but was now living in Sean MacDermott Street. Though the reason given for requesting

50   Death letter of Sister Paul Cooke; death letter of Sister M. of St Joseph Carton (Marie Thérèse), d. 30 Oct. 1989, aged 88 years (DARGS, OLC1/6/4).

51   'Parents, other relations or intimate friends shall be allowed to visit the children at convenient times, to be regulated by the committee or manager. Such privilege is liable to be forfeited by misconduct or interference with the discipline of the school by the parents, relatives or friends. The manager is authorised to read all letters which pass to or from the children in the school, and to withhold any which are objectionable'. Regulation no. 16, Rules and regulations signed 14 Feb. 1927.

this transfer is that the older girl, now aged 15 years was 'still rebellious and troublesome', it is more likely that it was intended to place them beyond the father's reach, as much is made in the register of his violence towards them. Very many children recorded as unmanageable or incorrigible nevertheless continued in St Joseph's through to their 16th birthday. Fears for the moral safety of girls on discharge were not without foundation, as the mother was dead, the father of 'bad character' and the address which he gave was too well known (in 1940) for its associations with prostitution.

## Discharges by Ministerial Order and 'on Licence', St Joseph's Industrial School, 1927 to 1952

Any parent or parents, married or unmarried, who had previously consented to the committal of a child to an industrial school ('being unable to support the child'), under the Children Act 1929 could apply to the Minister for Education to discharge the child into their care, once they could satisfy the minister that they were now able to support the child.[52] This provision was seen in operation in St Joseph's where the numbers of children discharged by ministerial order before the expiration of their sentence time was 53 out of all admissions from 1927–52, that is, 17% (where the total is 315, figure 5.1). More than a third of these children (21, or 40%) were returned to the father alone (the mother having died or the father being otherwise the sole parent); another third (19 or 36%) were released to the mother alone; only four children were returned to the mother and father (that is, both parents were mentioned in the register).[53] Six children were formally discharged before their sentence was up into the care of other relatives (aunt or grandmother), and two others into the care of persons who do not appear to be relatives but were known to the child. One child was legally adopted, a route possible only after the passing of the Adoption Act of 1952. A final discharge order was still needed before application could be made by the prospective adoptive parents to the Adoption Board (An Bord Uchtála). This in effect meant that no child could be adopted directly from an industrial school, even where eligible for adoption, suitable parents had come forward and the school manager was in favour, as the Department of Education spelled out in a circular of September 1953. Application for a final discharge order had to be accompanied, where possible, by the written consent of the child's mother or guardian (legal adoption was confined to children of illegitimate birth or whose parents were both dead). Only when that first hurdle was overcome, and the child was no longer detained in the school by court order, could the prospective parents make an application to An Bord Uchtála under the Adoption Act 1952.[54] The discharge order or licence loomed large over every move to

52  Department of Education to Whitehall Industrial School, 16 Aug. 1929 (DARGS, SJ/4/1/1 no. 3).
53  This analysis is based on entries in the Register for St Joseph's Industrial School, 1927–73, insofar as they can be interpreted; it should not be taken as definitive, in that it is impossible to know if, for example, a child released into the care of the mother would be supported by the father also.
54  M. Ó Siochfhradha, cigire, Department of Education, to the Resident Manager of the Industrial School named in envelope (*sic*), 10 Sept. 1953 (DARGS, SJ/4/1/1 no. 27)

take a child out of an industrial school, no matter how much it could be shown to be in the child's interest. No parent could remove a child without a discharge order or licence. Though only three instances have been found among the cohort admitted to St Joseph's from 1927–52 of the police either bringing a child back to the school or ordering the parent to bring her back (one child 'taken' by a parent, two 'absconded'), it is safe to presume that all relatives and other interested parties knew – or very soon found out – that they could be prosecuted if they took matters into their own hands in defiance of the law.

That the school could not block a ministerial order for the release of a child was evident in several register entries, where the school had a dissenting opinion. The discharge of one child was opposed by the sisters 'who said she would be friendless in England' (as did indeed turn out to be the case), but the intervention of an unnamed 'very important person' secured the order. There is another instance in 1952, where the school expressed the strongest possible opposition to two girls (then aged nine and ten years) being returned home on the basis of a 'very bad account of the mother', underlining (most unusually) in red that 'the children are on no account to be allowed to go to her'. In this case, the school prevailed and the girls were placed, in due course, in service employment.

The number of widowed fathers who applied successfully for the return of their children before the expiration of their sentences is noteworthy. Some had remarried or had other relatives who would assist in the rearing of the children, but all had to demonstrate that they were financially capable of supporting their children. A widowed and unemployed father married again; 'he never rested until he had the discharge of his two children' is the final note in the register. There are several cases of a father simply showing up, taking the child away there and then – to the consternation of the manager – and applying retrospectively for an order discharging the child into his care. These entries are included in the figures, but there were also at least three additional cases where 'Father came and took her away' without any discharge order, either current or retrospective. That some of these girls on discharge under ministerial order immediately became the carers, rather than the cared-for, can be deduced, on occasion, from the register.

Of the full intake under court orders from 1927–52, family contact – living with one or both parents or with another near relative (grandmother, grandaunt, aunt, adult sister) after time spent in St Joseph's – can be ascertained for 154 children (49%, where the total number is 315). If the ten children who were transferred out of St Joseph's to another industrial school, and whose 'final destination' is therefore not part of this record, are excluded, the proportion of children returning to family reaches 50%. This figure includes those children whose family made direct and successful application to the Minister for Education to have the children returned to them (45). Brief notes are entered on each case: the widow whose child was eight months in St Joseph's (1927) 'afterwards obtained employment and being then in a position to support the child she applied for her discharge'.

The majority of the children who returned to family did so not under ministerial discharge, but under licence or supervision certificate. This was subject to the approval of the school manager, who might also seek the advice of the school inspector. It could be before the expiration of the child's sentence at the request of a parent, who first had to give evidence that the child would be properly cared for and an undertaking that the child would attend a named local school regularly. The legal formula was: 'licensed on condition of her receiving adequate care and attention and home conditions continuing to be satisfactory. Failure to comply with this condition is to result in recall'. 'Release on licence' could be at any age but was usually shortly before the expiration of the sentence, that is, before the 16th birthday, when the young person returned to live at home but remained under the supervision of the school until her 18th birthday (or until her 19th birthday for those children committed to a reformatory). That the Department of Education insisted on strict compliance with the licence as 'the instrument to exercise supervision or to recall a child, should such course be necessary' is evident from its many circulars on the matter, its checks on individual children, and the effort invested in the printing of books of blank certificates to be filled in by the schools.[55]

For the other 50% or so of all admissions under court order from 1927–52, there is no evidence of return to family on leaving St Joseph's. Among the children of illegitimate birth (74/315, that is, just under a quarter of all the children admitted), the percentage who returned to their mother or grandmother was about 23% (17/74). Where the mother had never told her family of the birth of an illegitimate child, it was unlikely that she would seek her return, as in the case of two girls born in England to a Galway mother and left to the care of St Joseph's as the mother was back living with her parents, 'who know nothing of the two children'. Although children of illegitimate birth were statistically less likely to be re-united with their birth family, the register shows that parents or grandparents could, and did, apply to have children discharged into their care by making application to the Department of Education using the standard process open to all parents and concerned relatives. In most of these eight cases, either the mother had married in the meantime and was now in better circumstances or the grandmother was prepared to support the child. In one case, a mother – now married in Birmingham – came in person to retrieve her two children, with an approving note entered in the register that she appeared 'good living'. That these particular children, who had spent the greater part of their childhood at St Joseph's (nine years), visited frequently afterwards when on holiday and corresponded with their old teachers can be taken as a happy outcome all round. But they had the unusual advantage of an aunt resident in Dublin who visited them throughout their time in St Joseph's, and so were never as cut off from their birth family as most of the other children entered as illegitimate.

A simpler route towards being re-united with a daughter, which did not require a ministerial order, was for the birth mother (or grandmother) to request that the child be placed on licence with her. If all appeared to be working out in the child's interest (insofar as the school could judge), the child would be formally discharged into her care at the end of the detention period. Birth status was not a reason for granting – or refusing – such a request, at least insofar as can be deduced from the register. A child admitted in 1929 aged six years

55   See for example, Department of Education, Reformatory and Industrial Schools Branch, to the Manager, Whitehall Industrial School, 1930–31 (DARGS, SJ/4/1/1/ no. 5).

and of illegitimate birth (the father, a pedlar, 'makes no effort to earn a living'), was placed on licence to her mother, with the consent of the school inspector, when she turned 13: 'Though the parents are not married and have never separated, the mother is attached to the children and evidently wants them to be good'. When this girl turned 16 she was recorded as living still with the mother and working in Abbey Clothing Factory at 12s per week, her conduct 'satisfactory'. A later case, dated 1952, was the youngest admission ever to the school, an infant aged 8 months and discharged when aged four years by ministerial order into the care of the mother and her sister living together in the Regina Coeli Hostel run by the Legion of Mary in North Brunswick Street. Of the other children whose birth was registered as illegitimate and whose birth family successfully requested their return, one was placed on licence with her mother who had left a TB sanatorium, another on licence to care for her grandmother.

Whether or not the child had relatives to take her for the annual July/August home leave might be taken as an indicator of active family engagement in the child's welfare and interest in her future prospects.[56] Home leave was allowed, in a small number of cases, from 1924, but a circular issued in August 1934 extended the provision 'to all suitable children who have been *three* months in school'.[57] This new regulation was implemented from summer 1935 in St Joseph's, when there were 36 home leaves out of a school population of 78 in detention. Though the number and percentage going on home leave fluctuated from year to year, the privilege became standard policy from then on, and was applied in the way insisted on by the department. There is some correlation between those who returned to live with family on or before their 16th birthday and those who went on a home holiday in earlier years – though each case is, as always, unique. The percentage of children who went on home leave – to mother, grandmother, father, aunt, uncle, 'friend', former foster mother – between 1935 and 1952 ranged from 20% to 46%, that is, between 14 and 28 children on home leave out of a school total (in detention) of between 57 and 82 children.

During the time of detention, a 'Report of character and conduct' for each child was completed twice yearly in the register. These brief, confidential notes are full of harsh moral judgements and mixed praise, and were, of course, never intended to be seen by anyone other than the school inspector and the school manager:

> 'conduct improved, still deceitful, progress very good'
> 'spoilt, bad-tempered but nice disposition withal'
> 'improved, backward at lessons and sometimes idle often very good'
> 'very reliable and earnest, not very intelligent but anxious to do well'

---

56   Regulation 15 refers to holiday leave, 'Rules and Regulations for the Certified Industrial Schools in Saorstát Éireann, approved by the Minister for Education under the 54th Section of the Act, 8 Edw. VII, Ch. 67', signed by Agnes McVeagh and T. Ó Deirg, 4 Feb. 1933 (DARGS, SJ/4/1/1/ no. 3). Hereafter, Rules and regulations 1933.
57   W.F. Walshe, Department of Education, to the Manager, Whitehall Industrial School, 3 Aug. 1934 (DARGS, SJ/4/1/1 no. 11). Emphasis as in the original.

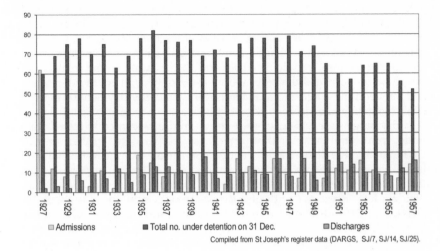

Compiled from St Joseph's register data (DARGS, SJ/7, SJ/14, SJ/25).

**Figure 5.3** St Joseph's Industrial School, Whitehall, admissions, detentions and discharges 1927–57

The greatest emphasis, from infancy onwards, was placed on honesty and truthfulness, with a view to the girl's future employment when so much, it was felt, depended on how well these virtues had been inculcated. Not answering back was another trait to be encouraged, and every effort to 'overcome faults' was praised. The reports on some of the children post-release were much more positive than the school dared hope. The facility of recall (excluding those children committed for non-attendance at school) when still under licence or supervision certificate could also be to the child's advantage. One child was entered as 'Improved, often extremely good but temperamental' in her final school report, after two years of more troublesome behaviour. Allowed out on licence to the stepmother (who was recorded as having grievously neglected the child and her sisters), the placement lasted just three days. The girl was recalled to St Joseph's and quickly placed as a children's maid with a family in Ballsbridge. Two years later, there were 'excellent reports, same place, most reliable and capable', and after she married and moved to work in England, reports continued to be most satisfactory.

## Placement and Employment Under Supervision and Final Discharge, St Joseph's Industrial School, 1927 to 1952

Practically all the girls who came to St Joseph's industrial school via the District Court were sentenced for the full length possible under the law, that is, up to the day before their 16th birthday. The pattern of discharges (figure 5.3) reflects the number of girls who reached that birthday in any given year. At the end of this period, the school manager was obliged to record in the register 'Particulars as to leaving the school by licence or discharge', with a final column dedicated to 'Report of conduct after discharge'. Under the Children Act 1908, the industrial school child was to 'remain up to the age of 18 years under the supervision of the managers of the school'.[58] Where the school was not happy with the child's conduct or had reasons to fear for her welfare, it could recall her, but it was statute-bound to place her out again on licence at the latest within three months. It could not retain a child beyond these age and time limits nor would any payment be made.[59] Children detained because of non-attendance at school were excluded from post-discharge supervision, as were those children returned to their family under ministerial order or transferred at an earlier date to other schools. Children simply taken away – 'went on home leave to aunt and father took her to England' – were obviously beyond any chance of supervision, as the school register makes clear. But even when these groups are excluded, that still left St Joseph's with post-discharge responsibilities for about 240 girls (of the 315) admitted through the District Court from 1927–52. Some of these children had come, by court order, at a very young age and without family contacts, making St Joseph's the only childhood home they would ever know. A small number had physical or intellectual disabilities or severe health problems, that made it unlikely they would ever support themselves independently. Some had relatives who were anxious to do all they could to make a home for the girl on discharge, but others would find their birth family unwilling – or unable – to make space for them, or (in a few extreme cases) the school thought they would be better off having nothing at all to do with them. All this added to the moral as well as legal responsibilities placed on the school manager in deciding where each girl might be placed on discharge.

The request by the Department of Education made of all school managers in July 1930 for information in connection with the licence and discharge of children, and the draft reply by the Whitehall school manager (typed on the reverse), shows the department's role in monitoring child welfare post-release and the difficulties the school faced, not least because the religious community running it was bound by enclosure. Among other points, the department wanted to know the steps taken to ensure that the child was being sent to 'a respectable and trustworthy employer' and the means taken to ensure that the stated wages 'are paid with regularity and direct to the child by the employer'. The school manager replied that 'we send children to employers who are known personally to us, or if not, we get information respecting them from a priest to whom they are known'; 'in no case has it come to our knowledge that wages were not paid regularly and directly to the child'.[60] The girls did have some protection in labour law, as set out in section 62 of the Conditions of Employment Act 1936. This stated that all the foregoing provisions of the Act, such as limitations on work hours and the right to annual leave, applied as much to institutions 'carried on for

---

58    Children Act 1908, section 68.

59    W.F. Walshe, Department of Education, to the Manager, St Joseph's Industrial School, 20 July 1940 (DARGS, SJ/4/1/1 no. 19)

60    M.R. Whelan, Department of Education, to the Manager, Whitehall Industrial School, 29 July 1930; draft of reply on reverse, 30 July 1930 (DARGS, SJ/4/1/1/no. 6).

charitable or reformatory purposes' as to ordinary employers.[61] Under the National Health Insurance Act 1924 and Widows and Orphans Pensions Act 1935 employers were obliged to pay combined contributions for all employees between the ages of 16 and 70. The industrial schools were circulated in 1944 to instruct their girls to get an insurance card immediately on taking up outside employment. They were also to see that any girl aged 16 years or older kept on in the school as an employee held an insurance card and had it stamped regularly.[62] The careful note taken of wages agreed, and the stamping of cards by the institute itself where past pupils aged 16 were employed for a spell show these safeguards in operation. For the school, the best source of information on the girl's behaviour, character and circumstances during the period of supervision was the girl herself, who was expected to return on visits.[63] The sodality was, from at least 1939, an important means by which the sisters could maintain that 'frequent and direct communication with children during their period of supervision' that was required of them under the law, and insisted on with great energy by the Department of Education.[64]

The post-discharge experiences of St Joseph's court-order children in the period 1927–52 are recorded in very brief notes in the register, from the first work placement or 'situation' of each girl on reaching her 16th birthday to the end of formal supervision on her 18th birthday. Later visits to the school, holidays and attendance at sodalities by some of the girls could be taken as an extension of that supervisory and parental role. The analysis here excludes those transferred to other schools or to family under ministerial order (as the school had no responsibility for them from the date of the order), and those detained for non-attendance at school. While each case is unique, and the record is much fuller for some than others, nevertheless the number and detail of register entries is sufficient to allow patterns to be identified. Some girls had multiple placements over a short period, and were recalled to – or returned themselves to – the school in between. Others found their own jobs after the first placement and the school had to catch up on their whereabouts to close off the register entry, in some cases through third party information. Still others went 'off to England', leaving no contact or forwarding address, at least when the register entry was closed on their 18th birthday. Some had their first employment arranged for them by family members, most usually where the girl was discharged under licence or supervision certificate into the care of a parent or other relative. But in other cases, even though the girl was going to live at home, it fell to the school to try and find suitable paid employment for her. Allowing for these complications, it is still possible to rank the fields of employment of the girls admitted from 1927–52 to St Joseph's during what was seen as the transition to independence between 16 and 18

61   M.R. Whelan, Department of Education, to the Manager, St Joseph's Industrial School, 3 June 1936 (DARGS, SJ/4/1/1 no. 12).
62   P. Ó Muirieartaigh, cigire, to An Bainisteoir Comhnuitheach, Scoil Saothair Fionnbrugh, 31 Deire Fóir 1944 (DARGS, SJ/4/1/5). Also spelled Fionnbrúigh, Fionnbrúgha, Fionnbhruigh, Fionnbhrugh.
63   Whelan to the Manager, Whitehall Industrial School, 29 July 1930; draft of reply on reverse, 30 July 1930.
64   S. Murphy, Inspector, Department of Education, to Whitehall Industrial School, 2 June 1933 (DARGS, SJ/4/1/1 no. 10).

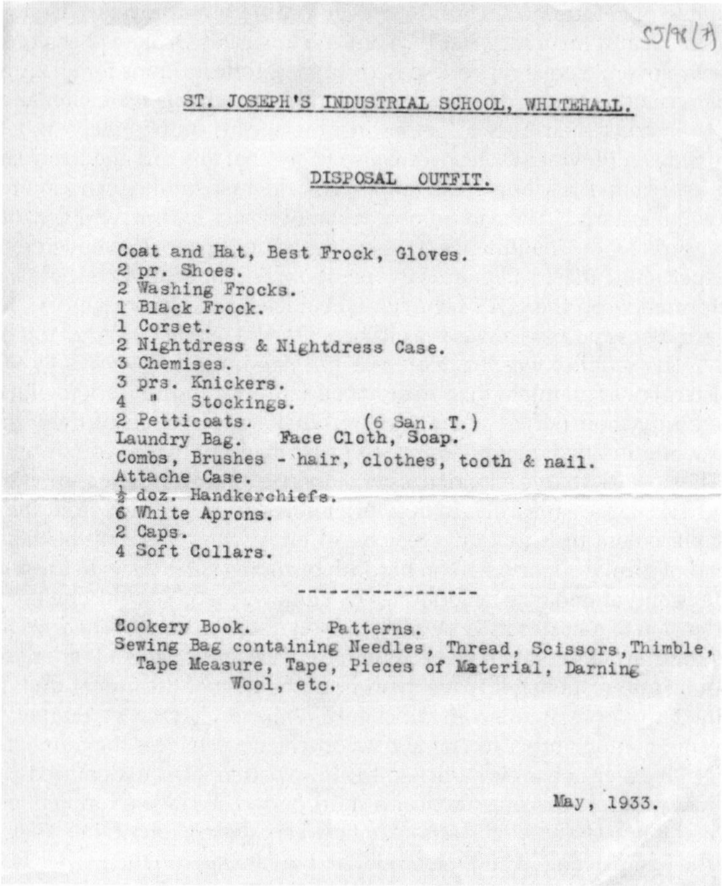

SJ/4/(7)

ST. JOSEPH'S INDUSTRIAL SCHOOL, WHITEHALL.


DISPOSAL OUTFIT.


Coat and Hat, Best Frock, Gloves.
2 pr. Shoes.
2 Washing Frocks.
1 Black Frock.
1 Corset.
2 Nightdress & Nightdress Case.
3 Chemises.
3 prs. Knickers.
4  "   Stockings.
2 Petticoats.          (6 San. T.)
Laundry Bag.    Face Cloth, Soap.
Combs, Brushes - hair, clothes, tooth & nail.
Attache Case.
½ doz. Handkerchiefs.
6 White Aprons.
2 Caps.
4 Soft Collars.


-------------------


Cookery Book.        Patterns.
Sewing Bag containing Needles, Thread, Scissors, Thimble,
   Tape Measure, Tape, Pieces of Material, Darning
         Wool, etc.


May, 1933.

**Figure 5.4**   Outfit on leaving St Joseph's Industrial School, Whitehall, May 1933.
(DARGS, SJ/4/1/1 no. 9).

years of age, while the starting wages and other brief notes give a hint of the relative attractiveness of posts.

By far the largest field of opportunity was seen to be domestic employment, either indoor or as a 'daily worker'. The 'disposal outfit' with which each girl was typically provided in 1933 (figure 5.4) included white aprons and 'washing frocks', the sort of clothing required of a parlour or general maid.[65] Where the girl had no home other than the school, placement with a family had the obvious attraction of accommodation and security. For those returning to live with their mothers or other family member (grandmother, aunt, father), outdoor domestic work was the usual means of livelihood, or factory work, but that was not an option for a 16-year-old expected to sup-

65   St Joseph's Industrial School, Whitehall, Disposal Outfit, May 1933 (DARGS, SJ/4/1/1 no. 9).

port herself entirely on her own. Of all the girls admitted through the District Court from 1927–52 and still in the care of the school coming up to their 16th birthday and not returning to live with family, the great majority were placed with private families in domestic service. These placements could break down very quickly for any number of reasons – 'recalled, mistress in hospital and did not need her', 'recalled, place not suitable', 'recalled, owing to illness', 'recalled, owing to loneliness', 'the work was too heavy for her' – but another placement would usually be found within the short time allowed by the legislation. One girl – recorded as 'strongwilled and good', 'upright and intelligent' but not physically strong – had six placements in the period 1941–44 before she settled down. Her case was not unique. Some of the recalls and re-assignments might have resulted from the obligation placed on the girl to report back within at most a fortnight as to how she was being treated, and if the terms agreed were being met. How well these safeguards operated is impossible to know, but the fact that so many returned from domestic service – or were recalled for their 'own safety', before another post was found for them within the short time allowed by the legislation -- indicates that the girls were instructed to keep in touch, and that the obligation to maintain contact was taken seriously by the school.

Wages in domestic service were much the same across Dublin at any point in time, at least according to this register, where the going rate between 1932 and 1940 ranged from £12 to £19 per year. Most of St Joseph's past pupils started out at the lower end of the scale. What mattered more was how well the girl was treated and whether she was sufficiently content to stay. She too could walk out and return to the school, as several did, assured of being taken back, at least for a short period. The difficulties in finding a place with reasonable conditions of service, and then keeping it, do not seem to have deterred the school managers from preferring indoor domestic service for St Joseph's girls in the transition to independence. The other area of paid employment was domestic service in institutions, usually a hospital, nursing home or boarding school. Though small in number (and far more girls were always sent into private domestic service), these openings were important to St Joseph's as they too offered live-in, full-board accommodation, close supervision and what were seen as training opportunities. For a girl whose job with a family had collapsed – for whatever reason – a job with an institution gave her another chance and a roof over her head, at least while waiting for something else to turn up.

Between 1940 and 1953, a total of 21 former St Joseph's girls spent some time as indoor domestic servants in the Dominican Convent, County Wicklow, a girls' boarding school, making it the single most important institutional employer of past-pupils. For some, this was one of a succession of short placements or an interim post between jobs in private domestic service; for others, this was their first paid employment now they had reached 16 years of age. A typical case is of a girl in 1940, sent first to a family in Inchicore as a servant – 'position not suitable, recalled for her own protection' after one month – then sent to the Dominican Convent in Wicklow, where she earned the same wage as she had with the family, £1 per month. Two years later, aged 18 years and due for discharge from supervision, she was still working with the Dominican sisters and earning £1 10s per month, before marrying shortly after. In another typical though later case, the girl's first situation was with the Dominican Sisters, commencing January 1953 (at the rate of £1 per week). She returned to St Joseph's for the Christmas holidays 'but did not wish to go back to Wicklow'; three weeks later, an opening was found for her with a family in Ballsbridge, but that lasted only three days – 'returned because she was lonely' – and she had two further placements before finally leaving the school and making her own way in the world. In certain cases, the Wicklow convent was used as a trial to see if the girl was capable of holding down a job outside the closeted environment of the school. 'Recalled, not capable of employment' was the verdict in at least one case, though most of the others seem to have left of their own volition and found other jobs, with or without the assistance of the school. The Wicklow employees with the longest service who had come from St Joseph's (during the period of this study) were there for two years and three years respectively. For the other workers, the length of stay ranged from a few days to under two years, and was clearly a staging post on the way to something better or to employment of their own choosing. The rates paid by the Dominican Convent in Wicklow in 1940–52 reflect war-time wage inflation and are a useful baseline against which wages of young women in other sectors might be compared. The annual wage was £12 in 1940, £15 in 1944, £18 in 1946, £24 in 1947–50, £36 in 1952–5, with full board and lodging also.[66]

St Michael's Guesthouse, opened in the grounds of High Park in 1919 by the sisters as a retirement home for elderly women, played a small but important role in the training of St Joseph's past-pupils over the period of this study. There were 16 girls on licence accepted as temporary employees between 1938 and 1948 inclusive; of these, 14 came straight from the school. 'Placed for training in St Michael's Guesthouse, wages 15s per month' is the entry for a 16-year-old who worked there for four months in 1938, before going to the first of two indoor situations (and a wage of £1 per month). That the primary field of employment envisaged in that decade for the girls was indeed domestic service is amply borne out by the register. The two girls who had 'situations' before their training stints in St Michael's are the exception; one girl had survived for four days only in her first situation ('readmitted from licence, was not strong enough'), and the note 'recalled, post only temporary' is entered shortly after her employment in St Michael's. One of the girls who worked in St Michael's did so until her application to enter a convent in England was accepted (she entered the novitiate but left before profession). The wage rate for St Michael's can be tracked: it was £1 per month in 1931–43 inclusive (excepting one instance of 15s); it was £1 10s in 1944–5; in 1948, it was £2 per month and, by 1956–60, it had reached £6 per month, all with full board and accommodation, and the girls' insurance cards stamped, as the law required.[67] These figures are exactly in line with the wages offered in the Dominican Convent, Wicklow, and no less than the going entry rate for housemaids and parlour maids, if the register is taken as a fair survey of domestic service openings in the greater Dublin area in the 1940s.

66   Register for St Joseph's Industrial School, 1927–73.
67   The approximate weekly wage of unskilled workers (housemaids) is given as from 6s to 7s per week (in addition to board and lodging) in 1930, according to the notes on reverse of the circular dated 29 July 1930 (DARGS, SJ/4/1/1/no. 6).

Hospitals were another important institutional employer because of the accommodation that came with the job. Indeed, any live-in employment would be given favourable consideration on that score alone. Jervis Street hospital employed four girls on licence between 1939 and 1946; the indoor rates of pay are similar to those to be found elsewhere, with another girl working as an outdoor maid.[68] Throughout the 1940s, three girls worked as indoor servants in Highfield hospital near High Park. Another girl found a post for herself in Mercer's hospital, two were placed as domestics in the asylum for the blind, Merrion, and another (after a rather mixed career) worked as an indoor servant in the Dominican convent, Sion Hill.[69] An aunt working as housekeeper in a boys' boarding school arranged employment, in turn, for two nieces who lived with her in the lodge while still under the supervision of St Joseph's (they had previously spent the summertime 'home leave' in the college with her). There are two instances of girls sent across the yard to the High Park convent to be employed as housemaids or parlour maids, at the standard rate of pay and insurance 'stamps'.[70] The first, it appears, stayed a very short time, but her next place of employment is not recorded. That the school manager had difficulty in placing the second girl is evident from her register entry, but an indoor post was eventually found for her in St Anthony's Convalescent Home, Merrion. The last entry in St Joseph's register is 'Attends sodality. Still impossible'.

A small percentage of the girls admitted from 1927–52 were to be found in second-level education or undergoing a course of training when they reached 16 years (and excluding the training in domestic work already discussed). Ten girls attended school or commercial college beyond the age of 16 and therefore needed to have their term of detention extended to be allowed to continue at St Joseph's. The earliest case is dated 1943, when a girl was first sent (aged 12) to the Presentation College, Mountmellick, as a boarder to receive a secondary education but, 'not making good progress' after one year, was recalled and sent as a day pupil to the Dominican College, Eccles Street. The permission of the minister was sought, first to allow her to complete the Intermediate Certificate (1947) and again to 'continue studies' which she did for another two years before (aged 19) she commenced nurse training in Derry (Londonderry). The 1943 experiment of placing this child in an ordinary boarding school was in line with a memorandum circulated by the Department of Education to all industrial schools in October 1942 drawing attention to section 12 of the Children Act 1941, whereby children 'who show promise' could be given the opportunity of a second-level education. The capitation maintenance grant payable by the state (through the Department of Education) and local authorities could be redirected to meet boarding school fees, and the child's period of detention could

68 The indoor rates of pay in Jervis Street hospital ranged from the standard £12 per annum in 1939 to £24 per annum in 1946; the outdoor maid was paid 7s per week in 1940, Register for St Joseph's Industrial School, 1927–73.
69 The rates of pay in Highfield Hospital were £12 per annum in 1942, £20 per annum in 1946; in Sion Hill they were £24 per annum in 1946, Register for St Joseph's Industrial School, 1927–73.
70 The girl who was a housemaid in the convent in 1934 was paid £18 per annum; the girl employed in 1948 was paid £24 per annum, Register for St Joseph's Industrial School, 1927–73.

be extended to allow him or her to complete the course of study or training.[71] The Department of Education rowed back on this enlightened approach with a later circular warning that this provision was strictly 'in the interests of the brighter type of boy or girl capable of benefiting from such education or training and whose future prospects would be enhanced thereby'. Each case needed the approval of the Minister for Education and was not to be applied 'to children who are not of exceptional mental or vocational capacity, and have been following the normal school curriculum as prescribed by the courts'.[72] Fortunately for St Joseph's school children, the manager had already embraced the more inclusive understanding and persevered in sending at least some girls on to second-level who (in her judgement) would benefit from the opportunity. By the early 1950s, the official mood had changed again. Those industrial schools that did give 'clever children' the chance of secondary or vocational training were commended in a letter of August 1952 (which would include St Joseph's, based on the documentary record), but the very many which had made no effort were urged to get a move on and report back to the minister in detail on the provision made to date and for the coming school year.[73] St Joseph's had the enormous advantage of being within easy reach of a selection of second-level schools with a range of training opportunities, which allowed also for the girls to be sent individually in ones and twos, not en masse as a group. In August 1952, one girl was midway through a commercial course at the Dominican Convent, Eccles Street, and another was about to start a commercial course at Marino Technical School.[74] Over the coming years, these two schools would feature most frequently as the educational providers for St Joseph's girls, along with King's Inns Street, and as discussed in chapter 9.

## Placement and Employment Under Supervision and Final Discharge, St Joseph's Industrial School, 1927–52

From among the intake to St Joseph's from 1927–52, eight girls went on for nurse training. Admission to training for children's nursing, the most popular field among this small sample, does not appear in the 1930s to have required more than a good sixth-class primary standard of education, accommodation was in the hospital and a small stipend was provided. The drawback was the registration fee required at the start by most – if not all – hospitals. Employment on completion could be with a family, but the wages would be higher than for domestic service; one girl ('a foundling') who completed nurse training in 1938 in St Ultan's, Charlemont Street, was employed with a family in Upper Clanbrassil Street at £36 per annum. Two girls did their nurse training in Norwich in England, but this was as a result of the mother's involvement as she lived there, and the costs involved for one girl at least were met by the Society of St Vincent de Paul. Similarly, the girls who trained in hospitals in Northern Ireland had relatives locally who supervised them, though the school was still responsible

71   Referring to section 12, Children Act 1941, Department of Education circular, 12 Aug. 1952 (DARGS, SJ/8/3 no. 4).
72   An Roinn Oideachais, Explanatory memorandum on implementing sections 2 to 5, 8, 12, 14, 15, 21 and 22 of Children Act 1941 (DARGS, SJ/4/1/1 no. 20).
73   Department of Education circular, 12 Aug. 1952 (DARGS, SJ/8/3 no. 4).
74   Draft of reply, on reverse of circular dated 12 Aug. 1952 (DARGS, SJ/8/3 no. 4).

while they were on licence. In a most unusual case, one girl was left £91 on the death of her mother which was used to fund her training as a children's nurse in Temple Hill infants' hospital, Blackrock; she graduated in 1941 as a staff nurse, earning £40 per annum (and 'married well' shortly after).

Those girls who had family to return to were in a position to take up 'outdoor' employment, with the business address and the rate of pay recorded in the register for as long as the girl was still under the supervision of the school. One girl took up a job in a laundry at Harold's Cross and a visitor reported of her home at Pembroke Lane 'that it is all that can be desired' (1938). Another girl worked as a barmaid in a club – the school played no role in securing that post. Several got 'day work' as domestics. One worked as 'packer' in a chemist, another in a confectioner's, another as a grocer's assistant, and two others in a print works. There were openings in factory work in a city that had a small but varied manufacturing sector, and at least 28 girls found some sort of factory employment on returning to live with their families. Most of this work was in clothing, tailoring, shirt-making and hosiery; occasionally, the employer offered live-in accommodation also. The wages (compared to those in domestic service) appear pitifully small, but for some at least it is specified that the wage is while training, and there was potential for higher earnings later. A rate of £6 per annum ('in addition to food, lodging and clothing') was offered to a hosiery employee in 1931, about half what she would get in domestic service at that time. Wages in hosiery in Balbriggan, once famed for this industry, seem a little higher, with two sisters returning to live there with their mother and taking up a post with Messrs Smyth and Company in 1939. 'Wages vary according to work, 10s to 18s 9d per week, commenced at 8s per week'. There were a number of clothing factories in and around Abbey Street in Dublin which employed several past pupils in the late 1930s and 1940s. The best factory wages by far in this small sample are for work in Jacob's biscuit factory, which was paying 16s 6d per week in 1936 to a trainee, rising to 35s per week when trained (1940). Rates of pay for factory work in England are not recorded but may be presumed to be, on the whole, higher than in Dublin. Several past pupils joined family in England and readily found work, one in a motor cycle factory in Birmingham (1949), another in the GEC factory (1955), also in Birmingham. A good illustration of how much family connections and introductions mattered in the small, over-supplied labour market of Dublin is found in the case of four sisters discharged in turn, between 1944 and 1956, who found employment in the brush factory where their widowed father worked before his untimely death, with each sister 'training in' the next.

For most of the girls labelled 'mentally deficient', in poor health or with other disabilities, paid employment was found on discharge though their placement involved additional care and effort; they are included in this analysis. But there was also a number of girls among the 1927–52 court intake who were deemed incapable of holding down employment, and for whom the worst was feared should they be thrown on the world. For these girls, some sort of supervised, protected, residential placement was sought, either temporarily or long-term. In this analysis, they are termed 'protective placements' and 20 have been identified among the 250 or so discharges that were still under the supervision of the school on their 16th birthday (from the court admissions

1927–52). The single case of a girl retained in the school dates to 1950 and she is described as 'unfit for employment, mentally deficient'. This child had been in the school since the age of nine and had perhaps one of the saddest personal histories of neglect and starvation – 'utterly uncivilised and hardly able to articulate' on admission, father dead and mother, then disabled, to die while the child was detained in St Joseph's. The reason for her continued retention is entered in the register – 'not fit for outside' – but her quiet, peaceable demeanour was probably another factor in her being allowed to stay in the school (until death), 'gentle and pious' being entered after her name at a later date.

Transfers to the Good Shepherd home in Limerick could be placed under the heading of transfers to magdalen refuges and residential homes, or alternatively under 'institutional employment', to continue the categorisation created for this research. The one case that came directly from St Joseph's School is of a girl persistently described as 'wayward and uncontrollable' and therefore 'incapable of taking a situation'; she was employed as laundress in the Good Shepherd home at a salary of £24 per annum (indoor) in 1941. Around the same time, another girl who had held several situations but 'did not get on well' was placed in Limerick, where she stayed for a brief time only before taking up a job as a waitress, indoor, at 10s per week (1940). Sending a 17-year-old girl as far away as Limerick was unusual, and even more so one of such good conduct and character (according to the school record), but this was probably to keep her at a distance from the mother whom the register condemns as 'known to be very immoral'. A later placement of a girl in the same Good Shepherd convent in Limerick 'for further training', though counted as a protective placement, could probably be considered as temporary institutional employment and a parallel to what was being done for girls in St Michael's guesthouse. All of the other 'protective placements' took place after the girl had already been in service, and most for the standard reasons: 'for her own protection', 'placed there because of mental deficiency', 'she is not capable of looking after herself'.

The practice of sending industrial school girls 'whose weak mentality and want of competent guardians is perilous' to magdalen refuges or asylums on reaching 16 was common throughout the country, according to a survey the Department of Education conducted in 1931. The 'invariable custom' of the school sending the girl was to 'keep up correspondence and send small presents occasionally to encourage these weak minded or unstable girls to stay in safety'. The department neither approved of nor condoned the practice, stating simply that 'It is only where there is no alternative place where protection could be assured that this course has to be adopted. Until provision is made for special homes for this class of girl, the County Home offer the only other solution of the problem.'[75] The undesirability of committing children 'unlikely to be trained to the stage of becoming self-supporting' due to learning difficulties to an ordinary industrial school was highlighted by Justice Cussen in his report published in 1936. His recommendation, that they be committed to a 'mental colony' such as St Vincent's Institute, Cabra, or St Augustine's Colony, Obelisk Park, Blackrock, was slow to be taken up.[76]

75   Department of Education, 'Reports from Magdalen asylums and kindred institutions, compiled in 1931' (DARGS, SJ/4/1/50).
76   Cussen report, para. 132.

Troublesome cases of this type were not a priority for the new state. There are five cases of girls discharged directly from the supervision of St Joseph's, Whitehall, to a magdalen refuge or residential home; in four of these cases, the labels 'congenital imbecile' or 'mentally deficient' are used and the same or similar derogatory terms feature in their school reports for the preceding years. The reason given is always the same: 'for their own protection'. These transfers – two each to Gloucester Street and to St Patrick's Refuge Dun Laoghaire – date between 1930 and 1941. The earliest is to an unnamed 'institution for preservation' in 1933 (which is neither of the OLC Dublin refuges).

Two girls travelled together to the 'Girls' Home' attached to the OLC convent at Redcliffe, Ormskirk (near Liverpool), in June 1937; one was a model of propriety (according to the school reports) and it appears was sent to accompany the other girl, who had a difficult history. The last known address of this girl's mother was in Liverpool; the girl herself had incipient TB, from which she was dead a year later. At least eight girls were sent for a spell while still under licence to the Girls' Home (Our Lady's Home) at Henrietta Street run by the Daughters of Charity of St Vincent de Paul for older girls and young women. All of these girls had experience already of service employment and had not coped well, for whatever reason. Henrietta Street was intended to be short-term only and girls who did not return to family or find employment at the end of their term of supervision could be moved on, especially if the managers decided there was little hope of progress. One of this cohort transferred from Henrietta Street to St Patrick's Refuge in Dun Laoghaire (1944). Another case in the list of 'protective placements' is of a 17-year-old who, having lost her service job 'through bad behaviour', decided to enter the Gloucester Street Refuge, 'as she did not feel able for work outside' (1942).

## St Joseph's, Whitehall, and the Issue of Remand

The use of St Joseph's, Whitehall, by the courts as a place of remand for children whose cases were yet to be decided dates from 1910 (following on the Children Act 1908). The managers expected that its role as a remand centre would cease when it became an industrial school in 1927, but its reformatory school licence was not withdrawn at the time by the Department of Education. 'Of course, it is to be understood that we shall only continue to take those Remand children until such time as other arrangements can be made for their reception' was the sisters' position in 1929.[77] In the absence of 'other arrangements' being made by the state for girls, the courts continued to remand children to St Joseph's, Whitehall, and to pay for their maintenance. The school manager continued to accept them, though putting on record several times, with both the Department of Education and the Department of Justice, that the community saw this as a temporary arrangement.

The difficulties in extricating the school from this 'interim arrangement' are illustrated in an embarrassing climb-down in 1952. Having absolutely refused to accept any further remand cases – 'We regret, our decision is final, our first duty is to the children under our care'[78] – the sisters were forced

77  Draft of reply, 29 Mar. 1929 (DARGS, SJ/4/1/2 no. 3).
78  Draft of reply, Resident Manager to Department of Education and to Department of Justice, 23 Feb. 1952 (DARGS, SJ/4/3),

six days later to reverse their position under pressure from the archbishop, Dr McQuaid.[79] The sisters had found the level at which the maintenance payment was set well below what it cost to provide the service, based on the figures for the 12 months to December 1950, when 97 children were sent on remand to Whitehall for periods ranging from two days to one month. No matter how short the period of remand, each child had to be provided with clothing (a school uniform), 'as a means of identification in the event of their absconding' and, more often than not, their clothing on arrival was in such a state that 'they depart in clothing supplied by us'. All the remand children, staying overnight, required to be bathed and cleansed, 'and suffice it is to say that the majority receive medical attention for their skin sores and ailments'.[80] But the decision to discontinue was not based on money alone:

> We have every reason to believe that these older girls sent on remand are often of a character calculated to do grievous harm to the innocent. As we have constantly endeavoured to raise the morale of the school, we feel that our efforts are being hampered and the fruits of our labours destroyed by this evil contact.[81]

Acknowledging the welcome increase in the capitation grant that came into force on 1 April 1952, and reversing her earlier absolute decision, the superior made sure to put on record – using the same formula employed on earlier occasions – the order's determination to withdraw from remand as soon as it could be managed (that is, as soon as the archbishop might allow).[82]

The first child to be admitted to St Joseph's on remand arrived on 16 February 1910. Practically all were sent from the Dublin Metropolitan Police district, under which heading the Department of Justice paid for their keep, settling the account on a quarterly basis. The rate of payment in 1910 was 1s per day. On independence, the eight-day rate was set at £1 1s 6d (1923) but this was reduced to £1 in September 1926. This continued until April 1948 as the standard rate, despite petitions from the school.[83] The number admitted on remand fluctuated from year to year, and even throughout the year; a single court sitting could result in several girls, perhaps siblings or friends charged with the same offence, being sent on remand to St Joseph's, while weeks – or even months – could elapse before the school received another remand case. The school operated on 'standby', accepting girls without prior notice brought directly from the court. Occasionally a girl was remanded more than once before her case was dealt with – these are indicated in the register, with the dates of each period of remand. Some were up before the district justice several times a year, and each case involved a distinct period of remand, so that the

79   F. C. Connolly, Department of Justice, to the Resident Manager, St Joseph's Industrial School, 29 Feb. 1952. Same to same, 1 Aibreáin 1952 (DARGS, SJ/4/3).
80   Draft of reply, in pencil, 27 Feb. 1951 (DARGS, SJ/4/1/2 no. 2).
81   Ibid.
82   'Copy of reply', 29 Mar. 1952 (DARGS, SJ/4/1/2 no. 2)
83   M. Ó Siochfhradha, cigire, An Roinn Oideachais, to An Bainisteoir Comhnuitheach, Scoil Saothair, Fionnbhruigh, 2 Aibreán 1946 (DARGS, SJ/4/1/2 no. 2).

number of register entries is greater than the number of girls sent on remand to the school. The smallest number of entries in the period 1927–52 is for 1936 (eight remand entries) and the highest number is for 1944 (122 entries). The remand figures are higher in the 1940s and 1950s than in the 1930s but, even within each decade, there are substantial swings: in 1940 there were 89 remand entries, in 1941 there were 23; in 1950 there were 97 remand entries, in 1951 there were 23. Whitehall was used as a place of remand for girls of all ages. Of those sent in 1927–52, the youngest was an infant of 18 months, the oldest a girl of 17 years, but the vast majority were in the age bracket 13 to 16 years. That St Joseph's played a significant role in the judicial system is evident from the large number of remand orders involved, which totals 1,267 for the period 1927–52, and probably accounts for the anxiety of the Department of Justice (and the archbishop) that it should continue to accept remand cases.[84]

The period of remand depended entirely on the court timetable and case management. Many were two, three or four days, some were 12 or 14 days, and the vast majority were eight days or fewer. One of the longest was a 16½-year-old girl, 'sent here for 14 days, remained as not called for' (in 1951), evidently because of some mix-up in the court system. After a total of 32 days, she was sent out by the school manager who had 'secured employment for her as domestic' (though regrettably, she proved 'unsatisfactory'). There was one case of very young sisters held on remand for 65 days (1938), and two 13-year-olds held on remand for 36 days (December 1936/January 1937), but these lengths of time were well outside the norm, which for most girls was between two and eight days.

Most girls of 16, 16½ or 17 years of age sent on remand to St Joseph's completed their short time there without note or comment but, technically, a girl of 15 or over was beyond the age of admission to an industrial school, and managers always had the right to refuse a child they could not cope with, irrespective of age. Of the 1,267 entries in 1927–52, seven or eight girls first 'named' to be remanded at St Joseph's found themselves in St Mary's, of whom three were underage for an adult refuge. The unsuitability of St Joseph's as a remand home was the subject of comment in 1941 by a proba-tion officer, who pointed out that it was not a remand home, but simply an industrial school into which children on remand might be detained:

> In order to keep these girls as far apart as possible from the pupils in the school, they are generally relegated to a portion of the house little frequented by the latter, for instance, the kitchen – an arrangement not to be commended but perhaps unavoidable under the circumstances.[85]

---

84   Calculations are based on entries that are numbered, that is, treated as distinct periods of remand for payment purposes and not consecutive periods of remand ordered by the court of the same girl, which are a single, bracketed entry.
85   E. M. Carroll, probation officer, 'Memorandum re: women and girls who come before the Central Criminal Court on serious charges – and other relevant matters', 7 July 1941, p. 6. Reprinted in *Final report of the Inter-Departmental Committee set up to establish the facts of State involvement with the Magdalen Laundries* (Dublin, 2013), appendix 5. Online at www.justice.ie.

These girls feature in the entrance register to St Mary's, as well as the remand register of St Joseph's. As remand cases, all were short-stay and remained the responsibility of the court. None of these girls stayed beyond the date of their return to court, so no more can be deduced. St Joseph's remand register records only the bare minimum of name, age, dates, length of remand and the payment due; it does not record the crime the child is accused of, nor the outcome of court proceedings. It does not compare with the register for the industrial school children which, for all its limitations, carries valuable family and other background information, as well as notes on the destination of the child on first leaving the school.

## Rules and Regulations for Industrial Schools 1933, as Implemented in St Joseph's

The rules and regulations for industrial schools that were formally adopted by the 'Committee of Managers' for St Joseph's on 8 February 1927 were re-issued in 1933 with minimal changes and duly signed once more, this time by Agnes McVeagh (Sister Mary of St Cecilia), who succeeded as superior in 1930.[86] Under these rules, the type of education to be provided had to be both 'literary' and 'industrial', and the progress of the children in both branches would be tested from time to time by examination and inspection.[87] The day was to begin and end with prayer and, on Sundays and holy days, the children were to attend public worship in a convenient church or chapel.[88] A timetable showing the hours of rising, work, school, instruction, meals, recreation and retiring was to be drawn up, approved by the inspector, displayed in the schoolroom 'and carefully adhered to on all occasions', with any important deviation from it to be recorded in the school diary.[89] Discipline and order were to be maintained in the school, and the children themselves were required by the official regulations 'to be respectful and obedient to all those entrusted with their management and training'.[90] Running a reformatory school for almost 70 years, the Sisters of Our Lady of Charity had already provided literary instruction and industrial training, religious and moral formation at St Joseph's, and structured the day to fit in with the many demands of that state system, so this was nothing new. The business of St Joseph's Industrial school, as summarised in the community circular letter for 1935, was written up in compliance with these regulations:

> We keep the children until they are 16 years of age, and give them a thorough religious, secular, and domestic education.

86  'Rules and Regulations for the Certified Industrial Schools in Ireland, approved by the Minister for Education under the 54th Section of the Act, 8 Edw. VII, Ch. 67', signed by Elizabeth Byrne and J. M. O'Sullivan, 14 Feb. 1927; 'Rules and Regulations for the Certified Industrial Schools in Saorstát Eireann, approved by the Minister for Education under the 54th Section of the Act, 8 Edw. VII, Ch. 67', signed by Agnes McVeagh and T. Ó Deirg, 4 Feb. 1933 (DARGS, SJ/4/1/1/ no. 3).
87  Regulation no. 10, Rules and regulations, 1933.
88  Regulation no. 11, Rules and regulations, 1933.
89  Regulation no. 20, Rules and regulations, 1933.
90  Regulation no. 27, Rules and regulations, 1933.

> When they leave us they are fully trained and in a position to
> gain a good livelihood as domestic servants.[91]

True to its origins in the mid-19th century juvenile reform movement, a substantial portion of the day was to be spent in industrial work or manual labour. The regulations the sisters signed up to stated that, excluding only those of 'tender years', no less than six hours per day were to be spent in industrial employment. The balance between industrial and literary training for both boys and girls was revised in the 1933 regulations, where industrial training was not to exceed three and a half hours daily for juniors (under 14) and not to exceed six hours per day for seniors (over 14).[92] The time allotted for literary instruction and study was to be not less than four and a half hours per day (under 14 years) and three hours per day (over 14 years), on weekdays, at least two-thirds of that time to be between breakfast and dinner, 'when the most beneficial results are likely to be obtained'. Religious education could be counted in the hours devoted to literary instruction, 'and in the case of seniors, reasonable time may be allotted to approved general reading'.[93]

The industrial employment of girls – listed as needlework, laundry work, cooking and housework in 1927 – was rephrased in 1933 as training 'in accordance with the Domestic Economy syllabus', that is the syllabus prepared by the Department of Education for use in national schools. The girls were to be taught also, where practicable, 'the milking of cows, dairy husbandry and the management of pigs, poultry and bees, as well as cottage gardening', revised downwards in 1933 to 'the milking of cows, care of poultry and cottage gardening'.[94] An up-to-date list of the occupations making up the 'industrial training' of the children and the qualifications of the instructors had to be submitted to the Department of Education.[95] Despite the expectation that girls would be trained to do farm and other outdoor work, the sisters in Whitehall were to restrict their ambitions for 'industrial training' to instruction in cookery, housewifery, laundering and needlework.[96]

The March 1933 timetable approved for St Joseph's adhered tightly to the spirit and letter of the regulations (figure 5.5), with very early rising followed by prayer, Mass, make beds and eat breakfast. All spaces in the day were filled, with 'household duties', class, needlework, meals, recreation, studies and drill, 'dressing room' and prayers. The seniors spent most of Monday morning and Tuesday afternoon each week in the school laundry, and the afternoons of Wednesday and Friday in 'cookery work'. The timetable for Saturdays differed in that the morning was taken up with confession, household duties and baths; the afternoon was divided between music, 'duties and

91   High Park, circular letter, 15 Aug. 1935, p. 18 (DARGS, OLC1/3/1 no. 27).
92   Regulation no. 9, Rules and regulations signed 14 Feb. 1927, also Rules and
regulations, 1933.
93   Regulation no. 7, Rules and regulations, 1933.
94   Ibid.
95   Regulation no. 9, Rules and regulations, 1933.
96   Report for 1954, Scoil Saothair Whitehall, 31 Iúil 1954 (DARGS, SJ/1/4/1/5).
Hereafter, Report for 1954.

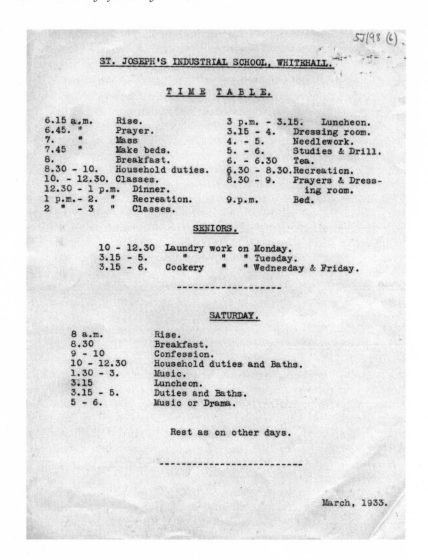

SJ/98 (6)

**ST. JOSEPH'S INDUSTRIAL SCHOOL, WHITEHALL.**

**T I M E   T A B L E.**

| | | | | |
|---|---|---|---|---|
| 6.15 a.m. | Rise. | 3 p.m. - 3.15. | Luncheon. |
| 6.45. " | Prayer. | 3.15 - 4. | Dressing room. |
| 7. " | Mass | 4. - 5. | Needlework. |
| 7.45 " | Make beds. | 5. - 6. | Studies & Drill. |
| 8. | Breakfast. | 6. - 6.30 | Tea. |
| 8.30 - 10. | Household duties. | 6.30 - 8.30. | Recreation. |
| 10. - 12.30. | Classes. | 8.30 - 9. | Prayers & Dress- |
| 12.30 - 1 p.m. | Dinner. | | ing room. |
| 1 p.m.- 2. " | Recreation. | 9.p.m. | Bed. |
| 2 " - 3 " | Classes. | | |

**SENIORS.**

10 - 12.30   Laundry work on Monday.
3.15 - 5.        "        "    " Tuesday.
3.15 - 6.   Cookery   "    " Wednesday & Friday.

--------------------

**SATURDAY.**

8 a.m.          Rise.
8.30            Breakfast.
9 - 10          Confession.
10 - 12.30      Household duties and Baths.
1.30 - 3.       Music.
3.15            Luncheon.
3.15 - 5.       Duties and Baths.
5 - 6.          Music or Drama.

Rest as on other days.

--------------------

March, 1933.

**Figure 5.5** School timetable, St Joseph's, Whitehall, March 1933. (DARGS, SJ/4/1/1 no. 3)

baths' and drama.[97] Times of rising and retiring were a little easier by 1940, but a very early start was still made by all. No child was expected to rise before 8.30am on Saturdays, and on Sundays, holydays and, during the holiday periods, it was 8am.[98] Silence (as reported in 1940) was imposed in the dormitories, 'to ensure speed and order in the mornings; order and rest at

97   St Joseph's Industrial School, Whitehall, Timetable, Mar. 1933 (DARGS, SJ/4/1/1 no. 3).
98   Draft of letter, Manager to the Inspector of Industrial Schools, 30 May, 4 June 1940 (DARGS, SJ/4/1/1 no. 15).

night' and also at breakfast and teatime, 'to facilitate the supervision of table manners'.[99] Asked to list the disciplines imposed in 1954, under the heading, 'Methods used to train character', the school principal maintained that the overall approach, 'based on Christian principles', was kindness and charity, using prizes and rewards ('naughty girls are sometimes deprived of this'). When necessary, 'senior girls are deprived of privileges, forfeit recreation, slapped with cane, kept apart from companions, and in extreme cases deprived of lunch or supper'. There were no abscondings or 'special difficulties' that merited mention.[100] The maintenance of discipline was vested in the school manager under the Children Act 1908. That corporal punishment was widely used in Irish schools in the 1960s is well documented.[101] It was not banned until 1982, so that it is not surprising to find caning still among the punishments listed in 1954.[102] The removal of regulation no. 11, titled 'A spirit of industry to be cherished', is the only major deletion in 1933 from the pre-existing rules. This regulation stated that 'the manager shall see that the children are constantly employed, and that they are taught to consider labour as a duty, to take kindly to it, to persevere in it, and to feel a pride in their work'.[103] There were many good reasons for its deletion – aside from the impossibility of fulfilling it – but the underlying philosophy, that the child ought to be kept constantly occupied under supervision and within a tightly regimented day, according to a written timetable, was embedded in the system. Games were to be encouraged (from 1933), both indoor and outdoor, and the required equipment to be provided, but all closely supervised, to ensure that all children take part.[104] The school manager made sure the department knew that, during 1938/9, 'we have devoted all the spare time to Swedish and Keep Fit exercises, under the guidance of Miss Medlar of the Medlar School of Drill and Dancing'.[105]

One significant part of the life of St Joseph's that was not covered by the 1933 revision of the rules and regulations for industrial schools (or by any earlier version), nor by the Children Act 1908 (or its amendments) was the nursery. Infants and toddlers, brought before the District Court for the same reasons as older children (begging, wandering, unsupervised), were committed to Whitehall from 1927. Very young children were frequently brought to St Joseph's at the end of the court sitting to be kept overnight before they began the long journey to the industrial school down the country to which they had been committed. Among the remand cases, which were for two or three days only, there were infants and toddlers also. This added to the difficulties faced by the nursery, as these children must have been upset by the

99  M.R. Whelan, Department of Education, to the Manager, Whitehall Industrial School, 19 June 1940; Manager to the Inspector of Industrial Schools, 24 June 1940 (DARGS, SJ/4/1/1 no. 16).
100  'Methods used to train character', Report for 1954.
101  Diarmaid Ferriter, *The transformation of Ireland 1900–2000* (London, 2004), pp 588–9.
102  Children Act 1908, section 54; Department of Education, Primary Branch, R.R. 144329, Circular 9/82, copy provided by Marion Rogan N.T.
103  Regulation no. 11, Rules and regulations signed 14 Feb. 1927.
104  Regulation no. 14, Rules and regulations, 1933.
105  Memo, 8 Jan. 1940, 'Reply to inquiry as to the number of fire drills held in the year 1938/9' (DARGS, SJ/4/1/1 no. 8).

unfamiliarity of all that surrounded them and the presence of strangers.[106] The Department of Education does not appear to concern itself much with these very young children until they reach national school age, that is six years, from which birthday the state first paid the industrial school capitation grant. But they were nevertheless a very real part of St Joseph's from 1927 onwards, with 13 children aged under six years in the nursery in 1954.[107] One of the few references to nursery care is from the obituary for Sister Mary of Blessed Oliver Plunkett O'Neill (Margaret), who was given charge of the babies on the opening of the industrial school, 'Often she was to be seen with a baby in her arms, in true motherly fashion'. Her skills as a nurse are extolled and the 'splendid order' in which she kept the children's wardrobes and dormitories, giving special attention to the 'personal cleanliness of the children'. On Christmas morning 1939, as was customary according to the obituarist, 'she visited the dormitories dressed as Santa Claus, and distributed gifts to all the children', and on St Stephen's day (visiting day), 'as she passed in and out of the room where the children had their friends, she had a cheery word for all.'[108] She died unexpectedly, aged 39 years, of pneumonia on 28 December 1939, hence the Christmas focus in her obituary. But it does give at least a glimpse of the nursery work that is otherwise passed over.

## The Commission of Inquiry into the Reformatory and Industrial School System 1934–36 and its Concerns

In the early 1930s, public and political concern with the operation of the reformatory and industrial school system is evident from the more active engagement of the Department of Education. The sisters running St Joseph's reported that the system of inspection had become 'more intense and demanding' than previously, and numerous reminders and questionnaires were circulated to the schools in the name of the minister.[109] This concern culminated in the appointment in May 1934 of the Commission of Inquiry into the Reformatory and Industrial School System in Saorstát Éireann under the chairmanship of Justice Cussen, Dublin District Court; its report was signed off on 17 August 1936. In the first of its 51 recommendations, the commission strongly endorsed the continuation of the industrial and reformatory school system, subject to a number of modifications. It also recommended that the schools should remain under the management of the religious orders, which had already undertaken the work. Most of the commission's key concerns with the industrial schools had already been articulated in circulars and data-collection exercises undertaken by the Department of Education. Progress in, or obstacles to, the implementation of its recommendations can be tracked in its correspondence with the school managers and with the association that represented their interests, the Association of Resident Managers of Industrial and Reformatory Schools. That so little notice was taken of its

106   Draft of letter, Resident Manager to Departments of Education and Justice, 23 Feb. 1952 (DARGS, SJ/4/3).
107   Report for 1954.
108   Death letter of Sister M. of Blessed Oliver Plunkett O'Neill (Margaret), d. 28 Dec. 1939 (DARGS, OLC1/6/4).
109   High Park, circular letter, 15 Aug. 1935, p. 18.

recommendations is evident from the complaints of a Mrs M. Macauley of the Adoption Board in 1955, and she was by no means the only well-informed and independent observer to express frustration with the response to Cussen.[110]

Out of a total of 52 industrial schools then in operation, the Cussen commission undertook formal visits to nine. St Joseph's, Whitehall, was probably the first to be visited, as its inspection was carried out on 4 June 1934.[111] It can be identified for certain in some of the points made in the final report, particularly in relation to the standard of spoken Irish and the acting of Irish plays.[112] A brief contemporaneous account of the visit picks up quite perceptively on matters that would feature in the commission's final report:

> The whole school building was left absolutely at their disposal. The time table was followed and the literary classes were in progress. Everything was examined, the routine of the day closely questioned, the food, clothing, beds and mattresses etc., our arrangements with doctors, dentists and oculists, was it by contract? The fees paid, the after care of children discharged, the 'mental deficient' was most exactly questioned, visiting days, letters written and received, the recreations, outings etc. A very extensive questionnaire was sent a few days later on, concerning recreation grounds, play fields, library, fire drill, and many other matters.[113]

The commission's review of statistics across all industrial schools in the five years 1930–34 inclusive revealed that on average, 89% of children were there due to 'poverty and neglect', 5% were there for 'serious offences' and 6% for failure to attend school.[114] The vast majority were there for no fault of their own and therefore merited at least as good attention as – if not better than – what was on offer in the ordinary national school. The commission was anxious that the full school day be devoted to literary subjects, with occupational training for children from 12–14 years to be on Saturdays, or otherwise outside the ordinary hours of instruction. Payments for children retained in the school to complete a course of study or training (to 17) were proposed. The extension of home leave, the nurturing of family links and more contact with the outside world generally were urged, along with better aftercare or post-discharge supervision. A more varied and suitable diet

110   Mrs M. Macauley, 'Our children', *Christus Rex,* ix, no. 2 (1955), pp 126–33.
111   The visitors consisted of the chairman Justice Cussen, Fr John Flanagan (parish priest of Fairview, who died before the report was published); Dr P. MacCarville, Mr O'Tierney head inspector, Senator Mrs Clarke, Mrs Mary E. Hackett, Doctor (Miss) M.M. O'Leary, and the secretary, Mr W.F. Walshe, clerk of the Industrial Schools' Office. The school manager stated the other commission member present was either Mr Hanna, Principal Officer, Department of Finance, or Mr Seamus O'Farrell of Raheny House. Incidental school register, St Joseph's Industrial School, 1889–1966, also loose memo.
112   Cussen report, para. 96.
113   Incidental school register, St Joseph's Industrial School, 1889–1966.
114   Cussen report, para. 25.

was recommended, as was more care to be taken with safety. The medical examination of children before committal, fuller and more systematic medical care while in the schools and the extension of medical inspection to cover the premises generally were promoted by the Cussen commission, as was the better provision of bathrooms and recreation spaces, both indoor and outdoor. The industrial school setting was held up by the commission as entirely unsuited to children with special learning needs (what it termed 'mental defectives'), but more suitable schools or homes would first need to be certified in the same way as the industrial schools, so that they could be paid state and local authority grants.[115] The reduction of school size to 200 pupils (with 250 pupils the maximum) was urged, and the break-up of Artane boys' school into separate units was strongly recommended, its exceptional size placing it in a class of its own (certified for 800 boys, average number 700). The significant proposal that the appointment of managers be made subject to the approval of the Minister for Education was abandoned, due to the implacable opposition of the Industrial School Managers' Association.[116] Nor was Artane broken up into smaller, manageable units, as urged by Justice Cussen. But agreement among managers with the majority of the recommendations was carefully noted by the department and most eventually found their way into the system, either through changes in the regulations or, where necessary, through legislative change.[117]

## St Joseph's, Whitehall, as a National School, 1941–55

The standard of teaching and learning, the qualifications of teachers and their conditions of pay and service, and whether or not Irish should be a required subject as it was in national schools, was a central concern of the Cussen commission. Under the regulations of 1933, the national school programme was to be followed in all industrial schools, and the manager could arrange, if he or she wished, for the children to attend a local national, continuation, secondary or technical school, on condition that no increased cost was incurred by the state.[118] In its deliberations, the Cussen commission had access to the reports of the inspectors of national schools on the primary education given in the industrial and reformatory schools so, despite the limited number of their visits, the members did have a basis for their denunciation of the standards to be found in very many schools.[119]

That the standard of what was called the 'secular programme' was as good in St Joseph's as it was in other primary schools prior to its incorporation as a national school (in 1941) may be judged from its success in a number of outside competitions. The school was awarded first prize in 1934 and 1935 in the drama section of the Dublin Feis, a concept which needed explaining to those outside Ireland: 'In ancient Ireland the Feis was as important a

---

115   Cussen report, para. 132.
116   Memorandum from the Industrial School Managers' Association meeting, Clery's, 10 Dec. 1940, concerning the Children Bill 1940 (DARGS, SJ/8/6).
117   Copy letter, Proinnsias Ó Dubhaigh, An Roinn Oideachais, to Revd Br T.M. Lennane, secretary, Industrial School Managers' Association, 29 Meitheamh 1937 (DARGS, SJ/4/1/4).
118   Regulation no. 8, Rules and regulations, 1933.
119   Cussen report, para. 93.

function as the Olympic Games were in Greece; its chief object in modern Ireland is the revival of Irish culture'. This was an open competition, against all the 'most efficient' primary schools in the country, 'but in spite of this our children had no difficulty in carrying off first prize', and repeatedly. Individual children were also entered for different competitions, and some won prizes, most frequently in poetry recitation and conversation. The report for 1935 recalls the praise of the adjudicators for the prize-winners, their school and their teacher, Sister Mary of St Finbarr Dowling, who had also written the play; 'our little ones, though not from Irish-speaking districts, learn their native language without the least difficulty and speak it fluently'.[120]

The 'taking into connection with the national school system' of industrial schools throughout the country was one of the tangible outcomes of the Cussen report and expressly designed to bring the second-rate teaching the commission found in many of the industrial schools closer to the national average. The intention of the Department of Education (Primary Branch) was to ensure that all teachers held recognised qualifications and were subject to inspection. 'Exceptional recognition' could be extended to teachers already teaching satisfactorily in the schools, but all persons proposed for appointment in the future would have to possess 'full qualifications as national teachers'.[121] The advantage to the industrial schools was that teachers now received salaries directly from the Department of Education (Primary Branch), at first through monies voted in the budget each year but, from 1 April 1946 onwards, the aid was to be received 'on the same basis as other National Schools', that is, on either a classification or a capitation basis, whichever option the school chose (St Joseph's chose to be paid on capitation).[122] The transition to full national school status meant that years of service were now recognised in the usual way (for a teacher's pension), though the schools were already subject to all the usual regulations of the department and to its inspection regime.

St Joseph's was 'taken into connection' in 1941, with the first salaries paid from 30 June 1941.[123] The first Primary Certificate group was entered in 1943; only one child passed all three subjects – Irish, maths and English – but each of the other children passed in one or two subjects, and the pass rate did improve, though not always year on year. Of the eight children taking the Primary Certificate in 1953, seven passed in all three subjects, with the other child failing Irish.[124] The school followed the usual national school timetable and programme in the morning and early afternoon. It fulfilled its legislative obligation to provide industrial training – which had not been revoked – by running domestic economy classes in the afternoon for different groups of girls, Monday to Saturday inclusive, as communicated to the primary schools branch of the Department of Education in 1943 by Mrs Margaret Burke

120 High Park, circular letter, 15 Aug. 1935, p. 18.
121 Department of Education (Primary Branch) to Sister M. Anna Jennings, re Whitehall Industrial School, 14 July 1942 (DARGS, OLC 1/3/8 no. 1).
122 'Vote for Primary Education to Reformatory and Industrial Schools', P. Ó Muirieartaigh, circular letter, 6 Mar. 1946 (DARGS, SJ/4/1/2 no. 3).
123 'Salaries' is entered as paid from 30 June 1941, Leabhar tuaraimí an chigire (DARGS, SJ/8/2 no. 3).
124 Primary Certificate examination results, 1943–54 excluding 1950, 1952 (DARGS, SJ/8/3 no. 2).

(Mother Mary of St Ignatius).[125] The report for 1954 refers to four 15-year-olds and one 16-year-old, 'doing complete domestic course and receiving further instruction in Christian Doctrine and English Literature', with four prizes recently obtained in the Gas Company cookery competition.[126] The tutor by then was Sister Mary of St Francis Thérèse Blackmore, who had trained as a home economics teacher before joining the community in 1933.

A very full religious education programme was implemented, with reports of the diocesan examiners repeatedly awarding the school a 'pass with merit' and full marks for the singing of sacred music.[127] Preparation for the sacraments of First Communion and confirmation was given pride of place. The spiritual association, the Apostleship of Prayer, was seen as a means of enlivening the faith among sisters, women, children and past pupils alike, with a new register started for the school in January 1941.[128] The Sodality of Our Lady, with junior and senior sections, was a vehicle for moral and religious instruction. It became the single most important means through which contact was kept with past pupils, whether on licence or discharged, throughout the 1940s and 1950s.

At the first inspection held on 23 November 1942, with which the report book (Leabhar tuaraimí an chigire) opens, there were three teachers on the staff: the principal, Sister Mary of St Finbarr Dowling (Charlotte, born 1881), who taught the senior girls, from 5th to 8th class inclusive (28 girls); Sister Mary of St Aloysius Pilkington (Sara, born 1911), who came on the staff in 1935, taught a middle group (4th class, 20 girls), while the remainder, from 3rd class down to junior infants (38 children) were taught by a newly-appointed assistant teacher, Miss Síle Ní Siochtháin, aged 22, who held her teaching qualification from Limerick (1940–42).[129] At the first inspection (mórfhiosrú) for Iníon Ní Siochtháin, her work was commended ('tá obair chreidiúnach ag déanamh ag an oide seo'), with some points of advice, such as to give more time to penmanship. At the Mórfhiosrú of the two experienced teachers, held 29 and 30 March 1943, the solid foundation these teachers were giving the children, and their personal zeal and devotion, was commended: 'Tá díbhirce agus dúthracht ag baint le saothar na múinteoirí seo agus tús maith déanta ar ghnáth-chlár na mbunscolatha'. Sister Finbarr was a graduate of the model training school in Marlborough Street (1903–5, diploma 1909). There are no formal qualifications after the name of Sister Aloysius and she was most likely recognised by the department as a junior assistant mistress, a term that belied her many years' experience.

125    Labhras Ó Muirthe, leas-rúnaithe, an Roinn Oideachais, to Mrs Margaret Burke, Whitehall Industrial National School, 27 Feb. 1943 and 2 Mar. 1943 (DARGS, SJ/4/1/5).
126    General council of the Federation, Minutes, 22 June 1955 (DARGS, OLC5/5/1 no. 1). Sister Frances Thérèse Blackmore (Margaret), born 17 May 1911, entered 2 Oct. 1933, received 11 Apr. 1934, professed 25 Apr. 1936, d. 27 July 1999 (DARGS, OLC1/6/3–5).
127    High Park, circular letter, 15 Aug. 1935, p. 18.
128    'Register, Apostleship of Prayer, list of members', midway, 'St Joseph's Industrial School, Whitehall', Jan. 1941, Feb. 1944, Jan. 1947, June 1956, Apr. 1960, Aug. 1962 (6pp); near end of book, 'Past Pupils, St Joseph's Industrial School', June 1941, Aug. 1941, Feb. 1944, 1947, Nov. 1952, 1956 (DARGS, OLC1/7/6 no. 9).
129    Leabhar tuaraimí an chigire (DARGS, SJ/8/2 no. 3). The spellings Sighle and Siothcán are also used.

Different inspectors continued to praise the teaching standard in the school – 'an obair ag gabháil ina cinn go sásamhail' – and to give advice on points of the curriculum and teaching methods, right up to the final inspection on 18 January 1956.

The confidential reports on each of the five teachers on the staff for various periods between 1942–51 are unremittingly positive.[130] In September of 1950, Sister Teresa Coughlan arrived on the staff following the two-year training programme in Carysfort college (1948–50); she replaced Sister Finbarr Dowling from September 1950 to September 1953 and, like all newly-qualified national school teachers, her classroom work was inspected on two occasions before she was awarded her final diploma.[131] All the teachers here, whether experienced or newly-qualified, faced the same 'adverse circumstances', namely the lack of early schooling among some of the children – a deficit, the inspector maintained, that would be difficult, if not impossible, to make up. In the Mór Thuairisc of 1951, the work of the school as a whole was deemed satisfactory, 'sásúil', and the improvement in manners and general deportment of the children was singled out for praise. The teaching of all subjects was good, but music and handiwork were deemed very good. The quality of penmanship was excellent, more care could be taken with spelling, oral command of Irish was outstanding ('Sí an Ghaeilge an ghnath-theanga scoile') but was not quite matched by the written Irish, where care was needed with grammar.[132] The obituary for Sister Mary of St Finbarr Dowling in 1953 refers to her family background as an active member of the Gaelic League and to her published poems and plays in Irish for children, 'greatly admired for their simplicity and poetry'. She communicated with the Department of Education in fluent Irish on the most difficult, technical issues and there can be no doubting her role in making possible the demonstrably high standard of Irish at the school throughout the 1930s and 1940s.[133] An early play was *An tobar naofa, dráma beaga chun na leanbh* (1925); a book of games was titled *Fá bhrat Bhrighde* (1940). A copyright agreement for *Caisleáin Ordha* was drawn up in 1940 and there are notes of royalty payments, though few outsiders were likely to make the connection between the author, Searlot Ní Dhúnlaing, and Sister Finbarr of High Park.[134] When sanction was granted in 1954 to transfer the children to the girls' and infants' national schools at Larkhill (Scoileanna an Leinbh Íosa, Cailíní agus Naíonáin), ending the period of St Joseph's as a national school, there was no reason to worry about whether or not the children would be able to hold their own with their peers.[135]

130 Staff reports, 1941–51 (DARGS, SJ/8/5).

131 Sister Teresa Coughlan OLC had to resign from teaching in Sept. 1953 due to lung trouble. Personal communication, 4 Mar. 2014.

132 Staff reports, 1941–51 (DARGS, SJ/8/5).

133 Death letter of Sister M. of St Finbarr Dowling (Charlotte), d. 31 Aug. 1953, aged 72 years (DARGS, OLC 1/6/4).

134 Department of Education to High Park, relating to the 'royalties on certain books by the late Sister Mary of St Finbarr [Searlot Ní Dhúnlaing] published by the Department of Education', correspondence dated 1940–53 (DARGS, OLC1/6/5 no. 7).

135 [Illegible signature], Department of Education, to Sister M. of St Eithne O'Neill, High Park Convent, 10 Aibreán 1954 (DARGS, SJ/4/1/5).

## Home or Holiday Leave, Post-1934

The issues of home leave and more family contact generally were tackled by the Department of Education while the work of the Commission of Inquiry into the Reformatory and Industrial School System was still in train. In response to a query about visiting, St Joseph's school manager responded that 'All bank holidays are the appointed visiting days. When parents or relatives come at other times, as very frequently happens, they are always allowed to see the children.' As a city school, with 'the great majority' of children from Dublin, the manager continued, letter writing was confined to Christmas and Easter and other times when necessary, with children always receiving any letters sent to them.[136] No register was kept of visits from family or friends, so it is impossible to know exactly who had visitors and how often, but that visiting was an established part of the routine, for some at least of the children, can be inferred from asides in other documents.[137] The issue of home leave can be established with greater authority, as the school had to submit names, numbers and dates to the department on a quarterly basis.

Under the regulations of 1933, the privilege of holiday – or home – leave of no longer than seven days annually was limited to 'well conducted children' who had already completed at least one year in detention. It was subject to the approval of the inspector, 'and provided the home conditions are found on investigation to be satisfactory'.[138] Under the revised regulation announced in August 1934, home leave could be offered to children who had completed three months' detention, at the discretion and on the responsibility of the manager, with the approval of the inspector.[139] The department hoped this would greatly increase the number of children benefiting from a holiday at home. The attraction to the school was that the state maintenance grant would not be cut for the duration of the holiday leave – unlike, for example, a spell in hospital, when the grant would be stopped immediately for whatever number of days was involved.[140] The loosening of the rules in 1934 did indeed increase the uptake of home leave in the case in St Joseph's. From two or three children on leave in the early 1930s, there were 36 home leaves out of a school population of 78 in detention in 1935, the first year of operation. The recommendation of the Cussen commission that annual home leave be increased from 14 to 21 days was put into force by a circular of May 1937. It was strongly endorsed by the Department of Education,

---

136　Manager, St Joseph's Industrial School to W.F. Walshe, Industrial Schools Office, 30 May 1934 (DARGS, SJ/4/1/4).

137　For example, see death letter of Sister M. of Blessed Oliver Plunkett O'Neill; draft of letter, Manager, St Joseph's Industrial School, Whitehall, to the Minister for Education, Hume Street, 8 Mar. 1939 (DARGS, SJ/4/1/5).

138　Regulation no. 15, Rules and regulations, 1933.

139　M.R. Whelan, Department of Education, to Whitehall Industrial School, 7 Dec. 1934 (DARGS, SJ/4/1/1 no. 11). A memo to this effect was pasted into the incidental school register (DARGS, SJ/8/1 no. 5).

140　The school paid the extern hospital per day out of the capitation grant and was obliged to return any excess to the Department of Finance in 1932, but in later years it appears that the hospitals had the state and local grants paid directly to them. Whichever arrangement was in place, no child was paid for in two institutions simultaneously. M.R. Whelan to the Manager, Whitehall Industrial School, 17 Feb. 1932 (DARGS, SJ/4/1/2 no. 2).

which directed the schools to ensure that parents and guardians were made aware of the home leave privilege. It expressed the view that the schools should provide holiday facilities for those children with no suitable home or relatives, 'in view of the undoubted benefits of a holiday for such children'.[141]

The commitment of the Department of Education to home leave, and the slowness of the industrial schools generally to take full advantage of the latitude offered under the revised regulation, is evident in the circulars issued 1942–54. Managers were urged to take steps to keep the home leave scheme in operation, despite war-time fuel shortages, 'for the benefit of the children and in furtherance of the family contacts which the scheme is intended to establish and maintain'.[142] In 1944, a robustly-worded circular insisted that the minister was in full sympathy with the 'strong public feeling' that had grown in recent years, 'that committal to an industrial school should not be allowed to sever a child's family ties, except in cases where they would exert a definitely bad influence'. It said that children should be placed in schools near their homes 'so as to allow of frequent visits by their parents and relations', and that all children should have a holiday at home at least once a year. The full holiday was to be allowed to all children 'unless the parents' or relatives' character and environment are known to be unsatisfactory'. Dublin children detained in country schools were the minister's particular concern and, so that no child would be deprived of a holiday at home solely because his or her family could not afford the fare, the department would refund any excess spent by the school on return bus or train fares over the state grant for the child for the holiday period.[143] Representations made to the minister by poor parents in the early summer of 1944 that they could not afford the fares involved made it obvious that some, at least, of the 'country schools' were not co-operating with the scheme. In a reply to the department, the manager of St Joseph's stated, in the language of the circular just received, that it was co-operating in full with the minister 'in doing all in our power to ensure holidays at home for the children where such holidays would not be prejudicial with the children's welfare'.[144] Long distance travel was not an issue for St Joseph's, as the vast majority of the children came via the Dublin Metropolitan Court and had home addresses, if any, in the greater Dublin area. What limited the home leave from St Joseph's, according to the manager, was the fact that so many had no home to go to. Responding to a circular criticising the numbers on home leave in 1944, when only 16 of the total 76 in St Joseph's went on home leave (21%), the manager responded that 46 children (57%) had no homes to go to, a further 14 had parents of 'criminal habits' or the mother was dead, and there were three parents too poor to take the children.[145] In the latter cases, the fare home was not the issue. Another exhortation was issued in June 1945, urging that 'every child for whom suitable

141    Cussen report, para. 77; M.R. Whelan, Department of Education to Whitehall Industrial School, 6 May 1937 (DARGS, SJ/4/1/1 no. 11).
142    F. Mac Lochlainn, cigire, Department of Education, to Whitehall Industrial School, 6 July 1942 (DARGS, SJ/4/1/1 no. 11).
143    P. Ó Muirieartaigh, cigire, An Roinn Oideachais, to Scoil Saothair Fionnbhrúigh, 17 Meitheamh 1944 (DARGS, SJ/4/1/1 no. 11).
144    Draft of reply, 12 July 1944, appended to circular of 8 Iúil 1944 (DARGS, SJ/4/1/1 no. 11).
145    Draft of reply, 24 Nov. 1944, appended to circular, P. Ó Muirieartaigh, cigire, An Roinn Oideachais to Scoil Saothair Sheosamh Naomhtha, 18 Samhain 1944 (DARGS, SJ/4/1/1 no. 11).

arrangements can be made' would be allowed home for the full holiday period of three weeks which, from the summer of 1948, could be extended to a full calendar month (31 days, not necessarily all together).[146] Repeated also was the expectation that those children not granted home leave might be provided with 'holiday camps, outings, picnics, trips to seaside etc.'[147] St Joseph's 'holiday arrangements exclusive of home leave' were listed a few years later as 'excursions to seaside in summer', and in winter 'outings to pantomime, their own concerts and Xmas tree party'.[148] But lest the legal restrictions of the system be overlooked, the importance of issuing supervision certificates in respect of every child going on holiday outside the school was repeatedly stressed:

> On a child's failure to return by the stipulated time the certificate will have been forfeited by breach of the condition and the absentee could then be arrested without warrant under Section 67 Children's Act 1908, as amended by Section 13, Children Act, 1941.[149]

There was nothing spontaneous or open-ended about home leave; it was planned for and closely regulated, built on – rather than undermining – the 19th-century foundations of the system.

The numbers going on home leave from St Joseph's in the later 1940s increased to almost 40% of the total number in detention. Under the inspector's close scrutiny, a good reason would have to be given, in writing, to block a child with family from spending the summer holiday with them. The figures submitted by each school were subject to comparative analysis, all of the books were open to inspection and there was certainly pressure from the inspectorate, which quoted the minister, the Dáil, social workers and 'public opinion' in favour of extending home leave to the greatest possible extent. Nevertheless, St Joseph's school manager of the time thought lengthy home leave had its drawbacks, as is evident from an internal response to a 1949 proposal to increase home leave to six weeks. After 21 days, she maintained, the children return 'run down in health and in a good many cases disimproved in conduct' and she could see no advantage, for most, in doubling the length of time they were outside the school.[150]

## Diet, Safety, Medical Care and the Issue of Funding

The breadth of the Cussen inquiry and the wide range of issues at least touched on in the final report is reflected in the diverse nature of the follow-up. Requests were sent out to the schools 'for inspection and record purposes' for

146  M. Ó Siochfhradha, cigire, An Roinn Oideachais, to an Bainisteoir Comhnuitheach, Scoil Saothair Fionnbhruigh, 7 Meitheamh 1945 (DARGS, SJ/4/1/1 no. 11)
147  M. Ó Siochfhradha, cigire, Department of Education, to the Resident Manager, Whitehall Industrial School, 23 Meitheamh 1948 (DARGS, SJ/4/1/1 no. 11)
148  Report for 1954.
149  M. Ó Siochfhradha, cigire, Department of Education, to the Resident Manager, Whitehall Industrial School, 21 Apr. 1950 (DARGS, SJ/4/1/1 no. 11)
150  Draft of reply, 7 May 1949, appended to circular, J. J. Kelly, Association of Managers of Industrial Schools, to Revd Manager, 2 May 1949 (DARGS, SJ/4/1/1 no. 11).

copies of the current 'dietary' (regulation 6) and the timetable (regulation 20). Recommendations for improvement in the diet were returned to each school in a standard format. Whitehall industrial school was told to increase the milk allowance per child from ¾ pint of milk to 1 pint per day but otherwise the daily menu or diet (figure 5.6) was approved.[151] Great stress was laid on health and safety throughout the 1930s and 1940s. Orders to see that there were 'effective safeguards' to banisters on landings and staircases were issued, and that open fires and other dangers were properly fenced off. The frequent and systematic practice of fire drill was demanded (in accordance with regulation 14) in 1933 and again in 1941.[152] The fire at St Joseph's orphanage, Cavan, in February 1943, in which 35 children and an elderly woman died, increased the pressure on school authorities to see to the safety of residents, with a fire survey of all premises ordered by the Minister for Local Government and Public Health in February 1944.[153] The outbreak of fire in an unnamed industrial school later that month, though it did not result in loss of life, coming so soon after the Cavan tragedy, was used by the department to underscore 'the grave responsibility' resting on each manager to ensure there was no fire through negligence, and the need for unremitting vigilance.[154]

The 'Emergency' of 1939–45 brought additional and very real safety concerns; air raid precautions were issued to the schools, along with notes on elementary fire fighting.[155] Nobody could predict how long the war would last and its outcome was far from certain. The schools were given orders in June 1940 to stockpile 'essential commodities', namely fuel, flour, tea, sugar, medical and surgical supplies.[156] In March 1941, they were told to use turf instead of coal or, if not, to explain why this was not feasible.[157] In February 1943, they were given orders relating to the conservation of fuel[158] and the disposal of waste paper.[159]

Perhaps the greatest shift post-Cussen, and not requiring a change in legislation or an increase to the maintenance grant, was the emphasis on each child's physical health. Schools had to submit the name of their medical doctor from 1938 and the fees paid to him or her. A female medical inspector,

151   M.R. Whelan to the Manager, Whitehall Industrial School, 14 Feb. 1940 (DARGS, SJ/4/1/5).

152   M. McNeill, Department of Education, query re fire drill, 27 Mar. 1933; V. F. Walsh, Irish Red Cross, 'Firefighting', circulated Oct. 1941 (DARGS, SJ/4/1/1 no. 8).

153   P. Ó Muirieartaigh, cigire, An Roinn Oideachais, to the Resident Manager, Whitehall Industrial School, 2 Feabhra 1944 (DARGS, SJ/4/1/1 no. 8).

154   P. Ó Muirieartaigh, cigire, An Roinn Oideachais, to An Bainisteoir Comhnuitheach, Scoil Saothair Fionnbrúgha, 28 Mar. 1944 (DARGS, SJ/4/1/1 no. 8).

155   Department of Defence/British Home Office, *The protection of your home against air raids* (Dublin, n.d.); *Air raid precautions, memorandum no. 17* (Dublin, 1941); Ministry of Home Security, *Air raids, what you must know, what you must do* (London, 1940) (DARGS, SJ/4/1/1 no. 14).

156   W.F. Walshe, Department of Education, to the Manager, Whitehall Industrial School, 27 June 1940 (DARGS, SJ/4/1/1 no. 18).

157   S. MacLochlainn, cigire, Department of Education, to the Manager of the Industrial School named in the address, 24 Mar. 1941 (DARGS, SJ/4/1/5).

158   Copy letter, J. Cassidy, Roinn Tionscail agus Trachtála, to the Secretary, Department of Education, 27 Feb. 1943 (DARGS, SJ/4/1/5).

159   Copy letter, Seán Ó Muimhneacháin, Department of Finance, to J. O'Neill, Department of Education, 23 Feabhra 1943 (DARGS, SJ/4/1/5).

SJ/182(2)

ST. JOSEPH'S INDUSTRIAL SCHOOL, WHITEHALL.

DIETARY TABLE - NOVEMBER, 1939.

**Breakfast** - Porridge, Bread (brown & white), Margarine, Tea (¼ pt.)

**Dinner** -

Sunday - Brown Soup, Sausages, Potatoes, Vegetables in season (i.e., Cabbage, Cauliflower, Spinach, Parsnip, Swede and White Turnip, French Beans, Peas, Lettuce, Vegetable Marrow).

Steamed Suet Pudding (Fig & Date), Sauce.

Monday - Irish Stew & Vegetable, Milk Pudding, varied when possible with additional stewed fruit, dried or fresh according to season.

Tuesday - Mutton Broth, Boiled Mutton, Potatoes, Vegetables,

Fruit & Custard Sauce.

Wednesday. Vegetable Soup, Roast Beef, Potatoes, Vegetables,

Milk Pudding.

Thursday- Soup, Brown Stew, Potatoes, Vegetables, Baked Bread Pudding.

Friday - Lentil Soup, Fish (Steamed Cod or Whiting) & White

Sauce; or Scrambled Egg; or Buttered Beans or Peas,

Mashed Potatoes & Milk Pudding.

Saturday- Soup, Shepherd's Pie, Milk Pudding.

Very young children's dinners, i.e., 2 years - 7 years,

Soup, Eggs, Mashed Potatoes, Vegetables, Milk

Pudding.

Home made Bread (Brown) 4 days per week.

**Lunch** -      Bread & Margarine.  Milk for small and delicate children - ¼ pt.

**Supper** -     Bread, Cocoa (½ pt.), Margarine or Dripping.

EXTRAS.

On special annual occasions, numbering about twenty, the following extras are allowed:- Fruit - Oranges & Apples (2 on average). Confectionery - 3 Pastries. Sweets. Jam. Cake. Plum Pudding.
Delicate children get Cod Liver Oil, Parishe's Food, Eggs, and other additional nourishment as recommended by the Medical Officer.

**Figure 5.6**  Set diet for schoolchildren, St Joseph's, Whitehall, November 1939. (DARGS, SJ/4/1/5)

Dr McCabe, was appointed 4 April 1939 to the industrial and reformatory schools section of the Department of Education. A full medical form had to be filled out at admission, including a medical history (where known), and a continuous record of the child's health was to be kept during his or her stay, with weight and height taken four times per year.[160] In reply to a request for the medical officer's name, present remuneration, general conditions of service and duties, the Whitehall school manager gave the name of Dr Edward Eustace, who – though he lived in Stillorgan – worked in a private hospital

160   Medical forms (DARGS, SJ, individual files).

close to High Park, and was the school's named medical officer from 1932. But having a resident doctor as a member of the community – Sister Mary of St Joseph Carton – 'Dr Eustace's services are only required for quarterly examination and for consultation'. His rate of pay in 1948 was £3 3s for each quarterly examination and 15s per consultation (unchanged from 1932).[161] All schools were asked to increase their payments in line with Medical Association of Éire recommendations in 1948, with which St Joseph's, and no doubt others also, complied.[162]

The difficulty of providing all that was asked of the schools within the tight constraints of the maintenance grant was the complaint of all managers before the Cussen inquiry – and even more so afterwards. The Industrial School Managers' Association highlighted the absence of any after-school grant to support the schools in fulfilling the supervision obligations placed on them by statute. It also sought the extension of the Schools Medical Service (of the local authorities) to the industrial schools, and made repeated – though unsuccessful – demands throughout the 1930s and 1940s for an increase in the basic grant.[163] The issue of funding, which the Cussen commission side-stepped (except to say that the schools were managed 'very economically'), was difficult for all sides.[164] The maintenance rates payable by the local authorities were raised in 1942: 5s per week for each child aged under six years, 7s 6d per week for six to 16 years and also 7s 6d for those children whose period of detention had been extended beyond 16 years under the Children Act 1941.[165] But the state grant was reduced, leaving the combined grant unaltered and the schools no better off. All the time the Department of Education did what it could to claw back any excess. Payment from parents of committed children (a minor item, if it featured at all), and payments from 'voluntary pupils' had to be reported.[166] A child returning to school, for example, after the first day of the quarter, after a period in hospital, would not be paid for in that quarter.[167]

An industrial or reformatory school could receive the state maintenance grant only for the number covered by the school certificate, which for Whitehall in 1927 was set at 50 girls, half the school's approved capacity of 100 girls. Children committed by the courts over its certified number were not paid for by the state, nor was there any state payment for children under the age of six years. The local authority portion, the other half of the maintenance grant,

161   M. Ó Siochfhradha, cigire, An Roinn Oideachais, to the Resident Manager, Industrial School, Whitehall, 1 Sept. 1948, notes in reply to same, 4 Sept. 1948, (DARGS, SJ/1/4/1/5).
162   P.J. Delaney, The Medical Association of Eire, to Dear Sir, 3 Nov. 1948 (DARGS, SJ/1/4/1/5).
163   Memorandum from the Industrial School Managers' Association meeting, Clery's, 10 Dec. 1940, concerning the Children Bill 1940 (DARGS, SJ/8/6). Department of Education, Reformatory and Industrial Schools Branch, Talbot House, Talbot Street, to An Bainisteoir Comhnuitheach, Scoil Saothair Fionnbhrugh, 2 Apr. 1946 (DARGS, SJ/4/1/2).
164   Cussen report, para 38.
165   Children Act 1941 (section 21) Regulations, 1942, para. 2 (a).
166   [Indecipherable signature], cigire, Department of Education, to Resident Manager, St Joseph's Industrial School, 24 May 1951 (DARGS, SJ/4/1/2 no. 7).
167   Department of Education, Industrial Schools Branch, to the Manager, St Joseph's Industrial School, 3 July 1936 (DARGS, SJ/4/1/2).

was paid for these classes of children, but the loss of the state grant (which was handled centrally and did not require the school to pursue each local authority) was a grievance that Cussen did nothing to address. Writing in 1939, the Whitehall school manager returned the number 'in excess' over the previous 12 years as averaging 23, for whom only the local authority capitation grant of 4s 6d (or, in a few cases, 5s per week) was received. Having been 'always been most generous in everything that regarded the children's welfare', the natural consequence was expenditure running ahead of income.[168] The reason the manager gave for the excess number was the willingness of the school to facilitate court officials and inspectors of the National Society for the Prevention of Cruelty to Children 'who do not, as a rule, like to send children where they cannot be conveniently visited by their relatives'. A case from the previous week was cited in support of this point, where the sisters obliged Inspector McGinn of the NSPCC who could find no vacancy in any other Dublin school and 'did not wish, if at all possible, to send the children where they could not be visited by their old father'. The school had the space and, in conscience, could not turn the girls away. 'The objection to our numbers being increased has been that the country schools have not got their numbers' was the manager's reading of the situation – and, in this, she was correct. The cap on numbers was to ensure the viability of the system throughout the country, a policy which had always had the effect of directing some children to schools far distant from home and making it nearly impossible for parents or other relatives to visit.[169] An increase of 20 in the certified number was sought; an increase of ten was allowed from 1 January 1940, and a further increase of ten from 1 April 1943, bringing the certified number up to 70, It was a satisfactory outcome from the school's perspective, considering that the Department of Education said 'no' to practically all requests that cost money.[170] A further endorsement of Whitehall's childcare record to date was its approval, in 1948, for 'public assistance cases', that is, children whose maintenance would be paid by the health board – the total of all children in the school still not to exceed 100.[171]

Payments for children sent on remand to Whitehall were always more straightforward. These came from the Garda Síochána section of the Department of Justice and can be tracked from the remand register. The rate of payment in 1910 was 1s per day; from 1 April 1948 it was 3s 6d per day, and from 1 April 1952 it was 7s per day. The eight-day rate was 7s 6d in 1918 but was almost doubled to 13s 6d in 1919. After independence, the eight-day rate was set at £1 1 6d (1923), but this was reduced to £1 in September 1926. A long-overdue increase came into force on 1 April 1952, when the rate was set at 7s per day.[172]

168    Draft of letter, Manager, St Joseph's Industrial School, Whitehall, to the Minister for Education, Hume Street, 8 Mar. 1939 (DARGS, SJ/4/1/5).
169    Ibid.
170    M.R. Whelan, Department of Education, to the Manager, St Joseph's Industrial School, 9 Oct. 1939 (DARGS, SJ/4/1/5); Inspections book.
171    Approved under section 47 of the Public Assistance Act 1939, N. Twohig, Department of Health, to An Bainisteoir, St Joseph's Industrial School, Deire Fomhair 1948 (DARGS, SJ/4/1/5).
172    Ó Siochfhradha to An Bainisteoir Comhnuitheach, 2 Aibreán 1946.

The failure of the industrial schools generally to engage with the world outside their own boundaries was raised by the Cussen inquiry, and followed up in due course by the Department of Education. Bound by their rule of enclosure, the Sisters of Our Lady of Charity were no doubt one of the groups against whom this charge could be fairly laid. A circular in June 1940 communicated the minister's wish that managers would provide 'all reasonable facilities for social intercourse outside the schools', with organised games with the children from local schools, 'and other suitable forms of social activities including shopping (especially for girls)' listed as means of giving the children 'confidence and experience'.[173] St Joseph's manager promptly replied that they fully concurred with the minister's wishes and were well ahead in promoting such contact 'as will be beneficial to the children', giving a summary of how the school was trying to meet this broader aim:

> To encourage a sense of responsibility, the senior girls are entrusted with the care of the younger ones who are extern patients of the hospitals. They take turns in conducting them there, and give and receiving messages from the nurses and doctors. The bigger girls shop, while young and old are allowed out to spend their pocket money in shops in the vicinity. The children also visit places of interest, i.e., the Museum, Botanic Gardens, Collinstown Aerodrome, etc., where they are given freedom to examine and ask questions of caretakers and those in charge. Suitable films are shown in the school about six times per year, depicting places and scenes of geographical, industrial and topics of current interest. Games such as baseball [basketball], cricket and camogie are played and encouraged in the school, and camogie matches are refereed by a member of the Camogie League.[174]

Changes to the legislation governing industrial schools post-Cussen were minimal, leaving the Children Act 1908 untouched in its essentials. Changes brought in under the Children Act 1941 dealt with the grounds for committal of children and young persons, rather than with the operation of the system itself. It raised the upper age limit for committal to an industrial school from 14 to 15, for committal to a reformatory school from 16 to 17 years. There were some shifts in language; the title 'resident manager' (section 5) was employed from 30 October 1942, and the term 'release on licence' to be superseded by 'release on supervision certificate' (sections 14 and 15).[175] The pivotal role of the resident manager was stressed; he or she was not merely an assistant, but was 'the person responsible for carrying out the duties of control and supervision of the school in all matters connected with

173  M. R. Whelan to the Manager, Whitehall Industrial School, 21 June 1940 (DARGS, SJ/4/1/1 no. 17).
174  Copy letter, Manager to the Inspector of Industrial Schools, 25 June 1940 (DARGS, SJ/4/1/1 no. 17).
175  S. MacLochlainn, cigire, Department of Education, to the Manager, Whitehall Industrial School, 1 July 1942 (DARGS, SJ/4/1/1 no. 20).

the Children Acts'.[176] (It was under section 12 of the Children Act 1941 that the period of detention could be extended to enable a child to complete a programme of education or training.)

## Grants for Building Improvements and Vocational Equipment, 1946

While there was no extra money in the 1940s for an increase in capitation, for the first time ever there were to be state grants for capital investment in physical, and therefore visible, improvements in industrial schools. After a process of consultation, a scheme was announced on 1 October 1946 whereby a building grant could be drawn down on the basis of the number of children in residence 'chargeable to the state grant'.[177] The urgent need for repairs, improvements and additions to many of the buildings used as certified schools had been acknowledged by Cussen and by the department, which also had files of letters protesting that the schools could not meet these costs without state assistance. Sanitary annexes, dormitories, bathrooms, play halls, classrooms 'and the necessary equipment for vocational training' were all listed as needing urgent investment.[178] The grants announced in October 1946 were not meant to cover the full cost of new building and improvements, but only a portion, 'not less than one-third to be carried by managers'. They could not be used for ordinary maintenance, painting and repairs, but were ring-fenced for new and substantial improvements that had been through a lengthy approval process. The grants were tightly controlled, with sanctions for failure to complete the approved work within the time agreed, and the repayment of grants should the premises no longer be used as an industrial school. The standards of accommodation for dormitory, refectory, classroom and playground were fixed by the Department of Education in consultation with the Department of Local Government and Public Health with, if desired, technical assistance from the Office of Public Works. The placing of contracts was the business of the school but was subject to the prior approval by the minister of the plans and estimates, with dire consequences (such as the discontinuation of payments to the school) should there be any deviation from what was agreed in advance.[179]

St Joseph's, Whitehall, participated in the new scheme, which required first the preparation of full building reports detailing the dimensions of each room and its light, ventilation and heating systems. The numbers accommodated in each dormitory and classroom were entered, and showed that the internal arrangements of 1946 were much as when the building was opened in 1874: the first floor dormitory accommodated 42 children, the second floor dormitory took 34 children and there was an infirmary for ten children, an isolation room for five children and a bedroom for the teacher. The babies' dormitory was one of the three areas into which the second floor was divided. There were three classrooms, the largest one doubling up as the indoor

176   Circular, An Roinn Oideachais, 4 Nov. 1942 (DARGS, SJ/4/1/1 no. 20).
177   M. Ó Siochfhradha, An Roinn Oideachais, to Br S. Ó Ceallaigh, Runaí, Cumann na mBainisteiori gComhnuitheach, 13 Nollaig 1945 (DARGS, SJ/4/1/2 no. 3).
178   M. Ó Siochfhradha, cigire, An Roinn Oideachais, to An Bainisteoir Comhnuitheach na scoile atá luaite i gclúdach na litre seo, 6 Meán Fomhair 1946 (DARGS, SJ/4/1/2 no. 3).
179   Building and equipment grants, instructions for the guidance of managers, enclosed with letter of M. Ó Siochfhradha, 6 Meán Fomhair 1946 (DARGS, SJ/4/1/2 no. 3).

recreation room also, with space for 60 children. Outside, playground provision was more generous, with eight acres for games, sports and general recreation, and also a concrete playground with shed for inclement weather about 40 yards from school, and a small school yard for recreation between classes. The 'scheme of improvement' successfully put forward by the school was for new toilets and bathrooms which, when completed, gave the building a total of 16 lavatories, 14 washbasins, and eight bathrooms, bringing it right up to the standard of the time.[180] A report in 1950 recommended the provision of a separate, indoor recreation room and a separate domestic economy classroom (the school kitchen was still used for these lessons).[181]This was done, but not for another three years or so, when the transfer of the children to the local national schools at Larkhill freed up space within the 1874 building.

## Post-discharge Supervision and the Sodality of Our Lady

The public scandal of industrial school children released on licence being exploited by cruel employers was raised in 1933 in the Dáil; the Department of Education's response was to order school managers to 'take steps to ensure that when children are placed out in employment, the employers shall strictly observe the conditions of such employment as previously arranged'. Managers were to instruct children to communicate to them within a fortnight, 'reporting as to their treatment'. Should a child fail to do so, the manager was to write to the child, enclosing a stamped addressed envelope for a reply and, should there still be no contact, the manager 'should communicate with the local priest or garda officer asking for a confidential report as to [the] child's welfare and conduct'.[182] The drastic failure of many schools to take an active interest in the welfare of their past pupils featured in the Cussen report also, though it did find the girls' schools made a better effort and were more successful, on average, than the boys' schools.[183]

The single most important means through which the sisters running St Joseph's school, Whitehall, maintained the 'frequent and direct communication with children during their period of supervision' that was required of them under the law – and insisted on with great energy by the Department of Education – was the Sodality of Our Lady.[184] From at least 1939, and throughout the 1940s and 1950s, this was the principal route through which past pupils, whether discharged or still on licence, maintained contact with the school and with the sisters who had (in many cases) reared them from early childhood. The Sodality of Our Lady was already known in secondary schools, parishes and youth groups in Ireland and Britain, having crossed from continental Europe – especially France – where it was part of Jesuit-inspired schools. As Margaret Mac Curtain has explored in her study of female spirituality in 20th-century Ireland, 'the initiation into and practice of the Sodality signified a mid-adolescent rite of passage into a position

180   'Form A, Scoil Saothair Fionnbrugh, Accommodation for the use of children under detention', n.d. but 1946 or early 1947 (DARGS, SJ/4/1/2 no. 3).
181   M. Ó Siochfhradha, cigire, Dept of Education, to Mother Mary Imelda Jennings, resident manager, Industrial School, Whitehall. 30 Nov. 1950 (DARGS, SJ/4/1/2 no. 3).
182   Murphy to Whitehall Industrial School, 2 June 1933.
183   Cussen report, paras 120–1.
184   Murphy to Whitehall Industrial School, 2 June 1933.

of leadership and responsibility in the upper school', while admittance to its ranks 'conveyed an aura of dignity and conferred status, even privilege, on a class educated into middle-class virtue'.[185] Associated with fee-paying privilege – the prestigious Sacred Heart school in Dundrum, County Dublin, was possibly the earliest adopter in the diocese[186] – there was certainly no industrial school or reformatory stigma about sodality membership. What was required of the member was spelled out in the guidebook or Manual of the Child of Mary, as was its internal organisation and record-keeping, all of which were admirably straightforward.

The Whitehall sodality had a junior section, for girls still in school, which met weekly on Thursday evenings, but under the direction of some senior members. The senior section met on the second Sunday of each month. The meeting was an important social forum and means of peer support, with the sodality grounded on the 'good example' and encouragement that the members would give to each other. The extant minutes, from 1946–53 (the sodality was founded in 1939), illustrates the aims and structures of the sodality, the roles taken on by its young officers and members, and something of the content of the lecture delivered at each meeting by the spiritual director or directress, as it was the secretary's task to write up a summary.[187] The senior girls met in the school but walked in procession to the chapel for special events, such as the reception of new members. Attendance in 1946–53 ranged between 16 and 30 girls, with most meetings attended by 20 or 22 girls. The roles of secretary, sacristan and treasurer were held for a few months only, and whatever particular project was then under way also had its designated leader.

The first aim of the sodality member, according to the Child of Mary manual, was personal holiness. The second aim – to save and sanctify the neighbourhood – would only be advanced if attention was given to the first. At each meeting, both spiritual and temporal work was assigned; the spiritual work usually consisted of intentions to be prayed for, along with reflection on a section of the sodality manual or rule. To fulfil the rule of spiritual reading, the Whitehall branch started a pamphlet library (in September 1947) with Catholic Truth Society booklets, costing 1d each, the first stock donated by the priest director, Fr C.F. Lee. Visits to sick members and schoolchildren were arranged, with Crooksling TB sanatorium and Jervis Street hospital featuring most often on the rota. The resolutions had a practical, as well as spiritual, ring: 'To make an effort not to curse, to use language that befits a Child of Mary'; 'Each sodalist is to buy one pamphlet per month and read it'.

The 'temporal work' for this group in the 1940s encompassed both overseas mission support and local parish involvement. One group collected and sorted used postage stamps, which they sent on to St Stanislaus College, Tullamore, County Offaly, the fundraising centre for the Jesuit Mission to China. They also sold raffle tickets for this and other missions. Another group

185    Margaret MacCurtain, 'Fullness of life: defining female spirituality in twentieth-century Ireland', reprinted Margaret MacCurtain, *Ariadne's thread, writing women into Irish history* (Galway, 2008), pp 176–7.

186    M. Kelly, Sacred Heart convent, Dundrum, to Dr Cullen, 14 Aug. 1872 (DDA, Cullen, 335/1 file III, nuns, no. 25).

187    Sodality minute book, Feb. 1946 to Sept. 1947; Sodality minute book, Oct. 1947–Nov. 1953 (DARGS, SJ/7/1 nos. 2, 3). The discussion which follows is based on these two volumes.

remodelled and cut down old clothes for poor children, knitted garments and whatever other sewing and handiwork they could manage with the materials and funds at their disposal, working towards a Christmas deadline. The results were distributed through the national school in the parish (Corpus Christi girls). Occasionally they extended their efforts further afield, as in June 1946 – following on a moving appeal 'from the suffering people of Hungary' for old clothes – the donations to be brought by a set date to the Clothing Guild Centre of the Catholic Social Services Council, City Quay.

The 'Dramatic Section' put on plays once or twice yearly, with volunteer teachers, Miss Aileen McManus and Miss Freda Nolan, acknowledged for their role in productions in the later 1940s. 'Tarcisius', a Eucharistic play, was performed in May 1946, but the others appeared to be secular productions or fairy tales for children, and included 'The Singer' (1946), 'Prince Floizell, detective' (1948), and 'The Missing Prince' (1949). For Sodality Day, 8 December 1953, the feast of the Immaculate Conception, a cast list headed 'The Pupils, Past and Present of St Joseph's School, Whitehall' presented a stage version of Jane Austen's 'Pride and Prejudice', with Miss Colette Redmond as producer.[188] The Sodality World Day in May was the annual highlight, a day of special ceremony when the girls wore their blue cloaks, ribbons and Child of Mary medals, formed a semi-circle around the altar to Our Lady in the chapel, sang the *Salve Regina*, then recited together the Act of Consecration. The day was further marked by a netball challenge between the junior sodalists and the school team, and given serious treatment in the minutes.

The spiritual lectures were given by the priest director or, in his absence, by the sister directress, who up to her death in 1953 was Sister Finbarr Dowling. The lecture was intended to be timely and relevant to the sodalists; it could fit in with a forthcoming feast-day ('On the faith brought by St Patrick'; 'On the courage of Mary'), the gospel of that Sunday ('The Good Shepherd'), the liturgical year (Lent, Holy Week), or on some point of Christian doctrine ('On the importance of prayer'). Other titles indicate a strong moral content, as in 'What is a nice girl?', 'On work difficulties in life', 'Self-respect', 'Dignity of womanhood', 'The power of good example', 'On the choice of a state of life'. On his return from Lourdes in July 1948, the priest director of the time, Fr C.F. Lee, spoke to the girls on the shrine of Lourdes and distributed souvenirs. On another occasion, there was the novelty of a film strip, titled 'The Mass understood' (1951). Whatever the focus, the lecture was written up in summary form by the young secretary that the lesson might be reinforced at the next meeting when the minutes were read aloud. The lecture of Pope Pius XII to an assembly of 200,000 girls at a youth rally in Rome, in August or early September 1948, was recalled in the minutes: 'We were particularly impressed by His Holiness's portrait of the Catholic girl, "modest but not timid, with shining and pure eyes, with direct glance, with frank and friendly but if necessary firm answers".'

The format of the sodality meetings varied somewhat over the period, but they always opened with prayer and concluded with the singing of the *Salve Regina*. Congratulations were extended to newly-wed sodalists, and recent brides (with husbands) came back to visit the group. Meetings, plays, enrolments, basketball games and other sodality events were rounded off with 'a nice tea

188  Programme, 'Pride and Prejudice, a play in three acts by Helen Jerome, from the novel by Jane Austen. 8 Dec. 1953' (DARGS, OLC1/7/6 no. 12).

and re-union in the school', with thanks recorded for the tea to Mother Frances Thérèse Blackmore, the home economics teacher. There is a moving tribute by the sodalists on the death of Sister Finbarr Dowling, 31 August 1953, 'our beloved teacher and our friend who worked for us unsparingly and prayed for us too'.

In the school report submitted to the Department of Education for 1954, the working of the sodality is summarised: the discharged girls met monthly, had use of the playing field, produced an annual play and exhibition of needlework. However, the core purpose was to bring the girls back to Whitehall that contact might be maintained:

> When ill or out of employment they may come here to stay, and many spend their summer holidays with us. Contacts are frequent and maintained long after period of supervision has expired. In the school year 1953–54, twelve ex-pupils returned to spend holidays.[189]

## Conclusion

The application of the Sisters of Our Lady of Charity to turn their reformatory school into an industrial school in 1927 was processed by the Minister for Education without drama or delay. The sisters signed up to operating under the Children Act 1908 and the department's own rules and regulations, revised in 1933 and brought to the attention of school managers through frequent circulars, inspections, questionnaire surveys and other demands for information. The system they agreed to implement was highly prescriptive and tightly regulated, involving repeated form filling and return of statistics. It placed huge emphasis on exact numbers, the physical care of the children, the dimensions of the rooms – all areas that lend themselves most readily to outside scrutiny.[190]

Analysis of St Joseph's school register of children admitted 1927–52 reflects the general pattern of committals by the courts across the industrial school system nationally. A departmental memorandum, dated November 1944, gives a total average across all schools of about 60% of children committed on the grounds of parental poverty (a further 17% for 'parental unsuitability', 12% for failure to attend school, and 10% for indictable offences).[191] The majority of children committed by the District Courts to St Joseph's, as to other industrial schools, were there for the 'crime' of family poverty and what Moira Maguire terms the extraordinary preference for institutionalisation, at public expense in Ireland.[192] Official policy, at both local and central government levels, well into the 1950s, was to remove children from the care of their parents, rather than provide assistance to keep families together.[193] Though the pro forma registers provided by the department did not allow for much beyond the minimum

189    Report for 1954.
190    Form A, Scoil Saothair Fionnbrugh, Accommodation.
191    P. Ó Muirieartaigh, cigire, An Roinn Oideachais, to Scoil Saothair Sheosamh Naomhtha, 18 Samhain 1944 (DARGS, SJ/4/1/1 no. 11).
192    Maguire, *Precarious childhood*, p. 42.
193    Ibid.

information given on the committal order, reports on progress at school and discharge under supervision, there are occasional hints at the pain of family separation, and brief but explicit acknowledgements in other documents. After the name of one girl, who had two sisters also in the school, is added the note, 'she suffers from great depression and longing for her mother (who does not want her)'. 'In kindness and charity we try to make up the loss of home life' is entered by the school manager under one of the headings prescribed by the department for its end-of-year report.[194] The industrial school system of 1868, derived from a reformatory school model and intact in all essentials in the 1950s, was always one of confinement to allow industrial or work-directed training. The psychological and emotional well-being of young children was far from the mind of its creators and advocates, whose starting point was the adult prison, not the family home. Once in place, there was no dislodging it.

St Joseph's, Whitehall, did manage to have at least some warmth and normality and that is probably down to several factors, rather than any single overriding cause. Its numbers were in its favour: the total was never more than about 70 children, from infants to upper second-level, and always well below its registered capacity of 100. The very small role it played in the industrial school system nationally is evident from the enrolment numbers: in May 1957 (figure 5.7), it had 2% of all the girls resident in industrial schools in Ireland on that day (and slightly more than 2% of the total capacity). In earlier decades, its percentage of all industrial school girls was even less (as some schools had closed by 1957). Always one of the smaller girls' schools, it occupied a compact if old-fashioned building (by 1952) that records show was kept in good repair, and had its own games fields and hard-surface playgrounds with shelters. Its accessible location, in the developing north city suburbs, made it easier for the children to attend local schools as day pupils (from 1953). When the Department of Education urged second-level attendance on all school managers, St Joseph's was already in the vanguard. Good public transport, along with small numbers and mixed age groups, made possible some of the 'exceptional recreations' it boasted of in 1954, including picnics to the seaside, visits to Spring and Horse shows, outings to films and pantomimes, matches arranged with school teams outside.[195] Post-discharge employment opportunities were better in Dublin than in small towns and rural areas, once a girl was taken on her own merits. The network of contacts assiduously built up by the school meant that most Whitehall girls got at least a first chance.

The school was frequently inspected and recommendations followed up, as can be judged from the extensive documentary record, and it was certainly easy to reach Whitehall from the Talbot Street and Marlborough Street offices of the Department of Education. The confidential reports on the school teachers, sisters and lay staff, speak of highly-motivated but also effective teachers who appeared (as stated by the inspector) to love their charges. The sisters employed in St Joseph's were appointed by the High Park superior. They were not drawn from other houses or re-assigned arbitrarily, therefore long terms of service were common. This brought stability and continuity to the children's environment and was an advantage

194   Report for 1954.
195   Ibid.

**Figure 5.7** Industrial schools in Ireland, statistics 1 May 1957 (DARGS, SJ/4/1/5)

| | Girls | | | |
|---|---|---|---|---|
| Year founded | School name | Certified number | No. in school on 1 May 1957 | No. not committed |
| 1886 | Athlone, Summerhill | 200 | 80 | 25 |
| 1878 | Ballinasloe | 100 | 74 | 14 |
| 1882 | Benada Abbey, Sligo | 106 | 87 | 22 |
| 1886 | Ballaghderreen | 100 | 93 | 35 |
| 1870 | Birr | 100 | 78 | 14 |
| 1870 | Booterstown | 96 | 90 | 9 |
| 1869 | Cavan | 100 | 76 | 3 |
| 1869 | Cashel | 125 | 69 | 9 |
| 1872 | Clifden | 120 | 118 | |
| 1869 | Clonakilty | 180 | 96 | 3 |
| 1870 | Cobh | 60 | 60 | |
| 1870 | Cork, St Finbar's | 200 | 78 | 10 |
| 1880 | Dundalk | 100 | 44 | 13 |
| 1869 | Dundrum, Tipperary | 80 | 76 | 2 |
| 1875 | Ennis | 110 | 56 | |
| 1856 | Goldenbridge | 165 | 161 | 14 |
| 1869 | Kinsale | 180 | 32 | 6 |
| 1869 | Killarney | 98 | 85 | 2 |
| 1873 | Kilkenny | 130 | 102 | |
| 1869 | Lakelands | 110 | 92 | 9 |
| 1864 | Loughrea | 100 | 65 | 3 |
| 1869 | Lenaboy, Galway | 88 | 88 | 11 |
| 1870 | Limerick, St George's | 170 | 86 | 6 |

| | | Girls | | |
|---|---|---|---|---|
| Year founded | School name | Certified number | No. in school on 1 May 1957 | No. not committed |
| 1880 | Mallow | 80 | 57 | 4 |
| 1870 | Monaghan | 140 | 60 | 14 |
| 1875 | Moate | 74 | 71 | |
| 1869 | Newtownforbes | 145 | 82 | 24 |
| 1867 | New Ross | 100 | 48 | 10 |
| 1879 | Pembroke, Tralee | 85 | 54 | 3 |
| 1871 | Sligo, St Laurence's | 200 | 90 | 28 |
| 1870 | Templemore | 70 | 48 | 1 |
| 1858 | Whitehall | 100 | 60 | 4 |
| 1871 | Westport | 117 | 59 | 26 |
| 1871 | Waterford | 200 | 103 | 13 |
| 1869 | Wexford | 146 | 58 | 2 |
| **Total, girls** | | **4455** | **2811** | **355** |
| **Senior boys** | | | | |
| 1870 | Artane | 830 | 566 | 48 |
| 1884 | Clonmel | 200 | 200 | 10 |
| 1872 | Glin | 220 | 150 | 22 |
| 1874 | Greenmount | 235 | 129 | 6 |
| 1887 | Letterfrack | 190 | 100 | |
| 1876 | Salthill | 208 | 190 | 30 |
| 1860 | Tralee | 150 | 125 | 37 |
| 1889 | Upton | 250 | 174 | 39 |
| **Total, senior boys** | | **2283** | **1634** | **192** |

(*Continued*)

**Figure 5.7**   (Continued)

| | | | Girls | |
|---|---|---|---|---|
| Year founded | School name | Certified number | No. in school on 1 May 1957 | No. not committed |
| **Junior boys** | | | | |
| 1875 | Drogheda | 150 | 103 | 44 |
| 1879 | Kilkenny | 186 | 173 | 6 |
| 1873 | Cappoquin | 75 | 75 | 22 |
| 1872 | Killarney | 50 | 50 | 2 |
| 1882 | Passage West | 80 | 73 | 4 |
| 1900 | Rathdrum | 110 | 104 | |
| **Total, junior boys** | | **651** | **578** | **78** |
| | | Certified no. of places | Total no.in schools on 1 May 1957 | Vacant places |
| **Total, girls & boys** | | **7389** | **5023** | **2366** |

*Note:* an error in the arithmetic is corrected on the MS and the correction given here (DARGS, SJ/4/1/5).

where the carers were suited to – and able for – the work. The motherliness of the sisters who worked in the nursery, dressing room, kitchen and throughout the house more generally is also a matter of written record. St Joseph's late launch as an industrial school – in 1927 – may have made the sisters more open and amenable to suggestions, and they had long been open to outsiders seeing for themselves how their schools and homes were conducted. The childcare facilities they knew most about were those run by their own order in France and England, which were subject to close state monitoring in return for rather more generous state funding, as reported in the circular letters which were the means of updating the other houses on progress elsewhere. That up to 30 past-pupils returned for the monthly sodality meeting run by their own committee throughout the 1940s and early 1950s, when no force could have been exerted on them, might well be taken as a willingness among some of the girls to maintaining contact (at least temporarily) with those who had reared them, as well as with their peers.

The Cussen commission started its inquiries into the reformatory and industrial schools system in June 1934 with a free run through a small, much-inspected girls' school in operation (as an industrial school) for just over seven years. It had several exceptionally well-qualified and experienced individuals among its care staff and teachers. It is impossible to say how this first impression coloured Justice Cussen's final report and recommendations, but Whitehall may not have been the best place to begin.

# Chapter 6

# The Remaking of Gloucester Street Magdalen Asylum and Convent as a Monastery and Refuge of Our Lady of Charity, 1887–1949

## Mecklenburgh Street/Gloucester Street Asylum 1822–87

On 17 February 1887, six sisters from High Park arrived to take charge of an asylum in the north inner city of Dublin. The address was 104 Gloucester Street Lower (now Sean MacDermott Street), but this incorporated premises numbered 76 and 77 Mecklenburgh Street (renamed Tyrone Street and later Railway Street).[1] Flanked on the west by Gardiner Street, a high-status residential street then in decline, and on the east by the station and yards of the Dublin to Belfast railway on Amiens Street (figure 6.1), this compact district had long been notorious for prostitution, and there were no indications in the 1880s that the social trajectory would be other than downwards. The three-storey premises numbered 76 Mecklenburgh Street, titled 'Magdalene Asylum' on the Ordnance Survey five-foot plan of 1847 (figure 6.2), had been leased to a local Catholic clergyman, John Vincent Holmes in 1823, and established as a trust in the name of the 'Female Penitents' Retreat' in 1833.[2] A charitable widow named Brigid Burke first opened an asylum either in this premises or (more likely) nearby in 1822, which she ran with her daughter. A later account describes it as a 'humble dwelling' where women seeking to renounce a life of prostitution took shelter, 'doing penance for their

1 Both spellings Mecklinburgh and Mecklenburgh are used throughout the period.
2 The earliest lease is dated 27 Sept. 1817, Nugent Brooker to John Reade. A lease dated 24 July 1823, John Fowler to Revd John Vincent Holmes, probably marks the opening of the asylum, but it may not have been formally established until 1833, see renewal, 8 Nov. 1833, Arthur Perrin to Anna Maria Holmes, and 'Declaration of trust relating to the Female Penitents' Retreat Mecklinburgh (sic) Street', 27 Dec. 1833, listed in memorandum from Thomas F. O'Connell Rooney and Co., 17 Feb. 1931 (DARGS, OLC2/9/1 no. 17). The Valuation Office cancelled book Dublin, North Dock, vol. dated 1906–15, has 'apr [approximately?] 1823' in the margin opposite 63 to 72 Gloucester Street North Lower, in the name of the Sisters of Charity (sic), reps John Moore and J.D.B. Duncan. In 1890, it was stated that the asylum was founded 70 years ago, which would make it an 1820s foundation, Gloucester Street, circulaire, 24 avril 1890, p. 9 (NDC Caen, Archives Rennes). The Gloucester Street annals were not transferred to the OLC Irish regional archive at Beechlawn (DARGS) and are feared lost; their content may be partly reconstructed through the circular letters.

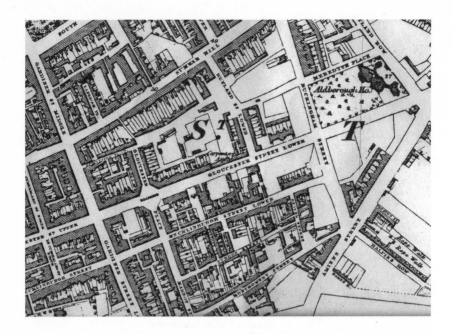

**Figure 6.1**  Location of magdalen asylum, 76 Mecklenburgh Street, Dublin, founded 1823 (OS six inch Dublin sheet 18, 1837)

lives of sin and occupying themselves in laundry work'.[3] It was this modest enterprise that Fr Holmes supported in 1823, leading to the appointment of trustees in 1833 and the employment of a matron.

The publicity and fund-raising surrounding the Mecklenburgh Street asylum in its early decades recall the classic magdalen discourse of the period (chapter 2). A charity sermon preached in 1848 sought support for the 33 'children of wretchedness' then resident in the home.[4] All others, it was claimed, were the objects of sympathy – the aged, the child, the sick – 'everyone has a friend here and a home hereafter but one, and that one is the poor, degraded, fallen penitent'.[5] The example of Christ was repeatedly invoked as the reason why this most miserable class ought to be assisted; He who would not drive away the weeping Magdalen from the hall of the Pharisee, 'but said that much was forgiven her because she had loved much'. Listeners (and readers) were reminded that Mary Magdalen was not only found in tears at the feet of Jesus, but 'she was the last that saw Him on the mountain's top and the first that met him on the glorious day of His

3  *Souvenir of golden jubilee of Monastery of Our Lady of Charity of Refuge, Gloucester Street, Dublin* (Dublin, 1937), p. 16. Hereafter, *Golden jubilee*. The first burial from the asylum was in 1822, see Sister M. Bartholomew McDonnell to Mr Coyle, n.d. but 1888, Copy letters 1887–1931, pp 26–7 (DARGS, OLC2/5/2 no. 3). Hereafter, Copy letters.
4  *Sermon preached by the Reverend Dr O'Brien of Limerick on behalf of the Female Penitents' Retreat, Mecklenburgh Street, on Sunday 15th October 1848* (Dublin, 1849), p. 12. Hereafter, *Sermon*.
5  *Sermon*, p. 4.

resurrection'.[6] The imminent threat of an outbreak of cholera (in August 1848) was put forward as another very good reason to give alms; who could say whether he would have the opportunity to contribute this time next year?[7] But despite the example of Christ Himself in welcoming the penitent, and the eloquence of the appeals made in the name of this refuge, it was a small-scale charity that always struggled merely to keep open.

The original 76 Mecklenburgh Street asylum was expanded in October 1863 to include the adjoining three-storey house, number 77, and the row of very poor cottages (occupied by Sylvester Moore's lodgers) behind this premises. In November 1868, the rest of the land and buildings to the rear of numbers 76 and 77 Mecklenburgh Street were also in the name of the Female Penitents' Retreat (figure 6.2).[8] Numbers '68 to 72 Lower Tyrone Street taken into asylum 1892' was later entered by a surveyor from the Valuation Office.[9] (The renaming of the street as Lower Tyrone Street, and later as Railway Street, is illustrated in figure 6.2). At the start of 1869, there were 45 women resident in the home maintained by their own labour and the proceeds of a charity sermon – though it had have excellent frontage onto Gloucester Street Lower and space for building, debt weighed heavily.[10] Its sorry state was known to the Good Shepherd sisters in Limerick who were looking out for a foundation in Dublin city in 1871 and cited the Mecklenburgh Street asylum as a possible location, with a certain 'good Mr Devereux' named as informant and potential bene-factor.[11] The archbishop, however, approached the Mercy sisters who, in 1873, agreed to take charge, re-naming it 'St Mary's Retreat'.[12] Thirteen years later, the Mercy sisters were anxious to relinquish management, on the grounds of not having the special vocation for the work, and pressing demands else-where in Dublin.[13] Their own constitution obliged them particularly to con-centrate on the instruction of the poor, and sisters from Gloucester Street were already teaching in the docklands area of Townsend Street.[14] During their term, the Mercy sisters managed to purchase a derelict site next door (the Brewery Yard), which was later to become the site of the chapel.[15] While they did receive public support in legacies and donations,[16] they appear to have

6   Ibid. p. 7.
7   Ibid., p. 15.
8   Mecklenburgh Street, Valuation Office cancelled book, Dublin, North Dock, vol. dated 1855–69 (Irish Life Centre, VO).
9   Gloucester Street Lower, Valuation Office cancelled book, Dublin, North Dock, vol. dated 1906–15 (Irish Life Centre, VO).
10   Statement of income and expenditure, Female Penitents' Retreat, Lower Gloucester Street, 26 Jan. 1869 (DDA, Cullen, 321/2 laity, no. 15).
11   Sister M. of the Immaculate Conception, Good Shepherd convent, Limerick, to Dr Cullen, 13 Feb. 1872 (DDA, 335/1 file III nuns, no. 6).
12   Sister M. Bartholomew McDonnell to Mr Toomey, n.d. but 1887 or 1888, Copy letters, pp 23–4.
13   High Park sent three choir sisters, two *converse* and two *tourière*, Sister M. Bartholomew McDonnell to My hon. and dear Mother, 29 June 1887 (NDC Caen, Archives Versailles).
14   *The rule and constitutions of the religious called Sisters of Mercy in Italian and English* (Dublin, 1863), ch. I, of the object of the congregation, pp 3-4. Hereafter, Mercy rule.
15   Brewery Yard was purchased in 1878, VO cancelled book, Dublin, North Dock, vol. dated 1855–69.
16   The Mercy sisters, over the 13 years to Feb. 1887, received £6,642 3s 3d in legacies and do-nations, 'as extracted from their accounts', Memorandum concerning proposed new buildings at Gloucester Street Magdalen Asylum, n.d. but July 1888, Copy letters, p. 29.

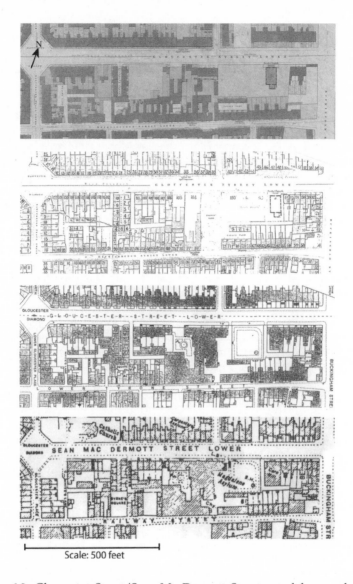

Scale: 500 feet

**Figure 6.2**  Gloucester Street/Sean MacDermott Street magdalene asylum as
mapped 1847–1939. Sources: OS 1:1056 Dublin sheet 9 (1847); VO
1:1056 Dublin (1854); OS 1:1056 Dublin sheet 18–48 (1909); OS
1:2,500 Dublin sheet 18–7 (1939)

been overwhelmed by the constant labour 'under very depressing circumstances' and the impossibility of generating sufficient regular, weekly income
to make ends meet, let alone to repay borrowed monies.[17] It was they who

17    Sister M. Bartholomew McDonnell to Mr Toomey, n.d. but 1887 or 1888, Copy letters,
pp 23–4.

approached the Sisters of Our Lady of Charity in High Park in December 1886 and secured the sanction of the archbishop, Dr Walsh, for a transfer of management.[18] They very speedily yielded possession of the property and all involvement in this work.[19]

On arrival in Gloucester Street, the founding OLC superior, Sister Mary of St Bartholomew (Mary McDonnell) and her five companions were briefed by the outgoing Mercy superior, Sister Mary Gertrude Howell, shown the asylum accounts (all current bills paid up to date, and some laundry monies due), asked if they had any questions (they had none), and then left to manage as best they could.[20] The women residents had had no inkling of this change. They were assembled to be told that these were the new sisters appointed by the archbishop to take care of them. The earliest description of this transfer recounts that, although the women received the sisters well, 'they found it difficult to conform to our rules and customs, being almost entirely left to themselves, the close supervision which our holy rule requires was irksome to them but by degrees they are becoming more reconciled'.[21] Reflecting on the first three years of operation, the superior recounts that the women were greatly distressed by the departure of 'the good Mercy sisters' to whom they had become attached, but no rebellion ensued, and after a short time they accepted the change with docility and surrender. The outgoing chaplain, Fr Healy, noted for his rapport with the women and great influence over them, was credited with helping to smooth matters over.[22] It was from among the older women, those longest resident, that the new sisters feared dissent, and at least some – Hilda and Mary Michael are named – resented the takeover. Hilda became reconciled 'after a short time' while Mary Michael was censorious and resentful to the end, according to the obituarist.[23] There may have been others who chose to leave the asylum, rather than submit to a new system, but as the early Mercy register has not survived it is not possible to say. It appears that the majority of the residents, after some upset and grumbling, decided that there was nothing to be gained by going against the government and went along with the new regime.[24]

The location of the asylum was ideal from the perspective of a congregation devoted to the rescue of 'penitent women'.[25] According to the earliest description of the venture, because they could be found in the very heart

---

18  Gloucester Street, *circulaire*, 24 avril 1890, p. 1.

19  Ibid.

20  Sister M. Gertrude to Mother M. Bartholomew, 30 July 1887, Copy letters, pp 20–1. The new OLC superior, M. Bartholomew, signed herself 'Sister' but was referred to as 'Mother' by the sisters after her election. The title 'Sister' is used here for consistency.

21  Gloucester Street, circular letter, 8 Dec. 1887 (NDC Caen, Archives Versailles).

22  Gloucester Street, *circulaire*, 24 avril 1890, p. 2.

23  Mary Michael died in 1898, Hilda died in 1901, 'Entrance of the penitents and their leaving, Convent of Our Lady of Charity of Dublin, commenced the 17th day of February 1887' (DARGS, OLC2/8/1 no. 2), hereafter, Women's entrance register, Gloucester Street; Gloucester Street, circular letter, 15 Aug., 1901, p. 10 (DARGS, OLC2/3/1 no. 7).

24  Gloucester Street, *circulaire*, 24 avril 1890, p. 2.

25  'Règles et constitutions pour les religieuses de Notre-Dame de Charité, édition entièrement conformé au texte original [1682] avec des introductions et des notes', *Oeuvres complètes de Bienheureux Jean Eudes*, x (Vannes, 1909), Constitution i, De la fin de cet institut, et des motifs qui doivent porter celles qui le professent à en faire de bon cœur les fonctions, p. 80. Hereafter, *Constitutions*.

of the city (*au ventre de la ville*), many women sought admission. Moreover, being in the centre of the red light district, the premises was perfectly sited to steal poor souls from the eternal damnation that would otherwise be their lot.[26] It was near a major railway terminus, Aldborough military barracks and the port, all of which contributed to the concentration of prostitution in this small area;[27] both female prisons (Grangegorman female penitentiary and Mountjoy women's prison) were also close by. Its persistent association with this poorest strata of society is evident from the notes made by the Ordnance Survey officers on the squalor and desperation they encountered as they conducted research into the local placenames in 1837.[28] By the time of the OLC takeover in 1887, prostitution was entrenched locally, and there are references throughout the records of the convent to the proximity of 'houses of ill repute', and to girls fleeing such houses in the immediate vicinity of the asylum. Women drawn into prostitution 'are sometimes touched by sudden grace' and so a place of retreat within easy reach was imperative, presumably before the grace of the moment wore off.[29] The location of the asylum was always part of its appeal to subscribers: 'We are in the centre of a neighbourhood that too often requires immediate help, and *this* alone has already appeared a most important fact in the eyes of the charitably disposed in our city'.[30]

But there were also complications about accepting a city-centre asylum that had been in operation over seven decades. The first issue was its name. The title by which it was popularly known, and the name recorded on the OS maps, is 'Magdalene Asylum'; the new OLC administration tried to continue with the Mercy name, 'St Mary's Retreat'. The reason given was that this was closer to the 'old name' used by the 1833 trustees (Female Penitents' Retreat), though it might be expected that OLC would introduce their own traditional term of 'refuge'.[31] But it was difficult to force a name change while simultaneously insisting on its unique status as the sole and only Roman Catholic 'magdalen asylum' in the city of Dublin and the historic continuity which entitled it to legacies made in the name of its predecessor bodies. They quickly found that by using the title 'Gloucester Street Magdalen Asylum' in public advertising, 'this merciful object speaks for itself'.[32]

There were difficulties around outstanding bills and the debts with which the house was encumbered. Without a written legal agreement 'concerning the assignment of this convent' it was not clear which community was responsible for the payment of bills submitted months in arrears, or from what date repayments on a loan for £500 taken out by the Mercy

26    Gloucester Street, *circulaire*, 24 avril 1890, p. 4.
27    Tadhg O'Keeffe and Patrick Ryan, 'At the world's end: the lost landscape of Monto, Dublin's notorious red-light district', in *Landscapes*, 10 (1) (2009), pp 21–38.
28    Jacinta Prunty, *Dublin slums 1800–1925, a study in urban geography* (Dublin, 1998), p. 297.
29    Sister M. Bartholomew McDonnell to My Lord Archbishop, 26 July 1888, Copy letters, p. 30
30    Same to Mr Toomey, n.d. but 1887 or 1888, Copy letters, pp 23–4. Emphasis as in the original.
31    Ibid.
32    'Preliminary notice', for bazaar to be held Dec. 1899, Copy letters, p. 65.

sisters became the responsibility of the new proprietors.[33] There was about £110 due to the laundry at the handover but the Mercy superior explained that these were monthly or quarterly accounts and 'we could not make the customers pay that at once to suit us'.[34] Clergy from Westland Road were already serving the asylum on Sundays and holy days, but there was the embarrassment of who was liable for the cab hire.[35] Some outstanding bills, such as gas and water, which were paid quarterly, had to be met; 'we left you the means of meeting them *we* would have had', explained Sister Gertrude.[36] The means the Mercy sisters had would have been inadequate, and were still inadequate for the new proprietors. On transfer, only the sum of £40 was at the disposal of the institution.[37] These 'trifling matters we are both anxious to settle' nevertheless dragged on for months, awaiting the preparation of the written agreement by Mr O'Hagan the solicitor.[38] As the departing Mercy superior counselled, 'Lawyers are noted for being slow, so both sides have to exercise patience before the matter is brought to a conclusion'.[39]

The laundry business, which was supposed to finance the day-to-day running of the asylum, was more of a drain on resources than a generator of income. The charges being made for laundry work were derisory, but there was only so much the new proprietors could do with existing contracts for fear of losing the business altogether.[40] The standard of work left much to be desired.[41] Sister Bartholomew McDonnell soon understood that the inability of the Mercy sisters to raise Gloucester Street from 'the degraded position' they found it in was, in large measure, 'owing to work undertaken at price which it was impossible to execute'.[42] On taking charge she did revise the charges per article for the domestic, weekly customers and refused to countenance deductions, replying to a householder in Mountjoy Square that 'I beg to assure you it would leave a loss to do them [for] less, and but for our anxiety to keep the work you are kind enough to send we would refuse a new washing on the same terms'.[43] She made every possible effort to get people to pay outstanding bills, sending as emissary one of the earliest and most loyal of her lay supporters, the unflagging Patrick Kennedy, on what was not a pleasant job: 'I ask you to settle it within the week, else I shall be

33 Correspondence between Mother M. of St Bartholomew McDonnell and Sister M. Gonzaga Whelan (bursar), also Sister M. Gertrude, July 1887, Copy letters, pp 5–7, 18–19.

34 Sister M. Gertrude to Mother M. Bartholomew, 30 July 1887, Copy letters, pp 20–21.

35 [Mother M. of St Bartholomew McDonnell] to Fr Conlan, n.d. but July 1887, Copy letters, p. 8.

36 Sister M. Gertrude to Mother M. Bartholomew, 30 July 1887, Copy letters, pp 20–21. Emphasis as in the original.

37 Sister M. Bartholomew McDonnell to Monsignor, 3 Feb. 1891, Copy letters, p. 79.

38 Same to Sister Gertrude 31 July 1887, Copy letters, pp 6–7.

39 Sister M. Gertrude to Mother M. Bartholomew, 30 July 1887, Copy letters, pp 20–21.

40 M. McDonnell, superioress, to Mrs Mooney, Mountjoy Square, 20 July 1887, Copy letters, p. 10.

41 Memorandum concerning proposed new buildings, n.d. but July 1888, Copy letters, pp 28–9.

42 Sister M. Bartholomew McDonnell to Fr Baxter, n.d. but 1887, possibly July, Copy letters, pp 22–3.

43 Same to Mrs Mooney, Mountjoy Square, 20 July 1887, Copy letters, p. 10.

obliged to put the affair into the hands of our solicitor'.[44] Pressure was placed on the asylum by customers of all types – clerical, institutional, commercial and private – to undertake work for half nothing – that is, for the rates they were used to.[45]

The biggest challenge, however, was replacing the simpler, lay-run and Mercy traditions with a time-honoured monastic culture. The *asile* tradition of Notre Dame de Charité was based on the creation of an oasis of peace, quiet, order and routine within which sisters, 'penitents' and others associated with the monastery (such as boarders and schoolchildren) could work out their salvation. Ample grounds, landscaped gardens and boundary fences helped make this separation explicit in High Park. Ingenuity, as well as funding, would be required to make the cramped Gloucester Street premises, overlooked on all sides by crowded tenement houses (figure 6.2), a 'refuge from the world' in the sense understood by the Sisters of Our Lady of Charity. As well as the obligation of preserving enclosure, the new sisters had to carry a much heavier liturgical load than the Mercy sisters, whose constitutions obliged them only to the recitation of the Little Office of Our Lady.[46] The choir sisters of Our Lady of Charity had the daytime cycle of monastic hours to complete, though the founding group numbered merely three sisters of that rank. The various offices or employments within OLC came with rather heavy job descriptions, due to the centrality of the rule in their tradition, the accretion of customs and practices over more than two centuries and the relentless efforts made to model practice on what was done at Caen (and Paris). Putting the laundry on a sound footing would require the efforts of sisters at every stage of the process. Trying to establish a zone of quiet around even the chapel would be difficult, with the women crowded in with so little open yard space or garden in which they could sit to chat without being heard 'quite distinctly'.[47]

In many respects, the Sisters of Our Lady of Charity could, and did, start afresh, as in the brand new register of admissions to the asylum, ruled and filled up in the High Park (and Caen) tradition. They were not lacking in ambitions for this new foundation. But the long pre-OLC history of the asylum could not be overlooked. The residents had the right to expect that they could stay forever if they chose, and these undoubtedly included infirm and elderly women whose care needs were greatest. There would be no 'lead-in' period in terms of planning for residents as they aged; these women were already in place. The new management would benefit from legacies made in the name of the old asylum, and from public goodwill towards an established charity, but they would also have to sort out countless small matters that predated their involvement, such as claims for legacy duty from the

44   Same to Mr Goulding, 12 Mar. 1891, Copy letters, p. 95.
45   See for example, McDonnell to Baxter, n.d. but 1887, possibly July, pp 22–3; Sister M. Bartholomew McDonnell to Fr Healy, 6 Apr. 1891, Copy letters, p. 77.
46   Mercy rule, ch. IX, of the office and mental prayer, pp 18–19.
47   Gloucester Street, circular letter, Aug. 1905, p. 2 (DARGS, OLC2/3/1 no. 8).

Revenue Commissioners.[48] There was already a laundry business but, as noted already, some of the customers were more trouble than their washing was worth, disputing bills, ignoring repeated demands for payment and blaming the sisters for mix-ups that were in fact the customer's own fault.[49]

The premises facing onto Mecklenburgh Street was already more than 60 years in operation as an asylum and bore all the marks of hard usage and age. The brewery yard adjoining 104 Lower Gloucester Street (figure 6.2) had potential for building but, at this stage, was full of old cabins and sheds. Outrageous prices would be asked for ruinous houses and derelict yards in proximity to the asylum by owners and leaseholders. There was a complicated history of trusteeship behind the asylum of 1887: transferred into the archbishop's hands only in 1863, the multiple leases on the premises generated legal paperwork for OLC for decades after they took charge.[50] There was some support for an asylum – evident in the legacies and bequests received by the Mercy sisters – but there were many competing charities in the city.

The asylum and the laundry (*la buanderie*) were in a very sorry state at the handover in February 1887, particularly the loss-making laundry. It was in a dreadfully dark yard, with several old and derelict buildings needing to be renovated. This was the brewery yard and associated outhouses which had been acquired by the Mercy sisters.[51] The new superior, Sister Bartholomew McDonnell, took the initiative of requesting the archbishop to call and see for himself what was, after all, the only Catholic asylum of its kind in the north inner city. Dr William Walsh was conducted around the premises on 15 March 1887, accompanied by his chaplain, Fr Denis Petit, and declared himself so shocked at the state of things that he ordered the return of the sisters to High Park, for health's sake, pending the necessary renovations.[52] Although this order was quickly overtaken by events – a small plot of land nearby came up for sale, relieving the immediate crisis – the house was undoubtedly in a very poor state. Two of the sisters working in the condemned laundry were struck with typhus fever in September 1887, which was all the more alarming, as there was not enough space to isolate them.[53] The effect on Sister Elizabeth Kenny was 'loss of former vigour', and it is unlikely her

---

48   For example, handwritten statement of legal fees from John O'Hagan, solicitor, 9 Harcourt Street, relating to costs incurred in 'resisting the claim put forward by the Commissioner of Inland Revenue to legacy duty on legacies bequeathed to the Magdalen Asylum, Lr. Gloucester Street' from Hugh Blayney, deceased, 9 Feb. 1890 (DARGS, OLC2/9/1 no. 4).

49   M. McDonnell, superioress, to Mrs Mooney, Mountjoy Square, 20 July 1887. Same to same, 21 July 1887, Copy letters, pp 10–11.

50   Copy assignment 19 Feb. 1863, conveyance 23 Dec. 1878, Joseph Doyle, David Cunningham, Michael Lyons, Revd. Paul Cullen; in total, 49 documents dated 1817–1931 are listed for the Gloucester Street and Lower Mecklenburgh Street premises by Thomas F. O'Connell Rooney and Co., 17 Feb. 1931 (DARGS, OLC2/9/1 no. 17). The core premises, later numbered 80 Lower Tyrone Street and No. 106 Lower Gloucester Street, was held under lease dated 22 Sept. 1817 from Nugent Booker to John Read; this property was not conveyed to the OLC sisters until 1902, see Thomas F. O'Connell & Son, solicitors, 28 Bachelor's Walk, to Revd Mother Prioress, North Gloucester Street (*sic*), 26 Aug. 1924 (DARGS, OLC2/9/1 no. 14).

51   Reference made to 'conveyance of premises in Lr. Gloucester Street dated 23 Dec. 1878' in Thomas F. O'Connell & Son to Revd Mother Prioress, 26 Aug. 1924.

52   Gloucester Street, *circulaire*, 24 avril 1890, p. 4.

53   Gloucester Street, circular letter, 8 Dec. 1887

companion made a full recovery either.[54] Although none of the other sisters or the women succumbed to the fever, the health of all residents must have been adversely affected by the crowded and damp conditions.[55]

No doubt the illness that stalked the house in its first months under OLC management concentrated the mind of the superior on the matter of burials. As a lay asylum, from 1822 onwards, burials were in the Mecklenburgh asylum plot in Glasnevin cemetery. By the time of the transfer from the Mercy sisters to the sisters of Our Lady of Charity in 1887, this plot was long filled, and deceased residents were buried in what were termed the usual 'poor ground' plots in Glasnevin, at the 'considerate sum' of 1/6 per burial. An early appeal was made to the Cemeteries Committee for the continuance of this charitable financial arrangement and, in addition, to grant a burial place (also situated in 'the poor ground'). OLC 'would have a granite base stone erected round the plot, similar to other burial places devoted to charitable institutions'. There would be no financial loss to the cemetery (the offer to enclose the plot would in fact be an enhancement, at no cost to the committee), and the 'poor inmates' of Gloucester Street would have the spiritual comfort of knowing that they would be buried together, rather than being buried 'promiscuously', that is buried in whatever plot was opened at the time of their death.[56] The eloquent appeal was granted.[57]

## Establishing Gloucester Street as an Autonomous Monastery of Our Lady of Charity

The way of life that the new community introduced to Gloucester Street convent and asylum in the late 1880s matched, in essentials at least, that of any of the OLC houses which were wedded to the 'primitive rule' of the founding refuge of Caen. The principles and practices of the OLC system have already been discussed in the case of High Park (chapter 3); what follows concentrates on what was particular to the local situation of Gloucester Street, or where the Gloucester Street records are exceptionally full.

The first reality was that the new community was on its own. On leaving High Park for Gloucester Street in February 1887, the founding sisters described the wrench in heartrending terms, their only consolation the assurance that they were answering the call of the Good Master who was always to be relied on.[58] For their part, the High Park sisters comforted themselves on their loss with the knowledge that the 'little apostolic band' had 'accomplished the Divine Will in this extension of their zeal for poor erring souls', but have nothing further to say concerning the fortunes of 'their'

---

54    Death letter of Sister M. of St Elizabeth Kenny (Anne), died 23 Jan. 1941 (DARGS, OLC2/6/4 no. 13).
55    The deaths of women residents in 1890 were reported to be from consumption, and from old age and diseases related to a lifetime of alcoholism, Gloucester Street, *circulaire*, 24 avril 1890, p. 3.
56    Sister M. Bartholomew McDonnell to Mr Coyle, n.d. but 1888, Copy letters, pp 25–6.
57    Grant of right of burial in Prospect Cemetery, no. 17680, to Mother Mary McDonnell, 2 May 1888 (DARGS, OLC2/8/1 no. 4).
58    Gloucester Street, *circulaire*, 24 avril 1890, p. 2.

**Figure 6.3** Our Lady of Charity of Refuge, Gloucester Street, superiors 1887–1948

| Order | Date of election | Superior | | Assistant |
|---|---|---|---|---|
| 1 | 3 Feb. 1887 | Mother Mary of St Bartholomew McDonnell | Insufficient no. of capitular sisters (3) for election, reappointment of Mother M. Bartholomew by Dr Walshe, archbishop | Sister Mary of St Vincent Markey |
| 2 | 13 May 1890 | Mother Mary of St Bartholomew McDonnell | | Sister Mary of St Vincent Markey |
| 3 | 18 May 1893 | Mother Mary of St Ignatius Ryan | Came from High Park | Sister M. of St Vincent Markey d. August 1894; succeeded 12 Sept. 1894 by Sister M. of St Bartholomew McDonnell |
| 4 | 19 May 1896 | Mother Mary of St Bartholomew McDonnell | d. 22 June 1898 | Sister M. of the Angels McCabe, returned to High Park; succeeded 12 Aug. 1896 by Sister M. of St Aloysius McCabe |
| 5 | 15 July 1898 | Sister Mary of St Aloysius McCabe | Professed 2 July 1890, Gloucester Street | Sister M. of St Stanislaus Masterson; resigned, succeeded Mar. 1899 by Sister M. of St Francis Xavier Leamy |
| 6 | 21 May 1901 | Sister Mary of St Aloysius McCabe | | Sister Mary of St Stanislaus Masterson |
| 7 | 19 May 1904 | Sister Mary of St Francis Xavier Leamy | Professed 3 July 1895, Gloucester Street | Sister Mary of St Stanislaus Masterson |
| 8 | 16 May 1907 | Sister Mary of St Francis Xavier Leamy | | Sister Mary of St Stanislaus Masterson |
| 9 | 12 May 1910 | Mother Mary of St Aloysius McCabe | | Sister Mary of St Stanislaus Masterson |
| 10 | 8 May 1913 | Mother Mary of St Aloysius McCabe | d. 4 Feb. 1918 | Sister Mary of St Stanislaus Masterson |

*(Continued)*

**Figure 6.3**   (Continued)

| Order | Date of election | Superior | | Assistant |
|-------|------------------|----------|---|-----------|
| 11 | 8 June 1916 | Mother Mary of St Francis Xavier Leamy | | Sister Mary of St Stanislaus Masterson |
| 12 | 5 June 1919 | Mother Mary of St Francis Xavier Leamy | | Sister Mary of St Stanislaus Masterson |
| 13 | 1 June 1922 | Mother Mary of St Stanislaus Masterson | Professed 13 July 1892, Gloucester Street | Sister Mary of the Immaculate Heart Walshe |
| 14 | 3 July 1925 | Mother Mary of St Stanislaus Masterson | | Sister Mary of the Immaculate Heart Walshe |
| 15 | 24 May 1928 | Mother Mary of St Francis Xavier Leamy | d. 2 March 1931 | Sister Mary of the Immaculate Heart Walshe |
| 16 | 11 April 1931 | Mother Mary of the Immaculate Heart Walshe | Professed 26 April 1906, Gloucester Street | Sister Mary of St Stanislaus Masterson |
| 17 | 17 May 1934 | Mother Mary of the Immaculate Heart Walshe | | Sister Mary of St Stanislaus Masterson |
| 18 | 13 May 1937 | Mother Mary of St Stanislaus Masterson | | Sister Mary of the Immaculate Heart Walshe |
| 19 | 9 May 1940 | Mother Mary of St Stanislaus Masterson | | Sister Mary of the Immaculate Heart Walshe |
| 20 | 10 June 1943 | Mother Mary of the Immaculate Heart Walshe | | Sister Mary of St Stanislaus Masterson |
| 21 | 6 June 1946 | Mother Mary of the Immaculate Heart Walshe | Served as superior again 1955–58, d. 7 Jan. 1963 | Sister Mary of St Stanislaus Masterson, d. 23 Feb. 1951 |

5 November 1948, Federation of High Park Drumcondra, Gloucester Street and Kilmacud, from which date superiors were appointed, not elected

*Note:* The title Mother was reserved to the superior during her term of office; the same person was known as Sister when she served as assistant. Sources: XIX Book of the elections of the Convent of Our Lady of Charity of Dublin, commenced and established February 1887 (DARGS, OLC2/5/2 no. 1); obituaries, Gloucester Street (DARGS, OLC6/2).

first foundation.[59] There is a reference to High Park supplying milk for six weeks during 1887, for which the new community was eternally grateful, but it was in the spirit of sisterly support during a fever crisis, rather than of obligation.[60] When a successor to Sister Mary of St Bartholomew McDonnell was needed, and Sister Mary of St Ignatius Ryan, 'hidden in the shade of her lovely convent home' at High Park was elected, her transfer to Gloucester Street is described in melodramatic terms: 'she heroically left all to follow her Divine Master into exile'.[61] Only a few miles south of High Park – within walking distance – this project was an entirely separate foundation, and the sisters appointed to Gloucester Street had no right of return, or indeed any expectation that they might see High Park again, even to visit. It was not a branch house but an autonomous foundation; it would be united to the other houses of Our Lady of Charity through faithful observance of the 'rules, constitutions and customs of our holy institute', rather than through the government of a superior general or any other form of centralised administration.

In the tradition of Our Lady of Charity of Refuge, the role of the superior was crucial, and even more so when coupled with the honour and responsibility of foundress. The first act of Sister Mary of St Bartholomew McDonnell, dated 3 February 1887, was to swear solemnly, in writing, 'to live and die in the observance of the Rules, Constitutions and Customs of our holy Institute'. This was confirmed at the first chapter assembly on arrival in Gloucester Street, and presided over by Fr McMahon.[62] Her next official act was to oversee the election of an assistant superior. This was not a complicated task, as there were only two eligible candidates, the two choir sisters who had accompanied her: Sister Mary of St Vincent de Paul (Catherine Markey), and Sister Mary of St Angela (Jane Frances McCabe). Vincent Markey was duly elected assistant to Bartholomew McDonnell, in which role she 'seconded her every effort', as well as filling the office of mistress of penitents.[63] She was to serve in Gloucester Street for seven years until her death at the age of 50 years. The other choir sister, Sister Angela McCabe, was a niece of Bartholomew McDonnell and had endured for ten years 'all the hardships' incidental to a new foundation, acting in turn as sacristan, *économe* (bursar) and assistant, returning to High Park in 1896 where she died a year later, aged 42.[64] Local leadership in Gloucester Street would be headed by a very small number of sisters taking turns as superior and assistant for more than six decades (figure 6.3). Other members of the founding group were two lay sisters (*converse*), Sister Mary of St Anthony (Mary Daly) who was aged 47 at the time of the foundation,[65] and Sister Mary of St Elizabeth (Anne Kenny), a novice aged 31 or 32 who was to make her profession of vows in Gloucester

59  High Park, circular letter, 24 Mar. 1887, p. 6 (DARGS, OLC1/3/1 no. 15).

60  Gloucester Street, circular letter, 8 Dec. 1887.

61  Gloucester Street, circular letter, May 1896, p. 1 (DARGS, OLC2/3/1 no. 4).

62  Preamble, 'XVII Book of the Chapter of the Convent of Our Lady of Charity Dublin, Gloucester Street, commenced and established 17 February 1887' (DARGS, OLC2/5/2 no. 2).

63  Gloucester Street, circular letter, May 1896, p. 3.

64  Gloucester Street, circular letter, 15 Aug. 1901, pp 1–2; death letter, of Sister M. of St Angela McCabe (Jane Frances), d. 30 July 1897 (DARGS, OLC1/6/4 no. 73).

65  Death letter of Sister M. of St Anthony Daly (Mary), died 15 Feb. 1914 (DARGS, OLC2/6/4 no. 5).

Street and to spend her life in the laundry, kitchen and refectory.[66] There was one outdoor (*tourière*) sister, whose name has not been confirmed, but this may be Margaret Bailey (or Baily), who made her oblation or promises in High Park in 1884 (aged 24), and was in Gloucester Street during 1888 and 1889, at which point she returned to High Park.[67] Sister Bartholomew was elected assistant on 12 September 1894 due to the unexpected death of Sister Vincent Markey; 'the council [to the superior] was not elected, owing to the Sisters still being in the novitiate'.[68]

The setting up of the record-making and record-keeping systems in accordance with OLC tradition dramatically underlines the autonomy of the new house. It now had responsibility for securing funding, acknowledging benefactors, negotiating contracts and holding property in its own name. It would recruit postulants, receive and train novices and elect its own superior at three-year intervals (no superior could serve more than two terms consecutively). It would have to distribute the duties or offices of the house among its few members, and see that they kept these roles, as prescribed in the rule and customs book. It started its own annals, as was done by the first monastery of Caen and for the same purpose: 'to immortalise the conduct of Providence in their establishment and their progress', to engrave upon the hearts of the sisters 'the eternal memory of so many wonders wrought on their behalf' and to instruct and inspire succeeding generations.[69]

Separate registers were started, to record receptions and professions (book III), examination of the novices before profession (book IV), chapter decisions on admission of candidates to the noviceship (book XVII), the elections of superiors (book XIX) and the admission of penitents (book X). Setting up the register of benefactors was to prove far more complicated in the case of Gloucester Street than even John Eudes could have foreseen, as there were so many small benefactors, giving repeatedly and generously in kind, money and services.[70] Those who had contributed to the asylum in its earlier manifestations had to be remembered also, in perpetuity.[71]

What happened at Gloucester Street was grafted onto the Caen tree through the record-making and record-keeping practices. A translation

---

66   Death letter of Sister Elizabeth Kenny.
67   Electronic database, 'Residents of women's asylum' (DARGS, OLC2/8/1 no. 1), created from the women's entrance register, Gloucester Street (DARGS, OLC2/8/1 no. 2).
68   'XIX Book, elections of superiors' (DARGS, OLC2/5/2 no. 1).
69   'Annals of the Order of Our Lady of Charity instituted by Revd. John Eudes where are recorded the most remarkable events that have happened in the Monastery of Caen as well as in the other monasteries of the same order with the characters of several of the Religious who have been distinguished for their virtues. Compiled by order of the Council of the Monastery of Caen on 1 March 1722' (2 vols), MS, trans., commenced in High Park 1853, and continued in 1887 at Gloucester Street (DARGS, OLC2/1/1 nos. 1, 2). Hereafter, Annals of Caen.
70   *Constitutions*, p. 170.
71   'Annual Sacred Heart', list dated 1884–88, names and addresses of subscribers to the Sacred Heart lamps, Copy letters, pp 45–54; 'Immaculate Heart of Mary, Annual', names and addresses of subscribers, list starts 21 Aug. 1884, Copy letters, pp 133–8; second list 'Immaculate Heart of Mary, Perpetual', starts 19 Oct., no year but 1891 or earlier, Copy letters, pp 91–2.

of the annals of Caen, recording the founding days of the order from 1635 onwards (volume 1), had been started in High Park in 1853 (and continued in several hands). This copybook was given to mark the foundation of Gloucester Street in February 1887 and immediately used to enter the names of the first well-wishers and benefactors, the 36 'Ladies who attended the meeting' (undated). A subsequent numbered list of 135 items, with donors' names and addresses, is probably associated with the first 'grand bazaar' held in December 1888.[72] This was more than merely making economical use of blank pages; it was a conscious effort to connect the new foundation and its struggles with those of the 'cradle' of the order and its founder John Eudes, though Caen played no active part in the Gloucester Street foundation. The new foundation story would be written into the order's larger history, 17 February 1887 inserted into the roll of OLC house foundation dates and its struggles viewed against the larger canvas of OLC history – indeed, of salvation history. Clarification on countless small points of observance would be sought directly from Caen, seen by Gloucester Street (as indeed by High Park) as the model of 'best practice'.[73] In addition, Gloucester Street undertook to foster that 'mutual interest in each other's joys and sorrows' advocated by the founder through the long-established expedient of circular letters.[74] Taking on the weight of history and tradition, the Gloucester Street community worked hard to present itself as the latest branch of the 'old root' though its generous Dublin supporters understood it as a contemporary response to the compelling problem of prostitution in the city.

## Organising the Life of Gloucester Street Convent and Asylum in Accordance with the Principles, Practices and Spiritual Heritage of Our Lady of Charity of Refuge

On her appointment as its first superior, Sister Bartholomew McDonnell set herself the task of 'raising up' Gloucester Street magdalen asylum after decades of neglect.[75] The primary challenge, as she saw it, was to organise religious life and the life of the asylum according to the distinctive system of Our Lady of Charity of Refuge, as set out in the rule and customs book and embodied in the routines of the first monastery of the order in France. Arising from this overall aim were particular projects: the building of a new convent and asylum, requiring serious fundraising, and the 'marketing' of the charity to the Dublin public; the erection and furnishing of a new chapel, to be the spiritual heart of the house; fostering the spiritual life in the traditions of the order, as set out by the founder, John Eudes; the modernisation of the laundry (on which the financial viability of the enterprise depended); and the promotion of a devotional 'ambience' (or religious atmosphere) both inside and outside the house, albeit in a densely-built complex where open or garden space was always rather limited. Kindly, motherly concern coupled

---

72  See Annals of Caen, ii.
73  No title, n.d., copybook, in numbered question and answer format, section titled 'Confessions and Communions', item no. 6 (DARGS, OLC2/5/1 no. 9). Hereafter, Copybook, questions and answers.
74  Gloucester Street, circular letter, May 1896, p. 1.
75  Sister M. Bartholomew McDonnell to Lord Mayor, Dec. 1888, Copy letters, p. 37.

with a zeal for the perfect living out of 'the rule' by all who lived under her authority – sisters, novices and women residents alike – were expected of the new superior, and she expected it of herself. Charity, obedience, self-sacrifice, penance and mortification were expected of all.

The new foundation was within easy reach of so many religious communities that the services of a priest were readily secured for Mass, confession, the last sacraments, retreats and spiritual talks (*des prédicaleurs*).[76] Priest relatives also helped out on occasion.[77] The location of the house, beside the major transport nodes of port and rail, near the residence and offices of the archbishop, and close to the seminaries of All Hallows and Holy Cross College Clonliffe, ensured that the community had a stream of Irish and overseas clerical visitors seeking to celebrate Mass, and willing to address both the 'poor penitents' and the sisters. At least one bishop, Bishop Mannix of Melbourne, took advantage of the welcome to press for a foundation in his own diocese, but to no avail.[78]

Organising the recitation of the Divine Office in common – the duty of the choir sisters – was not so easy as the numbers were small, but nevertheless the principal daytime hours were recited from the outset: matins, lauds, terce, vespers, compline. Whatever liturgical books – missals, breviaries, vesperals – were decided on or sponsored by Caen, the Gloucester Street community took as carrying an imprimatur for use in their monastery.[79] Not only on the larger issues, but also in smaller matters of liturgical decorum – where and when to stand, sit, kneel, kiss the ground, incline the head; the portions of the office said 'in high psalmody' and those said 'straight voice' – the small Gloucester Street community sought faithfully to reflect the hallowed practices of the first monastery.[80] In the preparation of the annual 'spiritual account', covering 'the practice of the observances and advancement in virtue' of the community 'and the progress made for the salvation of souls', the template provided by Caen was followed: 'we have during the year ___– (so many penitents) ___ – so many approached the sacraments in good dispositions___ – so many died___ – so many left or returned to their friends etc.'[81]

Regular visitations of the convent and asylum by the archbishop or his deputy were in place from the first year.[82] While the reports focused on spiritual matters – such as 'the faithful observance of rule, regularity of the

---

76   Priests were drawn from the following communities over the period of this study: Dominicans, Jesuits, Capuchins, Vincentians, Augustinians, Redemptorists, the missionary seminary of All Hallows, the diocesan seminary at Clonliffe and the pro-cathedral parish of Marlborough Street.

77   These included the first superior's brother Paul McDonnell, a Carmelite priest, and nephews, John and Joseph McCabe (brothers to Sisters Angela (Jane Frances) and Aloysius (Bridget)), also Carmelite priests; Gloucester Street, circular letter, Aug. 1905, p. 3.

78   Gloucester Street, circular letter, May 1913, p. 3 (NDC Caen, Archives Versailles).

79   For example, see reference to vesperal sent from Caen, 'conformable to that used by our Holy Mother the Church', Gloucester Street, circular letter, 15 Aug. 1901, p. 7.

80   Copybook, questions and answers, first section, 'The Divine Office and Meditations', 107 items.

81   Ibid., section titled 'The Father Superior, Confessor, & Visits', item no. 1.

82   Gloucester Street, circular letter, 15 Aug. 1901, p. 3.

exercises, and careful instruction of our penitents'[83] – the inspectors had access to all parts of the asylum and convent and free access to all residents, sisters and women alike. In many respects, throughout the first decade, the house fell short of what Sister Bartholomew McDonnell intended it should be. Despite her zeal for the full implementation of all the standard practices of OLC religious life, she had an insufficient number of choir sisters (seven were required) to have a proper chapter and elections and, until the new building was ready, they had no space to admit new candidates.[84] So few and inexperienced were the numbers that they had to petition High Park for a superior to replace McDonnell when she had completed the maximum of two terms (six years). Sister Mary of St Ignatius Ryan came from High Park in 1893 to succeed her, but on the completion of one term, the founding superior was re-elected to the office and continued until her death two years later.[85]

Organising – or rather, re-organising – the women, *notre classe de Ste Madeleine*, was even more problematic. There simply was not the space to 'arrange' or group the 54 women recorded as resident in August 1890 according to the OLC tradition. Besides, they were already following well 'their own rule', which was probably an amalgam of the arrangements that pre-dated 1873 and the Mercy rule. There is a brief account of the system in operation in the four years or so before the Mercy sisters took charge. As a lay asylum, under the direction of Miss Coonan, the women assembled for morning and night prayers, heard Mass on Sundays and holydays in their own little oratory, and were frequently visited by priests who took a 'kindly interest' in the penitentiary, both Vincentian priests from Phibsborough and diocesan clergy from Marlborough Street. The laundry work occupied them all day and 'often far into the night', as there was no machinery; 'consequently all the washing and ironing was done by hand'.[86] The Mercy rule warned sisters against being too curious or censorious about the previous lives of applicants to their House of Mercy, so it is likely that the practice of accepting women without close questioning – and keeping the barest minimum of personal information on file – was already the norm.[87] The new sisters recognised that there were already long-established routines and customs, and moved cautiously. The first initiative to be reported was the introduction of the sodality of the Children of Mary, after the retreat of 1888, which the other houses were told was warmly received; more than one woman sought to wear her Child of Mary medal on her deathbed.[88] This was followed in 1890 by creating the 'Class of Perseverance', which involved taking on a consecrate or magdalen name and undertaking to follow a rule of life, paralleling religious life (as discussed in chapter 2); the first admitted were three

83  Gloucester Street, circular letter, 18 Dec. 1892, p. 1.

84  It was stated that three choir sisters came on the foundation, Gloucester Street, circular letter, 18 Dec. 1892, p. 1. In January 1890, the only professed members were one choir sister, one lay sister and two outdoor sisters but, by Aug. 1890, there were four professed choir sisters, two lay sisters and two outdoor sisters, with a further five novices and postulants across all ranks. Gloucester Street, *circulaire*, 24 avril 1890, p. 5.

85  Gloucester Street, circular letter, 15 Aug. 1901, p. 1.

86  From account of an 'aged penitent' who entered the house in 1869, *Golden jubilee*, p. 16.

87  Mercy rule, ch. IV, of the admission of poor women, pp 12–13.

88  Gloucester Street, circular letter, 15 Aug. 1901, p. 9.

long-resident women. One of these was already a golden jubilarian of the asylum and the hope was held out that her good example would encourage other residents to consecrate themselves to the loving hearts of Jesus and Mary.[89]

Accounts of life in the asylum dwell heavily on the spiritual supports offered to the women, including annual retreat, weekly confession and Sunday sermon. Marian processions, exposition of the Blessed Sacrament, benediction and other para-liturgies also feature, along with 'sacred recitations and tableaux of an instructive character', put on by friends of the institute on feast-days.[90] Redemptorist or Vincentian priests, allowing some continuity with the previous regime, usually gave the retreats to the women, and it was a matter of pride that they were never deprived of these opportunities, even when the house was under pressure and the sisters had to forego theirs.[91] A decade after taking on the asylum, the OLC community scribe reported that there were, on average, 70 women in residence and, 'excepting an occasional burst of temper, there is no serious fault to be met with'.[92] A spirit of docility and simplicity was the boast of the asylum, as it was of the convent. The women were to be pitied, rather than censured; with the women newly entered, 'we try to gain them to God by kindness as they are seldom corrected by rigour'. The day was punctuated by prayer and devotional exercises, and the women were expected to keep the 'great silence' of a religious house when the bell for 8pm was rung.[93] Celebrations were tied into the cycle of the liturgical year, with its feast-days and solemnities. Major feasts were preceded by retreats and novenas; the celebration itself was often spread over a triduum and the appropriate statue, altar or chapel was decorated in the most lavish and imaginative way – candelabras, alabaster vases, rich lace and fresh flowers are all mentioned.

The circumstances around the deaths of two of the residents in 1890 give glimpses into the new regime as it was being established, and the ways in which religion was incorporated into daily life. When Alphonsine, a young girl, died in January 1890 of consumption, she had spent some time in the infirmary, surrounded with all the consolations of religion. The other women, during their customary procession to their recreation room held in honour of Our Lady, this day decided to make the procession to obtain for her the grace of a happy death; the obituarist recounted that she gave up her soul to God only when her companions arrived at the infirmary, their hymns and prayers to Mary giving every reason to hope that the Blessed Virgin would indeed be her intercessor in heaven. The other 1890 death was that of Jerome, of a 're-spectable family', who had battled with alcoholism all her long years as a resident in this asylum. Her remarkable piety, fidelity to daily Mass and frequent recourse to the sacraments, her excellent work ethic and reluctance to enter the infirmary until she was visibly weaker, were all cited in her obituary.

The asylum routine as established by the sisters of Our Lady of Charity at High Park was introduced here in its essentials, and step-by-step superseded the Mercy system. The women were given house names on entry to

---

89   Gloucester Street, *circulaire*, 24 avril 1890, p. 5.
90   Gloucester Street, circular letter, May 1896, p. 3.
91   Ibid., p. 2.
92   Ibid., p. 3.
93   Copybook, questions and answers, section titled 'The Penitents', items no. 2 and 7.

ensure their anonymity ('Alphonsus' was given out 11 times in the first few years).[94] The daily routine was punctuated with prayer, devotional exercises and religious instruction, with set times for rising, meals, work and recreation in common. There was a separate infirmary, to which those past their working lives and the ill were transferred, and nothing was neglected that might better prepare the dying for their final moments. This included the attentions of the chaplain, who brought Holy Communion and administered extreme unction,[95] and the presence of a sister at the bedside to watch their final passing 'to the silent land, we hope to the light of heaven'.[96] A moving and flowery obituary, sketching in some facts (where known) of the woman's background, playing heavily on the sufferings and temptations she had endured and the story of her journey in faith, with focus on the final illness, the bedside vigil and the moment when the soul was yielded up to God, were composed in the OLC tradition (and as was done for the sisters). These real-life stories were meant to inspire others to trust in the infinite loving-kindness of God and to praise Him 'for all His mercies in time and eternity'.[97]

## First Major Building Phase and Fundraising, Gloucester Street Monastery and Asylum, 1888–98

The need to enlarge the asylum was evident to the sisters of Our Lady of Charity from the day they took over from the Mercy sisters. Far more applicants sought entry than the house could hold, and large numbers had to be turned away.[98] Even as essential (and expensive) repairs to the existing premises were undertaken, ambitious plans were drawn up for a new building and a separate chapel. In July 1888, it was reported that, over the preceding year and a half, about £2,000 had been spent on the asylum buildings exclusively, including £218 'paid architect and measurer for new plans now submitted to His Grace'.[99] Another report of about the same date boasts that 'we are making efforts very successfully to raise it after 70 years' abject poverty to an important home for many who require it'.[100]

The development of the campus was to be incremental, dependent on the acquisition of adjoining plots from owners, leaseholders and their representatives who, understandably, saw this as a once-off opportunity to profit handsomely and set outrageous prices for ruined houses and derelict yards. The means to embark on a major building plan so quickly came through the willingness of a Mr Kelly to make an advance of £500, at 5% per annum interest. This money was transferred to the sisters on 15 September 1887 (he had previously lent the Mercy sisters £500, at the same commercial rate of

94   Other names which feature repeatedly as house names include Anne, Annunciata, Augustine, Barbara, Berchmans, Bernadette, Borgia, Brendan, Charlotte, Christina, Clare, Columba, Cortona, Cyril, Dominica, Elisabeth, Emily, Finbar, Francis, Gabriel, Genevieve, Hilda, Isidore, Joachim, Joan, Josephine, Martha, Rebecca, Sophia, Veronica.
95   Copybook, questions and answers, section titled 'The Penitents', item no. 1.
96   Gloucester Street, circular letter, May 1896, p. 3.
97   Annals of Caen, i, preamble.
98   Sister M. Bartholomew McDonnell to Dear Madam, n.d. but Sept. 1888, Copy letters, p. 57.
99   Memorandum concerning proposed new buildings, n.d. but July 1888, Copy letters, p. 28.
100  Sister M. Bartholomew McDonnell to Fr Donegan, n.d. but 1888, Copy letters, p. 38.

interest).[101] The facts are somewhat at variance with the popular account, which was that a gentleman donor had promised to give 12,500 francs (£500) to enlarge the monastery if this sum could be matched by a sufficient number of smaller donations.[102] What was by any calculation an audacious project was made possible by the readiness of the sisters – in practice, of the superior, Sister Bartholomew McDonnell – to carry a massive debt, trusting that Divine Providence would in time give them the means to extinguish it. Having the building work in progress was, she felt, the surest way to generate interest: 'It is reasonable to expect when the Public see a real effort being made that donations to at least a moderate amount will be received'.[103] Fundraising events could be timed to coincide with the stages of the building. Thus in July 1888 she negotiated with the Hibernian Bank to advance £5,000 for three years at 4.5% interest, 'which will meet the contractor's demands pending the Bazaar, a collection at the laying of the foundation stone, and another collection at a meeting proposed to be held after the convent and chapel have been roofed'.[104] By September 1888, Sister Bartholomew could report 'the building has been begun, but at a cost of £8,000 all of which has yet to be obtained'.[105]

In the competitive market that was the Dublin charity scene, there were huge difficulties in attracting funds for an asylum for destitute and 'fallen' women. The sisters of Our Lady of Charity had the further difficulty of being confined to the enclosure, unlike (for example) the Mercy or Holy Faith sisters, whose superiors could (and did) call in person to conduct their business. Sister Bartholomew McDonnell's fundraising strategy was to rely on the written word and on the close collaboration of trusted intermediaries, both of which she accomplished with remarkable success. The numerous copy letters in her hand – including letters to people she had met before, however briefly, when she was superior in High Park (1872-8) – testify to the power of her pen. One of those she most actively involved in promoting the interests of the new project was Mrs Sims, the sister of Sister Mary of St Stanislaus Brennan (High Park, assistant 1866-72) who, with her husband, were counted among 'the unfailing and faithful friends' of Gloucester Street, as they were already of High Park.[106] Patrick Kennedy who had rendered 'inestimable services' to High Park and now Gloucester Street, acted as debt collector, donor, clerk of works, financial adviser and public relations consultant. In brief, 'his efforts to lighten our difficulties, and to remove all obstacles that might impede the success of our Foundation, were unsparing. … from morning till night he was at his post

101    [Superior] to Mr Kelly, 2 Nov. 1887, Copy letters, p. 12.
102    Placing of monastery under the protection of St Joseph, 30 June 1887, 'Book in which the Sisters of the Congregation of Our Lady of Charity write the years and the days of their vows and the annual confirmations which they make in this monastery of Gloucester Street Dublin and which has been established the 17 February 1887' (DARGS, OLC2/6/1 no. 1); hereafter, Gloucester Street profession register.
103    The winning tender was that of Mr Meade, for a total of £8,335. Memorandum concerning proposed new buildings, n.d. but July 1888, Copy letters, p. 28.
104    Ibid.
105    Sister M. Bartholomew McDonnell to Dear Madam, n.d. but Sept. 1888, Copy letters, p. 57 (DARGS, OLC2/5/2 no. 13).
106    Mr and Mrs Sims donated £300 to the construction of the new convent at High Park in 1885, High Park, circular letter, 24 Mar. 1887, p. 4 (DARGS, OLC1/3/1 no. 15)

superintending the workmen and was utterly regardless of his own needs'.[107] He died on 17 February 1897, ten years to the day on which the OLC sisters arrived in Gloucester Street, and his passing was noted with real sorrow.[108]

The readiness of relatives of the sisters and key friends outside the enclosure to get involved was important to the asylum project, but McDonnell also needed to identify its strongest selling points, and to secure some 'headline' donors who would set an example to the wider public. The status of Gloucester Street as the only Catholic magdalen asylum in the city was in its favour, as was the example of Jesus Himself in reaching out to the woman who was a sinner. Despite being in existence for some decades, it was a very poor institution ('without exception, the very poorest in Dublin').[109] All of these points were used to argue its entitlement to some small share of the generous alms disbursed annually in Dublin, especially at Christmas. In December 1887, the attention of the 'good Christians' of the city was drawn to the 'forsaken inmates of Gloucester Street', a class of persons 'who have little sympathy except from those who seriously reflect on the love of Our Lord bestowed on Mary Magdalen'.[110] The support of the archbishop and of other Dublin notables was particularly important in the face of public hostility towards – or disinterest in – the fate of destitute and 'fallen' girls.[111] Archbishop Walsh expressed both 'confidence and generosity' towards the new venture, with a contribution of £300 in September 1888 and subsequent donations up to his death.[112] Generous new donors were sought, and found, among the family connections of the sisters.[113]

The names of supporters of standing in political, ecclesiastical and business circles were shamelessly used to encourage others to be generous. Sister Bartholomew McDonnell went to endless trouble to secure the attendance of the Lord Mayor Mr Sexton at the blessing of the foundation stone, underlining 'what a benefit and advantage our Lord Mayor can bestow by his valuable presence'.[114] Prospective wealthy donors were circulated with the information that 'His Grace will perform the ceremony and, you will be glad to hear, has given ample proof of his interest by subscribing the munificent sum of £1,500'.[115] Bishops were informed that the asylum offered shelter to women 'from every diocese in Ireland', it was a work in which the archbishop was actively interested and it was their 'gracious presence' at the forthcoming ceremony that was sought, rather than monetary help.[116] The time and energy invested in advance paid dividends by all accounts, with effusive

---

107    Gloucester Street, circular letters, 8 Dec. 1896, p. 1 and 15 Aug. 1901, p. 1.
108    Gloucester Street, circular letter, 15 Aug. 1901, p. 1.
109    M. McDonnell, superioress, to Mrs Mooney, Mountjoy Square, 20 July 1887, Copy letters, p. 10.
110    Christmas appeal, n.d. but Dec. 1887, Copy letters, pp 16–17.
111    Sister M. Bartholomew McDonnell to Fr Donegan, n.d. but Sept. 1888, Copy letters, p. 40.
112    Same to Fr Petit, Sept. 1888, Copy letters, p. 32; Sister M. of St Aloysius Morris to Dr Walsh, Christmas 1900 (DDA, Walsh papers, Religious, 1900).
113    For example, Sister M. of St Aloysius McCabe to My dear sister, Dec. 1898, notebook, 'copy of letters' (DARGS, OLC2/5/2 no. 4).
114    Sister M. Bartholomew McDonnell to Lord Mayor, n.d. but Sept. 1888. Copy letters, pp 41–42.
115    Same to Fr Donegan, n.d. but Sept. 1888, Copy letters, p. 40.
116    Same to 'Their Lordships', 6 Sept. 1888, Copy letters, p. 35.

thanks to the attendees for 'helping to lay the foundation of a happy home for many who are too anxious to enter it'.[117] The success of the day, however, lay in the exposure it gave to a charity that was relatively unknown until then, rather than in the total sum raised.[118]

Possibly more important to Gloucester Street as a steady, annual source of income was the bazaar and the charity sermon, staples of charity fundraising throughout Britain and Ireland. The drawing power of a bazaar could be enhanced by the patronage of titled personages; some might be prevailed on to furnish a stall, and even to act as sellers on the day.[119] Letters to Lord French and to Sir Richard Martin requesting their patronage include a list of 'the names of other gentlemen I am asking a similar favour of', presumably in the hope that one would put pressure on another to do the generous thing and allow their names to be associated with the charity.[120] The new superior called a meeting of the 'ladies', headed by Countess Plunkett, and ambitious plans were put in train for the first bazaar. This appears to have been held in December 1888, in Leinster Hall (later the site of the Theatre Royal, Hawkins Street), in advance of which Sister Bartholomew McDonnell wrote to Arnotts department store and other companies looking for prizes, and got the indefatigable Patrick Kennedy to approach people to allow themselves to be named as patrons. An Augustinian priest, Fr Alphonsus Walsh, presided over several preparatory meetings of the 'lady stall-holders', encouraging them 'to work earnestly for the charity'.[121] Getting the archbishop, Dr Walsh to approve the November 1889 bazaar tickets before printing was but one of the numerous ways in which he was kept abreast of developments by the astute superior.[122] At the bazaar of November 1895, named patrons included the Countess of Cadogan, the Countess of Arran, Lady Inchiquin and the Lord Mayor and Lady Mayoress of Dublin, all of whom 'took a personal part in it, which tended much to its success'.[123] Raffles were associated with each bazaar; a Mr Andrew Keogh and his 'influential friends' were credited in 1898 for securing excellent prizes.[124] The first charity sermon under OLC management was held in St Francis Xavier's, Gardiner Street chapel, on 16 October 1887; the preacher was Revd N. Walshe, who had already helped out in High Park,[125] and various dignitaries were solicited to favour the occasion 'with your presence and influence'.[126]

---

117   Same to Dear Sir, July 1888, Copy letters, p. 31.
118   Days after the foundation-stone ceremony, donations stood at £450 (including the archbishop's most recent donation of £100). Sister M. Bartholomew McDonnell to My dear Lord Archbishop, Sept. 1888, Copy letters, p. 34–5.
119   Sister M. Bartholomew McDonnell to Dear Sir, n.d. but Oct. or Nov. 1888, Copy letters, pp 43–4.
120   [Superior] to Lord French; to Sir Richard Martin, n.d. but early 1889 Copy letters, pp 68–9.
121   Gloucester Street, circular letter, 18 Dec. 1892, p. 2.
122   [Superior] to Fr Petit, 1 Mar. 1889, Copy letters, p. 69.
123   Gloucester Street, circular letter, May 1896, pp 2, 3.
124   Gloucester Street, circular letter, 15 Aug. 1901, p. 5.
125   [Mother M. of St Bartholomew McDonnell] to Fr Walshe, n.d. but Oct. 1887, Copy letters, p. 14.
126   [Superior] to Lord Mayor, n.d. but Oct. 1887, Copy letters, p. 9.

The most successful, at least in terms of emotive appeal, seems to have been that of October 1896 when 'Our claims were put before the public in words of pathetic eloquence, which powerfully affected them and influenced them to give a practical sympathy with our work'.[127]

The size of the network established to support the Gloucester Street asylum in 1887, when it was effectively re-founded under OLC management, is evident in the multi-volume manuscript 'Registry of the founders and benefactors of the community'.[128] The first major refurbishment and building phase, from 1887 through to the late 1890s, resulted from the efforts of a very large number of persons, drawn from all parts of the city; their memory was kept alive through the recitation in the community each year of their names and gifts.[129] Generous supporters were to be found among the middle classes, professional families and shop-keepers of the north city, including from Blessington Street, Great Britain Street, Eccles Street, Dorset Street, Geraldine Street, Clonliffe and Drumcondra. Support was drawn from the immediate environs of the asylum, including Lower Gloucester Street itself, Fizgibbon Street, Amiens Street and the North Strand. A Miss Costelloe of St Lawrence Hotel, Howth, is recorded as a benefactor, as are a number of residents in the south city townships of Rathmines and Rathgar. The most striking feature is the geographical spread, with practically every part of the city represented. Efforts to advertise it as a metropolitan charity appear to have been successful.[130]

Something of the teamwork and excitement behind the bazaars and raffles of the late 1880s can be glimpsed from a numbered list of 135 items.[131] These include 'an exquisite cameo set in gold of the Virgin and Child', 'an antique oil painting of the Last Supper', 'a stained glass panel of Irish scenery', 'a fancy basket china and glass', '*biscuitère*', 'Canadian sewing machine family hand', 'splendid double-barrelled gun'. Mrs Sims gave a 'cosey beautifully crewel worked', while Lady C. Bellingham donated 'a pair of Roman cameo ear-rings'. One of the novelty items was 'a Musselman pipe (£35) Mrs T. Farrell O'Connell Street', while the 'splendid porcelain thermometer hand-mounted in bronze' presented by Patrick Cahill, optician, of Wellington Quay, was probably in the same category. The name of the donor of 'a real seal coat perfectly new cost £25 guineas' is left blank ('presented by ___ ').

127  Gloucester Street, circular letter, 8 Dec. 1896 (DARGS, OLC2/3/1 no. 4)
128  See 'Book 5, Registry of the Founders and Benefactors of the community of Our Lady of Charity of Refuge Dublin', entries dated 17 Feb. 1887 to Apr. 1974 (DARGS, OLC2/9/4 nos. 1 to 5).
129  High Park put the following question to Caen in Sept. 1896: 'Our dear Revd. Mother wants to know if the reading of the benefactors' book may be divided into two or three parts as we find it very difficult to finish it at one chapter, it requiring nearly 3 hours to read it entire (High Park)'. 'Ans: Twenty years ago we were much in the same case, but we abridged it in uniting together the different gifts of the same family, precising (*sic*) however the different dates. This allows us to make the reading in about half an hour. Each year we enter the fresh gifts', Copybook, questions and answers, section titled 'Different points of observance, item no. 38. In practice, the 'large benefactors' book' was recited each Sept., the 'small benefactors' book' each March.
130  See 'Book 5, Registry of the Founders and Benefactors of the community of Our Lady of Charity of Refuge Dublin', entries 17 Feb. 1887–Apr. 1974 (DARGS, OLC2/9/4 nos. 1 to 5).
131  List of items donated, back of bound volume, Annals of Caen, i.

Convent. Gloucester Street North. Dublin.

**Figure 6.4**  Monastery of Our Lady of Charity of Refuge, Gloucester Street, Dublin, undated postcard but *c.* 1925.

Rural contributions included 'a large fat sheep presented by Mr John Carroll, Queen's County'.

## Devotional Life and the Completion of the House and Chapel of Gloucester Street, 1887-1910

The first new building, the convent, was described on its completion in 1890 as a simple, solid building of three storeys, about 80 feet long and 20 feet wide, and facing onto Gloucester Street (figure 6.4). The ground floor had three parlours, the refectory, the community laundry and a wide corridor. The second floor held the community room, the novitiate, the bursar's office and two other small rooms. The top storey consisted of 20 cells or small bedrooms, and bathrooms. In terms of health, the new sanitary arrangements were described as perfect. Niches for life-size statues were part of the interior design.[132] The high quality of the construction was attributed in part to the close supervision of their loyal friend Patrick Kennedy, who attended the building site to ensure that all was done in the best and most durable way.[133] But the city-centre location, with its noise and dirt and frequent intrusion by burglars, was still far from the monastic ideal. The best that could be done was to block the city out from within, and to improve the outer defences. The superior elected in 1898, Sister Mary of St Aloysius McCabe, tried to enhance 'that feeling of enclosure so dear to religious souls' by

132    Gloucester Street, circular letter, 15 Aug. 1901, p. 6.
133    Gloucester Street, *circulaire*, 24 avril 1890, p. 5.

**Figure 6.5**  High altar and sanctuary, Monastery of Our Lady of Charity of Refuge, Gloucester Street, Dublin, undated postcard but *c.* 1925.

having the windows covered with 'handsome coloured tracery', as well as getting the floors stained and polished so that none of the 'poor penitents' would need to be employed scrubbing the convent floors.[134] It was also under her orders that 'crystal glass screens' were placed in all the windows: 'these screens attract the light, and at the same time they shut out all view from the streets, this we appreciate very much'.[135] It was she who had an iron fence of 'ingenious design' erected around the garden, 'which screens us from being overlooked by the dwellers in the neighbourhood', besides which 'it adds also to the picturesque appearance of the surroundings'.[136] This was but the first of many railings; by 1910 'a very high expanded metal railing' was erected to keep out intruders.[137] Major new laundry buildings were still in process of erection in 1913 under the energetic leadership of Aloysius McCabe; several 'useless old houses' at the rear of the convent chapel facing Mecklenburgh Street/Lower Tyrone Street were torn down (figure 6.2). The new building was to include 'bathroom, receiving room with wardrobes, workroom with large presses', its ground floor to consist of 'sacristy stores, carpenters' workshops, van sheds, harness room, soap stores and stoving room',[138] the latter presumably indicated by the chimney on figure 6.2 (1939). The household was reported to be exactly 150 in 1913, made up of 26 professed sisters and one novice, 115 women ('penitents')

134   Gloucester Street, circular letter, 15 Aug. 1901, p. 6
135   Gloucester Street, circular letter, Aug. 1905, p. 2.
136   Gloucester Street, circular letter, 15 Aug. 1901, p. 7.
137   Gloucester Street, circular letter, May 1910, p. 3.
138   Gloucester Street, circular letter, May 1913, p. 4.

and eight men (a chaplain, foreman, stoker, two vanmen, a gardener, a carpenter and an errand-boy).[139] It had come a long way between foundation and silver jubilee.

It was the chapel which was at the heart of the monastery (figure 6.5). The new church, under Mr Byrne as architect and Messrs Meade as builders, was described as a 'very beautiful example of classic architecture'.[140] The late 19th-century descriptions still hold for the most part. The plan was simple, with the nave divided by a single aisle, with 'well-made benches', and a block of choir stalls on either side. The women's benches were ranged in front facing the altar. There was never need for a grille or divide, as the women and sisters were all within the enclosure. There was a semi-circular apse, the full height of the church, within which the tabernacle and altar were set as a single unit (until the liturgical reforms following the Second Vatican Council). The roof was barrel vaulted with a geometric design of panels, the four windows on each side were set high in the walls. This allowed the carved wood stations of the cross ('delicately coloured and mounted in drab and gold') to be at eye level.[141] Colour was suffused through the stained glass windows, and the many niches – in the classical tradition – were occupied with statues. The church was entered through the avant choir or small chapel, over which the organ gallery protruded into the church. Off the organ gallery were two small rooms, with glazed openings to the church and their own tiny fireplaces. These rooms were used by invalids to unite with the church services happening below.

When construction had advanced to the point of roofing the chapel, the sisters issued an explicit invitation to a Mr Murphy to consider donating the cost of the bell, namely £54. The request was timed with exactitude, as the erection of a bell 'can never be done hereafter without much additional expense'. The significance of a chapel bell pealing several times a day over a district notorious for poverty and prostitution was stressed: 'Great importance is attached to the erection of this bell which may often soften many a heart in the degraded streets surrounding our Asylum'.[142] Whether it was this Mr Murphy, or someone else, who paid for the bell has not been determined, but it would have been difficult to resist such an appeal, and a bell was erected over the chapel.[143]

On the blessing of the chapel and the first Mass on 27 March 1892, it was immediately the home of the 'Adorable Sacrifice' and the focus of household devotion, both personal and communal.[144] The first midnight

139   Ibid., p. 6.
140   Sister M. Bartholomew McDonnell to Mr Murphy, 1890, Copy letters, pp 76–7; Gloucester Street, circular letter, 18 Dec. 1892, p. 1.
141   These were donated by Mr Murphy who died in 1896, and cost £150. Gloucester Street, circular letter, May 1896, p. 2.
142   McDonnell to Murphy, 1890, Copy letters, pp 76.
143   There is a very full record of larger donations and bequests for this period but, to date, none relating specifically to the chapel bell has been identified, see 'Book 5, Registry of the Founders and Benefactors'. The Mr Murphy whose death was mourned in 1896 had previously donated stations of the cross for the chapel and may be the person who was petitioned about the bell, but the name is too common to be certain. Gloucester Street, circular letter, May 1896, p. 2.
144   Gloucester Street, circular letter, 18 Dec. 1892, p. 1.

**Figure 6.6**   Chapel of St John Eudes with shrine encasing his relics, Monastery of Our Lady of Charity of Refuge, Gloucester Street, Dublin, undated postcard but *c.* 1925.

Mass was held Christmas 1893 when, as reported to the other houses, all approached the altar for Communion, the music was beautifully rendered 'and the calm spirit of which the angels sung seemed to have rested on all hearts'.[145] The furnishing of the chapel advanced incrementally up to 1910. Practically every significant item of sacred furniture or fittings – silver-gilt tabernacle, stained glass, marble altars, altar rail and brass gate, sanctuary lamp, stations of the cross, sacred vessels, monstrance, altar linen, lace, candelabra, vases and much more – was the gift of a friend, relative or group of friends, and recorded in the 'registry of benefactors', rather than on inscribed plates or in any other public way.

Improvements to the lighting, painting and ventilation were made and unmade.[146] In 1893, the newly-elected superior, Sister Ignatius Ryan, found the chapel 'unpleasantly lightsome' and introduced tinted glass, 'thus imparting that dim religious light so suitable to holy ground'.[147] This temporary work was replaced by the insertion of eight stained glass windows of heavy tracery, 'with an angel in the centre of each, holding in his hand some emblem of the Passion'.[148] A later superior, Sister Aloysius McCabe,

145   Gloucester Street, circular letter, May 1896, p. 2.
146   About two feet of the glass in the lower part of each of the eight windows was 'brazed into a square frame, hung on brass pivets' (*sic*) to rectify the lack of ventilation. Gloucester Street, circular letter, 15 Aug. 1901, p. 5.
147   Ibid.
148   Ibid., p. 3. The windows in the nave (from the back of the chapel, right side) are of St Thérèse of the Child Jesus, St Mary Magdalen, St John Eudes and the Immaculate Heart of Mary, matched on the left by St Anne, St Augustine, St Joseph and the Sacred Heart of Jesus.

found the chapel unduly dark and added five stained glass windows in the dome of the central apse, representing the four evangelists, with the Holy Ghost in the centre. She too was responsible for having the walls and dome 'artistically painted' in April 1903 with adoring angels and flights of cherubs, the stucco work picked out in gold.[149] But it was the windows, 'real works of art in design and colouring', that were most frequently extolled by commentators: 'they throw a beautiful mellow light on the altars and sanctuary'.[150]

The furnishing of the chapel was completed with the installation of a high altar and two side altars, the gifts of named friends and relatives of the sisters. The first proper high altar was installed a week before Easter 1901, containing 'a beautiful figure of the dead Christ, which looks most effective'.[151] This was shortly afterwards replaced by another marble altar depicting St Mary Magdalen washing the feet of Jesus in the house of Simon the leper. The first altar was moved to the side, as St Joseph's altar, where the representation of Christ's death is flanked by carved side panels showing the hearts of Jesus and Mary intertwined. At the other side is Our Blessed Lady's altar, with the Annunciation in the centre, and lilies in the side panels.[152]

One further project was the transformation of the avant chapel (1903-4), which was little more than a porch where the sisters assembled in their choir cloaks, before processing into the church. The spiral staircase leading to the organ gallery above was removed entirely – access via the first floor of the convent being judged sufficient – allowing this 'objectionable and inconvenient' space to be transformed into a small chapel (figure 6.6). Decorated in green and gold, this was furnished with a stained glass window showing the founder John Eudes in one of his best-loved poses: kneeling at the feet of the Blessed Virgin who carries the infant Jesus ('the design taken from a marble group by M. Valentine').[153]

## Fostering the Devotional Life in the Tradition of Our Lady of Charity at Gloucester Street Monastery and Asylum

The building, decoration and furnishing of the chapel was integral to the establishment of the monastery of Our Lady of Charity of Refuge at Gloucester Street, but efforts to create a thoroughly religious ambience extended to all parts of the complex, indoor and outdoor, to all times of the day and to the cycle of the year. The overall aim, using the language and theology of John Eudes, was to arouse an emotional response towards the heart of Christ, font of tender love and compassion, who most desires and cherishes

149  Gloucester Street, circular letter, May 1910, p. 4.
150  Gloucester Street, circular letter, 15 Aug. 1905, p. 4.
151  This was the gift of a Mr Thompson, Gloucester Street, circular letter, 15 Aug., 1901, p. 7.
152  The high altar, with the image of Mary Magdalen washing the feet of Christ, was funded by Mr P.J. McCabe, brother of the superior Sister Aloysius McCabe. Mass was said on it by their brother, Fr Joseph McCabe, in the presence of the extended McCabe family on 21 June 1904. Our Lady's altar was the gift of Mr Andrew Keogh, 'relation of dear Sister Assistant', Gloucester Street, circular letter, Aug. 1905, pp 4–6.
153  Ibid., p. 2.

the poor sinner.[154] Every possible means was directed towards that end. The celebration of the Eucharist in the chapel spilled over into processions and benediction, while private daily visits to the chapel were expected of all who had the privilege of living under the same roof as the Blessed Sacrament. It was in the chapel that the Way of the Cross could be made, but invitations to contemplate the passion of Christ could be found throughout the house.[155] Hymn-singing and the recitation of prayers was not confined to the chapel but could be heard in workrooms, in the recreation hall and in the dormitories. Linking the chapel to the asylum infirmary by a small glazed passage was a spiritual union with the sick, as well as a practical means of enabling the priest to bring Communion to the sick without crossing an open yard.[156] Encouragements to devotion were strategically placed throughout the convent and asylum; en route to their refectory the women passed four new life-size statues added about 1907 (the Blessed Virgin, St Joseph, John Eudes and St Mary Magdalen) and, reportedly, 'are very pleased and grateful to have them, as they help very much their devotion'. On the first landing of the convent was a life-size statue of St Francis Xavier, 'cross in hand, on a carved oak pedestal, a very commanding figure'.[157] Such was the scale and positioning of religious art that nobody could move though the buildings without being conscious that they were in a 'house of God'. The rich spiritual heritage of the Eudist tradition was presented as the heritage of all who were, alike, children of Our Lady of Charity. As with the postulants who presented themselves at the convent door, the women who came to Gloucester Street were introduced to the story of John Eudes, his teaching and example, and met him frequently during their stay.

The primary devotion was, of course, to Jesus Christ, son of God and son of Mary, and to the Mass or Eucharist, understood by Catholics as making present the ultimate sacrifice of the Son of God on the cross.[158] Devotion to the Eucharist was promoted under all its guises: Mass, 'holy exposition of the Blessed Sacrament', private visits to the chapel where the Blessed Sacrament was reserved and processions where the Blessed Sacrament was carried in honour through the house and grounds, culminating in benediction or blessing of all present with the Sacred Host. Frequent reception of Holy Communion, by women and sisters alike, was promoted.[159]

After the Blessed Sacrament, the Sacred Heart was the image of Christ given most prominence in Gloucester Street. The iconic image, where Christ displays his beating heart, burning with love, and looks directly at the poor sinner for whom He died, had an irresistible appeal for countless Catholics in 19th century Ireland. But it was a devotion which had been championed much earlier by the founder of the order, John Eudes, as explained in the preamble to the registry of vows of the sisters of Our Lady of Charity. The sisters' vocation,

154 'Particular intentions', Gloucester Street profession register, p. 2.
155 Gloucester Street, circular letters, May 1896, p. 2; 15 Aug. 1901, p. 8; Aug. 1905, p. 3.
156 Gloucester Street, circular letters, Aug. 1905, p. 2.
157 Gloucester Street, circular letter, May 1910, p. 4.
158 'The Eucharist is the memorial of Christ's Passover, that is, of the work of salvation accomplished by the life, death and resurrection of Christ, a work made present by the liturgical action', *Catechism of the Catholic Church* (Dublin, 1994), art. 1409.
159 Gloucester Street, circular letter, May 1896, p. 2.

'to labour for the salvation of strayed souls', was described as taking its origin 'in a particular manner from the most charitable Heart of Jesus, all inflamed with love for these souls'.[160] The feast of the Heart of Jesus was inaugurated by John Eudes on 20 October 1672 and celebrated on that date in Eudist circles until the post-Vatican II revisions brought this feast into alignment with that of the Sacred Heart (Friday after the second Sunday after Pentecost). It is not surprising therefore that the image of Jesus as the burning heart of love featured throughout Gloucester Street convent and asylum, including gardens and workrooms.

Mary, Mother of God, was an ubiquitous presence in Gloucester Street under her various titles, including the 'Heart of Mary', favoured by John Eudes who established this feast on 8 February 1648. Devotion to the Hearts of Jesus and of Mary was presented by John Eudes as a single or matching devotion: 'the most charitable heart of Jesus', aflame with love for erring souls, 'is but one and the same heart with that of his Blessed Mother'.[161] The congregation had been consecrated to the Heart of Mary by the founder:

> so that those who are received into it may anxiously endeav-
> our to impress on their hearts an image and perfect resem-
> blance of the most holy life and most excellent virtues of the
> most sacred Heart of their best Mother, and by this means
> make themselves worthy to be the true children of the most
> loving Heart of the Mother of true love.[162]

In the church, the statue of the Immaculate Heart of Mary in the niche to the right of the main altar, was the match of the Sacred Heart statue on the other side, and similarly with the stained glass windows closest to the sanctuary. Mary also appears in her own right, en route to the women's refectory, on a pedestal in the women's garden, and at the very back of the chapel.[163] The feast of the Immaculate Conception was marked with high Mass, solemn benediction and a sermon: 'every altar and statue of Our Blessed Lady through the convent was dressed and lighted up for the day and during the whole octave; it was a real feast in every sense'.[164]

The Children of Mary sodality, developed under the Jesuits and widely used in schools and parishes throughout Europe (as discussed in chapter 5), was one of the vehicles through which the sisters of Our Lady of Charity hoped to 'win' souls for Christ. This sodality group was granted its own oratory in what was 'formerly the damping room', holding its first meeting there on the first Sunday in March 1901: 'having a nice altar, strips of carpet, seats, and some devotional pictures. The walls are coloured blue, with an exceptionally pretty paper dado'.[165] A new floor was laid a decade later, the walls plastered and panelled, and the gloomy chapel declared to be a 'perfect gem of

160  'Particular intentions', Gloucester Street profession register, p. 2.
161  Ibid.
162  Ibid.
163  Gloucester Street, circular letters, May 1910, p. 4 and Aug. 1905, p. 2.
164  Gloucester Street, circular letter, May 1910, pp 2–3.
165  Gloucester Street, circular letter, Aug. 1905, p. 2.

light and beauty'.[166] Girls and women were received into the Children of Mary sodality, or upgraded to the next stage (blue ribbon, black ribbon) in private ceremonies held in this oratory at intervals throughout the year. Devotion to Mary under the title of Our Lady of Lourdes can be dated to the creation of a 'miniature grotto' with cascade, in the convent garden in the 1890s; this devotion was greatly advanced when the mother general of the Bon Secours sisters ('who has a great interest in our good work for souls') completed the tableau with the gift of a 'quaint figure' of Bernadette:

> She is clothed in a terra-cotta dress, white apron, and part-coloured shawl, a white veil on her head, and holds a taper in her hand. She has a lovely face, and is looking up with pleading, earnest eyes towards Our Blessed Lady.[167]

The cult of St Joseph was embraced by the founders of Gloucester Street with as much – if not more – fervour as in High Park. It was under his protection that the ambitious building project was formally placed on 30 June 1887, and the first choir novice to enter Gloucester Street, Miss Frances Carroll, was given that name.[168] He was to be met with in chapel, cloister and garden. St Mary Magdalen was another special saint as the inherited patron of the asylum. She was represented most beautifully in the marble carving of the high altar where she was depicted washing the feet of Jesus in the house of Simon, and in the small panels on either side, where she was weeping over her past sins, and holding aloft a skull, as she contemplated mortality and the eternity beyond death. A life-size statue of St Mary Magdalen was one of the four added to enhance the cloister, and she was also to be found occupying a pedestal in the women's recreation ground, completed in 1905.[169] The sisters of Our Lady of Charity prioritised devotion to the loving hearts of Jesus and of Mary over the tradition of St Mary Magdalen, but nevertheless much was made of her feast-day on 22 July. It was preceded by the annual preached retreat for the women – invariably described as making 'a deep and lasting impression' – and culminated in a special Mass followed by a party.[170]

The first decades of the Gloucester Street re-modelling as a monastery of Our Lady of Charity were marked by an enormous zeal to make their founder, John Eudes, known and revered. This continental saint was little known in Dublin, if at all outside High Park. The beatification in 1909 gave an impetus to this movement, but it was well under way from the day of the sisters' arrival in 1887. His statue was among the first four to grace the cloister, though this was relocated to the main chapel to mark the beatification (St Ignatius was moved to make room for him).[171] The avant chapel (already

---

166  Gloucester Street, circular letter, May 1913, p. 3.
167  Gloucester Street, circular letter, 15 Aug. 1901, p. 7. These statues have been re-erected in the grounds of Beechlawn Nursing Home, Grace Park Road.
168  'Promise made by Sister Mary of St Bartholomew McDonnell in her name and in that of the community', Gloucester Street profession register, p. 5.
169  Gloucester Street, circular letter, May 1910, p. 4.
170  Gloucester Street, circular letter, 15 Aug. 1901, p. 8.
171  Ibid., p. 4.

dedicated to John Eudes, figure 6.6) was used for the founder's relics, presented to Gloucester Street in 1909 by the reverend mother of Caen. These were placed in an exquisite alabaster shrine, above which two angels were painted holding a scroll with the founder's motto: 'If we live, let us live for Jesus, and for the souls He died to save'. Before this, a lamp was placed to burn night and day, in alabaster ('of a unique and very elegant classic design'). Close by was a stained glass window showing the founder praying before a statue of the Blessed Virgin, who holds the child Jesus.[172]

The celebrations which marked the beatification of the founder John Eudes on 25 April 1909 give some insights into the devotional culture of the house. While the reverend mother and her assistant were in Rome (attending the beatification and a subsequent assembly in Caen, see chapter 7), the local community 'united in spirit, tried to do honour to the glorious event in our own small way'. The 'window of our blessed founder' and his statue 'were beautifully dressed, and ablaze with lights for three days'. The women carried a statue in procession to their own recreation room, where there was an altar ready. A succession of clerical visitors called to venerate the founder and to deliver an appropriate few words; in the recreation room, the women sang 'our blessed Father's hymn' and knelt to receive the priest's blessing.[173] The full-scale triduum of celebration in Gloucester Street culminated on 8 February 1910 with the traditional Eudist feast of the Heart of Mary. The first two days were reserved 'for our own and our poor children's devotions'; Mass, private prayer before the Blessed Sacrament and benediction were the principal events. On the second day, the families of the workmen were present at Mass. On the third day, 'the convent, asylum and grounds were open to all', as was the chapel. The panegyric on John Eudes was delivered by Fr Matthew McMahon of Clonliffe College, and the choir was made up of priests and seminarians from Clonliffe whose services helped to render the ceremonies 'impressive and attractive'. Banners illustrating episodes in the life of John Eudes hung from the pilasters and, over the high altar, a very large picture of the founder was placed, 'a facsimile of the one used in St Peter's at the time of the beatification' nine months earlier. There was no end to the flowers and candles, and 'extra lights hung suspended round the whole interior of the church'. The local triduum closed with a procession of the relics, to the 'beautiful little shrine erected for them where they were placed, and then incensed'. The cloister, convent and asylum were also 'tastefully decorated', with the additional note: 'our poor penitents were present at all the functions which took place during these three days of grace and thanksgiving'.[174]

## Gloucester Street Asylum as Home and as Workplace, 1887–1911

Analysis of the register of admission of women (discussed below and in chapter 9) reveals that the vast majority of the women who came to Gloucester Street asylum from 1887 onwards used it as a temporary, emergency or

172  Ibid., p. 3.
173  Ibid., p. 5.
174  Gloucester Street, circular letter, May 1910, p. 2.

short-term shelter, a finding that is substantiated by a critical reading of the obituaries.[175] However, the sisters themselves always referred to it as a home, and it was only as a home, not as a hostel or training school, that it was advertised. Subscriptions were urged in 1888 towards 'the home that is now being built to accommodate at least fifty additional poor girls who anxiously seek a rest from a hard, hard life'.[176] The extended asylum was to be 'a larger and happier home for many poor Magdalens'.[177] The vulnerability of girls driven by misfortune or destitution to living on the streets was the constant theme, so that assisting 'poor girls who have no home, no friends, or sympathisers' would assuredly bring blessings.[178] Homelessness in itself was presented as the greatest danger young women faced, leading inexorably, as it did, to other problems.

On taking charge of the Gloucester Street asylum in 1887, and having conducted the archbishop through the building to see for himself its sorry state, the sisters of Our Lady of Charity under Sister Bartholomew O'Donnell drew up ambitious plans for its development.[179] The matter of size is easiest to track. In August 1890, the number of women in residence was 54; three years later a new dormitory was opened, 'the number of applicants being most pressing'.[180] By December 1896, the house was operating at its full capacity of 70 women.[181] When the archbishop undertook a visitation in person in December 1897, 'he expressed himself greatly astonished and very much pleased at the wonderful change that had taken place in the asylum since his last visit', and complimented the superior 'on the visible proofs he saw of her wise and prudent administration'.[182] Other, less pretty but no less necessary, works were undertaken, with the excavation of large, open drains to take the new sewers laid in October 1899.[183] As the numbers seeking admission increased, the constricted site required that the asylum be built upwards, as well as outwards. To extend the dormitory space and to upgrade the infirmary accommodation, to allow for a total of 115 beds, 'the roof of the dormitory had to be raised, another storey added, and a good deal extended, and to the broad stair case, which only reached half way, two flights of stairs were added'. The massive remodelling was, all agreed, well worth the effort: 'The infirmary is now a very bright, spacious and airy room, supplied with every possible convenience. Windows

---

175   For example, of the seven women who died between 1910–13 and for whom there are obituaries, six had come and gone before finally dying in the asylum and most, if not all, would not have stayed (according to the obituarist) but for poor health. Gloucester Street, circular letter, May 1913.

176   Text of appeal, 'St Mary's Magdalen Asylum, Lower Gloucester Street, Xmas 1888', Copy letters, p. 61.

177   Sister M. Bartholomew McDonnell to Fr Delaney, n.d. but Oct. 1888, Copy letters, p. 42.

178   'Preliminary notice', for bazaar to be held Dec. 1899, Copy letters, p. 66.

179   Gloucester Street, *circulaire*, 24 avril 1890, p. 4.

180   Gloucester Street, circular letter, May 1896, p. 4.

181   Gloucester Street, circular letter, 8 Dec. 1896, p. 1.

182   Gloucester Street, circular letter, 15 Aug. 1901, p. 3.

183   A woman fell into one of the open drains in the course of construction, on 24 Oct. 1899, but was unhurt, Gloucester Street, circular letter, 15 Aug. 1901, p. 8.

are on both sides, one side of which overlooks their [the women's] own garden.' It also enabled an upgrade in the sanitary accommodation; the dormitory underneath the newly-extended dormitory 'which years ago had been a mangle room, is now converted into a spacious bathroom and lavatory'.[184]

The enlarged women's recreation room, with its five windows, polished pine flooring and wainscoting of the same timber, was hailed as the most handsome room in the house by 1910.[185] Pride was also taken in the refectory,'a large, bright, healthy, cheerful room' with 'hot and cold water and every want amply supplied'. The basement kitchen was similarly extolled in 1910 due to recent investment: the scullery had been extended and a meat safe, lined inside with white tiles ('which keeps the meat perfectly fresh and cool, even in the hottest days of summer') had been built. New also was a 'large white enamelled trough, with hot and cold water taps for the washing of vegetables'. The basement floors were newly tiled, the heating pipes had been renewed, the boiler replaced and, it was declared, 'the whole surroundings in perfect order and neatness'.[186] Not surprisingly, there was a perpetual cycle of painting and decorating, with renewal of one part of the premises quickly overtaken by the need to update another.

The repeated references to the garden or 'recreation ground' is to be expected from an order with a rule of enclosure that sought to create the atmosphere of a place apart, a spiritual retreat or oasis of stillness and quiet where souls might be restored to peace. The scrap of garden that came with the house in 1887, the sisters would have liked to have to themselves, but were obliged to share with the women.[187] In 1905, a 'spacious recreation ground' was provided for the women on the site of 105 Gloucester Street, a lime yard and sheds occupied by a Mr Michael Flood, on the opposite side of the convent to the chapel.[188] Though the term 'spacious' rather overstates the facts, the laying of grass and the placing of statues of saints already well-known from the chapel and around the house did effect a spectacular transformation, the old yard 'now transformed into a garden, with handsome garden plots, concrete walls, and a fountain in the centre':

> Here and there through the grass plots are pedestals, on which
> are very fine statues of the Sacred Heart, Our Blessed Lady, and
> St Mary Magdalen; they add much to the surroundings. The
> garden is separated from the drying yard by a wire fence.[189]

While fundraising accounted for the major infrastructural projects, the weekly receipts from the laundry were crucial to the day-to-day maintenance of the entire campus, convent and asylum. Investment income from

184  Gloucester Street, circular letter, May 1910, p. 4.
185  Gloucester Street, circular letter, 15 Aug. 1901, p. 4.
186  Gloucester Street, circular letter, May 1910, p. 4.
187  Gloucester Street, circular letter, Aug. 1905, p. 2.
188  Tyrone Street Lower, Valuation Office, cancelled book, Dublin, North Dock, vol. dated 1887–95 (Irish Life Centre, VO).
189  Gloucester Street, circular letter, Aug. 1905, p. 2.

the dowries of the choir sisters was also important, but the size of that income flow depended on the number of choir sisters and the wealth they brought with them; the rate of return on railway shares or other 'safe' investments was always modest, and the capital could not be touched until after the death of the sister. The expectation was that every person, sister and woman resident alike, would be employed in some daily task towards the common good, excepting only those who were ill or enfeebled by age, in which case they would still be making a contribution through their prayers and their good example of suffering patiently borne. Work was seen as contributing towards the upkeep of the community as a whole, rather than being individualised employment. Idleness was not an option; to have 'sufficient work' to keep the women (as well as the sisters) well employed was regarded as 'a blessing for which we can never be sufficiently grateful'.[190]

Housework, helping with the sick and work in the laundry were the principal occupations.[191] In the census of 1901, of the 79 women named in the household returns, 56 had the occupation 'laundress' and another eight have more specialised laundry skills, namely, shirt ironer (5), collar ironer (1), and collar starcher (2). Other occupations returned for 1901 were seamstress (6), clerk (3), domestic servant (1); five were returned as having 'no occupation'.[192] In the census returns for 1911, there were 83 names, of whom all except four were returned as 'laundress'.[193] On occasion, the skills of a particular woman were the subject of comment, such as those of Mary Stephen, 'a most refined girl', praised for the 'delicate fancy work that came from her hands'.[194] But for most of the women residents, and for most of the sisters, work each day involved the processes of a commercial steam laundry: checking, sorting, marking, washing, starching, drying, folding (or ironing and folding), packing and dispatching (figure 6.7).

Both the lay-run and Mercy-run asylums that predated the OLC asylum had hand laundries.[195] The outdated technology, inefficient systems and ruinous costs of the Mercy system were tackled immediately by Sister Bartholomew McDonnell, but it was only under her niece, Sister Aloysius McCabe, that her grand plans came to fruition.[196] On her election in 1898, she undertook to increase the debt to introduce 'the latest modern machinery to enable us to carry on our work in the best possible manner'. This, she calculated, was the only way to put the business on a sound commercial

---

190  Gloucester Street, circular letter, 8 Dec. 1896, p. 1.
191  Gloucester Street, circular letter, 15 Aug. 1901, p. 6.
192  The women entered as 'no occupation' are aged 84, 70, 29, 28, 18 years in the 1901 returns. Form A, Return for members of family, 6 pp, enumerated by Patrick Heffernan, signed by Mary McCabe, superioress. Household census returns for 1901, City of Dublin, Poor Law Union Dublin, District Electoral Division North Dock, Parish St Thomas (NAI).
193  Household census returns for 1911, City of Dublin, Poor Law Union Dublin, District Electoral Division North Dock, Parish St Thomas (NAI).
194  Gloucester Street, circular letter, 15 Aug. 1901, p. 9.
195  *Golden jubilee*, p. 16. Sister M. Gertrude to Mother M. Bartholomew, 27 July 1887.
196  Memorandum concerning proposed new buildings, n.d. but July 1888, Copy letters, pp 28–29.

**Figure 6.7**   Packing room, Our Lady of Charity of Refuge, Gloucester Street, Dublin, undated postcard but *c*.1925.

footing.[197] By 1901, as she started her second term of office, it was reported that the laundry had undergone a complete transformation:

> It is now one of the finest laundries in Ireland, and is furnished with the latest modern improvements. The machinery comprises three large brass washers, two hydro extractors, large vats for hot and cold water, zinc troughs for boiling soap and making steam, machine for starching collars, and one copper boiler for making the starch. There is a large air fan in centre of laundry, which takes away all the exhaust steam; one closet for airing shirts and collars before sending them into the packing room; a drying closet, containing 13 galvanised horses, with pitch pine doors wrought in solid; this closet dries and bleaches from 60 to 70 dozen clothes in 20 minutes by hot air pressure and a cold air fan; the latter has the same effect as bleaching in the open air.[198]

By then, it was at the leading edge of steam-powered, high-technology laundries, with internal systems more akin to factory work than to the washboards and back-breaking sinks of its predecessors. Improvements continued, with a report a few years later that 'a splendid new brass double washer' had been

197   Sister M. of St Aloysius McCabe to My dear Lord [archbishop], 18 Aug. 1898, notebook, 'copy of letters' (DARGS, OLC2/5/2 no. 4).
198   Gloucester Street, circular letter, 15 Aug. 1901, p. 3.

installed, also a large steam mangle, 'as the one we had was not sufficient to turn out the work quick enough to meet the demands of our customers'.[199] A spacious new ironing room was also opened in 1901 and, though ironing systems are less amenable to automation than washing processes, some new technologies were introduced here also:

> The ironing room contains one large cylinder, two collar machines, six tylers for glazing shirts, three double tables with ten gas irons and a glazier on each, 10 shirt boards furnished with irons, and large table with two irons for ironing curtains.[200]

The efficient receipt and dispatch of the laundry was crucial to its smooth running and profitability, as customers could – and would, over the most trifling matter of a wrong handkerchief or missing sock – take their business elsewhere. The 1901 report described the efficient way in which the van shed, the sorting room and the packing room were adjacent: an 'enamelled cloister' or corridor separated the packing room from the 'very large and spacious sorting room', as illustrated on one of the 'thank you' postcards issued by the convent. Both sorting room and packing room had large rolling doors leading directly into the van shed, which opened out into Gloucester Lane. The superior, Aloysius McCabe, got her brother, Peter McCabe, to bring his influence to bear on the city councillors to induce them to repair the laneway, which 'was in a dreadful state, and utterly unfit for traffic'. This they readily did, 'and showed a further interest in our institution by shutting up some objectionable houses in the vicinity'.[201]

## Gloucester Street Monastery and Asylum, Recreation 1887–1937

Recreation was an integral part of the daily timetable for all in the enclosure of an OLC monastery, women and sisters alike. The weekday work regime of all residents was interspersed with set breaks for prayers, meals and recreation in common (figure 6.8), while the yearly cycle of feast-days and holidays brought a welcome change in routine, and opportunity for creativity. It was laid down in the rule that the women get a 'lunch and recreation' to mark the feast of their first and second mistresses, 'some convenient day' on or after the feast,[202] while St Mary Magdalen, on 22 July, and other feasts of the order, were also to be marked spiritually, materially and socially. The feast of the Epiphany (6 January) was marked by homely traditions of French origin, with a king and queen, drawn by lot, to preside over the celebrations for the day.[203] The Foundation Day for Gloucester Street was 17 February. The titular feast was that of the Immaculate Heart of Mary, 8 February, which was also the day on which, despite numerous obstacles and

---

199    Gloucester Street, circular letter, May 1910, p. 4.
200    Gloucester Street, circular letter, 15 Aug. 1901, pp 3–4.
201    Ibid., p. 4.
202    'Observations on the sisters in the different employments', item no. 9, MS notebook, n.d. (DARGS, OLC2/5/1 no. 11).
203    Sister M. of St Aloysius McCabe to Dear Hugh, 3 Jan. 1899, notebook, 'copy of letters' (DARGS, OLC2/5/2 no. 4).

**Figure 6.8**    Recreation room, Our Lady of Charity of Refuge, Gloucester Street, Dublin, undated postcard but c.1925.

'contrary to all human expectation', the order was founded.[204] The founder, John Eudes, was commemorated on 19 August. The Feast of the Presentation of Our Lady, 21 November, was the day on which the sisters confirmed their vows. Christmas, Easter, St Patrick's Day and each of the other major feasts were marked, as they came round, with a celebration appropriate to its rank in the Church's calendar and its traditional importance within the order.

There is a lengthy account of the celebration of the feast of St Bartholomew in 1897, but probably because the superior of that name (and the foundress) was seriously ill at the time. The feast was marked by an octave of celebration, during which 'our poor Penitents gave her much pleasure by performing a little play in her honour'. The sisters (her 'devoted children') gave her small gifts they had made themselves, and her nephew, Fr John McCabe, pastor of Bridlington, Yorkshire, called by and gave all, women and sisters alike, 'the pleasure of enjoying some of his beautiful selection of sacred music and entertaining recitations'.[205] Both of Sister Bartholomew McDonnell's nephews, the Carmelite priests John and Joseph McCabe, frequently came to brighten up an evening with their musical talents. As brothers of the later superior, Aloysius McCabe (superior 1898–1904 and 1910–16), they continued to sing for the 'poor penitents' during their holidays for more than two decades.[206] Joseph was posted to Australia sometime before 1912 but never failed to spend time in Gloucester Street with the sisters and the women on visits home.[207] Another brother, Hugh, seems to have been forced into delivering

204    'Particular intentions', Gloucester Street profession register, p. 2.
205    Gloucester Street, circular letter, 15 Aug. 1901, p. 3.
206    Gloucester Street, circular letter, May 1910, p. 4.
207    Gloucester Street, circular letter, May 1913, p. 2.

'entertaining recitations' also, at least on occasion.[208] The sister, Aloysius McCabe, was an accomplished organist in her own right.[209]

The custom of making up plays for in-house entertainment is recorded from the first decade of OLC administration, and may be earlier. As was done for recreation in High Park, novices and women undertook to compose poems and put words to well-known tunes for the concerts that were held to mark the feast-days of the local superior and of the various 'mistresses' – of novices and of penitents.[210] While plays and concerts were usually an internal affair, the beatification of John Eudes in 1909 gave the women residents the opportunity of performing for a larger audience, on this occasion made up of clergy, friends and benefactors of the house. While the subject of the play is not stated (no doubt it was of a moral, uplifting character), the audience was enchanted, and congratulated the women on their 'artistic powers'.[211] The women had their own piano from 1903, presented by 'the kind-hearted and generous priest Fr James Williams' on the Feast of the Immaculate Heart of Mary; this 'very valuable semi-grand piano in walnut (cost 90 guineas)' was kept in the recreation room (as illustrated in the postcard, figure 6.8) and 'the poor penitents are very proud of it and prize it very highly'.[212] Any resident who could play the piano was a particularly welcome addition to the circle. However, the women could be unreasonable in their demands; one very good pianist, with the house name Alphonsus, 'when in good disposition gave up her leisure time to playing on the piano for our poor penitents, but [as] the latter becoming exacting and requiring her to play when she was far from well, she gave up doing so except at the request of her mistress'.[213]

The practice of outsiders coming to put on concerts seems to be of long standing; the Christmas holidays of 1900, for example, were reported as 'passing very pleasantly' for the women 'as numerous friends come to entertain them'.[214] The fullest report is of the entertainment offered Christmas 1927 when an amateur drama group, under the direction of a Fr Gleeson, put on what appears to be a sacred tableau. The Nativity was 'carried out with such refinement and ease by the artists acting in perfect harmony and looking so picturesque in their most attractive and appropriate costumes'. It was a 'rare treat' and left a lasting impression, it was reported, on the women.[215] The following Easter, Fr Gleeson directed a performance in which Judas was the acknowledged star; 'everyone is talking of the perfection with which he played his part'. Both men and women were involved, with thanks extended to all from 'the composer of the drama to the tiniest 'Florette'', including 'your very artistic lady (Mrs Coates) who designed the costumes', the stage manager, the electrician, a Miss Tilly McLaughlin and a Miss Vera Traynor. As before, 'its

208   Sister Aloysius McCabe to Dear Hugh, 3 Jan. 1899.
209   Gloucester Street, circular letter, May 1910, p. 3.
210   'Verses of the Mother's Feast', MS collection of songs, poems and letters, 24 Aug.
1870 – July 1888; Feastday greetings, handwritten, 31 May 1892 – Feast of the Immaculate
Heart 1934 (DARGS, OLC2/5/4 nos. 1, 2).
211   Gloucester Street, circular letter, May 1910, p. 6.
212   Gloucester Street, circular letter, Aug. 1905, p. 3.
213   Gloucester Street, circular letter, May 1910, p. 7.
214   Gloucester Street, circular letter, 15 Aug. 1901, p. 8.
215   [Superior] to Revd Fr Gleeson, n.d. but probably Jan. 1928, Copy letters, p. 115.

effects on our poor Children is bound to be everlasting'.[216] On another occasion thanks is extended to a Mr Fee, who appears to be a university student, for 'the thoroughly enjoyable evening you and your kind friends secured for us'; the women and the sisters will try to repay through their prayers.[217] Probably the most professional and public of the entertainments was the musical comedy 'Tangles' performed on three occasions in April 1937 to mark the golden jubilee. In the printed programme, the cast of 13 are named (the house names are used) and there is a synopsis or 'argument': the play is set 'a very long time ago' and involves a prince in disguise, multiple suitors, the carrying off of the wrong girl by 'freebooters' and a final resolution, where all the characters marry off in the best fairy tale tradition.[218] It could not be described as a religious tableau by any stretch of the imagination. A newspaper review claimed that 'The choral singing was really fine; the dancing perfect, and some of the parts were played with an élan and a skill that professional players might well envy', to the delight of a very large audience.[219]

## Gloucester Street Magdalen Asylum, Admissions and Departures 1887–1947

There is no record of exactly how many women the asylum could hold under the Mercy sisters but, if the later dormitories are stripped out, a maximum of about 30 women on any one night seems reasonable. Short-term, voluntary stays were the expected pattern under Mercy management, as set out in their rule, and an asylum in the heart of the city was likely to have a frequent turnover of residents, at least when compared with more isolated, rural retreats.[220] In 1887, the first year of operations under OLC management, 75 women are entered on the register of admissions, but this probably included women who had previous experience of the Mercy asylum and thus were not 'first entrants' in the way that can be established for later years. All except two of these 75 women had left again within two years, so that the Eudist policy of running a 'voluntary' system appears to have been in place from the first year of the new administration. Account must also be taken of the pressing demand for short-term accommodation among women, as well as men, in the poorer parts of the city, as recounted by the social reformer and founder of the Legion of Mary, Frank Duff, whose knowledge of the reality was probably unrivalled. He has left a vivid account of the squalor of Dublin's 'cheap lodgings' in the 1920s, the beds 'dirty and swarming with vermin' beyond what anyone would believe.[221] In his analysis, the problem of prostitution, despite appearing at first to be different, 'is in reality, the same down and out problem',

---

216    Sister M. Stanislaus [Masterson] to Revd Fr Gleeson, 16 Apr. 1928, Copy letters, loose leaf enclosure.
217    Same to Mr Fee, 25 Mar. 1928 Copy letters, p. 123.
218    'Programme, Golden Jubilee Entertainment, 13th, 14th· 15th April 1937' (DARGS, OLC2/10/1).
219    'Golden Jubilee of a Dublin convent…', *The Standard*, n.d. but Apr. 1937 (DARGS, OLC1/11/1 no. 1).
220    Extract from *Guide for the Religious called Sisters of Mercy* (London, 1866) reprinted as document 20 in Maria Luddy, *Women in Ireland 1800–1918, a documentary history* (Cork, 1995), p. 59.
221    Frank Duff, *'The Morning Star; the theory and practice of a great experiment'*, Commission on the relief of the poor, statement of Frank Duff (Dublin, 1928), p. 1.

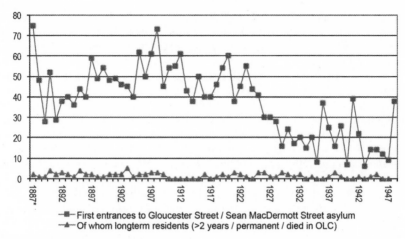

—■— First entrances to Gloucester Street / Sean MacDermott Street asylum
—▲— Of whom longterm residents (>2 years / permanent / died in OLC)

*1887 includes women already in residence in the asylum

**Figure 6.9**  Admission of women to Gloucester Street/Sean Mac Dermott Street asylum, 1887–1949.

the life of a woman involved in prostitution 'shocking in its hardship'.[222] The 'casual wards' of the union workhouse, 'by extinguishing the last flickering gleams of self-respect killed every prospect of uplift'.[223] Seeing prostitution in this light, he offered a remedy that he claimed from experience would have a 'success list' of about two out of every three of those reached: 'supplying wants which are common to all the class, that is, a decent bed, facilities for cleanliness, clothing, work, sympathy, encouragement'.[224] While the Legion of Mary women's hostels are not to be confused with the magdalen asylums – the former facilitated mothers, married or not, to keep their own children, and were essentially open, lay-run establishments – both offered emergency accommodation outside the union workhouse to women of the 'down and out' class described by Duff. Evidence for movement between hostels and asylums has been found in the OLC registers, while Legion members took on various volunteer roles in OLC homes, as discussed in chapters 9–13. There was a pressing demand on Gloucester Street asylum for bed places in the 1920s and 1930s, as indeed there was on facilities offered elsewhere in the city.

Across the study period of 60 years – from 1888, its first full year of operations, to 1947 inclusive – the average number of first entrances per year to Gloucester Street is 38 women (figure 6.9). However, this number masks a wide range from year to year, from a high of 73 in 1908 down to single figures.[225] Across the first 50 years, the average of 38 entrances needs to be further broken down: from 1888 to 1904 inclusive it was 44 women; from 1905 to 1930

222   Ibid., pp 2, 5.
223   Ibid., p. 20.
224   Ibid., p. 9.
225   There were six first-time entrances in 1943, seven in 1940, eight in 1935 and nine in 1947, women's entrance register, Gloucester Street.

inclusive it was 61; from 1931 to 1947, it was 18 first entrances on average per year. Very many factors can be called on to explain the wide disparity from year to year, which included the capacity of the house (when extra beds were added, and the space freed up by departures and by deaths), what the state and charitable organisations offered in terms of bed and board or outdoor assistance; the wider economy and the position of women who needed to support themselves within that economy. When a large number was admitted within a short time, there was a reduction in the number of free beds unless there was an exodus, and the economic reasons that drove some women into the refuge were exactly the same reasons that kept other women there beyond the immediate crisis – the dearth of paid work and affordable accommodation for vulnerable women without (at that time) too many safe alternatives.

The number among each year's first-time entrances in the period 1888-1947 who can be classified as permanent or long-term residents (figure 6.9) is more consistent. This number is made up of all women of that cohort who have been identified as remaining for two years or longer in the refuge, who returned to the refuge on a later occasion or who died in the care of the refuge regardless of length of stay. Of the first 75 entries in the register, only two (it appears) remained long-term. Over the period 1887 to 1947 inclusive, just under 4% (88) of all first-entrances (out of a total of 2,310) can be placed in this category. It appears that no more than one, two or three women out of each year's intake stayed long term, but in some years, none at all can be identified. From 1910 to 1917 inclusive, there were 381 entrants, of whom only two women can be identified as staying permanently. From 1922 to 1930 inclusive, there were 283 entrants, out of whom 16 women can be identified as staying permanently. From 1931 to 1947 inclusive, there were 307 entrants, of whom 13 women have been identified as staying for two years or more, or until they died, or returned to the refuge on a later date (sometimes when ill or dying). Statistics based on the register of admissions to the asylum must be treated with caution, even when – as in this case-study – the register information is augmented or confirmed from other records (such as obituaries, burial records, sodality notebooks, the 1901 and 1911 census, and the register of deaths in the General Register Office). It is likely that the percentage of entrants who stayed long-term is higher than research will ever be able to yield definitively. Women who entered under several names feature under each name (unless 'return' or 'here before' is entered in the register), and there are very many instances of the same name (such as, Mary Murphy, Margaret Kelly), each of whom must be treated as a separate person unless there is evidence to the contrary. Several 'return' cases have been found in the course of this research which are not specified as such in the register. But what can be relied on is that the number who stayed for two years or longer or unto death (including those who arrived straight into the infirmary to die shortly after) was a very small percentage of the full cohort of entrances in any one year.

Though the core number of permanent residents was always small, it was augmented in a steady way by a small number of women out of every year's intake over the period of this study staying for longer than two years. As most of these women would live for several decades more, admissions were always well ahead of losses through death. Of the entrants for whom it is known that Gloucester Street became their long-term home (that is, for two years or more), there was a still smaller group to whom the term 'magdalen' was properly reserved; these were the 'consecrates'. There are ten women (from a total of 2,928 entrants, 1887-1966) for whom magdalen names are recorded in the Gloucester Street register (and not to be confused with house names, which were assigned to every entrant). All of these women made their consecration between 1892 and 1926, and all but one continued in Gloucester Street until death. There may have been two others in the 1890s who left or died before their consecration name was recorded in the register or in any other document.[226] These older, 'steady' women carried out some of the more responsible duties in the house with the sisters, such as the night-time checking of doors and locking up, though the principal expectation laid on them seems to have been to give good example to the younger girls.[227] The traditional house devotions are reflected in the names taken by some of the women on their consecration: Magdalen of the Sacred Heart, Magdalen of the Holy Heart of Mary, Magdalen of St John Eudes, while there is also a strong devotion to the sacred passion of Christ: Magdalen of the Passion, Magdalen of the Holy Face, Magdalen of the Wounded Shoulder, Magdalen of the Five Wounds.[228]

The bulk of the database entries 1887 to 1948 inclusive to Gloucester Street allow analysis of age on admission and exact date (where the total was 2,181). The oldest entrant in that period was 70, the youngest was aged 14, but these are exceptions at the extreme ends. Almost half the women (1,028, or 47%) were aged 20 to 29 years on admission and a little under a third were aged 30 and upwards (691 or 32%). Girls 17, 18 and 19 inclusive made up 18% of admissions (390), while 16-year-olds made up 2% (50 girls). The cut-off age appears to have been 17 years, with younger girls (aged 16, 15 and 14 years) making up 72 entrants, or three in every 100 admissions. Children aged under 14 found destitute or begging, 'wandering and not having any home or settled place of abode, or visible means of subsistence', were eligible for committal to an industrial school under the Children Act 1908.[229] All the 14-years-olds admitted to Gloucester Street predate the Children Act 1941, when the upper age limit for committal to an industrial school was raised from 14 to 15.[230] Any 15- or 16-year-old who found herself homeless and destitute was, however, still in a limbo, too old for an industrial school and not the responsibility of the local authority, which may explain the presence of these younger girls, though each case needs to be

226  There is a reference in the circular letter for 1901 to three women recently 'consecrated to the class of perseverance' but these do not appear to have continued, Gloucester Street, circular letter, 15 Aug. 1901, p. 8.
227  Gloucester Street, circular letter, 15 Aug. 1901, p. 8.
228  The other magdalen names recorded for the Gloucester Street refuge were Magdalen of Patience, Magdalen of Repentance, Magdalen of St Brigid; women's entrance register, Gloucester Street.
229  Children Act 1908, section 58 (3).
230  S. MacLochlainn, cigire, Department of Education, to the Manager, Whitehall Industrial School, 1 July 1942 (DARGS, SJ/4/1/1 no. 20). The exceptions were one 14-year-old who came from the Sacred Heart School, Drumcondra, in 1952 and left, and another who was accommodated en route to St Anne's, Kilmacud in 1966.

taken on its own merits. The 14-year-old admitted in 1896 was dead within a fortnight. She had been accepted as an act of charity to her parents to give her the comforts of religion in her final days and to carry the expense of her burial.[231] All the other 14-year-olds left after a short stay, as indeed was the position of the vast majority of the women or girls, regardless of age.

For the majority of the women and girls, there is nothing in the register to hint at the reasons why they came to Gloucester Street, nor is there anything about why they left or where they went to. Names, dates of entry and exit, age on entry, parents living/ not living, place of birth and house names are all that can be relied on, and even this minimal information is not complete for everybody. Obituaries are rather more spiritual than biographical and cover only the small percentage of entrants for whom Gloucester Street became their final home. They are not extant for all women (nor sisters) who died in the convent, but they do offer occasional glimpses into personal circumstances, the general operation of the refuge and the virtues that were heavily promoted. Most of the women who died in Gloucester Street from 1887–1947, as reported to the other houses, had a history of leaving the house and returning, before what is invariably described as suffering meekly borne, culminating in a holy, happy and edifying death: 'she died after receiving all the Sacraments with the sentiments of a true penitent' (Columba).[232] The reasons why women entered or returned to the house varied (according to the obituarist), but homelessness, temporary or long-term, was the most common factor. Behind this were individual stories of alcohol addiction, misfortune, expulsion from home, seduction, violent abuse by a partner or relative, illness, mental or physical disability and entrapment into prostitution (often 'not so much from malice as ignorance'), each case with its own sad mix. Alphonsus left the asylum to live with her sister, 'but after six months finding her sister had no welcome for her, but on the contrary treated her unkindly, she returned to us and remained with us till her death'.[233] Mary Amelia, the daughter of 'respectable parents of the farming class', stayed briefly in the asylum, and returned again 18 years later to escape a violent relationship; she would have left again, 'but her sight becoming affected, and rendering her unable to do anything for herself, she was obliged to remain here'. Bedridden as well as blind for the last six years of her life, 'she gave great edification and for a long time before her death she was looked upon as a saint', as indeed were many others in their old age, if the obituarist is to be believed.[234] The death of both father and mother left some girls with nowhere to turn. Clare, 'the child of a worthless father, whose wretched life compelled his poor wife and children to take refuge in the poor house', wandered homeless after her mother's death, until she was taken into a Protestant home. 'Clad in the uniform of that institution', she sought admission to Gloucester Street, aged about 21 (and suffering from TB): 'she had a most attractive appearance, and was full of an innocent

231   This is most likely the young girl mentioned in the Gloucester Street circular letter dated 15 Aug. 1901.
232   Gloucester Street, circular letter, May 1910, p. 1.
233   Ibid., p. 7.
234   Ibid., p. 9.

humour that was pleasant to witness' – and fortunately, her faith had not been 'tampered with'.[235]

Some entrants were described as 'simple-minded' and had been placed by relatives. They did not come of their own accord: 'Paul was a good hearted but hot-tempered girl, who had gone through much hardships in her early days owing to the unkindness of her relations. Being half-witted, they played upon her, and at last got her placed with us to save themselves from all responsibility concerning her'.[236] Other women stayed because their illness or disability precluded all chance of managing outside. Hilda, a resident from the Mercy days, was paralysed by a stroke two years after the OLC takeover and found herself 'an unwilling prisoner to the mercy of God'. Though declaring that it was her affliction alone that kept her in the house, she was another of those who was reported as edifying all by the resignation with which she bore her sufferings: 'Every morning saw her at Mass, and many of our poor Penitents would have yielded to sloth were they not ashamed at the sight of poor Hilda on her way to the chapel'.[237] The only fault of the 'gentle and unassuming' Francis of Assisium was her 'inordinate love for intoxicants'. She sought admission 'anxious to be saved from herself' and lived for six years in the house; her devotion to prayer and frequent reception of the sacraments were recorded in her obituary, while she also did her work 'in a conscientious and superior manner'.[238] Very few appear to have had the blessing of family visits, though the occasional reconciliation with a parent is noted when illness struck and death approached. Madeleine's mother visited her frequently from her admission through to her death (from 'decline', or consumption), 'always trying to bring her some nice presents which she distributed most freely among her companions'. Madeleine had sought admission on returning from a position in England and in the throes of alcoholism.[239] Brendan was 'pardoned and blessed' by her father on her deathbed and buried, at his expense, in the family plot, in reparation perhaps for his 'hardness of manner' while she lived in Gloucester Street.[240] Teresa, whose life had been 'very reckless', had returned to Gloucester Street about a year and a half before her death. When the young woman was laid out, her brother appeared, and thanked the sisters 'for being instrumental in obtaining for his sister such a happy death'.[241] There is no record of his coming to visit any earlier.

## Former Prisoners and Women on Probation at Gloucester Street Convent, 1887–1940s

The presence of former prisoners and women on probation in the Gloucester Street asylum merits attention as it was a recurring feature of this house's intake, albeit the absolute numbers were very small. The earliest case of a woman with experience of prison that has been identified is a 35-year-old

---

235   Gloucester Street, circular letter, 15 Aug. 1901, p. 9.
236   Ibid.
237   Ibid., p. 10.
238   Gloucester Street, circular letter, May 1896, p. 4.
239   Gloucester Street, circular letter, May 1910, p. 8.
240   Gloucester Street, circular letter, May 1913, p. 6.
241   Gloucester Street, circular letter, 15 Aug. 1901, pp 8–9.

'sent from prison by Mrs Dillon' in October 1887. Two later entries refer to Fr McMahon, a prison chaplain in Mountjoy. On Christmas Eve 1906, a 33-year-old native of Belfast who 'came from prison' was admitted and stayed five nights. The following day, Christmas Day 1906, a 29-year-old Dublin woman who also 'came from prison' was admitted and stayed for one month. Of the entrants in 1887-1921, ten 'came from prison' (one further woman 'left for prison'). From a total intake of 1,727 over this period, the percentage with a recognisable or recorded prison connection is therefore well under 1%. Four of these ten women returned on multiple occasions to Gloucester Street, with one girl, Columba, entering at least 12 times.

Post-1922, mixed in with the general intake, occasional entries with the note 'came from prison' point to the use of Gloucester Street as a place of probation by the new state, while it continued to provide short-term accommodation for a small number of women on first discharge from prison. The initiative around probation appears to lie with those parties familiar with the OLC general practice of admitting all comers, no questions asked and no money involved. Under the Probation of Offenders Act 1907, an enlightened piece of legislation, a judge had the discretion to keep from prison a person whose youth, below-average intelligence, sad family history or other factors made it seem just that he or she be spared the stigma and hardship of a prison sentence, particularly where it was their first encounter with the criminal justice system.[242] A person who failed to comply with the conditions of his or her probation order was liable to be arrested and brought back before the court, where they would be convicted or sentenced for the original offence.[243] The incentive to comply with the probation order therefore was very strong. Under section 8 of the Criminal Justice Administration Act 1914,[244] which made more practicable the provisions of the 1907 Act,[245] a judge could impose conditions that he thought might keep the offender before him from repeating the crime or committing others, such as staying at a given address, keeping curfews, avoiding alcohol.[246] From 1914, therefore, it was lawful for the district court, when making a probation order, to include a requirement to live at a given address as a condition of probation. The address could be that of a family member, a place of indoor employment, a hospital (where the offender needed

242   Probation of Offenders Act 1907, section 1 (2).
243   Ibid.
244   An Act to diminish the number of cases committed to prison, to amend the Law with respect to the treatment and punishment of young offenders, and otherwise to improve the Administration of Criminal Justice, 4 & 5 Geo. 5, ch. 58.
245   See the McAleese report, part 3, chapter 9, for an exploration of the legislative basis on which girls and women were referred to the magdalen laundries through the criminal justice system, understood in its broadest context to include the relevant government departments, as well as state agencies (An Garda Síochána, Probation Service, Prison Service) and the courts. Girls were placed on remand, on probation, on temporary release and on early release from prison, as well as through informal placements by the gardaí and probation services, typically due to homelessness. *Final report of the Inter-Departmental Committee set up to establish the facts of State involvement with the Magdalen Laundries* (Dublin, 2013). Online at www.justice.ie. Hereafter, McAleese report.
246   Criminal Justice Administration Act 1914, section 8, amending section 2 (2) of the 1907 Act.

medical treatment) – or, indeed, any address that satisfied the judge. It was under this requirement that Gloucester Street came to be used on occasion as a place of probation – along with numerous other hostels, night shelters, refuges, convents, schools, homes and hospitals, in the care of religious congregations, voluntary societies and private bodies, Catholic and Protestant alike.[247] The first Gloucester Street case likely to be under this provision is dated 27 September 1922. A girl from Dublin who 'came from the courts' was given the house name Mel, and later left; the girl's age and date of departure are not recorded. Three years later, in August 1925, a woman aged 29 similarly 'came from the courts' and the same person features in the register 'sent by the courts' exactly one year later. A more complicated case is that of 19-year-old Eleanor from County Monaghan who, on 14 July 1941 was 'sent from court'. She was 'sent again from court' on 16 January 1942 and placed on probation 2 September 1942 for 12 months. In between, she had also spent time in the refuge in Dun Laoghaire, and returned again to Gloucester Street of her own volition on 12 March 1945 (but later left). Doing the rounds of different asylums and shelters, in between short prison sentences, was all too familiar a story.

The Gloucester Street sisters did not seek approval of their asylum as a recognised place of probation under section 7 of the Criminal Justice Administration Act 1914, which meant that they were not entitled to state funding towards the costs involved in accommodating these girls. In nearby Henrietta Street, Our Lady's Home (under the Daughters of Charity of St Vincent de Paul) did achieve this recognition, its origins in the Discharged RC Female Prisoners' Association giving it a particular focus on women in contact with the justice system.[248] By staying outside section 7, the OLC sisters were spared the trouble of having to name the superior or another sister as the probation officer and taking on all that role involved. Both OLC refuges, at High Park and Gloucester Street, were to receive girls under the more general heading of section 8, that is, at the discretion of the judge, with named conditions. The recognisance was the legal obligation the person entered into before the judge to do, or not to do, some particular act. A young person might state before the judge that she would reside at a given address for the duration of the sentence (which could not be longer than three years) and, on the strength of that recognisance, the judge might decide to give her the benefit of the Probation Act, rather than imprisonment. There was, however, nothing automatic – probation could be refused – and the girl had to give her consent. At all stages, the agreement was between the girl and the judge; the Gloucester Street convent was not a formal party to the arrangement. The justice system appointed a female probation officer to supervise each girl; the officer's role included ensuring that the girl knew the date of expiry of her term of probation, and informing the court should the girl break the conditions under which she had been granted the benefit of the Probation Act.[249] How the system worked

247  Ibid.
248  Jacinta Prunty, Bríd O'Neill and Eileen Devlin, 'Our Lady's, Henrietta Street, accommodation for discharged female prisoners', in Jacinta Prunty and Louise Sullivan (eds), *The Daughters of Charity of St Vincent de Paul in Ireland, the early years* (Dublin, 2015), p. 181.
249  McAleese report, ch. 9, p. 258.

out in practice can be better understood from the court records – for example, the case of a 16-year-old, convicted in 1936 of 'loitering and soliciting
for the purposes of prostitution' and ordered to reside in Gloucester Street
for 12 months, 'subject to the supervision of the Rev. Mother'. This she duly
did, after which the probation officer reported on her excellent conduct and
that she had stayed on voluntarily in the home (though she left some time
after).[250]

The use of convents generally by the courts as places of probation for
older girls was raised by the Cussen inquiry of 1934-36 which complained
that there was no place for female offenders aged 16 to under 21 other than
prison, as there was no equivalent of the male borstal. Judges were reluctant
to commit young girls to prison but had no legal power to order detention
otherwise. To get around this, the offender would be sent to a home or refuge conducted by a religious order, provided the girl consented and the home
agreed to accept her:

> In our view, this procedure is undesirable for obvious reasons,
> chief among them being the absence of specific powers
> enabling the judges and justices to commit to these homes.
> Further, the courts have to rely on the generosity and co-oper-
> ation of the religious orders conducting these institutions who
> accept such cases without payment.[251]

Although she had given an undertaking to reside at the convent up to a
certain date, a girl could not be detained by force, which Justice Cussen
considered to be most unsatisfactory: 'As matters stand, a girl who elects to
go to a home may leave at any time.[252] In a lengthy and thoughtful report
for the archbishop, the probation officer Miss E.M. Carroll spelled out the
many problems she saw first-hand with the use of magdalen asylums by
girls on probation. If 'difficult to handle and unbiddable', the girl will not
be kept, but even if she does settle in, religious training directed to 'a permanent renunciation of the world' was hardly appropriate for a young person who would leave the moment her sentence expired and 'without any
steps being taken to give her a fresh chance to earn an honest living'.[253] A
larger sample of court records would allow a fuller picture, but the worries
around the presence of young female offenders in adult asylums expressed
in the early 1940s appear to be well founded. There is ample evidence that,
for good or ill, in the OLC asylum at Gloucester Street (as in High Park) into
the 1940s, there was no separation on the basis of age or mode of referral.
The girl's name, age and parents, living or not, was entered in the register, and the standard practice of assigning house names implemented. The
girls coming from the courts shared the same living quarters and followed

---

250   Quoted in McAleese report, ch. 9, p. 271.
251   *Report of the Commission of Inquiry into the Reformatory and Industrial School System,*
*1934–1936*, para. 183. Hereafter, Cussen report.
252   Ibid., para. 184.
253   E. M. Carroll, probation officer, 'Memorandum re: women and girls who come before
the Central Criminal Court on serious charges – and other relevant matters', 7 July 1941, p. 5.
Reprinted as appendix 5, MacAleese report.

the same regime as everyone else. All took part 'in the ordinary routine work of the institution', including the public laundry, sewing, mending and cleaning.[254] The only clue that these girls had come to the attention of the justice system is a note in the register such as 'came from the courts', and sometimes even this is not present.[255] There is never a mention of the crime of which they were accused, convicted or exonerated, nothing of their past life is recorded by the sisters of Our Lady of Charity, just as practically nothing was recorded of the previous experiences of the other girls and women who sought admission.[256] No formal application was made by the Department of Justice to Gloucester Street or High Park (or at least, no trace has yet been found). No court papers were handed over to either institute (as the arrangement was legally between the girl herself and the court) and, as no money was given towards the girl's maintenance, there are no financial records. The issue of girls on probation in magdalen asylums, as well as the need for the state to provide a remand home for females, came to the fore in the 1950s and is taken up again in chapters 8 and 9 (dealing with younger women and girls) and in chapters 11 and 12 (the remodelling of OLC women's refuges).

## Golden Jubilee of Gloucester Street Monastery and Asylum, 1937, and its Aftermath

Anyone who called to Gloucester Street during the jubilee year of 1937 could not fail to notice the poverty and dereliction of the district, with the convent about the only premises that bore evidence of investment and repair. But, according to the jubilee souvenir record, 50 years earlier this locality had been even worse, a 'moral plague spot, the haunt of vice, the home of the city outcasts of the street'. Mecklenburgh Street had been 'so unsavoury' that the city corporation had changed its name first to Tyrone Street and later still to Railway Street. 'Yet it was on such unfavourable soil that the tiny mustard seed was planted....'[257]

To mark the jubilee, an account of the foundation, derived from the annals, was grafted on to the 300-year-old story of the order and its revered founder, St John Eudes. Like the sisters of Caen, High Park and other OLC houses, the Gloucester Street sisters, 'have gone forth in the steps of Him who trod the highways of the world in search of those who were lost, that they might heal them'.[258] The unerring hand of Divine Providence was seen in its development, from humble beginnings to the proportions it now held,

---

254 Ibid.

255 The McAleese inquiry identified a number of cases referred by the courts where the OLC registers did not include any source of referral, which bears out this point. McAleese report, pp 267, 269.

256 The annual reports of the Probation Service for the 1930s mention some of the crimes for which women were given the benefit of the Probation Act providing they lived, for a set period (usually 12 months) in the refuges of High Park or Gloucester Street; 'loitering and soliciting', committing an act 'contrary to public decency', infanticide and stealing are all listed. The vast majority of cases where women were required to reside at a magdalen laundry as a condition of probation involved 'minor' offences, such as larceny, not the more serious crimes. McAleese report, ch. 9, p. 263.

257 *Golden jubilee*, p. 16.

258 Ibid., p. 14.

sheltering 135 penitents, 'voluntarily making reparation for past wrong-do-ings, and endeavouring with the aid of Divine Grace, to follow anew in the footsteps of Him who "is the way, the truth and the life"'.[259] In the hands of the unnamed clerical author, the story loses nothing in the telling, with much made of the measureless, divine love of the Good Shepherd and the perseverance of 'Magdalen of Bethania'. A similarly romanticised treatment is to be found in the popular *Father Matthew Record* for May 1937, which adds, however, that the 'little hand-scrubbing laundry enterprise' of 50 years' earlier has given way to 'a fully equipped plant' in which the women conduct 'an able laundry business'.[260]

The golden jubilee was an opportunity to promote knowledge of and devotion to the founder, who was still barely known – if at all – out-side the walls of the two Dublin monasteries of the institute. An account of the triduum of thanksgiving held in Gloucester Street to mark the be-atification of John Eudes on 25 April 1909, and the elaborate celebrations to mark his canonisation on 31 May 1925 is given in full. There is an ar-chitectural description and photographs of the convent chapel, with full credit given to the Irish artists and Irish builders who created it and the generous donors who made it possible. The chapel itself is described as 'much visited' by outsiders, 'a source of gratification to the Com-munity and a priceless haven for the souls committed to their care'.[261] The cult of the founding mothers takes shape in the chapter titled 'Our Three Mothers', in which each is dealt with in turn and at great length – Bartholomew McDonnell, Aloysius McCabe and Francis Xavier Leamy (fig-ure 6.3); the one-trimester superior who came from and returned to High Park, Ignatius Ryan (1893-6), is overlooked. The final chapter is a compen-dium of death-bed scenes, selected and reworked from the obituaries of the women, each a pathetic story of failure and struggle and trial but, invariably (in the author's opinion), through the action of divine grace, each resulting in 'the attainment of sanctity in a life hidden with Christ in God'.[262]

The jubilee booklet closes with an appeal for vocations to this order and for funds to extend the building to meet the ever-increasing number of women 'seeking a home and salvation' in the asylum and to solve the cur-rent overcrowding and attendant inconveniences.[263] In terms of vocations, there had never been an influx and most circular letters refer to 'novices disrobed' and postulants left, with the blanket phrase 'not having the quali-fications for our community'. Each circular also referred to deaths, frequent-ly of young professed sisters, of whom much was expected. A well-recom-mended young women with a dowry (£500 was the 'usual dowry' required

259   Ibid., p. 15.
260   T. J. Molloy, '1887–1937, Monastery of Our Lady of Charity of Refuge, Gloucester Street, Dublin, Golden Jubilee Celebrations', *Father Matthew Record and Franciscan Mission Advocate*, vol. 30, no. 5 (May, 1937), p. 279.
261   *Golden jubilee*, p. 27.
262   Ibid., p. 52.
263   Ibid.

of a choir postulant in 1899)[264] could choose from any number of religious orders long established in Dublin with better-known and more visible ministries, while those without a dowry were not short of openings either. But a sufficient number of sisters did make it beyond the noviceship to enable the house to continue, with a total of 33 sisters (17 choir, ten lay, six *tourière*) returned in 1937.[265] The last of the six Gloucester Street pioneers died in January 1941, Sister Mary of St Elizabeth Kenny (Anne), a lay sister. Her death letter closes with the note: 'This severance with the last link of the Foundation Days leaves an unexplainable void.'[266]

The 1937 jubilee appeal for funds to extend the asylum or refuge was badly-timed, though nobody could have foreseen that. The outbreak of war in 1939 led to a shortage of building materials and other privations, but also great uncertainty about what might be the future of the Free State – an Allied victory was by no means assured until late in the war. Much-needed and long-planned municipal housing projects were postponed or abandoned; the Gloucester Street diamond was one of the casualties.[267] But the delay in advancing public building projects did allow the convent to extend along Railway Street (Mecklenburgh Street), from where the laundry business was carried on, and along Gloucester Street, the principal frontage, in the process further complicating the history of landholding in this compact area (figure 6.2).[268] One small vacant plot was purchased from the city corporation in July 1938 and put to immediate use as a recreation ground, described as 'urgently needed', since the number of women was now 130.[269] Another quarter acre of the 'unoccupied square' (with frontage to Gloucester Street) was purchased in 1946[270] with the intention of enlarging the recreation area, extending the laundry and erecting a new counting and packing

---

264  Sister M. of St Aloysius McCabe to Fr Kennedy, May 1899, notebook, 'copy of letters' (DARGS, OLC2/5/2 no. 4).

265  Gloucester Street, circular letter, 1 Sept. 1937 (DARGS, OLC2/3/1 no. 11).

266  Death letter of Sister Elizabeth Kenny.

267  Prunty, *Dublin slums*, pp 315, 338.

268  From rent demands, receipts and an apportionment document, all dated 1954, the following may be deduced about previous ownership: 83–86 Railway Street (Corporation); 81 and 82 Railway Street (purchased from the Corporation 1944); 80 Railway Street, and 72 and 72A Lower Sean MacDermott Street (Crawford estate); 78 and 79 Railway Street, 78A Railway Street, 71A Lower Sean MacDermott Street (Crawford estate, formerly Duncan estate); 64 to 70 Lower Sean MacDermott Street, 73 to 75 Railway Street (both Smyth and Crawford estates, unclear); 71 Lower Sean MacDermott Street also 76 and 77 Railway Street (held free of rent); 68 to 72 Railway Street, 68A and 63 Lower Sean MacDermott Street (Crawford estate, formerly Duncan estate) (DARGS, OLC2/9/1 no. 19). Nos. 73–80 Railway Street were occupied by the community by 1921, see correspondence dated June 1921 (DARGS, OLC2/9/3 no. 16). The purchase of 60–67 Railway Street was closed in 1963 (DARGS, OLC2/9/1 no. 26).

269  Sister M. of St Stanislaus Masterson to Fr Glennon, 23 July 1938, letter marked 'Permission granted 27/7/38' (DARGS, OLC2/2/2 no. 5).

270  Sister M. of the Immaculate Heart Walshe to Dr McQuaid, 29 Aug. 1944, note added by archbishop, 'Agreed – Mgr. Walsh your ecclesiastical superior has been requested to consider details' (DDA, OLCR, Gloucester Street no. 1); Michael P. O'Connell, secretary, to Mother Superioress, acknowledging receipt of letter of 29 Aug. 1944 (DARGS, OLC2/2/2 no. 5).

room to cope with the orders from city restaurants and hotels.[271] However, the archbishop's permission, the architect's plans, the builder's estimates and the readiness of 'kind friends' to pay the costs all came to nought with the refusal, in May 1947, of a building licence by the Department of Industry and Commerce because of a shortage of cement.[272]

By the time the development of this vacant piece of land came up for consideration again, Gloucester Street convent would find itself part of the Irish Federation of the Sisters of Our Lady of Charity (created in 1948). It would also find itself caught up in the movement towards modernisation that would take hold in Ireland in the aftermath of World War II, advancing slowly but inexorably in the 1950s. The original Mecklenburgh Street 'Female Penitents' Retreat' and its Mercy successor were overtaken by the enclosed, OLC system of monastery and refuge, though these early associations were still important to the charitable public, as was its city-centre location. What was held up for public approbation in the golden jubilee year of 1937 was, in essence, the spirituality, rule and customs of OLC High Park which were ultimately (via Paris and Rennes) those of the refuge of 1640s Caen and its much-loved founder, John Eudes. The documentary evidence points to zealous implementation of this tradition as understood by the founding sisters, and especially by the superiors and assistants, and how it might be worked out in the particular circumstances of the second monastery of Dublin.

---

271   Unsigned memo, Gloucester Street, 25 Nov. 1946 (DDA, OLCR, Gloucester Street no. 1).
272   Michael P. O'Connell to Revd M. Immaculate Heart, to note that the archbishop, 'having once given his approval, will not permit an unauthorised change of plans', 4 Feb. 1947 (DDA, OLCR, Gloucester Street no. 1). Envelope postmarked 25 Nov. 1946, from W. H. Byrne, architects, 20 Suffolk Street, annotated 'estimate for new building and archbishop's letter' (DARGS, OLC2/2/2 no. 5). Sister M. of the Immaculate Heart Walshe to Fr Glennon, 3 Feb. 1946 [1947] enclosing Mr J. P. Donnelly's revised estimate, 18 Nov. 1946, proposed extension to ironing and dispatch rooms, and new enclosed recreation yard and same to Dr McQuaid, 21 May 1947 (DDA, OLCR, Gloucester Street no. 1).

# Chapter 7

# Upheavals Internationally in the First Institute Founded by John Eudes and the Role of the OLC Monastery of Caen, 1902–49

In August 1902, news of the impending beatification of the founder, John Eudes, was broken by a jubilant superior in Caen to all the monasteries of Our Lady of Charity in Europe, North America and Mexico:

> The sitting of yesterday [26 August 1902] has been a success. In December there will be a general Assembly in presence of the Holy Father, and in January the Decree for the Virtues. Alleluia! ... This letter has been to our hearts as a bright sunbeam in the midst of the storm.[1]

That Rome's first communication was expressly 'for the ancient monastery of Caen'[2] – ahead even of communication with the Eudist fathers – was a matter of satisfaction to the sisters in Caen who had played an active part in the advancement of the cause, and was a welcome acknowledgement of its special status as the cradle of the order. The reference to 'a storm' was aptly chosen, for the announcement came at a time of upheaval for the Catholic Church in France. The context for the beatification was the long-running tension around the separation of Church and state in France, and the various steps along the way to beatification in 1909 and canonisation in 1925 were weighted with political overtones.

But not all the storm clouds could be blamed on outside forces. Some were very much the product of long-standing rivalries within the Eudist family. The forthcoming beatification, which might have been expected to be a time of unreserved celebration for all who called themselves sons and daughters of John Eudes, was approached with some trepidation in OLC circles. The beatification would bring all three families of St John Eudes – the Sisters of Our Lady of Charity (founded 1641), the Congregation of Jesus and Mary priests (founded 1643) and the Sisters of Our Lady of Charity of the Good Shepherd, Angers (generalate approved 1835) – to papal, as well as

---

1 Caen, circular letter, 30 Aug. 1908 (DARGS, OLC1/3/2 no. 14).
2 Ibid.

public, notice. As an order of autonomous monasteries (to use the language of the documents), Our Lady of Charity had been held together since the 17th century by faithful adherence to a common rule and the veneration of the one founder. However, what was viewed by the 'old houses' of the Refuge as the 'breakaway' congregation of the Good Shepherd cherished the same rule, wore the same habit, venerated the same founder and had the same end. Organised around a generalate at Angers under its founding superior Mère Marie de Ste Euphrasie (Rose Virginie) Pelletier (venerable 1897, blessed 1933, saint 1940), by 1902 it had a much greater reach internationally – and larger numbers – than its parent, the order of Our Lady of Charity. Numbers were attracted to the Good Shepherd that OLC could only dream of.

Novices were trained in large numbers at the Good Shepherd general novitiate at Angers, some to be returned to their home countries but very many at the disposal of the superior general to be sent wherever in the world she decided. The noviceship numbers returned in December 1900 to 1914 ranged from 76 to 129, with an average of just over 100. As each provincial house also had its own novitiate, the number of Good Shepherd sisters making profession each year was several times greater.[3] In Ireland, the provincial house and novitiate were in Limerick and there were houses also (in order of foundation date) in New Ross, Waterford, Belfast, Cork and Derry. The numbers returned in December of 1900 to 1914 from the Limerick novitiate ranged from eight novices to 21 with an average of 14 novices at any one time. Irish girls had been entering the Good Shepherd congregation in small but steady numbers since the mid-19th century and by 1900 they made up a significant proportion of the membership: 952 religious were returned as Irish in 1900 (13% of the membership) and 1,048 in 1922 (12% of the membership), of whom the great majority worked outside Ireland.[4] The cover of *Bulletin du Bon Pasteur*, produced in Angers as a means of circulating information on new ventures and other matters of common interest, carries a quotation from the venerable mother foundress: 'Our device ought to be zeal, and this zeal ought to embrace the whole world'. How seriously this motto was taken is demonstrated in the contents of each succeeding issue. But the Sisters of Our Lady of Charity in the Dublin diocese – or indeed elsewhere – did not need access to the other institute's official returns and internal communications to be well aware that, statistically speaking, the future of the Good Shepherd looked much brighter than theirs; they knew from word of mouth, from their own network of correspondents and from the newspapers.

On the OLC side, at least in Caen and houses closely allied to it, a deep distrust of the Good Shepherd congregation was in evidence at the opening of the 20th century, even though the Eudist fathers had an explicit policy from 1865 of promoting closer relations between all three branches.[5] Suspicion of

---

3   There were 32 Good Shepherd novitiates in 1900 that had been properly – that is, canonically – erected as the various provinces were established from 1855 onwards. Not all had novices all the time, but all were entitled to admit novices. Statistiques de la Congrégation de N.D. de Charité du Bon Pasteur d'Angers, 1900–21, p. 119 (BP, Archives historiques, R. 24).
4   Ibid., pp 11, 255.
5   Paul Milcent, 'Notre-Dame de Charité, relations entre maisons', unpublished typescript, Nov. 1998, p. 11 (NDC Caen).

Angers is more apparent than cordiality in the OLC archival record leading up to the beatification in 1909 and the canonisation in 1925 of their common founder. There was a basis in statistics for this distrust, though numbers alone were not the issue. During the generalate of Marie Euphrasie Pelletier (1835–68), 33 foundations had been made in France and 77 in other countries; her successor, Marie Pierre de Coudenhove (1868–92), is credited with a further 85 foundations, mostly outside France, while the next elected to the role, Marie Marine Verger (1892–1905) oversaw the opening of another 66 houses. At the opening of the 20th century, there was a Good Shepherd house on each of the five continents. The statistics for 1900 list houses in France (37), Italy (24), Holland (6), Belgium (5), England (9), Germany and Austria (22), Ireland (4), Spain and Portugal (3), Algeria and Egypt (8), Asia (10), Mexico (1), Canada (7), United States (45), Chile, Argentina and Brazil (35), Peru, Bolivia, Ecuador, Colombia (8) and Australia (4).[6] There seemed to be no halt in sight. Certainly the Good Shepherd was holding true to the expansionist vision of its founder, as the marble slabs inscribed with the names and dates of new foundations marking the tombs of the first five superiors general make strikingly clear.[7] The statistics of 1 January 1903, as sent to Rome, give the number of sisters (professed religious and *tourière* sisters) at 7,394 and '*personnel des œuvres*', the women and girls in the various institutions run by the congregation, at 43,701. There were 245 monasteries divided between 24 provinces, an increase of 17 houses over the figures from two years earlier.[8]

The attractive patronym 'Bon Pasteur', carried by all the Angers houses, barely needed to be translated, and its use internationally gave the congregation what today might be termed 'brand recognition'. The OLC monasteries, however, were frequently better known by the house dedication, such as St Michael, St Cyr, St David, which did nothing to assist the public perception of the order as a whole.[9] Under headlines such as 'Founder of the Good Shepherd order raised to the altars', newspaper coverage of the beatification of John Eudes in August 1909 added to the confusion, with more than one reporter describing the Order of Our Lady of Charity as 'developed into' the Good Shepherd nuns, and reducing the representation at the papal audience that followed the beatification to just the Eudist fathers and Good Shepherd nuns.[10] Each house, whether Good Shepherd or of the Refuge, held its own triduum of celebrations, but the weight of newspaper publicity came

6   Statistiques, 1900–21, pp 13–22 (BP, Archives historiques, R. 24).
7   The fourth superior general, Mère Marie de Ste Domitille Larose (1905–28) is credited with 52 foundations; the fifth, Mère Marie de St Jean de la Croix Balzer (1928–40) with 44 new foundations and the reunification of 11 monasteries of the Refuge with Good Shepherd, Angers. These tombs, and plaques to later holders of the office, as well as tributes to Mère Marie de Ste Euphrasie Pelletier from houses on all continents are to be found in the Immaculate Conception chapel in the grounds of the mother house at Angers.
8   'État des œuvres de la Congrégation de Notre-Dame de Charité du Bon Pasteur d'Angers', 1903 (CIVCSVA, A-7 (2) /2 no. 5).
9   Caen urged houses to try and obviate this confusion in the public mind by using 'our title of nobility, Our Lady of Charity' in all correspondence and advertising. Caen, circular letter, 24 Apr. 1913 (DARGS, OLC1/3/2 no. 59).
10   Newspaper cuttings, n.d., relating to the beatification of John Eudes in 1909, including extracts from the *Monitor and New Era* and *The Catholic Times* (DARGS, OLC1/7/4 no. 12).

down very much on the side of the Good Shepherd.[11] A lengthy report in the *Irish Catholic* newspaper on the celebrations held in the Good Shepherd house in Cork in honour of Eudes makes no mention of the order of Our Lady of Charity.[12] The booklet produced by High Park to mark the beatification makes no mention of the Good Shepherd of Angers, or its claim on Eudes as founder.[13] For Caen and the monasteries which followed its lead, the success of Angers and its network was something to be concerned about, rather than celebrated: 'as you know the Good Shepherd is in much esteem at Rome and [that] the Sacred Congregation of Bishops and Regulars tend to re reunite in one branch the divers divisions of an Order.'[14]

The awfulness of being forced to emulate the Good Shepherd congregation by altering the constitutions to allow centralised government is a recurrent theme in letters from Caen to the other OLC houses from the later 19th century through to the 1930s. Any such change was construed as an assault on the exact and perfect observation of the constitutions as handed down by John Eudes, a betrayal somehow of 'the ancient root of the blessed tree of our Holy Institute'.[15] In this general opinion, Dublin, and many other houses, followed Caen's lead. But a more immediate threat was posed by houses simply asking Angers to accept them into its fold. In 1895, the monastery of Park Place, Oregon, in the US defected to the Good Shepherd sisters, opening up the horrific prospect of further desertions. In the circular announcing this scandal, Caen informed the loyal OLC houses that the Oregon monastery had been led astray by the 'secret projects' and 'spirit of independence' of the superior, Mother M. of St Alphonsus Stüffler, and all lived to regret their unhappy choice.[16] Houses in difficulty which chose this path need not look to Caen for understanding, let alone support.

The political context for the beatification of John Eudes dated back decades, if not to the French Revolution itself. The success in 1879 of a secular, republican government, committed to the concept of *laïcité*, led immediately to a concerted campaign to drive religious congregations out of education, where they were by far the principal providers.[17] The Jesuits were targeted in a law of 1879 which banned unauthorised religious orders from teaching in secondary schools. Legislation in 1881 and 1882 made primary education compulsory, free and non-denominational for both girls and boys. Religious

---

11    See, for example, local accounts and reprinted newspaper reports in Bulletin du Bon Pasteur/Bulletin of the Congregation of the Good Shepherd of Angers, 17th year, no. 4 (July 1909) to no. 8 (Dec. 1909) inclusive (BP, Archives historiques). (Hereafter, GS Bulletin).

12    *Irish Catholic*, 6 Nov. 1909, reprinted in GS Bulletin, 17th year, no. 7 (Oct. 1909) pp 523–31.

13    *Sketch of the life of Blessed John Eudes, apostolic missioner, founder of the Congregation of Jesus and Mary, of the Order of Our Lady of Charity of Refuge, and of the Society of the Most Admirable Heart of the Mother of God, promoter of the liturgical worship of the Sacred Hearts. Translated from the French by a Religious of Our Lady of Charity, High Park* (Dublin, n.d. but 1909 or 1910) (DARGS, OLC1/7/4 no. 11).

14    High Park sent £20 to Valence as a token of solidarity. Caen, circular letter, 11 Aug. 1908 (DARGS, OLC1/3/2 no. 13).

15    Caen, circular letter, 14 July 1902 (DARGS, OLC1/3/2 no. 12).

16    Ibid.

17    See Claude Langlois, 'Féminisation du Catholicisme', pp 283–92 in *Histoire de la France religieuse*, ed. Jacques Le Goff and René Rémond, iii, 'Du rois Très Chrétien à la laïcité républicaine XVIIIe–XIXe siècle' (Paris, 2001), pp 283–4.

instruction was now to be provided outside the classroom at the parents' request. Under a law of 1886 aimed at the laicisation of the teaching profession, more than half the nuns and brothers teaching in primary schools were removed by the early 1890s.[18] Claims that religion was inherently destructive of human liberty and that religious orders hindered the good of society were vigorously disputed.[19] The government of René Waldeck-Rousseau was formed in June 1899 with a strong anti-Church agenda, and passed a law on association in 1901 that required religious congregations to receive authorisation from parliament.[20] This new law was used by the anti-clerical education minister Émile Combes to evict tens of thousands of monks, friars and nuns from their communities between June 1902 and January 1905. A third of the schools run by religious were closed; others survived by being taken over, nominally at least, by lay persons, and under what has been described as 'an exhausting variety of semi-legal manoeuvres'.[21] A law of 7 July 1904 closed off these loopholes when it ordered the phased exclusion of authorised, as well as unauthorised, orders from teaching in any school, however owned or administered.[22] The way in which the sisters of Caen re-classified their younger girls, making a new category, under a new patron, the Angel Guardian, for the purposes of training in industrial skills, is an example of how orders tried, unsuccessfully, to circumvent the rules.[23] The separation law of 9 December 1905 ended the payment by the state of salaries to Catholic clergy (and to Protestant pastors and rabbis), and ordered the transfer of Church property to 'cultural associations', representative bodies made up of local parishioners, the formation of which was in turn banned by Pope Pius X (1903–14), placing the local Church organisations in a perilous position *vis à vis* property ownership.[24]

The discourse around the beatification and canonisation of John Eudes was closely tied to contemporary political developments. The decree allowing the cause of John Eudes to proceed, published on 6 January 1903, advertised how timely it was, when the Church was beset with troubles, to contemplate the virtues and the glories of those founders of religious orders whose blessings, for the Church and for civil society, persisted through their successors (*leur descendance*). Making reference also to Julie Billiart (1751–1816), foundress of the Soeurs de Notre Dame de Namur in 1804, and whose cause for beatification was allowed to proceed just before that of John

---

18   James F. McMillan, 'Catholic Christianity in France, 1815–1905', in *The Cambridge history of Christianity: world Christianities c. 1815–c. 1914* (Cambridge, 2006), viii, p. 228.

19   Leo XIII, *Testem benevolentiae*, on the dangers of activism, 22 Jan. 1899, no. 3 in *The states of perfection according to the teaching of the Church, papal documents from Leo XIII to Pius XII*, ed. Gaston Courtois, trans. John A. O'Flynn (Dublin, 1961), p. 2; Gérard Cholvy, *Christianisme et société en France au XIXe siècle, 1790–1914* (Paris, 2001), pp 167–8, 174.

20   Cholvy, *Christianisme et société en France au XIXe siècle*, pp 171–2.

21   Maurice Larkin, 'Religion, anticlericalism, and secularization', in James McMillan, ed., *Modern France 1880–2002* (Oxford, 2003), p. 210.

22   Cholvy, *Christianisme et société en France au XIXe siècle*, p. 173.

23   *Dans la charité du Christ: Vie de la Très Honorée Mère Marie de Saint Ambroise Desaunais* (Caen, 1939), p. 82. Hereafter, *Vie de la Mère Marie de Saint Ambroise Desaunais*.

24   Due to this ban the Church did not exist as a legal entity capable of taking control of its own property until 1924, which resulted in the loss of much Church property to municipal uses, see McMillan, 'Catholic Christianity in France, 1815–1905', p. 231.

Eudes, Pope Pius X referred to the excellent virtues of these two venerable servants of God, both with France as mother, newly-raised as intercessors or protectors before God for their storm-ravaged country.[25]

The persecution was experienced in France most pointedly between 1902 and 1905, but continued to 1911. It drove religious men and women overseas to houses of the same congregation where that was feasible, but also to establish places of refuge, where a small community might manage for a few years until circumstances allowed a return. Some houses had to transfer allegiance. Others had no choice but to disperse, their members seeking shelter wherever they could get it. The dissolution of the Eudist congregation of priests, the dispersal of its members, the closing down of its works and being thrown out onto the street, including its sick and elderly men, without any resources, was expected daily throughout the later part of 1902.[26] Many had already taken to the road, with Canada, Colombia and Mexico becoming important refuges for some of the able-bodied. The Good Shepherd house at Nancy became the subject of outrageous claims and was forcibly closed; reports on the affair filed in Rome give some sense of how newspaper coverage and pamphlet literature – sensationalist, vindictive and reasoned – quickly spiralled out of control, with anti-Catholic activists and pro-Catholic conservative opinion adopting irreconcilable positions on matters well beyond the initial issue.[27] Although most Good Shepherd and OLC communities in France did in fact continue, all operated under the very real threat of imminent closure.[28] Cardinal Vivès, the cardinal-protector, wrote from Rome for Easter 1903 assuring the Good Shepherd sisters that their bonds with the Divine Pastor, Jesus Christ, could not be broken: 'you will be religious in spite of dispersion, separation and persecution'.[29]

25    'Décret relatif à la cause de Béatification et de Canonisation du Vénérable Serviteur de Dieu, Jean Eudes, missionnaire apostolique, instituteur de la congrégation de Jésus et Marie et de l'Ordre de Notre Dame de Charité', Congrégation des Saints Rites, Rome, trans. Angé le Doré (DARGS, OLC1/7/4 no. 7). Julie Barrett, foundress with Françoise Blin de Bourdon, of the Soeurs de Notre-Dame de Namur, was beatified on 13 May 1906 and canonised 22 June 1969.
26    Angé le Doré to Ma réverende mère, 1 septembre 1902 (DARGS, OLC1/2/3 no. 5); A. Pinas to Ma réverende mère, 12 novembre 1902 (DARGS, OLC1/7/4 no. 6). For an earlier expectation of dissolution, see Bishop Poirier, Bayeux, to Mes chères confrères, Mes très chères soeurs, n.d. but 1861 (DARGS, OLC1/2/3 no. 1).
27    The Good Shepherd superior general forwarded to Rome in 1903 a bound volume of letters of commendation from the bishops in whose dioceses the sisters worked (including letters from the bishops of Limerick, Ferns, Cork, Waterford & Lismore, Down & Connor) along with the statistics for that year, most likely to counter the damage done by the claims made by M. Turinaz, the bishop of Nancy, in the summer of 1896 which led to investigations by both state and Church. Published papers relating to the affair include M. Henri Joy, 'L'affaire du Bon Pasteur du Nancy' in *La Réforme Sociale* (16 June 1903) and *L'Affaire du Bon Pasteur d'Annonay* (17 May 1903) in which Joy recalls the Nancy affair, summarises the evidence on both sides and draws his own conclusion. 'Congrégation de Notre Dame de Charité du Bon Pasteur d'Angers, Œuvres – Statistique, appréciation de nos Seigneurs les Evêques de France et de l'Étranger sur les divers Établissement du Bon Pasteur dans leurs diocèses respectifs', 1903 (CIVCSVA, A-7 (2) /2 no. 5).
28    Nancy is among the French houses in the statistical returns for 1902 when it had a household of 253, but is absent for 1903. Reference is made to calumnies and injustices suffered by this community throughout the Good Shepherd bulletin for 1903.
29    Cardinal Vivès to Mother General, Easter Sunday 1903, reprinted in GS Bulletin, 11th year, nos. 2 & 3 (Apr. and June 1903), pp 123–5.

Among the OLC houses, it was only the financial support given by the overseas monasteries, including Dublin, towards Valence that saved it in 1908 from being joined by the bishop to the Good Shepherd congregation.[30] The OLC community at Rennes circulated overseas houses in early 1904 seeking refuge for a number of sisters, should the present persecution make that necessary. High Park regretted that it did not have accommodation but advised of a suitable premises for purchase in Waterford, and noted that other French monasteries were making investigations in England.[31] As Rennes had been involved in the foundation of the first monastery of Dublin, it might have hoped for a more positive response but the Irish houses did assist in a roundabout way by taking on the house in Mold, North Wales, established by a group of Caen sisters as a refuge should the persecution in France require the whole community to go into exile.[32] It was difficult to refuse the request to assist with Mold when Mère Desaunais herself undertook a dreadfully stormy crossing of the Irish Sea to visit High Park in late 1910. There, according to her biographer, she was fêted in every possible way and had touching proofs of the deference which Dublin gave to Caen.[33] Even after the Caen sisters moved back to their beloved monastery and were enjoying what seemed to be a more benign political climate, there was an underlying anxiety that persecution of religious institutes could resume without warning.[34] By 1913, St David's, Mold, formerly a gaol, had been sold to the Jesuits, and the remaining OLC sisters and residents moved to Ormskirk, Redcliffe, at the invitation of the bishop of Liverpool where there were certainly far more openings, and the community was supplemented by sisters from Ireland.[35]

The account by the community at Nantes of the various trials they suffered from 1903 to 1912 can be taken as fairly typical of what happened to OLC and Good Shepherd houses throughout France.[36] Nantes was subject to what the superior described as 'close and disagreeable' visits from the lady inspector of works, who insisted on entering when she wished and found fault with everything. There were heavy-handed inspections from 1904 by the Prefecture four times yearly under the heading of residents' welfare. Immediate entry and full access to all parts of the building could be demanded

30 Soeur M. de St Ambroise Desaunais to Ma très honorée et très chère Sœur (Besançon), 28 août 1908 (DARGS, OLC1/3/2 no. 17).
31 Soeur M. de Ste Genevieve Byrne, High Park, to Rennes, 20 Apr. and 5 May 1904 (DARGS, OLC1/3/3 no. 21).
32 Described as 'un asile en cas de malheur', the sisters from Caen, 'nos chères Exilées', found the foreign language, the change in manners or customs and usages, the dearth of subjects and the lack of resources to be insurmountable obstacles, Caen, *circulaire*, 15 janvier 1911 (DARGS, OLC1/3/2 no. 39). Among the sisters who helped in Mold for a few years was Sister M. of St Liguori Daly of Buffalo, New York, see Caen, circular letter, 15 Oct. 1912 (DARGS, OLC1/3/2 no. 54).
33 Late 1910 has been deduced from the context, *Vie de la Très Honorée Mère Marie de Saint Ambroise Desaunais*, p. 91.
34 Caen, *circulaire*, 13 janvier 1912 (DARGS, OLC1/3/2 no. 53).
35 Caen, circular letter, 15 Oct. 1912; Sister M. of St Aloysius Morris, High Park, to Archbishop Walsh, 10 Mar. 1913 (DARGS, OLC1/2/2 no. 13). Sœur Marie de St Ambroise Desaunais to Ma très honorée et très chère Sœur, 28 août 1914 (DARGS, OLC1/3/2 no. 67).
36 'Nous connaissons trop la situation précaire de la plupart de nos monastères en France', Soeur M. de St Ambroise Desaunais to Ma très honorée Sœur, Besançon, 28 août 1908.

at any time, whereupon the register was viewed and residents questioned, especially those aged 16 to 18. Ongoing harassment was complained of, with three young sisters forced to take their vows privately in the chapter room; the sisters reportedly found some parallels between their situation and that of the early Christians in the catacombs. Only in 1908 could sisters again make vows publicly. There was a malicious burning of the monastery on 12 August 1904, and a dramatic midnight evacuation of all dormitories. In 1905, facing the likelihood of future closure, the Nantes community contemplated a refuge in England, and also began negotiations, which would ultimately prove successful, with Monsignor Donahue, the bishop of Wheeling, USA. In search of a new house, two sisters left the enclosure on 16 January 1907 without, in their own words, any guide but their Angel Guardian and the light the Star of the Sea.[37] In the crisis year of 1908, the community described its situation as so desperate that it looked as if it would soon be offered up as an oblation or sacrifice, presumably for the good of the Church in France.[38]

Under such an onslaught from the state, which showed no sign of abating, with mounting debts and little possibility of meeting them, and with so many obstacles to further vocations, OLC communities throughout France had good reason to fear for their future as stand-alone, autonomous houses. There was also pressure from Rome under the new canon law of 1917 which tightened up on the making of new foundations and brought some standardisation to the regulations governing religious life. Centralised government seemed the only way to cope administratively with the relentless increase in the number of institutes, forcing autonomous houses to consider at least the possibility of some kind of amalgamation; the loose federation engineered for the Irish houses in 1948 was in response to that pressure. The assembly called for Caen in May 1909 (scheduled to allow sisters from North America and other distant places travelling to Rome for the beatification of the founder to be present), and in July 1931 (convened to bring the constitutions into line with revisions in canon law), would deal expressly with the threat of centralised government. The conflagrations which engulfed continental Europe in 1914 and again in 1939 would profoundly change the world in which religious institutes operated. The upheavals of 1902 to 1949 need to be read against this larger canvas, though there is still an internal, self-contained history over which the shadow of a Good Shepherd 'takeover' looms, however unreasonable this fear was even at the time. In this history, the beatification of John Eudes in 1909 is a major landmark; the canonisation in 1925 is another.

## The Cause for the Beatification of John Eudes

The beatification of John Eudes was first broached in the Congregation of Jesus and Mary in 1847, but it took an expression of interest by Pope Pius IX in 1861 for steps to be taken towards that end.[39] The first or diocesan stage, the process to establish the reputation for sanctity of the nominee, was held in Bayeux on 12 October 1868. The next stage required by Rome was extensive research into

37    Nantes, *circulaire*, 15 février 1912.
38    Ibid.
39    Père Angé M. le Doré to Ma réverende Mère et mes très chères Soeurs, 4 juillet 1868 (DARGS, OLC1/2/3 no. 2).

all that had been written by or about the person now officially titled 'servant of God'.[40] It was at this point that the monastery of Caen came to the fore. Its library was found to hold previously-unknown manuscript materials in the hand of the founder.[41] It already had the unrivalled honour of preserving in the chapel the relics of the founder.[42] Through to the beatification in 1909, and indeed to the canonisation in 1925 and beyond, the Caen community would take an active role in all that pertained to the honouring of Eudes and the acknowledgement of his sanctity. This was under the long-serving superior Soeur Marie de St Ambroise Desaunais (died 1937), but also under Soeur Marie de St Pacôme Mathis (died 1914), who alternated with Desaunais as superior for short periods.[43] The soliciting of donations to meet the costs involved, the promotion of publications about Eudes, the commissioning of portraits, sculptures and holy pictures, the composition of prayers to advance the cause, all were handled by the mother house of Caen, which also took on itself the duty of keeping the other OLC houses abreast of developments, no matter how minor.[44]

Angers did not lag behind Caen. It too gave financial backing, circulated prayer cards and other aids to devotion and provided its own sisters with full transcripts of the relevant documentation through its *Bulletin*.[45] The first vice-postulator, Père Angé le Doré, undertook the work in the name of the three congregations founded by Eudes.[46] He was a frequent visitor to Angers, where he gave the latest update on the process to the assembled sisters and novices, which were then disseminated to the Good Shepherd sisters internationally through their *Bulletin*.[47] His efforts to deal even-handedly with both OLC and Good Shepherd are evident throughout the 40 years that the process would eventually take, supplying both Caen and Angers with French translations of the Latin documents issued by Rome and witness accounts of each of the ceremonies as they occurred, which they could then send on to the other monasteries in their respective networks.[48]

The decree for the cause of the beatification and canonisation of the Venerable Servant of God John Eudes (1601–80) was published on 6 January 1903 by the Vatican's Sacred Congregation of Rites.[49] French and English

40   Ibid.
41   Sœur Marie de St Ambroise Desaunais, supérieure, NDC Caen, to Ma très honorée et bien chère Sœur, 13 juillet 1868 (DARGS, OLC1/2/3 no. 2).
42   The coffin of John Eudes had been translated to the old Jesuit church of Notre Dame de la Gloriette, Caen, in 1810, at which time the skull and two femurs were given as relics to the monastery chapel of Notre Dame de Charité in Caen. The penetration of lime destroyed most of the relics held in the Gloriette, so that the relics held by the sisters in their chapel choir assumed enormous significance. Paul Milcent, *Un artisan du renouveau Chrétien au XVIIe siècle, Saint Jean Eudes* (Paris, 1985), p. 565.
43   *Vie de la Mère Marie de Saint Ambroise Desaunais*, p. 199.
44   Ouvrages du Eudes, Manuscrits (DARGS, OLC1/2/3 no. 2).
45   These included holy cards, booklets, postcards, écussons, medals and statues, GS Bulletin, 17th year, no. 2 (Apr. 1909), pp 144–5.
46   Angé le Doré, letter dated 6 Jan. 1909, reprinted in GS Bulletin, 17th year, no. 1 (Feb. 1909), p. 27.
47   For example, concerning visit of Père le Doré to Angers in Dec. 1908, see GS Bulletin, 17th year, no. 1 (Feb. 1909). p. 42.
48   GS Bulletin, 17th year, no. 4 (July 1909).
49   'Décret relatif à la cause de Béatification et de Canonisation du Vénérable Serviteur de Dieu, Jean Eudes', trans. Le Doré.

translations were quickly made, with the Good Shepherd *Bulletin* of February 1903 carrying the full text, as well as the circular letter from Angé le Doré, now superior general of his congregation. Described as apostolic missionary and founder of the Congregation of Jesus and Mary and of the order of Our Lady of Charity, the decree opens with the central question: did John Eudes practise to a heroic degree the theological virtues of faith, hope and love of God and neighbour, and the cardinal virtues of prudence, justice, fortitude, and temperance? Before going on to describe how he did indeed live these virtues, the Congregation of Rites considers how timely this reflection is at a time when the Church is under attack. Stress is laid on Eudes as a Frenchman, truly sent by God to be a model of justice and of holiness at a time when France was falling into the worst excesses. Stories are recounted of his pious upbringing and early desire to consecrate himself exclusively to the service of God, his commitment and success in mission preaching, and his truly heroic service to the plague-stricken of Caen in 1634 when, to avoid bringing infection to others, he retired each night to a barrel in a field outside the town, which became known as the meadow of the saint (*le pré du saint*). The unrelenting hostility that followed the setting up by Eudes of a society of priests which had for its end the preaching of missions and running of seminaries is recalled, and the exemplary patience with which he bore all manner of opposition, calling those who opposed him 'friends' and 'benefactors'. There is a succinct treatment of his many initiatives and sufferings crowned with a holy death, his passing marked by spontaneous outpourings of grief and devotion among huge crowds. The decree concludes with a summary of the meetings held to adjudicate on the virtues of this venerable servant of God, culminating in the meeting at which Pope Leo XIII declared that, not alone was Eudes an illustrious man whose holiness of life shone through but, through his intelligent zeal for the salvation of souls, and above all through the institutes he had founded, he was an example, in all countries and in all ages, of service to mankind.[50] The political overtones of the Pope's comments were unlikely to be missed by his contemporary audience.

The publication of the decree on the virtues of John Eudes in January 1903 set in motion the build-up towards the decree of beatification.[51] A critical point was reached with the acceptance on 5 May 1908 of the certainty of the three miracles which the diocese of Bayeux, as promoter of the cause, had submitted to Rome.[52] A moment of pure theatre was provided on 22 October 1908 by the solemn exhumation of the remains and their canonical verification, *la reconnaissance des reliques*, as captured in the lengthy account by Soeur Ambroise Desaunais circulated to all the OLC houses.[53] Angers brought the

50   The meetings were dated 14 Nov. 1899, under Cardinal Miecislas Ledochowski; 18 Dec. 1900 and 26 Aug. 1902, Palais du Vatican; 16 Dec. 1902, in the presence of Pope Leo XIII, with Cardinal Dominique Ferrata and others. 'Décret relatif à la cause de Béatification et de Canonisation du Vénérable Serviteur de Dieu, Jean Eudes', trans. Le Doré.

51   The decree, along with a letter of Père le Doré, were reprinted in GS Bulletin, 17th year, no. 1 (Feb. 1909).

52   'Décret de béatification et de canonisation du Vénérable Serviteur de Dieu, Jean Eudes', trans. Le Doré.

53   Caen, circular letter, 28 Oct. 1908 (DARGS, OLC1/3/2 no. 16).

drama into the Good Shepherd convents through a special edition of its *Bulletin*, a very full account similar in essentials to that of Caen.[54]

Soeur Ambroise Desaunais herself had a starring role in the ceremonies of 22 October 1908. Not alone was she superior of the premier monastery but, as a pupil in the Caen boarding school, she had witnessed the placing of the relics under the grille of the sisters' choir in 1884 and so could testify to the accuracy of the account in the monastery's annals.[55] The bishop formally sought admission to the enclosure, and entered 'with all the tribunal', three doctors and two lay people – a local notable and a distant descendant of John Eudes. All were sworn in. The workmen who were to remove the marble slab were also sworn in and undertook not to add or take from the relics. The boxed remains, consisting of a skull and thighbones fixed together with pitch and resin, were broken apart over three hours with a chisel by one of the doctors, with the sisters and tribunal members as silent witnesses. The doctors were called 'to give their opinion on the state of the relics, their appreciation on the stature, constitution and intelligence of our good Father'; they signed a report attesting to the 'great intelligence' of the deceased whose height was likely to be between four feet 10 inches and five feet 2 inches (1m 50 to 1m 60). During all this, Desaunais sat beside the bishop 'in order to be the first in rank', while to her was given the honour of wrapping up the relics in white silk, an honour she graciously shared with the vice-postulator, Fr le Doré. The whole drama took more than four unbroken hours, and culminated in a procession: first the sisters with lighted tapers, then the coffin, placed upon a brancard decorated with silk, lace and flowers and carried by the two Eudist fathers who were chaplains to Caen, and then the tribunal.[56] They passed along the cloister and upstairs to a little oratory created to be the honoured but hidden receptacle of the precious remains 'until the moment of the Beatification'.[57] Before giving his final blessing, the bishop directed the sisters to honour the founder in the best possible way: 'to imitate his virtues and penetrate yourselves more and more with the spirit which he gave to your Institute remaining such as he established it'.[58]

## The Beatification Ceremony of John Eudes in Rome, 25 April 1909

Nothing was left wanting in the build-up to the grand day of the beatification of John Eudes, even before the date itself was confirmed. Art works were commissioned by Caen, of which the most important was the portrait to be unveiled at the very moment of the beatification, the *apothéose*, in the splendid setting of St Peter's.[59] As a special favour, in November 1908, a likeness of the

54  GS Bulletin, 17th year, no. 1 bis (Jan. 1909), pp 30–40.
55  Milcent, *Un artisan du renouveau Chrétien au XVIIe siècle, Saint Jean Eudes*, p. 565. Trans., 'Letter of the Rev. Père le Doré on the occasion of the ceremonies of beatification of the Blessed John Eudes' to 'My very rev. Fathers and my dear Sisters', p. 12 (DARGS, OLC1/7/4 no. 18). Hereafter, Le Doré, Letter concerning 25 Apr. 1909.
56  Caen, circular letter, 28 Oct. 1908.
57  Sister M. of St Ambrose Desaunais to Dear Sister, 28 Oct. 1908 (DARGS, OLC1/3/2 no. 15a).
58  Caen, circular letter, 28 Oct. 1908.
59  Soeur M. de St Ambroise Desaunais to High Park, 16 Nov. 1908. The picture of John Eudes planned by High Park is to go behind the high altar; she describes in particular the picture being prepared for the *apothéose* of the beatification (DARGS, OLC1/3/2 no. 18).

**Figure 7.1**   Souvenir postcard to mark the beatification of John Eudes, 25 April
1909. (DARGS, OLC2/12/4 no. 11)

Venerable Eudes, the first sketch of the engraver, was forwarded to High Park;
this was held to be the earliest known image and quite true to life.[60] Souvenir
postcards were published (figure 7.1). New hymns were composed, one with
the opening line, '*O Jean Eudes, ô prêtre de France, à qui Dieu de son cœur dévoila
les splendeurs*', which dwelt on Eudes' role as zealous formator of the clergy in
France at a time when error reigned.[61] Letters of permission to travel to Rome
were secured from the local bishop, as it involved leaving the enclosure;[62] the
larger question of whether sisters should be present in Rome had already been
mediated by Caen.[63] OLC sisters from France, Italy, England, Ireland, Spain,
Canada, the United States and Mexico, and the superior general and European
provincials of the Sisters of the Good Shepherd of Angers, began the long journey to Rome. Mère Marie de Ste Domitille Larose (elected 30 June 1905) headed the Good Shepherd delegation. Also invited were representatives of the
Daughters of the Heart of the Admirable Mother of the Congregation of the
Sacred Hearts, established at Notre-Dame des Chênes at Parame, 'for they regard themselves with good right as the Daughters of the Blessed John Eudes'.[64]
The representatives from High Park were Mother Mary of St Genevieve Byrne

---

60   J. Dauphin to Ma réverende mère, 29 novembre 1908 (DARGS, OLC1/2/3 no. 6).
61   Hymns to Blessed John Eudes, in French, n.d. but prepared for 25 Apr. 1909 (DARGS,
OLC1/7/4 no. 15).
62   Bartholomew Fitzpatrick, Permission to travel, 13 Apr. 1909 (DARGS, OLC1/2/2 no. 12).
63   *Vie de la Très Honorée Mère Marie de Saint Ambroise Desaunais*, p. 209.
64   Le Doré, Letter concerning 25 Apr. 1909, p. 8.

and Sister Mary of the Sacred Heart Pilkington[65] and, from Gloucester Street, Mother St Francis Xavier Leamy and Sister Mary of Aloysius McCabe, who was accompanied by her two nieces, the Misses McCabe.[66] Pilkington created a lengthy and entertaining narrative out of the rough notes she made while travelling, drawing also on the postcards and letters she sent from abroad.[67] In London, they were entertained by Lady Morley, the mother of Sister Mary of St Agatha Ayling (High Park), at Flowermead, the family's 'handsome residence' outside Wimbledon.[68] The superior of Waterlooville, Mother Mary of St Paul Carroll (who had made profession for High Park), joined the party before they travelled via Dover and Calais to Paris. The itinerary was stretched to allow a visit to every monastery of the order that could possibly be included. High Park had a special affection for Chevilly, a town about nine miles outside Paris, to which the community of rue St Jacques had removed.[69] On the longest single portion of the adventure, a train journey of some 36 hours from Paris to Rome, they were joined by sisters from the French and American houses, making 40 sisters in all, including Soeur Desaunais of Caen. She was described on first meeting as 'a fine woman, tall and stout, having a square face, I should think she is very capable'.[70] During their time in Rome the Irish sisters were spellbound by all they witnessed, with St Peter's itself meriting special praise: 'Everything is colossal and magnificent beyond description, the statues, monuments, all of the most lovely of marbles.'[71]

The beatification ceremony was held in St Peter's basilica, Rome, on Sunday 25 April 1909 commencing at 9.30am, with a further liturgy, including benediction, at 5pm.[72] Very full accounts of the moving ceremony, but with slightly differing emphases, can be found in the records of OLC and Good Shepherd.[73] As the *Te Deum* was intoned, every eye was fixed on the picture of John Eudes which hung over the high altar, 'in a halo of glory with his hands crossed on his breast, looking up to heaven surrounded by angels, some holding harps and another a heart'. As the electric lights spread around the church, 'it seemed as if countless stars had burst into light'.[74] At the afternoon ceremony, the French pilgrims took over, filling the basilica

---

65   The election by the local chapter usually took place just before Pentecost and so the period of superiorship (*supériorité*) usually dates from mid – or late – May. Mother M. of St Genevieve Byrne was superior of High Park 1901–07 and 1914–20; she died 23 Mar. 1930. Mother M. of St Aloysius Morris was superior of High Park 1895–1901 and 1907–14; she died 21 Apr. 1917.

66   Mother St Francis Xavier Leamy was superior of Gloucester Street 1904–10, 1916–22 and 1928 to 2 Mar. 1931, when she died; Sister M. of Aloysius McCabe was superior 1898–1904, 1910–16, and died 4 Feb. 1918.

67   Sister M. of the Sacred Heart Pilkington, 'Sketch of our journey from Dublin to Rome on the occasion of the beatification of our venerable founder, Père Eudes', 14 Apr.–8 May 1909 (DARGS, OLC1/7/4 no. 19). Hereafter, Pilkington, 'Sketch of our journey from Dublin to Rome'.

68   Ibid., p. 5.

69   Ibid., pp 30–32. The founding sisters of the first monastery of Dublin were from Paris and Rennes, see chapter 1.

70   Ibid., p. 13.

71   Ibid., p. 17.

72   Entrance tickets to the ceremonies in St Peter's, 25 Apr. 1909 (DARGS, OLC1/7/4 no. 15).

73   For Good Shepherd account, see GS Bulletin no. 4, 17th year (July 1909).

74   Pilkington, 'Sketch of our journey from Dublin to Rome', p. 20.

with devotional singing, 'a fitting outpouring of the hearts in gratitude for having bestowed upon their country and their nation so great a favour'.[75] The next morning's highlight was the audience with the Pope. After Pius X met descendants of John Eudes, Père Angé le Doré, superior general of the Congregation of Jesus and Mary, presented a group representing his own congregation, the Eudist fathers (himself and Fr Mallet), the Sisters of Our Lady of Charity (the superiors of Caen and Rennes) and the Good Shepherd Sisters (the mother general and her assistant). In separate but nearby rooms, the Pope then greeted members of these three institutes, all of whom venerated Eudes as founder, and whose virtues he urged them to imitate.[76] The significance of this joint presentation to the Pope was to be heavily stressed by Le Doré, who felt that the occasion made it clear in the eyes of the Church that together they formed but one single family, 'all of us living with the same heart and spirit which was the spirit of our common Father'.[77] Le Doré spoke of two different observances but one single order, which was not canonically correct – the Good Shepherd had been a fully-fledged congregation in its own right since 1835 – but there can be no doubting the sincerity with which the old man spoke, having himself worked with unflagging zeal for more than 40 years to bring the parties to see themselves in this light.[78] Three further days of ceremonies followed in the Jesuit church of the Gesú, with the picture from over the high altar in St Peter's used again as a striking backdrop and the façade of the church lit up and surmounted by the Eudist caption, '*Vive Jésus et Marie*'.[79] In the panegyric given on the final day, much was made of the Good Shepherd of Angers, of its founder Euphrasie Pelletier and her zeal for souls, of her lay supporter and friend Count de Neuville, of houses of refuge to be found in every land and how the confidence of John Eudes was to be seen in the life of Pelletier, another 'pearl' of the French Church whom the speaker, H. Pasquier, apostolic protonotary, hoped would soon be beatified also:

> The daughters of the Good Shepherd have carried his [Eudes']
> apostolic spirit to all lands. Like the Catholic Church, no
> obstacle can hinder their course; differences of language,
> rigours of climate cannot damp their zeal. If we make a tour of
> the world, we shall find them established under the broiling
> Indian sun, in the new fields of Australia and New Zealand, in
> the plains and on the mountains of the two Americas.[80]

While the autonomous monasteries of OLC which traced their origins to Caen were not exactly overlooked, no one could misread Rome's regard for the expansionist Good Shepherd congregation, its dynamic, centralised government in Angers, and its embodiment of the charism of John Eudes.

75    Ibid., p. 21.
76    Ibid., p. 22.
77    Le Doré, Letter concerning 25 April 1909, p. 10.
78    Milcent, 'Notre Dame de Charité, relations entre maisons', p. 11.
79    Pilkington, 'Sketch of our journey from Dublin to Rome', p. 27.
80    GS Bulletin, 17th year, no. 6 (Oct. 1909), p. 363.

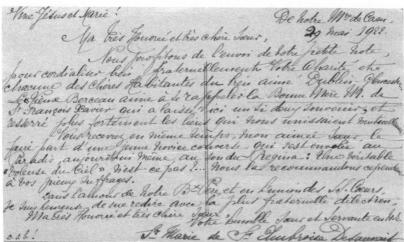

**Figure 7.2** Souvenir postcard noting that the relics of Blessed John Eudes are held by the monastery of Our Lady of Charity of Refuge, Caen; letter on reverse by the superior of Caen, Mother Mary of St Ambrose Desaunais, 29 May 1922. (DARGS, OLC2/12/4 no. 11)

To extend the celebrations beyond Rome, all houses which claimed John Eudes as founder and friend were given the right to celebrate a triduum, with indulgences attached, over the following 12 months and involving the faithful.[81] Accounts of local Good Shepherd celebrations were published in successive volumes of the *Bulletin*[82] while OLC celebrations were made known

81  Le Doré, Letter concerning 25 April 1909, p. 10.
82  Accounts of local Good Shepherd celebrations in honour of Blessed John Eudes are to be found in GS Bulletin, 17th year, nos. 6, 7, 8 (1909).

to the other autonomous monasteries through the long-established medium of the circular letter. The prayers proper to the Mass for the beatification and subsequent triduum were published, and hymn sheets, prayer leaflets, holy pictures and medals honouring John Eudes were widely circulated.[83] The distribution of relics of the newly-beatified was undertaken by the Eudist father general, in conjunction with the superior of the first monastery of Caen and the Bishop of Bayeux.[84] The first Dublin monastery was honoured with a first-class relic, '*ex ossibus et ex cineribus*' of the founder.[85] In Caen itself, on 15 May 1909, the principal relics (at least, the skull and one of the femurs – the other was held by the Bishop of Bayeux) were deposited anew in the monastery chapel (figure 7.2), where the first triduum outside Rome was held on 17, 18 and 19 May 1909, with every possible solemnity and extravagance.[86]

## The 1909 General Assembly at the Monastery of Caen

The beatification in Rome of the founder, John Eudes, offered an unprecedented opportunity for an assembly of sisters drawn from all the autonomous monasteries of the order he founded. There was also a pressing need to agree some changes to the constitutions to bring them into line with revisions in canon law, most especially around the powers of the superior of a religious community and the frequent reception of Communion. The initiative was taken, not surprisingly, by the superior of the first monastery of Caen, Mère Marie de St Ambroise Desaunais, who convened a general assembly for May 1909. In the preparatory correspondence, it was presented as a re-run of the famous 1734 Caen assembly of deputies from all the houses, which resulted in the four-part customs book, approved by Pope Benedict XIV in 1741. Such an assembly, it was claimed by Desaunais, had long been 'earnestly wished for by all houses', but knowing that the beatification was coming up made it opportune to await that moment.[87] The hope was held out that this assembly – only the second in the history of the order – would be a powerful means of renewal in the spirit of Our Lady of Charity, both individually and collectively, and lead to greater esteem for and love of this 'admirable vocation'.[88] Its more practical objective was 'to decide many points requiring a solution', for which purpose a questionnaire was

83   Mass text proper to the beatification and triduum, *In solemnis beatificationis Ioannis Eudes conf. et subsequentibus Triduanis Festivitatibus*, issued by the secretary to the Sacred Congregation of Rites, 14 Apr. 1909, and printed with imprimatur of P. Fages, Paris, 3 May 1909 (DARGS, OLC1/7/4 no. 10).

84   Some relics were distributed after the beatification in 1909, others after the canonisation in 1925, see Milcent, *Un artisan du renouveau Chrétien au XVIIe siècle, Saint Jean Eudes*, p. 565.

85   Le Doré, Letter concerning 25 April 1909, pp 12–13; 'Authentic (*sic*) of the large relic of our Blessed Founder, John Eudes, brought from Caen after the Assembly by our Honoured Mother Mary of St Aloysius Morris, May 27th 1909'. Certificate in the name of Thomas Paul Henry Lemonnier, archbishop of Bayeux and Lisieux, 9 June 1909, also M. Flavell and E. Deslamby (DARGS, OLC1/7/7 no. 23).

86   The femur held in the cathedral sacristy from May 1909 was returned to the monastery in 1924 when it was installed in a new altar dedicated to John Eudes. *Vie de la Très Honorée Mère Marie de Saint Ambroise Desaunais*, pp 214–5, 217–8.

87   Sister M. of St Ambrose Desaunais to Dear Sister, 28 Oct. 1908.

88   Same to Ma très honorée et très chère Sœur, Besançon, 6 Apr. 1909 (DARGS, OLC1/3/2 no. 21).

circulated requesting superiors to identify, by number, which constitutions needed to be revised or discussed at Caen.[89] Before debate got under way, all were reminded that the assembly was for the purpose of maintaining and strengthening unity and exact conformity between their different monasteries and the exact observance of the rule laid down (*tracé*) by their blessed founder, John Eudes.[90] Its overriding aim was to extinguish all consideration of a generalate that the status quo – autonomous monasteries – might be preserved in essence and in detail. Everyone present knew that Rome looked favourably on centralised structures; they also knew the mind of Caen, as the superior of the first house of the order had made it the subject of circular letters and private correspondence in advance of the meeting:

> It has been insinuated that the Holy Father wished and asked for a generalate that, by the fusion of all, there would be many great advantages. Do not think so – roses were never found without thorns! And if we will really reflect seriously, we shall be convinced, that our Ven. Father Eudes was animated by a spirit of wisdom and prudence and really enlightened when he gave us this legislation which, in truth, we can say is our strength, our life and our assurance.[91]

With an increasing number and variety of religious houses to be found in any single diocese, the bishop found it more efficient to deal with major superiors, that is, superiors general, provincial and regional superiors who would handle the difficulties that had a tendency otherwise to fall to him to solve. Caen was well aware of the pressure that bishops were putting on Rome in this regard but maintained that the Pope's wishes were what mattered above all, namely, 'that the religious families live in peace, union, fidelity and holiness!'[92] The other matters which might arise at the 1909 assembly were insignificant in comparison with this core question of governance.

Fifty-three sisters assembled in Caen in May 1909, representing 30 monasteries (as listed in appendix A; there were in all 40 OLC houses at that date). In most cases, it was the superior and one other (the assistant or another councillor or the previous superior). The delegates were listed in order of the foundation date of each house, making for 14 French houses (there were four sisters from Caen, and two from the others, making 30 delegates), then came High Park, the first of the overseas houses, represented by Mère Marie de Saint Aloysius Morris (superior) and Soeur Marie de Ste Genevieve Byrne (*déposée*), followed by the American (Buffalo, New York), Canadian and Mexican houses, then by England (Waterlooville) and the second monastery

---

89 'Aperçu des questions à étudier à l'Assemblée Générale', n.d. but 1909 (DARGS, OLC1/3/2 no. 19).
90 'Les actes ou procès verbaux des sessions de l'Assemblée Générale des Soeurs de Notre Dame de Charité du Refuge, tenne au Monastère de Caen, première session, 27 mai 1909' (CIVCSVA, B79/1). Hereafter, Les actes ou procès verbaux des sessions de l'Assemblée Générale.
91 Caen, circular letter, 14 July 1902.
92 Ibid.

of Dublin, Gloucester Street, which sent Mother St Francis Xavier Leamy (superior) and Soeur Marie de St Aloysius McCabe (*déposée*).[93]

The absentees are of interest, and again are listed in order of foundation dates: La Rochelle, for unspecified serious reasons; Bilbao, in the Basque region of Spain, for language reasons; Salzburg, Austria, prevented by the bishop; the second house in Marseilles, because of the illness of the local superior. Of the three monasteries in England, only the superior of Waterlooville participated in the assembly; the superior of Bartestree, an Irish woman, Sister Patrick O'Dwyer, died on arrival in Caen, and the superior of Northfield (Birmingham), Sister Stanislaus Roche, accompanied the body back to England for burial. Five recent foundations in the US were not in a position to send a representative.[94] Questions to be considered at the assembly had been previously invited from each superior. From what was submitted, Caen compiled a single list and circulated it in advance of the assembly to each superior or deputy who was expected to attend.[95]

The archbishop of Bayeux, Bishop Lemonnier, took a prominent role in the proceedings on the basis that Caen was in his diocese and under his jurisdiction. It was he who proposed the formidable Mère Marie de St Ambroise Desaunais, superior of the Caen monastery, as president; she was elected to the role by acclamation. A council of four sisters elected by secret ballot became a sort of 'steering committee', made up of a sister each from Ireland (M. Aloysius Morris), England (M. of the Blessed Sacrament Gouillard), US (M. St Rose Tittling) and Canada (M. Eudes of the Heart of Mary Johnson); the three secretaries elected were French, but an English-speaker was added on day two. The archbishop presided in person, insisted on the secrecy of all the discussions and counter-signed the documents that were subsequently sent on to Rome via his chancellery.[96] Two priest consultors or theologians were approved for the assembly, Père Angé le Doré, the Eudist superior general, and Père Dauphin, also a Eudist priest.

The very first proposition presented to the assembly, once the secretarial and other organisational matters were sorted, was designed to settle the matter of a generalate once and for all. The proposition stated that, out of respect for the form or structure given by the blessed founder and because the sisters were not convinced of the advantages of a generalate over the inconveniences such a modification would involve, the assembly was not of a mind to group the monasteries under the authority of a single superior general, and preferred that the houses conserve their independence and their autonomy. The proposition went to a secret ballot: 51 votes in favour, two against, a result so heavily weighted in favour of the status quo that it rendered further debate unnecessary. With the possibility of a centralised government so completely removed from the agenda at the first business session, the assembly then went on to suggest some ways in which the widely-dispersed OLC monasteries, described as faithful to the spirit and

---

93   List of persons present, General Assembly, Caen, 27 May 1909 (DARGS, OLC1/3/2 no. 24).
94   Les actes ou procès verbaux des sessions de l'Assemblée Générale, première session, 27 mai 1909.
95   'Aperçu des questions à étudier à l'Assemblée Générale'.
96   Les actes ou procès verbaux des sessions de l'Assemblée Générale, deuxième session, 27 mai 1909 (CIVCSVA, B79/1).

work of Blessed John Eudes, might be supported, and the overall prosperity, unity and stability of the institute assured.

The other propositions covered internal communication, especially with Caen as the cradle and 'mother house'; the fostering of closer connections with the Eudist priests (*une rapporte d'une manière toute spéciale*), as both shared the one founder; the extension of the spiritual rights and privileges of Caen (as the founding house) to the other houses; and the appointment of a cardinal-protector in Rome to underline the subordination of the institute to Rome and to render its relationships with Rome easier and more 'regular'. All of these were allowed without much opposition, at least, insofar as can be deduced from the annotations on the manuscript. However, the proposal that there might be assemblies every ten, 12 or 15 years – the first to be held in Caen to emphasise the filial respect that the institute owes to the mother house, with the decisions submitted to Rome – was flatly rejected.[97] The proposition was for a type of general chapter, with two Eudist fathers as consultors and following the prescriptions in their constitutions for meetings. But, in the absence of a generalate or any other centralised government and the uncertainty around the status of its decisions, it is not surprising that Rome rejected it out of hand.

The fifth and final proposition was in answer to the vexed question of relations with the Sisters of the Good Shepherd, and the expectation by Rome that these sisters of a common founder would have some sort of formal union. Noting the approbation given by the Holy See to the Sisters of the Good Shepherd as being part of the order of Notre Dame de Charité, and in memory of the role they had played in the beatification of John Eudes, and referring to the audience held with Pope Pius X in the Vatican rooms when he jointly blessed all three institutes, the union that was proposed by the assembly was to be a spiritual union, a union of prayer, merits and cordial charity, to be marked annually on 19 August, the feast of the founder. No objection could be raised to this proposal, but it certainly fell far short of what had been expected to result from the first-ever gathering of the heads of the three institutes and their shared benediction by no less than the Pope himself. All of this ('*une union générale de prières et une communication des mérites et de bonnes oeuvres*') had already been established in 1889 when the three institutes had agreed to hold the anniversary of the death of the founder as the feast-day in common.[98] Whatever the impression of progress or of newness this final proposition may have been intended to convey, it was in fact a reiteration of what was already in place.

The first proposition, disposing of the matter of a generalate, and the five minor propositions, dealing with communications, future assemblies and spiritual union, were all proposed and adopted unanimously by the assembly on day two, by raised hands.[99] Only the requiem Mass for the sister from Bartestree who died on arrival prevented these ready-made proposals being voted on even earlier. That there was undue haste on the part of the president, Mère Ambroise Desaunais of Caen, is evident from the following day's minutes, where the character and status of the meeting – whether a *réunion*

97   Ibid., troisième session, 28 mai 1909 (CIVCSVA, B79/1).
98   Angé le Doré, Paris, to Mes bien-aimés pères et mes très chères sœurs, 12 Février 1889, p. 3 (DARGS, OLC1/2/3 no. 4).
99   Les actes ou procès verbaux des sessions de l'Assemblée Générale, troisième session, 28 mai 1909.

*fraternelle* or a general assembly in the canonical sense – is questioned by the archbishop of Bayeux and the two Eudist consultors. As members of a congregation with a well-defined central government, they had experience of how a general chapter ought to be run.[100] All was suspended until the authority of those present was verified. Letters of obedience from the respective bishops, and letters of procuration or permission to act as proxy, signed by the council of the monastery, were demanded of all delegates. The superiors of St Brieuc and of Vancouver assured the assembly they had the necessary authorisation, but needed to write home to procure letters of obedience. Of the eight absent communities, six had written in advance that they would concur with whatever decisions were made; the two missing English houses (Bartestree, whose superior was dead three days, and Northfield, whose superior had travelled back to England with the body), had their documentation fully in order, but were not now part of the assembly. It was only after this investigation that the assembly could be declared valid, legitimate and canonical, and the decisions taken at the previous sessions allowed to stand.[101]

Following what must have been a worrying interlude, what the sisters on the steering committee had identified as the issues to be addressed were grouped under four headings: the modifications required to the constitutions to conform with recent decrees of the sovereign pontiff and norms issued by the Sacred Congregation for Religious; the numerous small articles in the customs book and directory which needed to be altered; a more complete and precise rule for the *tourière* sisters; the penitents' rule, which was described as needing to be revised from top to bottom. Overwhelmed by the impossibility of covering this work in the required detail over a few days by a body of 53 persons, the assembly voted unanimously to name a commission of four sisters whose arduous and delicate work would be informed by the summaries already made of the sisters' observations and by the discussions of the assembly, carefully minuted. They were to carry out this work under the direction of the two Eudist priests already acting as advisers to the meeting, Père le Doré and Père Dauphin.[102] The four persons named were the superior and assistant from Caen, and the assistant superiors from Lyon and from Nantes, and they would meet in Caen, to which house all correspondence would be directed.[103] But pending the completion of that important work and its ratification by the Sacred Congregation for Religious, the Caen assembly went ahead and voted unanimously for the observation of the enclosure exactly as set out in the constitutions, with recourse to the cardinal-protector in case of difficulty in any place, and applying to the local ordinary or bishop, who had a duty to protect the enclosure, for dispensations from enclosure in particular and temporary cases.[104] That its agenda was overwhelmingly defensive was obvious to all present, even if the voting records suggest some dissent.

---

100    Ibid., quatrième session, 29 mai 1909.
101    Ibid.
102    Ibid.
103    Loose-leaf postscript to *circulaire* from Caen, n.d. but 1909 (DARGS, OLC1/3/2 no. 37).
104    Les actes ou procès verbaux des sessions de l'Assemblée Générale, quatrième session, 29 mai 1909.

The modifications suggested by the assembly were written up by the commission of four sisters in the form of parallel texts: *texte ancien* and *texte proposé*. It was also necessary to submit up-to-date statistics on the order as a whole; the houses were petitioned over the summer and autumn of 1909 to forward the information to Caen, which Père Dauphin put together in a single-sheet format (appendix A).[105] The accompanying letter, dated 30 December 1909, was signed by Soeur Marie de St Ambroise Desaunais, superior of the monastery of Caen and president of the general chapter held in the first house of the order, and countersigned by the Bishop of Bayeux, through whom the document was sent on to the Sacred Congregation for Religious in Rome, where it appears to have lain, untouched or at least without annotation or comment, for at least 12 months.[106] The requested changes appear on close examination to be the minimum required to implement decrees recently issued by Rome that were applicable to the faithful more generally. The modifications requested and approved included exhorting the sisters to daily Communion, freeing the sick from the need to fast before the reception of Holy Communion and removing from sisters the obligation to reveal matters of conscience to the superior.[107] The powers of the extraordinary – or outside – confessor were curtailed somewhat, as his advice was no longer required before a sister could approach the altar rails.[108] The Little Office of the Blessed Heart of Mary could now be said privately in the mother tongue, as well as in Latin.[109] The outright ban on instrumental music was lifted; the organ could now be used during any of the religious services – insufficient voices in choir was pleaded – but with the comment that the sisters would endeavour always to respect the simplicity recommended by the founder and to prefer Gregorian chant to all other types of music.[110]

Few of the undoubtedly numerous small articles in the customs book and directory which needed updating were tackled. There were limits placed on 'extraordinary and public penances' (they were effectively banned); the annual retreat could start on the day of the superior's choosing, not necessarily on the feast of St Michael; the need to carry work to do at weekday recreation (*'en parlans'*) was ended; the lengthy instruction on deportment was cut down to the advice that sisters keep their hands under their scapulars when out walking.[111] The distance of the grille was to be defined as 16 to 18 centimetres, rather than six or seven inches (*pouces*) – that is, no change.[112]

---

105    Soeur M. de St Ambroise Desaunais, Caen, to Ma très honorée et très chère Sœur, Besançon, 12 août 1909 (DARGS, OLC1/3/2 no. 29); Caen, *circulaire*, 1 septembre 1909 (DARGS, OLC1/3/2 no. 32a).

106    Soeur M. de St Ambroise Desaunais, address, in French, Soeurs de Notre Dame de Charité dit du Refuge, united in general chapter in their first house, Caen, with postscript signed by Bishop of Bayeux, 30 décembre 1909. Another handwritten copy of the same text with the same changes is dated 10 janvier 1911 (CIVCSVA, B79).

107    Proposed revisions, *Texte ancien* and *Texte proposé*, bound copy, pp 24, 27, 71, 99, 120, 131, 132, 135 (CIVCSVA, B79). Hereafter, Proposed revisions.

108    'In accord with the decree *Quemadmodum*, 17 Oct. 1890', Proposed revisions, p. 24.

109    Proposed revisions, p. 33.

110    Ibid., p. 21.

111    Les actes ou procès verbaux des sessions de l'Assemblée Générale, quatrième session, 29 mai 1909 (CIVCSVA, B79/1), pp 38, 45, 93, 94.

112    Ibid., p. 61.

The indeterminate position of the *tourière* sisters – essential to the outdoor business of the convent, but without the full privileges of religious life – was the one issue that the 1909 assembly brought to a successful close.[113] The requests made at the end of 1909 were granted: *tourière* sisters, zealous for the saving of souls, were to make the fourth vow of the order just like the lay and choir sisters.[114] They were to be dressed simply and modestly in black, in a uniform manner, rather than what the original constitutions proposed, namely that they be supplied with sufficient to dress themselves 'honestly'.[115] Their reception ceremonial was to be the same as that of the lay sisters, with a two-year noviceship and admission to vows by a majority of votes, with vows taken annually for five years (later changed to three years) and then perpetual vows.[116] In short, they were to become incorporated fully as sisters and treated no differently in all that pertained to the convent than the lay sisters. The lay sisters were no longer to be referred to as *les soeurs domestiques* but as *les soeurs converses*, with a note added to the constitutions that they were to be treated no differently than the choir sisters; the fact that they would still have neither active nor passive voice in the monastery's internal elections was taken as understood.[117]

The penitents' rule, which had been described at the start of the assembly as needing to be revised from top to bottom, was barely touched on. The principal modification was described as a more precise articulation of the end or aim of the institute, still described as the rescue of penitent women who voluntarily sought refuge in the house. Another sentence was needed to cover the work of 'preservation' of young girls that had in fact been long exercised by the order, but was not explicitly stated in the first constitution.[118] The addition stated that the sisters work also to preserve from vice young women or girls who were particularly exposed or vulnerable, and who were confided to the care of the sisters by their parents, or those acting in the role of parent.[119] Minors or youngsters who were brought by their parents or guardians might also be received, insofar as the means of the house permits.[120] The house is on no account obliged to receive any person brought by force or under restraint, a long-standing protection for the monastery against being used as a prison.[121] The women residents, rather than 'perfectly' keeping the enclosure,

---

113   'On demande pour les Sœurs Tourières l'uniformité de costume, qu'elles soient traitées comme les Sœurs Converses, pour les vœux, le chapitre, les constitutions, les entretiens de communauté, les exercises etc. Leur constitution semble devoir être refaite en entire'. In 'Aperçu des questions à étudier à l'Assemblée Générale'. For the arguments in favour of these changes, and the slow progress, see Caen, *circulaire*, 10 mars 1910 (DARGS, OLC1/3/2 no. 40).

114   Proposed revisions, p. 2.

115   Ibid., p. 186.

116   Ibid.; Caen, *circulaire*, 27 mai 1911; *circulaire*, 3 novembre 1911 (DARGS, OLC1/3/2 nos. 46, 51).

117   Proposed revisions, pp 17, 24.

118   Les actes ou procès verbaux des sessions de l'Assemblée Générale, cinquième session, 29 mai 1909 (CIVCSVA, B79/1).

119   Proposed revisions, p. 4.

120   Ibid., p. 10.

121   Ibid.

were now to keep the enclosure 'in so far as possible'.[122] After the usual night prayers and examination of conscience (the 'examen'), they were to retire to the dormitory (*leur dortoir*) rather than to individual rooms (*leurs cellules*).[123] The ban on contact with outside bodies while resident in the home was not to extend to parents, and a woman resident liable to set the house on fire during the night was not to be confined under lock and key.[124] The ban on admitting any woman while pregnant was unchanged, as was the right to refuse a woman with a disease likely to infect the other residents.[125]

Quite unexpectedly, it was the invitation to the Sisters of the Good Shepherd of a spiritual union, in the name of their common founder, the newly-beatified John Eudes, that was the most contentious outcome of the assembly. The proposal had been adopted unanimously by the general assembly and Soeur Marie de St Ambroise Desaunais, in her role as president of the assembly, had been mandated to write on behalf of all the 42 houses of the order then re-united in Caen; the letter was sent about three weeks later. The invitation itself could not have been more inoffensive: to join each year with the sisters of Our Lady of Charity and with the priests and brothers of the Congregation of Jesus and Mary on the anniversary of the founder's death, 19 August, to pray for each other's intentions. The letter opened with a strong affirmation of the legitimacy of the modifications introduced to Notre Dame de Charité by Vénérable Mère Marie de Ste Euphrasie Pelletier. It recalled how, at the recent beatification in St Peter's, OLC and Good Shepherd sisters had co-operated with affection, finding themselves united in the one sentiment of joy, gratitude and devotion. They had knelt together before the Pontiff, the mother superior of Angers, *au nom de votre Observance*, the superior of Caen, *au nom de l'Observance primitive*, and the superior general of the Congregation of Jesus and Mary (the Eudist fathers). An idyllic picture of mutual goodwill and spiritual support was painted, with the final note, that each institute would assist the other to walk in the way which Providence had assigned to it, a form of words that that made it clear that nothing further than this union of hearts was offered or expected.[126]

The sisters of Our Lady of Charity rightly expected that their Good Shepherd counterparts would receive the letter 'as spontaneously and cordially as we had written it'.[127] But before circulating it to her own membership by having it published in the *Bulletin*, the Good Shepherd superior general made some editorial changes and added the 'signature' of Soeur Marie de St Ambroise Desaunais, all of which was taken as very bad form indeed. In a memo marked 'confidential', Soeur Ambroise Desaunais of Caen complained of the changes, circulating to each OLC house a copy of the original letter she herself had

122   Ibid., p. 12.
123   Ibid., p. 13.
124   Ibid., p. 15.
125   Ibid., p. 10.
126   Soeur M. de St Ambroise Desaunais, superior, Caen, 'Copie de la lettre d'association écrite au Bon Pasteur d'Angers (rédigée par le T.H. Père le Doré)', 22 juin 1909 (DARGS, OLC1/3/2 no. 25).
127   Caen, *circulaire*, postscript marked *Confidentiel*, 1 septembre 1909.

signed side-by-side with the version circulated by Angers, that the full extent of the deception might be understood.[128] The matter came to the attention of the Caen superior only because the Good Shepherd superior general had forwarded her amended version to Père le Doré without realising that he was the real author of the well-crafted letter.[129] Maximum offence was taken by Soeur Ambroise Desaunais on behalf of the entire order: 'A most cordial and gracious advance loses its charm assuredly if it is not received in the same spirit.'[130]

The Caen letter sets up a dialectic between the houses of the 'original' or 'authentic' order (*'les monastères de l'observance primitive'*), that is, Our Lady of Charity, and the houses of 'the other' (*'les monastères de votre observance'*), that is, the Good Shepherd.[131] Angers scrapped all references to 'observance' and used the terms *'Religieuses de Notre Dame du Refuge'* and *'Congrégation du Bon Pasteur'*. The *union cordiale* that Caen hoped to cement between *nos deux observances* was rephrased by Angers to *cette union cordiale de nos deux familles*. Assigning to Our Lady of Charity the title *de l'observance primitive* was defended as the true, official and canonical term, and employed in that sense 'in all simplicity' by Le Doré. The Good Shepherd sisters, *de l'observance d'Angers*, objected to the older institute being given the title of honour, it was claimed, because it humiliated them, and would lead them – and outsiders – to suppose that their observance was second-rate and less 'regular'. In a further postscript – claimed to be from a reliable informant – the Good Shepherd sisters were accused of deliberately not telling their subjects that they are of the 'second observance', and it is only after profession that the difference which exists between 'our order' and 'their congregation' is understood.[132]

The superior of the Caen monastery immediately sought the views of the superior of each OLC monastery and its local council, stating that Caen's position was to hold fast – come what may – to the title 'of the Primitive observance'.[133] In this they were supported by the houses in France, England and Ireland, with only three French houses recorded as disagreeing with Caen.[134] Responses from the American houses had not been received at the time the general consensus was communicated.[135] High Park was passionate in defence of this 'legitimate and canonical distinction under which we have lived, loved and laboured for over two and a half centuries and which we will defend and maintain to the last breath of life'.[136] Gloucester Street did not reply, nor did Waterlooville in England, but it was presumed by Caen that

---

128  'Copie de la lettre d'association écrite au Bon Pasteur d'Angers (rédigée par le T.H. Père le Doré); Copie de notre Lettre, modifiée par la Réverende Mère Génèrale du Bon Pasteur, où elle se proposait de publier ainsi dans le Bulletin de sa Congrégation', 22 juin 1909 (DARGS, OLC1/3/2 no. 26).

129  Caen, *circulaire*, 1 septembre 1909.

130  Ibid.

131  'Copie de la lettre d'association écrite au Bon Pasteur d'Angers'.

132  Caen, *circulaire*, 1 septembre 1909.

133  Ibid.

134  Soeur M. de Jésus Martial, Caen, to Ma très honorée et bien chère Mère, High Park, 20 septembre 1909 (DARGS, OLC1/3/2 no. 33).

135  Caen, *circulaire*, 25 septembre 1909 (DARGS, OLC1/3/2 no. 34).

136  High Park, 'Copy of letter to Caen: Important'. 26 Sept. 1909 (DARGS, OLC1/3/2 no. 32b).

they would be of the same opinion as High Park, both having been founded (or, in the latter case, 'refounded') from High Park.[137]

Suspicion of the younger branch of the Eudist family was surely augmented by the letter writing to which the controversy gave rise, while pushing OLC houses to take a stand on the matter made for more extreme positions and a greater focus on distinctiveness. The rather unseemly quarrel was of course patched up, with the invitation to a union of prayers and of merits issued once more by Our Lady of Charity and the message passed on by the Good Shepherd superior general to her sisters in her own terms.[138] The gracious tone of the Christmas circular of 1909 from Angers was no doubt intended to defuse tensions; the OLC sisters were assured of the unceasing religious affection of the Good Shepherd sisters, an affection which been rendered even more lively and ardent by the joy they shared in the recent beatification of their founder.[139] Death notices were exchanged and other non-contentious communications quickly established.[140] While it is unlikely that there was any intention to cause upset, the re-editing on the Good Shepherd side, and the grave offence taken on the OLC side, undoubtedly put back progress towards friendly and open communications (let alone union) between these two daughter institutes of John Eudes.

## The Role of Caen in the Aftermath of the 1909 General Assembly

The build-up to the beatification of John Eudes, the general assembly of 1909 and all the business which ensued, enhanced Caen's role of communications hub. On the appointment of the cardinal-protector (requested by the 1909 assembly), Caen undertook to communicate with its first holder, Dominique Ferrata OP, in the name of all, on those matters that affected every monastery.[141] These logistical arrangements, in addition to its unique status as the first foundation, would bolster Caen's authority over the other autonomous houses and see it take on functions that in other institutes were reserved to the generalate. This was probably not intended but quickly came to be the *de facto* situation, an irony that seems to have been lost on the person who led the campaign against changes to the constitutions that would allow any sort of union, Soeur Ambroise Desaunais, superior of Caen for 27 years.[142]

As Desaunais herself explained to the sisters, the role of the cardinal-protector was to guard the position of the order at Rome, to safeguard their privileges and protect their interests against undue force.[143] Ferrata's hope on appointment was, reportedly, to affirm the sisters in the exact practice of their holy constitutions and to make themselves more and more faithful to all that they prescribed or recommended.[144] What would prove significant was

137  Martial to High Park, 20 septembre 1909.
138  Caen, *circulaire*, 7 janvier 1910, postscript headed 'Confidentielle' (DARGS, OLC1/3/2 no. 38).
139  Monastère Générale de N.D. de Charité du Bon Pasteur, Angers, circular letter, 20 décembre 1909 (DARGS, OLC1/2/5 no. 1).
140  Caen, *circulaire*, 20 mai 1910 (DARGS, OLC1/3/2 no. 41); Caen, *circulaire*, 8 décembre 1910 (DARGS, OLC1/3/2 no. 44).
141  Caen, *circulaire*, 21 juin 1910 (DARGS, OLC1/3/2 no. 42).
142  Caen, *circulaire*, 8 décembre 1910.
143  Caen, *circulaire*, 28 mars 1911 (DARGS, OLC1/3/2 no. 45).
144  Caen, *circulaire*, 8 décembre 1910.

Ferrata's decision to keep as assistant the Eudist priest, Père Gabriel Mallet, who had succeeded as vice-postulator of the cause of John Eudes and was resident in Rome; Ferrata's praise of Mallet as greatly attached to OLC and active in its regard would certainly be proved true.[145] As would have pleased his predecessor, Père le Doré (died 1912), the Good Shepherd sisters were also utilising the services of Mallet to conduct business on their behalf in the Vatican.[146]

The basis for Caen's authority rested first on article V of the 1738 customs book which called for 'the closest union of charity, a complete conformity and a constant intercommunion' between Caen, from which every house directly or indirectly had been founded, and for whom Caen continued to model how the first rule was to be lived 'in all its pristine vigour and perfection'.[147] Through its 'inalienable attachment' to the other monasteries and loyalty in communicating with them, Caen had long acted as the conduit through which correspondence could be forwarded to other houses, and appeals for moral and practical assistance made. Its opinion was sought, and filed for reference, on particular points of the rule, customs and ceremonial. The superiorship of Caen therefore, in the words of the sister who best knew the weight of it, Soeur Ambroise Desuanais, was of *'un charactère tout special'*.[148] So well-organised was Caen that, by at least 1902, it had its own printing facility, a type of ink roller with a metal press (*une planche métallique*) which it used to make multiple copies of its handwritten obituaries, feast-day greetings and longer *circulaires*, in both French and English. The sister secretary even produced an advice sheet for the other houses on the processes involved and the skills needed to get the best possible results.[149]

The channelling of communications with Rome via Caen was set out in friendly but firm language. To spare Ferrata, the newly-appointed cardinal-protector, from being inundated with correspondence, no-one was to write to him except for something exceptional that required his intervention.[150] Caen would handle general queries and so much more. The general assembly had sought to have the spiritual rights and privileges attendant on Caen extended to all houses; the rescript for the canonical erection of each house of the institute came back to Caen.[151] More significantly, from 1912 Caen was entrusted by Rome with the privilege of processing applications for dispensations from dowries for choir sisters (no dowries were required in Canada or the US).[152] Rome also gave Caen a rescript of sanations (dispensations given after the act has taken place) that allowed the leadership (up to

145   D. Card. Ferrata to Ma Réverende Mère, 21 juin 1910 (DARGS, OLC1/3/2 no. 43a).
146   Caen, circular letter, 15 Oct. 1912.
147   Article V, Union between the monasteries, *Customs and usages of the Congregation of Our Lady of Charity, order of St Augustine, with the formulary of the clothing and the profession of the religious*, iii, p. 173, text of 1738, trans. Peter Lewis (Aberdeen, 1888), (DARGS, OLC1/5/1 no. 12).
148   Soeur M. de St Ambroise Desaunais to Ma très honorée et très chère Soeur, 3 juin 1914 (DARGS, OLC1/3/2 no. 65).
149   La soeur sécretaire, Caen, 'Une leçon d'expérience', n.d. but estimated 1910 (DARGS, OLC1/3/2 no 35).
150   Caen, *circulaire*, 8 décembre 1910.
151   Caen, *circulaire*, 28 mars 1911.
152   Caen, *circulaire*, 23 janvier 1912. However, see also Fr Gabriel Mallet to Superior, High Park, 28 Nov. 1922, concerning dispensation from dowry (DARGS, OLC1/2/1 no. 21).

8 February 1912) to bring into accord with current canon law anything that had been irregularly done prior to that date in the matter of admitting choir subjects without dowries, or admitting persons who had previously been members of another institute and had not been dispensed from their vows. The rescript would regularise the position of any of these sisters and 'ease conscience'.[153] With elaborate detail, Caen explained all that concerned these rescripts, and how dispensations from dowries could be secured in particular cases.[154] While Caen had set its face resolutely against a generalate, it had no problem acting as the central depôt and clearing house, seeing it as an extension of its traditional role of animating all the houses of the order in the faithful following of what the founder had laid down.

Post-beatification Caen continued to play a leading role in the promotion of the cult of John Eudes, describing itself, quite rightly, as the 'old reliquary' of the founder (figure 7.2). The superior of Caen worked with the Eudist fathers on getting the Mass and office of the founder approved by Rome, arranged for the Gregorian notation, updated all OLC houses on its progress through the printing press and handled the orders for missals and breviaries.[155] Long the authority on matters liturgical and ceremonial, Caen played a significant role in the retention and promotion of the feasts of 8 February (Heart of Mary, established 1648) and 20 October (Sacred Heart of Jesus, established 1672).[156] An English-language edition of a history of the order published in 1891, *Les origines*,[157] was longed for by Caen, and a tip-off that the sisters in Buffalo, New York (founded 1855 from Rennes), had started the task was passed on to High Park, knowing that the Irish sisters would encourage the project.[158] Caen was not to be found wanting when the local *curé* of Ri, Orne, the birthplace of the founder, sought financial support to preserve the original chapel from ruin and to make it a fitting place of pilgrimage. In addition, Caen quickly canvassed all OLC houses, noting that the reverend mother general of the Good Shepherd of Angers had already 'addressed the warmest appeal to each of her houses' and no doubt OLC would want to do its best also.[159]

In the post-1909 revision of the constitutions and customs book, and in countless smaller matters, it was Caen that sought the views of all the houses with the phrase 'the majority of the opinions will give the answer'. It was Caen that kept the houses abreast of the very slow but satisfactory progress of OLC business at Rome post-1909 – all was just a matter of

153   Caen, *circulaire*, 23 janvier 1912.
154   The bull was dated 20 Dec. 1912. Certificate of dispensation from dowry, issued 27 janvier 1914, signed by the superior and secretary of the Monastery of Caen (DARGS, OLC1/3/2 no. 55). Caen, circular letter, 24 Jan. 1913 (DARGS, OLC1/3/2 no. 57).
155   Caen, *circulaire*, 10 juillet 1910 (DARGS, OLC1/3/2 no. 43b).
156   Caen, *circulaire*, 15 janvier 1911.
157   Joseph-Marie Ory, *Les origines de Notre-Dame de Charité ou son histoire depuis sa fondation jusqu'à la Révolution* (Abbeville, 1891), with a foreword by Angé le Doré. This study is noteworthy for its research basis, namely newly-discovered archival materials held in the monastery of Caen.
158   Sœur Marie de St Ambroise Desaunais to Ma très honorée et très chère Sœur, 14 juillet 1914 (DARGS, OLC1/3/2 no. 66). This was published as *The origin of the order of Our Lady of Charity or its history from its foundation until the Revolution, translated from the French of Father Joseph Mary Ory by one of the Religious of Our Lady of Charity of Buffalo, New York* (Buffalo, 1918).
159   Caen, circular letter, 21 Oct. 1913 (DARGS, OLC1/3/2 no. 61).

time.[160] Explaining why certain changes to the constitutions were refused and others imposed by Rome, Caen finally arranged for the English translation to be done at Bartestree (founded 1863 from Caen) which had French sisters, as well as English-speakers.[161] In these and in so many other matters, Caen kept running accounts for each house: what it owed for office books and other publications, for holy pictures, for sheet music (Gregorian chant). It calculated, and collected, what each house was to contribute per annum towards the expenses of the cardinal-protector in Rome and of his assistant Père Mallet.[162]

Following on the decision of the 1909 assembly to treat the *tourière* sisters as lay sisters, Caen modelled what should be done by giving its nine *tourière* sisters the guimpe and veil at the Mass for the renewal of vows on 21 September 1909.[163] It subsequently provided all houses with the ritual of how exactly these sisters would make their profession, where they would sign and in what form.[164] Caen promised to send on a photograph to every OLC house to illustrate the very minor modifications made to the habit at the 1909 assembly, that it might serve as reference or *'une Perpétue'*.[165] The photo recalled the prank played by Mère Desaunais during one of the recreation periods at the 1909 assembly which, while harmless in itself, carried a message also. She had placed the large, 238-year-old mannequin dressed in the habit of the order, *'Soeur Perpétue'*, in the community room while the delegates were taking the air, and then had them summoned in haste to greet a newly-arrived sister from abroad, she herself holding forth with the dignified and modest – but immobile – figure until the sisters exploded with laughter.[166] Caen was the guardian of the habit in the most literal sense, and treated this role as a sacred trust.

Around everything to do with the keeping of the enclosure – 'which to us must be our life' – Caen held tenaciously.[167] Uncertainty about its status was expressed in 1909, whether papal or enclosure,[168] and about whether the vows were simple or solemn.[169] The issue of the enclosure was settled in 1912, when Rome delivered its judgment on the documents submitted in the wake of the 1909 general assembly: the enclosure was episcopal, not papal and, despite some hand-wringing about what was perceived as an ignominious loss of 'ancient privileges', the judgment had to be accepted as unequivocal.[170] The bishop could not suppress the enclosure but 'he is at liberty to make it more or

---

160   Caen, *circulaire*, 10 mars 1910.
161   Caen, *circulaire*, 23 janvier 1912.
162   'Monastère de Dublin – High Park, au 1er mai 1913', statement of account with Caen, (Avoir/Doit) (DARGS, OLC1/3/2 no. 56); Caen, *circulaire*, 15 janvier 1911.
163   Caen, *circulaire*, 7 janvier 1910.
164   Proposed revisions, p. 186; Caen, *circulaire*, 27 mai 1911 (DARGS, OLC1/3/2 no. 46). Caen, *circulaire*, 3 novembre 1911 (DARGS, OLC1/3/2 nos. 51, 52); English summary of extracts from Caen (DARGS, OLC1/3/2 no. 5).
165   There were modifications to the choir cloak, *le camail*, and to the amount of fabric in the habit, *le robe à sac*. Caen, *circulaire*, 7 janvier 1910.
166   *Vie de la Mère Marie de Saint Ambroise Desaunais*, pp 239–40.
167   Caen, circular letter, 15 Oct. 1912.
168   Proposed revisions, p. 58.
169   Ibid., p. 63.
170   Caen, circular letter, 15 Oct. 1912.

less strict'; he could not be obliged to sign every permission for entry and exit, which it was expected would be in the hands of the mother superior under a 'general permission'.[171]

## The Great War, 1914–18

The outbreak of war in 1914 had an immediate impact on Caen. In August 1914, Soeur Ambroise Desaunais reported on expulsions from Brittany and the impending ruin of France. Their former boarding school was overwhelmed with streams of refugees of the most diverse types – wounded, reservists, native and German refugees, families from Belgium and from northern France fleeing from the invasion. Expelled religious men and religious women were returning to their beloved France, the men to fight for her defence, the women to tend her wounded.[172] The noise of war was all around and the fear was that, as a world war, the victims would be without number.[173] By December 1914, the menaces of war were bearing down on Caen, with all men aged 18 to 45 to be called up. Practically every sister had a brother or nephew under arms, some dead or injured in battle, others missing or imprisoned by the enemy. According to Soeur Ambroise, there was some small comfort to be found in how dearly the soldiers in the trenches held to their Catholic faith.[174] Although the French were reported as confident of the final victory, the price in blood would be enormous; by April 1915, the desire for peace was ever sharper and, though not in the theatre of hostilities, Caen was still close enough to know all about it.[175] By 24 May 1915, it was hoped that, with the new alliance, the final victory was now close.[176] Tragically, this would not be so and the numbers of dead, injured and displaced would be far beyond the darkest predictions.

Even as a world war waged around it, the monastery at Caen continued to offer its advice to the other houses on how the constitutions of the order might be interpreted. A desire by the monasteries of Dublin to branch out into a new field of work, the care of young, single, pregnant girls, was dismissed out of hand by Caen as incompatible with the spirit of the order and against the desire of the founder. The 'end of the institute' expressly excluded those who were pregnant; the rule was formal and allowed for no exceptions. The lengthy argument that Dublin had offered about 'the end of the institute' being to work 'for the salvation of souls' was countered in the one line that this did not allow them to undertake all manner of good works. But rather than extinguish what was obviously something that the Dublin monasteries felt strongly about, Desaunais made the suggestion that they might communicate with the Sisters of St Raphael, a Eudist institute in Paris newly-founded for that important and precious work, where the sisters took vows but did not wear a religious habit, and already had several houses.[177]

Under the pressure of wartime destruction, there was a small but genuine

171   Ibid.
172   Desaunais to Ma très honorée et très chère Sœur, 28 août 1914.
173   Ibid.
174   Sœur Marie de St Ambroise Desaunais to Ma très honorée et très chère Sœur, 15 décembre 1914 (DARGS, OLC1/3/2 no. 70).
175   Same to same, 8 avril 1915 (DARGS, OLC1/3/2 no. 71).
176   Same to same, 24 mai 1915 (DARGS, OLC1/3/2 no. 72).
177   Ibid.

reaching out to the Good Shepherd sisters. Mère Desaunais, with a travelling companion, had left Caen in 1916 on a round of visits to OLC houses that were in crisis, most notably Tours, but she also included Le Mans, Blois and Nantes on her itinerary. She decided to call without notice on the Good Shepherd mother general, Mère Marie de Sainte Domitille Larose, in Angers some time before 7am on 18 March 1916. According to Desaunais' biographer, the sister *tourière* on glimpsing the white robes underneath the travelling garb of the two strange sisters asked who would she say was calling, to be told the reverend mother of Caen, whereupon bells were furiously rung and the startled mother general and the first assistant positively galloped down to welcome the visitors.[178] The Good Shepherd *Bulletin* carried an account of the cordial and lengthy visit, which closed with the two Caen sisters kneeling to pray before the tomb of Venerable Euphrasie Pelletier. Both sides presented the event to their own constituencies as cementing the union of hearts and of prayers that that had been forged between the two institutes at the beatification of their founder in Rome in 1909.[179] To reciprocate, an invitation to visit Caen was issued to the superior of Angers on the feast of John Eudes in 1922, which was taken up on 14 September 1922. This first-ever visit to the 'old cradle' was especially treasured by the Good Shepherd side, who had never slackened in devotion to the founder and to the 'wishes' he had articulated for the sisters. Reports from the leadership of both institutes spoke of how the visit strengthened spiritual links – but there was not the least mention of political union.[180]

It is likely that the delay in inviting the Angers superior general to Caen was not just down to wartime destruction, but had to do with tensions generated within OLC by the revival of the debate around centralised government. In the summer of 1918, news reached Rome of the desire of many of the OLC houses in North America, backed by their local bishops, for a generalate modelled along the lines of Angers.[181] One of the factors behind this desire was the provision in the new code of canon law whereby Rome now reserved to itself the foundation of an independent monastery; this effectively banned any OLC house from making a new foundation without lengthy recourse to Rome. Gabriel Mallet CJM, as vicar to the cardinal-protector, was unequivocal in his dismissal, reminding the sisters that the desire for change was most usually the work of the devil and yielding to temptation brought trouble and even ruin in its wake.[182] While acknowledging that the generalate was undoubtedly the more common form of organisation and had many advantages for communication, and that the Good Shepherd sisters were models of virtue and their work manifestly blessed by God, he declared there was no good reason for the sisters of the 'primitive observance' to abandon their independence. Indeed, he continued, Rome had never ceased to protect those independent monasteries in which so many had arrived at the highest perfection,

178    *Vie de la Mère Marie de Saint Ambroise Desaunais*, p. 240–1
179    Ibid., p. 242
180    Ibid., pp 243–5.
181    Gabriel Mallet aux Monastères de N.D. de Charité dite du Refuge, à Buffalo, Ottawa, Allegheny, Toronto, Green Bay, Vancouver, San Antonio, Salthill, Wheeling, Monterrey, Pittsburg, Hot Springs, Dallas et autres villes d'Amérique, 29 septembre 1918 (CIVCSVA, B79/3).
182    Ibid., p. 2.

even to being listed among the catalogue of the saints, as brought to mind in the newly-revised code of canon law (1917). As vice-postulator of the cause for the canonisation of John Eudes, Mallet was also involved in promoting the cause of the first superior-general of the Good Shepherd sisters, Euphrasie Pelletier, and assured the American OLC sisters that two generalates, each under its own 'Mother Pelletier', simply would not work.[183] Invoking the authority of the cardinal-protector and of the Pope himself, to the Good Shepherd communities, Mallet directed fidelity to the mother house of Angers; the OLC sisters were to continue as they were, the faithful guardians of the tradition.[184] What Mallet did warn against was the multiplication of the houses of the order; at least 40 sisters were required for the rule to be kept in all aspects. Before any house could consider founding a daughter house, it would need to have at least 40 or 50 sisters and more than 100 residents, as well as the permission of Rome. Should a house not have the resources to continue and no other OLC community be able to assist, and should the good of souls require that the work be continued, and with due regard to the rights of the individual religious, another institute could be asked to take over. In such a case, the Good Shepherd might be preferred above any other order, with the surviving sisters of Our Lady of Charity withdrawing to the foundation monastery (or monasteries) of that particular house.[185] Mallet recalled a directive issued in 1909 by Cardinal Vivès as prefect for religious and cardinal-protector of the Good Shepherd sisters and now reiterated by the present cardinal-protector, Louis Billot, and sanctioned by the Pope himself: there was to be absolutely no question of an OLC sister or a community transferring to a Good Shepherd house or vice versa.[186] The question of a generalate was thus shelved, but not with the finality that Mallet expected.

## The Canonisation of John Eudes in Rome, 31 May 1925

The canonisation of John Eudes in 1925 and its immediate aftermath recalls in many respects the beatification ceremony of 1909, but on a grander scale. The difference, as described by a Eudist priest present at both events, is that the beatification 'means or signifies the departure for glory, not the entrance into glory', while the canonisation signifies the end point of this journey:

> To accompany Saints into heaven, the Church must employ all its splendors and magnificence, all its lights and illuminations, the mixture of all its lights coloring the pomp of all its processions; it is obligatory that the Pope himself preside so that all the beauty of the Church Militant conduce to conduct to the Church Triumphant one of its children.[187]

While the canonisation was undoubtedly 'more beautiful, more gorgeous

---

183   'Nous pouvons vous assurer que deux Mères Pelletier ne se recontrent pas aisément', ibid., p. 1.
184   Ibid., p. 2.
185   Ibid.
186   Ibid., pp 2–3.
187   Ibid., p. 2.

still' than the beatification, most of the elements were the same.[188] As before, the acceptance by the Church of two miracles attributable to the intercession of the saint-to-be was the final hurdle to be crossed. Banners depicting these miracles dominated the gospel side of the altar during the ceremony on 31 May 1925, Pentecost Sunday.[189] The canonisation ceremony had strong French overtones, with St John Marie Vianney and St John Eudes jointly honoured, and a 58-strong delegation of the French parliament in attendance.[190] From the balcony of St Peter's hung the *gloire* showing both saints on their knees in ecstasy and carried to heaven on the wings of angels, Vianney (the *curé d'Ars*) in white surplice and stole, 'with a bearing emaciated by austerity and transparent with sanctity', Eudes in his long black mantle and holding a heart in his hand.[191] The procession to the basilica was truly 'a spectacle without equal' with its long line of cardinals, bishops, Eudists, religious of other orders and diocesan clergy, priests of the different Eastern rites, members of the Roman congregations and many more dignitaries, both secular and clerical, accompanying the banners of the new saints to the basilica. The standard of Eudes was preceded by a delegation of Eudist priests; that of Vianney by 200 priests of France; the procession was brought up finally by Pope Pius XI flanked with his household and splendidly-armed guards. The gorgeous costumes, richly-coloured vestments, lighted candle and cheering crowds were overwhelmed by a tumult of singing – 'in Latin, Greek and Chinese, the Ave Maris Stella, psalms and hymns, terrific discord, immense ocean of human sound, singularly tumultuous, uniting together, acclaiming the new saints'.[192] Silver trumpets sounded as the Pope was carried on the *sedia gestatoria* through the basilica to the papal altar, the procession alone taking more than one hour. As with the beatification, at the heart of the ceremony was a simple question-and-answer exchange. The attorney for the canonisation, Cardinal Vicoy, approached the Pope requesting that the names of John Eudes and John Mary Vianney be inscribed in the catalogue of the saints; three times the request was made, and each time all present were led to implore heaven for guidance on so momentous a matter. Finally, Pius XI pronounced that both Eudes and Vianney would be inscribed in the catalogue of saints of the universal Church, their memory to be celebrated 'with pious devotion' on the anniversaries of their death each year, which for Eudes was 19 August.[193] The pronouncement was immediately followed by the singing of the *Te Deum* and the invocation of the new saints, after which the papal Mass continued with all the solemnity and

188    Ibid.
189    Death-bed cures, both in Colombia, were authenticated on 8 Feb. 1925: that of Bonaventure Romero, a young employee at the seminary of San Pedro, Bolivia, suffering from a fractured skull and peritonitis, who had been left a relic of John Eudes on his pillow just as a novena to the Blessed had been announced for the morning, and that of Sister Jeanne Beatrix Londino of the Presentation Sisters of Tours at Bogota, suffering from advanced diabetes, who awoke on the last day of a novena held in honour of John Eudes to find herself cured. *St John Eudes* (Dublin, 1927), p. 31.
190    'Feasts of the Canonisation', typescript account of the canonisation of John Eudes, Rome, 31 May 1925, unsigned but by a Eudist priest who was probably Canadian, p. 1 (DARGS, OLC1/7/4) no. 24. Hereafter, 'Feasts of the Canonisation'.
191    Ibid., pp 1–2.
192    Ibid., p. 3.
193    Ibid., p. 4.

splendour that Rome could muster for such an occasion. The illuminations both inside and outside St Peter's were 'simply splendid', beyond words, though postcards issued at the time did try to give an inkling of the effect.[194] On the day following, the 'whole family' of Père Eudes was summoned to a papal audience; reported as 'short but satisfactory', representatives of the Eudist priests, the sisters of Our Lady of Charity and the sisters of the Good Shepherd were greeted and blessed, about 300 persons in all. The one disappointment recorded was that Père Albert Lucas, the superior general of the Eudists, was not given a chance to deliver the address he had prepared, due to pressure on the pontiff's time in what was a jubilee year.[195] Later that day, at an audience for more than 2,000 pilgrims, the Pope eulogised 'our dear France' who had given to the Church yet two more saints, urging the priests present 'to imitate these two beautiful models of all sacerdotal virtues'.[196] The Eudists gathered in Rome, numbering about 40 men, met for a lively celebratory meal hosted by the superior general Fr Lucas; the contrast with the dark mood of 1909, when their position in France was indeed perilous, is noteworthy.[197] The sisters of Our Lady of Charity, 42 in number representing 26 houses, also held a celebration separately, in the same restaurant; heading the attendance list were Mother Mary of St Teresa Montreuil and Mother Mary of St Ambrose Desaunais of Caen. From Dublin came Mother Mary of St Genevieve Byrne and Sister Mary of the Sacred Heart Pilkington (High Park), and Sister Stanislaus Masterson and Sister Mary of St Francis Xavier Leamy (Gloucester Street).[198] Three of these four sisters had been present in 1909, an illustration of how the same person was so often re-elected to the office of superior in Dublin – and indeed in other monasteries of the order.

Following the pattern of the beatification in 1909, a triduum in honour of St John Eudes took place in the Jesuit church in Rome, the Gesú, on 2, 3 and 4 June 1925; the banner carried in the procession to St Peter's was given pride of place behind the high altar. The morning Masses, afternoon vespers and benediction, including panegyrics on the virtues of the new saint, were carried out by a succession of eminent Churchmen and attended by large numbers of the Roman public, with the music, chanting and illuminations reported as splendid and brilliant, fervent and confident.[199] The closing of the Rome celebrations was but the beginning of the celebrations to be held in France and the universal Church, led in most cases by the various branches of the Eudist family. As before, Caen would take the lead on behalf of the monasteries of the 'primitive' or old observance, holding its triduum in June 1925 and forwarding to the other monasteries postcards showing

194    Ibid., p. 8; G. Felici, Roma, 'Canonisatione dei Beati Vianney et Eudes', postcards nos. 1093 and 1096 (DARGS, OLC1/7/4 no. 25).
195    'Feasts of the Canonisation', p. 9,
196    Ibid.
197    Ibid., pp 10–11.
198    The OLC houses represented were Caen, Rennes, St Brieuc, Tours, Chevilly, Versailles, Nantes, Lyon, Toulouse, Le Mans, Blois, Montauban, Marseilles, Besançon, Dublin (High Park), Buffalo, Marseilles, Valognes, Toronto, Waterlooville, Dublin (Gloucester Street), Salzburg, Bitterne, Troy, Ormskirk, 'Feasts of the Canonisation', p. 12.
199    'Feasts of the Canonisation', p. 13.

its decorated shrine and cloisters.[200] High Park would open its triduum on 20 October 1925, the feast of the Sacred Heart, and Gloucester Street on 8 February 1926, feast of the Immaculate Heart of Mary. Though nowhere near the scale and grandeur of the celebrations in Rome, these would not be lacking in terms of liturgical solemnity, artistic creativity and outpouring of devotion.

## Campaign for Centralised Government in the Order of Our Lady of Charity, 1929–34: Generalate, Union, Federation

An early request for a centralised government of some sort in the order of Our Lady of Charity was made by the American houses in 1918 with the backing of their local bishops. Although dismissed out of hand, the desire for a generalate on the part of several OLC houses did not go away. It was from England in 1929 that the prefect of the Sacred Congregation for Religious, Alexis Henri Marie Lépicier, who also happened to be the OLC cardinal-protector, next heard formally of the desirability of some sort of union between OLC houses; in this case it was a joint petition from the archbishops of Cardiff, Birmingham and Liverpool to make what they termed a province of the autonomous houses in their dioceses.[201] Rather than recounting the many problems these houses faced individually, the bishops focused on some key areas: the role of superior was impossible when the outgoing superior still lived in the house and could head a faction opposed to the new regime; office holders continued, though no longer capable; the junior sisters got no training for the duties they had or would have; there were few sisters fit to be appointed to the role of novice mistress and the novices, few in number, were not being kept apart from the community, as canon law required. The solution the English and Welsh bishops offered – the only solution, they claimed, and one which they held John Eudes would approve were he alive – was to have a capable provincial superior with the authority to oversee the convents, to send sisters to other houses as needed for the glory of God and the good of religion, and to appoint superiors and remove outgoing superiors, so that they might not hinder the work of the next. A general novitiate was needed where the novices might be properly trained to be more independent and more capable of benefiting those who would be in their care. High Park was proposed as the formation house, as it appeared to be well-conducted with a good spirit, and also many of the religious in England were of Irish birth.[202] The reasons given with such frankness by the archbishop of Cardiff and his fellow bishops for a layer of centralised government were repeated, more or less, by individual North American and other OLC monasteries in their submissions, so that Cardinal Lépicier, on whose desk all this correspondence would eventually arrive, determined to tackle the matter in a concerted way. The general assembly at Caen in July 1931, convened for the purposes of making changes to

200    Postcards, 'Caen at triduum, June 1925', 'Cloister of Caen at triduum, June 1925' (DARGS, OLC1/7/4 no. 25).
201    The diocese of Portsmouth was also named in the application but its bishop was not one of the signatories; Francis, archbishop of Cardiff; Thomas, archbishop of Birmingham; Richard, archbishop of Liverpool to Eminentissime Princeps, 1929 [dated 24–29] (CIVCSVA, B79/3).
202    Ibid.

the constitutions to align them with current canon law, and involving all the houses (though not every house sent a representative), provided him with the ideal opportunity – or so he thought.

It was no secret that the Sacred Congregation for Religious in Rome actively supported the creation of centralised government structures of different types – generalate, union, federation and variations thereof. But while the Congregation carried enormous authority in its work with religious institutes, it could not impose its preferences. Nor indeed had the local bishop the authority to alter the constitutions of a house in his diocese, even though many bishops thought they had. Any change to the status of a religious house required the full and free consent of the overwhelming majority of the professed members, and that could be done only by reasoned argument and after open discussion involving all the sisters affected in any way. The arguments in favour of an OLC generalate were to be presented at the 1931 assembly in Caen by Fr Gauderon CJM, delegated by Cardinal Lépicier as head of the Sacred Congregation for Religious to preside on his behalf.

While Fr Lépicier was undoubtedly used to handling difficulties within and between institutes in his role as cardinal prefect of the Sacred Congregation for Religious, and Fr Gauderon, a spiritual son of John Eudes, must have had some knowledge of the culture of OLC monasteries, neither man appears to have expected the intensity of opposition that greeted the proposal, and that became more organised and intractable over the following three years. At the opening session of the assembly on 29 July 1931, Gauderon read aloud Lépicier's letter which dealt with the gravity of the situation felt by many OLC monasteries with absolute autonomy, and how a more centralised structure, adapted to the particular needs of OLC, would be a source of mutual aid. The matter was to be discussed openly and the needs of each monastery were to be heard; then, for the greater good of the whole order, a decision was to be taken and the results forwarded to the Holy See. Though the term 'generalate' is used, only a 'mitigated' or limited type of central government was under consideration. There was no chance of anything more ambitious surviving long as an agenda item. Discussion went on for a full week and, as summarised by one well-informed source, the superiors in favour of a generalate based their arguments on important facts.[203] Those in favour of autonomy did not respond to facts, but based all their opinions on sentiment and tradition. A vote was taken: 19 in favour of a generalate, 16 against, a disappointingly slight or weak majority (*'une grosse déception'*) that tied the hands of the Sacred Congregation for the time being.[204] However, some houses, including High Park, did read the result as a sign of the direction things were going, which they ought not to block without good reason.

Lépicier re-launched the process just over a year later under continuing pressure from OLC sisters who desired a generalate. The petitions were worded in similar terms: recounting ongoing trials and their need of his assistance

---

203   Untitled typescript, 11 pp, in French, summarising the lead-up to the 1931 assembly at Caen and the discussions to *c*.1934 around a generalate for OLC (CIVCSVA, B79/3). English summary by Sister Teresa Coughlan OLC, Rome, Oct. 2005 (DARGS, OLC1/2/1 no. 40). Hereafter, Summary of discussions, pre-1931 assembly to *c*.1934.
204   Ibid.

as being enclosed and autonomous, they could not take concerted or joint action.[205] This time the Sacred Congregation for Religious contacted each house separately, through the local ordinary. By a circular letter dated 3 December 1932, all bishops in whose diocese there was an OLC house were instructed to conduct a ballot of the sisters, choir and lay, to see if they were in favour of the union now proposed. The essential features of this union were summarised as the submission to a superior general and the creation of a general council to govern the institute. Sisters would not be moved from the house of their profession unless sent elsewhere for reasons of government or other need; autonomy in terms of property, bequests and finance would continue, but the new superior general would have to be provided with a residence. There would be no change to the rule of enclosure; the existing fundamental rules of the institute would be observed as before and, in due course, houses with 12 or more sisters could propose names for the role of local superior.[206] A very full analysis of the benefits which would accrue to OLC from a generalate was submitted,[207] developing the points already made by the English bishops[208] such as appointment of more capable superiors, lessening the isolation of superiors, giving sisters a point of contact where a superior was over-controlling and, through the general chapter, enabling the exchange of ideas and updating of lifestyle. Local elections, with all their clans and cabals an endless source of trouble and upset, would be suppressed. The more serious and longer training that a central novitiate would allow was perhaps the strongest argument in its favour, ending the 'too easy' acceptance of candidates with no life experience and giving 'mediocre' girls the chance to mix with novices of a higher class or of a better type to the long-term benefit of the order. Overwork of all– novices, sisters, women residents – was set out as a feature of several really poor monasteries, to the neglect of the spiritual life, and depriving the women residents of the 'refuge' which they expected. Under a generalate, sisters could be lent as necessary, while a change of milieu could also help sisters physically and spiritually.[209] Zeal for the salvation of souls required the adaptation of the work to the needs of the time; this was to include the re-education of the women residents, as well as the better training of the novices. The major superior would get to know the resources and needs of each house through canonical visitation and her role would include the promotion of necessary changes. A generalate would also be a great comfort and protection for a house in times of revolution or persecution.[210] A generalate would undoubtedly open the door to change; there was no question of that.

An angry report from the superior of Besançon, Soeur Marie-Aimée de Jésus Lemercier, reveals the strategies employed this time round to try and achieve the 'correct' result. Realising that someone needed to talk directly to the voters, to answer questions and to assuage fears, Cardinal Lépicier now

205   Ibid.
206   Ex Secretaria Sacrae Congregationis de Religiosis, printed circular (N. 7493/32), signed by Cardinal Vincent La Puma, 3 Dec. 1932 (CIVCSVA, B79/3).
207   Summary of discussions, pre-1931 assembly to *c.*1934.
208   Francis, archbishop of Cardiff; Thomas, archbishop of Birmingham; Richard, archbishop of Liverpool to Eminentissime Princeps, 1929.
209   Summary of discussions, pre-1931 assembly to *c.* 1934.
210   Ibid.

sent his envoy Père Gauderon to visit as many convents in person as was humanly possible, and as often as seemed necessary. The father-protector of the order, through Père Gabriel Mallet, was also recruited to press the case. Although welcomed by some houses, the superior of Besançon took Gauderon's visit as an outrageous intrusion, and the cardinal-protector's follow-up as a further affront. She described how, at the first evening meeting, Gauderon read aloud the letter from the cardinal-protector conferring on him, Gauderon, the oversight and direction of the discussion, and expressing the desire that the sisters would see their way to accepting a generalate. The commentary which followed amplified their astonishment as the 'desire' was packaged as an order and the requirement to discuss it could not be shirked.[211] At all stages perfect secrecy was to be maintained within the community; no-one outside the chapter room was to be consulted, not the bishop nor anyone else. This was, of course, exactly what the cardinal-protector and his delegate wanted: a free and open vote cast without outside interference, as they saw it. Despite the Besançon community's wholehearted rejection, the project was pursued with tenacity by the cardinal-protector who re-presented it under two simple headings: a generalate was the desire of Rome, as it wished to unite religious orders and, through a generalate, obstacles to the progress of the institute would be overcome. The strategy seems to have backfired in Besançon at least, with Soeur Marie-Aimée de Jésus complaining that the whole process was set up to exploit their ignorance and have them voting in the dark, and she herself became a strident champion of the 'no' side.[212]

Voting across all houses of the order took place in spring 1933. The total number of *votandi* and the numbers voting for and against the motion were returned directly to the Sacred Congregation for Religious in Rome where they were collated; most also had a covering letter from the bishop, whose opinion did not necessarily match that of the sisters.[213] The result, at least as it stood April 1933, was a significant increase on the yes side: 24 monasteries were in favour of a generalate despite the diminution of autonomy that would bring, and a further five monasteries had failed to reply.[214] In May 1934, the number in favour of a generalate appeared to be 27, but few houses had been won over from the other side, which was variously reported as 43, 44 or 46 monasteries. The number of religious for and against – what might be termed the 'popular vote' – was more evenly balanced. Of the approximately 2,000 OLC sisters who voted, about half were in favour of the generalate.[215]

Of the 18 houses in France, six were in favour of a generalate while 12 were in favour of continuing with autonomy. In all but one case the result was unanimous, or practically so. The French houses hoping for a generalate – or at least willing to go along with it – were Valognes, Lyon, Le Mans, the two houses in Marseilles and Valence, all with troubled histories stretching back for several decades. The community at Valognes saw in the proposed

211  Soeur Marie-Aimée de Jésus Lemercier, Besançon, to Mon Révérend Père, 30 avril 1932 (CIVCSVA, B79/3).
212  Ibid.
213  MS notes on voting for and against proposed union, n.d. but May 1934 (CIVCSVA, B79/3).
214  Summary of discussions, pre-1931 assembly to *c*.1934.
215  Gabriel Mallet, Rome, Mémorandum, mai 1934 (CIVCSVA, B79/3).

generalate the opening of new horizons for their few young sisters who were seriously overworked, their spirits weighed down by the interminable crises.[216] The superior of Lyon, writing in July 1931 of '*l'imminence de peril*', '*ce pénible dilemme*', saw the speedy acceptance of a generalate as a matter of life and death for them, though they were pained at finding themselves voting contrary to what Caen wished.[217] For Le Mans, the proposed new generalate would be the saving of those communities in decline while also injecting new vitality into the order. This perfect submission to the wishes of Rome would surely draw down countless blessings. Unusually, Caen comes in for explicit criticism by another house as having fallen into an inertia, not merely deplorable, but prejudicial to the good of the institute.[218]

The two Marseilles houses, Boulevard Baille and Du Cabot, saw the advantages of a general novitiate, the greater choice of superior and the possibility of moving sisters to other houses as reasons to vote for a generalate, despite lobbying by Caen. Having stated their position, they now abandoned themselves entirely to whatever Rome might decide.[219] The Valence community had a long history of internal crises and the choice was now between an OLC generalate or the Good Shepherd of Angers.[220] Apprehensive about finding themselves subjected to Caen or to St Brieuc, and frustrated by the indecision around the proposed OLC generalate – for which they had already voted in good faith more than three years earlier – they were now in communication with Angers.[221] What set Rennes apart from the other houses in France was that the voting was not hopelessly skewed in one or other direction: out of 74 sisters, 52 voted for a generalate.[222] It was listed on the yes side but with a note that this was in the context of other needs (*favorable à généralat à course des autres besogneux*). The other continental houses that supported the generalate project were Salzburg (voting 62:1 in favour), and the sole Italian house, Lorette, which was consistently in favour of some form of centralised government.[223]

Of the 16 North American houses, 14 voted strongly in favour of a generalate.[224] Wheeling, established in 1900 (from Toronto) as a refuge house for Nantes, held fast to autonomy. The sisters of Sandwich, Ontario, were not

216    Soeur M. du Divin Coeur Milcent, Valognes, to Eminence, 22 août 1932 (CIVCSVA, B79/3).
217    Sœur Marie de l'Incarnation Vialle, Lyon, to Eminence, 24 octobre 1932, 11 mars 1934 to Très Saint Père, 19 mars 1934 (CIVCSVA, B79/3).
218    Soeur M. de St Leon Papin, Le Mans, to Très Saint Père, 5 novembre 1932 (CIVCSVA, B79/3).
219    Sœur Marie de St Thérèse Bonnel, Marseilles, to Cardinal Lépicier, 6 septembre 1932 (CIVCSVA, B79/3); Marie du Cours, Marseilles, to La Puma, 21 avril 1933 (CIVCSVA, B79/2).
220    Camille Pio, bishop of Valence, to Cardinal Lépicier, 12 février 1933 (CIVCSVA, B79/2).
221    'La seule planche de salut que nous semblons surs est le Généralat du la Bon Pasteur d'Angers', Soeur Agnes Toncherey, Valence, to Cardinal Lépicier, 5 avril 1934 (CIVCSVA, B79/3).
222    Renatus Migner, bishop of Rennes, to Eminence, 13 janvier 1933 (CIVCSVA, B79/2); in the May 1934 list the votes are recorded as 53 in favour of a generalate (CIVCSVA, B79/3).
223    MS notes on voting for and against proposed union, May 1934.
224    In favour of a generalate: Pittsbug (Lincoln Avenue), Pittsburg (Lowrie Street), Rochester, Edmonton, Ottawa, Toronto, Vancouver, San Antoine, Buffalo, Dallas, Green Bay, Monterrey, Little Rock, El Paso, MS notes on voting for and against proposed union, May 1934.

radically opposed to the idea of a generalate, 'but until they know just what it involves they are unwilling to surrender their autonomy', fearing the imposition of French ideals and customs under a French mother general – or at least a mother general living in France.[225] The other four OLC houses in Canada were placed on the 'yes' side, but the underlying reasons varied. Edmonton was strongly in favour of a proposal the sisters judged to be for 'the general good of our holy order', adding frankly that, if the French 'understood the conditions of our fields of labor here in Canada and the U.S. they too would be of the same opinion'.[226] From whatever point of view the Vancouver community considered the subject, 'the generalate affords advantages not found in autonomy': the interchange of sisters, the better training of novices, all 'would likely bring about a broadening of ideas, and would infuse new life into our communities'.[227] For the sisters in Toronto, the fact that it was Rome's preference carried huge weight; after the voting (49:3 in favour of a generalate) the superior reported that all 'experienced an extraordinary feeling of peace' which they were convinced came from having carried out the wishes of the Holy Father.[228] Explaining what was behind the rather mixed message from the French-speaking community of Ottawa (24 for the generalate, ten against), one sister claimed that the superior and her relatives had voted en bloc, all ten against the motion, and moreover the superior (and presumably her relatives) were fully in favour of a generalate until the speech of Soeur Marie de St Ambroise Desaunais at the assembly in Caen.[229] Another sister thought it was the fear of being swamped by English, and of alienating French-language vocations, that led some Ottawa sisters to vote no, rather than any real objection to the concept of a generalate.[230]

Buffalo, New York, the first house in North America and 'well established' in all respects, felt bound to support the generalate 'in so far as it would benefit the entire Order of Our Lady of Charity of the Refuge', though it had questions that would need to be addressed in due course.[231] Pittsburgh strongly urged that the generalate house be in Rome, that an English-speaking consultor be part of the new arrangements and, should an assembly be necessary, that it might be held in the US or Ireland, 'as the English-speaking sisters are at a disadvantage in France, not understanding fully what transpires, not understanding the French language'. The voting sheets from the two houses in Pittsburgh (Lowrie Street 37:2 and Lincoln Avenue 16:1) include in full the reasons given by each sister for her vote, demonstrating the seriousness with

225  Sister M. of St Alphonsus Sullivan and others, Sandwich, Ontario, 18 Jan. 1933 (CIVCS-VA, B79/2).
226  Sister M. of St Aloysius Buck, Edmonton, to Cardinal Lépicier, 7 Oct. 1932 (CIVCSVA, B79/3).
227  Sister M. Eudes, Vancouver, to His Eminence 17 Oct. 1932 (CIVCSVA, B79/3).
228  Sister M. of St Magdalene, Toronto, to Cardinal Lépicier, 7 Mar. 1933 (CIVCSVA, B79/2).
229  Sister M. of St Benedict Russell, Ottawa, to Cardinal Lépicier, 9 Nov. 1932 (CIVCSVA, B79/3).
230  'Deux langues son ici en usage, le français et l'anglais, et notre Communauté est la seule en Canada qui se serve des deux idioms', Soeur M. of St Jean Berchmans, Ottawa, to Eminence Lépicier, 20 octobre 1932 (CIVCSVA, B79/3)
231  Sister M. of St Stanislaus Dietz, Buffalo, to Cardinal Lépicier, 7 Dec. 1932 (CIVCSVA, B79/3).

which this remarkable exercise in democracy was treated. Some respondents followed logically through from a yes vote to suggesting an 'entire' or 'proper' union with Bon Pasteur, 'into one grand congregation'.[232] Rochester, the newest of the OLC houses (founded 1930 from Buffalo), backed the motion (seven in favour, one against) and, when nothing happened, lobbied forcefully for 'the complete revolution of existing conditions' that was required to enable the sisters to cope with the exigencies of the times and 'to reap the fruits of the work of our holy founder'.[233] Rochester went so far as to place the work under the joint guidance of St John Eudes and Blessed Mother M. of St Euphrasia, 'for no-one understands better the entire affair than these two zealous lovers of souls'.[234] All five Spanish-speaking sisters in El Paso, Texas, entrusted their future entirely to the decision of the Holy See, wishing only to live for the salvation of souls as the humble daughters of St John Eudes – though they, too, got anxious when they heard nothing of progress towards a generalate.[235]

In Britain there was a 4:1 split: Ormskirk (Liverpool), Northfield (Birmingham), Bartestree (Cardiff) and Waterlooville (Portsmouth) were in favour of a generalate, while Bitterne (Portsmouth) held out against it. Bitterne was too closely attached to its founding house, St Brieuc, Montbareil, to contemplate anything other than following the example of the oldest French monasteries.[236] High Park and Gloucester Street negotiated as one; the yes vote that was delivered in October 1932 in favour of a generalate 'should the Sacred Congregation of the Religious judge the thing more opportune for the common good of our order', was withdrawn in December under the instructions of the archbishop of Dublin, Edward Byrne.[237] He complained of the 'importunate insistence' of the Eudist priest Père Gauderon who had prevailed on the assistant superior in High Park, 'a scrupulous and nervous person', to write to Cardinal Lépicier, 'saying that if it were judged necessary they of High Park would not hold out in opposition'. This, according to Byrne, 'in no way reflected the mind of the community or even of the writer herself from whom it was really extorted unfairly.'[238] He returned the newly-taken Dublin votes: High Park, two for, 68 against and Gloucester Street, eight for, 22 against, warning of vehement local opposition.[239] One important convert to the concept of an OLC generalate was Père Gabriel Mallet, who had so strongly opposed the whole idea in 1918. In the 1930s he viewed it as the salvation of this 'ancient branch' of the order so

232    Sister M. of St Richard Troy, Pittsburgh, to Cardinal Lépicier 10 Mar. 1933 (CIVCSVA, B79/2).
233    John Francis O'Hara, Bishop of Rochester, to Cardinal Lépicier, 14 Feb. 1933 (CIVCSVA, B79/2).
234    Sister M. of St Agnes Zimmerman, Rochester, to Cardinal Lépicier, 4 May 1934 (CIVCSVA, B79/1).
235    Sister M. of the Immaculate Conception Escobar and others, El Paso, Texas, to Cardinal Lépicier 11 Oct. 1932 (CIVCSVA, B79/3). Same to same, 1934 (CIVCSVA, B79/1).
236    Sister M. of St Gabriel Rabbilard, Sup. Bitterne, Southampton, to My Lord, 9 Dec. 1932 (CIVCSVA, B79/2).
237    Sister M. of St Cecilia McVeagh (High Park), Sister M. of the Immaculate Heart Walsh (Lower Gloucester Street) to Eminence, 10 Oct. 1932; Sister M. of St Cecilia McVeagh to My own dearest Sister, 7 Dec. 1932 (CIVCSVA, B79/3).
238    Edward Byrne, archbishop of Dublin, to Cardinal A. Lépicier, 3 Dec. 1932 (DARGS, OLC1/2/1 no. 39).
239    Same to same, 1 Feb. 1933 (CIVCSVA, B79/3).

beloved of John Eudes and put the case for it in terms that convinced the sisters in Vancouver and El Paso, and undoubtedly elsewhere also.[240]

Arguments against a generalate or union were marshalled by the no side which was led, not surprisingly, by the old cradle of Caen, but there were articulate and influential standard-bearers in other houses also, most notably in Besançon. The bishop of Bayeux faithfully returned the Caen vote (73 to retain autonomy, nine for a union) but he himself could see many advantages in union.[241] The 'no surrender' position taken by Caen was well understood in Rome, where 'autonomy at any price' was pencilled in after its name by whoever tabulated the voting returns of May 1934.[242] Successive superiors had warned sisters in the other houses against the least deviation from the 'exact observance' of the rule and constitutions: 'Let us ever venerate our ancient customs, let us keep our holy Rules and our holy Rules will keep us.'[243] Yielding to a generalate was seen as a betrayal of the founder's wishes for the institute, as articulated in these 'primitive constitutions' and sanctified by nearly 300 years of use. The arguments were contradictory, but that made them no less compelling. The other houses in France holding fast to autonomy were Besançon, St Brieuc, Blois, Montauban, Chevilly, Toulouse, Nantes, La Rochelle, Tours and Versailles. Bitterne in England, which saw itself as inextricably tied to St Brieuc and to Caen, and Bilbao, the only Spanish house, also held steadfastly to the status quo.

The fullest array of arguments against the proposed generalate was advanced by Besançon, where the cardinal-protector had tried valiantly to reverse the community's no vote by re-presenting the issue under two clear headings: a generalate was the desire of Rome as it wished to unite religious orders and, through a generalate, obstacles to the progress of the institute would be overcome. These difficulties were listed as the choice of superiors, the recruitment of postulants, the formation of novices and the safeguarding of the health of sick sisters. Each of these claims was demolished in turn by the superior of Besançon, Soeur Marie Aimée de Jesus Lemercier – who, in addition, felt the whole process was underhand from start to finish.[244]

The single strongest argument against an OLC generalate was that there was simply no need. Through their long and scrupulous observation of the same constitutions there was a uniformity across all houses of the order, and what was variously termed '*une unification morale*' or '*une union de charité*', in accord with article V of the 1738 customs, was already in place. There were lots of instances where monasteries had helped out others in difficulties: St Brieuc had sent vocations from its '*juvenat*' to Caen, Chevilly, Blois, La Rochelle and Montauban,[245] while Chevilly had recently assisted Versailles

240   Sister M. Eudes, Vancouver, to His Eminence, 17 Oct. 1932; Mallet, Mémorandum, mai 1934; Sister M. of the Immaculate Conception Escobar and others, El Paso, Texas to Cardinal Lépicier 11 Oct. 1932 (CIVCSVA, B79/3).
241   Bishop of Bayeux to Cardinal Lépicier, 22 janvier 1933 (CIVCSVA, B79/3).
242   'Autonomie à tout prix', MS notes on voting for and against proposed union, May 1934.
243   Caen, circular letter, 14 July 1902.
244   Lemercier, Besançon, to Mon Révérend Père, 30 avril 1932, p. 2.
245   Soeur M. de la Misercordiae, St Brieuc, to Monseigneur, 3 octobre 1932 (CIVCSVA, B79/3).

with personnel and money.[246] Nantes had sent eight sisters, a novice and a postulant to Tours in 1920, which had enabled it to continue.[247] None of this had required a generalate.

Houses that were flourishing saw no need at all to gamble on a generalate. Besançon drew numerous solid vocations from an extensive and Christian region and was supported by the archbishop and the civil authorities. Loss of autonomy would threaten these happy relationships, while redistributing resources, including personnel, to a poor house would undermine the stability of a well-endowed, flourishing community.[248] Montauban feared the opposite outcome: that in a generalate, the prosperous and large monasteries would work against the interests of the smaller houses in crisis, and saw its 'no' vote as protecting against this.[249] Forcing a generalate on St Brieuc, it was felt, would bring a loss, not a blossoming, of vocations from Brittany, where the locals appreciated the enclosure and the autonomy of the house.[250] The superior of Toulouse described her monastery as fervent, well conducted and in order (*régulière*), permeated by a great religious spirit and, thanks to God, its works prospering; why would anyone seek to upset this?[251]

Having a parallel generalate to that of Angers opened up all sorts of contradictions. The Good Shepherd managed as the houses were filiated or subject to the mother house for many years. They had always had a common noviceship, and the process of expansion had happened progressively, but there was no way the same could happen in OLC. How would it appear to outsiders to have two institutes, with the same founder, the same constitutions and the same end, operating from two generalates? And if OLC went with a generalate, to which institute would candidates be drawn: to the flourishing one, Good Shepherd, or to the one which appeared to be in decline, Our Lady of Charity? Such a reversal in status could not be countenanced, while the advantages of local over distant control were argued with passion and wholeheartedly endorsed by the local bishop (at least, in several cases).[252]

The unarguable fact that autonomy was the 'antique tradition' in the Order of Our Lady of Charity was presented by all communities who voted 'no' as a reason for preserving the status quo. The dearest wish of the monastery of Blois was to stay exactly as the holy founder had established

246  Sœur Marie de Ste Madeleine Combat, Chevilly, to Revd Seigneur, 23 novembre 1932 (CIVCSVA, B79/3).
247  Soeur M. de Saint Francois d'Assise Guérin, Nantes, to Excellence, 24 novembre 1932 (CIVCSVA, B79/3).
248  Soeur Marie-Aimée de Jésus Lemercier, sup. Besançon, to Monseigneur, novembre 1932 (CIVCSVA, B79/3).
249  Clément Roques, évêque de Montauban, to Eminent. Domine, 11 février 1933 (CIVCSVA, B79/2).
250  Soeur M. de la Misercordiae, St Brieuc, to Monseigneur, 3 octobre 1932.
251  Sœur Marie du Coeur de Jésus Lola, Toulouse, to Mgr La Puma [S for reject], 21 novembre 1932 (CIVCSVA, B79/3).
252  Lemercier, Besançon, to Mon Révérend Père, 30 avril 1932, pp 2–4; Henricus Briset, Besançon to Excellency, 23 janvier 1933 (CIVCSVA, B79/2).

the order.[253] Similarly with Nantes.[254] The autonomous monasteries of the 'cloistered orders' – the Poor Clares, the Carmelites and the Visitation Sisters – were left in peace; so too another ancient order, the Sisters of Our Lady of Charity, should be allowed to continue in fidelity to holy Church and to its *'anciennes traditions'.*[255] Furthermore, as Toulouse darkly warned, some of the overseas houses had strayed from the perfect practice of the constitutions and customs of OLC, making any sort of union with them impossible – the 'little colony' founded from Dallas, Texas, was called to mind.[256]

As the voting papers were returned to Rome, those charged with overseeing the ballot could have been in no doubt as to the certainty and immovability of the 'no' side. And while Caen's opposition carried the greatest weight, and the determination of its longest-reigning superior Soeur Marie de St Ambroise Desaunais to hold fast could not be doubted (she herself travelled twice to Rome in 1932),[257] other houses were just as determined to hold out against any sort of centralised government and felt they had history on their side. Chevilly vowed to hold onto autonomy, come what may: this was what the founder had ordained and the community, through its many vicissitudes, had been blessed for its fidelity. From its foundation in 1724 in Paris, through the revolutions of 1793, 1830 and 1848, the commune of 1871, the expulsions of 1907 when it transferred to Chevilly, its fervour and regularity had never slackened, its work had never been compromised. It was hardly now going to surrender the constitutions and rule.[258] Tours, founded 1714, also cited its cruel sufferings under religious persecution; it had no appetite for the upset and distress that a generalate would cause and wished only to be left in peace.[259] Toulouse was adamant that an OLC generalate (or union) was not alone unworkable, but that it was the quickest and most certain route to destroying the order. Its additional claim, that this position was taken in 'perfect union' with Caen, St Brieuc, Chevilly and the other large French monasteries, made clear the futility of trying to force a change of course.[260] Historic linkages between houses are noted in the voting papers and summary, with the pre-Reformation houses and those founded directly by them holding fast to tradition (see figure 1.2): St Brieuc and Besançon would go with Caen (*'auton[omie] comme Caen'*), as would Chevilly and Versailles. Tours, which was reliant on Nantes

253 'De garder son Autonomie et de rester tel que notre Fondateur Saint Jean Eudes nous a établi', Soeur M. des Anges Chapeau, Blois, to Monseigneur, 23 novembre 1932 (CIVCSVA, B79/3).
254 'Nantes veut rester ce qu'il a été fondé', Soeur M. de Saint François d'Assise Guérin, Nantes, to Excellence, 24 novembre 1932 (CIVCSVA, B79/3).
255 Lemercier, sup. Besançon, to Monseigneur, novembre 1932 (CIVCSVA, B79/3).
256 Sœur Marie du Coeur de Jésus Lola, Toulouse, to Mgr La Puma [S for reject], 21 novembre 1932 (CIVCSVA, B79/3).
257 *Vie de la Mère Marie de Saint Ambroise Desaunais*, pp 246–51.
258 Soeur M. de Ste Madeleine Combat, Chevilly, to Revd. Seigneur, 23 novembre 1932 (CIVCSVA, B79/3).
259 Sœur Marie de Saint Bernardin de Sienne Gendrou, Sup. N.D. de Charité de Tours, to Excellence, 29 novembre 1932 (CIVCSVA, B79/3).
260 'Il serait le plus court chemin pour arriver au démembrement de notre Institut'; 'En parfaite union avec les Monastères les plus importants de notre Ordre'; Toulouse: pro autonomie 38, pro union three, declaration by all sisters (no signature), 16 janvier 1933, (CIVCSVA, B79/2).

for help, would follow whatever the latter decided ('*d'abord de Nantes*').[261] The Bitterne sisters, England, could not in conscience do anything that would separate them from St Brieuc, Montbareil, to which community they owed everything.[262] The much-troubled community of Versailles, whom one might reasonably expect to embrace the concept of a generalate – and whose bishop certainly thought they should take that road – gave the most eloquent account of the influence wrought by Caen. As the cradle of the order, and the sacred repository or *depôt* of the founding spirit (quoting article V, customs), Caen was – and would always be for Versailles – the subject of veneration. This fidelity was the assurance they had that God would bless the community and keep them in safety just as they had been established – that is, with no change to their autonomy.[263]

As the consultations dragged on interminably and there was still no prospect of an OLC generalate, the head of the Sacred Congregation for Religious, Vincent La Puma, pushed forward what was believed to be the preferred option all along of Pope Pius XI: that the houses of the Sisters of Our Lady of Charity would place themselves under the Angers generalate.[264] The superior general of Bon Pasteur d'Angers, Mère Marie de St Jean de la Croix Balzer (elected 9 July 1929), fully expected that the talks in Rome would lead to the establishment of an OLC generalate. But in the meantime, she found herself in the rather uncomfortable position of being unable to conclude negotiations with OLC applicant houses pending Rome's decision on the future of government in OLC. She made an exception for Salzburg, as its situation was unique: the only house of the Refuge in Germany and founded by sisters from Bon Pasteur, it became part of the Angers network in 1934.[265] But it was clear by then that only under Angers could the advantages of a centralised government be realised, and the Good Shepherd found itself handling multiple requests for the transfer of houses.

A list of 11 OLC houses, under the heading 'Réunion des Monastères du Refuge', is inscribed on the funerary monument to the fifth superior general of the Good Shepherd institute, Mère Marie de St Jean de la Croix Balzer (1929-40), under whose leadership the transfers were effected. The list is headed 1934 Salzburg and ends 1938 Ottava (*sic*); six are French houses which had been in crisis for some years (if not decades) already and whose dire need for long-term support was already widely known. The last four to transfer are in Canada.[266] A brief note informing the congregation at large appeared in the Good Shepherd *Bulletin* shortly after each transfer; in most cases, this is simply an expression of thanks 'for the maternal welcome ex-

261   MS notes on voting for and against proposed union, May 1934.

262   Sister M. of St Gabriel Rabbilard, Sup. Bitterne, Southampton, to My Lord, 9 Dec. 1932 (CIVCSVA, B79/2).

263   Sœur Marie de St Coeur de Marie Douzenel, Versailles, to Excellence, 24 novembre 1932 (CIVCSVA, B79/3).

264   Milcent, 'Notre-Dame de Charité, relations entre maisons', p. 13.

265   Soeur M. de St Jean de la Croix, Angers, to Mon Très Révérend Père, 13 novembre 1934 (CIVCSVA, B79/3).

266   The inscription on the memorial in the Chapel of the Immaculate Conception, Bon Pasteur, Angers, is: 'Réunion des Monastères du Refuge, 1934 Salzburg; 1935 Valence, Lyon, Valognes, Marseille, Marseille le Cabot; 1936 Troy, Vancouver, Windsor; 1937 Toronto; 1938 Ottava' [Ottawa].

tended by the mother general' and the 'bright hopes' all now have for the future as part of a larger body.[267] In the case of Valence, the first French house to transfer, there is a fuller account. Deprived by the state of much of its property in 1906 (its schools demolished to make way for a railway), decimated by the influenza epidemic of 1918, by the 1930s its vast choir was practically empty of sisters and it requested affiliation with the Good Shepherd as 'the only means which could give life back to the monastery'. The rescript from Rome was issued on 4 February 1935 and the mother general came to visit a month later. The two last novices set out for Angers in July, bringing to an end 117 years of autonomy. The 'motherly kindness and loving sympathy' extended especially towards those 'in the evening of life' was publicly acknowledged, though the change here and elsewhere was hardly as smooth as these tributes might tempt one to believe.[268] The sisters of Valognes joined the Good Shepherd later in 1935, where they were required to start their novitiate all over again.[269] The language of the Good Shepherd account matches the enormous wall painting in the motherhouse depicting the spreading of the congregation in all directions from the trunk of Angers: 'After the example of Salzburg and Valence, Valognes, Lyon and the two Houses of Marseilles also hastened to attach their leaf to the big tree of the congregation'.[270] By the end of 1938, leaves representing Troy in France and Vancouver, Windsor, Toronto and Ottawa in North America had been added to the ever-spreading tree.

## World War II and Separate Federations of Houses of Our Lady of Charity in the US, France, Britain and Ireland

By 1936, the best efforts of the Sacred Congregation for Religious to persuade the different OLC houses to accept a generalate had collapsed entirely. With the permission of Rome, the Good Shepherd congregation had already begun accepting those OLC communities who saw in the generalate structure their best – perhaps their only hope – of survival, and who had given up on any move to that end within OLC. In February 1936, the Sacred Congregation for Religious received a request to approve the minimal modifications made to the OLC constitutions at the Caen assembly held five years earlier. The covering letter, by Soeur Ambroise Desaunais, notes once more, for the record, how attached the sisters of the 'first house' are to the primitive observance, and their unrelenting opposition to union.[271] Desaunais herself died on 25 December 1937 and was buried in the monastery chapel, an honour well merited by more than four decades protecting the position of Caen and the inviolability of the early constitutions. But the dark clouds of fascism had already gathered over Europe. The outbreak of war in 1939, the German occupation of parts of France and the collaboration of the Vichy regime, the imprisonment of the Pope in the Vatican, the levelling of Caen, including the monastery, in the

267　GS Bulletin, 44th year, no. 4 (Aug. 1936), p. 407; for accounts of Toronto and Vancouver, see GS Bulletin, 46th year, no. 2 (Apr. 1938), pp 150, 158; for Windsor see GS Bulletin, 47th year, no. 2 (Apr. 1939), pp 173–4.
268　GS Bulletin, 44th year, no. 4 (Aug. 1936), pp 402–4.
269　Milcent, 'Notre-Dame de Charité, relations entre maisons', p 13.
270　GS Bulletin, 44th year, no. 4 (Aug. 1936), p. 407.
271　Soeur M. de St Ambroise Desaunais, Caen, to Eminenza [in Italian], 4 Feb. 1936 (CIVCSVA, B79/3).

bombardment of 6 June 1944, and the catastrophic loss of life, destruction of property, displacement of people and extinction of hope in humanity and the onward march of progress that came with this second world war would change the landscape entirely.

The fire-bombing of Caen, including its OLC monastery, started on the afternoon of 6 June 1944. The response of the German troops to the Allied bombardment reduced the town to ruins with enormous loss of life; the monastery itself burned without pause for four days and four nights and 20 residents were killed.[272] As the bombs rained down, the occupants were evacuated to a religious house, Bon Sauveur, at the other end of town: 'We were 500 defiling in the obscurity, what a mournful procession'.[273] The community and the permanent women residents, the perseverants, numbering close to 200 in all, were further evacuated on 16 July to Bayeux, from where the superior managed to send an appeal, via High Park, to the English-speaking houses for aid in their distress. In the burning of the monastery, all was lost: the archives and library, furniture, paintings, statues, all that had been accumulated over 300 years of unbroken residence.[274] The building itself had been designed and constructed during the lifetime of the founder, while the chapel, though not architecturally distinguished, was the devotional heart of the house and held many fond associations: 'From our dear cradle, it stays nothing only some parts of wall calcined'.[275] The daring rescue at the height of the bombardment of the relics of John Eudes (figure 7.2) and of the small statue of Our Lady of Charity dating to 1641 was the one bright spot, and taken as a portent of the continued care of the founder for the order.[276]

The destruction of the historic monastery of Caen forced the sisters and the women and children still in their care to join the streams of refugees seeking shelter; after Bayeux, they found refuge in Trouville, in the chateau d'Aguessau, where the realisation dawned that there would never be a return to the Quai Vendoeuvre. Not alone was the site poisoned, but its location meant that it would be needed for port activities once the rebuilding of the city got under way. A radical solution was embraced: building from scratch an enormous but modern complex on a 12-hectare site at Cormelles-le-Royal just outside the built-up area of Caen, publicly funded and with conspicuous political and ecclesiastical support.[277] The first phase of the construction was celebrated on 19 August 1949, by which date the sisters had taken up residence in their new home.[278] But the new house did not mean a return to the old dispensation. A federation of the French houses was created out of necessity in July 1945,

272    Caen, circular letter, to be forwarded to houses in America, England and High Park, 20 July 1944 (DARGS, OLC1/3/2 no. 110).
273    Ibid.
274    René Dubosq, *Le nouveau 'berceau' de Notre-Dame de Charité du Refuge de Caen* (Caen, n.d. but 1948), p. 3.
275    Caen, circular letter, to be forwarded, 20 July 1944.
276    High Park, circular letter, 8 Dec. 1944 (DARGS, OLC1/3/1 no. 17). P. Mouton is credited with saving one of the femurs and the skull, the other femur was rescued from the debris afterwards, see Milcent, *Un artisan du renouveau Chrétien au XVIIe siècle, Saint Jean Eudes*, p. 565.
277    Dubosq, *Le nouveau 'berceau'*, pp 4–5, 7.
278    Ibid., p. 10.

with Chevilly as the residence of the superior general, assuming many of the functions that had once been carried out by the superior of Caen.[279]

The matter of governance had taken on a more urgent character under the pressures of war. Seven monasteries in the US had already gone ahead with a federation in 1944: Erie, Buffalo, Rochester, Pittsburgh (two houses), Dallas and San Antonio.[280] France was the second to have a federation, composed of 13 monasteries in 1945. The desire of several English bishops to have the OLC houses in their dioceses under centralised government wanted only the war to be over before it could be reactivated. The Good Shepherd congregation had already demonstrated its ability to accept, on a case-by-case basis, OLC houses which 'presented' themselves to Angers (the term that was employed)[281] so that the threat of a Good Shepherd 'takeover' had not gone away. Both the American and French federations were similar in structure, under the direction and control of a superior general and her council.[282] But these groupings embraced only some of the houses, nor were there any connections between the federations. This time round it was Père François Lebesconte, superior general of the Eudist fathers, who took upon himself in 1946, as successor to John Eudes, the impossible task of getting all OLC houses to agree to a centralised government:

> In my visit to the different monasteries in the US, whether they belong to the union or not (a few have not joined yet), I spoke to all of them of the advantages which would result to the Order should both the two unions (the French and the American) and the other monasteries still keeping apart join together and form one grand general federation.[283]

Buffalo, the oldest OLC house in America, was perhaps the most set against any diminution of autonomy. The superior later complained privately to High Park of how Père Lebesconte had visited them repeatedly and, displeased with their intransigence, 'insinuated that we may be pressed to join with France', something that she maintained none of the American bishops would countenance.[284] Overtures were made by Lebesconte to the Dublin houses in October 1946 when he planned to visit, through a deputy, to discuss the subject in full, anxious to assist 'in all these efforts towards a general union of all your monasteries'.[285] The response from a furious Dr John Charles McQuaid, archbishop

279   From 1945–62, the French mother general lived in Chevilly; from 1962–81, she lived in 'Le Mesnil' in Longpont sur Orge, a suburb of Paris.
280   'Events which led up to the forming of the Federation', preamble to minutes of federation council meetings, Union of the three monasteries of the order of Our Lady of Charity of Refuge in the archdiocese of Dublin, amalgamated 5 Nov. 1948, p. 32 (DARGS, OLC5/5/1 no. 1).
281   For example, in relation to Valence, GS Bulletin, 44th year, no. 4 (Aug. 1936), p. 402.
282   'Events which led up to the forming of the Federation', p. 32.
283   Père Lebesconte, Paris, to Revd Mother, High Park, 14 Oct. 1946 (DDA, OLCR, Amalgamation no. 1). He was the 16th superior general of the Congregation of Jesus and Mary, 1937–53.
284   Mother M. of St Agnes, Buffalo, to V.H. Mother, High Park, n.d. but 1947, transcribed in preamble to minutes of federation council meetings.
285   The deputy was Fr Sebillet; Lebesconte to Revd Mother, 14 Oct. 1946.

of Dublin, left him in no doubt as to what he thought of his presumption, and he had no choice but to withdraw. McQuaid asserted his authority as ecclesiastical superior of the institute both in common law and according to the constitutions of the institute.[286] He dismissed the apology proffered by Lebesconte, that he was only trying to give information, in a brotherly way, on something that Rome may perhaps wish for all houses of the order in the future: 'I think you will agree that any intention or desire of the Holy See will be duly communicated to me by the Sacred Congregation for Religious'.[287]

The notion of 'one grand general federation' – so beloved of successive Eudist superiors general and so slow to gain favour in OLC – was followed up by the French federation under the pretext of an assembly at Chevilly planned for April 1948 and under the presidency of Père Lebesconte. By means of a *circulaire*, it extended an open invitation to the High Park and Gloucester Street communities, to the new US federation and to those houses on both sides of the Atlantic not yet part of any federation:

> As besides adaptations of statutes with new necessities, there may be special needs for different nations, local questions may be considered in sub-commissions, on the one hand all American houses, on the other English and Irish ones, and a third group with French, Italian and Spanish ones, In the case of union of those houses, it might be well to look at three corresponding provinces. More than ever, we feel the truth of the French quoting, *L'union fait la force.*[288]

A copy of this invitation from Chevilly, with all that implied, arrived on the desk of the archbishop of Dublin by the very same post that brought an invitation to the Irish houses to be part of a British federation.

Overtures from England for a British and Irish union or federation predated Dr McQuaid's episcopacy. As early as 1929, the archbishop of Cardiff, Dr Francis Moyston, pressed the case, supported by the bishops of Birmingham, Liverpool and Portsmouth.[289] The implacable opposition of the Dublin archbishop, Dr Edward Byrne, to what he called the 'Provincia Hiberno-Anglia', closed down that project but the discussion was overtaken in any event by the more ambitious plans for a generalate sponsored by Cardinal Lépicier in Rome.[290] Dr Moyston's successor in Cardiff, Michael McGrath, had succeeded in his previous post in getting the Mercy sisters in the diocese of Menevia to amalgamate with the Mercy province of Birmingham.[291] As bishop of Cardiff, he now turned his attention to the OLC convent

286   J.C. McQuaid to Père Lebesconte, 6 Nov. 1946 (DDA, OLCR, Amalgamation no. 1).
287   Ibid.; Père F. Lebesconte to Dr McQuaid, 13 Nov. 1946 (DDA, OLCR, Amalgamation no. 1).
288   Soeur M. de Jésus le Levier, Chevilly, to Mother M. of St Ignatius Burke, High Park, 8 Dec. 1947, transcribed in preamble to minutes of federation council meetings, pp 1–3.
289   Francis, archbishop of Cardiff; Thomas, archbishop of Birmingham; Richard, archbishop of Liverpool, to Eminentissime Princeps, 1929 [dated 24–29] (CIVCSVA, B79/3).
290   Edward Byrne, archbishop of Dublin, to Cardinal A. Lépicier, 3 Dec. 1932 (DARGS, OLC1/2/1 no. 39).
291   M. McGrath, Cardiff, to Dr McQuaid, 10 Jan. 1948 (DDA, OLCR, Amalgamation no. 1).

in Bartestree, Herefordshire, where he found that the idea of amalgamation was a live issue and, moreover, had widespread support in the other convents, providing only that High Park, Dublin, also joined.[292] In July 1947, he called in person on Dr McQuaid to press what was by now, in his opinion, a convincing case involving five English houses and High Park.[293] Gloucester Street was not mentioned, but the presumption was that, if High Park joined, then Gloucester Street would too, and (for those who knew it existed) the third monastery of Dublin, St Anne's, Kilmacud, also. The arguments in favour were similar to those given before: it would preserve the order for the future, there would be less responsibility on the local superior and, when required, a superior could be taken from another house, a central novitiate would cover the problem of some houses having no new subjects, and a change of sisters, when necessary, would be possible.[294] On a personal note, he had found that, with amalgamation, 'a harassed Bishop is spared subsequently many pin-pricks which are normally earned by the new Superior General'.[295] High Park was at all stages proposed as the mother house and central novitiate, and the greater scope for recruitment in Ireland was certainly one of the reasons behind its inclusion, with Ormskirk, Liverpool, already expecting High Park to send sisters, and the superior protesting that none cared to go 'and certainly I could not *send* them!'[296] By December, Dr McGrath reported that 'things are moving strongly at our side in connection with it', 'all the convents very anxious for it' and their respective bishops and vicars general were on board also.[297] By January 1948, McGrath had compiled a lengthy document setting out the history thus far of his involvement, the views of the ordinaries on the matter (from the dioceses of Liverpool, Birmingham, Portsmouth, Cardiff), the views of the convents and sisters concerned and the 'loose' type of amalgamation envisaged which would not be part of any larger French or Eudist project and would not impinge on the financial independence of the houses. As had been the case in the voting 1929–34, four of the English houses were overwhelmingly in favour (Ormskirk, Northfield, Bartestree and Waterlooville), with Bitterne's 'no' vote softened by the postscript 'God may show a different light and we only want to do what He wills'.[298] McGrath had also broached the matter on a recent visit to Rome with Monsignor Fossato, prefect of the Sacred Congregation for Religious, and received assurances that the matter would receive every attention once brought before it.[299]

It was the coincidence of receiving, in the same post in January 1948, evidence of the multiplicity of approaches being made to the OLC houses in his

292  'Suggestions for a projected amalgamation of the five convents of the Sisters of Our Lady of Charity (Caen origins) in England and Wales with the Irish convents in Dublin', n.d. but Jan. 1948 (DDA, OLCR, Amalgamation no. 1).

293  M. McGrath, Cardiff, to Dr McQuaid, 20 Dec. 1947 (DDA, OLCR, Amalgamation no. 1).

294  Unsigned memo, on Bartestree notepaper, n.d., 'Suggestions for Amalgamation of Five Houses in England with Dublin' (DDA, OLCR, Amalgamation no. 1).

295  M. McGrath, Cardiff, to J.C. McQuaid, 7 Oct. 1948 (DDA, OLCR, Amalgamation no. 1).

296  Sister M. Ignatius, High Park, to Fr Glennon, 9 Oct. 1947 (DDA, OLCR, Amalgamation no. 1). Emphasis as in the original.

297  McGrath to McQuaid, 20 Dec. 1947.

298  'Suggestions for a projected amalgamation of the five convents of the Sisters of OLC, n.d. but Jan. 1948.

299  McGrath to McQuaid, 10 Jan. 1948.

diocese that forced Dr McQuaid to act decisively.[300] These unsettling proposals for amalgamation McQuaid summarised as: High Park with Gloucester Street; both with England; both with France; both with the Good Shepherd; and both with whatever grandiose scheme the Eudists had in mind.[301] At the recent canonical visitation of High Park, his vicar general reported, the sisters had made it quite clear that they wanted nothing to do with the scheme to amalgamate with the convents in England. Closer to home, many of the sisters in High Park were ready to go under the Good Shepherd institute, rather than amalgamate in any way with the monastery of Gloucester Street which, the vicar general felt, did not augur well for collaboration within the city, let alone across international borders.[302] The approach from France had thrown the superior of High Park, Mother Mary of St Ignatius Burke, into the greatest consternation, as she was coming to the end of her term of office and felt personally unable for a long journey to France; she divulged the contents of the letter to the superior and assistant of Gloucester Street before laying all before the archbishop and seeking his advice.[303] McQuaid had taken such a dislike to the Eudist fathers and their assumed authority over the Eudist sisters in his diocese that nothing emanating from that quarter was going to be tolerated.[304] McQuaid assured the sisters that 'I will leave nothing undone to assist you, both here and in the Holy See, to come to a decision that will safeguard your interests'.[305] He was as good as his word insofar as he managed the process from start to finish, with such a knowledge of canon law and internal Church procedures that it could not be challenged on grounds of haste, tumult, misunderstanding or undue influence. The danger of 'second thoughts' was pre-empted by moving speedily but carefully. The preamble to the minute book of the Irish federation, a 30-page account of all that led to its creation, including transcripts of key documents and eyewitness accounts of the many meetings involved, bears witness to the time, thought and personal energy invested by McQuaid, but also to the anxiety of the sister secretary to leave for posterity a complete and authoritative account of all that happened, step by step. When McQuaid's correspondence with other bodies and personal notes of meetings are also considered, he comes across as a skilled canon lawyer who knew how to use his authority and personal charm. High Park and Gloucester Street were, after all, autonomous monasteries that had had practically no dealings with each other to date, while St Anne's, Kilmacud, of which he could rightly claim to be the founder and patron (chapter 8), had only six sisters and was still a branch house of High Park and dependent on

---

300　J.C. McQuaid to Mother Mary St Ignatius, High Park, 26 Jan. 1948, copy letter (DDA, OLCR, Amalgamation no. 1).
301　Same to M. McGrath, Cardiff, 26 Jan. 1948, copy letter (DDA, OLCR, Amalgamation no. 1).
302　Unsigned, n.d. but on notepaper headed Parochial House, 34 Aughrim Street, Dublin (DDA, OLCR, Amalgamation no. 1).
303　Sister M. Ignatius, High Park, to Dr McQuaid, 15 Jan. 1948 (DDA, OLCR, Amalgamation no. 1).
304　See, for example, J.C. McQuaid to Fr Lebesconte, 6 Nov. 1946, 23 Nov. 1946; memo of meeting 4 Mar. 1947 with G.J. Fitzgerald CJM to M. McGrath, 26 Jan. 1948 (DDA, OLCR, Amalgamation no. 1).
305　John Charles McQuaid to Revd Mother, High Park, 26 Jan. 1948, transcribed in preamble to minutes of federation council meetings, pp 3–4.

it in countless ways. Getting the superiors on board mattered not a whit if the membership took umbrage. The ordinary sisters had rights in canon law that they may not have fully understood, but they knew well enough to vote 'no' should they feel patronised or bullied. Having as model what Dr McGrath of Cardiff had done to date was also useful, as practically all was applicable to the Dublin houses taken on their own.

Dr McQuaid, accompanied by the chancellor of the archdiocese Revd Richard Glennon, visited High Park on Tuesday 10 February 1948 at 3.30pm to meet the leadership of the three monasteries, High Park, Gloucester Street and Kilmacud, 'to decide the matter one way or another'. The outreach from France was the first item for consideration. Referring, erroneously, to the letter from France as 'invitation from Caen to go to General Assembly', he made his own opinion clear: 'I regarded the position as unsettling in view of the Eudist General's intervention, the English proposal to amalgamate Ireland into England, the latest movements for union in the USA and also the suggestions in Ireland for union with the Good Shepherd'.[306] In response to the question of attendance at the assembly in Chevilly, according to McQuaid, 'All present decided that they saw no useful purpose in going', which closed down that avenue, though the minutes show that, at the outset, some were keen to send a representative. McQuaid's assurance that laws and statutes made at Chevilly would not apply to them without his consent, and the difficulties of following proceedings in French, even with interpreters, were persuasive arguments against attending. All three superiors said they would not attend, 'His Grace seemed pleased at the decision'.[307]

With the French question disposed of – and with it any possibility of a larger union encompassing Europe and North America – McQuaid then proposed leaving aside all other matters and considering only the issue of an Irish federation, mooted now for the first time. He himself would call in person to each of the monasteries to explain what was involved, a week would be devoted to prayer and consideration ending with a secret vote and a formal report to the Holy See. Should other questions arise ('such as qualifications for their work in teaching or domestic economy'), these could be dealt with after the amalgamation. Thoughts of a union with the Good Shepherd sisters – whom everyone present well knew to be involved in the same kind of work, living under the same constitutions and cherishing the same founder – were not to be entertained: 'If further, any sister thought still of union with Good Shepherd, I would advise such to leave and join the Good Shepherds and I would gladly obtain for them an indult.'[308]

Dr McQuaid was true to his promise to explain to all the sisters, in person, the advantages that would arise from such a union; before the end of the week he had met with High Park and Gloucester Street communities, the Kilmacud community dividing up between the two. The following

306  J.C. McQuaid, Memo, 'Amalgamation of High Park, Gloucester Street and Kilmacud, 10 Feb. 1948 at 3.30pm' (DDA, OLCR, Amalgamation no. 1). Herafter, Memo, amalgamation.
307  'Discussion regarding invitation to French assembly', Preamble to minutes of federation council meetings, Union of the three monasteries of the order of Our Lady of Charity of Refuge in the archdiocese of Dublin, amalgamated 5 Nov. 1948, p. 5.
308  McQuaid, Memo, amalgamation.

Wednesday at 3pm, he presided at the secret ballot in the chapter room of
High Park, his two secretaries (Dr Michael P. O'Connell and Fr Christopher
Mangan) acting as scrutineers and the community of Kilmacud (six sisters)
voting as one body with High Park. The result was 54 in favour of amalgamation, 13 against, one null. The archbishop and his entourage then proceeded
directly to Gloucester Street for 4pm where the voting was 31 in favour, three
against. Within days of the voting, he communicated all that had happened
to date to a well-placed colleague in Rome, seeking his advice on who exactly should make the appeal to Rome, the three superiors or himself. While
regretting all the upset caused to the sisters by the 'secret and surreptitious
suggestion of union', he spoke glowingly of the sisters themselves: 'I am
happy to say that these three religious [communities] are among the best in
the diocese: of very good families, well-educated, excellently trained in the
Religious Life, hard working and tranquil'.[309] McQuaid duly composed the
formal petition for union which each superior would sign, on 20 March 1947,
in the name of her monastery and including the result of the secret ballot.
When a query came back from the Sacred Congregation for Religious on the
precise form of union or amalgamation requested, he insisted on a formal
consultation of all the professed sisters before the type of union which in-
fringed least on the traditional autonomy of the houses was confirmed.[310] On
8 July 1948, he was able to announce that 'the rescript enabling me to form
the Union of the Houses has come from Rome, exactly as we had asked for
it'.[311] This specified the type of federation, its overall purpose and the powers
of the superior general:

> the monasteries will be independent, each of the others, and all
> will be under the direction and control of the superior general
> and her council, the more aptly to secure the canonical forma-
> tion of candidates to religious life, and the technical training
> of the sisters-in-charge for the fulfilment of their works.[312]

It had taken just under five months from first proposing to approval, which
by Rome's standards must be described as lightning fast. It was not until 5
November 1948 that the formal reading aloud of the decree of amalgamation,
by which it was brought into effect, was held in the Sacred Heart parlour of
High Park convent. McQuaid, by the faculties granted him to inaugurate the
federation, oversaw all arrangements for a general chapter, the election of
delegates and the election of a superior general and her council. He presided
at the first general chapter, held in the choir of High Park chapel on 23 November 1948, at which Mother Mary of St Eithne O'Neill was elected superior

309  J.C. McQuaid to Rev Mgr Augusto Fidecicchi, 22 Feb. 1948 (DDA, OLCR, Amalgamation
no. 1).
310  'Enquiry from Holy See regarding precise form of union requested, 8 June 1948', 'Visit
of His Grace in regard to the above enquiry', 'Second form of union preferred', preamble to
minutes of federation council meetings, pp 8–9.
311  'Letter from His Grace. He has received rescript enabling him to form the union',
preamble to minutes of federation council meetings, p. 9.
312  'Decree of amalgamation', preamble to minutes of federation council meetings, p. 13.

general: 'The big bell was rung to summon all the sisters to the choir. They approached, and kissed the hand of the newly-elected superioress-general on bended knees. Meanwhile, the *Te Deum* and *Ave, Maris Stella*, were sung. At the close of the ceremony, the signal was given, and the sisters left the choir'.[313] This was followed the next day by the election of the general council on which all three houses were represented as McQuaid had urged.[314] Mother Eithne O'Neill's first duty was to read aloud the decree of amalgamation, and appoint High Park as the seat of the mother house and of the common novitiate. No objections were raised. Amendments to the constitutions, she said, would be considered in due course.[315] For good or ill, the Irish federation was now a reality and the door was shut on other options, despite efforts in late 1948 by the archbishop of Cardiff to get his own monastery of Bartestree knitted into the new arrangement.[316] Mother Eithne O'Neill would continue as federal superior until 1971, excepting only a four-year interval 1960–64 (appendix B), resuming responsibility on the untimely death of her successor in office. The five British houses would announce their own federation in December 1957, almost a decade after McQuaid had scuppered the possibility of an Anglo-Irish federation.[317] Interference from the Eudist congregation or from any other OLC union, of whatever type, existing or yet to be created, was forestalled by the announcement, worded by McQuaid, that 'amendments to be inserted in the constitutions by reason of the amalgamation will be carefully considered, and submitted through His Grace the Archbishop of Dublin to the Holy See for revision and approval'.[318] Most OLC sisters outside Ireland probably learned about the federation for the first time in the Christmas circular of 1948, when attention was drawn to the happy timing of its proclamation, 5 November, the eve of the first Saturday, consecrated to the Immaculate Heart of Mary, and the vigil of the feast of All the Saints of Ireland: 'May we not regard it as a special dispensation of Divine Providence, a presage of success of the union of our three monasteries?'[319] The upheavals around governance which shook the institute internationally from 1902 onwards, involving the monasteries of High Park, Gloucester Street and Kilmacud, along with every other OLC house, came to a very certain close under Dr McQuaid. Questions about closer integration and a larger union would not – and could not – be raised again in Ireland for decades.

---

313   'Concluding address of His Grace', preamble to minutes of federation council meetings, p. 23.
314   Ibid.
315   Preamble to minutes of federation council meetings, p. 27.
316   M. McGrath, Cardiff, to Dr McQuaid, 29 Sept. 1948 (DDA, OLCR, Amalgamation no. 1).
317   Bitterne, circular letter, 19 Dec. 1957 (DARGS, OLC1/3/3/ no. 41).
318   'Circular sent to all the monasteries of our order and to the general of the Eudists', preamble to minutes of federation council meetings, p. 30.
319   High Park, circular letter, 8 Dec. 1948.

# Chapter 8

# Foundation and Early Decades of St Anne's Reformatory School and Monastery, Kilmacud, 1944–70

A third monastery of Our Lady of Charity in Ireland was opened in 1944, but without a women's refuge or magdalen asylum, the traditional work of the order. As the sisters explained to their houses abroad, they had been asked by the archbishop to create and manage a new residential school for girls aged 12 to 17 that the existing reformatory and industrial schools simply would not take.[1] As OLC ministry had always been carried out within the enclosure, the new school required the foundation of a new monastery. Set up as a branch house of High Park – with a sister-in-charge, not a superior – and with limits under canon law on what it could borrow or purchase in its own name, St Anne's, Kilmacud, was nevertheless, from the outset, a regular monastery of Our Lady of Charity.[2] The new community of five sisters, under their first local leader Sister Mary of St Carmel Staunton, had for their model of religious life what they knew from High Park, which was itself modelled on Caen – albeit via Paris and Rennes, and (by 1944) at some remove in time, as well as geography. Much that has been covered in terms of daily regime and devotional culture for the existing monasteries of High Park and Gloucester Street is relevant here also, though Kilmacud had the advantage over these houses of starting out without residents *in situ*. It is the establishment and early decades of St Anne's reformatory school that receive the greatest attention in this chapter, reflecting the reason for the foundation and the weight of the documentary record. Changes in governance, with the move to autonomy in 1950, are treated in some detail as particular to the history of this house and the development of its mission.

The leading role in the making of Kilmacud monastery and school was taken by the archbishop of Dublin, Dr John Charles McQuaid. It was he who initiated the project, drafted some and oversaw all of the correspondence signed by the sisters, inspected and blessed the premises on its purchase, advised on its name, said the first Mass in the house, furnished the oratory

---

1    High Park, circular letter, 8 Dec. 1943 (DARGS, OLC1/3/1 no. 17).
2    The High Park, diocesan and departmental records relating to St Anne's are extensive, while there is also a large body of official correspondence, reports, registers and circular letters in the St Anne's collection (DARGS, OLC3) from 1943 onwards. There are no minutes of local council meetings extant from Sister Carmel Staunton's time as superior (it is possible none were kept); volume 1 opens on 27 May 1971, St Anne's, Kilmacud, minutes of council (DARGS, OLC 3/5/2 no. 1).

with 'a good altar and safe tabernacle', steered the project though the Department of Education so that it became a recognised reformatory school, approved the borrowing necessary to its purchase and furnishing, and himself contributed generously to its foundation.[3] The Department of Education badly wanted the school, and thus allowed it to be grant-aided on a rather more generous basis than other certified schools. The sisters of Our Lady of Charity saw the proposed school as fitting well with their fourth vow, the salvation of souls, and their dual tradition of 'preservatory' and 'reformatory' work with girls and women. The archbishop knew in person the superior general, the local superiors and the work of the refuges at High Park and Gloucester Street (Sean MacDermott Street), while the inspectors and medical officers of the Department of Education had first-hand knowledge of their work with children in St Joseph's, Whitehall. From the very full archival record, it appears that the institute had, in the person of Sister Carmel Staunton, an exceptionally capable and creative local leader in whom the archbishop had confidence,[4] along with a small core of sisters who would make of St Anne's their life's work.

There had been official concern over a number of years about the position of young girls turned out of reformatory and industrial schools on the pretext of 'corrupting' the other children. These discussions provide something of the larger context for the creation of St Anne's, Kilmacud, and what would be expected of it. There was also unease about the use of convent asylums as places of probation, despite the fact that a girl who agreed before the judge to reside at that address could leave at any time, the judge having no powers of committal, and the convent no power – or indeed reason – to restrain her (there was no grant forthcoming towards her keep). These facts had been publicised in the Cussen inquiry of 1934–36, which also pressed for the opening of a state-funded female remand home, as had already been done for boys.[5] Ongoing complaints were made about the impossibility of ensuring that a girl on probation resided at the address named in the court order – in the case of a magdalen asylum, 'if the subject is difficult to handle and unbiddable, she will not be kept'.[6] The subheading 'Immoral conduct – girls & young women' was given to the Department of Justice collection of official notes relating to the

3    John C. McQuaid to Revd Mother, 22 Oct. 1943 (DARGS, OLC3/4/3 no. 1).

4    Appointed sister-in-charge in 1946, Carmel Staunton served as superior 1950–56, Mother Eithne O'Neill to Dr McQuaid, 29 Jan. 1953 (DDA, OLCR, Kilmacud, no. 2); reappointed in 1956 with Dr McQuaid's support (an indult was required from Rome), 'foundation is recent, of very special type, and has been excellently directed by Mother M. Carmel, who is very well viewed by the Government', Mother M. Eithne O'Neill to Dr McQuaid, 5 Jan. 1956, with MS annotation by McQuaid; McQuaid to O'Neill, 25 Jan. 1956 (DDA, OLCR, Kilmacud, no. 3). Staunton was out of office 1959–61 but appointed again as soon as canon law allowed, completing two more terms 1961–68 as superior. Application was then made to permit a further term of office, giving for reason, 'the precarious condition of the times regarding schools, etc.'. The community consultative vote was unanimously in favour, Mother Eithne O'Neill to Mgr Boylan, 22 May 1968 (DDA, OLCR, Kilmacud, no. 3). Sister Carmel Staunton died 19 July 1986 aged 85.

5    *Report of the Commission of Inquiry into the Reformatory and Industrial School System, 1934–1936*, paras. 183, 184.

6    E. M. Carroll, probation officer, 'Memorandum re: women and girls who come before the Central Criminal Court on serious charges – and other relevant matters', 7 July 1941, p. 5. Reprinted as appendix 5, *Final report of the Inter-Departmental Committee set up to establish the facts of State involvement with the Magdalen Laundries* (Dublin, 2013). Hereafter, Carroll, Memorandum.

numerous meetings and consultations dating from January to April 1942 involving probation officers and other officials in the Department of Justice and the Department of Education, judges – who, it was hoped, might have a particular concern for the young women who came before them in court – An Garda Síochána and the Catholic archbishop of Dublin, Dr John Charles McQuaid.

In a letter to the Garda Commissioner, on the subject of making better provision for the detention, education and reformation of girls aged between 12 and 17 convicted of offences involving 'immorality', the Department of Education sought information on the likely numbers involved and whether, therefore, the establishment of a special reformatory school could be justified. Drawing on expert opinion and on newspaper coverage, the department concluded that 'the number of actual convictions is not a safe guide, because the well-known absence of a suitable reformatory may lead Justices not to convict – it may well make Gardaí reluctant to prosecute, because they may argue, with great force, that there is no use starting something that will lead nowhere'. The 'melancholy conclusion' shared by all concerned parties was that, though the numbers were uncertain, 'we have only too many young girls of this class at large who ought to be in a Reformatory'.[7]

All parties were in agreement that a term in prison conferred no benefit at all on the young or first-time female offender. This was spelled out in 1941 by a woman particularly well-placed to comment, a female probation officer. According to Miss Carroll, in the women's prison there were no educational facilities, no practical training and no organised system of aftercare. There were no medical facilities for the up-to-date treatment of venereal disease or for blood tests, necessary 'in certain suspected cases of disease'. There was no segregation of offenders, so that young girls, even those on remand who ought to have been in a separate unit, 'are able to meet and converse with hardened offenders "doing time" whose vile influence is seen in the changed attitude of the newcomer even after a few days'. A girl convicted for a first offence, 'becomes embittered, hardened and morally decadent' through the free association with what the probation officer called 'the depraved characters who form the normal population of our prisons'.[8] In the absence of a state-funded, state-inspected remand home for young female offenders, with educational and training facilities, 'conducted on approved lines' and with post-discharge supervision ('under some form of licence or restraint'), vulnerable girls were ending up in adult refuges.[9] Giving the girl the benefit of the Probation of Offenders Act 1907 did spare her the ignominy and damage of prison, but the adult refuges of Our Lady of Charity were never designed for teenagers, as the sisters running them in the 1930s and 1940s were only too well aware.[10]

The inter-departmental discussion resulting in the decision to sponsor a new reformatory school was, however, precipitated by one particular and very public case. Two girls, aged 12 years and 13, were convicted in Limerick

7    S. A. Roche to Garda Commissioner, 21 Feb. 1942, copy letter (DDA, McQuaid Papers, Department of Justice).
8    Carroll, Memorandum, p. 3.
9    Ibid., p. 7.
10   The vast majority of cases where women were required to reside at a magdalen laundry as a condition of probation involved 'minor offences', such as larceny. McAleese report, ch. 9, p. 263.

district court in 1941 of 'being common prostitutes, loitering and importuning for purposes of prostitution'. Prosecutions were also brought against a number of males 'alleged to have been guilty of complicity in immoral offences with these girls'.[11] The girls were placed by the Department of Education 'on licence' in the adult Good Shepherd homes in Waterford and Cork, an arrangement that was admitted at the time to have 'obvious defects' – but the only alternative was their unconditional discharge, which no-one believed was in the girls' best interest.[12] In addition, because the refuges were not certified as schools, no state grants could be paid towards the maintenance of children sent there on licence, or indeed for children who arrived there by any other route:

> The present procedure is simply a fortuitous arrangement made possible by the good will and charitable disposition of the Members of the Religious Order concerned [the Good Shepherd sisters].[13]

In the Limerick case, the manager had admitted the girls, but soon wished them removed, using the terms 'only too well versed in immorality' and likely to corrupt the other children, whose crimes were 'merely' larceny and petty theft. Though representative of a very small number of cases annually (that is, 'after conviction and committal by the courts'), the Limerick case exposed a most serious flaw in the existing reformatory system and the legislation under which it operated.[14] It also reveals how young girls were held to be culpable for what would, in the 21st century, be termed child sexual abuse, a dark area of Irish social history that is the subject of recent and ongoing research.[15] The children in the Limerick case were found guilty of criminal offences and were sentenced to a reformatory school, where the managers refused or were unable to hold them. But there were other children in a similar predicament against whom no criminal charge was brought. The Children Act 1908 (section 58) expressly allowed for committal to an industrial school where a child was found frequenting the company of a reputed thief or reputed prostitute, or found in any circumstances 'calculated to cause, encourage or favour the seduction or prostitution of the child'. The legislation itself made the position of such children doubly difficult; it allowed a child committed to a reformatory to be held in an industrial school, once the court was assured that the 'character and antecedents' of the child were such that he or she would not exercise an 'evil influence' over the innocent children already in residence.[16] Industrial schools could, and did, refuse children on grounds of the bad influence they feared they would exert on the other children and now reformatory schools were advancing the same reason – namely, their duty of care to the children already in the school.

11    Proinnsias Ó Dubhthaigh, assistant secretary, Department of Education, to Secretary, Department of Justice, copy letter, 12 Feb. 1942 (DDA, McQuaid Papers, Department of Justice).
12    Ibid.
13    Ibid.
14    Ibid.
15    See for example, *Final Report of the Commission to Inquire into Child Abuse dated 20th May 2009*, 5 vols (Dublin, 2009). Hereafter, Ryan report.
16    Children Act 1908, section 58 (3).

The Department of Education could not stand over the continued committal of young girls to adult refuges and saw, in the establishment of one new special school, a solution to its problem. The archbishop of Dublin fixed upon Our Lady of Charity as the religious order in his diocese best equipped to further his plan – or, at least, the group most willing and able at the time to go along with it. The sisters got involved because, in their own words, 'We feel it is a cause very dear to the Sacred Heart and to our holy Founder, to uplift and train these girls spiritually and temporally to take their rightful place in the world'.[17]

## The Foundation and Approval of St Anne's Reformatory School, Kilmacud

The first formal, written approach to the Department of Education on the matter of a 'reformatory for young girls, aged about 11 to 14 years, whose moral life is in danger, and who have been committed for sexual offences' is dated 25 June 1943. The sisters of Our Lady of Charity were willing to undertake such a work, 'within the diocese of Dublin and close to the city'. This letter was dictated in Archbishop's House by Dr McQuaid, and signed by Mother Mary of St Ignatius Burke of High Park convent.[18] The proposal was well received by the secretary of the department, Seosamh Ó Néill, who added that 'The Minister notes His Grace the Archbishop has been in communication with you and has consented to grant you a new foundation should the Department agree to entrust such an institution to your care'. Subject to the provision of suitable premises and equipment, and providing that the proposed institution was conducted in accord with the Children Acts 1908 to 1941 (the statutory provisions dealing with the committal of children and youthful offenders aged 12 to 17 to reformatories), the Department of Education was prepared, in principle, to pay grants 'at the same rate and on the same conditions as in the case of similar existing institutions'.[19] The department's inspector of Industrial and Reformatory Schools, Mr P. T. Moriarty (P. Ó Muirieartaigh) was instructed by his superior officer to call to High Park to discuss the proposal. He brought with him the medical officer, a woman, Dr McCabe.[20] Moriarty took great pains to explain the process by which an institution became a reformatory. The first step was for the sisters to write to the Minister for Education 'to have the premises certified as a Reformatory School under Part IV of the Children Act 1908 as amended'. On receipt of this request, the minister would direct an inspector and a medical officer 'to examine into the conditions and regulations of the school and its fitness for the reception of youthful offenders or children to be sent there'.[21]

But the first task was – obviously – to secure suitable premises. The building selected was a large, old house in Kilmacud, called St Kevin's Park,

17   High Park, circular letter, 8 Dec. 1943.
18   Mother M. Ignatius Burke to Mr Joseph O'Neill, Secretary, Department of Education, 25 June 1943, with pencil note, 'This is the <u>first</u> letter we sent – at the request of His Grace. (Dictated at Archbishop's House)' (DARGS, OLC3/4/3 no. 1).
19   Seosamh Ó Néill, rúnaí, Department of Education, to Sister M. St Ignatius Burke, High Park, 3 Iúl 1943 (DARGS, OLC3/4/3 no. 1).
20   P. Ó Muireartaigh to Sister M. Ignatius Burke, 16 July 1943 (DARGS, OLC3/4/3 no. 1).
21   P. Ó Muireartaigh, cigire, Industrial and Reformatory Schools Branch, Department of Education, 12 Feb. 1944 (DARGS, OLC3/4/3 no. 1).

recently vacated by the technical school, which had moved to Cathal Brugha Street in the city centre.[22] It had a garden, 25 acres of land 'and prospect of more later on'.[23] A preliminary inspection of the Kilmacud premises was carried out by Mr P. J. Moriarty and Dr McCabe on 15 September 1943; in their positive report, they did warn that the issue of a formal certificate could not be considered until the premises had been made 'fit to receive youthful offenders'.[24] The sisters went ahead with the purchase and shortly after invited the archbishop to see the house for himself.[25] It was at this point that Dr McQuaid, alert to the danger of having the new foundation confused with St Kevin's boys' reformatory school, Glencree, advised on its name:

> I should say that "reformatory" is a harsh name in Ireland. "Home" would be more gentle. "St Anne's" alone would perhaps be best. Your neighbours are never spoken of except as "St Philomena's".[26]

A brief but accurate summary of all that had led to this unexpected new project was included in High Park's Christmas circular of 1943, with the role of the archbishop, 'intensely interested in all social projects for the benefit of his flock, especially the children', given the first place.[27] Although 'essential repairs and improvements' to the property were ongoing, the sisters moved in on 2 February 1944.[28] The first Mass was celebrated, as promised, by Dr McQuaid, and the house blessed on the feast of the Immaculate Heart of Mary, 8 February 1944.[29] After a second inspection by the same two officials – Mr Moriarty and Dr McCabe – on 19 April 1944, the department declared itself satisfied. The statutory notice of the certification of the school was published in *Iris Oifigúil* on 12 May 1944. The managers – Sisters of Our Lady of Charity – had to appoint a resident manager within one month of the issue of the certificate; Mother Mary of St Carmel Staunton was appointed by the community, and the necessary form duly filled in and returned.[30] From first tentative proposals to occupation and state approval had taken just 11 months.

The house was purchased, renovated and equipped at the expense of the sisters of Our Lady of Charity. Sanction to borrow £6,000 to pay for 'essential

22   Resident manager to Mr Moriarty, 10 Sept. 1943, copy letter (DARGS, OLC3/4/3 no. 1).

23   High Park, circular letter, 8 Dec. 1943.

24   P. T. Moriarty to Mr Byrne, c/o Messrs. Carton O'Meara and Kieran, Solicitors, 15 Sept. 1943, copy letter (DARGS, OLC3/4/3 no. 1).

25   On 20 Oct. 1943, the balance of the purchase money was paid; on 24 Dec. 1943 the redemption price of the portion of Land Commission subdivided holding was paid. Chronology referring to St Anne's, n.d. (DARGS, OLC3/1/1 no. 10); John C. McQuaid to Revd Mother, 15 Oct. 1943 (DARGS, OLC3/4/3 no. 1).

26   Same to same, 18 Oct. 1943, 22 Oct. 1943 (DARGS, OLC3/4/3 no. 1).

27   High Park, circular letter, 8 Dec. 1943.

28   P. Ó Muireartaigh, cigire, to Mother M. St Ignatius Burke, High Park, 24 Feb. 1944 (DARGS, OLC3/4/3 no. 1).

29   John C. McQuaid to Revd Mother, 3 Feb. 1944, Oct. 1943 (DARGS, OLC3/4/3 no. 1).

30   P. Ó Muireartaigh, cigire, Industrial and Reformatory Schools Branch, Department of Education, to A Bhean Uasal Oirmhidnigh, 10 Bealtaine 1944 and 18 Bealtaine 1944 (DARGS, OLC3/4/3 no. 1).

repairs' was given by the archbishop 'in view of the extreme urgency of the work'.[31] He himself sent a cheque for £1,000 'for initial expenses of this foundation'.[32] Expenditure was reported as 'far higher' than the community's income, and an application for an equipment grant was turned down, the minister regretting that 'there are no funds at his disposal from which he could make a grant for this purpose'.[33] The archbishop was loyal in his support, though it did not always appear in monetary form; tokens of his interest and concern included a piano, carpet for the oratory, cart loads of turf when coal could not be got, a large ham.[34] He made Christmas and other visits in person and directed government officials and other useful people to visit St Anne's to judge for themselves what was under way.[35]

## Committal, Remand and Reform at St Anne's

From the outset, there were tensions between what the Department of Education wanted of St Anne's, what the archbishop of Dublin had in mind and how the sisters perceived the mission of the house. There were also legal impediments to what all parties wanted. Alongside the core work of St Anne's, the opening of this special school was seen by the sisters of Our Lady of Charity as an opportunity to relieve their industrial school at Whitehall, St Joseph's, from a class they had long wished would be kept away from their main intake of 'destitute but innocent' children.[36] But children on remand had not been convicted of any offence, and the very point of sending remand cases to industrial schools was to keep them separate from convicted, reformatory-school children. St Anne's, as Archbishop McQuaid pointed out, was intended expressly, and solely, as 'a house of detention for juveniles committed for immoral charges'. McQuaid was anxious to protect against the places being taken up by children who were outside 'the class for which St Anne's was founded'. His suggestion was that the sisters examine with the Department of Education 'the feasibility of sending to St Anne's both remanded and committed juveniles of an immoral character'. The advantage of such a scheme was that it would preserve 'the homogenous character of St Anne's' while, at the same time, 'leaving High Park free to receive other types of remanded juveniles and destitute children'.[37] There was never a formal agreement with the state departments involved, merely an undertaking to 'suggest to the court authorities that these older girls [on remand] should be sent to St Anne's'.[38] This was to be an ongoing problem, however, as district justice and court officials, quite rightly, did not discriminate between cases when remanding juveniles, and most cases continued to be sent to St Joseph's. The school managers could not re-arrange matters to their mutual

31   John C. McQuaid to Revd Mother, 17 Dec. 1943, Oct. 1943 (DARGS, OLC3/4/3 no. 1).)

32   Chronology referring to St Anne's, n.d.

33   M. Breathnach, Industrial and Reformatory Schools Branch, Department of Education to An Bainisteoir Comhnuitheach, 20 Mí na Samhna 1944 (DARGS, OLC3/4/3 no. 4).

34   Sister M. Carmel Staunton to Dr McQuaid, 20 June 1944, 27 Nov. 1944, 20 May 1946 (DDA, OLCR, Kilmacud no. 1).

35   Same to same, 26 Dec. 1945, 8 Aug. 1957 (DDA, OLCR, Kilmacud nos. 1, 3).

36   John C. McQuaid to Revd Mother, 4 Apr. 1944 (DARGS, OLC3/4/3 no. 1).

37   Ibid.

38   Typed memorandum summarising meeting of 7 Apr. 1952, n.d. but postscript indicates written before 10 May 1952 (DARGS, OLC3/2/2 no. 8g).

satisfaction, nor could they direct the judge in what he did. St Joseph's wanted all juvenile delinquents on remand banished to St Anne's, while they would continue to receive 'the destitute on remand'. St Anne's was more than willing to take whomsoever the court sent, as its numbers were always perilously low, but that did not matter.[39] A court order was just that, a court order. The solution proffered as ideal in 1952 was for the state to fund a new, independent remand home in the grounds of St Anne's (in converted outbuildings) which would allow the segregation that was supposed to be the hallmark of a remand facility, but there was not the least danger of the state taking on that expense.[40]

The Department of Education wanted this special reformatory school – St Anne's – to fulfil a very distinct function. According to its own briefing document, and in the language the department employed at the time, the problem was how to deal with girls between the ages of 12 to 17 who 'a) have had sexual intercourse or b) are living in circumstances which may reasonably be expected to lead to their downfall'. The industrial schools flatly refused to admit or retain girls who had had sexual intercourse, despite existing law allowing them to be admitted. A girl over 15 could not be committed to an industrial school. It was almost as difficult to have such a girl admitted to a reformatory school. First the girl had to be convicted of an offence 'punishable in the case of an adult by penal servitude or imprisonment'. It would be extremely difficult to secure convictions against young girls on grounds such as keeping a brothel or procuring for a prostitute. In the calendar years 1941 to 1943, there were only two committals to a reformatory school for what the department termed 'sexual offences', and these were both following conviction on the grounds of 'loitering for the purpose of prostitution'. The industrial school could seek to have a child over 12 years of age transferred to a reformatory 'if she is found to be exercising an evil influence over the other children', but this rarely happened, as it was 'common knowledge' that the only girls' reformatory school – St Vincent's, Limerick – 'would not accept sexual cases'. But it was self-evident that there were numbers of girls who had been the subject of sexual assaults or were sexually active. Court convictions of men for having sex with underage girls, the evidence of medical examination (where the girl was found to be pregnant) and the girls' own admissions or complaints to An Garda Síochána, social workers or other 'responsible parties' all demonstrated (to the department) a category of girls urgently 'in need of committal to a suitable institution'. The Department of Justice estimated that 'an average of at least 85 girls under 17 are defiled annually' but, by its own admission, these figures, based on formal complaints, were only the tip of the iceberg.[41]

39    Mother M. of St Eithne O'Neill to My Lord Archbishop, 10 Apr. 1952; St Joseph's High Park to the Minister for Justice, 22 May 1952 (DARGS, OLC3/2/2 nos. 8c, 8e); High Park local council, minutes, 21 Apr. 1952 (DARGS, OLC1/5/2 no. 1).
40    Typed memorandum concerning remand question, n.d., also copy of letter sent to Msgr Boylan on 10 Apr. 1952 (DARGS, OLC3/2/2 no. 8c).
41    Department of Education, untitled memorandum beginning, 'The problem is to deal with young girls who either a) have had sexual intercourse or b) are living in circumstances which may reasonably be expected to lead to their downfall'. n.d. but between 1944 and 1948 (DARGS, OLC3/4/3 no. 9).

Soon after its establishment as a 'special reformatory school' in 1944, it became clear that there was a legal impediment to St Anne's fulfilling the role envisaged for it by the Department of Education – and indeed by Archbishop McQuaid – while the sisters themselves always wanted to admit a broader category of children not merely committed or 'criminal' cases. The first issue was those girls described as 'class b' in the Department of Education's briefing document, girls living in circumstances which may reasonably be expected, by the court, to lead to their downfall.[42] The two inspectors, Mr Moriarty and Dr McCabe, at a meeting in the school, inquired if St Anne's would be willing to accept girls 'charged with larceny but guilty also of immorality, girls in dangerous surroundings with a marked tendency in that direction'. If the department could be certain that the school would not turn away such cases, then, according to Mr Moriarty, 'the certificate for St Anne's would be issued without delay'.[43] The legislation already allowed for children found in unsafe circumstances to be confined in an industrial school so all that was needed was to get St Anne's inscribed on the industrial school register, while at the same time continuing as a reformatory.[44]

In the meantime, Sister Carmel Staunton sought permission to have the school included on the list of institutions to which local authorities could send children, paying for their care under the Public Assistance Act 1939.[45] The Department of Education had no objection to this move, provided that the managers of St Anne's obtained the prior permission of Dr McQuaid to the proposal that no less than 18s per week be sought per child from the local authorities (the minimum rate already prescribed), and that 'only girls of the class for which St Anne's was established' would be received.[46] Dr McQuaid endorsed these attempts to move beyond the confines imposed by its reformatory status: 'I see many reasons which would make it useful for the girls to enter your institution without any reference to the police. And in the case of these children, it is their ultimate welfare that we must keep in view'.[47] McQuaid added that:

> I was deeply impressed by the liberty which the officers of the Department of Education unhesitatingly gave you in your methods of dealing with the girls. Such generosity is a great tribute to the Department and a telling answer to the frequent and very ignorant charge of undue interference by Civil Servants.[48]

The generosity of the department in paying the school 'on a notional figure of forty' for the first year was acknowledged; there is no record of it being reviewed in March 1946, as was supposed to happen, and the funding was

42  Ibid.
43  Sister M. Carmel Staunton to Dr McQuaid, 19 Apr. 1944 (DDA, OLCR, Kilmacud no. 1).
44  Children Act 1908, section 58 (3).
45  National schools and reformatory schools were expressly outside the list of 'approved institutions' in which local authorities could maintain children.
46  M. Ó Siochradha, cigire, to Mother M. Carmel Staunton, resident manager, 21 Deire Foir 1946 (DARGS, OLC3/4/3 no. 5).
47  John C. McQuaid to Revd Mother M. Carmel, 18 Nov. 1946 (DARGS, OLC3/4/6 no. 2).
48  Ibid.

simply allowed to continue, though the superior at least was aware that this could be cut back at any point.[49]

McQuaid astutely noted the 'divergence of view' between the legal experts of the Department of Education and the Department of Local Government and Public Health,[50] and he was proved right: getting legal authority to allow St Anne's reformatory school to take in a broader class of girls was to be a lot more complicated than first envisaged. On one side of the struggle was Dr Ward of the Department of Local Government and Public Health, who maintained that 'girls addicted to sexual immorality are more or less mental and should come under the Mental (Treatment) Act 1945 whereby they receive scientific treatment for six months and further periods of six months, not exceeding two years' and, furthermore, that such cases should be left to parents and guardians to bring to the notice of the Garda. Dr McCabe of the Department of Education was firmly in the opposite camp and rejected as dangerous nonsense the claim that 'all girls guilty of sexual immorality are more or less mental'.[51] In this, she was strongly supported by Sister Carmel Staunton who insisted that there were currently eight girls of this class in St Anne's 'who are all perfectly normal'. To add weight to this opinion, she undertook her own statistical analysis, though in language that would now be considered objectionable. Of 23 cases admitted to St Anne's to date, 'at least 11 girls have acted in a completely normal way while here' and, of the other 12, 'the majority are intelligent though somewhat unstable and we believe their age and lack of supervision had a good deal to do with their trouble, while three or so could be considered a bit abnormal or subnormal'.[52] Mental illness was not, according to Staunton, an issue in any of these cases, nor indeed would it be in the future, with one case only in the 1940s or 1950s of a girl discharged to a mental hospital, balanced by at least one case of a girl who got on well in St Anne's, having previously spent six months in Grangegorman mental hospital. The Department of Local Government and Public Health held strongly to its views, but was eventually overruled by the Department of Education, which had the archbishop on its side also.[53]

Two years were lost in drafting a Bill establishing a new category of 'guidance schools' before this route was abandoned in favour of 'a shorter and simpler Bill' which would allow St Anne's to be certified as an industrial school, without losing its reformatory status.[54] An amendment to the Children Acts 1908 to 1941 was required to allow St Anne's 'to discharge more fully the purpose for which it was established'. Titled the 'Children (Amendment) Act 1949', this statutory instrument was operative from 1 October 1949.[55] Between 1944 and 1949, only girls aged between 12 and 17 'who have been charged with and found guilty of indictable offences, and who are known to have been

49   Sister M. Carmel Staunton to Dr McQuaid, 15 Oct. 1947 (DDA, OLCR, Kilmacud no. 1).
50   McQuaid to M. Carmel, 18 Nov. 1946.
51   Sister M. Carmel Staunton to Dr McQuaid, 27 Feb. 1946 (DDA, OLCR, Kilmacud no. 1).
52   Ibid.
53   T. Ó Deirg to Dr McQuaid, 4 Feb. 1947 (DDA, OLCR, Kilmacud no. 1).
54   The term 'Guidance School' was dismissed by the archbishop as 'rather strange. A school which does not "guide" is not a school at all'. M. Ó Siochradha to Mother M. Carmel Staunton, Meitheamh 1946 (DARGS, OLC3/4/6 no. 2).
55   Children (Amendment) Act 1949, statutory instrument no. 231 of 1949.

associated with sexual immorality' could be admitted to St Anne's. After this date, girls could be admitted on the broader grounds applicable to industrial schools. The 'Explanatory memorandum' issued by the Department of Education in connection with the Children (Amendment) Act 1949 spells out why it was necessary to take the unusual step of having St Anne's Reformatory School certified as an industrial school also. This was so that the courts might be authorised to send 'girls under 15 years whom they may commit to industrial schools but who are of the class for which St Anne's was established'. St Anne's, therefore, was to receive girls on remand (awaiting sentencing), girls found guilty of indictable offences and sentenced to a period of detention and girls who had no association whatsoever with crime. The sole common factor was that they had been 'defiled' (or to use modern language, were the victims of sexual abuse), or were living in circumstances likely to lead to defilement or sexual abuse.[56]

## Admissions to St Anne's, Kilmacud, 1944–58

The annual reports required of Scoil Ceartúcháin, Cill Mochudha, by the Department of Education, and faithfully returned from 1944 through to 31 July 1958, provide some insights into the daily regime over this period from the admittedly limited perspective of the school management. The headings are tied closely to the Children Act 1908 and the amendments to the legislation in force at the time and under which St Anne's, like other certified schools (reformatory and industrial), was subject to inspection by the department. Along with the register evidence and correspondence, the annual reports can be used to determine the pattern of admissions and discharges over the first 15 years of operation, and to track changes in the curriculum, teaching methods and childcare policies, as recounted by Sister Carmel Staunton.[57] They can also be used to probe whether it did, in fact, answer the very specific need it was expected to meet.

With respect to admissions, the numbers committed by the courts and chargeable to the local authorities was always very small (figure 8.1). Over the first six years of operation, when it was restricted to admitting girls sent by the district courts either on committal orders or on remand orders, the total numbers described as 'under detention' ranged from eight in the first half year (February to July 1944), to a total of 17 in July 1946, the highest number ever in residence that came directly from the courts. Of this group, 12 had come from Dublin city or county and the remainder from a mixture of counties (Donegal, Kerry, Kilkenny, Leix, Louth). It listed its 1946 'total ordinary contributions' from public bodies at £217 3s 8d; there were 13 cases for whom payment came from the responsible county and borough council, with a further £2 income from its role as a place of detention for girls on remand from the courts. In the total admissions via the courts 1944–58, at least

56 An Roinn Oideachais, 'Children (Amendment) Act 1949: Explanatory Memorandum', Mean Fomhair 1949 (DARGS, OLC3/1/1 ). See also correspondence dated 30 Bealtaine 1949 in this file.

57 Annual proforma report for the Department of Education from Scoil Ceartúcháin, Cill Mochudha, earliest covers the 12 months to 31 July 1944, latest covers the 12 months to 31 July 1958 (DARGS, OLC3/4/3 no. 2). The registers utilised in this analysis are St Anne's Reformatory Register, 1944–81 (DARGS, OLC3/8/1/1 no. 3) and Register of St Anne's Reformatory School, 1944–79, quarterly incidental returns (DARGS, OLC3/8/1/1 no. 4).

**Figure 8.1**  St Anne's, Kilmacud, admissions 1943–58

| School year | Committed by the courts | Voluntary & Public Assistance cases | Total no. of girls in residence |
|---|---|---|---|
| 1943/44 | 7 | 0 | 7 |
| 1944/45 | 13 | 0 | 13 |
| 1945/46 | 17 | 1 | 18 |
| 1946/47 | 11 | 5 | 16 |
| 1947/48 | 6 | 4 | 10 |
| 1948/49 | 7 | 5 | 12 |
| 1949/50 | 12 | 8 | 20 |
| 1950/51 | 11 | 8 | 19 |
| 1951/52 | 8 | 11 | 19 |
| 1952/53 | 13 | 11 | 24 |
| 1953/54 | 11 | 6 | 17 |
| 1954/55 | 15 | 14 | 29 |
| 1955/56 | 17 | 8 | 25 |
| 1956/57 | 18 | 9 | 27 |
| 1957/58 | 19 | 13 | 32 |

*Source:* Return of discharges for the year [1943/44 –1957/58] (OLC3/4/3 no. 16)

16 counties (and 19 separate local authorities) are mentioned. The average number of Dublin children in the school in the 1940s and 1950s was consider-ably over half the total – 'and all of the poorest', according to the person best placed to comment, Sister Carmel Staunton – but that said, St Anne's was never an overwhelmingly Dublin institution in the way, for example, that St Joseph's, Whitehall, was.[58]

The minimum age of 11 or 12 years for St Anne's made for an older intake than in St Joseph's, where the absence of a lower age limit meant that infants and toddlers were also sent by the courts. Girls from 11 years of age could be committed to the industrial school, and girls from 12 to 17 to the reformatory. Girls up to 16 years were always accepted on remand. Between 1 August 1943 and 31 July 1958, ten school years, 87% of the girls admitted (out of 70) were aged 14, 15 or 16 years (figure 8.2). There was one girl aged 11, another aged 12, and seven aged 13 years. No girl had reached her 17th birthday on admission. The single largest cohort was aged 16 years, that is, 39% (27/70). The length of stay for most girls, though not as long as in other industrial or reformatory schools, was not short either, and account must be taken of the period of post-discharge supervision also which, for those who

---

58   Sister M. Carmel Staunton to Dr McQuaid, 26 Dec. 1956 (DDA, OLCR, Kilmacud no. 3).

**Figure 8.2** St Anne's, Kilmacud, total pupil numbers 1943–58.

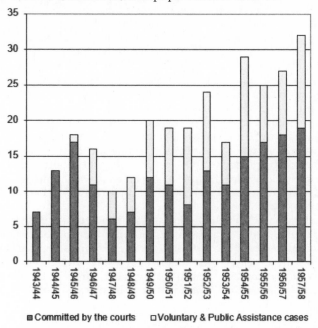

■ Committed by the courts ☐ Voluntary & Public Assistance cases

*Source:* Return of discharges, 1943/44 to 1957/58 (DARGS, OLC3/4/3 no.16)

had come following conviction for an indictable offence, was until their 20th birthday, and for others until their 18th birthday. By the end of February 1946, a summary of the 23 girls admitted to date was broken down into 11 charged with larceny, seven wandering abroad and sleeping out, two prostitution, two in surroundings reasonably expected to lead to their downfall, committed to an industrial school and transferred to St Anne's and 'one completely normal girl – attempted murder of her father – whom she accuses'. What they had in common, according to this report, was 'sexual immorality, or knowledge of, in all cases' – what, in the 21st century, would be defined as criminal sexual abuse or defilement of minors.[59]

Practically all of the 'court girls' committed to St Anne's in the 1940s and 1950s had been found guilty of larceny, petty theft and vagrancy (which included begging, sleeping out, gaming, found in enclosed premises, possessing picklocks). One girl was committed for housebreaking and shop-breaking. At least two children were committed under section 4 of the Children Act 1949, which allowed the courts to order a child convicted of an offence to be sent to an industrial school (instead of a reformatory). Only one girl was committed expressly for prostitution (1957); the other two girls reported in 1946 as having worked in prostitution must have been admitted under some

59   Same to same, 27 Feb. 1946 (DDA, OLCR, Kilmacud, no. 1).

other charge. There was ample scope, with the crimes of larceny, petty theft and vagrancy, to bring charges against any young person found in the company of persons suspected of – or known to be involved in – prostitution, so it is impossible to know if there were any other cases besides these. Two girls admitted in 1946, aged 15 and 16 years, were found to be pregnant and were sent on to a mother-and-baby home.[60] One girl diagnosed with syphilis in 1948 was treated in hospital: 'she is back at school free from infection and receiving weekly injection at hospital'. When the brief admissions information is put alongside the points made in the annual reports and the correspondence around its establishment, it is difficult to avoid the conclusion that these early court committals included girls who had been the victims of sexual assault, or were considered to be in grave danger of sexual assault through the company they were keeping or being generally out of control or without supervision.[61] But the intake was far from the 'homogenous' class of girls that Dr McQuaid had been concerned with, if such a class could be said ever to have existed.

The extension of the admissions criteria is noted in the circular letter of 1950 where the other OLC houses are told that, though the majority of the girls are committed by the courts, 'we are at liberty to accept voluntary girls provided we do not exceed the number for which the school is certified'.[62] This liberty did not, in fact, translate into greater numbers, but the small size could be cast in a positive light, for that at least was a point on which 'all Departments are of one mind'.[63]

## St Anne's School Programme, 1944–60

Under the rules and regulations pertaining to all certified schools, the type of education to be provided by St Anne's had to be both 'literary' and 'industrial', and the progress of the children in both branches would be tested from time to time by examination and inspection by the Department of Education.[64] The age profile of the girls admitted in the 1940s meant that most were too old to be allowed to sit the Primary School Certificate, reducing the incentive on all sides to follow the set programme in a systematic way. The department 'proposed a modified form of the ordinary Primary course, giving Domestic Economy subjects first place'.[65] The sisters thought the proposed course 'suitable and workable', in view of the limited literacy of the majority of the girls, with a few unable to read or write at all.[66] They had their own ideas too, with Sister Carmel maintaining that, with a little research and reading, 'I believe we could plan out our own programme, and so have

60   Ibid.
61   Scoil Ceartúcháin, Cill Mochudha, annual reports for the Department of Education, earliest covers the second half of the school year ending 31 July 1944, latest covers the 12 months to 31 July 1958 (DARGS, OLC3/4/3 no. 2). Hereafter, St Anne's, annual school reports, 1944–58.
62   St Anne's, circular letter, Christmas 1950 (DARGS, OLC 3/3/1 no. 1).
63   St Anne's, circular letter, Christmas 1951 (DARGS, OLC 3/3/1 no. 2).
64   'Rules and Regulations for the Certified Industrial Schools in Saorstát Eireann approved by the Minister for Education under the 54th Section of the Act, 8 Edw. VII, Ch. 67', signed by Agnes McVeagh and T. Ó Deirg, 4 Feb. 1933, regulation no. 10 (DARGS, SJ/4/1/1/ no. 3).
65   Sister M. Carmel Staunton to Dr McQuaid, 4 Sept. 1945 (DDA, OLCR, Kilmacud no. 1)
66   Ibid.

something to show besides the ordinary school curriculum'.[67] But whatever amendments to the programme were made, the instruction hours could not be shortened, and all the girls (excepting only those aged 16 years and older) had to attend school for the full time required by the programme for national schools. None of the sisters in Kilmacud in the 1940s or 1950s was a trained national school teacher. Nor, from the extant documentation, does it appear to have been a matter of concern either within the community or with the Department of Education, probably because the majority of the children were well beyond sixth class age and the recognition of teacher qualifications in the voluntary post-primary sector was still largely the preserve of the schools themselves. St Anne's status as a reformatory school meant that there could be no question of attending classes outside, which placed it a disadvantage to, for example, St Joseph's, Whitehall, which was able to offer its older girls education and training opportunities in the local secondary and vocational schools that could never have been provided in-house from existing resources. The report for 1944 on the literary ambitions of St Anne's is a succinct summary of what was attempted over the next decade or so:

> Ages range from 15½ to 16½ years – majority read and write imperfectly. It is proposed to teach these girls to read and write – and simply to fit them for the ordinary everyday life – giving them a fair idea of addition and subtraction in L.S.D. [pounds, shillings and pence]. We hope to fit them to write a letter, read a newspaper and take their part in ordinary, everyday life. If there are girls who can do more, we shall give them every opportunity, typing etc.

Those of the girls who had already achieved Primary Certificate or sixth class standard were quickly advanced to courses in commercial or secretarial skills. Book-keeping and typing were taught from the outset (by a lay teacher in the first year), followed in 1947 by shorthand, and these subjects would continue to be taught into the 1960s. The major focus was always on the training in 'domestic subjects', namely cookery, dress making, needlework and general household skills which incorporated 'housemaid's duty', laundry, scullery and 'training as parlour maid' and, occasionally, 'dairy work'. A trained domestic science teacher, a lay woman, was employed in the early years until there were sisters capable and confident of undertaking that work themselves, and there is ample evidence that very high standards of teaching and learning were achieved in this field.[68]

The school was always small, with 20 children the maximum reached in its first decade of operations; in three subsequent years only did it exceed 25 children (figure 8.3). But small as it was, throughout the 1940s and 1950s, it was always divided into two. The younger girls, from 12 to about 15 years, had a separate class-room, refectory and dormitory.[69] They attended what was termed the 'full time literary programme' for the same hours required of

67  Same to same, 1 Nov. 1946 (DDA, OLCR, Kilmacud no. 1).
68  St Anne's, annual school reports, 1944–58.
69  St Anne's, circular letter, Christmas 1950.

**Figure 8.3**   St Anne's, Kilmacud, 1943-57, age on committal by the courts

| Age in years | Number of girls |
| --- | --- |
| 11 | 1 |
| 12 | 1 |
| 13 | 7 |
| 14 | 15 |
| 15 | 19 |
| 16 | 27 |
| 17 | 0 |

*Source:* St Anne's school register (DARGS, SA/B/1 no. 1)

national school children and to a set timetable approved by the Department of Education. The number enrolled in school classes ('literary work') was 18 in 1946; the same or fewer were to be found in class over the next decade. One, or perhaps two, younger girls are described in most years as 'unable to concentrate' and needing special educational arrangements; the report to the department states that they were variously occupied in the sewing room, workroom or garden. The younger girls, as a group, received classes in cookery, knitting and sewing also, but most of that tuition, the 'full time domestic subjects', was reserved for the older girls, many of whom, it was reported, 'do not take kindly to formal lessons but they show a marked talent for needlework of all kinds'.[70] Older girls could also be kept full-time at the ordinary school programme where they had missed out previously, but not beyond 18 years at which point they were judged 'too old to follow literary programme' and would find their time taken up with the 'full time domestic subjects' and general housework.

From 1952, there was a little more variety to the handicrafts taught in the school, with rug-making, machine knitting and 'plaster made and painted' listed, as well as embroidery and knitting.[71] The production of goods by sisters and girls for the annual exhibition and sale of work, held each May, was not merely a date to work towards and a chance for the girls to show their skills, but 'helps to defray a small portion of our expenditure'.[72] The proceeds for 1954 were £268 – 'the best we have had so far' – and a respectable sum even today for a sitting-room sale of handicrafts.[73] By 1960, this was described as 'the usual happy reunion of friends and benefactors'

---

70   Ibid.
71   St Anne's, annual school reports, 1944–58.
72   St Anne's, circular letter, Christmas 1950.
73   Sister M. Carmel Staunton to Dr McQuaid, 31 May 1954 (DDA, OLCR, Kilmacud, no. 2)

and the girls' work, as before, 'the wonder and admiration of the visitors', with the stalls well cleared by evening.[74] Another annual event from the mid-1950s was the cookery competition run by the Gas Company and open to all schools. In 1957 'six prize winners spent an enjoyable afternoon in the City at the distribution'.[75]

Music was a named subject in the first annual report – or, at least, there was a music teacher listed among the staff. There is nothing more on record until 1959, when the girls staged their first operetta, 'Snow White and the Seven Dwarfs',[76] to be followed a year later with a production of 'Pearl the Fishermaiden'. The characters in the latter play, according to the reviewer, afforded much merriment and laughter, 'so great at times that we had to call a stop so as not to miss any of the wit'. The young actors and production team of sisters and drama teacher were applauded, 'considering the long passages that had to be committed to memory, and the many solos and chorises that had to be learnt'.[77] 'Physical culture' was a required part of the programme from the outset, taking up two hours every day and some longer weekly sessions. Sister M. Veronica McCarthy is listed as the games mistress from 1946 to 1957; though without 'official qualifications', she taught dancing, drill, skipping, games and Swedish drill.[78] A Mr Milliard makes a first appearance in 1957 as games-drill master; 'as many sisters as possible attend these twice weekly classes so that they may be able to take over at a later date'.[79] The general health of the institution was reported on in writing each year by the medical officer, who in the 1940s and 1950s was Dr Henry A. Hanna. His reports mention eczema (scabies when admitted), a case of septic blisters, the case of syphilis already mentioned and 'occasional tonsillitis, real or suspected'.[80] One child died in 1945 after three months in the Mater Hospital 'under treatment (including operation) for osteomyelitis acute'. He had the highest possible praise for the 'sympathetic and successful management of the children' that he witnessed and repeatedly noted how 'the excellent health together with their cheerful manner and contented appearance reflects the greatest credit on the superior and her little community'.[81]

## Religious Instruction in St Anne's school, 1944–60

There was no heading for religion in the Department of Education's template for the annual school report, but there was no danger that it would be neglected at St Anne's. After all, it was intrinsic to what the sisters were about and why they had taken on this work. The standard devotions provided in High Park, Gloucester Street and other houses of the institute to all who lived under the banner of Our Lady of Charity, were introduced to Kilmacud and

74  St Anne's, circular letter, Christmas 1960 (DARGS, OLC 3/3/1 no. 9).
75  St Anne's, circular letter, Christmas 1957 (DARGS, OLC 3/3/1 no. 6).
76  St Anne's, circular letter, Christmas 1959 (DARGS, OLC 3/3/1 no. 8).
77  St Anne's, circular letter, Christmas 1960. Spelling as in the original.
78  St Anne's, annual school reports, 1944–58.
79  St Anne's, circular letter, Christmas 1957.
80  St Anne's, annual school reports, 1944–58.
81  Ibid.

outward signs of devotion (which was all that could be assessed) read as hopeful signs of interior progress in the spiritual life:

> The girls too have had their Retreats, attend daily Mass and have
> a weekly instruction from one of the Carmelite Fathers who act
> as chaplains at St Anne's and Kilmacud. It is in this respect that
> our girls afford us most consolation – even the most difficult
> among them are prayerful and respectful in the Oratory.[82]

Preparation for the sacrament of confirmation involved several girls each year, but occasionally girls as old as 15 years had to be prepared for first confession and First Communion.[83] The annual cycle of the Church's year was followed, with the sisters and girls together participating in the Holy Week ceremonies 'in their new form' in 1950.[84] The great number of feast-days celebrated by the institute – there were 22 named holidays by one cal-culation, when the universal Church feast-days, OLC feast-days and the principal Irish saints' days were added together[85] – offered opportunities for spiritual teaching as well as a break from the usual routine and some small refectory treat and entertainment. A *Missa cantata* sung by the girls with the sisters, and later in the day exposition of the Blessed Sacrament, was held to mark 'our feast-days of grace', at which it was invariably reported that 'the fervour of the children is truly remarkable'.[86] A branch of the Sacred Heart sodality was started in 1946 by a local priest, Fr Brendan Carbery, at the re-quest of the superior. 'We hope that having been members here in St Anne's the girls will join a sodality outside, and as the Sacred Heart Sodality is so widely spread, they will be able to continue their membership more easily.'[87]

## School Recreations and Holiday Arrangements, 1944–60

The nature of the recreations offered to the children, the facilities available and the arrangements for holidays were among the matters the Department of Education troubled itself with most assiduously in its communications with certified schools. Much of this overlaps with what it termed 'physical culture'. The recreations at St Anne's in the 1940s were listed as games, danc-ing and walks, and the facilities as radio, piano, swings, tennis and baseball (basketball is probably meant). By 1955, the list had expanded to 'playing field with dancing platform, loud speaker from radiogram' and, shortly after, netball, hockey and a reading library are added. By 1958, the 'usual recreations' summary is thus:

> Reading (library). Radiogram with loud speakers in recreation
> hall and workroom. Playing field, Dancing platform loud
> speaker from radiogram. Films, concerts, picnics.

82   St Anne's, circular letter, Christmas 1950.
83   St Anne's, circular letter, Christmas 1956 (DARGS, OLC 3/3/1 no. 5).
84   Ibid.
85   St Joseph's Industrial School, Whitehall, dietary table, 1939 (DARGS, SJ/4/1/5 no. 4).
86   St Anne's, circular letters, Christmas 1951, Christmas 1952 (DARGS, OLC 3/3/1 nos. 2, 3).
87   Brendan Carbery to Dr McQuaid, 25 Jan. 1946 (DDA, OLCR, Kilmacud, no. 1).

The 'exceptional recreations' in the 1940s are listed as country walks, day's shopping, concert, film, excursions and 'days at the sea'. That the cinema had already taken hold of youth culture in Ireland by 1944 and would be blamed for so much can be deduced from a note on the first intake among whom was found 'a grave lack of self-control, a marked inability to concentrate, an imagination deeply impressed by the cinema'. The seaside excursions feature strongly under the heading 'holiday arrangements exclusive of home leave' from 1955 onwards. Some of the outings were facilitated by unnamed 'persons anxious to help in a work of charity', others by convents which put premises at their disposal over the summer months.[88]

The first residential seaside holiday was held for a fortnight in May 1957 in the holiday home of the Dublin Diocesan Catholic girl guides at Fernhill, Wicklow, 30 miles to the south of Kilmacud and close to the beach. The archbishop gave a one-word reply to the request: Excellent.[89] By the next year, the holiday was set for three weeks. On their return to St Anne's, the daily trips had to be resumed, the children, it was reported, having become so charmed by the sea (and the weather allowing). The Cenacle Convent, Killiney, is named as one of several nicely-situated host convents where the sisters were unfailing in their kindness to perhaps 30 young visitors.[90] Some trips were by train, others by bus, but however they travelled, the verdict was along the same lines, 'They enjoyed the bathing and swimming and came home each time sunburnt, tired and very happy'.[91]

While the school did what it could to make the six-week summer break from classes a real holiday, hardly any of the girls in the 1940s and 1950s went on 'home leave' to their families, and those who did went for a single day at a time. In 1945, ' five were allowed one day at home in Dublin, as reward', presumably for good behaviour, but that was about the largest number in any one summer. It is not until 1960 that home leave becomes the norm 'where circumstances permit' for the 'best-behaved girls'.[92] Outside of the home holiday, the seaside picnics and country walks continued for all, now augmented by lessons in local swimming pools and competitive games against outside teams (drawn from a local vocational school). The more relaxed summer regime was explained in terms of the new thinking on childcare:

> This represents in part our effort to co-operate with the approved modern tendency of lifting restrictions and lessening somewhat that rigid discipline which often has detrimental rather than re-forming effects on juvenile offenders. The Authorities are now even favouring shorter terms of detention for juvenile delinquents. If we may not altogether adopt the atmosphere of the 'open door' we endeavour at least to create an atmosphere of great freedom and a sense of home-life living.[93]

88  St Anne's, circular letter, Christmas 1956.
89  J.C. McQuaid to Sister M. Carmel Staunton, 28 Mar. 1957 (DDA, OLCR, Kilmacud no. 3).
90  Sister M. Carmel Staunton to Dr McQuaid, 30 June 1956, 19 July 1957 (DDA, OLCR, Kilmacud, no. 3).
91  St Anne's, circular letter, Christmas 1959.
92  St Anne's, circular letter, Christmas 1960.
93  Ibid.

## School Behaviour, Discipline and Discharge, 1944–60

Notes on the conduct of the children and their general behaviour were required by the Department of Education annually. The report on the first half-year of operations (1944) is 'good, considering their circumstances', quickly overtaken by 'conduct very good, in some cases excellent' (1947) or, more often, simply 'excellent'. Under 'methods used to train character', the approach set out in 1944 was confirmed in later reports, though the language varied: 'Girls are put in charge of a table in the refectory. They are allowed to choose their frock etc., to knit a garment for small brother or sister. Deprived of country walk or visit to place of interest' (1944). There was a system of 'weekly marks for good conduct, order, promptitude, duties', and rewards were 'positions of trust, badge given', 'prizes given after specified period', 'sent on errands to town', 'employed at responsible duties', 'divided into groups according to conduct', 'personal talks and difficulties discussed'.[94]

The nature of punishments for misconduct, which the department similarly required to be set out in the annual report, was articulated in the first year and continued largely unchanged into the late 1950s: 'Something less nice at mealtimes or less nice to wear for a day or two. Punishment has to be mild – except in extreme cases, where girls must be kept apart' (1944). Imposing silence, taking away good conduct marks, deprivation of favourite duties and 'in extreme cases application of cane to hands by resident manager' were all noted. As discussed in respect of St Joseph's, Whitehall (chapter 5), corporal punishment was not abolished in Irish national schools until 1 February 1982, so that its inclusion among the disciplines reported here is not surprising.[95] All of the girls who came via the courts knew, or very soon found out, that they were under a sentence of detention and were not free to leave as and when they chose. But however they felt about being detained, it was rare for a girl to abscond. In June 1945, it was reported that 'absconding by two girls were frequent at the beginning, none for six months'. Over the first 15 years, there were seven reported incidents of absconding, ranging from a two-hour absence to a week's absence before being readmitted.

The supervisory role of the resident manager of any certified school extended beyond each child's time of detention under the terms of the Children Act 1908. The Department of Education required detailed information on each girl as she was released on 'supervision certificate', including her first employment, address and rate of pay. The details of the girl's final discharge (usually after a short while on supervision certificate) also had to be reported. As the sisters explained to the other OLC houses

> The problem of the after-care of these girls is partly solved, in that, legally, they are under supervision until their 19th year – or in some cases their 21st year. In the event of their failure to make good, we are bound to recall them for at least three months.

---

94  St Anne's, annual school reports, 1944–58.
95  Department of Education, Primary Branch, R.R. 144329, Circular 9/82, copy provided by Marion Rogan N.T.

Actually in most cases they keep in constant touch with us – and this applies to many even who have left the Country.[96]

This breezy report glosses over the real crisis around discharge and aftercare, though the note on girls keeping in touch is borne out by correspondence and reports: 'Girls are required to write frequently, local clergy asked to be interested, girls become members of sodality in parish' (1946). In St Anne's, the resident manager also reported from 1948 that she herself visited their homes subsequent to discharge, which certainly did not happen at such an early date in the other convents of the order in the diocese (High Park and Gloucester Street). 'Letters exchanged and girls visit school regularly' was the summary report in 1955. The earliest report, for 1945, states that 'it is understood the girls may return for holidays'; it is known that this offer was taken up as two or three girls are noted each year in the 1950s as returning to the school for a holiday, while the practice of returning for a 'recreation evening' was in place by the second year of operations. Past girls would occasionally take a day off work to join their younger friends on a seaside or other outing.[97]

Analysis of the summary notes up to 1958 reveals that, of the first 72 girls placed on supervision certificate or discharged from St Anne's, almost half went straight into domestic work (34), and another 14% into factory work (ten girls).[98] Two of the girls taking up domestic posts were outdoor servants, but the rest were indoor. The principal attraction of domestic service as a first employment for girls leaving St Anne's, and indeed from other certified schools, was that accommodation was included and also an element of supervision with, it was hoped, a kindly interest in the girl. The high proportion of girls finding domestic posts is a reflection also of the well-to-do environs of the school, set in a developing and high-status suburban area with many large houses and villas. The school could mark up all these cases as 'discharging them to the trades which they were taught in school', to use the terminology of the Department of Education's industrial and reformatory schools' branch. There is one case each of employment in sewing and in a commercial laundry, and two as waitresses, which might conceivably be added to this category.

The high proportion of girls finding factory employment – to which group might be added the girl who got 'pottery work' – may have something to do with the training in handicrafts in the school. But the efforts to impart secretarial skills seem wasted if the first known employment of the girls is taken as the sole measure of success; one girl only went immediately to a clerical post. The numbers in domestic employment might be augmented by the girl who was 'at home helping mother', and perhaps others of the six who went straight home to parents. There were two past-pupils only about whom nothing was known, one of whom had left before this type of data-collection was in place. The other work opportunities varied: in 1945, one girl returned to her family, 'worked on the bog, said she received £3 19s per fortnight'

---

96   St Anne's, circular letter, Christmas 1950.
97   Sister M. Carmel Staunton to Dr McQuaid, 6 Aug. 1955 (DDA, OLCR, Kilmacud, no. 2).
98   Analysis based on official returns, taken from St Anne's, annual school reports, 1944–58; St Anne's Reformatory Register, 1944–81; Register of St Anne's Reformatory School, 1944–79, quarterly incidental returns.

which, considering the fuel shortages due to World War II, was not perhaps as unusual for a young woman as might first appear. One girl got work in a shop, another in a cinema, another got married on leaving St Anne's. One younger girl on returning to her parents attended a local school. A separate category was of Traveller girls, of whom six left during the period to 1958 with 'itinerant' after their names and nothing else; each, it appears, returned to relatives but it is impossible to learn anything further of what became of these girls (or indeed, of any others) after their time in St Anne's. There was one girl discharged to a mental hospital (1952), another 'retained in the school' (1951), and another (in 1958) 'awaiting employment'. The difficulties that past pupils faced on leaving the school, most especially those girls who were on their own as they tried to establish themselves in the world of work, is dealt with in chapter 9 under 'hostels and teenage welfare'.

## School Premises and Equipment, 1944–60

The built fabric was always of concern to the inspectorate of the Department of Education, for this at least was an area that could be readily assessed, with improvements (or lack thereof) and alterations recorded from year to year. The annual reports catalogue numerous small changes throughout the 1940s and 1950s: the installation of new sinks, kitchen presses and windows, plastering, tiling and laying of new pipes, fitting out of cloakroom and insertion of glass panels into doors, the installation of central heating in stages, the erection of swings, the replacement of 'dining hall equipment' and the endless round of painting and decorating that is demanded by a building in constant use. In 1946, the dormitories were divided 'and each bed curtained off, girls' sitting room furnished and shoe press in cloakroom'. The following year a glass case was installed in the sewing room, in which the girls' work was to be exhibited. The 'latest electric irons' were purchased for the laundry room in 1948. An outdoor hardcourt for games was laid in 1951 and, the following year, 'laundry remodelled and new play room built. New bathroom etc. in infirmary, dormitories and passages fitted with lino. New show cases in workroom'. Substantial internal re-ordering was carried out between 1954 and 1958 when the dormitories were painted and the school was 'divided into sections', a new classroom and dormitory was provided and the old 'centre building' was completely rewired, painted and decorated.[99]

The piecemeal additions to the school and the constant re-arrangement of the interior could not have done much to enhance the architecture of the building, which had already suffered at the hands of its previous occupants, the technical school. What visitors did comment on was the friendly atmosphere, the personal attention and the work carried out with the girls. At what must have been one of the earliest training courses in childcare, held in Carysfort College in the summer of 1953, an inspector from the Department of Education quite unexpectedly mentioned St Anne's. He was quoted as saying that 'if ever a school justified itself that school was St Anne's'.[100] There could hardly have been a more satisfying verdict for those involved in getting it under way.

99   St Anne's, annual school reports, 1944–58.
100   Sister M. Carmel Staunton to Dr McQuaid, 3 Aug. 1953 (DDA, OLCR, Kilmacud, no. 1).

## St Anne's Monastery and Autonomy, 1950

The purchase in 1943 of St Kevin's Park, Kilmacud, by the sisters of Our Lady of Charity for the use of a reformatory school involved the foundation of a monastery of the order along the lines set down by St John Eudes for the first house of Caen (1641) and, in its turn, High Park (1858). In the OLC tradition, ministry was to be carried out within the enclosure, an understanding that was questioned by 1960, but would continue to be the official stance until the revised constitutions came into force in 1973.[101] From the outset, the constitutions of the institute were put into practice insofar as the small number of sisters, the demanding work of the school and the tight internal arrangements of the house allowed. The Divine Office was recited in choir, the standard horarium was followed and the rule of enclosure respected. The monthly day of recollection and the cycle of private retreats and preached retreat in preparation for the annual renewal of vows on 21 November was established here, as in other OLC houses.[102] Sisters and girls all shared the one house – all were within the enclosure – with the convent quarters on the top floor.

St Anne's monastery was established subject to High Park, which announced it to the other OLC houses in its Christmas circular of 1943.[103] Aside from the donation by the archbishop, all the foundation costs were met by the first monastery of Dublin, which also met the shortfall in running expenses in the first few years. St Anne's had heavy debts and a modest income, and there were no signs that its financial position was likely to improve much in the foreseeable future. Autonomy was not an issue, for canon law demanded that a religious house be on a sound financial footing before Rome would even consider a request for independence. Canon law and their own constitutions required a sufficient number of professed members to be able to fill the different offices of the house, hold chapters and elect a superior, but with five choir sisters only by 1950, St Anne's was not a strong candidate on that point either.[104] The issue of governance is not raised in any of the extant documents prior to 1950, and for good reasons. The obstacles appeared insurmountable and there were plenty of other pressing matters around the mission of the house to be dealt with first.

However, the creation by Dr McQuaid of the Irish Federation of the Sisters of Our Lady of Charity in November 1948 (which was supported by St Anne's)[105] brought changes to the governance of all the houses. It undoubtedly brought the anomalous status of St Anne's to his attention, as it was now under both the superior of High Park and the new mother general. Though he himself had pushed for co-operation across all the houses – and, in that sense, worked against autonomy – it is possible that there were too many changes in personnel for his liking and that he feared a dilution of what he had planned for the house. In 1949, at least nine sisters were sent to or recalled from St Anne's (some more than once) by Mother Mary of St Eithne O'Neill

101   Same to same, 31 May 1960 (DDA, OLCR, Kilmacud, no. 3).
102   St Anne's, circular letters, Christmas 1950, Christmas 1956.
103   High Park, circular letter, 8 Dec. 1943.
104   Richard Glennon, chancellor, to Revd M. Superior-General, High Park, 30 Jan. 1950 (DARGS, OLC3/2/2 no. 5).
105   Sister M. Carmel Staunton to Dr McQuaid, 18 June 1948 (DDA, OLCR, Kilmacud, no. 1).

in her role as superior general, not just to work in the school, but also for a change of air, to recover their health or to recuperate from the strain of the work in the new school.[106] Whatever the reasons for the archbishop's alarm, the completion of six years in charge by Sister Carmel Staunton – what would have been two triennials, had she been superior – provided the archbishop with the opportunity of forcing a speedy and smooth transfer to full autonomy. As he had done before, Dr McQuaid took the initiative and pressed on with remarkable speed and scrupulous regard for procedure, so that there could be no challenge to the decision under canon law.

A week before the expiration of the six-year term of the first sister-in-charge, Dr McQuaid, through his chancellor Fr Richard Glennon, issued precise instructions on how to bring about the change he desired. With exactly seven days to go before the Feast of the Presentation of the Child Jesus, 2 February, when the current term of office of Sister Carmel Staunton would run out, speed was of the essence. While the superior general (with the consent of her council) could declare St Anne's an autonomous house and appoint its first superior, the votes of the superior and council of High Park were also required. Precise, numbered instructions and a timetable were issued to the superior general:

> Procedure therefore will be:
> 1. Meeting of superior and council of High Park and votes taken
> 2. Meeting of superior general and council and votes taken
> 3. Decision conveyed to His Grace the archbishop
> 4. On receipt of His Grace's written approval, the enclosed declaration is signed by all the persons mentioned.
>
> His Grace suggests that the meeting referred to in Nos. 1 and 2 above be held tomorrow or Monday, at latest, so as to give time to have the declaration signed and completed before Feb. 2nd.[107]

Helpfully, the archbishop also forwarded the formula to be used by the superior general in declaring the house to be independent and drafts of the letters she might post to him, with her signature and those of her councillors. The procedure was followed exactly. Some reservations about the heavy debts already contracted by St Anne's (and another unspecified point) were put to rest by the archbishop, after which the local council minutes state 'Unanimous vote in favour'.[108] The decision to make St Anne's 'a formal house' was conveyed to the archbishop on 29 January, written approval was received the following day and, on 1 February the document witnessing that 'the Branch House of the Monastery of High Park, known as St Anne's, situated at Kilmacud, shall henceforth be deemed to have the canonical status of an independent

---

106   General council of the federation, minutes of meetings, 12 Jan., 10 Apr., 18 Sept., 21 Sept., 30 Sept., 12 Nov., 8 Dec. 1949 (DARGS, OLC5/5/1 no. 1). Hereafter, Irish federation general council, minutes.
107   Richard Glennon, chancellor, to Revd M. Superior-General, High Park, 26 Jan. 1950 (DARGS, OLC3/2/2 no. 5).
108   High Park local council, minutes, 28 Jan. 1950.

House with the same juridical rights and obligations as the other Houses of the Federation' was signed by the superior general, the High Park superior and their councils.[109] The first superior was elected that day, took office the day following and was installed formally on 3 February. This was Sister Carmel Staunton, who had already held the role of sister-in-charge; she had an assistant (Sister Agnes Carlin), councillor (Sister Veronica McCarthy) and bursar (Sister Vincent Whelan).[110] The lengthy legal declaration states that the archbishop was petitioned by the superior general of the Federation – he *was* petitioned, but only after he himself put the process in motion – that the votes in favour of the petition were unanimous and that the superior general had given assurances 'after mature deliberation and having taken the votes of her council', that this branch house 'possesses all that is required by the Sacred Canons for religious observance, material maintenance, and the sufficient discharge of the work in question, namely, the education and training of girls whose morals have been in danger'. The local superior and council of High Park were removed from all involvement in St Anne's, while the final clause strengthened the hold of the archbishop over the house:

> Furthermore, We declare that this House cannot be suppressed or transferred, nor its work changed into that of another kind, without our express authorisation or that of our legitimate successors in the See.[111]

With the same person in charge before and after February 1950, the shift to autonomy was hardly disruptive, but there were new responsibilities, most importantly around land and property which were now held in the name of the community, while it could also borrow money on its own account. St Anne's was spared one of the most onerous duties of an autonomous house, the training of novices, as the federation of November 1948 had already created a common novitiate at High Park. The decree of federation had also created the role of superior general who, from 1950, acted towards Kilmacud in the same way as she acted towards the other autonomous houses of High Park and Gloucester Street (Sean MacDermott Street). One of her few functions was to undertake a formal or canonical visitation every three years and write a report. The thrust of the inspections of 1951, 1954, 1957, 1960 and 1963 is much the same:

> The community are very fervent and zealous for the observance of the rule and holy constitutions. They are doing a wonderful work for the souls entrusted to their care.[112]

---

109   Declaration of the independence of St Anne's, Kilmacud, 1 Feb. 1950 (DARGS, OLC3/2/2 no. 5).

110   Irish federation general council, minutes, 3 Feb. 1950.

111   Official declaration of the independence of St Anne's, Kilmacud, signed and sealed by John Charles McQuaid, and signed by Richard Glennon, chancellor (DARGS, OLC3/2/2 no. 5).

112   Sister M. of St Eithne O'Neill, Visitation by Superior General, St Anne's, Kilmacud, 5 Apr. 1957. See also 9 Sept. 1951, 28 Aug. 1954, 4 Apr. 1960, 29 Mar. 1963, Sister M. of St Eithne O'Neill, Visitation by Superior General, St Anne's, Kilmacud (DARGS, OLC3/5/2 no. 2).

Some strains might be picked up between the new and the old from the visitation reports; one complaint was around using the simpler form of the religious name already adopted by Sister Carmel Staunton and others in St Anne's. On her first visitation, 9 September 1951, the superior general, Sister Mary of St Eithne O'Neill, recommended formally that 'We should be careful when speaking, or writing of our sisters, to give them their proper religious title, Sister <u>Mary</u> of St ----. This is a very particular point to be observed. As we are daughters of her Immaculate Heart, and all receive the name of <u>Mary</u> with the Habit of Our Lady of Charity on their clothing day'. Another custom she found was ignored in St Anne's was that of announcing oneself at the different community exercises: 'we should say where we have come from in a low but audible voice (except in choir), for instance: Mother, we come from the school/guest house/kitchen etc. etc. Mother, permission to go to School, etc. etc. Mother, permission to disengage the reader, server'.[113] Concern with minor points of protocol would be lost in the sea of changes that was about to engulf both Church and society in the 1960s.

The first circular letter in the name of St Anne's dates from December 1950, sent out 'in the belief that Our Monasteries are glad to know how each Community endeavours to interpret our Holy Founder's ideals in these anxious days'.[114] Composed by Sister Carmel Staunton in the name of the community, the circular was not just a way of ensuring that St Anne's took its rightful place in the OLC network, but a means of presenting the work of St Anne's as faithful to the spirit of the order and relevant in the modern world. St Anne's letter-writing was reciprocated, with circular letters arriving in due course from far-flung OLC houses, telling of 'many projects in hand and many forward steps taken in our struggle to help those committed to our care, for all of which we thank God'.[115] That from St John's Villa, Carrollton, Ohio, was singled out for praise in 1958, but all were appreciated, and the fact of autonomy did not lessen the interest to be taken in each other's efforts, 'We take heart when we realise that we all share in the progress and good works of our Holy Order'.[116] The spiritual ties with Caen as the cradle of the order were acknowledged, though the original monastery and refuge had been destroyed in the bombardment of June 1944 (chapter 7). The raising up of Cormelles-le-Royal in its stead, and in time to mark the third centenary of the foundation of the order in 1651,[117] was interpreted in Kilmacud as 'a light to guide us on paths that are new, encouraging us to use God's gifts of nature as well as grace, to draw souls from the powerful attractions of the world'.[118] Far from holding the institute back, the spiritual heritage of St John Eudes was urged as directly relevant to the needs of the post-war world, requiring only to be put into practice in more modern ways as they were attempting to do in Kilmacud.

---

113   Sister M. of St Eithne O'Neill, Visitation by Superior General, St Anne's, Kilmacud, 9 Sept. 1951 (DARGS, OLC3/5/2 no. 2).
114   St Anne's, circular letter, Christmas 1950.
115   St Anne's, circular letter, Christmas 1956.
116   St Anne's, circular letter, Christmas 1958 (DARGS, OLC3/3/1 no. 7).
117   René Dubosq, *Le nouveau 'berceau' de Notre-Dame de Charité du Refuge de Caen* (Caen, n.d. but 1948), p. 10.
118   St Anne's, circular letter, Christmas 1951.

At the foundation, all the sisters lived in the same building as the girls, but the possibility of separating the school from the convent first arose, indirectly, in 1950 when a builder offered to purchase 15 acres of the land attached to Kilmacud House. The sisters had bought the house a year earlier for use as a guesthouse and as a place of training for girls before leaving (chapter 9). The timing was propitious as, with autonomy, the community had rights over how the windfall would be spent, though the approach to the archbishop for permission to sell the land would be done through the superior general in High Park. The debt on the school would first have to be cleared and expensive improvements made to Kilmacud House, but house-building would bring the advantage of mains water and drainage to their property.[119] At the time of the negotiations, an acre of land was given gratuitously as a site for a parish church and schools, which no doubt made for good relations at local level.[120]

Meanwhile the archbishop was insisting that the sisters establish a hostel which had, in any case, long been a cherished project of the superior Sister Carmel Staunton. Various expensive plans were developed – and abandoned – in favour of converting the top portion of the large house, currently used by the sisters, to a hostel for girls taking up jobs in the locality, as well as those employed in the guesthouse.[121] The building estimates for a small convent were considerably lower than what they had been quoted for a hostel, while it would also give the sisters, for the first time, a break from living totally in the school. Permission was granted, including permission to borrow from the bank, and the architect's plans marked (by the archbishop) with the comment 'the convent will certainly be simple'.[122] The sisters moved into the new convent on 15 September 1955 and the formal blessing and first Mass, in its little oratory, was said by the archbishop on 18 October 1955, with sisters from High Park and Gloucester Street also in attendance.[123] It was the chief item of news in the Christmas circular of that year, which explained how the sisters now came to the convent for all spiritual exercises, as well as for meals and recreation. Daily Mass continued to be celebrated in the school chapel for the benefit of all, but the greatest advantage was felt by those sisters who were duty-bound to sleep in the school, hostel or guesthouse, who could now, for one week in every three months, sleep in the convent, where they would have 'the quiet and recollection so necessary for those who work among seculars'.[124]

## St Anne's School from 1958 to the Kennedy inquiry, established 1967

St Anne's was held in high esteem in the late 1950s, with favourable comments on record from Mr O'Raftery, secretary in the Department of Education, and from a newly-appointed judge to the children's court, Justice Ó Riain,

119   Mother Eithne O'Neill to Dr McQuaid, 30 Aug. 1950 (DDA, OLCR, Kilmacud, no. 1).
120   R.J. Glennon to the superior general, 9 Oct. 1951 (DDA, OLCR, Kilmacud, no. 2).
121   Sister M. Carmel to Dr McQuaid, 1 May 1954 (DDA, OLCR, Kilmacud, no. 2).
122   William Fitzpatrick to Dr McQuaid, 5 May 1954; Dr McQuaid to Sister M. Carmel Staunton, 6 May 1954; Sister M. Carmel to Dr McQuaid, 13, 20, 24, 31 May 1954 (DDA, OLCR, Kilmacud, no. 2).
123   Irish federation general council, minutes, 18 Oct. 1955.
124   St Anne's, circular letter, Christmas 1955 (DARGS, OLC3/3/1 no. 4).

whom Sister Carmel Staunton described as 'extremely kind, very interested and anxious to help'.[125] The other OLC houses were told that 'the work at the School and at St Bernadette's [hostel] gives satisfaction to the Government officials.'[126] But the winds of change were gathering force; the decade 1958 to 1968 would see shifts in attitudes to childcare and juvenile reform and the introduction of new (and long overdue) practices. The 'grouping system' was not only approved of, but 'strongly recommended by the educational author-ities', according to the Christmas 1958 circular. 'Home leave' for the girls and the training and accreditation of staff were also expected: 'In all it is a peri-od of change, a fact which makes all important the giving to our sisters the maximum spiritual and educational aids.'[127]

At the very same time that the new thinking on child welfare was taking hold, and the profession of social work was making advances, there was the coronation of a new Pope, John XXIII; the sisters of St Anne's watched on tele-vision 'each wonderful phase of this glorious ceremony'.[128] Even before the convening of the Second Ecumenical Council, there is evidence of an aware-ness among the community at St Anne's about the changes under way in Irish society and in the Catholic Church (and the order) more widely. The Church's call for long-established parishes and religious orders to support evangelisa-tion in much poorer countries came to St Anne's with a visit from the arch-bishop of Nairobi, who told the community 'of the vastness of his diocese, and of the work there waiting to be done'.[129] Though the mission in Kenya would be led by the OLC sisters in England, the Irish houses – including St Anne's – would take an interest in its progress and provide support, including sending personnel, a small but real token of a wider engagement with the 'modern world'.[130] The hope for 1959 was that it be a year of 'blessing and progress for each house of our holy order'.[131] It was Sister Carmel Staunton whom the archbishop suggested should accompany the superior general to an as-sembly in Rome in 1960 (see chapter 13), which heightened interest in what was happening in other OLC houses.[132] En route home, Staunton stopped in Chevilly, where she was impressed by the French sisters' ability to modernise their work and yet stay true to their religious vocation, which she put down – tongue in cheek – to the extinction of the 'old cradle': 'They all appear able to combine great fervour in their own lives and a most progressive approach to the work of our Order. Caen was bombed, perhaps that is the explanation.'[133]

The opening session of the Vatican Council in 1962 turned all eyes to Rome. The proceedings were followed with intense interest at St Anne's, as they were in religious houses internationally (chapter 13). Two young American sisters, students in Rome during those eventful years, spent part of the summer of 1962 at St Anne's, sharing with the community 'the happiness

125   Sister M. Carmel Staunton to Dr McQuaid, 8 Aug. 1957 (DDA, OLCR, Kilmacud, no. 3).
126   St Anne's, circular letter, Christmas 1958.
127   Ibid.
128   Ibid.
129   Ibid.
130   St Anne's, circular letter, Christmas 1962 (DARGS, OLC3/3/1 no. 10).
131   St Anne's, circular letter, Christmas 1958.
132   St Anne's, circular letter, Christmas 1960.
133   Sister M. Carmel Staunton to Dr McQuaid, 10 July 1960 (DDA, OLCR, Kilmacud, no. 3).

and memories of life within the precincts of the Vatican' and continuing, on return to their studies, to keep the Irish sisters abreast of all that was happening in a lively and affectionate way.[134] In the circular for Christmas 1962, it was Pope John XXIII's plea for optimism and confidence that was taken hold of by St Anne's: 'we look into the past year with grateful hearts and into the future armed with hope and strength'.[135]

Key elements of the change in thinking about child and adolescent care (dealt with more fully in chapter 9) were the break-up of large numbers into smaller groups where a more relaxed, 'normal' family life might be possible, keeping the young child and teenager outside the court system insofar as that was possible, introducing psychological assessment and psychological services for children in care and encouraging professional training for those in childcare and special education. These new ideas were taking hold against a backdrop of mounting criticism of the industrial school system. The scathing articles published by Michael Viney in the *Irish Times* 27 April – 6 May 1966 were especially powerful in bringing to public notice how individual children experienced the system. In the internal review ordered by the Minister for Education, George Colley, in 1966, the harshness of the boys' schools in particular was highlighted.[136] The numerous failings of large-scale institutions for children were becoming a political issue at national level, and advocates for their closure were to be found among social workers and educationalists, lay and religious, as well as among medical personnel with first-hand knowledge of their operation.

The investigation of St Anne's by an *Irish Times* journalist, Mary Maher, published under the headline 'St Anne's, a home without rebels' on 1 March 1966 (figure 8.4), must be read within this context of public concern with residential childcare. Maher found much to praise in St Anne's, but also picked up on its underlying weaknesses. The line-by-line response by the school manager, Sister Carmel Staunton, to Justice Eileen Kennedy's report on the reformatory and industrial schools systems (the inquiry commenced in 1967) exposes tensions between the state and the local religious community around the operation of St Anne's.[137] It was meant to be a place of detention for (as the Kennedy report termed it) 'a certain type of girl', but was failing to fulfil this role. The school managers maintained that the Kennedy criticism was unfair and misrepresented the facts and, moreover, its 1944 mandate had been overtaken by developments in childcare and adolescent psychology. By the late 1960s, the future of St Anne's – and indeed that of other certified schools – was on hold pending the government response to the inquiry it had commissioned. But in the meantime the school community, sisters, staff and girls, got on with daily life.

St Anne's had never been other than a small group system by virtue of its numbers (figure 8.3), but there was scope to go further and to re-order the building internally so that each of two or three groups could have its

---

134   St Anne's, circular letter, Christmas 1962.
135   Ibid.
136   Dr C.E. Lysaght, Report on industrial schools and Reformatories, submitted to the Minister for Education, 11 Nov. 1966, quoted in Ryan report, iv, p. 290.
137   Typed memorandum, St Anne's School and Remand Home, 'Observations', date 1968 added by hand but this is an error; from content the memo is 1970 and 1971 (DARGS, OLC3/4/3 no. 13). Hereafter, St Anne's, 'Observations' c.1968–71.

THE IRISH TIMES, TUESDAY, MARCH 1, 1966

### ST. ANNE'S — A HOME WITHOUT REBELS

# The girls' school where boyfriends are invited

ESCAPING from St. Anne's School in Kilmacud is a simple proposition for the least guileful. The doors are not locked and the main gate is usually open. The supervision, if diligent, is admittedly informal.

Few girls attempt it, and those who do are usually the "court cases," delinquents sent there under court order. The others find quickly that an element of choice, an atmosphere of freedom, are the greatest deterrents to rebellion.

by
**MARY MAHER**

*A young seamstress shows her handiwork—an apron with a "Beatles" motif—to fellow-students in the handicrafts room.*

Mother Mary Carmel has run this Dublin school as nearly as possible on these principles since she was put in charge of it at its founding 22 years ago. She prefers that St. Anne's not be referred to as a reformatory or detention home, but the girls who live there are the ones no one else will take—the unruly, the emotionally disturbed, the minor criminal offender. They cannot be controlled in school or at home, but they are not unstable enough to be committed to a mental institution; they are not sufficiently bright, or academically conditioned, to keep of the normal school course, but they are not retarded.

There are not really many such cases in the country. St. Joseph's School, Limerick, is the only other school fulfilling the same role as St. Anne's. Neither school is filled to capacity; St. Anne's is certified to accommodate 80;

there are at present 25 girls in the school, and there have never been more than 40.

Because their numbers are few, the girls at St. Anne's enjoy a privilege that other children in institutions sometimes never realise; they live in a home, or a close approximation to it, and benefit from personal, individual attention.

The difference between St. Anne's and an industrial school of several hundred children is a matter of humanity. In the recreation room the girls play pop records and dance, squabble with one another and chatter with the nuns. They show almost none of the customary reticence that most convent-trained children display with religion.

The building itself is slightly riotous in colour with a profusion of flowered chintz, yellow and cream walls, winding stretches of cerise corridors. "I'm afraid our colours are a bit flamboyant," said Mother Mary Carmel, who is responsible for them. She has extended her theories on colour and cheer to things as elemental as pink facecloths in the washroom and flowered curtains on the lavatory windows.

The older girls sleep in single rooms. They are allowed to put out their personal belongings—tiny bottles of cologne, stuffed animals, an occasional transistor radio. Mother Carmel noted without surprise that nothing is ever stolen. "They are very fair with one another, and with us. Once in awhile I lose my temper and say something I regret, but when I apologise to a girl she'll say : 'It's all right, Mother, I know you didn't mean it.'"

It is remark that evidences something nearer a family bond than a pupil-teacher, or inmate-warder relationship. The nuns avoid regimentation or detailed organisation; the girls are assigned household tasks by the week and are permitted to accomplish them more or less when they choose, between class-hours and recreation. Bedtime is largely determined by the television schedule before 10 or 11 p.m.

#### No uniforms

Neither do the girls dress like penguins. There are no uniforms at St. Anne's. Sometimes a select committee of them will shop in town under the supervision of an older girl—frequently an ex-pupil—or the nuns will purchase samples to be approved or rejected.

The flexibility of regulations allows individual interpretation. Older girls are sometimes allowed to work outside during the day while still living-in. Visitors are permitted anytime outside of class-hours, and the girls are not only allowed to go out with boys, but encouraged to do so. "We do ask that the young men call here, and if they're nice lads they don't mind," said Mother Carmel. "It's a great help to a girl to have someone to care for her."

#### Training

Four mornings a week, the girls are instructed in reading, arithmetic, history and religion. They spend the rest of the time learning cooking, sewing, embroidery and arts and crafts. One of the three lay-teachers has a bachelor's degree, and one of the 11 sisters has a commercial-course certificate.

None of the sisters has had a formal training for the work she is doing; Mother Carmel seeks to have as many as possible attend lectures and take courses in psychology and sociology. Neither are they certified to provide vocational training, and careers as waitresses, scrubwomen, or maids are what the girls look forward to if they do not marry. Some become nurses' aides or beautician apprentices. Recently a course in typing—on six vintage machines—has been started and may soon produce several stenographers.

The Government now allots the school £3.10.6 per week per girl; the estimated operating expenses run to £9 or £10 per week per girl. The school has no psychiatric or counselling services, no remedial education programme, no trained staff or modern equipment necessary for teaching skilled or technological trades. Parents or guardians are asked to contribute what they can. In recent years, seven acres of land have been sold to meet expenses and more land will have to be sacrificed if the sisters do not receive more substantial aid.

Meanwhile the girls whom no one else can handle are living in something like a home, with the comforts of companionship and solicitous protection. It is a factor too important to be overlooked, but is it enough to equip them for the future.

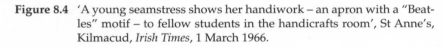

*Some of the girls are taking a course in typing.*

**Figure 8.4**   'A young seamstress shows her handiwork – an apron with a "Beatles" motif – to fellow students in the handicrafts room', St Anne's, Kilmacud, *Irish Times*, 1 March 1966.

distinct identity, as announced in 1962.[138] Though the school was certified to accommodate 80 girls, it had never had more than 40. When the journalist Mary Maher wrote her report in March 1966 the total number was 25 girls.

138   St Anne's, circular letter, Christmas 1962.

Accordingly, 'they live in a home, or a close approximation to it, and benefit from personal, individual attention'.[139] Other *Irish Times* coverage of child-care institutions gave Maher points of comparison, and she made much of the small scale of St Anne's:

> The difference between St Anne's and an industrial school of several hundred children is a matter of humanity. In the recreation room the girls play pop records and dance, squabble with one another and chatter with the nuns. They show almost none of the customary reticence that most convent-trained children display with religious.[140]

The bright colours of the building ('a profusion of flowered chintz, yellow and cream walls, winding stretches of cerise corridor') struck the journalist as did the 'pink facecloths in the washroom and flowered curtains on the lavatory windows'. The older girls had single bedrooms surrounded by their personal belongings ('tiny bottles of cologne, stuffed animals, an occasional transistor') and, in answer to the journalist's query if things were ever stolen, she was told no, 'They are very fair with one another, and with us'. What most surprised and impressed the journalist, according to the published article, was the family bond she detected, not the pupil-teacher or inmate-warder relationship that she had expected. The atmosphere was normal and relaxed:

> The nuns avoid regimentation or detailed organisation; the girls are assigned household tasks by the week, and are permitted to accomplish them more or less when they choose, between class hours and recreation. Bedtime is largely determined by the TV schedule before 10 or 11pm. Neither do the girls dress like penguins. There are no uniforms at St Anne's. Sometimes a select committee of them will shop in town under the supervision of an older girl – frequently an ex-pupil – or the nuns will purchase samples to be approved or rejected. The flexibility of regulations allows individual interpretation.[141]

The hostel arrangement for older girls (chapter 9) is noted, as is the open welcome to visitors outside of class-hours. To her evident surprise, she found that 'The girls are not only allowed to go out with boys, but encouraged to do so. "We do ask that the young men call here, and if they're nice lads they don't mind' says Mother Carmel. "It is a great help to a girl to have someone to care for her".'[142] Children from the OLC monastery of Waterlooville were brought on holiday to St Anne's in 1966, indicating that this Dublin house was not merely exchanging letters with its English counterparts, but actively

---

139 Mary Maher, 'St Anne's: a home without rebels', *Irish Times*, 1 Mar. 1966.
140 Ibid.
141 Ibid.
142 Ibid.

learning from the more progressive regimes to be found in Britain (as argued in chapter 9).[143]

The numbers reported by Mary Maher must have included every sister in the community, not just the five who are returned as 'religious staff' giving instruction in some capacity or another to the girls (according to the returns submitted in response to the Kennedy report).[144] By the mid-1960s, more than half of the sisters were providing what would now be termed home services to the community of girls and sisters and to the ladies resident in the guest house. Some of these sisters were past retirement age or in poor health and, while sisters could be moved between houses, under the federation that was very much the exception, and those who came to St Anne's could expect to live there for the rest of their days. The income for 1966 is reported by Maher at £3.10.6d per child per week; the capitation grant was raised in July 1968 and doubled in 1969 when it reached £8 13s per reformatory child.[145] The estimated operating expenses, according to the school principal, in 1966 were £9 or £10 per week per girl, so that even the increased grant left an operating shortfall.[146] The school had managed to meet expenses on the basis of being paid for a notional number of 40 girls (a privilege which was about to end), but also through the sale of land, a source of income which was also to close down.[147]

The programme offered to the girls throughout the 1960s was both academic and work-related, as it had always been, with four mornings a week spent attending classes in reading, arithmetic, history and religion, and the rest of the time 'learning cooking, sewing, embroidery and arts and crafts'. The typing course is described as newly-started in 1966 ('and may soon produce several stenographers'), but typing had been taught at least intermittently since the first year of operations. The lack of formal qualifications among the staff was noted by Maher ('One of the three lay-teachers has a bachelor's degree, and one of the 11 sisters has a commercial-course certificate'), while at the same time acknowledging that 'Mother Carmel seeks to have as many as possible attend lectures and take courses in psychology and sociology'.[148] The training of sisters 'for the fulfilment of their works' was one of the reasons given for the Irish federation of 1949.[149] Sisters from St Anne's did take advantage of the opportunities that were opening up, attending occasional lectures or short courses in a number of institutes, including the St John of God house

143   Sainte Anne, *circulaire*, janvier 1966 (DARGS, OLC3/3/1 no. 11). The French version of the circular letter for 1965, delayed until Jan. 1966, is somewhat fuller that the English version in the same file.
144   St Anne's, 'Observations' *c*. 1968–71.
145   *Reformatory and industrial schools systems report, 1970* (Dublin, 1970), p. 4. Hereafter, Kennedy report.
146   Maher, 'St Anne's: a home without rebels'.
147   Anthony M. Sherry, valuation of land attached to Kilmacud House, 24 Apr. 1962 (DDA, OLCR, Kilmacud, no. 3).
148   Maher, 'St Anne's: a home without rebels'. The teacher taking a typing class photographed here is Sister Vincent Whelan.
149   'Decree of amalgamation', Preamble to minutes of federation council meetings, Union of the three monasteries of the order of Our Lady of Charity of Refuge in the archdiocese of Dublin, amalgamated 5 Nov. 1948, p. 13 (DARGS, OLC5/5/1 no. 1).

in Stillorgan,[150] the philosophy department of University College Dublin (where psychology was taught)[151] and at the Holy Child Convent, Layton Hill, Blackpool, which was a leader in the training of childcare workers.[152] Research visits to model institutions outside Ireland were also seen, by Sister Carmel Staunton at least, as part of the sisters' ongoing education. But St Anne's was slow to release sisters for full-time training, to the frustration of the archbishop who, in granting permission to have part-time vocational teachers employed at the school in 1963, could not resist giving the superior a piece of his mind:

> May I ask why, after all these years of exhortation, your own sisters have not yet been prepared with every necessary qualification? Imagine having to borrow a teacher in literary subjects for these poor children! It may be that before I die some of my recommendations will be put into effect by the superiors. And two Sisters are now gone to study conditions in France! Much good may it do them![153]

Staunton's defence – that she wanted to release sisters from the heavy weight of teaching (which had always been done 'to the satisfaction of the Department of Education') so that they might be able to offer more time and energy to supervision, and that the girls would benefit from what lay teachers could bring to the school – resulted in a curt follow-up from Dr McQuaid as an educationalist: 'You are right about lay teachers, but you are quite wrong about Sisters. Nothing so gives a Sister entrance into the mind and heart of a child as teaching'.[154]

The principal criticism of St Anne's put forward by the journalist Mary Maher in 1966 was that the limited vocational training offered to the girls, by staff without formal qualifications, meant that 'careers as waitresses, scrub-women or maids are what the girls look forward to if they do not marry. Some become nurses' aides or beautician apprentices'.[155] The home-life that was provided for the girls, 'with the comforts of companionship and solicitous protection' was acknowledged by Maher as 'a factor too important to be overlooked', but the reader was still left with the question, 'is it enough to equip them for the future?'[156] That the same question also troubled the school leadership is amply documented. It would be one of the undisputed findings of the Kennedy inquiry across all reformatory schools, for girls and for boys, that 'no adequate system of vocational training exists in the Reformatories to provide the children leaving with saleable skills to enable them to take their place in society'.[157]

150  St Anne's, circular letter, Christmas 1950; Sister M. Carmel Staunton to Dr McQuaid, 12 Mar. 1962 (DDA, OLCR, Kilmacud, no. 3).
151  Irish federation general council, minutes, 16 Jan. 1957.
152  St Anne's, circular letter, Christmas 1952.
153  Dr McQuaid to Sister M. Carmel Staunton, 11 Aug. 1963, copy letter (DDA, OLCR, Kilmacud, no. 3).
154  Same to same, 16 Aug. 1963, memorandum (DDA, OLCR, Kilmacud, no. 3).
155  Maher, 'St Anne's: a home without rebels'.
156  Ibid.
157  Kennedy report, p. 38.

The response of the community of St Anne's to the hard-hitting Kennedy report, on its publication in late 1970, was, on the whole, positive; a heavily-annotated typescript records the initial reaction of the school manager. Many of the observations to the numbered points simply state 'in agreement', 'in complete agreement', 'this is a prevalent problem', 'recommendation agreed on in general'. There are a few suggestions as to how the recommendation might be made more forcefully ('why not to 14 years as in the European countries?) and some minor changes in terminology sought ('while the idea is good, the word overcompensated is not suitable'). Under administration, there is some criticism of Kennedy's recommendation that 'inspections should not be fault finding missions only':

> The word 'only' is revealing. Is the Inspection a fault-finding mission? Surely the persons who visit, would come mainly to exchange views and give advice, when the occasion arises.
>
> The word 'Inspector' is a come back from old ways and should be substituted.

The 'whole family' approach to the child that runs through the Kennedy recommendations found a resonance in St Anne's where Sister Carmel Staunton had already written on the need to support parents 'who are themselves emotionally disturbed and as a result are unable to understand or deal with their children in a balanced manner'.[158] Under the section on reformatories, the absence of information on the background of children was deplored; often there was nothing more than the child's name and approximate age.[159] The community of St Anne's strongly endorsed the idea of an assessment centre, as proposed by Justice Kennedy, Staunton adding that 'a professional team of psychologists, psychiatrist, career guidance expert, social councillor worker' needed to be provided immediately by the Department of Education, until such a team of experts 'becomes available in the neighbourhood'.[160] The sisters did, however, point out that they had been seeking exactly this facility for the past few years. The need to have children assessed by a trained psychologist was recognised in OLC circles as early as 1960, based on what sisters from Dublin saw at first hand in both France (Chevilly)[161] and England (London).[162] In the formal request to the Minister for Education for funding, they presented the assessment centre as a new way 'of contacting and helping the girls for whom St Anne's was founded'. Despite 'incessant efforts' to convince the educational authorities, no support was forthcoming, 'Already they approve the idea, its benefits, but the realisation of the project is a slow and laborious

158   Memorandum, 'St Anne's residential Approved School and Remand Home Kilmacud', n.d. (DARGS, OLC3/4/3 no. 21). Hereafter, Memorandum, St Anne's, n.d.
159   Kennedy report, p. 38.
160   Ibid.
161   Sister M. Carmel Staunton to Dr McQuaid, 10 July 1960 (DDA, OLCR, Kilmacud, no. 3). Chevilly Larue, *circulaire*, 5 janvier 1964 [refers to visit of 12 Sept. 1964, date of Jan. 1964 should read Jan. 1965] (NDC, Caen: Versailles).
162   The London visit was to an unnamed centre in Sept. 1964. Sister M. Carmel Staunton to Dr McQuaid 2 Sept. 1964 (DDA, OLCR, Kilmacud, no. 3).

work'.[163] The inquiry committee had been supplied with – and (according to Staunton) ignored – a full account of the Chevilly experiment in the assessment of troubled adolescents, hence the attention drawn to it once more in her line-by-line critique of the Kennedy report.[164]

The most contentious of the Kennedy findings, as read by St Anne's, was around intake. An undated memo, which may be placed somewhere between 1959 and the early 1960s, sums up the 'type of girl accepted' into St Anne's as the school manager saw it:

> Girls committed by the court, charged with petty larceny, wandering etc., and remain with us from six months to two years. Girls sent by the health authority whose foster parents are unable to exercise control; girls transferred from other schools. Girls brought by their parents or guardians who are worried by the girl's conduct; the usual complaint is that the girl is staying away from her home for longer or shorter periods. There is marked increase in this form of misbehaviour and the girls are usually emotionally disturbed and cause friction in the home. Accommodation for 40 [30] girls including those on Remand. The average number of girls in residence is 32.[165]

There were fewer court committals, and terms of committal were becoming shorter, according to the circular letter of December 1962.[166] But, from the outset, the school had tried to broaden its intake well beyond what the Department of Education had envisaged for it. This is borne out by the *Irish Times* interview in 1966 with the principal, Sister Carmel Staunton:

> She prefers that St Anne's not be referred to as a reformatory or detention home, but the girls who live there are the ones no-one else will take – the unruly, the emotionally disturbed, the minor criminal offender. They cannot be controlled in school or at home, but they are not unstable enough to be committed to a mental institution; they are not sufficiently bright, or academically conditioned, to keep of the normal school course, but they are not retarded.[167]

The statement in the Kennedy report that 'St Anne's is reluctant to accept girls who are known to be practising prostitution' was rejected by the school in the strongest possible terms.[168] First, the labelling of any child as 'practising prostitution' was considered outrageous by Sister Carmel Staunton: 'We are not prepared to comment on a statement of this nature, the good name and

163   Sainte Anne, *circulaire*, janvier 1966.
164   St Anne's, 'Observations' c.1968–71.
165   Memorandum, St Anne's, n.d.
166   St Anne's, circular letter, Christmas 1962.
167   Maher, 'St Anne's: a home without rebels'.
168   Kennedy report, p. 38.

welfare of those admitted to St Anne's is our chief concern.[169] As to why the school did not admit girls who on conviction are found to be pregnant – a fact which is not disputed – the response is simply that 'In our opinion, pregnant girls are best helped within a family'. This was indeed a common practice in Dublin in the 1950s and 1960s, whereby 'unfortunate girls' were offered family accommodation for the duration of their pregnancy, helping out with housework or babysitting but each an individual arrangement and for the purposes of protecting the girl's privacy and independence.[170]

A recent inspection had found only three girls on the rolls had been committed by the courts as delinquent. This was due to the school refusing to accept certain cases and, according to Justice Kennedy, 'It is obvious therefore that St Anne's is not fulfilling the purpose for which it was originally founded'.[171] These claims were strongly rebuffed, before and after the publication of the Kennedy report, but to no avail. Sister Carmel argued repeatedly that 'St Anne's had been misrepresented – they never refuse to take girls except in very exceptional circumstances. Any girl is taken on trial'.[172] The committal of girls to a certified school was and always had been the prerogative of the court; the school could do nothing to influence it. There was no evidence to support the claim that St Anne's had refused 'certain types of offenders', but rather there was ample evidence to prove the contrary:

> It would be worth while in the interest of justice to ascertain how often admission for committal was sought for by the courts and refused by the school authority from among the 341 girls on remand at St Anne's from 1965–70.[173]

That St Anne's was not fulfilling its founding purpose was dismissed out of hand; the world had moved on, and so should child welfare policy:

> It seems an opportune time to state that we consider the present legislation regarding young persons completely outmoded and futile. It is incredible that the same thinking would be expected in 1970 as in 1944.[174]

The right of school managers to admit or to refuse any young person was, St Anne's maintained, a principle that ought to be preserved; Justice Kennedy saw this as the nub of the problem whereby, if certain offenders were refused admission, 'the only course open to the courts is to place them on probation or to release them'. Girls charged with 'recurring sexual offences or found to be pregnant' were, Kennedy maintained, generally refused by the reformatory schools. The girls, knowing this, had little regard 'for the authority of the

169    St Anne's, 'Observations' c.1968–71.
170    The author has this information on the authority of her mother, Agnes Prunty.
171    *Reformatory and industrial schools systems report, 1970* (Dublin, 1970), p. 37.
172    Apostolate committee, minutes, 20 Aug. 1969 (DARGS, OLC5/5/7 no. 2).
173    St Anne's, 'Observations' c.1968–71.
174    Ibid.

courts'.[175] St Anne's claim, that it did not have a record of refusing girls in the first place, was not taken up. In any case, there were other girls' reformatory schools about which the criticism was most likely valid.

There was one further area of contention between St Anne's and Kennedy, namely the matter of funding. St Anne's took issue with the way in which its unique payment arrangements were presented, whereby 'payment is made on a notional number of 40, regardless of the number of girls actually detained there at a particular time'.[176] While the point was true, anybody reading the report would presume that, at present, the school was receiving payment for 40 girls, while there were only three in residence. The failure to take account of the 'voluntary' girls in the school or the remand cases was seen as a gross distortion of reality, with the postscript: 'in other circumstances these criticisms would have been challenged at a higher level'.[177]

The school's attitude to its statutory role as a place of detention can be deduced from its response to the Kennedy report, in which it states its agreement with its legal recommendations and endorsement of early intervention.[178] But this did not mean a complete break with short-stay remand girls aged under 17, which Sister Carmel Staunton at least continued to see as a service St Anne's could provide.[179] St Anne's followed up its response to the Kennedy report with an appeal to protect 'wayward children' from the stigma of a court appearance and a criminal label. This could be done, as in England, through a new structure that had the power to intervene before court proceedings became inevitable: 'With a properly organised team, the Family Court would we hope be a concrete means of keeping a family together, about which we all agree.'[180]

Sister Carmel Staunton need not have troubled herself with putting together such a considered response to the Kennedy report for, as a published document, its version of the story became the only one in circulation. But the misrepresentation of St Anne's – that it refused girls sent to it – rankled, to judge from the repeated rejection of the claim. Justice Kennedy found that there were at least 70 girls between the ages of 13 and 19 currently in convents or adult refuges 'who should properly be dealt with under the reformatory system'.[181] This was exactly what St Anne's had been set up to prevent, but to scapegoat St Anne's for the fact that it was still happening seems, from the documentary evidence, to be somewhat unfair.

St Anne's, Kilmacud, had been started in 1944 at the behest of the archbishop and to meet a specific need identified by the Department of Education. In practice, most of the children who ended up there via the district court were there for the same reasons that saw children committed to

175   Kennedy report, p. 38.
176   Ibid.
177   Typed memorandum, 'Submitted to Department of Education 14/12/'70' (DARGS, OLC3/4/3 no. 18).
178   St Anne's, 'Observations' c.1968–71.
179   Apostolate committee, minutes, 20 Aug. 1969; see also opposition to continuing remand, St Anne's local council, minutes, 26 June 1971.
180   Memorandum titled 'New legislation', appendix to St Anne's, 'Observations' c.1968–71 (DARGS, OLC3/4/3 no. 13).
181   Kennedy report, p. 39.

other reformatories and industrial schools – the poverty and failures of their parents and the historic preference in Ireland for institutional confinement over family or 'outdoor' social welfare assistance. The year the school opened, 1944, was also the year that children's allowances were introduced in Ireland. Though small and for third and subsequent children only, even that addition to the family income could make all the difference to a very poor family and carried no stigma (it was not means-tested or contributory).[182] While its impact cannot be quantified, it did play a role in decreasing the numbers of children ending up in industrial schools, while a greater reluctance among judges to commit children for lengthy periods, if at all, can be tracked from the 1940s onwards. Even as the new school opened its doors, therefore, the number in residential institutions generally was set to fall. In St Anne's, the 'court girls', from 1949 onwards, whether on committal orders or short-stay remand orders, were a small part only of what would turn out to be a more mixed intake which defies simple classification. By the late 1960s, the tide had turned against institutional care, and so much else had changed as well. The response of St Anne's community to the Kennedy report concluded with the statement 'We desire to participate in the formation of policy and the shaping of a new system.[183] The Kilmacud school had been a place for testing out new approaches to the care of teenage girls since its foundation and the sisters, under Carmel Staunton, had certainly moulded the 19th-century reformatory and industrial school system into something different, albeit no-one could quite decide how it might be categorised.

182   Moira Maguire, *Precarious childhood in post-independence Ireland* (Manchester, 2010), p. 45, note 43.
183   St Anne's, 'Observations' *c.*1968–71.

# Chapter 9

# Hostels and Other Initiatives for Teenagers at High Park, Sean MacDermott Street and St Anne's, Kilmacud, 1950–72

The winds of change that were blowing across a devastated Europe post-1945 did reach Ireland and the monasteries, magdalen asylums and reformatory schools of Our Lady of Charity of Refuge, though in ways that might not be immediately recognised.

The monastery of Caen had been wiped out by Allied bombing and would never be rebuilt.[1] The opening of a massive new complex in 1949 designed on modern and 'scientific' principles for displaced girls, and located in a new suburb at some distance from the old quayside, did mark the continuity of the work of the order, but now articulated in the most up-to-date language.[2] Caen, the bastion of tradition and guardian of the very spirit of the institute, was 'changed, changed utterly', and other OLC houses could see that for themselves. While it is impossible to make direct causal connections, post-war Caen would no longer act as a brake on innovation elsewhere. It could not halt the move towards closer collaboration between houses, with the exigencies of war forcing a federation on the monasteries of France, and moves already afoot in the US and Britain (chapter 7).

For OLC in Ireland, the small, new reformatory school of St Anne's, opened in 1944 (chapter 8), allowed for experimentation and the introduction of 'modern' ideas. Changes in the government structures of the congregation were intended to push forward change – in particular, to loosen the model of asylum or refuge within the enclosure, which was still the principal ministry of the two larger houses, High Park and Gloucester Street/Sean MacDermott Street. The federation of the three Dublin monasteries of Our Lady of Charity in 1948, forced through by archbishop John Charles McQuaid, was expressly to allow for the creation of a central novitiate and the better 'technical training' of the sisters. Interchange between the monasteries, it was hoped, would revitalize the works in each, if for no other reason than that the sisters would know something of what happened outside their own enclosure. The further education of the sisters 'for the fulfilment of their works' was expressly promoted, pushing open the door to qualifications in

---

1  Caen, circular letter, 'to be forwarded to houses in America, England and High Park', 20 July 1944 (DARGS, OLC1/3/2, no. 110).
2  René Dubosq, *Le nouveau 'berceau' de Notre-Dame de Charité du Refuge de Caen* (Caen, n.d. but 1948), pp 4–5, 7.

childcare, teaching, social work, nursing and other fields over the next de-cades.[3] The first, tentative step was travelling to outside lectures (from 1950); attendance at a course on psychology in 1957 given by Revd Dr O'Doherty to the Higher Diploma in Education students at University College Dublin was one of the earliest opportunities for professional training availed of by sisters from all three houses.[4] Federation did not change the core business of the institute, which had always been articulated in the language of the constitutions as working wholeheartedly with girls and women who had fallen into the disorder or confusion of a dissolute life and who, touched by the grace of God, wished to turn around their lives.[5] However, a short ad-dition to the first constitution, voted through at the general chapter of 1951, made it clear that the old system of offering a safe home or refuge, where the women worked alongside the sisters towards the upkeep of the house, would no longer be good enough: 'To achieve this purpose [of keeping girls from 'vice'] measures shall be taken to organise a system of instruction and education in keeping with modern needs, so as to fit the young persons for their life in the world'.[6]

The hostel was the new model of care that was being urged on the sisters at the start of the 1950s by both secular and Church authorities, and which they knew (from their circular letters) the more progressive OLC houses in France, USA, Canada and Britain were already experimenting with. In-structing them to press forward with their plans for a hostel at St Anne's, Kilmacud, in October 1953, John Charles McQuaid stated bluntly, 'All your Houses should have a Hostel and it will interest you to know that years ago I urged another Religious Community to have such a Hostel, for without it, they could do only a fraction of the good they ought to do'.[7] What was under-stood was a home to which young women would return after a day's work outside, paying something towards their keep, however modest their wag-es, and actively involving themselves in the management of the household through budgeting, shopping, cooking and cleaning. The hostel was intend-ed as a practical training in life-skills for those who were on the threshold of independent living or who, having failed already to manage for themselves (or never having been given a fair chance), needed some support as they tried to put their lives on track. The concepts of transition, rehabilitation, taking responsibility for self and showing responsibility towards those with whom

3   'Decree of amalgamation', Preamble to minutes of meetings of general council of the federation, Union of the three monasteries of the order of Our Lady of Charity of Refuge in the archdiocese of Dublin, amalgamated 5 Nov. 1948, p. 13 (DARGS, OLC5/5/1 no. 1). The minutes of the meetings are hereafter abbreviated Irish federation general council, minutes.
4   Irish federation general council, minutes, 16 Jan. 1957.
5   'Règles et constitutions pour les religieuses de Notre-Dame de Charité, édition entièrement conforme au texte original [1682] avec des introductions et des notes', *Oeuvres Complètes de Bienheureux Jean Eudes*, x (Vannes, 1909), Constitution i, De la fin de cet institut, et des motifs qui doivent porter celles qui le professent à en faire de bon cœur les fonctions, p. 80.
6   *Additions and amendments to the constitutions of the Order of Our Lady of Charity of Refuge, in accordance with the decree of the Sacred Congregation of Religious, dated 28 June 1948, and the rescript of the same Sacred Congregation dated 12 Feb. 1951* (Dublin, 1951), p. 43. Hereafter, *Constitutions, 1951 additions.*
7   John C. McQuaid to Revd Mother M. Carmel [Staunton], 1 Oct. 1953, copy letter (DARGS, OLC3/2/2 no. 9a).

they shared the accommodation, all featured in the internal explanations of what, for OLC, was the purpose of a hostel. It was always intended to be a temporary home for whatever number of month – or even one or two years – the girl needed, a point about which everyone was clear from the outset. As a step-up facility, it would meet the urgent need of the girl making the transition from institutional life (industrial school, reformatory or orphanage) to the adult world of work and who had no family or other support at this crucial juncture. It would replace the self-contained magdalen asylum for those who ended up there for the want of a more suitable alternative. This included young women aged 16 to 21 found guilty of offences, who needed to give the court an undertaking to reside at a fixed address before they could be given the benefit of the Probation of Offenders Act (1907). Up to now, they were using the asylums without anyone expecting that they would stay beyond the time of their sentence (if indeed they stayed that long) and without (it was feared) reaping much benefit from the time spent therein.

The after-care hostel run by the sisters of Our Lady of Charity in Bitterne, Southampton (diocese of Portsmouth), by an Irish woman, Sister Agnes Ennis, merits special notice, as it was held up as a model by John Charles McQuaid when he urged representatives from all three Dublin monasteries to visit in 1953 that they might to see for themselves how things could be different.[8] The new hostel was but part of the post-war modernisation of the magdalen refuge and reformatory school work then under way in Bitterne and supported by the UK welfare state. Through the annual circular letters faithfully compiled by Agnes Ennis, the sisters in all the Dublin houses already knew something of the high standards the sisters in Bitterne had set themselves and the progress made to date. In the hostel, the girls had their own bedrooms with hot and cold water (1949), went to outside work (1947), involved themselves in parish events (1949) and brought friends, including nice young Catholic men, back to the hostel where they had their own band to enliven social events (1949). Every aspect of the new system was, according to their own account, designed to encourage independent and upright living, but without prejudice to the spiritual good of the young women which would always be the first care of the OLC sisters. Catechetical instruction, retreat days, opportunities for Mass, Holy Communion and confession were scrupulously attended to, the Blessed Sacrament was reserved in the hostel, as well as in the convent, and there were frequent talks of an uplifting or encouraging nature given by priests and sisters. Underpinning this enlightened approach was an acceptance that all their sisters needed to hold recognised qualifications, with both younger and older members attending approved courses from at least 1947 in child welfare, teaching and nursing.[9]

8  Same to same, 15 Oct. 1953 (DARGS, OLC3/2/2 no. 9b); these were Sister Rita Cutler, bursar of High Park (and superior 1957–60), Sister Immaculate Heart Walshe, bursar of Gloucester Street (and superior 1955–8), and Sister Carmel Staunton, St Anne's, Kilmacud. They visited Bitterne, Southampton, 'in order to see how the hostel and other works there were organised', and also visited the monasteries of Waterlooville (also in Portsmouth diocese) and Bartestree (Cardiff diocese), before returning to Dublin on 6 Nov. 1953, Irish federation general council, minutes, 26 Oct. 1953.
9  Bitterne, circular letters, 1 Dec. 1946; 24 Dec. 1947; 24 Dec. 1948; 1 Dec. 1949 (DARGS, OLC1/3/3 nos. 31–5).

The hostel was a novel concept for the sisters of Our Lady of Charity in 1950s Dublin. It had greater potential for creative work with young people than the refuges for women where there were long-established routines, practically no state (and very little private) funding (hence the relentless pressure of generating an income, via the laundries) and a long-resident core population of older women and sisters, who could cope with incremental change, but not with anything touching on revolution. The very notion of a hostel was problematic in that it disrupted the stability, regularity, predictability and good order that was a hallmark of the cloistered religious life. Though not bound to it by solemn vows, the sisters had always observed enclosure, and the residential schools and refuges operated within the enclosure. A hostel, by definition, would involve comings and goings, personal freedoms and minimum timetabling, and the internal dynamics would depend more on the relationships among the girls resident at any one time than on anything the sister appointed to run the hostel might try to impose. But it was not alien to the spirit of the order, in that the sisters had always been concerned about providing a 'safe place' for girls and women at risk of ending up in crime and prostitution. Homelessness, as anyone could see for themselves, was the surest road to an unhappy end. The statutory obligation on the sisters to monitor and report on the progress of past-pupils of their industrial schools (to age 18) and reformatory schools (to age 19), was still in place, though it did not extend to non-court or 'voluntary' cases.[10] This oversight or 'friendly interest' worked only insofar as the girl herself was willing to keep in touch. But as some girls certainly did maintain contact, the sisters heard first-hand of the very real difficulties young people without good family, suitable friends or a kind employer faced, no matter what was done for them during their schooldays.

Although their primary responsibility was to their own past-pupils making the transition to independence, former industrial school girls from elsewhere were always among those who ended up in the refuges at High Park and Sean MacDermott Street. Under the Children Act 1908 a child was not to be sentenced to detention in an industrial school beyond their 16th birthday (as discussed in chapters 5 and 8). However, the same legislation placed the child under the supervision of the school up to the age of 18 years.[11] Under the Children Act 1941, the Minister for Education, in consultation with the school, could extend the obligation of post-discharge supervision to 21 years where it was deemed necessary for the 'protection and welfare of the young person'.[12] The managers of these schools were therefore obliged to ensure each child on leaving the school had a safe place to stay, at least until they were able to make arrangements of their own. Some of the schools throughout Ireland sent girls they could not otherwise place to the 'safety' of any one of a number of women's asylums in the bigger cities and towns.[13] The age of the girl, as entered in the High Park register, can be used to deduce whether she came directly from an industrial school or had

---

10    Children Act 1908, section 68.
11    The same regulation applied to reformatory school children up to the age of 19 years. Children Act 1908, sections 65, 68.
12    Children (Amendment) Act 1941, section 14.
13    *Final report of the Inter-Departmental Committee set up to establish the facts of State involvement with the Magdalen Laundries* (Dublin, 2013), chapter 10, para. 6.

misadventures in between. Other former industrial school girls came of their own volition when other arrangements (if there were any) had broken down and they found themselves without a place to sleep. However they arrived, it was only too obvious that former residents of institutions were an especially marginalised and friendless group, without the skills that would enable them to hold their own in a much-oversupplied labour market, and in need of the personal interest, aftercare and training in responsibility that the hostel aimed to provide.

There were developments in thinking around education, social welfare, religious life and missionary activity in the Catholic Church at large in the post-war and 1950s period and, though overtaken by the upheavals of Vatican II, it was already clear to many theologians and others that standing still was not an option. As noted elsewhere, federation in 1948 brought with it new reporting requirements that forced the Irish leadership of OLC to reflect at least on progress over the preceding five years and to submit to Rome plans or intentions for the further development of its mission.[14] The decrees of Vatican II, and the process of renewal it precipitated, turned the order on its head from the mid-1960s, as it did with other institutes also. The speed and scale of change that swept across religious institutes from about 1965 was without precedent, and contemporary changes in work and ministry must be viewed against this backdrop. But even before the whirlwind that was set in motion by the teachings of Vatican II, the signs of a widespread desire for – and expectation of – change can be read.

On the national scale, though not engaged militarily in the war, Ireland was not insulated from the social change and new habits of thinking that were gaining momentum in Britain and throughout the continent. The influence of newspapers, radio, cinema and television, allied to the reality of mass emigration, as Louise Fuller has explored, opened up the country to outside influences in a way that could not be controlled, much less halted.[15] Change on an unprecedented scale, and affecting especially the distinctive Catholicism of the independent state, was imminent. This, according to Fuller, was sensed by the Irish bishops who warned against the inroads that were being made by a more individualistic, secular, materialistic culture.[16] The more astute among them – which certainly included John Charles McQuaid – invested some of their energy in modernising projects which any educated Catholic could see were badly needed and long overdue. The Catholic Social Welfare Bureau was but one of the organisations over which McQuaid presided – in spirit if not always in person – and to which he introduced the OLC sisters, telling them to attend its meetings and update themselves on the new thinking in social welfare that it represented.[17]

A study of the hostels and homes for teenagers run by the sisters of Our Lady of Charity from about 1950 to the early 1970s must range over several different projects with different chronologies in four different parts of the city. Whatever the enthusiasm for the hostels, all of them dealt with much smaller numbers than the schools and refuges, which continued to operate

14   *Constitutions, 1951 additions*, p. 33.
15   Louise Fuller, *Irish Catholicism since 1950, the undoing of a culture* (Dublin, 2002), pp 37–51.
16   Ibid., p. 49.
17   McQuaid to M. Carmel, 1 Oct. 1953.

alongside them. There was never a question of abandoning or replacing the schools and refuges; the hostels were understood as a new layer of activity, the most up-to-date manifestation of the spirit of the order in Dublin, but not its principal or sole work and not the only field to which the sisters would have liked the epithet 'modern' to be applied. For John Charles McQuaid, the hostels marked 'the first breach' in the old asylum system in which the sisters had imprisoned themselves.[18] As McQuaid rightly understood, taking on this new work had a significance that went well beyond the small numbers involved. He himself had an unflagging enthusiasm for hostels and a belief in their efficacy, based probably on his involvement with the boys' hostel in Eccles Street, and there was no danger of his leaving the OLC sisters out of his plans for expansion, even when they themselves felt fully stretched.[19]

There are numerous parallels between the development of hostels for working girls, the provision of separate training and accommodation for the teenagers and younger women in the refuges, the upgrading and remodelling of the refuges themselves (chapters 11 and 12) and the implementation of new practices in childcare and after-care at St Joseph's industrial school Whitehall (chapter 5) and at St Anne's reformatory school Kilmacud (chapter 8). The system of 'family group homes', developed most fully in The Grange from 1956, is also part of the new thinking in OLC in Dublin and, with its hostel, merits discussion in its own right (chapter 10). Credit must also be given, in part at least, to the vision and energy of particular sisters who saw in the local situation how things might be different and made room for new ideas. Sister Carmel Staunton of St Anne's, Kilmacud (resident manager from 1944, sister-in-charge 1944–50, superior 1950–59 and 1962–71) was probably the lead player, and recognised as such by Archbishop McQuaid with whom she worked closely, as is evident from their extensive correspondence. She had a most able assistant at Kilmacud in Sister Veronica McCarthy. The principal mover in High Park was Mother Eithne O'Neill (federal superior 1948–60 and 1965–71) with the support of Sister Columba Cunningham (with the women) and Sister Aloysius Pilkington (with the children). In Sean MacDermott Street, it was the appointment of one of the first social science graduates, Sister Lucy Bruton, in 1970 that set in motion the long-overdue revamping of the welfare services on offer there. What was achieved – or at least attempted – in the hostels informed what was tried in other settings. Common to all the work with young people was a drive towards a more personalised experience in a more 'homely' setting, in line with the new thinking on child welfare and small groups.[20] The hostels, therefore, were more than small stand-alone projects; they were interconnected, philosophically and practically, with the other works of the federation that were going on at the time.

It is difficult to disentangle the hostel and other teenage welfare developments of Our Lady of Charity in Dublin in the 1950s and 1960s. The refurbishment of premises or portion of a premises, re-use under another title, the transfer of groups between buildings and the renaming which was

18    Ibid.
19    High Park, circular letter, 8 Dec. 1966 (DARGS, OLC1/3/1 no. 31).
20    'The coming year will see the progress of the grouping system, which is not only approved but strongly recommended by the Educational authorities', St Anne's, circular letter, Christmas 1958 (DARGS, OLC3/3/1 no. 7).

all part of the new was no doubt crystal clear to the parties involved at the time, but makes for a complex story at this remove. Added to this are ideas which, despite the many meetings, letters and architects' plans that were generated, did not reach fruition or were swallowed up in another project. Matters were brought up at council meetings, and were duly minuted, that had no follow-through. One issue that resurfaces periodically is an unease with having anything to do with remand, and the difficulties the sisters had in extricating themselves from historic and statutory arrangements, stretching their co-operation until the state had ready a new female prison with remand accommodation which, though promised for 1974 (in Kilbarrack) and earlier (on various sites), still had not happened.[21] The autonomy of each monastery must also be underscored; the type of federal structure accepted in 1948 by the three monasteries of High Park, Gloucester Street (Sean MacDermott Street) and Kilmacud, left the initiative to the local community. When The Grange was set up in May 1956, despite its small size it, too, quickly prided itself on its autonomy. The isolation of the houses was compounded by enclosure, which was maintained until the implementation of Vatican II reforms in the 1970s, and by injunctions not to tell the business of the house to outsiders which (it seems) was applied even to sisters from the other houses of the federation. The superior general could communicate the opinions or desires of the arch-bishop, of government departments and of others, but she did not – and could not – dictate what was to be done. She knew only whatever she was told or shown; she did not have the powers to enquire much further. Projects in each of the four monasteries (from 1956) therefore ran in parallel, rather than in concert. Not until the creation of the apostolate committee in 1969 in line with the new openness promoted by Vatican II was there a body to promote communication across the federation. That Sean MacDermott Street lagged behind High Park in terms of teenage provision, and that both lagged behind St Anne's, Kilmacud, in embracing the hostel model, is therefore no surprise. The introduction of legal adoption in 1952, for orphans and for children born outside marriage, marks a watershed in the history of childcare in Ireland, with the numbers of children ending up in the care of the state in industrial schools set to fall drastically. The year 1953, when all houses celebrated the centenary of the first Dublin community of High Park, was a landmark for the order in Ireland. Even while the docility and penitence of the asylum residents was being lauded in the handbook produced to mark the occasion, Mother Eithne O'Neill – in her role as mother general – was convening meetings at High Park and at Gloucester Street to see what local plans might satisfy the archbishop's insistence that they move towards modernising their methods.[22] The hostel for girls was but one step towards what McQuaid saw as the larger project of dismantling, 'as soon as we can, the present Penitentiary system'.[23] The publication of the report on reformatory and industrial school systems in Ireland in 1970 (under the chairmanship of Justice Eileen Kennedy) and its follow-up, the CARE report of 1972 – produced by a consortium of social workers, which included Sister Aloysius Pilkington of Our Lady of Charity

21   'Report on the work of the Apostolate Committee, appointed August 1969', 1972, p. 10 (DARGS, OLC5/5/7 no. 1). Hereafter, Apostolate committee report.
22   Irish federation general council, minutes, 9 Feb. 1953.
23   McQuaid to M. Carmel, 15 Oct. 1953.

(High Park) – throws light on what was generally agreed in social work circles at that time. The raising of the obligatory school leaving age to 15 years in 1972 also helped focus attention on the needs of vulnerable teenagers, while research papers of the mid-1970s on the 'subcult of the teenager' show how adolescent psychology and sociological studies on the influence of environment had come to prominence.[24] The early 1970s is a suitable point at which to close this discussion. What follows post-Kennedy requires a full study in its own right – based on an understanding of what had been done up to then and the new discourses and experiments of the 1960s.

## St Anne's Hostel, Kilmacud

The need to attach a hostel to St Anne's reformatory school, Kilmacud, as a step-up or transition facility was evident from its first year of operation.[25] In the formal review submitted to the Department of Education for the school year ending 31 July 1945, the resident manager noted that

> the after care of this particular type of girl is a problem – so many are unfit to stand alone. Were we in a position to allow those girls who are discharged and have no proper home, to take up daily work and live here, we believe good would be done.[26]

The same point is made in 1946 and again in 1947: 'the need of a hostel for the after-care of these girls is more apparent as time goes on'.[27] There was no movement on the part of the government department – and not surprisingly, as this would incur new costs for the taxpayer. But when Kilmacud House – the property of Colonel Dwyer, and sited across the road from St Anne's – came on the market in 1948, the sisters moved swiftly to secure the approbation of the archbishop for its purchase and use as a ladies' guesthouse. The principal advocate was Sister Carmel Staunton whose line of argument was: 'in time I hope Kilmacud House will keep the good work at St Anne's'.[28] The archbishop was persuaded. He commended their foresight and courage, noting that it would generate a steady income for St Anne's, create paid work opportunities for past pupils and 'supply a very serious need in the present condition of things, when so many aged ladies find it impossible to obtain

---

24  For example, see university paper titled 'The modern teenager in his environment, a project', study and research by Muriel Fortune, Sister Carmel Gorman, Mary Lee, Denis Cormican, Sister Mary Wall, Sister M. Aloysius, May 1975 (DARGS, OLC, Archives library).

25  St Anne's, Kilmacud was opened as a reformatory school on 2 Feb. 1944, received girls aged 12 to 17 on remand from the courts from 1945, and was further certified as an industrial school in 1949, without losing its reformatory status. See Children (Amendment) Act 1949, statutory instrument no. 231 of 1949.

26  Report for year 1 Aug. 1944–31 July 1945, Scoil Ceartúchain, Cill Mochuda, required by Department of Education, signed M. Carmel Staunton. The earliest extant report covers the 12 months to 31 July 1944, the latest covers the 12 months to 31 July 1958 (DARGS, OLC3/4/3 no. 7). Hereafter, St Anne's, annual school report [for named year].

27  St Anne's, annual school report for year 1 Aug. 1945 to 31 July 1946; for year 1 Aug. 1946 to 31 July 1947.

28  Sister M. Carmel Staunton to Dr McQuaid, 10 Nov. 1948 (DDA, OLCR, Kilmacud, no. 1).

domestic help'.[29] Council minutes recording the dates of the legal transfer reiterate the reasons behind its acquisition and use as a guest house.[30] As well as being a source of income to the community at St Anne's,

> it will be a means of extending the work for the reformation of the girls received in the school. Those who wish to remain on after their term of detention has expired, will be employed as maids in the guest house, and the sisters will thus be enabled to exercise supervision over them.[31]

The girls would occupy separate sleeping quarters in St Anne's, but other-wise 'enjoy all the amenities of girls earning for themselves'.[32] They were free to leave as soon as they wished or, for those who showed no inclination to move on, until such time as the sisters considered them fit 'to take their place in the world'.[33] Something similar was already in operation since 1919 at High Park, where past pupils of the school could find temporary employment in St Michael's guesthouse. From the end of January 1949, two of the eight sisters at Kilmacud moved into the new guesthouse[34] and, in April, the number was augmented by the transfer of Sister Mary of St Declan Leary from High Park to help with the work.[35] The oratory was blessed on 8 December 1949 by the chancellor of the diocese, Richard Glennon, and the Christmas letter for 1950 reported that 'Since then the house is full and while helping these old people to live comfortably and die happily we are encouraged to see our girls develop a sense of responsibility and an appreciation of true values'.[36] There was a steady demand among 'aged ladies' for places, according to internal correspondence, providing for its residents 'the care and tranquillity God sends as a reward at the evening of life'.[37] The reasons given for admission were reported as 'Ladies who have sold their homes; elderly ladies who do not want to live with their married sons and daughters'.[38]

There was a certain refinement about Kilmacud House which no doubt added to its attractions in the eyes of the women who made it their retire-ment home. It was architecturally impressive, with a flat roof, classical porti-co and large windows, an elegant wrought-iron staircase, moulded cornices and door surrounds, and distinguished fireplaces. The furniture was varied and comfortable, more akin to a private home than a nursing home. The

29   John C. McQuaid to Revd Mother M. of St Eithne, 3 Nov. 1938 (DARGS, OLC3/1/2 no. 3).
30   Mother Mary Carmel Staunton took possession of Kilmacud House on 2 Feb. 1949, 'and made arrangements for the necessary alterations.' Mgr Glennon, chancellor, with His Grace's permission, celebrated Mass in Kilmacud House on 8 Feb. 1949 and 'the dining room was prepared as an oratory for the occasion', Irish federation general council, minutes, 30 Jan. 1949, 2 Feb. 1949.
31   Irish federation general council, minutes, 30 Jan. 1949.
32   St Anne's, circular letter, Christmas 1950 (DARGS, OLC3/3/1 no. 1).
33   Ibid.
34   Ibid.
35   Irish federation general council, minutes, 8 Apr. 1949.
36   St Anne's, circular letter, Christmas 1950.
37   St Anne's, circular letter, Christmas 1951 (DARGS, OLC3/3/1 no. 2).
38   Apostolate committee report, p. 18.

privilege of having the Blessed Sacrament reserved in the oratory of the house was made much of, and there was the security of round-the-clock care in a house where usually two of the sisters slept overnight to be available to the residents.[39]

In 1960, Kilmacud House was described as 'a safe and profitable training ground for some of our girls during and after their period of detention in the school', the implication being that girls coming to the end of their time in the school could be sent there on work experience.[40] A new block of 24 rooms, the infirmary corridor, was in use by 1966, and the mission of the house was summed up as giving aid to persons aged, sick or infirm while, at the same time, serving as a preparatory centre for those young girls who were without a hearth ('*sans foyer*'), parents or friends.[41]

But as a place of transition, a stepping stone to independent living for those girls ready to leave St Anne's school, the guest house did not work out at all. The girls who started there 'are not anxious to change to outdoor employment, and oftentimes it is not desirable for them to do so'.[42] The problem was that it offered live-in domestic employment in a sheltered setting, which was all very well for those who would not be able to hold their own in the world of work, but was not to be confused with the ideal of the hostel for girls in proper 'outside' employment.[43] On a practical note, if few of the girls moved on, there would hardly be space for the girls coming up behind them.

That Sister Carmel Staunton left the guesthouse to work out as best it might – useful on its own terms, but not answering the after-care needs of the target group – is evident in a report of December 1951 on a 'class' or group independent of the school, working away at knitting machines, embroidery and rug-making. A girl was paid in proportion to the value of the finished article, the money lodged to her own account in the post office, a local shop agreeing 'to take any work we wish to dispose of before our Annual Display'.[44] The sale of handicrafts was hardly going to generate the kind of income these past pupils needed to support themselves independently, but the hope was expressed that it might sow the seeds of something more. For the present, at least, it would bring 'a measure of stability and security into the lives of those whom we are endeavouring to make safe for Heaven'.[45] On 1 October 1953, following a visit to Kilmacud, the archbishop gave unstinting approval in principle to the hostel, which Sister Carmel Staunton had been pushing for all along.[46] The initial plan was to alter and extend T-shaped outbuildings – stables, cowhouse, loft – into a hostel with 14 to 16 bedrooms, sanitary accommodation, recreation, kitchen and dining rooms. However, both the architect and the archbishop condemned the plans on numerous grounds, and the hostel girls were accommodated separate to

---

39   St Anne's, circular letter, Christmas 1950.
40   St Anne's, circular letter, Christmas 1960 (DARGS, OLC3/3/1 no. 9).
41   St Anne's, *circulaire*, janvier 1966 (DARGS, OLC3/3/1 no. 11).
42   St Anne's, circular letter, Christmas 1951.
43   St Anne's, circular letter, Christmas 1957 (DARGS, OLC3/3/1 no. 6).
44   St Anne's, circular letter, Christmas 1951.
45   Ibid.
46   McQuaid to M. Carmel, 1 Oct. 1953.

the other girls in the main house.[47] Only a classroom and laundry, in a one-storey building, were erected at the time – and they did not come cheap.[48]

The description 'St Bernadette's Hostel, where working girls are accommodated' is used in 1960, and its relationship to the school is spelled out:

> Generally speaking it is the ambition of the girls in the school to take up residence in the Hostel when their term of detention in the school has expired and we encourage this idea, especially for those whose return to unfavourable home-conditions would mean the undoing of the reform so hardly won during their period of detention, and also for some who are in fact homeless, and who would be ill-equipped as yet to live independently elsewhere.[49]

OLC reports on the hostel, as one would expect, emphasise the positive, but there is no avoiding the fact that few of the girls were able to manage outside employment, despite opportunities in the wealthy suburbs of south Dublin for those who could be recommended. The training on offer was practical rather than 'literary' or academic, with an emphasis on home-making, cookery, dressmaking and handicrafts and with the sisters themselves undertaking courses in dressmaking and crafts that they might have something more to pass on to the girls.[50] Spiritual helps were extended to the hostel girls, including weekly religious instruction and frequent access to the sacraments.[51] The older girls joined the younger schoolchildren on occasion for outings and films, and they all made their annual retreat together.[52] But far from requiring less of the sisters, the hostel girls presented with many problems, and 'training for this particular work is most necessary'.[53]

One further hostel or step-up facility developed on the Kilmacud campus was 'Girlsville', opened in May 1970 in a compact two-storey annex with space for ten or 12 girls, in the old stables that had been written off some years earlier. This was taking personal responsibility and community living quite a bit further than what was supposed to be the working girls' hostel, and much further than was ever expected of the guesthouse. The name 'Girlsville' was used to try to break the association with St Anne's: 'Over the years, we were conscious that when girls left St Anne's a shadow followed them; Girlsville is an effort to free them of this handicap'. While it was claimed that six of the first ten girls were already working, in reality only one girl held down an outside job, in charge of a laundrette in Blackrock. Five more were attending 'a type of sheltered workshop on our premises', probably a successor to the earlier handicraft enterprise, and the others were attending school at

---

47   John Aylward to Revd Mother M. Carmel, 'Proposed Girls Hostel', 10 Oct. 1953, copy (DARGS, OLC3/2/2 no. 9c); McQuaid to M. Carmel, 15 Oct. 1953.
48   High Park local council, minutes, 12 May 1960 (DARGS, OLC1/5/2 no. 1).
49   St Anne's, circular letter, Christmas 1960.
50   St Anne's, circular letter, Christmas 1957.
51   St Anne's, circular letter, Christmas 1956 (DARGS, OLC3/3/1 no. 5).
52   St Anne's, circular letter, Christmas 1959 (DARGS, OLC3/3/1 no. 8).
53   St Anne's, circular letter, Christmas 1957.

St Anne's. 'Girlsville' was to be run entirely by the girls themselves, 'one of whom will be selected by them to act as girl in charge', with the services of a 'highly qualified retired hospital matron' and one of the sisters available to them when needed.[54] That it was a lively but short-lived venture, at least in this unstructured form, is not surprising.

## High Park Teenage Group, Training Centre and An Grianán

The concept of a hostel for working girls was slower to gain favour in High Park, where sisters in the early 1950s were much more engaged with earlier stages, namely, trying to get some of the women in St Mary's Refuge ready and able to take up outside employment.[55] The particular concern was the youngest cohort, those girls aged 16 or 17 to 20 years. For the most part, they had few skills to bring to the jobs market and little prospect, as things stood, of setting up home for themselves. It was for these girls that the first modest training programme opened on 22 June 1955, with a teacher qualified in home economics and a first enrolment of 18 pupils.[56] The venue was a newly-equipped classroom on the ground floor of St Mary's to which the girls and younger women were taken for part of the day to give them the 'further training in cooking and sewing' that, it was hoped, would help them find employment on leaving St Mary's (see chapter 11).[57] What was termed 'emphasis on rehabilitation of teenagers in St Mary's' is dated internally to 1962.[58] It was among these younger girls that the 'group system' was first implemented in St Mary's when they were given their own dormitory sometime before 1965.[59] From 1971 the 'teenage group' had entirely separate living quarters in the first floor 'flatlet', and the title 'Grianán Training Centre and Semi-Liberty Hostel' was used to sum up its role.[60]

The reconfiguration of the building to create a separate teenage unit was undertaken only after more ambitious plans had fallen through. Efforts had been made as early as 1960 to remove the younger girls from the refuge entirely, but the funding application for what were termed 'units for teenage or problem girls' was not successful.[61] In early 1965, the archbishop was told that plans to reconstruct a portion of St Mary's had been delayed by the builders' strike, but would now go ahead; 'this will provide a home for the rehabilitation of our teenagers who will take up employment outside'.[62] In the summer of 1968, the erection of a purpose-built training centre, including hostel accommodation and funded through the sale of some land, was discussed with

54   Resident Manager [Sister Carmel Staunton] to Tomás Ó Floinn, Department of Education, 4 May 1970 (DARGS, OLC3/4/3 no. 24).
55   McQuaid to M. Carmel, 1 Oct. 1953; High Park local council, minutes, 3 Feb. and 16 Feb. 1953.
56   Irish federation general council, minutes, 22 June 1955.
57   High Park local council, minutes, 7 Mar. 1955.
58   Apostolate committee report, p. 2.
59   Extraordinary General Chapter of the Irish Federation of the Order of Our Lady of Charity of Refuge for the election of a superior general 25–7 Jan. 1965, minor petitions presented by the monasteries, p. 2 (DARGS, OLC5/1/4).
60   Apostolate committee report, p. 2.
61   High Park local council, minutes, 12 May 1960.
62   Mother Mary Eithne O'Neill to Dr McQuaid, 12 Feb. 1965 (DARGS, OLC4).

outsiders.[63] Testimony was given as to the unmet need for hostel places for 'problem and street girls'. The Sancta Maria hostel in Harcourt Street, run by the Legion of Mary, claimed that it was forced 'to turn away over 200 deserving girls in 1968, on account of lack of accommodation'.[64] Architectural plans were drawn up for (it appears) two houses with 12 girls in each. These were duly considered by the local council and submitted to the Commissioners of Charitable Donations and Bequests.[65] Contact was made with the OLC house in Northfield (diocese of Birmingham) for advice on how they might best organise the new training centre.[66] At the end of 1970, permission was received from the city corporation to go ahead with the building, but archbishop's house brought the project to a complete halt. Monsignor Cecil Barrett, liaising on behalf of the archbishop, completely misunderstood what was envisaged (according to the sisters) 'as he wondered why the children could not attend local technical schools'.[67] That girls from High Park had been attending the vocational school in Marino since 1950 shows how little he knew of what was intended, while he appears to have conflated the school, St Joseph's, with the refuge, St Mary's. But there was no misinterpreting the 'no' that came from the archbishop, and the new training centre was abandoned.

With no prospect of being allowed to start afresh in a new building, the sisters decided in 1971 to make the most of what they had in terms of the programme that was already in place, their staff resources, both internally and from outside the order, and the accommodation on the first floor of the old refuge, which was at least reserved entirely to the teenagers. They had already managed to get the services of a visiting psychiatrist and psychologist for the girls through the Dublin Health Authority, and now decided to apply to the same body 'for approval and recognition of our Teenage Group as a Training Centre for problem adolescents', which approval came in June 1971.[68] To bring the accommodation up to date, Sister Columba Cunningham proposed plans 'patterned on those she had seen in England' for the re-making of the first floor of the refuge into a 'flatlet' for this group.[69] Following a research visit to the Sacred Heart Home in Drumcondra in March 1971, which had already been reconfigured along these lines, the work of reconstruction began. The bedrooms were single cubicles and there was a kitchen, dining room, toilets and showers.[70] The new kitchen allowed the domestic science classroom, formerly the ground floor 'training centre', to be decommissioned, and made the unit even more compact and independent.[71] A new hall door was broken through on the ground floor and a new stairway installed making the 'teenage quarters' – including access – quite distinct from the

63  High Park local council, minutes, 19 July and 9 Dec. 1968.
64  Ibid., 28 Mar. 1969.
65  Ibid., 28 Mar. and 18 Apr. 1969, 29 June 1970.
66  Apostolate committee, minutes, 11 Sept. 1969 (DARGS, OLC5/5/7 no. 1)
67  High Park local council, minutes, 10 Nov. 1970.
68  High Park local council, minutes, 13 May 1970, 15 June 1971. On 9 June 1972, An Grianán, along with Sean MacDermott Street, and St Anne's, were registered as 'places of detention for the purposes of Part V of the Children's Act, 1908', general correspondence (DARGS, OLC1/3/8 no. 1).
69  High Park local council, minutes, 2 Mar. 1971.
70  Ibid., 2 Mar. 1971, 4 May 1971, 16 Mar. 1971.
71  High Park local council, minutes, 15 June 1971, 29 June 1971.

women's quarters. By July, the new self-contained 'Teenage Unit', with space for 13 girls, was ready to be painted and decorated.[72] All now operated under the bright new title 'Grianán' or sunny place, a placename dear to the Donegal-born Sister Columba, rather than particularly apt to the new rooms.[73]

The Grianán training programme was summarised in 1972 as covering 'special teaching in academic subjects, typing lessons, industrial training and home making'; the greater part of the day was spent in class, the remainder in 'work training', with swimming, 'physical education training', elocution and 'club facilities' (organised by voluntary workers) also included. Outings were allowed 'according to individual capacity for freedom', and pocket money of 50p weekly was given to the girls.[74] The programme received the standard industrial school maintenance grant from the Department of Health of £8.25 per child per week. Its certification in 1972 as a remand home – 'for a temporary period pending the building of a new state prison for women' – meant that it was also funded by the Department of Justice for each girl that was sent there while awaiting sentencing by the courts, at a rate of £1.18 per day, with rarely more than two remand girls in the centre, never more than four, and often none.[75]

## Martanna House, High Park

The development of the 'teenage unit' and training centre in St Mary's from 1955 onwards was all very laudable, but it was not a proper hostel – that is, a place for those of St Mary's girls who would be able to cope with the world of work and independent living if only they had some place to live while making the transition. This separate and distinct project got properly under way a decade after the archbishop had urged the sisters to move into hostels.[76] In the spring of 1964, time was spent searching for a 'suitable site' in their own grounds.[77] Eventually it was agreed that the counting and sorting room of the laundry, which was near the gate onto Grace Park Road, would be re-built and a storey added. It was recognised that, while expensive, there was so much spare capacity in St Mary's it seemed better 'to make the necessary adjustments' than to add another building to the sprawling complex.[78] The new hostel, to be called Martanna House, a combination of St Martin and St Anna, had 16 bedrooms, of which one was a double room and the rest singles.

Reports on the fundraising efforts of the lay committee set up to support the venture refer to 'our hostel for young girls in St Mary's who have been

---

72   Mr Treacy was awarded the contract worth £1,328. High Park local council, minutes, 13 July 1971.
73   This teenage unit was to continue in the same building until 1990 when it was moved to 369 Collins Avenue, a purpose-built residential home in the grounds of High Park, and formerly the Cuan Mhuire building, the children's home for Our Lady's Group.
74   Apostolate committee report, p. 6.
75   Federal superior's report, 'Report on the state of the Irish federation 1970–73, Federal chapter, Irish Federation of the Order of Our Lady of Charity, minutes, 5 Oct. 1973, preliminary session, pp 1–8a (DARGS, OLC5/1/7). Apostolate committee report, p. 7.
76   McQuaid to M. Carmel, 15 Oct. 1953.
77   High Park local council, minutes, 9 Apr. 1964.
78   Ibid., 22 June 1964.

rehabilitated'.[79] Where space allowed, and over time, the Martanna House intake extended beyond former residents of St Mary's to include young women with jobs, newly-arrived in Dublin and seeking short-term hostel accommodation until they found their feet. However, in its setting up, the client group was well defined, as was its role: to be a home to which young women in need of accommodation would return after a day's work or training elsewhere, and in the running of which they would play a full part. All was with the aim of developing personal responsibility and the skills necessary to managing their own lives and their own homes. The time of residence could vary from a few weeks or months up to about two years, depending on individual needs, but for all it was a transition facility, not a long-term or permanent home.

Construction work commenced a full year after the decision to re-build the counting and sorting room, the delay – in part at least – due to a builders' strike.[80] The architect was Simon Leonard and the builders Messrs Kiernan Brothers, Kells, both of whom had been employed on other OLC projects. The estimated cost at the outset was £30,300, but other bills outside this budget came in later, including for a chimney stack in connection with the heating system (another £513), tarmac for the entrance and folding doors for the recreation room, so that the final cost was probably as high – if not higher – than the cost of a completely new premises.[81] There was, from the outset, a significant measure of outside support, starting with groups who already had connections with St Mary's through putting on concerts and visiting the women (see chapter 11). But there were also neighbours who got involved for the first time, probably attracted by the fact that this was a modern venture with (it was hoped) tangible results. When the contract was signed, a group from the Knights of St Columbanus offered to fundraise 'by organising entertainments etc. to aid this new branch of our apostolate'.[82] When the construction was completed but before the formal opening, the neighbours and friends who had set themselves up (with the archbishop's permission) as a lay committee to support Martanna House held a bring-and-buy sale in the building.[83] This was reported to be a wonderful success; no doubt the chance to see inside drew the public, as well as the obvious merits of the cause.[84] While funded from the convent and with the monies raised by the committee, public money was also sought on the basis of 'the purpose and the class of teenage girls we intend catering for'.[85] Building grants of £600 were received from the Local Government Board and from the city corporation.[86] Later in the year, a grant for £1,250 was sanctioned by the Minister for Health (thanks to the lobbying of the lay committee), bringing the state contribution to £2,450 or almost 8% of the building costs and an important political and public endorsement of the venture.[87]

79  Irish federation general council, minutes, 4 June 1966. See also High Park local council, minutes, 21 June 1966.
80  High Park local council, minutes, 30 Oct. 1964.
81  Ibid., 8 June 1965, 4 Apr. 1966, 20 Sept. 1966, 30 Jan. 1967.
82  High Park local council, minutes, 8 June 1965.
83  Ibid., 21 June 1966.
84  Irish federation general council, minutes, 4 June 1966.
85  High Park local council, minutes, 4 Feb. 1966.
86  Ibid., 4 Feb. and 21 June 1966, 17 Aug. 1966.
87  Ibid., 25 Nov. 1966, 30 Jan. and 28 Mar. 1967.

Martanna House was formally opened by the Lord Mayor of Dublin, Alderman Eugene Timmons, on 12 June 1966, and was blessed by the local parish priest, Fr John Kelly, assisted by the young chaplain, Fr Laurence Forristal. 'The architect together with members of the committee, and a number of other persons interested, were afterwards entertained at table'.[88] Martanna House was completed in 1969 with the laying of an all-weather tennis court, at a cost of £650 to include tennis posts, sockets, net, paint markings and wire surrounds.[89] A short 'home movie' made on the occasion of the blessing displays the tennis skills of the girls, which wanted only the hard court to be allowed to develop. It is also a record of their considerable talent at dancing, as well as who was present on the day of the opening.[90]

Martanna House was truly the beginning of something new – as the archbishop had hoped. The first development was a 'Club for the girls of the parish' of Marino, opened and blessed on Sunday 27 November 1966.[91] For clubhouse, a room in St Mary's was given, along with the right to use the Martanna House sports facilities.[92] It was dedicated to the Sacred Heart, had its own chaplain and was under the direction of one of the sisters, four 'trained youth leaders' and some help on occasion from seminarians in All Hallows College.[93] Though not likely to make headlines, it was nevertheless a long-lasting engagement with parish life and an opportunity for the hostel girls to mix with other teenagers and to become better integrated socially.[94] A senior section was added in 1968 for the girls of working age in Martanna House and more generally for past pupils of their own OLC and other institutions, both boys and girls, along with other young parishioners.[95] Another development was in May 1967, on the first anniversary of the opening of Martanna House. The committee, that had done so much to engage public support for the hostel, 'expressed the desire of extending their social activities to St Mary's Home, so as to supply finance for the much-needed re-construction of the dormitories etc.'[96] The offer was accepted unanimously and a friendly, outside body became party to the modernisation efforts in the refuge (chapter 11). One further example was the decision made in September 1970 to buy a private house, 124 Grace Park Road. Though initially intended as one of three houses for the St Joseph's school children,[97] when that project fell through, it was used as an extension to Martanna House for teenagers graduating from An Grianán training centre and without homes.[98] This was closer to 'ordinary' family accommodation than anything yet developed, and moreover gave the

88    Irish federation general council, minutes, 12 June 1966.
89    High Park local council, minutes, 18 Apr. 1969.
90    'Seaside and Martanna House', July 1966, 16mm cine film (DARGS, OLC1/2/5 no. 7).
91    High Park local council, minutes, 25 Nov. 1966.
92    Ibid., 18 Apr. 1969.
93    Ibid., 18 Apr. 1969; Apostolate committee report, p. 11.
94    For a reflection on how the club assisted in the integration of the girls, see Apostolate committee, minutes, 5 Mar. 1973 (DARGS, OLC5/5/7 no. 1).
95    Apostolate committee report, p. 11.
96    High Park local council, minutes, 28 May 1967.
97    Ibid., 10 Nov. 1970.
98    Five girls from Martanna House and two sisters moved in to 124 Grace Park Road on 1 Nov. 1970. Report for Commission on the Apostolate, 1972 (DARGS, OLC5/5/7 no. 1). Hereafter, Report for Apostolate Commission on 124 Grace Park Road.

girls an address on a most respectable Dublin suburban road that could not be associated with an institution.[99] This was a step ahead of the Department of Education's circular on allowing residential homes (what remained of the 'industrial school' system post-1970) to 'have separate designations by name or street number and, where appropriate, separate addresses' – that is, for the girls to have home addresses that would not label them as 'in care'.[100] The house in Grace Park Road also accommodated working girls from the country whose families wished them to stay in a hostel until they 'get used to city life', which further helped 'to "normalise" the atmosphere of the house' and prevent – or at least reduce – the likelihood of the girls being stigmatised.[101]

## St Joseph's School Children, Past and Current, and Family Group Homes, High Park

The longest-running of all OLC childcare facilities was St Joseph's school, High Park, which opened first as a reformatory, in 1859, and was re-launched as Whitehall industrial school in 1927. It could still be used by the courts as a place of remand up to 1972.[102] The after-care of these school pupils was always a particular worry, not just because of the statutory obligation to report where they had been placed on leaving the school and the contact that had been maintained (or not) with them, but more simply because most had been reared from childhood on the High Park campus and knew no other home.

St Joseph's had a school population of 65 children in December 1950 (it had seven admissions and 16 discharges over the preceding 12 months). The children were accommodated in what was by then an old, three-storey school building (completed in 1874) with capacity for 100 children. It was the extra space within St Joseph's, and the relatively small and predictable numbers completing their schooling each year, that made possible the development of accommodation for past pupils. The residential school and its after-care facilities were kept separate in every way from the convent and from St Mary's refuge – from the teenage unit and training centre (from 1971 titled 'An Grianán') – and from Martanna House and its later, short-lived extension, 124 Grace Park Road (1970–74).[103]

St Joseph's had the physical space for a past-pupils' hostel; more importantly, the school's resident manager, Sister Aloysius Pilkington, was a staunch advocate of hostels, having watched for years for the opportunity to move the matter forward. The younger children had been attending the Holy Faith national school at Larkhill from 1953, and the older girls were enrolled in

99    Minutes of special meeting convened re purchase of small house on Grace Park Road, 18 Sept. 1970 (DARGS, OLC1/3/8 no. 1).

100   L. Ó Laidhin, Department of Education, to the Resident Manager, 4 Aug. 1972 (DARGS, SJ/4/1/2).

101   Report for Apostolate Commission on 124 Grace Park Road.

102   Apostolate committee report, p. 3. A girl who had reached her 15th birthday could not be admitted to an industrial school, but girls of 15 and 16 could be held on remand at St Joseph's.

103   A case in 1972 of a girl admitted to An Grianán, either through the district court or by the Department of Education, and whose maintenance was paid to St Joseph's School, the first instance of this arrangement, is described by the sister in charge as too complicated and not to be repeated, and the distinction between the two is emphasised. Copy letter, Sister Anne to Miss Roarty, 18 Dec. 1973 (DARGS, SJ/4/1/2 no. 18).

nearby vocational schools from 1950 onwards. The expectation that all would be making their own way in the world once they reached school-leaving age meant that the general spirit tended more towards real-world engagement and local integration than was the case (for example) in the adult OLC refuges of the time.

The 'group system' was in place at St Joseph's from 1961 and boys were accepted from 1963 when necessary, to keep the family unit together.[104] What was in fact the first hostel in High Park was created in St Joseph's in April 1964. This was the refurbishment of the 'babies' dormitory' on the second floor into a room for past pupils of the school 'who have clerical posts, but find it difficult to get accommodation, fitting room up with cubicles etc.'[105] Its successor, for a few of the girls at least, was the very small steward's lodge facing onto Collins Avenue known as 'Lourdesville' or simply 'the bungalow'.[106] This was occupied by three or four past pupils and one sister in April 1971 and continued until possession was taken of 124 Grace Park Road (displacing the St Mary's/An Grianán past pupils) in early 1974.[107] Plans to extend the steward's lodge into a fully-fledged hostel 'for the working girls from St Joseph's' were overtaken by other developments.[108]

Hostel provision in St Joseph's was linked to the opening of 'family group homes' for the schoolchildren. The Department of Education expressly urged the introduction of the 'group system' into industrial schools in the circular of 1958 announcing a long-overdue increase in the capitation grant:

> Under this system it is claimed that the children feel a greater sense of security, become more alert, make better progress at school, are generally more friendly and more easily overcome their handicaps.[109]

The 'small group' system had been recommended strongly to government departments by very many parties, including Archbishop McQuaid, over the preceding decade. The Commission on Youth Unemployment, in its report published in 1951, urged that, where institutional care is still found necessary, 'these units be re-organised on a small unit basis'.[110] The Department of Health made its preference for boarding out in foster homes over committal to an industrial school clear in 1954.[111] Sister Carmel Staunton of St Anne's, Kilmacud, proposed to the archbishop in December

---

104   Apostolate committee report, p. 2.

105   High Park local council, minutes, 1 May 1964.

106   There is a lengthy saga surrounding the repossession of the bungalow, let to an outsider, a garda, since 1965. See High Park local council, minutes, 1 June, 9 Oct., 10 Nov., 31 Dec. 1970, 11 Jan., 30 Mar., 4 May 1971.

107   Sister Teresa Coughlan OLC was the sister sleeping in 124 Grace Park Road in Nov. 1970 and the girls moved in after that date. Personal communication, 10 Oct. 2014.

108   High Park local council, minutes, 30 Mar. 1971, 4 May 1971, 15 Feb. 1972.

109   M. Ó Siochfhradha to the Resident Manager of the Industrial School named on the envelope, 14 Aibreán 1958 (DARGS, SJ/4/1/2 no. 2).

110   Quoted in the *Commission to inquire into child abuse, report* (Dublin, 2009), iv, p. 40. Hereafter, Ryan report.

111   Article 4, boarding out regulations, 1954, quoted in Ryan report, iv, p. 6.

1956 that St Joseph's industrial school children, 'a well-behaved, refined group', be removed entirely from the High Park campus to St Anne's, where something 'more in line with the English schools' could be developed. This would leave the old St Joseph's premises as a remand home, 'which it is in fact'. [112] The Catholic sociology journal *Christus Rex* published research in 1956 comparing progressive models of childcare in London with the bleak, single-sex industrial school that was still the rule in Ireland. Residential care was presented as the 'last resort' and, where it could not be avoided, only small numbers were to be reared together, in a cheerful, domestic setting, with each child having his or her own caseworker to see that the child's individual needs were recognised and to foster the child's relationships with his/her birth family during the time of separation. [113] Professional and public opinion was moving strongly in the direction of small group care, however that might be worked out in each situation. The remodelling of the first floor of St Joseph's into apartments in 1965, with family bedrooms, was the most visible manifestation of the effort to implement this type of residential care on the High Park campus. The children were placed in two groups, each with their own sister in charge: the Little Flower group and Our Lady's group, and each apartment was intended to be a self-contained – if rather large – family home.

The school principal, Sister Aloysius Pilkington, tried but failed to move the children out of the school building entirely in 1970. The superior and her local council committed the community to the purchase of 124 Grace Park Road in September 1970, a three-bedroom family home beyond the gates of High Park, but within easy reach and in excellent condition. [114] At the same time, a builder was erecting houses for sale on land opposite St Michael's guesthouse, and therefore also close to the High Park complex. The school principal consulted the builder, who was willing to make some alterations in the two houses earmarked for St Joseph's children; each had four bedrooms and cost £7,500, and all agreed 'that they were very suitable and reasonably priced'. [115] On being informed of these plans, which would have moved most – if not all – of the pupils into the kind of setting advocated by everyone with an interest in residential childcare, the wrath of archbishop's house descended. Permission was granted, grudgingly, for the acquisition of 124 Grace Park Road, as a contract was already in place, 'but we shall not be permitted to buy other houses in the area for the school children. We may build on our own grounds, after seeking approval from His Grace the archbishop'. [116] The effort to have the children in 'ordinary' houses facing onto the road had to be shelved for the moment, but the development of the two self-contained units (for the Little Flower group and Our Lady's group), each managing its own budget, was taken as 'a preliminary to moving to group homes later on'. [117] In the meantime, the rest of the old school building

112   Sister Mary Carmel to My Lord Archbishop, 31 Dec. 1956 (DDA, McQuaid Papers, Department of Justice).
113   Ann Kenny, 'The deprived child', *Christus Rex*, x, no. 2 (1956), pp 112–3.
114   High Park, minutes of special meeting, 18 Sept. 1970.
115   High Park local council, minutes, 4 Sept. 1970.
116   Ibid., 10 Nov. 1970.
117   Apostolate committee report, p. 15.

was cut off and used for staff quarters and an administrative office, but not for the children.[118]

The full implementation of 'family group homes' for the children of St Joseph's was achieved in 1978 when the schoolchildren were moved from the first floor apartments into two purpose-built houses on the northern edge of the High Park property, close to St Michael's guesthouse: the Little Flower group into Bláithín (the Irish form of the same name), facing onto Grace Park Road, Our Lady's Group into Cuan Mhuire (Mary's harbour), facing onto Collins Avenue.

## Teenage Training Centre/Ri Villa Training Centre, Sean MacDermott Street

Sean MacDermott Street refuge or asylum underwent a similar process of modernisation post-Vatican II, as did High Park, but the reconfiguration of the accommodation to support the new models of care – hostels, training centre, small and separate groups, aftercare – was especially complicated. There was little space in which to implement the new ideas, there was no spare land on which one might build anew (should the funds be there, which they were not) and there was a high turnover of residents, largely due to its city-centre location, with many of the girls and women interested only in short-term emergency accommodation.

The creation of a teenage group and training programme in the asylum or refuge at Sean MacDermott Street ran several years behind High Park but, once begun, the process gathered momentum. The move towards effective separation is reflected in the record keeping and in the provision of proper classes. From September 1959, information sheets or individual files were started for teenage girls whose names were also (up to November 1966) entered in the regular Sean Mac Dermott Street register. From November 1967, a separate register was started titled 'Junior Girls' to be continued under the title 'Ri Villa' from 1971.[119] In January 1966, it was recorded that 'cookery classes for the girls in Gloucester Street monastery were commenced'[120] and, in the same month, plans were made to build a new classroom adjoining the refectory 'to facilitate the holding of classes for the girls'.[121] Elsewhere, the year 1966 is given as the start of the 'semi-separation of teenagers for purpose of rehabilitation'.[122] As in High Park, the intention was to remove younger girls from the adult refuge and to educate them for an independent life. This group formed the core of what would be re-launched in 1970 as a self-contained hostel and training centre in the monastery; it was entered from Railway Street, in the building marked 'workroom' in figure 13.1. It was also known as the Ri Villa Training Centre, named after the Normandy birthplace of the founder of the order, John Eudes. As part of the more recent asylum story, this comes up under the 'introduction of modern methods'

---

118    Ibid., p. 14.
119    Small alphabetical book for Ri Villa titled, 'Junior Girls, Sr Euphrasia' on the inside cover, first entrance appears to be Nov. 1967 (DARGS, OLC2/8/4 no. 4); Ri Villa register, from 1971 (DARGS, OLC2/8/4 no. 3).
120    Irish federation general council, minutes, Jan. 1966.
121    Gloucester Street local council, minutes, 20 Jan. 1966 (DARGS, OLC 2/5/2 no. 7).
122    Apostolate committee report, p. 2.

to Sean MacDermott Street (chapter 12). In 1972, teenagers at Sean MacDermott Street could be found in any of three settings: in 'The Teenage Training Centre' (eight girls), in the 'Transition Hostel' (five girls) and among the remand referrals and those seeking short-term accommodation in the 'Casual Unit'.[123] Still in operation was the original Gloucester Street magdalen asylum or refuge for women but, working on the 'small groups' principle under the revised title, 'Our Lady of Charity Home' (from 20 January 1973) and from which teenagers were now excluded. Despite changes in name and the frequency of exits and re-entries common to all units, it is possible to disentangle the development of the teenage section from other parts of the Sean Mac Dermott Street complex.[124]

The Training Centre for teenagers, Ri Villa, was described as 'a separate unit with accommodation for 10 girls'. In 1972, there were eight girls aged 15 to 20 in residence. An internal review after just over two years of operation described it as 'homely and provides a relaxed and free atmosphere'. The varied reasons given for admission were listed as 'broken homes; parents unable to cope; sexually involved; on probation; vagrancy'.[125] Maintenance grants on a per day basis were received from the Department of Justice for those girls referred by the courts, that is, sent on remand (and no more than four at any one time), the convent having been certified as a remand home for women aged 17 and older from 1960, and as a junior remand home from June 1972. Where a teenager was sent on remand, she could be moved, for her own welfare, from the casual unit into the training centre, the mixing of older and younger women on remand always giving grounds for worry. The training centres in both Sean MacDermott Street and High Park were approved by the Department of Education and the Department of Justice in May 1973 as places to which the state could send troublesome young people for 'care and training', some of whom would be already on probation, and for whom maintenance would be paid.[126] The extension of the period of obligatory school attendance to 15 in 1972 and the political commitment to reform of youth services that came in the wake of the Kennedy report (1970), most fully articulated in the social workers' CARE report of 1972, helped focus political attention – and some resources – on the care of teenagers out of home. The approval of the training centres run by OLC can be seen within these larger political and sociological, as well as philosophical, contexts, but the sisters had also much practical experience and knowledge to draw on once given the freedom and resources to experiment. The training regime in the Sean MacDermott Street training centre, as listed in 1972, was much like what was already on offer at An Grianán, namely, 'part-time academic training and part-time work training', with 'classes in the 3 Rs, typing, cookery, dress-making,

---

123   Ibid., p. 6.
124   House council minutes do not appear to have been taken for the years 1969 to 1987 or, if they were, they have not survived; for dates before and after that, see bound volume DARGS, OLC2/5/2 no. 7.
125   Apostolate committee report, p. 8.
126   Superior General to My Lord Archbishop, 2 May 1973, copy letter (DARGS, OLC3/2/1 no. 34). From 9 June 1972, An Grianán, Sean Mac Dermott Street and St Anne's were registered as 'places of detention for the purposes of Part V of the Children's Act, 1908'. General correspondence (unlisted) (DARGS, OLC1/3/8 no. 1).

hygiene, home-making, Christian living'. There were also lessons in physical training, swimming and drama. 'Outings are allowed as reward system and depend on individual girls', with 50p pocket money weekly for each girl.[127]

## St Anne's Hostel/Transition Hostel, Sean MacDermott Street

An 'aftercare hostel' or 'Transition Hostel' for teenagers was opened in Sean MacDermott Street in 1966, though not on the scale or with the ambition of Martanna House in High Park which opened in the same year.[128] The 'Transition Hostel' was re-launched under the title 'St Anne's Hostel' after a break of some months, in January 1971. The leaflet produced to advertise the re-opening states that it caters for five girls aged between 16 and 20 who are in employment or in training, 'or at the time of entry have definite training or employment prospects within a reasonably short period of time'. The average length of stay was 12 to 18 months, though there could be some flexibility around that, depending on the girl's circumstances. The initial trial was for six weeks, at which point 'a contracted agreement regarding their future can be broached'. The aim of the unit makes it clear that this is a working girls' hostel, with no connection to the magdalen refuge:

> To prepare teenage girls for independent living; to provide a base where they learn basic life skills, e.g., budgeting, nutrition, socialising, coping with jobs and life; self management and responsibility.[129]

The training element was couched in rather vague terms, to be 'based on responsibility for self and responsibility for and towards those sharing accommodation with them'.[130] St Anne's was associated with the training centre for teenagers, in that 'the girls pass on to adjoining Transition Hostel when they commence open employment.' Indeed, girls from the casual unit could also be accommodated here if they were in work and temporarily in need of accommodation. There was room for seven girls in 1972, and the girls were expected to pay £3 per week, with overhead expenses paid out of the convent account. But to be truly successful, a working girls' hostel needed to have a social mix and a respectable address, both of which were possible for Martanna House and 124 Grace Park Road. Sean MacDermott Street had neither, and a report for the 1972 federal chapter advised that 'Extension of this unit is considered undesirable due to the unsuitability of the district for this type of work'.[131] A new register was started for St Anne's on 1 January 1973. Of the first 13 girls to use the service in 1973, six had come from the teenage unit, three from the casual unit, one came from High Park having formerly been in Dunboyne mother-and-baby home, another came from St Brendan's psychiatric hospital, another from the Mater hospital, and one girl was directed to St Anne's from 'Contact', the new drop-in advisory service for teenagers

127    Apostolate committee report, p. 8.
128    Ibid., p. 3.
129    Advertising leaflet, Jan. 1971 (DARGS, OLC2/8/3).
130    Ibid.
131    Apostolate committee report, p. 9.

started in 1972 as a project of the federation (see chapter 13).[132] There were no 'office girls' among the 1973 intake who could pay their way and, although the aim continued to be to support girls in outside employment or training, St Anne's hostel girls were never to be so easily categorised. The average age on admission in 1973 was 18, with the youngest girl 15 and the oldest 23.

## Casual Unit, Sean MacDermott Street

The 'Casual Unit' in Sean MacDermott Steet was opened in June 1971 as emergency accommodation for six females. According to its own mission statement it had two purposes. The first was to act as an assessment centre – or 'sorting out ground' – to which girls would be directed before being accepted into the training centres in High Park and Sean MacDermott Street. The theory was that this would allow their suitability and readiness to be assessed before either side made a commitment. In practice, the girls referred to the teenage units by social workers or by parents did not go via the casual unit, 'as the girls found it difficult to settle down in two places within a short space of time'. But the casual unit did act as a 'sorting out ground' in a more general sense, with all self-referrals and "casuals" admitted to this unit 'and from there to the service which seems suitable to them'. Thus a girl with a job but no accommodation might move into St Anne's for a spell, or a teenager who had been put out of her home could be admitted in due course to Ri Villa. It also served as a remand home for all who came from the courts, excepting the youngest women who were generally placed in the teenage unit and training centre. As was reiterated in relation to the remand services in High Park and Kilmacud, remand services at Sean MacDermott Street 'will be terminated in 1974 when the new Women's Prison in Kilbarrack is built which will contain a remand section'.[133] (The prison was never built).

Between June 1971 and the end of 1972 there were 223 admissions to the casual unit, of whom 38 were girls on remand – that is 17% of all admissions. The other principal purpose of the casual unit was exactly as its title implies, 'to cater for those who needed a night's lodging as being in the centre of the city and close to the rail, bus and boat terminals this service is in constant demand'. Providing separately for those women and girls who needed or wanted only overnight accommodation prevented a lot of upheaval in the refuge proper, and in the training unit and St Anne's hostel; it was facing up to current local demand, which was not for a long-term refuge or home, but for temporary crisis-driven accommodation. Maintenance for the remand girls was paid per day by the Department of Justice; others paid something if they could afford to (and very few did), with the bulk of the expenses 'paid from convent funds'.[134]

A summary report on the operation of the casual unit was made from 1 January to 17 November 1973 when 172 women and girls, including three children, went through. What all applicants had in common was an urgent need for free overnight accommodation in the city. Analysis undertaken by the founding director and social worker in charge at the time, Sister Lucy

132 Ibid., p. 19.
133 Ibid., p. 10.
134 Ibid. p. 11.

**Figure 9.1**  Casual Unit, Sean MacDermott Street convent,
1 January – 17 November 1973

| | |
|---|---|
| Remand from the courts | 31 |
| Past pupils between jobs or in trouble with accommodation | 7 |
| Garda referrals as runaways or stranded | 29 |
| Self referrals as runaways or stranded | 22 |
| Social service referrals: Contact, Simon Community, Samaritans, Society of St Vincent de Paul, Legion of Mary | 44 |
| Home troubles, temporary | 8 |
| Psychiatric illness, casual (moving between here and other free accommodation) | 6 |
| Longer term, 4 days to 2 months, 'received positive help' mostly with job placement | 29 |
| **Total** | **176** |

*Source:* Report on Casual Unit, January 1st to November
17th 1973 (DARGS, OLC7/5/5 no. 1)

Bruton, divided the girls and women into eight approximate categories (figure 9.1, where the total of 176 is accounted for by repeat visits). There were girls directed by a garda or local person, or by an organisation such as the Simon Community, Legion of Mary, Sherrard House or Samaritans, who arrived for one or two nights. Some were runaways from home (for whatever reason); others were simply stranded in Dublin, having missed buses and trains. Some were in search of a job but, as they wanted only a night's lodging, they were directed to the casual unit. A few came 'till home troubles were ironed out' and tempers had cooled: 'often this did not require positive negotiation, but just advising the girl how to go about going home and what to say, and leaving the way open for them to come back to me [Sr Lucy Bruton] if it didn't work'. Some were women on remand from the courts, of whom three were admitted to the teenage unit (Ri Villa). Three or four were 'deserted or "battered" wives looking for asylum'. Two were described as 'prostitutes from the picket workers', that is, girls sent on by the Legion of Mary who had been found working on the streets, but 'they didn't want help' and their presence among the younger girls was 'most unsuitable'. The largest group, 29 girls who 'received positive help and stayed longer periods' – the shortest being four days and the longest two months – were, on the whole, (according to Bruton) amenable to help, and she was able to fix these girls up in a job. Some needed to stay in the casual unit until they had saved enough money to pay for a flat. Others needed help due to pregnancy (which would have barred them from admission to the refuge proper). Others were teenagers 'who didn't, or wouldn't, fit into the teenage units but who needed help, for some time, until something else could be fixed up'. While some stayed no longer than one to three months in any place and were classed as 'unstable', the great majority were 'quite genuine and up from the country for jobs'. Some few were succinctly written off as 'chancers', not in real need nor intending to take up work, but simply taking advantage of the free accommodation. These were set up with a live-in job elsewhere and given the ultimatum of taking the job or leaving the hostel. The only group classed as hopeless were those poor women described as 'mostly psychopathic girls moving between here and other free accommodation', in and out of St Brendan's mental hospital, with many on probation from the courts. Nothing could be done for them 'as there is no psychiatric unit for such girls' and the casual unit could do no more than offer them a bed for the night. With so many using the casual unit, there was little chance of systematic follow through. In most cases, the best that could be done, the director explained, was to send the girls off to a job and to 'tell the girls that they know where I am if they are stuck again'.[135]

## Summary of Shifts in Childcare Philosophies, 1960s

Changes in approach in Ireland to the welfare of children in state care can be tracked from about 1950 and gathered momentum in the 1960s. The Tuairim report of 1965 was unequivocal in its demand that the Children Act 1908 be replaced with a new Children Act 'which would take into account the present needs of Irish society and contemporary theory and methods of childcare and protection'.[136] Many of its recommendations were seconded, privately, by the Department of Education, with the senior boys' reformatory and industrial schools judged to be most glaringly defective.[137] The Michael Viney *Irish Times* series on residential care published between 27 April and 6 May 1966 was a shocking exposé of the harshness that still characterised (in particular) boys' reformatory schools. Coverage of the initiatives of Our Lady of Charity by the *Irish Times* was limited to St Anne's school, Kilmacud, a few weeks earlier (chapter 8). Some journalistic licence must be allowed for the extensive praise heaped on the school and for the contrasts drawn between it and most of the other institutions investigated by the newspaper in 1966, but nevertheless there can be no doubting that St Anne's was held up as a model of what 'the new' could look like (with some reservations around its limited vocational training).[138] So, too – though perhaps not so

135  Report on 'Casual Unit', 1 Jan.–17 Nov. 1973 (DARGS, OLC5/5/7 no. 1).
136  London Branch Study Group, *Some of our children, a report on the residential care of the deprived child in Ireland*, Tuairim Pamphlet no. 13 (London, 1966), p. 33, quoted in Ryan report, iv, p. 287.
137  'Virtually all the convent schools are well-nigh excellent, the glaring defect in the senior boys' schools being the lack of the female hand in the domestic service. In the whole system, the most serious defect is the absence of official after-care machinery'. Internal Department of Education memorandum, 1966, quoted in Ryan report, iv, pp 288–9.
138  Mary Maher, 'St Anne's: a home without rebels', *Irish Times*, 1 Mar. 1966.

visible to the public – teenage care on the High Park campus and in the more crowded setting of Sean MacDermott Street began to be transformed in stages in the late 1950s.

By 1967, when the commission of inquiry was set up under the chairmanship of District Justice Eileen Kennedy, to carry out a survey of reformatory and industrial schools and to report and make a recommendation to the Minister for Education, everybody with an interest in children knew that the 19th-century institutional system of certified schools was long out of date. Among Kennedy's many criticisms of what she found was the practice of having 'certain types of girl offenders', between the ages of 13 and 19, placed by judges on probation 'with a condition that they reside for a time in one of several convents which accept them; in other cases they are placed on remand from the courts'.[139] That was certainly true of High Park in the 1930s, 1940s and 1950s – though after the opening of St Anne's, Kilmacud in 1944 (chapter 8), practically all younger girls found in the admissions register of High Park (up to and including 1971) were en route to Kilmacud, except for those who ran away or were removed from High Park within days, usually by a parent. Within High Park itself, the separation of teenagers from adults and the provision of training was under way, however modestly, from 1955. Similarly, though a few years later, a teenage group and training programme were in place at Sean MacDermott Street. That teenage girls should mix with adult women of all ages and backgrounds in magdalen refuges or asylums, no matter how short their stay or desperate their need for shelter, could not be defended, either internally or in public. Child and adolescent psychology, educational philosophy and applied social science were all in agreement that the child's emotional needs had to be met as much as – if not more than – the visible requirements of food, clothing, shelter and schooling. Though there was uncertainty about what the new care arrangements might look like, it would be built around small groups, in a homely setting with family involvement and a more individualised, flexible approach that did not cut the teenager off from the outside world. The involvement of Sister Aloysius Pilkington in the research and writing of the CARE report of 1972 has already been noted and probably accounts in some measure for the way in which quotations from Kennedy and from CARE became embedded in OLC internal research papers and policy documents. The Vatican II pastoral constitution on the Church in the modern world, *Gaudium et spes*, published 7 December 1965, was also extensively and repeatedly quoted by OLC in Dublin. Its call for the Church to engage fully with 'the joy and hope, the sorrow and anxiety of the men of our time, especially of those who are poor or afflicted in any way', and to 'continually examine the signs of the times and interpret them in the light of the gospel' gave an impetus towards modernisation that could not be denied.[140] In concert with other Vatican II pronouncements, as in the call to institutes to ensure that their members have 'a proper understanding' of mankind, of present-day conditions and of the needs of the Church, a greater openness

139   *Reformatory and industrial schools systems report, 1970* (Dublin, 1970), p. 39.
140   *Gaudium et spes, Pastoral constitution on the Church in the modern world*, 7 Dec. 1965, English trans., Catholic Truth Society (London, 1966), nos. 1, 4.

to change was fostered within OLC, as indeed within other religious institutes and the Church generally.[141]

But for OLC, change, though gradual, was under way before the public outcry around residential care gained momentum in the mid-1960s. The wartime destruction of Caen was a stark reminder, if such were needed, that there was no going backwards to old securities, while the after-care hostel developed by their own sisters in Bitterne, England, modelled how a thoroughly modern approach could still be faithful to the tradition of the much-loved founder, John Eudes. The archbishop of Dublin, Dr McQuaid, used his considerable personal and ecclesiastical authority to urge the sisters to modernise their approaches to the care of teenagers, The new federation structure of 1948, his own creation, gave him greater leverage over all the houses and, though he could not impose his will on the institute, through meetings and frequent correspondence with the sisters in charge, they were certainly appraised of his views on all that pertained to their work. All three houses that formed the federation of 1948 – High Park, Sean MacDermott Street and St Anne's, Kilmacud – developed their own services for older teenagers, involving small groups, in-house training and hostels for girls working in the city or suburbs, as did the new community at The Grange (from 1956). While each has its own local history and chronology, and its own network of generous supporters and advisers, in all cases these new ventures were developed in response to the needs of girls already in OLC reformatory and industrial schools – or likely to come their way – for whom the adult refuge or asylum was not suitable. The modernisation of the women's refuges, under way at the same time, did not change the basic principle that girls and younger women should be catered for separately from adult women. Past pupils of industrial schools were the single most identifiable group in need of aftercare and hostels, at least from what the sisters had learned thus far from their experience. Though the winding-down of the industrial school model was under way before Justice Kennedy published her report in 1970, there would continue to be out-of-home older teenage girls who were (for many and complex reasons) in need of accommodation and support. But there were not many groups or individuals volunteering to get involved in what was then, as now, a particularly demanding field.

---

141 *Perfectae caritatis, The decree on the renewal of religious life*, 28 Oct. 1965, Paulist Press edn, trans. Austin Flannery, commentary by Gregory Baum (New York, 1966), no. 2(d).

# Chapter 10

# The OLC Monastery of the Grange and the Development of the 'Family Group Home' System, 1956–70

On 23 November 1954, without any preamble, the archbishop of Dublin, Dr John Charles McQuaid, surprised the Irish Federation of Our Lady of Charity with the offer of a house that had recently been given to him, The Grange, Kill of the Grange, County Dublin (figure 10.1).[1] The question of 'rest and change for the sisters' was behind the offer and the house itself, and its location in an expanding and well-to-do suburb about five miles to the south of the city with distant views of the bay would certainly serve that purpose.[2] But The Grange was to be more than a rest house, as implied by McQuaid in his demand to be told 'the precise purpose for which it will be used, if it be accepted'.[3] To this, the response was given that it would be used as 'a house of preservation and as a training school for young girls', a rather general answer but sufficient – at the outset, at least – to satisfy the archbishop.[4] Three days after the offer was first made, a deputation representing each of the monasteries (High Park, Gloucester Street/Sean MacDermott Street and St Anne's, Kilmacud) travelled by car to see the house for themselves. The archbishop was there and later that afternoon he travelled to High Park 'to discuss matters relating to the property in question'.[5] Though without real plans or personnel – or indeed finance – in place, and without being allowed to tell their communities, the gift was accepted, the council minutes and annals stating that there was no way it could be refused, it being the archbishop's own idea. It was thus that The Grange became the fourth monastery of the Order of Our Lady of Charity of Refuge in Ireland. The archbishop saw it as a means of shaking the order into embracing more 'modern' approaches, hoping 'that the new house will bring fresh vigour

---

1   The official spelling 'Kill of the Grange' is used interchangeably with 'Kill o' the Grange', the popular local spelling, in OLC records. The official spelling is used here for consistency. See www.logainm.ie [28 Feb. 2017].
2   General council of the federation, minutes, 23 Nov. 1954 (DARGS, OLC5/5/1 no. 1). Hereafter, Irish federation general council, minutes.
3   John C. McQuaid to Mother M. of St Eithne [O'Neill], 13 Dec. 1954 (DARGS, OLC4). At the time of writing, the Grange papers had not been catalogued, hence the collection number, OLC4, is used for all items from this collection.
4   Mother M. Eithne O'Neill to Dr McQuaid, 16 Dec. 1954 (DDA, Cullen, OLC Kill of the Grange).
5   Irish federation general council, minutes, 23 Nov. 1954.

**Figure 10.1** Site of OLC, The Grange, Kill of the Grange, Dublin (Extract from OS 1:2,500, Dublin sheet 23.x (1939), annotations *c*.1964). (DARGS, OLC4)

into your Federation, especially into High Park', which he regarded (and in 1954 with good reason) as antiquated and overly large.[6]

   The Grange was not a gift without encumbrances. First, the freehold had to be purchased from the Espinasse estate, while the house itself would

6   John C. McQuaid to Mother M. of St Eithne, 17 Dec. 1954 (DARGS, OLC4).

require an immense amount of money to make habitable.[7] When set against the rateable valuation of the house, the sum required indicates serious dilapidation.[8] Over three floors and entered by steps at the first floor, it was dated by the historian Robert Simington to 1865. It was not a very old house but, left too long without a resident owner, it had become neglected.[9] There was a likelihood that the county council would take some of the three and a half acres of land that came with the house, and its gate lodge, for road widening at a future date.[10] The greater portion of the land to the south of the house, including its walled garden (figure 10.1), had already been purchased by the Bolands milling company (of Grand Canal Quay), which now paid a small rent twice-annually to the new ground landlords, the convent.[11] The house was purchased in the name of the federation, rather than as a daughter or branch of any one monastery, and the founding expenses were divided equally between High Park and Gloucester Street.[12]

Although the gift was offered by the archbishop and accepted by the federation at the end of November 1954, the legal transfer into the names of six of the sisters and the purchase of the freehold – with the elderly Mrs Espinasse in England advised by her agent to hold out for a higher price – was not closed until the last week of July 1955.[13] Nothing much could be done in the meantime. On becoming owners, the immediate priority was to get the collapsed part of the boundary wall repaired and also to take out fire insurance. The neighbouring landowner, Bolands Ltd, had also to be pursued about erecting a wire fence to stop the trespass 'by cattle and people on horseback' onto the land.[14] Attempts to persuade Bolands to sell the walled garden to the sisters ('it would be a great asset to us as we are an enclosed community') came to nothing, but at least they had tried.[15] The wilderness that was their own garden, and its glasshouses, were brought into line. Tables, a book press and other furniture that could be spared from the other houses were brought down.[16] The caretaking couple were difficult

7    The freehold would cost £2,750, the house repairs were first estimated at £15,000 or £16,000; John C. McQuaid to Mother M. of St Eithne, 13 Dec. 1954, 3 Feb. 1955, 8 Feb. 1955; Richard Ryan to Mother Eithne, 31 Jan. 1955; Mother M. Eithne O'Neill to James R. Ryan, 25 Apr. 1960 (DARGS, OLC4).
8    The rateable valuation of the house was £65 in 1955 and also in 1956, and that of the grounds £7 10s; R. Ryan to Mother M. of St Eithne O'Neill, 9 Mar. 1956 (DARGS, OLC4).
9    Robert C. Simington to Fr Aloysius, 28 Apr. 1955 (DARGS, OLC4).
10   John C. McQuaid to Mother M. of St Eithne, 13 Dec. 1954; Richard Ryan to Mother M. of St Eithne, 31 Dec. 1954; Vincent B. Gallagher to Rev Mother General, 19 Sept. 1955 (DARGS, OLC4).
11   R. Ryan to Mother M. of St Eithne O'Neill, 18 July 1955; see also rent receipts and correspondence, 1956–65 (DARGS, OLC4).
12   O'Neill to McQuaid, 16 Dec. 1954.
13   R. Ryan to Mother M. of St Eithne O'Neill, 31 Jan., 10 Mar., 2 Apr., 23 July 1955; John C. McQuaid to Mother M. of St Eithne, 13 Dec. 1954, 3, 8 Feb., 18 Mar. 1955 (DARGS, OLC4); Irish federation general council, minutes, 27 July 1955.
14   Vincent B. Gallagher to Revd Mother General, 4, 18, 26 Apr., 6 July 1955 (DARGS, OLC4).
15   Mother M. Eithne O'Neill to R. Ryan, 6 May 1955; R. Ryan to Mother M. of St Eithne, 17 May 1955 (DARGS, OLC4).
16   High Park local council, minutes 24 May, 25 July 1955 (DARGS, OLC1/5/2 no. 1).

to move on.[17] Both architect, and building contractor had already been engaged and were waiting only for the chance to get started. Building work
by Christopher J. Cooney began before the end of August 1955 under the supervision of the architect, Vincent Gallagher, who certified the work as payments fell due. The electrical work began the first week of September.[18] Time
was invested in the selection of light fittings and furniture, and the painting
scheme was decided only after Mother Eithne O'Neill, at the insistence of
her architect, visited Our Lady's School Templeogue in October 1955 to see
for herself how the light cream painting of the woodwork throughout had
given the entire building a 'great sense of unity'.[19]

Shortcuts taken with the drainage had to be rectified in spring 1960 – to
the great embarrassment of the community – after the pollution of a local
watercourse was traced by the county council directly to their old drains.[20]
The builder was blamed for a breach of contract and the architect for inadequate oversight, while both men protested that the superior had sought
economies as costs spiralled. In hindsight everyone saw what should have
been done the first time round, namely a completely new connection to the
main drainage.[21] The quarrel typifies the difficulties which were inherent
in managing a project at a remove. There was no resident superior on site
who might exercise some control over plans and costs. The superior general, Mother Mary Eithne O'Neill, lived at High Park in what was still an
enclosed community, and directed matters from there, trying to manage the
high expectations of the archbishop against what looks like a distinct lack of
enthusiasm from her councillors. While she did undertake some site visits,
it was not the same as being on hand, leaving her heavily reliant on what
could turn out to be poor professional advice.[22] The usual procedure was
for the architect or solicitor to call personally to High Park to confer or to
get Mother Eithne's signature, as the need arose. Similarly, the archbishop,
or a priest appointed by him, could call at short notice to confront her on
what she had – or had not – dared to do or say, or to respond to what he had
heard through his many contacts. Much of the business was conducted by
letter. Copies of outgoing correspondence were kept by all parties, meetings
were minuted and personal interviews were written up afterwards so that
the intricacies and conflicts are well documented. The position of Mother
Eithne O'Neill was certainly not an enviable one, saddled with a project
neither she nor the communities had ever asked for or knew what to do
with, on behalf of a federation of tightly autonomous houses with (in 1955)

---

17    Vincent B. Gallagher, Merrion Square, to Mother General, 4, 6, 18 Apr., 15 June, 2, 10 Sept.
1955 (DARGS, OLC4).
18    Christopher J. Cooney Ltd had addresses at Garville Drive, Rathgar, and Castle Park,
Monkstown, M. Wallace to Revd Mother General, 8 Sept. 1955 (DARGS, OLC4).
19    Vincent B. Gallagher to Revd M. Superior, 22 Oct. 1955 (DARGS, OLC4).
20    D. Delaney to Revd Mother General, 23 Sept. 1960; Mother M. Eithne O'Neill to Secretary,
Dublin County Council, 26 Sept. 1960; Mother M. Eithne O'Neill to James R. Ryan, 11 Apr.
1960, 25 Apr. 1960 (DARGS, OLC4).
21    Mother M. Eithne O'Neill to James R. Ryan, 11, 23, 25 Apr. 1960; J.R. Ryan to Mother
General, 20, 23 Apr. 1960; Vincent B. Gallagher to Messrs Arthur O'Hagan and Sons, 22 Apr.
1960 (DARGS, OLC4).
22    Mother M. Eithne O'Neill to Vincent B. Gallagher, 18 May 1955 (DARGS, OLC4).

complete control over their own finances and a very narrow view of what work was allowed by the constitutions.

The refurbishment of The Grange proceeded at an unhurried pace between August 1955 and spring 1956, with the sort of delays that attend any major project involving subcontractors and service providers. In the Christmas letter of 1955, occupation early in the new year was expected.[23] But the weeks passed. The delay in taking up residence came to a head in April 1956 when the archbishop wrote in fiery terms of the scandal caused locally by the costs of the repairs to a premises still lying empty and in which, to date, 'no work of public charity is performed'.[24] Weeks earlier, McQuaid had given his approval to the appointment of Sister M. of St Francis Assisi Smyth, aged 38 years, as 'sister-in-charge'.[25] Amid some haste and exactly one week from receipt of this ultimatum, five sisters (the minimum number allowed by the constitutions to form a new community) moved in, led by the young superior and accompanied by Mother Eithne.[26] On the Thursday following, Ascension Thursday, the bell was blessed and named 'John Eudes' in honour of the order's founder, and the house was blessed by Canon McMahon, the parish priest of Foxrock, of which parish the community was now part.[27] The sisters attended Mass in the local Christian Brothers' house of Carriglea until arrangements could be made to have the first Mass said in their own chapel.[28] Morning Mass and the recitation of the Divine Office in common structured the day here, as it did in all the houses of the order, while the liturgical seasons and feast-days, days of retreat and recollection, marked the passage of the year. The devotional life was shot through with the spirituality of John Eudes, with the loving hearts of Jesus and Mary represented in holy pictures and statues, and the favoured prayers and aspirations of Eudes embedded in the ordinary course of the day. The obligation under the constitutions to respect enclosure fostered a spirit of self-reliance, but it also limited interaction with the other, larger communities. The small size of the house, and the small numbers, meant that girls, children and sisters were never really separate. The foundation date of The Grange inscribed in the community books was 6 May 1956.

The slow start-up could be blamed on the wrangling of solicitors (on behalf of their clients) over the price to be paid for the freehold, which put everything on hold at the best time of the year for building and repairs. But without doubt the central issue was the 'purposes of public charity' for which the house was to be used. These had to come within the terms of

23   High Park, circular letter, 8 Dec. 1955 (NDC Caen, Archives Besançon).

24   John C. McQuaid to Revd Mother Superior General, 30 Apr. 1956 (DARGS, OLC4).

25   Sister M. of St Francis Assisi Smyth was too young in age and in years of profession, under the order's constitutions, to be superior, Mother M. Eithne O'Neill to Dr McQuaid, 6 Mar. 1956 (DDA, Cullen, OLC Kill of the Grange).

26   The founding community was Sister M. of St Francis of Assisi Smyth, Sister M. of St Lazerian Brophy and Sister M. of St Benignus Coyle, all from High Park, and Sister M. of St Louis Grignion de Montfort Goss and Sister M. of St John Bosco O'Connor, Gloucester Street; Irish federation general council, minutes, 4 May 1956.

27   Irish federation general council, minutes, 10 May 1956.

28   Mother M. Eithne O'Neill to Dr McQuaid, 4 May 1956; to Mgr Boylan, 4 May 1956 (DDA, Cullen, OLC Kill of the Grange). The first Mass was said on 19 June 1956.

the constitutions of the order.[29] What work would be carried out? And how would that work be funded? There was never any question of operating a women's refuge in The Grange; whatever need there might have been locally, there was not the slightest chance the archbishop would countenance another refuge in his drive for 'the new'. The refuges at High Park and Gloucester Street generated the income needed to keep them open through their laundries, while both St Joseph's (Whitehall) and St Anne's (Kilmacud) received maintenance grants from the state for most of their children. On what could The Grange rely from week to week? The initial response to the gift in November 1954 was that it would be used as 'a house of preservation and as a training school for young girls'; at the time of the move, 18 months later, the same plan was reiterated, this time with the age range 15 to 18 years specified.[30] But, in between, the archbishop came up with a very different idea. On the blessing of the new convent of St Anne's, Kilmacud (18 October 1955), he made known his wish that an ordinary primary school should be opened at The Grange.[31] He did not need to spell out the advantage that the security of one or more state-funded teacher's salaries would be to the struggling community, while the extent of housebuilding locally already guaranteed the demand for school places. However, meeting in council, the leadership would not hear of this, forwarding lengthy extracts from the founder's writings and the constitutions in which 'the scope of our work seems to be clearly and exclusively defined', namely, 'binding us to occupy ourselves in the conversion and instruction of erring souls'. Up to this point, their schools – meaning St Joseph's, Whitehall and St Anne's, Kilmacud – 'have been for those in need of care and protection'.[32] That they had only one sister with primary teaching qualifications at the time – and she was not going to be among those sent on the new foundation – made it well nigh impossible in practical terms. Displeased though he might be, he could hardly force them to operate outside their own rule, and he conceded the point.[33] That left them with their original, rather vague and financially shaky ambition of 'a house of preservation and training school for young girls', which could be construed, in McQuaid terms, as a hostel (chapter 9).

The novel status of the house also made for difficulties. Who was really in charge? To whom was the superior accountable? The Grange was under the federation, rather than the daughter house of a single monastery. But the federation, founded 1948, was a grouping of independent monasteries each jealously guarding its autonomy; it was far from the congregational model under central authority that the archbishop would have known from his own order, the Holy Ghost fathers, or that was already operating in the diocese, as in the Holy Faith sisters. As far as Dr McQuaid was concerned, The Grange was under the superior general. It was not an autonomous religious house of the order, and 'would not be a formal house for some years', hence

29   McQuaid to Superior General, 30 Apr. 1956.
30   O'Neill to McQuaid, 16 Dec. 1954. Same to same, 1 May 1956, copy letter (DARGS, OLC4).
31   Irish federation general council, minutes, 12 Dec. 1955.
32   Mother M. Eithne O'Neill to Dr McQuaid, 27 Dec. 1955 (DDA, Cullen, OLC Kill of the Grange).
33   John C. McQuaid to Revd M. Mary of St Eithne, 29 Dec. 1955 (DARGS, OLC4).

the title 'sister-in-charge' not superior.[34] McQuaid had no time for autonomous monasteries within his diocese, as is evident in the setting up of the
OLC federation and in his dealings with other orders with similar traditions
of independence. His understanding was that 'The Grange was meant to be
a Hostel mothered by the Gloucester Street Community', and it was certainly assisted generously by the latter with gifts in money and kind.[35] But, from
the outset, The Grange worked out of the OLC tradition of autonomy – and
not surprisingly, as the only model the sisters knew. It was spared some of
the burdens that come with autonomy under canon law, namely the election
of a superior, which was the responsibility of the mother general and her
council, and the management of a novitiate, as any recruits would automatically be sent to High Park for formation. Nor did it have to be self-
sufficient in terms of personnel or finance but could – and had to – rely on
the two large monasteries of High Park and Gloucester Street to stay afloat.
But in terms of managing its own affairs, seeking benefactors, liaising with
statutory bodies, fundraising, expenditure, investment and accounting, discussing plans or seeking advice, acquiring or selling land, it operated in the
spirit of a stand-alone, self-contained house. Its successful application, at
the *aggiornamento* or renewal chapter of 1969, for recognition under canon
law as an autonomous house within the Irish federation gave formal effect
to what had long been the reality.[36]

From June 1956 to December 1966 inclusive, the original idea – that is,
'the preservation and training of adolescents' – was the work of the house,
which had a maximum capacity of 16 places. Analysis of the register entries shows that 98 girls were admitted between 1956 and 1966 inclusive
(figure 10.2). Most girls were aged 13 to 16 years of age on entry. Seventeen
and 18-year-olds were among those admitted in the early years, up to and
including 1961. Younger girls, aged 13 or 14, were more strongly represented between 1964 and 1966. The number of new admissions ranged widely,
between a maximum of 16 new girls in 1959 to three in 1963, depending
on how many places had been freed that year by girls leaving (usually to
return to their families) or moving on to independent life. It is not possible
to do a full statistical analysis, as ages are not entered for just over a quarter of the girls. Most of these appear to be short-stay, older teenagers who
did not 'suit' the house or were inclined 'to wander off', but that cannot be
presumed in all cases. What is possible to deduce is a tendency to prefer
younger over older 'first time entrants' as the house settled down, and a
commitment to follow through into young adulthood those girls for whom
The Grange was indeed home. There were also seven girls admitted between
1956 and 1966 who were clearly outside the age criteria as they were 12
years of age or under. Some had older sisters in the house or were otherwise
short-term residents en route to another setting. The youngest of these girls,

34   Mother M. Eithne O' Neill to Dr McQuaid, 6 Mar. 1956 (DDA, Cullen, OLC Kill of the
Grange).
35   John C. McQuaid to Mother M. Rita, 15 June 1962 (DARGS, OLC4).
36   The rescript of the Sacred Congregation for Religious, Prot. N.200/55/69, is dated 9 Dec.
1969, Register of the Sisters of the Order of Our Lady of Charity in Ireland, p. 60 (DARGS,
OLC1/6/1 no. 4).

**Figure 10.2** Admissions to training school, The Grange, Kill of the Grange, 1956–66

| Year | Total numbers admitted | Age in years on admission | | | | | | | | | | | No age given |
|------|------|----|----|----|----|----|----|----|----|----|----|----|------|
| | | 18 | 17 | 16 | 15 | 14 | 13 | 12 | 11 | 10 | 9 | 8 | |
| 1956 | 8 | 1 | | 3 | 1 | | | | | | 1 | | 2 |
| 1957 | 10 | 2 | | | 2 | 1 | | | 1 | | | | 4 |
| 1958 | 15 | | | 2 | 2 | 1 | 1 | | | | | | 9 |
| 1959 | 16 | | 1 | 3 | 2 | 3 | 2 | | | | | | 5 |
| 1960 | 13 | | 3 | 3 | 1 | 4 | | | | | | | 2 |
| 1961 | 7 | 1 | 1 | | | | | 1 | | 1 | 1 | | 2 |
| 1962 | 6 | | | 3 | 1 | | | | | | | | 2 |
| 1963 | 3 | | 1 | | | | 1 | | 1 | | | | |
| 1964 | 9 | | | 1 | 1 | 4 | 1 | | | | | | 2 |
| 1965 | 4 | | | | | 1 | 3 | | | | | | |
| 1966 | 6 | | | | | 2 | 2 | 1 | | | | 1 | |
| Total | 97 | 4 | 6 | 12 | 12 | 17 | 10 | 2 | 2 | 1 | 2 | 1 | 27 |

*Source:* Admissions register (DARGS, OLC4)

an eight-year-old, was admitted at her mother's request in 1966 as the mother 'had suffered a breakdown some years previously' and was unable to look after the child. By this point, the concept of 'family groups' was gaining public acceptance, with Fine Gael naming as party policy the establishment of 'family group homes' in its document of 1965 titled *Towards a just society*.[37] Among the community of The Grange, plans for a 'family groups' admission policy were well advanced by 1966. The eight-year-old was probably admitted in the knowledge that she would shortly be joined by other very young children, which did indeed happen the following year.

Analysis of the intake, insofar as the limited register information makes possible, supports the summary given to the archbishop in 1960, that 'these girls mostly come from broken homes and industrial schools'.[38] This is reiterated in a confidential 1962 memo which makes the same point, adding to the list 'children threatened with disaster'.[39] Some of the industrial school girls were aged 18, but most appear to have been 15 or 16 on arrival and

37   Quoted in the *Commission to inquire into child abuse, report* (Dublin, 2009), iv, p. 286.
38   Mother M. Eithne O'Neill to Dr McQuaid, 28 Mar. 1960 (DDA, Cullen, OLC Kill of the Grange).
39   P. Boylan to Dr McQuaid, 29 June 1962 (DDA, Cullen, OLC Kill of the Grange).

they came from all parts of the country: Limerick, Lakelands (Sandymount), Kells, Dundalk, Loughrea, Monastereven. One industrial school 18-year-old, still legally under post-release supervision ('supervision certificate'), had been sent to work in St Vincent's hospital from Lakelands school by the Sisters of Charity; 'as she was keeping late hours we were asked to take her for a time' (1956). Another industrial school child, aged 16 years from Galway, could not settle down at all ('very troublesome, sometimes unbalanced', 1959) and was sent to St Patrick's, Dun Laoghaire but, 'given a second chance [in The Grange] she improved'. The mother of one industrial school girl in Munster was 'most anxious' that her daughter, on reaching 15 years of age, might come to The Grange. This mother had lived in the Donnybrook refuge for some years and had recently moved to Gloucester Street, so she had not reared the child herself. But that perhaps made her all the more anxious to do whatever she could to ensure her daughter got the best that was going, as she read the situation (1958). A few were day-pupils in Dublin with serious home troubles, where the school took sufficient interest to see if something could be done for the child. One 13-year-old had been expelled from her boarding school 'for leaving school with two companions late at night.'The mother had died giving birth to this child, the youngest of a large family, 'the father taking no responsibility'. It was the school chaplain who got her a place in The Grange where it was reported that she got on very well 'and became a receptionist bookkeeper' (1964).

Members of the Legion of Mary brought along girls on occasion, either via the Harcourt Street hostel or directly from wherever they met them in the city. In September 1959, a zealous legionary, Miss Celia Donovan, brought along a 15-year-old with a home address in the north inner city, 'in great danger as she was loitering on quays'. The same day, a 16-year-old using the Harcourt Street hostel was also admitted to The Grange, 'missing from home and found wandering in Dublin'. A distraught pregnant girl who 'left home when she discovered she was in trouble – found in Dublin' in 1957 was brought from Harcourt Street to The Grange. A near-identical scenario was played out in 1960 with another girl who 'ran from home as she was pregnant'. In both cases 'reconciled to her family, returned home' is the reported outcome. Neither girl was more than a few days in Kill of the Grange and could not have stayed there during the pregnancy. But for the legionaries who brought these girls along, it was a safe and 'respectable' place until things could be sorted out and an alternative to their own adult hostel. Practically all of the girls picked up by the Legion of Mary were gone a few days later, with the note 'left for home' or 'could not settle down'. The Grange did not have the stigma of the reformatory or asylum about it and did not carry a weight of historic prejudices. The label of 'underprivileged' was to be strictly avoided in all public appeals.[40] Even its setting, in one of the very best suburbs of the city, helped protect its reputation. All the girls were presumed to be of 'good character', anxious to make a future for themselves, but with some misfortune in their family or background that had necessitated their being in care.

---

40   Sister M. de Montfort Goss to Dr McQuaid, 29 Aug. 1963, with MS annotation (DDA, Cullen, OLC Kill of the Grange).

The breakdown of boarding-out or foster care arrangements was behind the admission of several teenagers. One very sad case was that of a Monaghan foster mother who had a stroke two years earlier. The two 13-year-olds she was caring for came together to The Grange in 1966; though not siblings, they at least had each other. A similar case was of a Cork 14-year-old (1964) whose elderly foster parents died within a short time of each other. The 'family did not accept Mary' and the child was admitted to The Grange (later 'went to England'). The foster mother of another 14-year-old admitted in 1964 had 'a very good relationship with her foster child'; the remarks on this child note that she attended the Dominican convent secondary school, later the commercial school and later 'returned home, doing well, married with family'. Another child admitted the same year, aged 13, had been boarded out at birth to an elderly couple and, aged four and a half, sent to the Sacred Heart Home. Though later adopted by a 'grown family' in Cabra, she had 'always been a problem', due perhaps to the adoptive mother's poor health and advanced age. The Grange seems to have given her the chance to thrive – at least, if the register can be believed: 'very intelligent, sent to secondary top Carysfort, later having the Leaving passed for Civil Service, still there'.[41]

The Grange was a training centre, not an ordinary school. Nor was it ever a reformatory or industrial school. It was very much the sisters' own creation, with the strengths and weaknesses of a solo initiative. In the house, the girls were given religious instruction, taught 'the usual literary subjects' and trained in 'the different branches of Domestic Economy'.[42] While a girl with what are now termed learning needs was not automatically excluded, the house was never intended as a sheltered workshop or long-term home. Nor was it a nursing care facility, though a child with a long-term medical condition or physical disability could be – and was – admitted. There had to be some evidence that the girl would benefit from the programme on offer, along with a willingness to at least try to co-operate. There could be no hint of compulsion or detention, nor could a girl who failed to 'settle' be kept. One young girl, named Mary, came from St Anne's, Kilmacud, in 1956 as part of the first cohort. She was described as 'mentally undeveloped' and 'could not grasp the way of doing the simplest household duty', and shortly returned to Kilmacud, where she was later 'employed in the guest house'. The Grange was similarly open to giving a chance to girls sent on by psychologists or from hospital. The child guidance clinic in the Mater Hospital (under the psychiatrist Dr Paul McQuaid, a nephew to the archbishop), and the St John of God Clinic in Orwell Road both occasionally directed girls to Kill of the Grange, as did the almoners or social workers in several hospitals, including St Kevin's and St Patrick's Mental Hospital. A girl from St Clare's orphanage, Harold's Cross, transferred to The Grange, from where she also attended Dr McQuaid's clinic (1964). The assertion that The Grange did not take girls out of the Gloucester Street refuge, 'but only girls who might be thinking of going to Gloucester', is also borne out by the

---

41   A 'secondary top' was a national school which was allowed by the Department of Education to offer a post-primary curriculum as far as the Intermediate Certificate.
42   O'Neill to McQuaid, 28 Mar. 1960.

register.[43] The very first admissions to The Grange were 'awaiting opening of here', namely, two 15-year-olds from Gloucester Street. There was one movement in the opposite direction, of a girl 'sent to Gloucester Street' after a four months' trial, but there is no other information on why she was in The Grange in the first place, where she came from or why it did not work out for her.

Of the 16 girls in residence in 1960, it was reported that six were 'employed in the district', one was attending a technical school and another the secondary school at Carysfort.[44] The other eight were being prepared for employment, in search of employment, between jobs or otherwise being kept busy in the house, while the sisters worried over their future path. Of the 16 girls in residence in 1964, six were attending secondary school at Tivoli Road, Dun Laoghaire, and two were attending the technical school at Blackrock. Five of the older girls were in outside employment, including as hair-dresser, shop assistant and seamstress, and the remaining three were 'occupied in the house in sewing, cooking and cleaning' pending their finding – and keeping – a place in the jobs market.[45]

Some girls did very well in life, insofar as staying on at school, completing a commercial course, undertaking an apprenticeship, graduating with the Intermediate or Leaving Certificate or being accepted for nurse training can be taken as measures of achievement. At least some success with the longer term goal – that each girl might find a job that would interest her sufficiently to persevere in it and pay her well enough to be worth the effort – can also be judged from the register under 'remarks', brief and incomplete though they are. One girl admitted in 1968 – no age given, but her mother was in England and 'unable to care for her' – was described as of average intelligence and good behaviour. She completed her Leaving Certificate in Rochford Manor and found employment as an assistant in a pharmacy. Several other girls from The Grange also completed the Leaving Certificate in this school. Another girl, whose foster care arrangements had broken down, lived at The Grange from aged 15 until her 21st year, 'boisterous, wild, good at school where she finally was employed by the VEC' (1967). She was not the only past pupil of The Grange to be employed by the Vocational Education Committee.

Nursing was the career path of several girls from The Grange, with some undergoing training (Jervis Street 1957; Temple Street 1961), and others working as 'assistant nurse', in 'private nursing' or in nursing homes (1958, 1956). One girl had already started an apprenticeship as a tailoress; 'continued and finished training', and later married, with the name of the husband and new address added, all in all a very satisfactory note on which to close an entry (1959). One girl, described soon after admission as 'not very bright, splendid worker' found employment some years later in a hospital (1960). Several local businesses were prepared to give a girl a fair trial such as 'Brendella' in Dun Laoghaire, which manufactured clothing, and Bolands, the milling company whose land adjoined the convent. One of the

43   Boylan to McQuaid, 29 June 1962.
44   O'Neill to McQuaid, 28 Mar. 1960.
45   Mother Rita Cutler to Dr McQuaid, 30 Jan. 1964 (DDA, Cullen, OLC Kill of the Grange).

youngest to be admitted to The Grange before the family groups arrived from 1967 onwards, was an 11-year-old of whom the register records her mother, an alcoholic, had asked The Grange to care for her. After secondary school, but still under the care of The Grange, she did a one-year course at St Anne's, Sion Hill, probably in household management, and found employment in a named company. Others were found work as live-in domestics and as 'mother's helps'. While the notes on the future paths of the girls who were admitted in 1956–66 are brief and incomplete, they do lend credence to the claim, that, 'as far as we can judge, those who have passed from under the care of the Sisters are doing satisfactorily'.[46] An outsider also wrote confidentially to the archbishop in 1962 that 'Apparently the Sisters have been very successful with the girls they have'.[47] The first reunion was held early in 1960 when, it was reported, most of the past-pupils came along.[48]

A few of the girls who were admitted to The Grange were Travellers – or, as the register enters, itinerants. Most were not inclined to stay, or got no encouragement from their families to stay, according to the school. One teenage Traveller was persuaded to come to The Grange by a well-intentioned housewife who had got to know her from calling each week 'for help'. She stayed for seven months, 'grandmother refused to allow us to teach her to read and write' and she was married, aged 15 or so, very shortly after returning to live with the grandmother (1960). Another Traveller child was willingly entrusted to The Grange as her family could not possibly care for her; she had been seven years a patient in Cabinteely hospital due to heart disease, 'a lovely child in every way, our angel'. Her time in The Grange was no more than six months when she was brought to the Mater Hospital, where she died (1959).

Where a girl was sent by the Catholic Protection and Rescue Society of Ireland (CPRSI), Anne Street, there is a possibility that she had placed a baby for adoption, but this is never spelled out in the register. Nor can it ever be presumed, as the CPRSI was also active in 'rescuing' those in what the organisation perceived to be moral danger. So, too, the Irish Society for the Prevention of Cruelty to Children (ISPCC) was involved in removing children from what its officers judged to be dangerous neglect or actual abuse. The Society of St Vincent de Paul directed a number of girls to The Grange over its first decade or so; one case was of a foster child in Harold's Cross who went to the Carysfort 'secondary top' where she passed her Intermediate Ccertificate in 1960 and was accepted for nurse training in Jervis Street hospital.

Parents, foster parents and guardians, where these were alive, known and in contact, appear from the records to have been generally supportive of what The Grange was trying to do for their child – or at least did not set out to purposely thwart it. There were exceptions, as in the case of a 13-year-old from Munster admitted on the advice of a local priest, where both parents were living in a 'very poor home', 'undeveloped physically and mentally, unable to read or write, smoking since she was six years of age, improved

46   O'Neill to McQuaid, 28 Mar. 1960.
47   Boylan to McQuaid, 29 June 1962.
48   O'Neill to McQuaid, 28 Mar. 1960.

in every way but parents removed her when she was 14 years' (1959). Not being part of the industrial school system, children were brought and removed without court orders. Even where there were ample grounds for believing there was neglect and mistreatment at home, the child could not be kept against the wishes of a parent or guardian. But the other side of the coin was that The Grange did not have to hold onto a child that would not settle, with notes 'needed her mother's attention'; 'unhappy being away from home' marked in the register before the child was returned home, even if other siblings stayed put.

Character-building of the girls was advanced as the principal aim of the work, 'so that they may become leaders in whatever walk of life they may find themselves'. To this end, every attention was given to their spiritual and moral formation, with opportunities for sodality membership, day retreats, meditation, spiritual reading and daily attendance at Mass.[49] Sister Mary de Montfort Goss, in particular, was very devoted to the ideals of the Legion of Mary and facilitated the organisation in holding retreat days and Patrician meetings at The Grange, which the resident girls could also choose to attend.[50] Good relations with the Legion also meant that young girls found wandering in the city and mistakenly sent to the Sancta Maria hostel, as noted already, could be brought to The Grange, which was in every sense a safer place for them.[51]

The financial underpinning of the house up to 1967 was precarious, to say the least. There was no regular, secure income and, when asked how they managed, 'the nuns speak of banking on Providence'.[52] The contributions from the girls at work were modest, and nothing at all came on behalf of those attending school or undergoing training in the house. 'The Sisters are making a great effort to contribute towards the upkeep of the house by various means: – the knit-wear industry, cake-making, the sale of flowers and fruit, etc.' reported the superior general when pressed.[53] Outside observers, including priests appointed by the archbishop to make inquiries into its viability, expressed surprise that it existed at all, and put it down to 'many generous and energetic friends'.[54] On this count, they were correct, as was set out for posterity in the register of benefactors.[55] Dr John Charles McQuaid, having donated the monastery, is termed 'its principal benefactor', while the monasteries of High Park and Gloucester Street are also given prominence. Clergymen, relatives and friends of the sisters and a large number of neighbours, both private parties and institutions, are credited with named gifts, services undertaken and gifts of sums of money. A Miss Reynolds furnished the dining room and the sitting room, as well as giving a piano and some other items. Mrs Doyle and family arrived with

49  Sister M. Francis to Dr McQuaid, 10 Feb. 1961 (DDA, Cullen, OLC Kill of the Grange).
50  O'Neill to McQuaid, 28 Mar. 1960.
51  Report of St Brigid's Training Centre, 18 Jan. 1964 (DDA, Cullen, OLC Kill of the Grange).
52  Boylan to McQuaid, 29 June 1962.
53  O'Neill to McQuaid, 28 Mar. 1960.
54  P. Boylan to Dr McQuaid, 14, 29 June 1962 (DDA, Cullen, OLC Kill of the Grange).
55  'Register of the founders and benefactors of the Monastery of Our Lady of Charity of Refuge, The Grange, Kill o' the Grange, County Dublin' (DARGS, OLC4). Hereafter, The Grange, benefactors' register.

ten pullets. Mr and Mrs Thomas Breaden of St John's Park, Monkstown, and proprietor of a soap-making works in Dun Laoghaire, gave them a 3½ foot statue of the Immaculate Heart of Mary in Sicilian marble, followed later by a matching statue of the Sacred Heart, an electric cooker and a radio.[56] A Miss Trewen was commended for all she did in 1959 when she gave 'much of her time to our girls, teaching the backward to read and write and often taking them for extra lessons in her own home'. Misses Annie and Bridie Brophy were thanked in 1960 'for giving us their time so generously to help us with our little knitting industry'. The Society of St Vincent De Paul 'gave gifts for our girls' at Christmas. A Dr Coffey pledged his medical services freely in September 1965.[57]

Foremost among the religious friends locally were the Christian Brothers, the Holy Ghost fathers and the Mercy sisters. The superior of Carriglea, who in the first two months had welcomed the sisters to Mass pending the blessing of their own chapel, 'sent two men with a tractor to plough and sow our land' twice yearly in 1957, 1958 and 1959. The principal of Blackrock College, Fr O'Farrell, not alone allowed his schoolboys to participate in flag days, but 'encouraged them to do their utmost to make their collections successful'. In January 1961, he gave '22 tickets for the film *Ben Hur* and also 12 tickets for the Savoy Cinema Show'. In March 1961, the thoughtfulness of the superior of the Mercy hospital at Rochestown Avenue, Dun Laoghaire, was recorded, as she 'on three occasions this month sent films and the use of her projector'.[58]

The first fruits of the local committee 'formed to organise functions to help this convent' is recorded for September 1957, namely, £750 raised from a bring-and-buy sale. This successful venture had Mrs O'Brien Twohig as chairman and Mrs Stokes as secretary, while 'the stalls were under the care of Mrs Smith, Mrs Walsh, Mrs Breaden, Mrs Goss [sister-in-law of Sister de Montfort] and Mrs Coyle [mother of Sister Benignus]'. Thereafter there was no end to the ingenuity and perseverance of the committee, with various members of the same core group of families helping out, and its second chairman, Mr Wallace, liaising directly with High Park on its ambitions.[59] 'Bring-and-buy', jumble sales, coffee mornings, afternoon teas, whist drives, dances, raffles, collection boxes in commercial premises and flag days in the borough of Dun Laoghaire were all part of their arsenal. In 1958, Mr Coyle, the father of Sister Benignus, first made calendars for sale in aid of the convent; by 1960, he had built up to 6,000 calendars, realising the very welcome sum of £200, and he continued with this project for several years. A radio appeal for 'our girls' was broadcast from 1963 onwards.[60]

With 16 spaces only and a waiting list, the development of the work was seen as dependent on more beds, and the archbishop was requested

56   Mother M. Eithne O'Neill to the Secretary, Department of Industry and Commerce, 25 Nov. 1955, copy letter (DARGS, OLC4).
57   The Grange, benefactors' register.
58   Ibid.
59   Boylan to McQuaid, 29 June 1962.
60   Sister M. de Montfort Goss to Dr McQuaid, 29 Aug. 1963 (DDA, Cullen, OLC Kill of the Grange).

in March 1960 to sanction the building of an extension.[61] His reply – that, as he had 'never been favoured with any report on the work being done at the Grange' and needed first to know 'what is being done and what it is proposed to do' – served rather to cool the enthusiasm of the sisters and lay committee.[62] So did the estimated cost of £22,000, which was well beyond the resources of the federation, let alone of The Grange.[63] The matter was brought up again in the summer of 1962, 'for the girls in the Grange who have started to earn their own living and who wish to remain under the guidance of the sisters'.[64] Permission was granted[65] only after Monsignor Patrick Boylan, then vicar general, drew up a confidential report on the matter, noting that the convent had no secure income and the residents of the proposed new hostel could not be expected to contribute much, but otherwise the proposal 'has everything to recommend it'.[66] The commitment by the general council that the monasteries of High Park and Gloucester Street 'are willing to bear the running expenses and repairs of the extension' satisfied the archbishop, together with the business acumen of the fundraising committee under Mr Wallace, which proposed 'to collect funds which they would invest, and after four or five years, if sufficient money had been collected for a beginning, plans could be made and submitted to Your Grace'.[67] Overlapping in time with these discussions, the dilapidated outhouses were inspected by an architect, who could not have been more dismissive of their potential for conversion into a hostel, no matter what money was spent.[68] A new building was the only option.

How exactly the plans, and permission, for a working girls' hostel on the grounds of The Grange became the plans, and assumed permission, for an entirely different work, is difficult to explain. But the delay in advancing the hostel meant it was overtaken by other developments. Getting 'recognised and approved' by the Department of Health in 1965 led to the admission of several girls under the aegis of a funding body for the first time.[69] But what the health authority really wanted was to place siblings needing care, both girls and boys, together, and its willingness to grant-aid institutions which made that possible had been grasped. Changes to the configuration of the land held by the sisters at Kill of the Grange also led to a shift in focus. The county council took two strips of land for its long-threatened road widening in 1964 (figure 10.1).[70] At the same time, the opportunity arose of purchasing a portion of the adjoining Carriglea land of the Christian Brothers. This was initially opposed by the general council, which felt it was unaffordable and

61  O'Neill to McQuaid, 28 Mar. 1960.
62  John C. McQuaid to Mother M. Rita, 24 Mar. 1960 (DARGS, OLC4).
63  High Park local council, minutes, 12 May 1960.
64  Mother M. Rita Cutler to Dr McQuaid, 8 May, 23 June 1962 (DDA, Cullen, OLC Kill of the Grange).
65  McQuaid to Cutler, 15 June 1962.
66  P. Boylan to Dr McQuaid, 14 June 1962 (DDA, Cullen, OLC Kill of the Grange).
67  Cutler to McQuaid, 23 June 1962.
68  Patrick Campbell to Revd Mother General, 5 June 1962 (DARGS, OLC4).
69  Mother Mary Eithne O'Neill to Dr McQuaid, 12 Feb. 1965 (DDA, Cullen, OLC Kill of the Grange).
70  J.R. Ryan to Mother St Eithne, 20 Oct. 1964 (DARGS, OLC4).

unnecessary.[71] The argument that the purchase of land 'would precipitate the erection of the hostel' and encourage the loyal fundraising committee – as they would see 'something concrete' happening – was dismissed; there was already ample space, and permission, to build.[72] However, persuaded that not to act would result in The Grange being tightly encircled by new housing, the general council relented, and the purchase was permitted by the archbishop 'to secure your property and to extend the work being carried out'.[73] It was a lucky move. The Grange now had an extensive new road frontage and an additional six acres.[74] With land prices soaring, it was the re-sale of portions of this land shortly afterwards that would make possible the building of the children's homes.[75]

In October 1967, the superior general informed the vicar general of the intention to undertake a new work, 'known nowadays as the Family Group System, which would entail the building of a house (or houses) for the accommodation of children from broken homes etc.'[76] Arguments in favour of this model of institutional care had been made in Ireland for more than a decade for those exceptional cases where the support of the birth-family, legal adoption or supervised foster-care were not workable solutions.[77] Small numbers, it was argued, allowed the individual interest and personal bonding that could never happen in a large institution, no matter how well intentioned, while the rearing of girls and boys together, attending ordinary day schools outside – with babies part of the group, rather than kept in separate nurseries – was promoted as benefiting all the children involved and well worth the extra finance that would be required to staff it properly.[78] Progress towards this novel system of mixed age-groups was already under way in The Grange before Archbishop's House was informed in October 1967. From the entrance register, 14 children had already been admitted, made up of three separate family groups (and two other girls, not related), while the health authorities were by then paying maintenance grants for most of the girls after sustained – and obviously successful – application by the local superior and, on her behalf, by the superior general.[79] The very first family group of boys and girls, ranging in age from two to ten years, arrived in January 1967 due, according to the register, to the mother being in hospital

71    Mother M. Rita Cutler to Revd C. Hurley, 22 Mar. 1964 (DDA, Cullen, OLC Kill of the Grange).
72    Sister M. St de Montfort to Dear Mother, 30 Dec. 1963 (DARGS, OLC4).
73    John C. McQuaid to Revd Mother General, 30 Mar. 1964, 12 June 1964 (DARGS, OLC4).
74    Mother M. Rita Cutler to Dr McQuaid, 30 Jan. 1964, 11 June 1964 (DDA, Cullen, OLC Kill of the Grange).
75    'In May 1970 sold on a portion of the land for £10,000 to Messrs Foxrock and Brewery Ltd, and in Oct. 1971 sold on another portion for £20,000', Sister de Montfort to Sister Anne, n.d. but June 1984 added in pencil (DARGS, OLC4); E.G. Gleeson to Revd Mother General, 25 Feb., 1 Oct. 1970 (DARGS, OLC4).
76    Mother M. Rita Cutler to Mgr Boylan, 3 Oct. 1967 (DDA, Cullen, OLC Kill of the Grange).
77    Ann Kenny, 'The deprived child', *Christus Rex*, x, no. 2 (1956), pp 99–114.
78    Ibid., pp 113–4.
79    Cecil Barrett to Dr McQuaid, 24 Oct. 1967 (DDA, Cullen, OLC Kill of the Grange); copy letter, Mother M. Eithne O'Neill to the Secretary, Dublin Health Authorities, 26 May 1965 (DARGS, OLC4)

and the father having deserted. The children were in the care of the Eastern Health Board. Later that year, a group of four sisters aged between seven and 14 years, another pair of sisters aged 13 and nine years, and another 13-year-old girl were transferred together, seven children in all, from an industrial school that was closing down, marking the continued effort of The Grange to 'doing something' for former industrial school children, while at the same time taking on the new model of family group care.[80] The maintenance grants being paid for these children would have transferred also, putting the new venture on a more secure financial footing. Sanction had been received from the Department of Health for an increase in the standard maintenance grant, pending only the permission of the archbishop for the sisters' involvement in the new family scheme.[81] Sister de Montfort Goss had already undertaken a study tour of Catholic residential homes in England, including some run by her own order, to see for herself how the new thinking in childcare was being worked out in practice.[82] It was the vicar general's opinion that the archbishop would have heard nothing about the switch of plan except that he, Patrick Boylan, happened to hear about it, 'by accident, more or less'. He was certainly correct in his reading of relations between the local, autonomous house and the leadership of the federation: 'I doubt if Mother General has much grip there at all'.[83] Well before the authorities were told about it, the 'family group system' was in operation at The Grange and making the case for a new purpose-built premises which, it was maintained, 'would leave space in the present building for conversion into a hostel for older girls'.[84]

The plan was to build a self-contained house to accommodate 12 children, boys and girls, in age groups one to ten for boys and one to 14 years for girls. The work would be in the hands of Sister M. of Perpetual Succour (Ann Marie Ryan), who had recently completed the British Home Office course for housemothers.[85] It was the inclusion of boys that most engaged the diocesan authorities – or, more exactly, what would be done with the older boys. To the first objection, Goss could draw on her research into homes in England: 'in all cases the Sisters in charge were very definite in saying that no problems existed provided the boys came to the Home at an early age'. Should there be an issue at some future date, there was a rather vague undertaking that 'places would be booked' in St Saviour's orphanage in Dominick Street, where 'Revd Fr McCormack is willing to accept these boys whenever we wish to transfer them'.[86] The problem, rightly identified by the diocesan authorities at the time, was that there would be no local authority maintenance grant with boys sent to St Saviour's or to the other possible alternative, St Vincent's orphanage, Glasnevin – they would be private or voluntary charity cases.[87]

80 Register, The Grange, 1967 (DARGS, OLC4).
81 Mother M. Eithne O'Neill to Mgr C.J. Barrett, 13 Dec. 1967 (DDA, Cullen, OLC Kill of the Grange).
82 Same to same, 30 Dec. 1967 (DDA, Cullen, OLC Kill of the Grange).
83 Cecil Barrett to Dr McQuaid, 6 Jan. 1968 (DDA, Cullen, OLC Kill of the Grange).
84 Same to same, 24 Oct. 1967 (DDA, Cullen, OLC Kill of the Grange).
85 Ibid.
86 Mother M. Eithne O'Neill to Mgr C.J. Barrett, 13, 30 Dec. 1967 (DDA, Cullen, OLC Kill of the Grange).
87 Mgr C.J. Barrett to Mother M. Eithne O'Neill, 15 Dec. 1967 (DARGS, OLC4).

The vicar general, Monsignor Cecil Barrett, spoke disparagingly of the local superior, whose judgement he did not rate highly, and expressed misgivings about the 'standards of the work'. He was equivocal about whether or not the project should be allowed to go ahead: 'I am still not terribly impressed, though I find it is difficult to say why exactly. However, it must be said in their favour that they are *trying* to lift themselves up'.[88] Another of the archbishop's advisers, Fr John Peirce of Cremore, Glasnevin, who was heavily involved in the Catholic Youth and Child Guidance Association for Residential Child Care, was much more positive in his assessment, but his judgement was in turn questioned by the vicar general.[89] The running costs would certainly be substantial and assurances were needed that High Park would underwrite them.[90] The fact that the superior general could point to having eight sisters currently attending the new year-long course in childcare held on Saturdays in the Institute for Adult Education 'for those already doing this work', and that the sister who would be in charge of the new family home already held a recognised UK qualification, seems to have swung the decision in favour of allowing the project to go ahead, but it was a closely-run thing.[91] The wording of the permission to build a family group home at Kill of the Grange 'thus allowing you to use the existing building as a Hostel for girls' shows Dr McQuaid holding tenaciously to what he had always taken to be the principal work of the house.[92]

Permission to build the first of what would be three family group homes, each with its own separate postal address and gateway, was granted in July 1968. Bartrès, called after the foster home of St Bernadette Soubirous, with the address 1 Pottery Road, was blessed by the archbishop on 24 January 1971 in the presence of local clergy, the Lord Mayor, the architects (Arthur Hickey and Patrick Campbell), the sisters and a great gathering of lay friends and benefactors. Of the final cost of £31,000, a substantial grant, £5,000, had come from the Department of Health.[93] A lengthy report, with photograph, in the *Irish Press* the following day lauded the 'normal home atmosphere' of the two-storey brick and timber house, 'a small and experimental project which is in line with the most modern thinking on the care of children from broken homes'.[94] The fact that they attended local primary, secondary and vocational schools was noted, as was the encouragement to develop outside interests: 'The children select their entertainment and their outings, in company with their school groups or friends from other houses in the district.' The house may have looked like a 'normal' family home to passers-by, but it was much larger, with seven bedrooms, two bathrooms, dining room, playroom, kitchen, laundrette, parlour and study for the house-mother. There was a very well-equipped outside play space,

88    Cecil Barrett to Dr McQuaid, 2 Jan. 1968 (DDA, Cullen, OLC Kill of the Grange). Emphasis as in the original.
89    John Peirce to Dr McQuaid, 3, 5 Jan. 1968; Cecil Barrett to Dr McQuaid, 6 Jan. 1968 (DDA, Cullen, OLC Kill of the Grange).
90    Same to same, 24 Oct. 1967 (DDA, Cullen, OLC Kill of the Grange).
91    O'Neill to Barrett, 30 Dec. 1967.
92    J.C. McQuaid to Rev Mother Eithne, 11 July 1968 (DDA, Cullen, OLC Kill of the Grange).
93    *Irish Press*, 26 Jan. 1971.
94    Ibid.

including sand pit and swings. The journalist was particularly taken with the role of the widowed mother of the first sister in charge of Bartrès, Sister Ann Marie Ryan, who came on visits from her own home in Cashel, County Tipperary, and was known and loved by all the children as 'Granny Ryan'.[95]

During its first year of operation, 1971, Bartrès had a minimum of six (two boys, four girls) and a maximum of 12 children (four boys, eight girls) in residence at any one time, and was grant-maintained by the Dublin Health Authority/Eastern Health Board.[96] Four sets of siblings were accommodated; the youngest child was an infant aged two. The underlying philosophy was very simply expressed: 'While the deprivation of a normal family can never be fully compensated for, we can best help the children to grow and develop in a setting that resembles as closely as possible an ordinary family group'.[97] Even as Bartrès was getting under way, work had started on a second house, also to accommodate 12 children (this was Cualann, 2 Pottery Road). Part of the original big house was being refurbished to cater for another group of 12 and the 'other part is being converted into flat-let accommodation for nine working girls who live in the original home'.[98] No doubt, pains were taken to make the continued existence of the hostel clear to the *Irish Press* journalist, lest the sisters be accused of abandoning what was their first work in The Grange and the cause for which funds had been publicly raised over the preceding decade.

The Grange came into the ownership of the Irish Federation of the Sisters of Our Lady of Charity at a time when new approaches to childcare were just beginning to take hold in Ireland. It was never part of the old, closely-regulated system of certified schools, with its committal orders and release on licence, and so did not have a weight of institutionalisation to shed. Nor was it ever a remand home for the courts, and the children were always part of the ordinary school population of the parish. In the traditional language of the order, it was intended to be a 'house of preservation' and a training school for young girls, but the shape this might take had still to be worked out at local level and without the advantage of any state funding.[99] For the first 15 years or so, the community kept a low profile and tried to avoid drawing the attention of the archbishop to its existence, even though he might rightly be listed as founder of the house and its first benefactor. Its work with adolescents up to 1966 was done, according to the documentary evidence, under the direction of the sisters within the local setting and without public fanfare; the sisters worked with small numbers, but followed each girl through to young adulthood in a way that more closely resembled family care than the traditional systems could ever achieve, no matter how well-intentioned their staff. The community was jealously protective of the reputation of its girls and past pupils, and this may perhaps account for

---

95   Ibid.
96   Monthly accounts, Bartrès, 1 Pottery Road, Kill o' the Grange, County Dublin (DARGS, OLC4).
97   'Report on the work of the Apostolate Committee, appointed August 1969', 1972, p. 14 (DARGS, OLC5/5/7 no. 1).
98   *Irish Press*, 26 Jan. 1971.
99   O'Neill to McQuaid, 16 Dec. 1954.

its keeping somewhat aloof from the other houses of the federation and requesting autonomy in 1969, a move which went in the opposite direction to all that was happening in the federation in the aftermath of Vatican II. The decision to become a children's home in 1966, admitting boys as well as girls whom the health board wished to place without breaking up sets of siblings, was a small shift, rather than a change in direction, and very much in accord with the new thinking. The opening of the first custom-built 'family group home' at 1 Pottery Road in January 1971 was the start of a new phase, but it did have precedents. There was already a history, though brief and little known, even within the order.

# Chapter 11

# The Irish Federation of OLC Monasteries 1948, the Centenary of High Park 1953, and the Modernising of St Mary's Refuge, 1952–72

The move towards 'modern methods' took hold in the 1950s among the sisters of Our Lady of Charity in Ireland, to use the term employed in the community's own records. The magdalen asylums, reformatories and industrial schools were upgraded and restructured, in a gradual, incremental way. By the 1960s, new models of residential care for children, teenagers and young women were started, namely hostels, training centres, small units and 'family group homes', as introduced already (chapters 8–10). The focus is now brought back to the founding work of the order, the refuge for women, looking first at St Mary's, High Park, and then at the asylum in Sean MacDermott Street. These parallel studies are then filled out with an exploration of how the OLC monasteries themselves engaged with the demands to modernise made by the Second Vatican Council and the changes to traditional practices and understandings that were asked of each sister in this unprecedented period of upheaval. The creation of the Irish federation of Our Lady of Charity in 1948 is taken as the opening date, and the implementation, *ad experimentem*, in 1973 of the revised constitutions as the closing date of this narrative. As has been explained at the outset of this study, the interconnectedness of the monasteries and the refuges, in all that pertains to their spiritual lives and temporal affairs, sisters and women residents, and as evident in the documentary record, requires that these three chapters in particular (11, 12, 13) be treated as overlapping or joint histories 1948–73, though presented separately.

## High Park at Federation, 1948

While much will be made of the significance of the creation of the Irish federation of Our Lady of Charity on 5 November 1948, it must be admitted that, on the surface at least, it brought little practical change to the three monasteries involved, namely, High Park, Sean MacDermott Street (Gloucester Street) and St Anne's, Kilmacud. The federation created of High Park a motherhouse and gave the superior general (see appendix B) the important role of visitation every three years, but the powers of the new central authority

**Figure 11.1** Emblem of the order of Our Lady of Charity: Mary with the Child
Jesus, circled by roses and lilies, set into a heart, representing the
love of God encompassing all. (DARGS)

were strictly prescribed and there were hardly any changes to the constitutions, beyond the bare minimum that allowed the federation to operate. The
preamble to the revised constitutions of 1951 states that the aforementioned
convents had joined the federation, such that 'the monasteries shall be independent each of the other, and all will be under the direction and control of
the Superior General and her Council, the more aptly to secure the canonical
formation of candidates to religious life and the technical training of the
Sisters-in-charge for the fulfilment of their works.'[1] The constitutions themselves warned the superior general 'to take diligent care that the authority
of the superiors of the monasteries is maintained', and to ensure that the
traditional rule of enclosure was not breached, excepting only – and with
her permission – journeys between the monasteries of the federation, and
where sisters were charged with works outside the community enclosure.[2]
The OLC constitutions, revised under Dr McQuaid, incorporated exactly
the spirit and the letter of the apostolic constitution *Sponsa Christi*, issued
by Rome in November 1950, which urged federation of religious houses to

1   Declaration by John Charles McQuaid, 3 Nov. 1951, *Additions and amendments to the
Constitutions of the Order of Our Lady of Charity of Refuge, in accordance with the Decree of the
Sacred Congregation of Religious, dated 28 June 1948, and the Rescript of the same Sacred Congregation dated 12 Feb. 1951* (Dublin, 1951) (DARGS, OLC1/05/1, no. 20). Hereafter, Additions to the
constitutions.
2   Additions to the constitutions. pp 32, 55.

overcome a lack of personnel, to provide 'mutual economic assistance' and 'the co-ordination of works', but 'without impairing essential autonomy nor in any way weakening the observance of cloister'.[3]

But federation placed High Park itself in an anomalous position, with two superiors, with different jurisdictions operating from offices on the same corridor.[4] The superior general (also called federal superior), the first councillor and the secretary of the new federation resided at High Park, and it was to High Park that the superiors of the other houses and their assistants were summoned for important meetings.[5] It was to the superior general at High Park that Archbishop McQuaid directed practically all his correspondence. High Park continued to have its own local superior, except for the period 1951–7 when Mother Eithne O'Neill held both the office of superior general and of local superior concurrently.[6] High Park was the training centre for all novices, the majority of whom were in fact its own. It was the best-resourced house in terms of property, funds and personnel numbers, so that any initiative by the new federation would depend on its support. But because of its long history, it also carried the heaviest burdens: outmoded systems of care and archaic buildings, heavy outgoings, few sisters with third-level qualifications and the federation's largest proportion of elderly and sick, sisters and women residents.

In what pertained to the daily religious life of High Park, the 1950s and early 1960s were marked by fidelity to long-established routines of early rising, set times of prayer, Mass, work, meals, times of silence and of recreation. The year still had its certain rhythm: 'In the spring we had the lovely days of "Quarant Ore" and the touching ceremonies of Holy Week', with monthly days of recollection held in both convent and refuge; the summer was marked by May and Corpus Christi processions, the week-long retreat for the women and the private retreats of the sisters; the sisters' preached retreat ended on the eve of the Presentation of Our Lady when they renewed their vows (21 November). The season of Advent led to the Christmas celebrations, the 'joys of the festive season' concluding finally on 2 February, the Presentation of the Child Jesus in the Temple.[7] The Children of Mary, the Franciscan Third Order, the Apostleship of Prayer,[8] each had their membership and their particular meetings, 'while all had their Triduum

3   *Sponsa Christi*, Pius XII, 21 Nov. 1950, in Lincoln T. Bouscaren and James O'Connor (eds), *The canon law digest for religious*, i, 1917–63 (Milwaukee, 1964), p. 335.
4   This continued until the opening of the federal house at Nutley Road, Donnybrook, in May 1975.
5   The second general chapter of the Irish federation held 24 Nov. 1954 decided that the first councillor might be permitted to live outside High Park. See 'Book of the elections of superiors of High Park from 1853 to 1948 and of the general council from November 1948' (DARGS, OLC1/5/2).
6   Additions to the constitutions, p. 33.
7   High Park, circular letters, 8 Dec. 1951, 8 Dec. 1957 (NDC Caen, Archives Besançon); 20 Dec. 1963 (DARGS, OLC1/3/1 no. 28).
8   Register, Apostleship of Prayer, titled 'The Penitents, St Mary's Asylum, High Park, Drumcondra, Dublin', Jan. 1941 to 3 Apr. 1964, but with note that first enrolments were in 1900 (DARGS, OLC1/8/1 no. 8).

in preparation for the Feast of the Most Holy Heart of Mary'.[9] For the sisters, the full recitation, in common, of the Divine Office continued, and going outside the enclosure was the exception, rather than the norm. The upgrading and remodelling of St Mary's refuge during the 1950s and 1960s took place against this background of stability. Change was to be incremental, at least until the later 1960s.

## High Park Centenary, 1953

The centenary of High Park, celebrated in September 1953 with a triduum of liturgical events, can be seen as a watershed: it celebrated the very visible success, on its own terms, of the asylum or refuge system created in 1640s Normandy and transplanted to the outskirts of Dublin in 1858. It was an opportunity to present the High Park refuge as a charity of the Dublin archdiocese, and the Irish Federation of the Sisters of Our Lady of Charity as especially favoured by the archbishop. The publication of an illustrated, 95-page 'centenary record' was the most ambitious effort yet made by High Park to engage in print with the larger public, and written in the self-congratulatory and rather overdone style of a work of its type and date.[10] This booklet emphasises the long tradition of the order and the distinctive spirituality that underpins its work; there is an explanation of the order's emblem – the silver heart engraved with an image of Mary holding the child Jesus, surrounded by lilies and roses – which dates from 1644 (figure 11.1). Devotion to the hearts of Jesus and Mary is to be the source of all the graces that the religious of Our Lady of Charity needs.[11]

The narrative of its foundation and development, appropriate to a centenary publication, placed the High Park of 1953 along a trajectory of development; it was under Providence that the dismal beginning gave way, by increments, to the splendid complex of 1953.[12] The tribulations through which the founder, Mother of the Sacred Heart Kelly, and her first companions passed were but a continuation of the mysterious workings out of the story started in 1640s Normandy; the modernisation that is boasted of in 1953 is but the latest manifestation of this unfolding story. In its reflection on the laundry, which occupied most of the sisters and of the women, and which its readers would be well aware was the institute's principal source of income, it paints a romanticised scene of 'prayer and work happily combined', with electricity and steam power having lightened the labour, and the 'merry chatter' of relaxation times.[13] The booklet concludes with a roll call of the houses of the order worldwide, starting with Caen in 1641. High Park is placed as the mother house of an expanding network, 'our daughter houses', and the connections with two English houses, although never part of the Irish Federation, are underscored: 'Waterlooville, re-established from High Park, 1900; Ormskirk, founded from High Park 1914'. High Park was

9    High Park, circular letter, 8 Dec. 1951.
10   *The Order of Our Lady of Charity of Refuge, 1853–1953, a centenary record of High Park Convent, Drumcondra, Dublin* (Dublin, 1953), hereafter *Centenary record*.
11   Ibid., p. 27.
12   Ibid., p. 60.
13   Ibid., pp 65–6.

now the central noviciate and the seat of the superior general.[14] Who was to say where and when it might be called on to graft a new branch onto the old tree?

## St Mary's Refuge, High Park and its Remodelling 1952–72

By 1953, St Mary's Refuge at High Park could accommodate almost 200 women and – it appears – there was sufficient work in the laundry, workshops, infirmary and general household to occupy the vast bulk of the women who, as always, were expected to work alongside the sisters towards their keep, excepting only the ill and elderly.[15] Surrounded by the 'holy atmosphere' of the house, it was prayer, silence, labour and the sympathy and kindness of the 'mothers' towards their 'dear charges' that the principal author of the centenary record, Fr O'Keeffe CM, credited with transforming even the most wayward soul.[16] The modernisation that was boasted of in the centenary year did not undermine the refuge system *per se* but served only to soften the edges – as, for example, with the recent introduction of the radio (figure 11.2):

> The Radio has been installed with extensions to every department and to the grounds. The poor invalids in the infirmary love to listen-in to the Holy Mass on Sundays and festivals, and indeed it is a delight for many who are not invalids to join them. The young people enjoy, during work hours, their favourite music, and often join in the familiar songs that are daily broadcast. Everything has been done to make them happy, for well the Sisters know that a merry heart makes a contented spirit.[17]

Even as friendly commentators celebrated what had been achieved to date, there was pressure to abandon the system entirely as outdated, albeit well-intentioned. The most insistent advocate of 'modern methods' was the archbishop of Dublin, John Charles McQuaid, and the diocesan federation in 1948 which he had managed from start to finish gave him the means – the superior general – through which he could communicate his views to each of the houses, in the expectation (not always fulfilled) that they would be implemented. At the election of a new superior general in 1954, he confirmed the sisters in their special vocation, which remained the same,

> What has however, changed, is the method of the Apostolate. Charity and patience may not change, but the demands of our times require many changes in the methods of the Apostolate. You can sanctify yourselves, you can faithfully fulfil your special vocation only when, in obedience to the Holy See and

---

14   An extension with at least 20 new cells or bedrooms had been completed in 1933. *Centenary record*, p. 67.

15   Ibid., p. 65.

16   Ibid., p. 26.

17   Ibid., p. 67. 'Radio licence' appears in the accounts from 1954.

**Figure 11.2** Women residents in the infirmary of St Mary's, High Park, listening to Sunday Mass on the wireless. (*Centenary record*, 1953)

the wishes of the Archbishop, you devote your best attention to the redeeming of penitents by methods suited to our present conditions.[18]

McQuaid closed his address with the prayer that, under the guidance of Our Lady, the sisters might 'realise the force of my constant exhortations'. None of the delegates present at the federation chapter could have failed to grasp the import of his message.[19] Follow-up meetings would make his determination even clearer.[20]

With federation, there was a more immediate and real connectedness with Rome, and a better knowledge of what Rome expected of religious institutes, a matter of enormous import with the calling of the 21st ecumenical or Church-wide council, Vatican II, announced on 25 January 1959. For the first time ever, the order in Ireland was obliged to submit to Rome lengthy and detailed five-year (quinquennial) reports.[21] This 'written *relatio*

18   Address given by His Grace John C. McQuaid to the members of the general chapter, 23 Nov. 1954 (DARGS, OLC5/1/2).
19   Ibid.
20   Meeting called for 3 Jan. 1957, J.C. McQuaid to Mother M. Eithne, 29 Dec. 1956 (DDA, McQuaid Papers, Department of Justice).
21   As prescribed by canon 510 of the 1917 code of canon law; a questionnaire or formula on which to base the report was later issued to the superiors general of religious congregations of simple vows approved by the Holy See, see 25 Mar. 1922, *Acta Apostolica Sedis*, XIV, 278.

of the disciplinary, economic and personal state of the Federation' was to be prepared by the superior general and her council, following a template prepared by the Sacred Congregation of Religious, and submitted via the local ordinary, the archbishop of Dublin.[22] The first OLC report from Ireland covers the years 1949 to 1953 inclusive, the following covers 1954 to 1958, and thereafter it continues at five-year intervals. In addition, the superior general had to make annual returns, the *Schema Annuale* to Rome, also via the local ordinary. With its requirement to return (under section 10) the qualifications of the members (noting whether university or internal degrees, name and type of degree, number of religious that have each degree, degrees from ecclesiastical universities; degrees from civil universities and educational institutions),[23] the scarcity of third-level qualifications among the sisters of High Park was evident, at least to the superior general and her council, and the Church's expectation that women religious would qualify themselves for their apostolic work was brought home. Learning 'on the job', however valuable in itself, would not meet outside expectations. Pointed questions on the future plans of superiors for the institute, what new activity had happened since the last quinquennial report, how Catholic Action[24] was being supported and the means the institute was using 'to attract and arouse vocations' all underlined that merely 'ticking over' was not what Rome expected.

The other key influence was the example of what was happening in OLC houses elsewhere. Despite their stand-alone character, they embraced the same constitutions, venerated the same founder and had the same special end: 'the conversion of girl and woman penitents, also the preservation and education of young girls'.[25] In the early 1950s, it was from sister houses in England that the Dublin monasteries learned something of how the call to 'move with the times' might be put into practice in an OLC setting, with reciprocal visits from English sisters hosted by High Park in the 1960s. The Irish Federation sent its superior general to an OLC meeting in Rome in 1960 with the grudging acquiescence of the archbishop. Despite his warnings ('You will need to be very watchful in regard to new proposals. Our conditions are not those of Latin countries'[26]) both then and on subsequent visits, lessons were learned directly from France on the care of young women and troubled teenagers, particularly from the OLC 'Observation Centres' of Chevilly and Le Mesnil. Though she had no governing powers outside her own Federation (established in July 1945), the considered opinion of the French mother general, resident in Chevilly, was taken as a reference point for OLC houses in Ireland. A tentative inquiry dated 11 February 1953 from the superior general of the Irish Federation, 'as to whether it is possible for

22   Additions to the constitutions, p. 33.

23   Loose memo, 'Annual Report form, translation of Forms', 1954 (DARGS, OLC1/2/1 no. 51).

24   In 1922 Pope Pius XI encouraged the Catholic laity to engage in organised religious activity, especially of a social, educational or quasi-political nature, and under the direction of the clergy; see 'Catholic Action', *Concise Oxford dictionary of the Christian Church*, ed. E.A. Livingstone (3rd edn, Oxford, 2013), online edn [20 Feb. 2017].

25   OLC Irish federation quinquennial report 1949–53, question no. 49, item no. 4 (DARGS, OLC1/2/1 no. 49). Hereafter, Irish federation, quinquennial report [year].

26   Dr McQuaid to Revd Mother Eithne O'Neill, 30 Mar. 1960 (DARGS, OLC5/5/2 no. 1).

a monastery of Our Lady of Charity to have a special section for unmarried mothers', was struck down by the French mother general following consultations with her councillors. They added for good measure that 'We think that this way of abiding in the spirit of our constitutions will draw down the blessing of the good God on works.'[27] But, despite that negative response, a more open, friendly exchange was developing; at a later date, the French mother general was hosted at High Park, where she showed 'photographic slides of the houses of the French Federation and their own Belle France'.[28] Similarly, the North American OLC houses did their part in fostering links with the Irish houses and keeping them abreast of new ventures. The mother president of the American federation extended an invitation to the Irish federation to send a sister to their extraordinary general chapter in 1958, in the role of observer or honoured guest.[29] Sisters from Dallas, Rochester and Wheeling all visited High Park on different occasions, en route elsewhere.[30] In April 1964, two sisters from San Antonio, Texas, made High Park their headquarters while endeavouring to recruit members in Dublin and various parts of Ireland: 'They returned to San Antonio on 3 November, bringing with them three postulants'.[31] Other outside perspectives came from OLC visitors from Buffalo, US, and from Edmonton, Canada.[32] The Buffalo refuge, founded 1855, was the closest in date to High Park; its centenary publication extols its quality training and comfortable, modern facilities, including a fully-equipped 'beauty salon' and typing room, with psychological, counselling and placement services available to the girls.[33] Nearer to home, there were also rare but friendly exchanges with the Sisters of the Good Shepherd: a once-off visit to their Limerick convent in March 1961[34] and a showing by a visiting Good Shepherd sister of pictures 'of their various English, Scotch and Welsh houses' in High Park in 1966.[35]

The changes that were afoot were in the context of massive upheavals in both Church and society, and the new thinking about 'the world' that the ecumenical council of Vatican II made possible. Exactly in line with the language of the council decrees, the circular letters of the 1960s are marked by warm references to dialogue with other OLC houses 'so essential for the good of our holy Order and the difficult apostolate in the modern world'.[36]

27    Minutes of meetings of general council of the federation, Union of the three monasteries of the order of Our Lady of Charity of Refuge in the archdiocese of Dublin, amalgamated 5 Nov. 1948, 8 Mar. 1952, referring to letter of Mother M. of Jésus le Levier, in response to a question sent by Very Honoured Mother [Mary of St Eithne O'Neill] (DARGS, OLC5/5/1 no. 1). Hereafter, Irish federation general council, minutes.
28    High Park, circular letter, 8 Dec. 1966 (DARGS, OLC1/3/1 no. 31).
29    Irish federation general council, minutes, 24 Feb. 1958.
30    Ibid., 22 July 1959, 30 July 1962, 5 Aug 1962, 25 Feb. 1963, 7 Aug. 1963.
31    The visitors were Sister M. of St Veronica and Sister M. of St Paul; Irish federation general council, minutes, 3 Oct. 1964.
32    High Park, circular letter, 8 Dec. 1966.
33    Souvenir booklet, *The Religious of Our Lady of Charity in Buffalo, 1855–1955, 485 Best Street* (Buffalo, 1955).
34    The visitors were Sister Aloysius Pilkington and Sister M. de Chantal O'Kelly, Irish federation general council, minutes, 28 Mar. 1961.
35    High Park, circular letter, 8 Dec. 1966.
36    Ibid., 20 Dec. 1963.

The overt concern with autonomy and with independence is superseded by what are presented as the obvious benefits of learning from other OLC houses:

> Besides, communication is now a very natural and indeed, in-dispensable part of human living: by it we learn more about our Sisters, and the best way of keeping in touch with a chang-ing world is a willingness to listen to what a different genera-tion has to say and try to channel the energies of modern ideas into constructive projects and desirable changes. We express the hope that the two-way process of intercourse in such a net-work may give to all a great deal of useful information.[37]

The most important and longest-standing affinity was between the inde-pendent monasteries of Our Lady of Charity in England, which always had Irish-born members, and the OLC sisters in Dublin. This was aside even from the past involvement of High Park in sending sisters to Waterlooville (1900) and to Ormskirk (1914), and the financial support extended to these houses over several decades.[38] The OLC community in Bitterne, Southampton, in the diocese of Portsmouth, was well ahead in terms of novel approaches to residential care. The shifts in thinking and the experiments tried in Bitterne were known to the High Park sisters as they unfolded through the annual circular letters, faithfully sent, of their go-ahead Irish-born superior, Sister Agnes Ennis, and through research visits by sisters from Dublin, the first of which was undertaken in October 1953.[39] The advances in Bitterne in respect of the teenage girls and women residents of the refuge involved sending them to night classes in the local technical school sometime before 1946, the provision of their own in-house training programme in domestic economy (1949), the payment of outside laundry workers (former residents) work-ing alongside their own (unpaid) trainees or temporary residents (from 1949), the introduction of new laundry technologies to lighten the labour (1950) and an increased engagement with the world outside the enclosure through seaside holidays, visits to the cinema and Saturday shopping excur-sions (1952). The influence of Bitterne can be read most directly in St Anne's, Kilmacud, but all the houses knew something of what was happening there, through the reading aloud of its circular letters in each community.[40]

Conscious of 'the changed social conditions' under which OLC sisters carried out their work in England, Sister Agnes Ennis of Bitterne ensured young sisters and some older members acquired recognised qualifications. From at least 1947, sisters were sent to undertake the course run by the

---

37   High Park, circular letter, 8 Dec. 1965 (DARGS, OLC1/3/1, no. 30).
38   Receipts and expenditure, Redcliffe Convent, 1 Jan. 1926 to 3 June 1930 (DARGS, OLC1/3/5 no. 8); death letter of Mother M. of St Genevieve Byrne (Elizabeth), d. 23 Mar. 1930 (DARGS, OLC1/6/4 no. 16).
39   The sisters visited Bitterne and Waterlooville (diocese of Portsmouth) and Bartestree (diocese of Cardiff); John C. McQuaid to Revd Mother M. Carmel, 15 Oct. 1953, copy letter (DARGS, OLC3/2/2 no. 9); Irish federation general council, minutes, 26 Oct. 1953.
40   Bitterne OLC convent, Southampton, circular letters, 1 Dec. 1946; 24 Dec. 1947; 24 Dec. 1948; 1 Dec. 1949 (DARGS, OLC1/3/3 nos. 31–5); 19 Dec. 1957 (DARGS, OLC1/3/3 no. 41).

Home Office in child welfare, with the inspection by this body of 'Voluntary Homes', commencing 1 January 1949, giving an added urgency to the
acquisition of appropriate qualifications. Throughout the late 1940s and the
1950s, there were sisters from Bitterne in training also as teachers of domestic economy and as state registered nurses, midwives and nursery nurses.
From 1949 onwards, Bitterne postulants had to reach school certificate standard before embarking on their novitiate year to ensure they were ready for
further training once professed, even though this could lengthen the postu-
lancy and (the superior admitted) releasing sisters for full-time training was
a big sacrifice by the rest of the community.

The level of involvement of the state in the provision of social welfare
in England (following the Beveridge report, 1942) was far beyond what was
politically or financially possible in 1950s Ireland, and the social work and
childcare professions in England were, as a consequence, much better developed. But the desirability of programmes of training for those in specific branches of social work – as hospital social workers, probation officers,
housing managers and childcare workers – was at least under discussion in
Ireland. There was a social studies diploma, with practical work and evening
lectures on offer in Trinity College Dublin (TCD) from 1934, developing rapidly in the 1940s when the diploma could be combined with a degree. The
obstacles to Catholic attendance at TCD (the permission of Dr McQuaid had
first to be sought) led to parallel developments in University College Dublin
(founded as the Catholic University), which had its own social science degree
course from 1954. Irish students also trained in Britain during these decades,
in some cases taking up jobs there 'and gaining valuable experience pending
the long-awaited openings in this country'.[41] There is direct evidence that
knowledge of 'best practice' in English OLC homes, subject to state inspection and in receipt of enviably generous state funding, influenced policy-
making and practice in High Park and decisions about where the sisters
might train. By the time of the fact-finding visit to Portsmouth in October
1953, all three Dublin monasteries had already introduced some elements of
'modernisation', and so their representatives were more likely to be open to
further learning. The refuge issues faced up to by Bitterne had their parallels
in Dublin, albeit in slightly different guises, and many of the new approaches
adopted in High Park in the 1950s and 1960s had been successfully tested in
England several years – if not decades – earlier. Home Office inspection of
'voluntary homes' in England dates from 1 January 1949,[42] putting OLC hostels and homes under the spotlight in a way which, considering the close connections between the social work profession in both jurisdictions, the High
Park sisters could reasonably expect would apply in Ireland in due course.[43]
Pressure from secular authorities in Ireland had not yet impinged much on
their particular area of work, but the matter of holding accredited qualifications could not be put on hold indefinitely when the archbishop of Dublin

41   Agnes McGuire, 'Some careers in social work', *Christus Rex*, ii, no. 3 (1948), p. 38. See also,
Agnes McGuire, 'Why almoners?', *Christus Rex*, vi, no. 3 (1952), p. 247.
42   Bitterne, circular letter 24 Dec. 1948 (DARGS, OLC1/3/3 no. 33).
43   Noreen Kearney, 'Social work education, its origins and growth', in Noreen Kearney and
Caroline Skehill (eds), *Social work in Ireland: historical perspectives* (Dublin, 2005), pp 24–30.

had expressly made it one of the driving reasons for the creation of the Irish Federation of Our Lady of Charity, and when he himself had given practical support to the development of degree and diploma courses in social science at University College Dublin.[44] Moreover, McQuaid repeated his insistence that the sisters needed to be trained, at every meeting he held with their superiors throughout the 1950s.[45]

## The Physical Refurbishment of St Mary's Refuge, High Park and the Introduction of the 'Group System'

The High Park sisters had stewardship of an enormous building, completed in 1880, but its size, design, materials, workmanship, internal layout and sheer capacity made its transformation into something that might serve the 'modern approach' a complicated and always very costly affair. Nevertheless, from the early 1950s onwards, under a succession of local superiors, the physical re-ordering of St Mary's Refuge was tackled. The upgrading of the sleeping accommodation, bathrooms, dining rooms and recreation areas, both indoor and outdoor, were the most obvious improvements, but there was also substantial investment in new heating and water systems, a fire-escape and an electric lift.

Making piecemeal changes to an old building was difficult. A building the size and age of St Mary's required ongoing maintenance, with matters such as leaking roofs, woodworm, wet rot, dry rot and broken boilers requiring immediate (and always costly) attention, as the tenders and invoices of numerous tradesmen testify.[46] Construction work in St Mary's in the summer of 1966 exposed the presence of dry rot; with considerable prescience, 'the superior said the treating of it, and the labour involved, would cost a considerable amount, the figure will be known later'.[47] Investigation of a leak in the roof over the cloister in St Mary's, the corridor linking the women's residence to the separate laundry buildings, led to the discovery of wet rot, the reappearance of damp only months after expensive repairs causing some alarm.[48] This was alongside the never-ending round of outside painting, new roofs on sheds and store houses, replacement of gutters and piping, and window cleaning that the enormous pile of St Mary's required.

The addition of extra toilets, handbasins and bathrooms in St Mary's was a major project between 1949 and 1954, with additions and repairs being balanced against the advantages of a whole new sanitary annex in 1963.[49] It was never just a matter of extra sanitary ware, plumbing and partitions; there were difficulties in ensuring adequate water pressure on the top

44   Kearney, 'Social work education, its origins and growth', pp 28–9.
45   For example, see record of meeting held 3 Jan. 1957 in J.C. McQuaid's hand, headed 'Girl Delinquents' (DDA, McQuaid Papers, Department of Justice).
46   Practically every local council meeting during the period of this study had to deal with maintenance and reconstruction issues, as recorded in the minutes.
47   High Park local council, minutes, 17 Aug. 1966.
48   Ibid., 3 Sept., 17 Oct., 9 Dec. 1968, 18 Feb. 1969.
49   Ibid., 15 Sept. 1949, 1 July 1950, 27 Sept. 1952, 12 Feb 1953, July 1954, 7 June 1963, 11 Oct. 1965, 4 Apr. 1966, 18 Feb. 1969; High Park Convent, daybook, 1954–79 (DARGS, OLC1/9/3 no. 114).

floor of St Mary's (it was, after all, built on a height, hence 'High Park'). Six new water tanks were installed in October 1965 'to provide sufficient water for baths in St Mary's'. Another 'absolute necessity' was the erection of a fire-escape for St Patrick's and St Brigid's dormitories, that is, from the top storeys down to the green.[50] The more interesting projects of reconfiguring dormitories into cubicles and making the dining room cheerful and welcoming must be set against the ongoing challenge of keeping the building itself in good repair, and these larger infrastructural projects.

Changes in the built fabric were an attempt by the sisters to make possible the implementation of their own version of what was called the 'group system', namely smaller numbers in a more homely setting, with greater personal autonomy and independence. At the 1965 chapter, it was proposed that the group system be introduced for all in St Mary's, implicitly acknowledging that it was already in place for some of the women.[51] This approach became official High Park policy in 1967, as recounted in the local council minutes:

> The architect is at present [1967] preparing plans for the re-construction of the institution building into smaller units. The smaller group system engendering the family spirit will lend itself to the therapeutic approach which is what we are trying to achieve.[52]

The groups in High Park were hardly small, with 30 and even 40 women at times recorded per group, but nevertheless the new system was to be qualitatively different to that which it replaced.[53]

The greater personalising of life in St Mary's began with the breaking up of the large dormitories. The first effort, begun in September 1954, was 'the erecting of curtained cubicles', with one small dormitory completed within a fortnight, and the remainder cubicled by November – just in time to allow for a report to the federation chapter on the progress made 'towards modernising our penitentiaries'.[54] A later memo refers to the need to get the girls to keep their cubicles in order; 'we realise if the Girls do not co-operate the plans for their comfort would be useless'.[55] Every effort to spruce up the sleeping quarters and make them more homely was complicated by the inherited deficiencies and age of the building, as in May 1963 when Mother Aloysius Pilkington was faced with replacing the worn-out wooden floors of the four large dormitories, the tradesman assuring her that they would take no more sanding and polishing.[56] This had to be done, irrespective of

---

50   The estimated cost was over £1,000 and the work was completed in 1964, High Park local council minutes, 7 June 1963.
51   Extraordinary general chapter of the Irish Federation of the Order of Our Lady of Charity of Refuge for the election of a superior general 25–27 Jan. 1965, minor petitions presented by the monasteries, p. 2 (DARGS, OLC5/1/4).
52   High Park, circular letter, 8 Dec. 1967 (NDC Caen, Archives Besançon).
53   High Park, daybook, 1954–79, accounts for 1971.
54   High Park local council, minutes, 14 Sept. 1954, 2 Oct. 1954; Irish federation general chapter 1954 record.
55   Ibid., 7 Feb. 1964.
56   Ibid., 3 May 1963, see also 5 Apr. 1965 when woodworm was reported.

the planned subdivision. She also had improvements in mind for the toilets
and baths, and did manage to convince her council of the need for 'more
hygienic mattresses', so rubber ones were procured: 'All agreed that these
improvements though very expensive are absolutely necessary'.[57] The purchase of 160 'tubular chairs' for the girls' dormitories in August 1965 gives
an indication of the capacity of the house, just a little down on the number
reported for the end of 1962, at 170 girls.[58]

The erection of curtains between the beds was quickly overtaken by a
council decision to replace the curtained-off beds with wooden partitions:

> With a view to adopting the 'Group System' in St Mary's it
> would be necessary to alter and divide our large dormitories
> so as to provide small rooms or cubicles for the Girls. This
> would create a more homely atmosphere, secure greater priva-
> cy, and should be an asset in our efforts to rehabilitate them.[59]

Providing each woman with what was in effect her own small bedroom tested
the ingenuity of the architect, Mr Dwyer.[60] How to ensure sufficient light and
space for each without sacrificing too many bed spaces? There had been a fall
in numbers from the 170 girls returned for December 1962, but there was still
a large household, and a significant number were likely to be permanently in
OLC care.[61] By April 1968, his plans for the conversion of one large dormitory
were accepted, 'This figure [£1,395] will provide 28 cubicles with wardrobe
and dressing-table in each'.[62] By the end of May, the carpenters were giving
way to the plumber and, by the end of June, tenders for the painting had been
approved and orders had been placed for new hand-basins.[63]

The women's dining room was the other area targeted for remodelling
in the 1950s, and further improved in the 1960s. Replacing the long refectory tables with smaller ones at the end of 1952 (under Mother Eithne O'Neill)
must have done much to reduce the institutional look and feel. The change
was made with deliberation: 'smaller ones being more modern or home-
like'.[64] Another minor landmark can be dated to October 1961 when the
superior of the day (Aloysius Pilkington) suggested some improvements
to the girls' refectory: first, to have the tables topped with Formika (*sic*) instead of the tablecloths and secondly, to have the tiled floor changed to a
wood-block or parquet flooring.[65] These changes, the other houses were
told, imparted 'a homely and comfortable atmosphere', while the 'up-to-
date equipment in their kitchen and pantry makes things easier for the

57   Ibid., 3 May 1963, 7 June 1963.
58   Ibid., 5 Aug. 1965; loose memos, returns for 1962 (DARGS, OLC1/2/1 no. 51).
59   High Park local council, minutes, 8 May 1967.
60   Ibid., 7 Aug. 1967.
61   Loose memo, preparatory notes for Irish federation quinquennial report, numbers for 1962
(DARGS, OLC1/2/1 no. 48).
62   High Park local council, minutes, 16 Apr. 1968.
63   Ibid., 24 May, 19 June 1968.
64   Ibid., 27 Sept. 1952, 12 Feb. 1953.
65   Ibid., 2 Oct. 1961, 6 Feb. 1962.

Cook'.[66] Spurred on by this success, in February 1962, Pilkington pushed a little further, announcing that she intended to have 'new tables and new delphware, all with a view of raising the tone of the girls. This, she reiterated, was 'all with a view of becoming more up-to-date, especially as all the other workrooms and dormitories have been modernised'.[67] One of the councillors dissented, but the motion was carried.[68]

What had always been described as 'the class' in St Mary's was, by 1967, divided into four groups, each with its own sleeping accommodation, recreation room and dining area, a craft room or workroom, with its own allotted 'house mother', its own schedule of outings, celebrations and holidays and managing – in a small way – its own purchases of clothing, shoes, other necessities and small treats. The physical subdivision of the premises into apartments would facilitate what was rather grandly described as 'specialisation in training'.[69] But the full process of 'grouping' took time to implement; by March 1969, the new bedrooms or cubicles were occupied and the four separate groups were in place, but two new sitting rooms still had to be fitted out. The full logic of separation was not carried through to four dining rooms, but rather it was agreed that 'the Refectory may be sufficiently segregated by means of tubular screens'.[70] Nor does it appear to have been carried through to the parlour or visitors' room, created in 1971, which the groups shared. Here the women could welcome their own visitors – it had its own outside door, necessitating the breaking through of an outer wall – and was conceived as another small step towards giving the residents of St Mary's a fuller sense of ownership of their home.[71]

In addition to the four groups in St Mary's, there was an additional group, the elderly and ill ladies of the infirmary who obviously had needs particular to them. The infirmary was always the pride of the house, and was not overlooked in the refurbishment of 1955, when the sink, presses and tables in the kitchenette were all renewed. Nor was it passed over when the painters were in – which, to the residents must have felt like most of the time, working on one or other portion of the vast building.[72] It was 'chiefly for the convenience of the older Girls and the semi-invalids who reside in the Infirmary situated on the third floor of the building' that a lift was installed in 1967, at an estimated cost of £2,300.[73] 'Extra sitting rooms' were provided throughout the building for the aged in the reconstruction of 1968.[74] A sister, if possible with formal nursing qualifications, had always been assigned to the infirmary. Sister Mary of the Seven Dolours Flynn, who was a qualified staff nurse and in charge of the nuns' private nursing home attached to the Mater hospital before she entered High Park in 1920,

66   High Park, circular letter, 11 Dec. 1961 (NDC Caen, Archives Besançon).
67   High Park local council, minutes, 6 Feb. 1962.
68   Ibid.
69   High Park, circular letter, 8 Dec. 1968 (NDC Caen, Archives Besançon).
70   High Park local council, minutes, 28 Mar. 1969.
71   Ibid., 28 Mar. 1969, 14 Dec. 1971.
72   Ibid., 26 Jan. 1955.
73   Ibid., Mar. 1967.
74   High Park, circular letter, 8 Dec. 1968.

spent more than three decades in charge of the penitents' infirmary.[75] The first outside nurse was appointed in 1970. Slight hopes were entertained at the time that the health authority (the Eastern Health Board) might carry the cost on the basis of 'the number of old and infirm and the total number needing occasional care'[76] but that was never likely, and the High Park community paid the nurse's salary in full, at £1,500 per annum.[77] Another of the groups in St Mary's consisted largely of women with mental or physical disabilities or learning needs – and referred to in the council minutes as the 'retarded group'. At the end of 1967, the health authority, for the first time, agreed a total grant of £2,500 per year towards the maintenance of these women, on the basis (it appears) of them needing full-time residential care.[78]

Changes in the uniform dress of the residents, and in the language to be used in their regard, marked another small but significant shift. A decision about dress, made at the federation chapter of November 1954,[79] was implemented in January 1956 when it was resolved:

> A modification or alteration was being made in the uniform of the hitherto called "Consecrates" or "Magdalens", in future to be called "Girls of the Class of Perseverance". All agreed as to the advisability of this change.[80]

Two months later, it is reported back that the modification has been implemented, but without specifying exactly how.[81] The formal or feast-day magdalen dress that was to be altered featured indistinctly in the centenary record of 1953 (figure 11.3) where, under the caption 'Our magdalens singing the praises of Our Lady, St Mary's Refuge', a group of women circle the Lourdes grotto, dressed in the white linen Normandy headdress that was a direct link with 1640s Caen (perhaps 17 are wearing the headdress; the remainder appear to be wearing Children of Mary veils). The same publication shows the other girls (the majority, those who have not taken vows as 'consecrates') variously posed in the gardens and workroom, with heads uncovered and wearing a neat collared, long-sleeved dress of uniform design and colour. No exact date has yet been found for when this dress, reminiscent of boarding school uniforms, gave way to more varied, 'ordinary' clothes, and it probably yielded over time, rather than on a particular date – the last quantity of navy dress material, 156 yards, was purchased in August 1955 and there is a reference in 1960 to the improvements in dress being 'highly appreciated' by all.[82] In the earliest surviving holiday film or 'home movie', recording a day

75  Death letter, Sister M. of the Seven Dolours Flynn, d. 8 Nov. 1960 (DARGS, OLC1/6/4).
76  High Park local council, minutes, 13 May, 1 June 1970.
77  Ibid., 15 June 1970.
78  Ibid., 6 Nov. 1967.
79  Irish federation general chapter 1954 record.
80  High Park local council, minutes, 30 Jan. 1956.
81  Irish federation general council, minutes, 1 Apr. 1956.
82  High Park, daybook, 1954–79, accounts for Aug. 1955; High Park, circular letter, n.d. but Dec. 1960 (NDC Caen, Archives Besançon).

**Figure 11.3** Women and girls gathered at the grotto to Our Lady in the grounds of St Mary's, High Park. (*Centenary record*, 1953)

trip to the beach at Rush, County Dublin, in July 1961, there is not the least hint of uniformity, with the women wearing floral and patterned skirts and dresses of every colour and design.[83] Bulk or central purchasing of clothes, and of large bales of material for dressmaking, had ended well before 1967, by which date each housemother endeavoured to supply the girls and women in her group 'with suitable clothing, shoes etc.'[84]

The decided suppression of the terms 'magdalen' and 'consecrate' at the local council meeting of 30 January 1956, to be replaced by the term 'Girls of the Class of Perseverance', merits notice.[85] This was part of a larger effort to expunge the judgemental terms 'penitent', 'magdalen', 'penitentiary' and 'asylum' from the discourse, and to offload the heavy baggage these terms carried. This was not at all an easy task, and was not made easier by the ubiquitous use of the terms among the public and in the print and broadcast media. Even within the community, it took time before it was entirely suppressed.[86] As the term 'Girls of the Class of Perseverance' implies, permanent, life-time commitment to an edifying life of prayer, work and penance within the enclosed setting of St Mary's Refuge was still held out as an ideal throughout the 1950s, even though the vast majority of those admitted were, as throughout its history, short-stay residents. The matter was listed on the agenda of the 1954 federation chapter, but it was decided to continue with the 'Class of Perseverance', with some modification of the

83    'Outing to Rush, July 1961', 16mm cine film (DARGS, OLC1/12/5 no. 1).

84    High Park local council, minutes, 30 Mar. 1971.

85    Ibid., 30 Jan. 1956.

86    The heading 'Penitents' Expenses' continues in the account books until Dec. 1971, High Park, daybook, 1954–79, accounts to 1971.

dress the girls wore.[87] Under this thinking, St Mary's was always open to receiving women who had left:

> Recently [1959] we were pleased to welcome back a few girls who, having left us in the dim past, now seek a haven of peace, away from the storms and tempests of the world, and we pray that they may remain with us until they have taken flight to their Heavenly Home.[88]

The goodness and fervour of the long-resident women was repeatedly extolled: their spirit of prayer and labour were as a 'beacon light' to their companions,[89] and their example 'a great incentive to the younger girls who have not much stability or spirit of work'.[90] Their edifying lives, extraordinary spirit of prayer, maternal interest in their companions' welfare and their saintly deaths led many others, it was claimed, to aspire to admission to the 'Class of Perseverance'.[91] In the quinquennial report of 1958, the phrase 'magdalens=auxiliaries' is entered in response to the question of who else, besides the professed religious, are dedicated to the institute without being members. Confirmation is given that 'provision is made in fairness and charity for their spiritual life, and also for their material security'. Furthermore, in reply to the query, 'Are there legitimately approved statutes for them?', the answer given is no; the penitents' rule, such an important appendix to the first constitutions, has been quietly allowed to slip into abeyance.[92] The last formal mention of admission to this class is found during the women's retreat of July 1954: 'three of their number merited the silver cross of perseverance, ten were admitted into the Sodality of the Children of Mary, others again were made aspirants'.[93] In the next sentence, it is noted that 'Many improvements have been made for their general comfort and happiness, in keeping with modern times',[94] which exactly sums up the 1950s: both old and new thinking were in operation simultaneously, despite contradictions.

It was the whole-hearted adoption of the 'group system' in 1967 that hastened the transformation of the physical structure of St Mary's and profoundly changed the dynamics of daily life. In a very real sense, it marked the end of the 'magdalen refuge', although its dismantling can be tracked over the previous two decades, and high-support residential care would continue for some women after that date, most obviously in the nursing home that succeeded it. Pressure to move away entirely from the old refuge model was coming from both within and without OLC. A series of lectures given in High Park in March

---

87    Irish federation general chapter 1954 record.
88    High Park, circular letter, Dec. 1960.
89    High Park, circular letter, 8 Dec. 1958 (NDC Caen, Archives Besançon).
90    High Park, circular letter, 12 Dec. 1950 (NDC Caen, Archives Besançon).
91    Ibid., 8 Dec. 1951. See also High Park circular letters Dec. 1960, 8 Dec. 1957.
92    See chapter 2. It appears that, even at the founding of the order, the penitents' rule was voluntary, not canonically binding. Irish federation quinquennial report 1954–58, questions 40, 141, 142, also note on page 1 (DARGS, OLC1/2/1 no. 48).
93    High Park, circular letter, Dec. 1954 (NDC Caen, Archives Besançon).
94    Ibid., Dec. 1954.

1967 by a much-respected lecturer from the Department of Social Science at UCD, Helen Burke, where three of the OLC sisters were registered students at the time, set out in uncompromising terms what was needed:

> She told us that the value of our work in the past cannot be over-stressed. However, the necessity of up-dating our present methods is of supreme importance. In linking the past work with present vigour and future promise we shall do a great service to those under our care.[95]

Her well-received lecture series ('Our admiration was tinged with no small share of envy for her knowledge') appears to have brought more of the sisters round to the new thinking that was necessary to the demise of the old refuge model.[96] Another contributor to the in-house lecture series at High Park in 1967 was a Mr McDonnell, described as 'a Rehabilitation Consultant to our Government', a 'well-read and convincing speaker' with 'wide experience of many countries'. His demonstration of the potential among people who appeared unable to benefit from rehabilitation initiatives struck a chord:

> His films portrayed the process of taking a psychiatric patient from custodial care and placing him in active employment: firstly in the institution, and later in society and provide in this majority of cases a return to normal living.[97]

While it is impossible to assess the significance of any one lecture or particular intervention, a succession of small but important changes can be dated to 1967, the year that the renewal called for by Vatican II began to take hold in OLC. In 1967 the practice of assigning house names to new entrants, to protect their anonymity, was wound down; there are intermittent usages of house names in the register for 1967, but none by 1968. The system of a single 'class' that was the general rule of any OLC women's refuge under the 1734 constitutions, with due allowance for age, disability and sickness only (and separate to the 'preservation' class of schoolchildren), was swept away. The large numbers that the old system allowed – indeed boasted of – were at an end, and a more relaxed daily regime, in a more homely and open environment, took hold, but in stages.

## Training, Education and Recreation at St Mary's Refuge, High Park

With respect to the laundry, outsiders would have been well aware that it was High Park's principal source of income and few, if any, in the 1950s would have disputed the right of the institute to require all able-bodied

---

95    Ibid., 8 Dec. 1967.
96    Ibid.,
97    Ibid.

residents to contribute to the costs of their own maintenance, considering that the refuge received no state grants. Even if the short account in the 1953 centenary record was overblown – lauding the up-to-date machinery, the happy combination of 'prayer and work', and 'the merry chatter of the relaxation times'– none of these points was factually untrue.[98] What nobody was claiming, neither sisters nor outsiders, was that the work routines of High Park – whether in the laundry, infirmary, kitchen, workrooms or on other household duties – constituted a structured vocational training programme. Of course it prepared girls for employment – those recorded in the High Park register as placed 'in situations' or otherwise gainfully employed on departure bear testimony to that – but this was only in a generic sense. It is no coincidence that, of the few former residents of St Mary's whose later place of employment is recorded in the register, a significant number found work in hospitals, colleges and similar institutions. There was little educational work outside literacy instruction (for some) which had always been among the responsibilities of the mistress of penitents and her assistants, as was religious instruction (for all).[99]

A resolution at the federation chapter of 1960 proposed that the existing facility for education be extended by recruiting other sisters not involved in St Mary's to take the women for classes on a Sunday afternoon.[100] But it was modern vocational and 'life-skills' training that was the pressing concern in the 1950s. By November 1954, arrangements were 'in prospect' for the inauguration of classes in domestic economy 'for the younger penitents, with a view to their re-establishment in the world'.[101] The shift in policy took practical form under Mother Eithne O'Neill when she announced in January 1955 that there would be 'some necessary changes' in St Mary's: 'a room being fitted up for the further domestic training of the girls, a gas cooker to be installed etc., as well as suitable tables and presses necessary for sewing classes'.[102] By March, it was reported that progress was well advanced on 'the new Domestic Training Room', to be formally opened on 22 June 1955 by Mother Eithne as 'St Philomena's Domestic Science School, High Park'.[103] There were 18 pupils present, and the first instructress was Sister M. of St Francis Thérèse Blackmore, who was well qualified for the task, having trained as a teacher of domestic science at Sion Hill before her entry to High Park. She was already working with the older girls in St Joseph's school.[104] Having recently completed a short course in childcare, she would spend that July on a revision course for teachers of domestic science.[105]

---

98   *Centenary record*, pp 65–67.
99   'Explanation of the Rule of the Penitents', pp 335–70 in 'Explanation of the Rules, Constitutions and Customs of the Religious of Our Lady of Charity …', p. 360 (DARGS, OLC1/3/1 no. 1).
100   'Report, third general chapter of the Irish Federation of the order of Our Lady of Charity of Refuge, November, 1960', item 3, p. 7 (DARGS, OLC5/1/3). Hereafter, general chapter 1960 report.
101   Irish federation general chapter 1954 record.
102   High Park local council, minutes, 26 Jan. 1955.
103   Ibid., 7 Mar. 1955.
104   Irish federation general council, minutes, 22 June 1955.
105   Ibid., 19 to 28 Aug 1953, 5 July 1955.

The first girls to undertake this new programme in 'all branches of cookery and household management' were, according to 'Sister Instructress', responsive and keen to learn.[106]

The beginnings of a formal training regime at St Mary's – at least for the younger girls and those deemed capable of benefiting from further instruction – can be dated to this 'domestic course' launched in 1955. That it was intended to be a proper, taught programme is evident from an inspection of the attendance register ('gnó speisialta – rollaí na rang cócaireachta a dheimhniú') in January 1956.[107] St Philomena's – effectively a single, well-equipped classroom – separated teenagers and younger women from the mainstream for at least part of the day, and was the origins of what came to be known as 'the teenage group' (chapter 9). It was expected that these girls would find work outside High Park, and from the first year of operations, this hope was realised in at least a few cases: 'the younger girls benefit much by their domestic training, and do very well in their situations'.[108]

A more comprehensive programme was introduced in September 1961; its rather clumsy title of 'classes for rehabilitation' does at least convey the understanding that these are girls destined to take up their place 'in the world'. Lessons included 'Christian Doctrine, personal hygiene, dress and deportment, music and graded classes in English and practical arithmetic', as well as lessons in all the branches of domestic economy (listed as sewing, cookery, housewifery and arts and crafts).[109] In March 1962, comments from Mother Aloysius Pilkington point to a further re-organisation of classes for the younger girls, specified as catechetics, cooking, sewing 'and some lectures in hygiene', all with the express purpose of helping the girls to move on: 'in order to fit them to take their place in the world'.[110] The following year, she allowed that 'naturally all have not the same capacity for full maturity'; however, the hope was still that 'several of this group may be rehabilitated as responsible, highly principled adults'. The girls 'are beginning to appreciate the benefit of education, realising how much time they wasted when at school' which, if true for all, would indeed be a signal achievement.[111] By 1966, the boast was that the modern new classrooms in St Mary's 'facilitate the re-education of the younger girls who respond admirably to their academic, social and domestic training in preparation for their future careers'.[112] There are further references to the 'domestic, commercial and academic classes' that were part of an overall 'therapeutic approach' geared to 'preparing the younger group to take their places in society'.[113] The first outside teacher, with a BA degree, was engaged in June 1968 to teach academic subjects in what was by then titled the 'Training Centre'. Her job

---

106    High Park, circular letter, 8 Dec. 1955 (NDC Caen, Archives Besançon).
107    An inspection of the cookery class on 18 Jan. 1956, as entered on the last page of Leabhar tuaraimí an chigire, was undertaken by the inspector who had previously visited St Joseph's as a national school (DARGS, SJ/8/2 no. 3).
108    High Park, circular letter, 8 Dec. 1956 (NDC Caen, Archives Besançon).
109    Irish federation general council, minutes, 1 Apr. 1959, 7 Sept. 1959.
110    High Park local council, minutes, 25 Mar. 1962.
111    High Park, circular letter, 20 Dec. 1963.
112    Ibid., 8 Dec. 1966.
113    Ibid., 8 Dec. 1967.

specification was to work five days a week from 9.30am to 3.30pm, and to place the emphasis on English, reading and writing, and arithmetic.[114] The 'commercial class' consisted of typing, shorthand and book-keeping, holding out the promise of office employment for those who could succeed in this field.[115]

Sewing and dressmaking was always a core subject and mentioned in dispatches:

> Though the results as yet would hardly merit a high place in the field of 'Haute Couture', their continued effort does finally bring immense satisfaction, whether it be a modest specimen of the familiar French seam (with a distinctive Irish touch) or a piece of fine embroidery from the more nimble fingered among them. They experience great joy in having their work admired, and it is with a certain impatience that they look forward to their annual display next April.[116]

The cookery classes were consistently popular and, from at least 1958, the girls were entered for cookery competitions sponsored by outside bodies, and with most attractive rewards: 'prize winners are treated to an outing which includes high tea and a film'.[117] The standards of 1963 must have been admirable as 'quite a number were awarded prizes by the Gas Company'.[118]

Religious formation was also approached from a more modern angle: 'the younger group have weekly talks and informal discussions on the every day problems of Catholic adolescents. Thus we hope to instil in them a sense of self-reliance and personal responsibility.'[119] St Philomena's was superseded in some respects by the creation of the High Park hostel (announced in June 1964) that came to be called Martanna House and by An Grianán and the other 'family group homes'. These were created primarily as step-up facilities for girls leaving St Joseph's school. St Anne's, Kilmacud was intended for girls aged 12 to 17, some of whom might otherwise find themselves in a magdalen refuge – a 15- and a 16-year-old were transferred from High Park to St Anne's on its opening in 1944, and three more girls aged 15 to 16 were transferred in 1959, 1964 and 1966 respectively. But even allowing for these developments, there were still younger women in St Mary's in the 1960s. These were in a separate group from at least 1967, the 'teenage group', with their own sitting room, bedrooms and 'other facilities'.[120] St Joseph's dormitory on the top floor was converted to a 'flatlet' for this group in 1971; Sister Columba Cunningham, their 'group mother'

---

114   High Park local council, minutes, 19 June 1968; this teacher appears to be Miss Clare Kavanagh.
115   High Park, circular letter, 8 Dec. 1967.
116   High Park, circular letter, 8 Dec. 1964 (DARGS, OLC1/3/1 no. 29).
117   Ibid., 8 Dec. 1958.
118   High Park local council, minutes, 7 Apr. 1963.
119   High Park, circular letter, 8 Dec. 1964.
120   High Park local council, minutes, 8 May 1967, 10 Nov. 1970.

at the time, 'proposed plans patterned on those she had seen in England'.[121] One of the first three OLC sisters to graduate (together) from UCD in 1969 with a degree in social science was immediately assigned to work with the teenagers as 'group mother'.[122] The cookery room was still reserved exclusively to them, and formal cookery classes continued, a policy that was reaffirmed in June 1971.[123] In her trenchant criticism of the admission of teenage girls to magdalen asylums, published in 1970, District Justice Eileen Kennedy acknowledges one unnamed magdalen institution where rehabilitation was under way, 'the handling of this problem is professional and practical because of the existence of trained staff'; it is possible this refers to the teenage unit at High Park.[124]

While the modernisation, subdivision and refurbishment of the refuge was in hand, the spiritual care of the women was also updated in several respects. As with the systemic changes in St Mary's, change came incrementally. In the Christmas circular for December 1964, there was a short account of the 'many helps' offered to the girls in St Mary's to enable them 'to live fully Christian lives', including their annual retreat and a talk at their monthly sodality meeting. The tentative introduction of new approaches without usurping the old 'spiritual helps' is evident. The reinstallation that year by Rome of the Mass of the Immaculate Heart of Mary (8 February) was greeted with delight, as there was no lessening of fervour for traditional Eudist devotions.[125] The introduction of Mass in the vernacular and congregational singing in 1965 was reported by the superior of High Park – in the language of the constitution *Sacrosanctum Concilium* (1963) – as having successfully led 'to that conscious and active participation by all the people in liturgical celebration which is rightly theirs'.[126] Earlier in 1965 compulsory attendance by the women at daily Mass had been ended, along with the noontime examination of conscience and what is cryptically noted as 'prayers to put on silence etc.', small but significant gestures towards the ending of what were acknowledged to be old-fashioned devotional practices.[127] In 1966, the girls in St Mary's 'have had their usual outings to the seaside and quite a number of them made pilgrimages to the famous Shrine at Knock, Co. Mayo'. In that year, all the traditional spiritual supports offered them – their yearly triduum, five days' retreat and a monthly day of recollection for the Children of Mary – were supplemented by a Saturday evening session when 'Sisters give instructions with the aid of religious films'.[128] It was through 'weekly talks and informal discussions' with the teenagers and young women that the greatest efforts were invested to make religion relevant to daily life.[129]

121    Ibid., 2 Mar., 4 May 1971.
122    Ibid., 13 Feb. 1971.
123    Ibid., 15, 29 June 1971.
124    *Reformatory and industrial schools systems report, 1970* (Dublin, 1970), p. 39. Hereafter, Kennedy report.
125    High Park, circular letter, 8 Dec. 1964.
126    Ibid., 8 Dec. 1965.
127    Extraordinary general chapter of the Irish Federation, minor petitions, p. 2.
128    High Park, circular letter, 8 Dec. 1966.
129    Ibid., 8 Dec. 1964.

The long-established in-house recreations of concerts, singalongs and amateur dramatics continued in St Mary's throughout the 1950s and 1960s, and were reviewed with effusive praise, the report for 1951 being typical:

> Gaiety and music had their part in making life happy for our dear children. Although we have no projector of our own, we nevertheless secured several good Cinema Shows. Plays and concerts were supplied by our many kind friends, and the girls themselves produced a very fine play, and for their Mistress' feast a delightful concert, including several items from "The Geisha".[130]

The mistress's feast-day in the following year was marked by a display of handiwork, namely 'beautifully embroidered tea-cloths, crochet and fancy work of all kinds', before the concert to crown the day.[131] Special mention was also made in the centenary record where one of the illustrations is titled 'Skilful fingers at work' (figure 11.4).[132] The 1961 display was a manifestation of 'the zest with which the pupils applied themselves' to classes in arts and crafts.[133] There had long been a consciousness of the need to ease the strain of routine; the diversions reported in 1964 'came in the form of films, variety concerts and gift parcels from generous benefactors'.[134] In successive years, the staff of the hosiery and underwear company, Glen Abbey Textile Company, brought 'most useful gifts, distributed by 'Santy' in person, much to the excitement of young and old.'[135] Thanks to a number of 'kind benefactors', including the Knights of Columbanus, what were termed 'various light entertainments for our girls' were brought into St Mary's.[136] Bingo was popular, organised – at least on occasion – by outsiders.[137] The feast-day of the mistress of the class, or her jubilee, called for a special effort, as did the golden and diamond jubilees of long-resident women. As noted already, the 1951 production included items from 'The Geisha'; the following year's concert consisted of items from 'The Mikado', 'which they acted very well and all enjoyed'.[138] In 1953, the girls and women produced 'The Miracle of Lourdes', judged to be 'a credit to all concerned and a fitting tribute to Our Immaculate Mother at the close of the Marian Year'.[139] In April 1956, the women presented 'their devoted mistress' of several years, a golden jubilarian, with a complimentary address followed by a concert, 'the main item being a display of folk-dancing which was truly admirable'.[140] In 1958, to mark the golden jubilee of four of the women, the usual 'crowning ceremony'

---

130   Ibid., 8 Dec. 1951.
131   Ibid., 8 Dec.1952.
132   High Park, circular letter, Dec. 1953 (NDC Caen, Archives Besançon).
133   Ibid., 11 Dec. 1961.
134   Ibid., 8 Dec. 1964.
135   Ibid., 8 Dec. 1966.
136   Ibid., 20 Dec. 1963.
137   High Park local council, minutes, 28 Mar. 1969.
138   High Park, circular letter, 8 Dec. 1952 (NDC Caen, Archives Besançon).
139   Ibid., Dec. 1954.
140   Ibid., 8 Dec. 1956.

SKILFUL FINGERS AT WORK

**Figure 11.4**  Four girls sewing with Sister Frances Smith, St Mary's, High Park
(*Centenary record*, 1953).

(with a wreath of flowers) was followed by a 'variety concert' put on by
their companions.[141] For the jubilee celebrations of Sister Madeleine in 1959,
the women put on the operetta 'The Enchanted Glen' for outside visitors,
as well as for the household while, in 1966, the jubilee celebrations for five
women residents concluded with 'an amusing production of that awful
tragedy, "the Babes in the Wood"!'.[142] The audience for these dramas was
largely – but not exclusively – drawn from High Park (women and sisters);
outside friends of the women, including members of the Legion of Mary
and of the Knights of Columbanus and other charitably-disposed persons,
attended. A note in 1957 states that the annual operetta was produced as a
thank-you for the kind benefactors who had organised the monthly film-
shows and other welcome entertainments.[143] Nor were the efforts at drama entirely amateur; it was noted approvingly in 1955 in reference to the
younger girls that 'they take an interest in their dancing and singing lessons
and from time to time can produce a nice entertainment'[144] and later:

> Our girls have the advantage of being trained in the art of
> dancing and singing by teachers from the Marian Art Society,
> and the production of a colourful operetta at Christmas [1957]
> reflected credit on both pupils and teachers.[145]

141   Ibid., 8 Dec. 1958.
142   Ibid., 8 Dec. 1966.
143   Ibid., 8 Dec. 1957.
144   Ibid., 8 Dec. 1956.
145   Ibid., 8 Dec. 1958.

Home movie shots of St Mary's girls dancing on a seaside outing in July 1966 – perhaps to keep warm on what looks like a breezy day – give a glimpse of their talents in this field and their evident enjoyment.[146] High standards in dancing and drama were no doubt encouraged by the exposure of the girls and women to the acclaimed productions of amateur societies. Several groups staged their current production in High Park; the highlight of the Christmas 1959 season was the Rathmines and Rathgar Musical Society's production of the opera 'Iolanthe'. In 1965, the same society gave what all agreed was 'a first class rendering of Gilbert and Sullivan's *H.M.S. Pinafore'*.[147] Both operettas, along with other items in the society's repertoire, were performed at intervals again in High Park.[148] The pantomime 'Sleeping Beauty' was reported to be the highlight of the Christmas 1966 season, but there is no record of which outside group was responsible.[149]

In terms of outdoor recreation, St Mary's had its own garden; this is the Penitents' Green referred to in 1954, when it was decided to close in the gate of open ironwork with corrugated iron 'to ensure more privacy for them'.[150] A new games area was opened in 1955 and, not surprisingly, was of most interest to the younger women.[151] A 'tar-mac-adam (*sic*) tennis court' was a welcome addition in 1959, and allowed the girls to host home matches with opposing teams, most likely from Dublin VEC schools: 'Here they have matched their skill with expert players and have carried off the laurels several times.'[152] St Mary's girls are filmed at ball games on the beach in the holiday movies that survive from 1961–66, and also skipping and playing tennis in a serious manner on the new tarmac courts at High Park.[153] A major investment was made in 1970 in a new recreation area for St Mary's; it included sheltered seating and was facing south.[154] The provision of a 'moveable platform for outside dancing' was requested and supplied, and once a drinking water tap was installed, the project was proclaimed a success.[155]

The first 'occasional day's outing' for the women can be dated to summer 1955.[156] Accounts of seaside holidays and day trips between 1957 and 1966 list Portmarnock, Malahide, Rush, Skerries, Sutton, Donabate and Balbriggan as the destinations, all on the north coast within easy reach of High Park. Some at least of these trips had the added interest of a short diversion to 'Collinstown air-port', as in the trips organised throughout the

146   'Seaside and Martanna House', July 1966, 16mm cine film (DARGS, OLC1/12/5 no. 7).
147   High Park, circular letter, Dec. 1960, 8 Dec. 1965.
148   *Iolanthe* was performed again in 1966, and *HMS Pinafore* Christmas 1967, High Park, circular letters, 8 Dec. 1966, 8 Dec. 1968.
149   High Park, circular letter, 8 Dec. 1967.
150   High Park local council, minutes, 2 Oct. 1954.
151   High Park, circular letter, 8 Dec. 1957.
152   High Park, circular letter, 8 Dec. 1959 (NDC Caen, Archives Besançon).
153   'Outing to Rush, July 1961', 'Skerries May 1962', 'Sutton Ascension Thursday 1963', 'Seaside and Martanna House 1966', 16mm cine film (DARGS, OLC1/12/5 nos. 1, 2, 4, 7).
154   The cost was £15,000, High Park local council, minutes, 9 Oct. 1970.
155   Ibid., 20 Apr. 1971; 4 May 1971.
156   Irish federation general chapter 1954 record.

summer of 1957.[157] In 1960, it was reported that 'The filming of their outings to the sea-side resort at Donabate was an added joy and is now the popular film of the season'.[158] From the addressee on the film boxes, Sister Columba Cunningham can be identified as the film maker.

In addition to the organised day trips, holidays with family or friends came for those whose family or friends invited them.[159] Once the group system was in place, it was the duty of the group mother to settle all aspects of the holiday for that group. In 1972, it was resolved that, 'if it were possible to find premises suitable for the retarded group, the effort to give them a holiday would be worth the trial of at least a year'.[160] This group too got the opportunity of an annual summer break away from High Park.

## High Park and the Legion of Mary

OLC engagement with the Legion of Mary, of which several sisters had been members before entering the convent, was broadly based and long-standing. The Legion of Mary features prominently in the organising of entertainments at St Mary's, but goes well beyond that. Sometime in 1965, the legionaries 'provided and served a delicious supper, followed by a concert and sing-song', described as but 'one of the many examples of their helpful co-operation in our apostolate'. The legionaries were 'constantly' visiting St Mary's, 'and in the summer bring some of the girls on pleasure trips, etc.'[161] Throughout the 1960s, legionaries were offering the most up-to-date entertainment they could put together to the women they had befriended in St Mary's. 'Visitors and girls danced to the modern music of a first class orchestra; interspersed with items by celebrated artists.'[162] It was the legionaries, appropriately enough, who first sponsored day-long outings to Our Lady's Shrine in Knock, County Mayo.[163] Good relations with the Legion of Mary date from its foundation by Frank Duff in 1925 and there was a longstanding connection with the Legion hostel in Harcourt Street, from where there were occasional introductions to High Park, with former High Park girls seeking refuge in Harcourt Street also.[164]

It was in the role of voluntary probation officer that some Legion members came to have a particular interest in and knowledge of girls on

157    High Park, circular letter, 8 Dec. 1957.
158    Ibid., Dec. 1960.
159    Ibid., 8 Dec. 1964.
160    High Park local council, minutes, 15, 18 Feb. 1972.
161    High Park, circular letter, 8 Dec. 1965.
162    Ibid., 8 Dec. 1966.
163    Ibid., 11 Dec. 1961, 20 Dec. 1963.
164    Of the two 16-year-olds brought by the Legion to High Park in 1936, one (Philomena) stayed permanently, the other (house names were Fintan, Maureen, Agnes, Monica) left and re-entered High Park and Gloucester Street multiple times before finally disappearing from the OLC records. Another girl (Agatha, aged 28) came from Harcourt Street in 1938 and stayed for a few days before returning there. A girl aged 14 was brought in Nov. 1940 by a legionary, Miss Lyons, and taken home to her parents sometime in Mar. 1941. A woman aged 39 (Constance) came in 1966 and stayed three weeks. Some of the cases 'brought by' a named woman probably involved Legion members, but this cannot be ascertained from the register alone.

probation from the district court or on early release from prison who were resident in High Park. The recruitment and training of Legion members as voluntary probation officers, the initiative of Judge H. A. McCarthy, dates to 1942, with 27 members agreeing to carry out the role of helper or assistant to the probation officer, divided between the six probation districts of the city.[165] Legion members worked primarily, but not exclusively, with children who had been before the Metropolitan Court. Early efforts included an evening call-in centre in Lower Abbey Street, where interviews were held in one room while the rest of the boys played games in the other. The Legion helpers also operated a library, met parents, held literacy and catechetical classes, ran excursions and outings throughout the year and organised an annual retreat 'very largely attended'.[166] In 1962, the scheme was re-invigorated and placed on a more official footing; the following year, two Dublin branches of the Legion of Mary, Praesidium Mater Salvatoris and Praesidium Virgo Potens, along with the Salvation Army (Women's Social Work), were granted formal recognition under section 7 of the Criminal Justice Administration Act 1914.[167] The voluntary probation officers from these organisations acted alongside, and in co-operation with, the very small number of probation officers paid by the state. They were recognised and then assigned cases by the courts, and granted powers to supervise young people on probation in precisely the same manner as the state's probation officers.[168] It was thus that certain Legion members came to befriend individual women who were to be found caught up in the general High Park numbers without distinction. The support was not all in the one direction; when the Legion put on a retreat day for its own hostel girls, it was High Park that offered hospitality.[169]

## The laundry at High Park: Technology, Management and Labour

The laundry at High Park underwent considerable change in the 1950s and 1960s, in terms of technology, management and labour. As a business, it had to contend with major upheavals in the larger society and economy, including the advent of gas and then electric washing machines and improved soaps and detergents, allowing household managers to choose to do their own laundry, rather than pay the real cost of having it done outside.[170] Although the High Park laundry was machine-driven from the 1890s, and the 1953 centenary record boasted of how 'electricity and steam power render labour less irksome and life more agreeable', it would need ongoing, substantial investment if it were to hold its customers.[171] Better machinery – faster, easier to use, more automated, less wasteful of power – was constantly

165   *Final report of the Inter-Departmental Committee set up to establish the facts of State involvement with the Magdalen Laundries* (Dublin, 2013). ch. 9, p. 235. Hereafter, McAleese report.
166   Justice H.A. McCarthy, 'The Children's Court', *Christus Rex*, ii, no. 4 (1948), pp 9–12.
167   McAleese report, ch. 9, pp 232, 240–4.
168   Ibid., ch. 9, p. 246.
169   High Park local council, minutes, 1 June 1970.
170   *Good Housekeeping's laundry book* (London, 1955).
171   *Centenary record*, pp 65–6.

coming to the market, and there was pressure to update.[172] An examination of the laundry expenses in any one year gives an inkling of the range of inputs required to operate a commercial laundry; labour and machinery were only the start of what was required.[173] There was a massive (and ongoing) outlay on new machinery, justified by the need 'to cope with present-day exacting standards and thereby to retain our many customers who want and deserve our very best'.[174] While the new technologies were installed to lighten 'the burden of the daily toil' for the workers, women residents and sisters, several decades of trouble-free use or a substantial increase in throughput would be needed before there would be any financial return on the investment.[175]

High Park was also faced with the much larger question of whether what was in effect a mechanised, factory setup could be incorporated into a modern 'rehabilitation' programme of the kind that was being urged on the sisters by the archbishop, and which they had some idea of themselves from their visits to – and ongoing contacts with – the order in England and France. The laundry was not, and never had been, the only place of work – there was ample opportunity in the kitchen and scullery, infirmary, sewing room and on general household duties – but the laundry was the principal, regular, year-round business from which the income to maintain the institute was generated, All other sources of income, including state subventions for a small number of girls through the health boards, the old age pensions of sisters and women and sales of farm produce surplus to the needs of the house were welcome, but very minor, items in comparison, and markedly so up to 1967. In the working of the laundry, the resident women laboured towards their upkeep, as did the sisters. St Mary's was their home, for life should they choose to stay (or have no alternative place to go), and work – in the laundry or elsewhere, for those who were able – was part of that life.

Throughout the 1950s and up to the mid-1960s, even though there was concern about decreasing receipts, there was not the least hint that the laundry might not continue as the primary source of income for the house.[176] The idea of having the resident women paid an individual wage only gradually came to the fore. A resolution that the women should receive 'some payment, however small, for the work they do for us' was made in November 1954, with the recommendation that 'a system of good marks' be introduced, with the reward 'in proportion to the marks received'.[177] A 'system

---

172  'The need for a more modern coat machine had arisen owing to the new design of coats worn by nurses. Messrs. Baker Perkins representative from Glasgow had offered a machine which would not only solve this problem, but would also eliminate the use of these old machines and thus reduce the number of workers and also lessen the consumption of steam. The cost of this machine is £3,000 approximately. The council sisters approved of the investment.' High Park local council, minutes, 20 Sept. 1966.
173  High Park Convent, daybook, 1954–79 (DARGS, OLC1/9/3 no. 114).
174  High Park, circular letter, 11 Dec. 1961.
175  Ibid., Dec. 1960.
176  Accounts examined, 'it was observed that the Laundry Receipts were not so good as formerly, owing we presume to the high cost of living and customers send out as little laundry as possible', High Park local council, minutes. 24 May 1955.
177  Irish federation general chapter 1954 record.

of remuneration in kind', operating in both High Park and Gloucester Street (Sean MacDermott Street), was described in 1960 as 'contributing much to the stability of the girls and gives general satisfaction'.[178] But it was not until 1967 that the issue of wages, not merely 'rewards' or discretionary pocket money, took centre-stage.

By 1965, advances in the life of St Mary's in the name of 'modernisation' were well under way: the upgrading of the living accommodation for the women, the 'classes for rehabilitation' or life-skills training programme for the younger girls, greater interaction with the outside world through outings and visits, radio and film. Education and training for those who it was thought could benefit removed them from the workforce in the laundry for at least part of the usual workday. Though the household was still large, it was patently clear that the direction of numbers was downwards, and that the laundry would have to manage with fewer hands.

The employment of an outside 'works manager', Gerry Carpenter, in January 1965 opened up a new chapter in the life of St Mary's, although the immediate reason behind his appointment was more technical than managerial, namely 'to instruct the sisters in charge how to manipulate the new machinery lately installed'.[179] Carpenter immediately decided that more machinery was needed and, over the next 18 months, succeeded in advancing the process of automation. Furthermore, he brought in new systems right through from where the laundry was checked, counted, marked, washed, folded (flannels) or ironed and packed ready for the return journey to its owners. This involved reconstructing the checking office and getting possession of an additional very large room as a laundry packing room.[180] He dealt with customers, managed the machinery, supervised the workers and generated business through his own network of contacts, carrying full responsibility for practically all aspects of the laundry. In time, he succeeded in introducing a new system of pricing and a quiet place in which this could be done, 'the present arrangement being very unsatisfactory'. The installation of a polymarking machine, hailed as revolutionary, was his initiative also; this replaced the intricate and tedious black ink and red thread marking-system in place for decades.[181]

In the 1965 end-of-year review, the superior of High Park, Sister Mary of the Nativity Kennedy, gave a lengthy account of the 'complete re-organisation' of the laundry that was under way, involving 'the installation of modern machinery and the introduction of new systems'. All of this was undertaken:

> because of our rapidly-changing present-day world and our desire to keep pace with the modern trend – making life less laborious and more pleasant for the worker, as also to facilitate the teenage group attending classes in a more leisurely way.[182]

178   General chapter 1960 report.
179   High Park local council, minutes, 14 Jan. 1965.
180   Ibid., 15 Mar. 1965; 4 Apr., 17 Aug., 20 Sept., 25 Nov. 1966; 30 Jan., 6 Mar., 7 Aug. 1967; 24 May 1968.
181   Ibid., 13 Feb., 12 Mar. 1971.
182   High Park, circular letter, 8 Dec. 1965.

In a good example of how the contradictions between the 'old' and the 'new' were held in tension, work in what was now the match of 'any modern commercial laundry' was presented as part of the training regime:

> It has been remarked, that indolent or discontented girls, when they compete successfully at these machines, have proved themselves interested and efficient workers. It is a social and vocational training so that the girls can later fit effectually into society and appropriate specialised occupation. However, further protection will be necessary in the form of residential facilities and for that we hope to open our new Hostel [Martanna House] in the coming spring.[183]

A hostel, that is, a home to which young women would return after a day's work outside, was to be developed in High Park as Martanna House. But once the concept had taken hold, it had implications for all the women resident in St Mary's. In a hostel, the women went out to work for which they were paid, however modestly, and they in turn paid towards their keep and were actively involved in the management of the household, through budgeting, cooking, shopping and cleaning. Above all, they handled their own money. The question as to why so many of the women in St Mary's, despite working a full day in the laundry, were not paid in their own right, and had no personal finances to handle or mishandle, could not be avoided. The fact that the women were in receipt of full board, clothing and health care (for life, should they choose to stay, including funeral service and burial), that they had companionship, recreations and outings and that automation had made laundry work much lighter, did not answer the fundamental question of why they were not paid a set weekly wage.

The question was squarely faced in March 1971, but there were particular events which led up to this. In preparation for the 1969 *aggiornamento* general chapter, called to revise the constitutions in line with the new teachings of Vatican II, frank discussion extended to all aspects of OLC life, including the apostolate. In a questionnaire survey collated in January 1967, at least one of the sisters submitted the proposition that 'our girls should be paid a just wage. Those working harder or taking a share in the responsibility of the work should get a higher wage'.[184] In January 1969 – still before the general chapter – the superior announced to the community (without much tact or sensitivity, it appears at this remove) that an outside supervisor was to be appointed to the ironing room for two reasons:

> 1) the sisters with social science degrees are unable to cope with the work in conjunction with social work among the girls; 2) there are few intelligent and reliable girls.[185]

183   Ibid.
184   'Compilation of the results of the discussions held by the Sisters of the Irish Federation on the response to the questionnaire which was sent out in January 1967', item no. 92a (DARGS, OLC5/3/1). Hereafter, Compilation of results of discussions, 1967.
185   High Park local council, minutes, 23 Jan. 1969.

Expecting a social science graduate, straight from university and full of new ideas, to work the old refuge model was simply not feasible. The renewal and modernisation called for by Vatican II was not to be sidestepped, and the new consultative structures and greater openness to new ideas meant that those who felt strongly on matters affecting the refuge had a better chance of being heard. The advantages of 'grouping' as tending to a 'more happy and normal life', 'modern standards' in accommodation, clothing and food, and the contentious issue of wages were recurring matters of discussion in the late 1960s.[186] The respect due to the individual that runs though the teaching of the council was seized on as very much in keeping with the original intention of the founder, and found expression in the demand that 'Opportunities, equipment and time for developing gifts of intellect and nature should be available to all, according to their capabilities; at present, only a select few are benefiting by such openings'.[187]

In the house, the introduction of the 'group system' for all the women, not just the younger girls, made considerable demands on those sisters who were willing and suited to being 'housemothers' and removed them from work in the laundry – which therefore required more paid, lay employees. Outside, opportunities for women had improved more generally, and for those with learning needs (described in the language of the time as 'retarded' or 'with mental handicap'), the development of specialist services, with some state funding, had reduced their likelihood of ending up in a magdalen refuge. Short-term accommodation alternatives, including OLC hostel developments in High Park (Martanna House), Gloucester Street/Sean MacDermott Street and Kilmacud, meant that the numbers of new entrants had declined sharply and those who stayed were unlikely to be managerial material.

Further lay staff were appointed to the laundry in 1970, despite the opposition of some of the sisters in the laundry who refused to co-operate with them, 'and as a result the girls were following their example'.[188] At the end of December 1970, new toilet and cloakroom facilities for 'outdoor female laundry staff' were planned.[189] By February 1971, the proposed appointment of one sister as house mother 'to the working group in St Mary's' gave rise to the problem of who would fill her position 'pricing at the laundry account books'.[190] Those who might take this on were already working as house mothers or otherwise fully stretched, and further lay appointments were inevitable. With a few paid employees only, and almost all men, the issue of wages for the internal workforce could perhaps be glossed over, but there was no way it could be avoided when paid and unpaid women were working alongside each other. There is also evidence that the small group structure had fulfilled its purpose of giving more scope for individuality and self-expression; in terms of clothes and shoes 'the girls were now anxious to make their own choice in these matters'.[191]

186  Compilation of results of discussions 1967, nos. 6, 56, 92, 92a; 100, 120.
187  Ibid., nos. 66, 114.
188  High Park local council, minutes, 10 Nov. 1970.
189  Ibid., 31 Dec. 1970.
190  Ibid., 13 Feb., 12 Mar. 1971.
191  Ibid., 30 Mar. 1971.

What was to be a landmark council meeting was held on 16 March 1971; 'the entire meeting was given over to discussing the problematic situation of not only those in the rehabilitation [teenage] group, but of all our girls':

> Due to the complete change over in their thinking, and attitudes to institutional care, Society is not slow in glancing askance and – perhaps erroneously, as Sr Columba [Cunningham] mentioned – making unfavourable comments on our old time system. It was agreed that very many in the working group, though capable of a day's work, were not fit to take their place outside, due to being now 'institutionalised'. These girls however, deserve our consideration, and should be receiving a remuneration for their services if not on a level, at least in some degree in proportion to their fellow workers, whom we employ under a compulsory wage system. Many sisters, at various times, have heard the comment that we do perhaps look after the girls, for which due praise is given, but there is a rising tendency to resent, at least by insinuation and more strongly sometimes, that we do not do justice to our girls when we do not allow them the dignity of handling money of their own.[192]

A fortnight later, the first version of the new system was proposed, working through the groups and their house mothers, the structure through which clothing and other requisites were already managed:

> All things being taken into consideration in today's rate of living, the sum of £2 per capita per month was decided upon as a reasonable amount to cover their personal expenses. Sister Superior said she would request Sister Bursar to furnish the necessary amount relevant to the number in each Group to the House Mother. It was agreed that Sister Colman [Cantwell] should have a stock press in the workroom and make the purchases for her group. (Also that the Leaders might have an extra amount for pocket money?)[193]

This was endorsed at the next meeting on a three-month trial basis, namely Sister Bursar 'to furnish approximately £2 per capita per month to meet the expenses of personal effects as required by the respective House Mothers for the girls in their groups'.[194] The special arrangement for Sister Colman's group, whereby she made the purchases on their behalf, was because these were the girls and women least able to manage independently (referred to as the 'retarded' group). The 'leaders' were the girls and women regarded as most dependable, who could take on the responsibility of bringing a companion to the health centre for a medical appointment or could accompany others to and from town on the bus.

---

192   Ibid., 16 Mar. 1971.
193   Ibid., 30 Mar. 1971.
194   Ibid., 20 Apr. 1971.

Under 'Penitents' Expenses', the accounts for May 1971 record the first of these payments: there were 38 women in Group 2, under Sister Colman, for whom £76 was paid, and 40 women in Group 3, under Sister Veronica Lennon, for whom £80 was paid. The teenage group was not included under this first arrangement, nor it appears were the elderly women in the infirmary. Just over a year later, in June 1972, this particular pocket money item ends and there is a new heading in the accounts, under 'Laundry', titled 'laundry workers'; the four-week wage bill came to £932, and employer's tax was also paid.[195] This would give an average figure of just over £6 per week per person, based on 38 girls employed (the number the preceding month), all of whom were full-time residents in St Mary's. The teenage group was outside these arrangements as the group 'are so far able to manage with the maintenance fee (the Dublin Health Authority contribution) being paid for some of the girls, whilst others are working'. Their personal needs and pocket money were already covered and under the supervision of their housemother and, should the necessity arise for paying these trainees, 'it was hoped the Dublin Health Authority would subsidise wages'.[196]

The payment of wages to all laundry workers (except the sisters, of whom there were still about 20 working full-time in the laundry in 1970) led to doubts as to whether or not the laundry was paying its way.[197] The outlook, deemed quite positive from a financial point of view at a review in November 1971, six months later turned bleak on the loss of three large hospital contracts, two hotels and others likely to be lost. The annual deficit was running at £11,000.[198] There were complaints in 1972 from several customers about items lost or damaged or poorly done, and furthermore about their complaints being ignored; the manager, while acknowledging that some queries had not been followed up, 'pointed out the immense difficulties against which they laboured in the setting where staff had to be selected to 'fit in' with our girls, and the staff are unobtainable'.[199] While outside staff could be dismissed, he could not sack the internal staff without some exceptional reason, and not every worker could – as he put it himself – 'fit in'. Having a long-experienced sister in charge of each stage of the process, with a ratio of about one sister to three girls assisting her (in the 1960s), had helped maintain the quality of the work, but this tight system was breaking down.[200] New entrants to the community were not being sent to work alongside women in the laundry, but were being trained for more ambitious roles, as social workers, nurses, teachers, and other professionals. Nor were 'new hands' coming from the ranks of the women who sought admission to St Mary's. Customers could also be simply unreasonable, a long-standing reality with laundry work.[201] The early 1970s

195   High Park, day book, accounts for May 1971 to July 1972.
196   High Park local council, minutes, 30 Mar. 1971.
197   Ibid., 7 Sept. 1971. The number of sisters at work in the laundry was between 20 and 30 in the 1960s. Personal communication, Sister Teresa Coughlan OLC, 9 Jan. 2011.
198   High Park local council, minutes, 16 Nov. 1971, 21 Mar. 1972.
199   Ibid., 4 Apr. 1972.
200   Personal communication, Sister Teresa Coughlan OLC, 9 Jan. 2011.
201   'Some customers send in laundry so soiled that no amount of bleach etc. can restore its appearance. When hearing these complaints, sisters should give the advice that the Manager would appreciate being personally contacted', High Park local council, minutes, 4 Apr. 1972.

were increasingly difficult: even if the capital investment was written off, the new-found ability of hospitals, hotels and institutions to look after their own laundry meant that High Park was unlikely to receive the volumes it required every week to ensure its commercial viability into the future. Meanwhile, the smaller, domestic customers, so difficult to please, were sending less and less.

Even while the laundry itself was on rather shaky ground, the transformation of St Mary's continued. This was in respect of all the women, not just the younger women, for whom the hostel Martanna House was intended and for whom a full training programme was already in place. In July 1971, Sister Columba Cunningham proposed that, 'as a precedent had been set by one girl from Group A taking up a job outside and continuing to live in St Mary's, the time had now come for consideration to be given to this group where others were likely to wish to do the same thing'.[202] While various proposals to build a separate unit were considered by the community, what is significant is the fundamental shift in the concept of St Mary's: it could continue as a home, but with an openness to its women residents finding jobs outside its walls and an active, up-front commitment to assisting them to integrate more fully into wider society. The matter of 'increased allowances and accommodation facilities' was put on the agenda by the 'group mothers' in February 1972 at the request of members of their groups, in which they were strongly supported by Mr Carpenter, the laundry manager.[203] All the women who worked in the laundry received the same allowance, enjoyed the same freedoms and suffered the same restrictions, yet clearly some had the capacity for much more autonomy:

> The manager strongly advised that some form of segregation be adopted for the Leaders who at present have not much further concessions than the retarded girl. He urged that they be granted further freedom at weekends and be allowed to 'Bingo' in the Blind Home [Rosminians] and other suitable entertainments occasionally. It was suggested that £1 increase might be experimented on for a while.[204]

Mr Carpenter's opinion, in this as in so many other matters, carried weight and the sister with direct responsibility, Sister Veronica Lennon, 'may be reminded of his suggestion that the working girls should receive extra pocket money and some fixed expansion and freedom in their recreation hours'.[205]

## Overview of Admissions to St Mary's Refuge, High Park, 1949–69

The total number of women at any one point between federation in 1949 and 1969, the last year in which women were admitted to St Mary's refuge in numbers (figure 11.5), decreased steadily, and was never to reach the peaks reported earlier: 211 women in December 1906, and 210 women in

202    Ibid., 13 July 1971.
203    Ibid., 29 Feb. 1972.
204    Ibid., 6 Mar. 1972.
205    Ibid., 4 Apr. 1972.

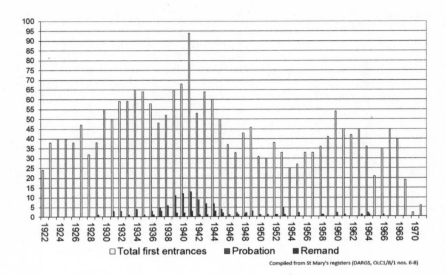

**Figure 11.5** First entrances of women, including on remand or on probation, to St Mary's Refuge, High Park, 1922–71.

December 1935. In December 1950, it was confirmed that 'the numbers in our Class of Penitents have somewhat gone down' and, in December 1951, there were 'about 180 girls', not so many as formerly but (as the other houses were always told), still affording the sisters 'wonderful consolation' through their devotion to prayer and edifying lives.[206] In December 1957, there were 165 girls resident in the refuge.[207] The total for 1962 is given as 170 girls.[208]

Analysis of the register between 1949 and 1969 inclusive shows a remarkably high number of first-time entrances, a total of 753 (of whom 25 were remand or probation cases). The number of first-time admissions each year (insofar as they can be distinguished from repeat entrances) ranges between 53 in 1960 and 19 in 1969. The average over the decade 1949 to 1959 inclusive was 40 girls per year, and between 1960 and 1969 inclusive, it averaged 38 girls per year (figure 11.5). Of these first-time entrants in 1949 to 1969 inclusive, a total of 19 girls have been identified as staying more than two years or becoming permanent residents. Only two of the girls who came on remand or probation (a total of 25 girls between 1949 and 1969 inclusive) might be added to this 'long-term' list; one stayed 28 months (given the house name Cyprian), and another entered multiple times (known as Pius and as Reginald). This analysis suggests that about three in every 100 of the girls who were admitted to High Park for the first time between 1949 and 1969 inclusive became long-term or permanent residents, that is, lived

206 High Park, circular letters, 12 Dec. 1950; 8 Dec. 1951.
207 High Park, circular letter, 8 Dec. 1957.
208 Loose memo, preparatory notes for OLC Irish federation quinquennial report, numbers for 1962 (DARGS, OLC1/2/1 no. 48).

**Figure 11.6** First entrances to St Mary's Refuge, High Park, 1937–67, and subsequent length of stay.

| Year | Total first entrances | Left within 1 month | Stayed 1–3 months | Stayed 4–12 months | Stayed 13–24 months | Left after 2 years | Left but no date of departure given | Stayed longterm / died in OLC |
|------|------|------|------|------|------|------|------|------|
| 1937 | 48 | 7 | 0 | 3 | 2 | 4 | 28 | 4 |
| 1947 | 33 | 0 | 1 | 0 | 0 | 2 | 28 | 2 |
| 1957 | 33 | 15 | 5 | 7 | 2 | 0 | 4 | 0 |
| 1967 | 45 | 25 | 4 | 0 | 5 | 1 | 7 | 3 |

Compiled from St Mary's registers (DARGS, OLC1/8/1 nos. 6-8)

more than two years in High Park. The exact figures must be treated with caution (for example, each instance of the same name is treated as a separate 'first entrance' unless there is evidence to the contrary, the same woman could be entered under both her single and married name and there are exits that are undated). It is the overall pattern that can be relied on, and all the evidence is that a very small percentage of each year's intake stayed long term (calculated as two years or more) – probably more than the 3% this analysis has arrived at, but not much more. A breakdown of the 1957 figures demonstrates the balance between short-term and longer-term residents (figure 11.6). Of the 32 women admitted that year, 15 left within one month, five within three months, seven within one year, and two more within two years. Three other women have simply 'left' after their name, and no date of departure; these were likely to be short-stay residents also. Nobody of the 1957 first-time cohort was to become a permanent resident. For comparison sake, of the 46 women in the 1937 intake, four left after being resident more than two years and a further four stayed long-term. Of the 1947 intake of 33 women, two left after more than two years, and a further two stayed long term. In 1967, out of an intake of 45 women, 25 left within one month, four within three months, five within two years, one person left after two years and three became long-term residents. There is nothing but 'left' written after a further seven women, who presumably were short-term also, but how short-term can only be speculation.

Age analysis is not a straightforward process, as the ages are not always given in the register. Many women left after an overnight stay or just a few days and there are entries with simply 'left' after the name. Nevertheless, an examination of the register shows that, of the 32 admissions in 1957, eight were aged under 21, five aged between 21 and 30 inclusive, and 17 were aged over 30 (two with no age given). Of the eight teenagers aged 15 to 19, all except one were gone after a short stay (three were overnight or less than a week; two stayed two months, one stayed three months, the other girl 'left'). The girl who stayed longest was there for 20 months before 'ran away' is entered after her name. Of the older women (aged more than 30) who are entered in the register for High Park in 1957, seven would seek shelter again in High Park on subsequent occasions, and two have the note 'entered previously'. In the admissions for 1967, the proportion of teenagers (aged 14 to 20 inclusive) is even higher, at 26 out of a total of 45 first-time entrants; but of these 11 are either overnight or less than a week on the premises, another stayed for a fortnight, a further seven for periods between one and 11 months, and three are longer term (also three 'left'). Two girls were sent on immediately to Martanna House, a 17-year-old and a 21-year-old. Only three of the 1967 teenage intake stayed long term: one 14-year-old stayed until she was 30 and was 'taken home'; a 19-year-old stayed until, aged 28, she was 'taken home by father'. The third girl, aged 17 on entry, stayed in High Park permanently, excepting a trial in Gloucester Street in 1980. These were among the younger girls who were kept largely separate from the main body of women and for whom the training programme was well established by 1967. From the register, it appears that the numbers fluctuated from week to week, but with a small, long-term core group. There was sufficient capacity in the system, in terms of bed places, to admit teenagers and older women to what might be termed emergency accommodation. The size of St Mary's was, in this respect at least, a major strength throughout the 1950s and 1960s.

With so few of the annual intake staying long-term, how could the end-of-year numbers be so large? These numbers do not take into account those women with pre-1949 experience of High Park who returned for days, weeks, months or to stay permanently over the period 1949 to 1969, and whose return was noted in the register after their first entry – or, indeed, were welcomed back without any note being made in the register at all. Although there are no statistics in the 1960 Christmas letter, it is reported that the refuge 'is filled almost to capacity', partly due to the return of a number of former girls who, 'having left us in the dim past, now seek a haven of peace, away from the storms and tempests of the world'.[209] By the 1950s, St Mary's had been in operation a full 100 years. The steady increment, year on year, of a small number of permanent residents was one of the factors leading to the large size of the household. Many of these were in their teens or early 20s on entry, and 40, 50, 60 and even 70 years later were still alive. Between 1922 and 1948 (pre-federation), an average of four girls from each year's new intake stayed permanently, to which must be added those who were previously in the refuge and returned in later life. Losses through death ran several decades behind the intake. The celebration of jubilees testifies to the longevity of quite a number of the women. In 1954, two of the women, both aged over 80 and both in the infirmary, jointly celebrated

209    High Park, circular letter, Dec. 1960.

their jubilees: 'poor Magdalen of the Assumption overdid it and was laid up next day', she had entered aged 30 in 1904 and was to die in May 1954; Magdalen of the Sacred Heart at the time of the jubilee 'is only awaiting God's time to take her to Himself', but contrary to predictions lived another three years.[210] Her case was typical of the multiple entries, first featuring on the register in 1914 (but with no age on admission), leaving and re-entering four more times, before her jubilee party in 1954, and death in 1957.

## Background to Admission 1922–71, including Probation and Remand

While there is occasionally some information in the register about what brought individuals to High Park, for a very large majority there is nothing more known outside date of arrival, 'left', age on admission, date of departure, parents living or not and the house name used in High Park (see figure 2.2); in some cases even that minimum is not known.[211] This significant limitation must be kept in mind. While the concern of this chapter is with the post-federation era of the 1950s and 1960s, some of the women residents had arrived in High Park decades earlier, making it necessary to push back the starting date of this analysis. The presence of women and girls on probation or on remand, though the numbers were small, is examined across the same period, to try and fill in the picture as completely as possible.

Over the period 1922 to 1971, some mention or hint of the girl's previous experience, or of how she came to arrive in High Park, has been identified in the register for 59 girls. (This is in addition to 137 girls who have been classified in this analysis on remand or probation). Out of a total intake of 2,219, this figure of 196 cases comes to less than 8%, hence the warning about treating these figures with the greatest circumspection. Nevertheless, a few trends can be identified. Several girls were 'brought by father'. 'Entered from hospital', and in particular from St Loman's hospital (for the treatment of women with mental illness and alcoholism) features strongly, while 'came from union' probably refers to the former South Dublin Union workhouse hospital, known as St Kevin's (now the site of St James's Hospital). Several women were 'sent from' or 'came from' a convent elsewhere; the Good Shepherd in Limerick is mentioned twice (1934, 1938), also the Presentation Fethard (1932), and Summerhill convent (1939). Several residents had been reared in an industrial school, having been 'sent by' – or 'was in' – a named institution; Booterstown, Clifden, Moate, Cork, Lakelands and Loughrea are each mentioned once, as is the 'mental handicap' institute in Glenmaroon and the 'special school' called St Philomena's, Kilmacud. On two occasions, women were recorded as 'sent from' the hostel in Henrietta Street (1934, 1936), once 'from Gloucester Street' (1937), once 'from Donnybrook (1956), while there were five instances of women coming from the Legion of Mary hostel in Harcourt Street, either

---

210    Ibid., Dec. 1954.
211    Eight women died or left between 1922 and 1952, and a further five died or left between 1952 and 1961, for whom no date of first entrance has been determined. These figures must be seen in the context of 2,219 entrances recorded between 1922 and 1971.

arriving on their own or 'brought by' a legionary. There is one instance of 'sent by' a named priest (1935), two instances of 'sent by' the mother-and-baby home of Sean Ross, Roscrea (1936), and a number who were directed to High Park by a named woman, such as 'Brought by Mrs Clarke', 'Sent by Mrs McNeill'. Between 1953 and 1956, four 'Italian refugees' entered High Park, one of whose place of birth was Yugoslavia, and another, born in Naples, who was in receipt of Red Cross help. The only conspicuous grouping is between 1 February 1962 and 9 December 1963, when a total of eight women of various ages transferred from St Patrick's Refuge, Dun Laoghaire, to High Park. It is not possible to extrapolate the larger picture from these few entries, but it does point out some trends which are confirmed by the examination of the Gloucester Street register where the entries are a little fuller.

Over the period 1922 to 1971, there is evidence in the register of admissions of girls and women coming to High Park after an encounter, of some sort, with the criminal justice system, understood in its broadest sense.[212] The numbers alone are discussed here, insofar as the records allow connections to be made. The role of OLC refuges in remand is considered more generally, with regard to Gloucester Street/Sean MacDermott Street (chapter 12), and again in chapter 13, where the co-operation of sisters with the state in the remand system, in the light of Vatican II, was a matter of internal debate. In this analysis, all entries which mention court, prison, Mountjoy, remand, probation, time or the terms Garda, guard, police, station, sergeant or their abbreviations have been extracted from St Mary's register. 'Miss Duffy' is taken to be a probation officer ('brought by Miss Duffy'). 'Time up' is understood as probation ('left as time up'). As already noted, there were 2,219 entrances to High Park from 1922 to 1971; of these, 137 have been identified as having some connection with the justice system. These 137 entries have been classified as on probation or 'time' 114; on remand 26, with one case excluded from the statistical analysis as coming via a probation officer in London. For 21 of the 137 entries, 'came from courts' is the descriptor; these are placed in the more likely category of remand or probation, depending on the length of time served or other hints, such as brought by a named person known to be a probation officer. Four of the cases were remand and then probation; others may also fit this dual description, but it is not stated in the register.

'On remand' meant anything from an overnight stay to seven days, the girl being held until the next court sitting at which her case would be decided. 'On probation', when the girl gave an undertaking to the judge to reside at a given address – on the strength of which the judge gave the benefit of the Probation Act, rather than a prison sentence – ranged from three months to three years, at least as it features in the High Park records (with one exception). It is known to have offered the same type of service more usually asked of

---

212  See the McAleese report, part 3, chapter 9 for an exploration of the legislative basis on which girls and women were referred to the magdalen laundries through the criminal justice system – understood to include government departments, state agencies (An Garda Síochána, Probation Service, Prison Service) and the courts. Girls were placed on remand, on probation, on temporary release from prison, and on early release from prison as well as through informal placements by the gardaí and probation services, typically due to homelessness.

Our Lady's Home, Henrietta Street, on at least two occasions, whereby a woman prisoner serving a life sentence could, with her own consent, be released 'on licence' to a named place and told the number of years in detention would be 'dependent upon her own conduct'.[213] As was the case with the general intake discussed already, there is no personal story or note of the person's encounter with the justice system to be found in the records of the asylum outside a phrase such as 'time from court 1 year', 'time 3 months', 'on remand for 2 days', '12 months probation'. As with all others who sought shelter, the barest minimum of name, parents alive or dead, 'native of', age, date of entry and house name are written up; it is only the note 'on remand' or 'time 2 years' that makes it possible to distinguish these entries from others. The subsequent history of the person is similarly scanty. Notes such as 'went to a situation' or 'went home to Wexford' are about as full as they get; for most, 'left' is all that is entered.

The formal approval of Gloucester Street/Sean MacDermott Street convent as a remand home in 1960 (and also of Our Lady's Home, Henrietta Street) removed the need for judges to use High Park for remand. Only one case, a girl of 18 from Wexford ('remand 3 days, then stayed 2 days until father collected her') features in the High Park register after this date. The numbers using High Park as their probation address also collapsed. The only girls who completed a time of probation in High Park in the 1960s were a 19-year-old Tipperary girl (entered 1960, on one year's probation, stayed two years and four months in all, 'ran away'); an 18-year-old Dublin girl (entered 1960, six months' probation, 'left'), and a girl from Cashel, aged 18 (entered 1961, on six months' probation but 'ran away').

The significant fact is that probation cases were always only a small fraction of the general intake (and the remand cases even smaller): about five in every 100 entrants used St Mary's refuge as their address while on probation, and one in every 100 were on remand between court appearances, making about 6% (136) of the total intake (2,219) between independence and 1971. Whatever the faults of the system, what the sisters of Our Lady of Charity operated here (as in Gloucester Street/Sean MacDermott Street) was a home into which cases from the courts were mixed with the general intake without distinction, with a constant throughput of girls, as most entered and left after short spells. Their own names were not used and, even if they were, no-one could tell other than the girl herself, while the stigma of a spell in prison was avoided.

## Education and Training Opportunities for Sisters of Our Lady of Charity, 1948–71

The better 'technical training' of the sisters was named as one of the key reasons for federation, which was itself pushed through by Dr McQuaid in 1948. Decisions around study were made at the level of the general council, but they also required local co-operation. By the chapter of November 1954, it was reported that 'an effort has been made', with one sister recently trained as a national teacher and two in household management.[214]

---

213  'Women on bail or early release from prison', McAleese report, ch. 9, pp 290–304.
The correspondence relating to High Park is dated 10, 16 July and 16, 18 Aug. 1930 (p. 294); 14, 16 Jan. 1941 (p. 304).
214  Irish federation general chapter 1954 record.

But once embarked on, there was no going back, with the move towards further education strengthened by the *aggiornamento* called for by Vatican II, a call to renewal and updating and the embracing of the modern world as the theatre within which Christians were to strive. The obligation on religious superiors to see that their members were properly equipped for the works in which they were engaged was the concern of more than Dr McQuaid, and pre-dates the Vatican council; it was surely brought home to the superior general and council of the new OLC federation in Ireland by the questions posed by Rome:

> Do superiors see to it that those involved in teaching receive adequate preparation for their work: scientifically, by acquiring knowledge which corresponds adequately to the grade of the class, and by obtaining degrees and certificates, even such as are recognised outside ecclesiastical circles; pedagogically, by the study and practice of the art of teaching; spiritually, so that they may exercise the office of teaching with a genuine zeal for souls and make it a means of sanctification for themselves and others.[215]

> With respect to those members of the institute involved in the corporal works of mercy, Do superiors diligently see to it that all persons who are to be engaged in various capacities in these institutions be competently prepared: scientifically, by obtaining even State certificates and other equivalent credentials, and b) by a practical period of trial.[216]

The answers of OLC Ireland to these questions were a lot more satisfactory by the end of the 1960s than on federation.

There was no obvious or single qualification for the work of an OLC sister in Dublin, but certain areas came to the fore, namely domestic science, child and adolescent welfare, nursing and social science. Training in household management was undertaken at Cathal Brugha Street and at Sion Hill, Blackrock.[217] A 'refresher course' in domestic science, held July 1955 in the Cross and Passion convent, Maryfield, was reportedly 'somewhat strenuous' but the greatest benefit derived by the attendees was perhaps 'confidence in their own capabilities'.[218] Sisters needing to be brought up to matriculation standard before admission to third-level education attended Maryfield College.[219] In September 1968, there were ten sisters, of varying ages, from High Park enrolled in night classes at the local technical school

215   Irish federation quinquennial report 1949–53, question 302.
216   Ibid., question 308.
217   Irish federation general council, minutes, 9 Jan., 28 Apr. 1950, 12 Sept. 1952, 31 Jan. 1954; High Park, circular letter, 20 Dec. 1963, High Park local council, minutes, 3 Feb. 1953.
218   Sister M. of St Francis Thérèse Blackmore, Sister M. of St Dominic Andrews, Sister M. of St Catherine Labouré Johnston, Irish federation general council, minutes, 5 July 1955; High Park, circular letter, 8 Dec. 1955.
219   Irish federation general council, minutes, 1 Apr., 7 Sept. 1959; High Park local council, minutes, 13 Sept. 1965, 29 Aug., 21 Sept. 1966, 16 June 1969; High Park, circular letter, 8 Dec. 1959.

in Marino, 'in advanced dress-making, and arts and crafts'.[220] The evidence is that these new-found skills, whether the fruits of part-time night courses or full-time programmes, were quickly tested.

In the allied areas of child welfare, child development and adolescent psychology, most of the training on offer – initially at least – consisted of short courses. A ten-day course in childcare held in Carysfort teacher training college, Blackrock, County Dublin, in August 1953 was well attended by OLC.[221] In January 1957, OLC sisters attended the first of a series of lectures on psychology by Revd Dr O'Doherty, University College Dublin.[222] A review of a later version of this programme lists the areas covered as personality, emotional and moral development, delinquency and psycho-sexual problems, all 'subjects so necessary to aid us in our specialised work'.[223] With Dr McQuaid visiting High Park in person twice in January 1957, no doubt the superior general was relieved to have this timely evidence of her institute's willingness to engage with new ideas. Doubts at the time as to finding young sisters suited to extra studies were overridden by the archbishop who insisted that 'once the Sisters would be known to attend such University courses as part of their apostolate, young girls attracted to the work would join in greater numbers from the ranks of social workers, legionaries and university students'.[224]

The Irish federation sent sisters to England to study, possibly due to the close contacts with OLC communities there who could vouch for the quality of the training on offer. The first to be sent to the Child Welfare Centre, Holy Rood House, London, commenced full-time studies in September 1959. But training opportunities in Ireland did expand, with (for example) the six-month specialist course 'For teachers of handicapped children' offered in nearby St Patrick's Training College, Drumcondra, in 1968 (one OLC student sister was among the enrolment).[225] Under the auspices of Dr McQuaid and the archdiocese of Dublin, the Child and Youth Care Group (CYCG) organised a number of courses in childcare,[226] delinquency[227] and adolescent psychology that were attended by High Park sisters between

220   High Park local council, minutes, 3 Sept. 1968; others schools attended were Loreto College, North Great George's Street (commercial course), Parnell Square ('arts and crafts' training, also 'academic studies') and St Mary's Technical School (dress-making). See Irish federation general council, minutes, 1 Apr., 3, 7 Sept. 1959, 22 Sept. 1967; High Park, circular letters, 8 Dec. 1959, 8 Dec. 1967.
221   Sisters Carmel Staunton (superior), Agnes Carlin (assistant), Ursula Fallon, Vincent de Paul Whelan, Dominic Andrews, Veronica McCarthy (St Anne's), also Sisters Aloysius Pilkington and Frances Thérèse Blackmore (High Park) attended, Irish federation general council, minutes, 19, 28 Aug. 1953.
222   Ibid., 16 Jan. 1957.
223   High Park, circular letter, 8 Dec. 1968.
224   MS notes dated 31 Jan. 1957, in J.C. McQuaid's hand (DDA, McQuaid Papers, Department of Justice).
225   Sister M. of Perpetual Succour Ryan, Irish federation general council, minutes, 7 Sept. 1959, 8 Aug 1960; High Park, circular letter, 8 Dec. 1959; High Park local council, minutes, 16 Apr. 1968.
226   A childcare course was held in Nov. 1967, High Park, circular letter, 8 Dec. 1967.
227   A course on delinquency to be held in Muckross Convent on 23 May 1970, High Park local council, minutes, 28 Apr. 1970.

1967 and 1971. The inspiration came from the full-time year-long courses approved by the Home Office in England, such as that in Holy Rood, London.[228] The other early provider of education for childcare workers was the diocese of Ossory where, under Bishop Birch and Sister Stanislaus Kennedy, one-year and shorter courses were availed of by at least three OLC sisters in the early 1970s.[229]

Nursing was a professional field with obvious applicability to the work at High Park in the 1950s and 1960s. There was one trained doctor, Sister Joseph Carton, who had qualified before joining the order in 1934; she had previously qualified as a nurse.[230] While several other nurses had entered the community over the years (Sister Dolours Flynn, Sister Ursula Fallon), the first person to undergo nurse training from High Park was Sister Mary of St Gemma Galgani O'Connor who began her training, still in first vows, at St Vincent's Hospital, Elm Park, in September 1958.[231] Others were to follow, although the opening of the OLC mission from England to Nairobi in 1959 (pioneered by Sister Agnes Ennis of Bitterne) was to draw several of the nurses trained for the Irish federation to Kenya.

The education of social workers made advances, most notably (for High Park sisters) with the establishment of a primary degree in social science at University College Dublin in 1954 and the postgraduate diploma in Applied Social Studies in 1968.[232] Two High Park sisters and one from Gloucester Street commenced the Bachelor of Social Science degree course in September 1965.[233] But even before these students registered, an interest in the future of the refuges had been taken by individual UCD lecturers, with Dr McKenna commended for her course of lectures on psychology at High Park in June 1961:

> Her charming personality won our attention and confidence from the beginning and our questions were answered with explanations as clear as they were enlightening. Sisters from our other houses of the Federation attended; the course should help us train our children (*sic*) to face courageously the many challenges of the modern world.[234]

---

228　The Kennedy report, 1970, complained that there were no active adequate courses in Ireland to give professional training in the sensitive field of childcare and, while there was a diploma course in childcare on the calendar of UCD for those who held a degree or diploma, the course had not run for some years due to insufficient applications. Kennedy report, p. 14.

229　These were Sisters Fidelma, Teresa and Elizabeth Burke, High Park local council, minutes, 7 Sept. 1971, 4 Apr. 1972.

230　Mary Thérèse Carton, born 24 Jan. 1901, first vows 30 Nov. 1936, died 30 Oct. 1989 (DARGS, OLC1/6/4).

231　Irish federation general council, minutes, 3 Sept. 1958; High Park, circular letter, 8 Dec. 1958.

232　Noreen Kearney, 'The historical background', in *Social work and social work training in Ireland, yesterday and tomorrow*, Department of Social Studies, Trinity College Dublin (Dublin, 1987), p. 14.

233　Sister M. of St Teresa Coughlan and Sister M. of the Divine Child Kerrane, from High Park and Sister M. of St Lucy Bruton from Gloucester Street convent, High Park local council, minutes, 13 Sept. 1965; see also Irish federation general council, minutes, 29 Aug. 1966, 21 Sept. 1966.

234　High Park, circular letter, 11 Dec. 1961.

The 1967 lecture series on the need for new methodologies in line with modern thinking. by Helen Burke was in support of the student sisters and the new ideas they were encountering in UCD. Two-month summer placements were unrivalled opportunities to see different ways of doing things: one student went to the Observation Centre at Chevilly, outside Paris, one to the Child Guidance Clinic at Rochester, New York, the third to a psychiatric unit in Buffalo, New York – all OLC initiatives.[235]

The hands-on involvement of Dr McQuaid in advancing social work and social work training in the diocese, and ensuring it was firmly tied to Roman Catholic structures and institutions, is evident in a general report on the events of 1968, when reference is made to the 'programmes of lectures and courses of immediate and practical interest' provided by the archdiocese 'in order to bring us abreast of current developments'.[236] The Dublin Institute for Adult Education, 62 Eccles Street, was the venue for the youth leadership course held in 1965, which several OLC sisters attended 'in order to have them better fitted for the extension of our apostolate'.[237] Study opportunities in spirituality, catechetics, prayer, sacred scripture, formation and all aspects of the renewal of religious life were also availed of (chapter 13).[238]

Traditionally, those who entered the OLC community were older and more experienced than, for example, recruits to teaching orders, and came with life experience and qualifications in a wide variety of spheres, as can be gleaned from the profession register, membership notes and obituaries. The difference now, for OLC, was that professed sisters would be sent to study in a lay environment to build on whatever skills or training they had entered with. Studies were undertaken, despite the tradition that outside training and qualifications were not really needed for the work in hand, despite long attachment to – and faithful observance of – a strict rule of enclosure and despite not knowing what scope might be given to new ideas and new learning. Not surprisingly, it was not always a smooth transition, with tensions around releasing sisters from full-time work 'between the lines' of council minutes.[239]

Study opportunities for sisters came with the federation of the houses in 1948. The community's commitment to updating its model of care – expected by Rome, pioneered by OLC houses elsewhere and tentatively expressed in the revised constitutions of 1951– was also in response to the relentless prodding of Dr McQuaid, whose determination to extinguish what he termed the 'penitentiary model' of residential care cannot be doubted. The upgrading and remodelling of the enormous building that was St Mary's Refuge that got under way in the early 1950s, against a background of stability in religious life, was incremental but tangible. Sleeping, living and working environments all bore witness to thoughtful and sustained investment. Smaller groups, in a more homely setting, with more

---

235    Ibid., 8 Dec. 1967.
236    Ibid., 8 Dec. 1968.
237    The students were Sisters Stanislaus Masterson, Columba Cunningham and Berchmans Casey, High Park local council, minutes. 1 Oct. 1965.
238    High Park, circular letters, 20 Dec. 1963, 8 Dec. 1964, 8 Dec. 1968.
239    For example, High Park local council, minutes, 13 May 1970, 13 July 1971.

personal autonomy and greater freedom to come and go, helped to change the culture of the asylum, as did the move to vocational training not merely offering a safe haven. Changes in the laundry itself were due as much to outside forces as internal pressures. The shift to a waged workforce was the final, and most protracted, part of its modernisation. The transformation from an essentially cloistered lifestyle to one more suited to an active apostolic life was to come with Vatican II, while its emphasis on engagement with the world and the autonomy of the individual would precipitate changes in OLC ministry beyond all expectations. But what was achieved in the decade before the Council needs to be acknowledged also.

# Chapter 12

## Introducing 'Modern Methods' to Sean MacDermott Street (Gloucester Street) Convent and Magdalen Asylum, 1949–73

In March 1949, the first canonical visitation of Gloucester Street (Sean Mac-Dermott Street) convent by the first superior general of the federation of the monasteries in Ireland of Our Lady of Charity was undertaken. The annalist records the impact of the visit:

> This coming left behind a feeling of great peace, concord and union, it also filled us with confidence that the happy amalgamation will, with the blessing of God, infuse new sap into the venerable branches of the Tree of Our Lady of Charity of Refuge, and that it will result in the obtaining of more numerous vocations to carry on the wonderful work of the restoration and reformation of souls, work more than ever necessary in these times.[1]

The visiting superior, Sister Mary of St Eithne O'Neill, recorded that here in Gloucester Street, after 62 years of autonomy, 'it was edifying and most consoling to find the constitutions and customs of our holy order so well observed in every detail'. This she credited to their spirit of unity, charity and great zeal for souls.[2]

Federation might reasonably be expected to lead to upheavals and remodelling, but the particular version adopted by the Dublin houses of Our Lady of Charity left so much of the existing structures in place that a smooth transition – at least on the surface – was indeed effected. The first visitation, far from threatening the monastery, confirmed the sisters in their living out of the traditions of John Eudes and of the founding monastery, the 'cradle' of Caen. Gloucester Street, like High Park and St Anne's, Kilmacud, continued

1   Annals or 'Book of the community', Gloucester Street. 1949 (DARGS, OLC2/5/2 no. 6). Hereafter, Gloucester Street, annals.
2   'Visitation by superior general, Union of the three monasteries of the Order of Our Lady of Charity of Refuge in the archdiocese of Dublin amalgamated on 5th November 1948', 7 Apr. 1949 (DARGS, OLC2/5/2 no. 9). Hereafter, superior general, visitation report, Gloucester Street.

to enjoy perfect autonomy throughout the 1950s and 1960s in all but the few matters it had subscribed to under federation. Building projects already in planning were brought to completion. The well-regulated routine of sisters and residents continued, but a little brighter and more varied than formerly. The fourth vow of the sisters – 'the wonderful work of the restoration and reformation of souls' – continued to be expressed in the provision of a home – not a hostel or training centre – for women in need of shelter. A small but steady stream of women continued to use it as their first shelter on discharge from prison, or as their address when on probation from the district court. Significant initiatives, including in 1960 the legal recognition of Gloucester Street as a place of remand for women prior to their sentencing by the court, and following a lengthy campaign by Dr McQuaid, were presented as refinements, improvements and further developments of this traditional ministry.[3]

Increasing the available accommodation, so that no applicant might be turned away – and their soul perhaps placed in jeopardy – continued to be the priority: 'The number of our poor Children is sometimes more than we can accommodate. Our one desire is to be able to enlarge in order to have more scope for our apostolic activities.'[4] In practice, the 1950s were marked by improvements in the *quality* of accommodation, rather than a simple expansion of numbers housed, and the gradual, small-scale loosening up of the asylum model in an effort to move – a little – with the times. The laundry work continued to be the principal source of income. The introduction of what was termed 'modern methods' into the asylum in the mid-1960s was a definite shift, marked first by the separation of the younger girls from the older, more settled women, and a new concern for training and education. This required the reconfiguration of the asylum accommodation, and a much more open engagement with the world outside the enclosure.

The pivotal role of the local superior, though now appointed by the superior general following the consultative vote of the community, was largely unchanged. Gloucester Street's novices were to be trained at High Park, but the impact of this important shift would not be felt for some years. Nor would new ideas and practices quickly arrive through the transfer of sisters from one house to another, as any sister professed before the date of federation was protected, by right, from being moved against her wishes. The exchange of sisters would be limited to a few, and mostly for short periods, far from what happened in a centralised congregation, such as the Good Shepherd sisters.[5] Federation did bring the occasional friendly exchange of visitors: a few sisters from High Park and from St Anne's, Kilmacud, travelled to Gloucester Street in May 1949 to attend a golden jubilee and, in September 1953, the Gloucester Street sisters attended the centenary celebrations in High Park, divided into three groups over the three days.[6]

3   Gloucester Street, annals, 1949.
4   Ibid.
5   Sister M. Benignus Coyle, a young professed choir sister, was sent from High Park to Gloucester Street for nine months in 1951, before being recalled for training. The same year, Sister M. Gertrude Whelan returned from High Park to her former community of Gloucester Street; Gloucester Street, annals, 1951.
6   Gloucester Street, annals, 1953.

But these were novelty outings and the 'rules of enclosure' were still to be observed, as the local superior found necessary to admonish her subjects.[7] The fact that enclosure was now defined as episcopal, not papal, made little difference in practice.[8]

Continuity, rather than change or transition, was underscored by the continuation in leadership roles of the same persons: the first superior of Gloucester Street appointed post-federation was Sister Mary of the Sacred Heart Conroy, who had previously been the second councillor, and her local assistant was Sister Mary of St Benedict Doran, previously councillor. The local council consisted of the previous superior (Immaculate Heart Walshe, now bursar as well), the previous assistant (Stanislaus Masterson) and the previous councillors (Alphonsus Penwarden, Blessed Oliver Murray).[9] The role of the council, to offer advice to the superior in frankness and humility and then to yield graciously to her decision, excepting only where it was judged she was bound on a course 'openly dangerous or evidently pernicious', did not change under federation.[10] The principal recorded business of the Gloucester Street council during the 1950s and 1960s was to 'examine and sign' the convent accounts twice-yearly as required by the constitutions, reinforcing the impression that, in the new federation, the real power continued to be vested in the local superior alone.[11] In brief, while the federation was more than a spiritual union, because so much of the status quo was left untouched, the developments of the 1940s and 1950s could fairly be presented as further flourishing of the OLC tree so well rooted in Caen in 1641.

The system of an annual, canonical visitation by the superior general did bring some outside influence to bear on what happened in Gloucester Street, as did the twice-monthly meetings of the general council. There was also the subtle influence of OLC houses elsewhere, so that the Dublin houses got updates through the annual circular letters and through accommodating visiting sisters of how other monasteries were trying – or not – to keep in step with the times. A more tangible outcome of diocesan federation was that it allowed for a strongly interventionist approach by the archbishop in the affairs of the order in Ireland. Through the mother general and her council, the archbishop could communicate his demands and expectations much more efficiently to all the houses. He frequently visited in person – and telephoned – the federation superior at High Park, whom he expected to secure the full co-operation of the sisters in whatever project he was trying to advance. The pressure brought to bear on the sisters of Our Lady of Charity was a small

7   'Minutes of the Council, Gloucester Street', 11 June 1955 (DARGS, OLC2/5/2 no. 7). Hereafter, Gloucester Street local council, minutes.

8   Minutes of meetings of general council of the federation, Union of the three monasteries of the order of Our Lady of Charity of Refuge in the archdiocese of Dublin, amalgamated 5 Nov. 1948, 15 Mar. 1951 (DARGS, OLC5/5/1 no. 1). Hereafter, Irish federation general council, minutes.

9   Preamble to Gloucester Street local council, minutes.

10   Typescript, 'Explanation of the Rule of St Augustine and of various points of the Constitutions of the Order of Our Lady of Charity of Refuge. For the Religious of the Irish Federation. Revised in 1953', constitution 37 (DARGS, OLC1/5/1 no. 21).

11   'A few business matters were proposed and discussed and more satisfactorily agreed to', Gloucester Street local council, minutes, 1 Feb. 1950, also 17 Feb. 1959.

part of the sustained lobbying undertaken by Dr McQuaid of the Taoiseach, ministers and civil servants, conducted through personal interviews, reports and letters, as well as on-site visits to institutions.

The insistence of Dr McQuaid on the professional training of the sisters was undoubtedly a key driving force towards the modernisation of OLC life in both convent and asylum. Having sisters well trained was in line with his larger ambitions for Catholic social work in the diocese; more particularly, it was one of the headings under which he forced the OLC federation through in 1948, and a point he returned to repeatedly to justify the trouble taken to amalgamate the three monasteries. He reiterated in 1951, when the minimum modifications to the constitutions necessitated by the new structures were approved by Rome:

> The rules, the discipline and the order would remain the same. The faith and religion had not changed since the Order was founded in 1641, but the people had changed, and the demands of the government would have to be complied with. This would involve the training of sisters for the different works of the Federation.[12]

In his earnest efforts to get the state to fund a girls' remand home, McQuaid saw the OLC sisters as the likely management, but only if they could demonstrate that they were up to the task professionally. If not, there were other religious orders to whom he could, and would, turn. But the opportunity of further education was not merely to prepare the Gloucester Street sisters for specific employments. It brought the chance of meeting and learning from laymen and laywomen, and from other sisters and religious brothers involved in social work, as discussed in relation to High Park. It was to be the first chance, for example, of any engagement with the Good Shepherd sisters who, despite having the same founder and being involved in similar work, were as little known to the sisters in Gloucester Street as those of any other congregation.

## Building Extensions and Structural Improvements to Gloucester Street (Sean MacDermott Street) Convent and Asylum, 1949–66

The Gloucester Street campus had expanded from its 1830s origins in the small asylum in Mecklenburgh Street (see figure 6.2) as adjoining plots and mostly ruinous buildings came on the open market, and the proprietors – the Mercy sisters from 1873 and the sisters of Our Lady of Charity from 1887 – grasped the opportunity to expand. Despite being tenement houses and abandoned yards, owners, leaseholders and their representatives sought the maximum possible return for all possible interested parties; none of the properties came cheap, or without a complicated history of leases and ownership.

Shortly before the decree of amalgamation bringing the federation into existence was read aloud on 5 November 1948, and with the active help of 'rich and influential friends', Gloucester Street rejoiced in the complete transformation of a 'small waste plot of land' adjoining the laundry with

---

12    Irish federation general council, minutes, 15 Mar. 1951.

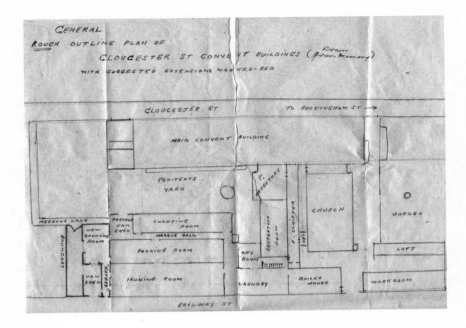

**Figure 12.1** Outline plan, convent, asylum and laundry buildings, Gloucester Street/Sean MacDermott Street, 'drawn from memory', n.d. but prior to 1944. (DARGS, OLC2/9/2 no. 44)

very necessary improvements: a new recreation ground for the women, a new packing room for the laundry and an extension of the ironing room.[13] The culmination of more than a decade of negotiations and changing plans, this is the site to the west of the boundary (figure 12.1) facing onto Railway Street and backing onto Gloucester Lane/Meehan's Lane, laid out with a flower bed and timber seating in 1946.[14] During 1948, new admissions were suspended but, in the following year, when additional bed spaces became available, there was a spike of 39 entrances (figure 12.2) before settling down to an average of about 27 entrances a year between 1950 and 1966. The confined city-centre site, its piecemeal assembly, the large number of resident women and sisters and the ground taken up by the laundry buildings and yards all placed a premium on open or garden space. In 1959, an extra piece of space was acquired, 'an old mill and other old buildings attached to it' and was immediately converted into an additional recreation ground for the women.[15] This is the site labelled 'Scots Church' in 1847 and, by 1935, 'corn mill' (figure 6.2).

13   Gloucester Street, annals, 1949.
14    W.H. Byrne, 'Magdalen Asylum, Sean MacDermott Street, Dublin, proposed walls and layout of yard on area recently acquired from the Dublin Corporation – mass concrete walls', 30 Oct.1946 (DARGS, OLC2/9/2 no. 45).
15   Gloucester Street, annals, 1959.

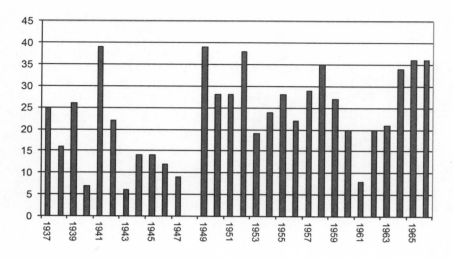

Compiled from register of admission, 1887–1966 (DARGS, OLC2/8//1 no. 2)

**Figure 12.2** Gloucester Street/Sean MacDermott Street refuge, first entrances 1937–66.

The acquisition of numbers 92 and 93 beside the laundry in 1948 was, however, celebrated for other reasons also. The site had formerly been occupied 'by houses of evil repute' and the takeover marked, symbolically, the triumph of good over 'sin and disorder', an 'almost unhoped-for transformation realised'.[16] The OLC annals associate the site with the exact houses first targeted by Frank Duff, founder of the Legion of Mary, in his crusade against prostitution in the 1920s and 1930s. Thus the dedication of the new buildings to Our Lady of Fatima was particularly apt in terms of iconography: 'where Satan once held sway, she who crushed the head of the serpent stands aloft in power and majesty'.[17] Finally, the insertion of a stone from the founding monastery of the order draws a direct line between Gloucester Street and Caen, the unbroken tradition of charity and zeal for souls that was the common heritage:

> Stone from the Monastery of Caen, founded 1641, placed here at the building of the new extension, 1948. Surely the spirit of our Holy Founder loves to linger here in this spot, redeemed by his daughters from the empire of Satan, and consecrated to the glorious work he founded over three centuries ago.[18]

When the ground rents of numbers 60 and 62 Lower Gloucester Street, adjoining the convent (to the west), came up for sale in 1955, 'the solicitor advised this

16   Ibid., 1949.
17   Ibid.
18   Ibid.

to be a desirable and opportune investment of £270' and the local council approved the purchase.[19] A separate and more complicated deal involved a plot 'with some disused out-offices at the rear entrance of our laundry', put up for sale in late 1955. Having consulted the superior general, 'it was advised to purchase this ground at any cost, if only to prevent undesirable purchasers'.[20] The vendors probably over-reached themselves, as no price could be agreed, and there was nobody else, in 1955, looking to buy a derelict plot in this part of the city. This was probably the same plot that came on the market again in 1962, described as 'a piece of waste ground which adjoined our garden'. The superior general forwarded the proposal to the archbishop, who advised its immediate purchase, and the solicitor, James Ryan, brought all to a speedy conclusion with a final note on its use: 'The ground needed to be cleared and enclosed by a high wall so that it will serve as an extension to our community garden'.[21] This marked the furthest extent of OLC property in Sean MacDermott Street Lower.

Alongside the new building and the expansion of the yard and garden spaces, and the erection of a greenhouse, there were ongoing improvements to the interior of the buildings throughout the 1950s and 1960s.[22] Some of it was routine maintenance, such as the repainting in 1952 of much of the premises, listed as three parlours, front hall, service room, the back stairs, sun room, 'children's dormitory', work rooms, stairs and robery.[23] New floors were laid in the kitchen and refectory also.[24] The asylum accommodation received a major upgrade in 1955:

> A beautiful new refectory has been built – also three extra bathrooms. The recreation room has been painted and looks very homelike with its new window curtains.[25]

The extension to the refectory covered much of the 'penitents yard' (figure 12.1);[26] it also brought new standards in catering, with the purchase of 'a hot plate cupboard' for the women in May 1955, the existing method condemned as 'unsatisfactory'.[27] Each improvement highlighted deficiencies elsewhere, with new bathrooms and toilets built in 1955 and 1958.[28] The installation of a lift in 1962 was perhaps the biggest investment up to then that was undertaken with an eye to the future needs of the older women residents and aged sisters.[29]

---

19   Gloucester Street local council, minutes, Sept. 1955.
20   Ibid., 17 Nov. 1955, Dec. 1955, 15 Feb. 1956.
21   Ibid., 19 Apr. 1962.
22   Ibid., 6 May 1959.
23   Gloucester Street, annals, 1952.
24   Ibid.
25   Ibid., 1955.
26   W.H. Byrne, 'Convent of Our Lady of Charity of Refuge, Sean MacDermot Street, Dublin, alterations and additions to refectory etc.', May 1954 (DARGS, OLC2/9/2 no. 47).
27   Gloucester Street local council, minutes, 25 May 1955.
28   Ibid., 11 June 1955, 30 Jan. 1958.
29   Ibid., 30 Mar., 19 Apr. 1962.

The laundry, the principal source of current income and the place of work of most of the women and sisters, was a business that required constant capital investment. The installation of new machinery can be tracked from the fire insurance certificates and from the service contracts, as in January 1953 when the insurance policy was renewed to include 'the new portion of ironing and packing rooms, oil tanks, and various new machines in laundry department'.[30] All the work was dried indoors and mostly by machine, with some of the remarkable new technologies which were bring developed all the time adopted by Gloucester Street, such as the installation of 'a set of sock driers' in May 1955.[31] Worn-out machines had to be replaced: a 'new Calendar to replace the very old one – beyond repair' approved for purchase in January 1960, or a 'new washing machine' approved, at an estimated cost of £1,000, in April 1963.[32] Outside or 'patent cleaners' were employed periodically to clean the ironing and packing rooms.[33] The painting and re-roofing of the various workrooms - boiler houses, wash house, ironing room, van shed – was a recurrent cost because of the steam and heat generated by laundry work. The maintenance and replacement of the laundry van had to be met immediately, whatever the expense.[34]

## The Routine of Daily Life in Gloucester Street (Sean MacDermott Street) Convent and Asylum, 1950s

The traditional OLC system of care, and the language in which it was presented, continued largely unchanged throughout the 1950s. Accommodation was given to those who sought it, with few – if any – questions asked, and little was entered in the register beyond date of entrance and of leaving.[35] The women were assigned house names and lived in the enclosure for however long they stayed, and there was no concept of outside assistance or aftercare – unless, of course, the woman returned to Gloucester Street. This is reiterated in a terse reminder to the sisters in Gloucester Street by the federation superior, Sister Eithne O'Neill, on the occasion of her first visitation in 1949: 'Once a penitent leaves the house, there should be no further communications with her except through the Superior and the sister who has been appointed Mistress of the Class'.[36] What the sisters regarded as their role was to keep an open door, that the woman would always have somewhere safe to return in time of crisis, and some certainly availed of that facility. A small number of women entered repeatedly, and some had experience of institutional life elsewhere, most usually as a child in an industrial school. But for the vast bulk of the entrants, there is no hint of their personal story outside the date of arrival and departure, and who – if anyone – was there for them in the 'outside world'. (Analysis of the entrance register is undertaken inso faras the data allows).

30    Ibid., 21 Jan. 1953.
31    Ibid., 25 May 1955; see also 6 May 1959, on the need of new machinery for the laundry.
32    Ibid., 20 Jan. 1960, 4 Apr. 1963.
33    Ibid., 15 Feb. 1956.
34    Ibid., 30 Jan. 1958, 20 Jan. 1960.
35    'Entrance of the penitents and their leaving, Convent of Our Lady of Charity of Dublin. Commenced the 17th day of February 1887' (DARGS, OLC2/8/1 no. 2). Hereafter, Women's entrance register, Gloucester Street.
36    Superior general, visitation report, Gloucester Street, 7 Apr. 1949.

There are pointed reminders throughout the 1950s about preserving the 'old ways'.[37] Despite – or because – of this, it is possible to track the introduction of changes which, though small, had the cumulative effect of loosening up the old system and bringing some welcome variety and colour. From 1958 onwards, the terms 'poor penitents' and 'dear Children' are replaced in the Gloucester Street convent minutes with 'girls', a change that was made in the High Park minutes from early 1956.[38] Most of the changes were ameliorations or minor improvements at the time but, in retrospect, they can be seen as preparing the ground for the self-conscious shift in 1965 towards 'modern methods'.

The annual cycle of the year continued, closely allied to the Church calendar, with feast-days and holy days marked ritually and with recreations including concerts. Christmas up to the feast of the Epiphany (6 January) was marked by 'the usual holiday concerts and festivities'.[39] Then there were nondescript 'routine weeks' until (in 1956) the month of March and visitation by the superior general from High Park.[40] These canonical visitations were treated as celebratory occasions: 'terminating with a little concert given by our children, which our honoured mother greatly enjoyed'.[41] Other visiting dignitaries were similarly, and frequently, entertained, while feast-days and jubilees – of the sisters and of the consecrates[42] – were further opportunities to show the talent to be found among the residents, both individually and collectively.[43] Sister John Eudes Giles is credited with having a large network of connections, including family members, who responded to her requests to contribute an 'entertainment', while Tommy Delaney , a talented local musician, frequently played what was called a 'Cordovox', a piano accordion with special effects.[44]

The most significant innovation, as it involved breaching the enclosure by women residents and sisters, was the introduction of holiday trips from 1956 onwards:

> June brought a welcome innovation in the lives of our dear children. They were allowed to spend a day at the seaside. They travelled in groups, by bus, on different days, accompanied by some of the sisters. These outings brought a real ray of sunshine into the lives of our dear children.[45]

Technological innovations also brought new experiences; from 1958 'the girls enjoy many film shows, now that we have our own projector'.[46] Handiwork for bazaars and sales of work occupied some of the women residents as well

---

37  For example, visitation report, Gloucester Street, warning re the enclosure, 11 June 1955.
38  Gloucester Street local council, minutes 30 Jan. 1956; High Park local council, minutes (DARGS, OLC1/5/2 no. 1).
39  Gloucester Street, annals, 1956.
40  Ibid.
41  Ibid., 1953.
42  Keernan and Mary Xavier celebrated silver jubilees. Gloucester Street, annals, 1951.
43  Gloucester Street, annals, 1953, also 7 Oct. 1957.
44  Memorandum titled 'On entertainment' by Sister Lucy Bruton, 8 Aug. 2011.
45  Gloucester Street, annals, 1956.
46  Ibid., 1958.

as the sisters – at intervals at least – while there are notes of women confined to the infirmary spending their time making 'pious objects', presumably in anticipation of a sale of work.[47] A major sale was held 9 to 11 November 1950 in the Catholic Club, O'Connell Street. This was the initiative of a Mrs Doherty, a 'very kind lady who is very interested in our work' and was to lessen the debt incurred through 'the various improvements and necessary works carried out in the laundry premises and the Penitents apartments'.[48] It was opened by Mrs O'Kelly, wife of President Seán T. O'Kelly, with other dignitaries in attendance, and drew sufficient popular support to realise the excellent sum of £3,400.[49]

## Music and Amateur Dramatics at Gloucester Street (Sean MacDermott Street) Asylum, 1950s

The follow-up celebrations to the successful sale of work held in November 1950 give a glimpse into how amateur dramatics was firmly established in Gloucester Street asylum, when a thank-you concert, 'a series of little plays', was held for all the helpers. Along with the usual effusive praise for the 'exceptional talent shown by the actresses', there is an additional acknowledgement:

> We owe a very large debt of gratitude to our kind friend Miss J. Marshall who spared no time or trouble to make the play a success. Every year she devotes two or three months to this work with the Children so that they were able to give a big surprise to their mistress.[50]

Miss Josephine Marshall, a teacher with the Loreto sisters in North Great George's Street, worked with the Gloucester Street girls as a volunteer musical director or choreographer from the late 1940s onwards. They worked towards one major annual performance, the concert to be held on the feast-day of the sister who had overall charge of the women's section, the 'first mistress', but the preparation extended over many months and the concert items themselves were re-presented on several other in-house occasions. Concert programmes, instructions for the piano accompaniment, manuscript and printed music scores (generally overwritten) and handwritten copies of the words to be sung to popular tunes all testify to the efforts of Miss Marshall, other lay helpers, the sisters and the women themselves in the production and performance of musical concerts at Gloucester Street. The names of some at least of the women performers are scattered throughout the sheet music and on memos and programme instructions, but regrettably hardly ever the date of the performance. A number of complete musicals were staged – 'Little

---

47    For example, Bernardine RIP, 'a great sufferer being afflicted with acute rheumatism. She passed long hours in the Infirmary making countless pious objects with her poor, crippled hands' Gloucester Street, annals, 1952.
48    Gloucester Street local council, minutes, 1 Feb. 1950.
49    Gloucester Street, annals, 1953.
50    Ibid., 1950.

Gypsy Jane' was one of the earliest, also Cinderella, while, in February 1950, 'The Rajah of Rajapore, or the Magic Ruby', was performed to great acclaim.[51] However, it appears to have been more usual to put together a concert from different musical sources, even where an overall title was assigned.

A typical concert opened with a band performance (figure 12.3); tambourine and drum music scores survive, and instructions for where the cymbals, triangle, combs, castanets, Egyptian bells were to come in, and where the 'hummers' were to play their part. The grand opening by the percussion band (with piano) was followed by perhaps 30 items, including individual and small group pieces, 'full stage', 'full choir', with Irish dancing set pieces, comedy sketches, two-part songs and the occasional solo. There was an eclectic mix of old music-hall favourites and new pop-songs, reflecting the mix of ages – and, no doubt, of stage abilities – among the women. Popular songs from stage and screen musicals were understandably among the favoured items, as they were inclusive – the chorus could take any number – and gave great scope for acting and dancing. The women made their own of certain theme songs from films, and songs recorded by the best-known artists and pop idols of the day. Humorous songs that needed to be acted out appear to have been preferred over straight singing, while no concert was complete without some traditional Irish melody, ballad or Irish musical sketch. Improvising costumes and getting made-up for the stage were all part of the experience, and rehearsals were spread over many weeks. A high standard of acting was expected of – and delivered by – the principals, according to one well-placed observer, but the dancing and singing routines gave everyone who wished (or could be persuaded) to perform an opportunity.[52] Although romance, melodrama and comedy were the standard ingredients, some of the more popular songs carried sound moral lessons which, no doubt, Miss Marshall, other helpers and the sisters hoped would be taken to heart by all participants, on stage and in the audience.

## Religious Devotions, Gloucester Street (Sean MacDermott Street) Convent and Asylum, 1950s

Concern for uplifting, light-hearted and 'improving' entertainments was not, however, at the expense of the spiritual good of the young women which was, after all, the first concern of the sisters. Training in music included learning new hymns and devotional pieces, and there were ample occasions, both inside and outside the chapel, when they could be sung.[53] Drama was used to enkindle devotion to Our Lady of the Immaculate Conception, with the women residents acting out a full-length play telling of the apparitions and messages to St Catherine Labouré (to whom the Miraculous Medal was revealed), complete with hymn singing, bell-ringing and special lighting effects.[54] The annalist records the fidelity of sisters and women to their annual retreats and to the monthly day of recollection.[55] Residents

---

51  For song titles see annotated scores (DARGS, OLC2/12/4 no. 12).
52  Bruton, 'On entertainment'.
53  See for example, 'Mother at your feet is kneeling' (Sister S.C.), 'Ave Maria, Mother most beautiful' (Crofts and Kearney), 'Lily of Lourdes' (Arthur J. Tucker).
54  'The miraculous medal', typescript, no author or date.
55  Gloucester Street, annals, 1960.

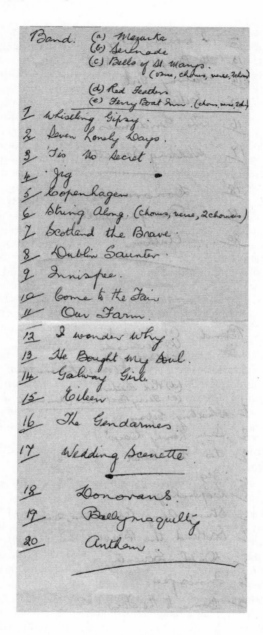

**Figure 12.3** Concert notes, undated but 1950s, Sean MacDermott Street refuge. (DARGS, OLC2/12/4 no. 12)

were introduced to devotions – predominantly Marian – that were receiving some coverage in Dublin or internationally, through the medium of visiting priests. Located so close to both Amiens Street railway station and to Dublin Port attracted many travelling clergymen to say Mass and to breakfast in the convent. To celebrate Mass at the John Eudes altar was a privilege especially cherished by visiting Eudist priests.[56] There were also other occasional visitors to Dublin with an interest in the order's work, who called to Gloucester Street as the most easily-reached of the houses.

In June 1949, all residents were given the chance to see the beautiful monstrance, made by a Mr Gunning of Dublin from the donations – including jewellery – of many devoted Irish Catholics, and to be presented to the Marian shrine of Fatima: 'an expression of faith and love made possible by generous sacrifices ... destined to hold in its shining circle the great Christ, and to show Him to the world in that hallowed place'.[57] The closing of the Holy Year of 1950 was marked in Rome with the proclamation of the dogma of the Assumption of Our Lady, closely followed on the wireless: 'It was with deep emotion we heard our beloved Holy Father's voice which gave us more intense love and devotion to our Heavenly Queen'.[58] Celebrations for the Marian Year of 1953–4 were built on the well-established devotional traditions of the house. Altars or shrines were decorated in honour of Mary in the chapel, cloister, the women's recreation room, and 'in each department of the laundry'; to mark the opening of this special year a priest led the sisters and women in procession 'to each of these shrines, saying the Rosary and singing hymns'.[59]

A frequent visitor – between 1951 and 1954 at least – was Fr Peyton, known internationally for promoting devotion to the rosary.[60] He seems to have gone out of his way to engage the women, as well as having to hand the very latest in promotional materials. On one visit, residents 'were given the pleasure of seeing the cinemathagraphic (*sic*) picture portraying the joyful and glorious mysteries of the Rosary'.[61] A later visit was effectively a full-length retreat as Peyton said Mass in the chapel for nine consecutive mornings.[62] He was to return again in 1954, when he also visited High Park.[63] Gloucester Street convent residents were certainly as well informed on the rosary crusade, and had probably seen more of the films associated with it, than any of their peers outside.

Devotion to Our Lady of Lourdes, long a favourite devotion in Gloucester Street convent, was given a particular boost in 1958, the centenary of the apparitions, when the new parish church was given this patronym. Dr McQuaid visited the convent on the day when he laid the foundation stone of the new church, practically facing the monastery.[64] Girls, women and sisters alike participated in parish events to venerate the Blessed Sacrament

56   Ibid., 1953.
57   Ibid., 1949.
58   Ibid., 1950.
59   Ibid., 1953.
60   Ibid., 1954.
61   Ibid., 1951.
62   Ibid.
63   High Park, circular letter, Dec. 1954 (NDC Caen, Archives Besançon).
64   Gloucester Street, annals, 1958.

and to honour the Mother of God through the Corpus Christi procession in June, and the May procession. Outside these traditional Eucharistic and Marian devotions, the new Holy Week liturgies, that were introduced by Rome in 1956, were probably the most noteworthy spiritual innovations of the decade: 'Rev. Father left nothing undone to carry through the Holy Week ceremonies with impressive solemnity'.[65]

One curious aspect of the spiritual life of Gloucester Street during the post-federation period that had nothing to do with the convent or asylum was the use of the chapel between 1949 and 1953 for the baptism and reception into the Roman Catholic Church of young German converts.[66] These young women were not residents of the asylum – the only person in the register who gives Germany as their place of origin was a 1912 entrant – but, according to the annalist, were from among the German refugee population in Ireland: 'a German Jesuit, who is interested in a colony of these displaced persons, performed the ceremony'.[67] The first such ceremony, of a German girl, was in July 1948 and a further four had been baptised by 1951. In all likelihood, these were Jewish girls, for Protestants would not have needed baptism to be received into the Catholic Church. In May 1950, an English girl (whose parents were 'bitter non-Catholics') was received 'into the true fold'. In 1952

> Again we witnessed, as on so many other years lately, the ever-moving ceremony of the reception into the church of several German Ladies, one of these has since entered a Carmelite monastery.[68]

A further two girls were 'received into the Church by a Jesuit father' in 1953, and another three in 1955, this time received by the chaplain. Their nationalities are not noted.[69]

## Efforts to Establish a State-Funded Remand Home 1956 to 1960

The creation of a remand home for older teenagers and young women at Gloucester Street/Sean MacDermott Street in 1960 was the outcome of concerted lobbying by Dr McQuaid, who saw it as one element in the modernising of penal services for young people, a field with which he had long been concerned. The sisters' themselves saw in the remand home an extension of their traditional work, though they themselves acknowledged the pressure exerted by the archbishop. Gloucester Street asylum had been used since the 1920s by small numbers of girls as a place of probation (as discussed in chapter 6). This had led to its rather uncertain status, as summarised in a short paper circulated in early May 1957 by the Department of Justice: it was not a remand home, nor industrial school nor reformatory, but 'simply an institution to which girls – primarily girls over 17 but occasionally girls

65   Ibid., 1956.
66   There is no register of baptism for Gloucester Street convent chapel and no information has been found outside the annals.
67   Gloucester Street, annals,1949.
68   Ibid., 1952.
69   Ibid., 1953, 1955.

under that age – are sent as a condition of their probation'; 'they need not go or stay there – they can choose to go to prison instead, and some of them do so'.[70] The only existing remand homes were for juveniles, whereas what now sought was intended for 'adult girls' who would otherwise be held in custody in Mountjoy Prison.[71]

Remand, that is, the detention of a person prior to trial, conviction or sentencing on the authority of the courts, is quite different to probation, even though often involving the same girls and the same institutions. Crucially, the girl's consent is not required for a remand. By definition, remand is always temporary and short stay as it depends on the court timetable and case management. The remand period could be for two, three or four days, up to 12 or even 14 days. The vast majority of remand periods (in this research) were for eight days or less. The new initiative was broached on 3 January 1957 when McQuaid convened a meeting at High Park, as the mother house of the Irish Federation of the Sisters of Our Lady of Charity, 'to discuss some aspects of *rehabilitation* of girls who appear before the Courts', with the aim of knowing 'what the OLC sisters can do' in this regard.[72] Dr McQuaid's own handwritten notes in advance of the meeting, and his summary afterwards, set out where the idea has come from and how it might involve OLC sisters. A project for delinquent boys, to replace the borstal, was in the process of being established at Mountjoy Prison, with its own special chaplain, and he was now turning his attention (once again) to the remand girls. He was satisfied, 'if they could have a period of remand in a special place, a great deal might be done to rehabilitate them.' He noted also that the children's court was 'very unsatisfactory'. Commenting on what had been done in each of the OLC houses recently, he noted they had 'modernised conditions' in both High Park and Gloucester Street, and had opened a hostel in St Anne's. He criticised what had been done at The Grange, 'renewed at what I can only call a sumptuous cost, but to what purpose I cannot say'. He renewed an earlier threat to replace the OLC sisters in the Dublin diocese with congregations more amenable to new approaches:

> Good Shepherd are very anxious to come in; you know how they have modernised their methods. Notre Dame have several times asked me to establish a Clinic such as Glasgow Clinic and they have done great work. Can you establish such a Clinic, by training your sisters abroad?[73]

70   J. Boland, private secretary, to Minister for Justice, to Private secretary to Roinn an Taosigh (*sic*), 6 May 1957 (NAI, Department of An Taoiseach, S13290 A/1).
71   Department of Justice, internal note titled 'Our Lady's Home, Henrietta Street, and St Mary Magdalen's Asylum – proposed use of as remand institutions for girls', 20 Oct. 1960, quoted in *Final report of the Inter-Departmental Committee set up to establish the facts of State involvement with the Magdalen Laundries* (Dublin, 2013), ch. 9, p. 220. Online at www.justice.ie. Hereafter, McAleese report.
72   J.C. McQuaid to Mother M. Eithne, High Park, 29 Dec. 1956 (DDA, McQuaid Papers, Department of Justice). Emphasis as in the original.
73   MS notes, in J.C. McQuaid's hand, headed 'Girl Delinquents, High Park, 3rd January 1957', 2 pp (DDA, McQuaid Papers, Department of Justice).

Giving the sisters until the end of the month to formulate a response, he returned on 31 January 1957 to learn of a general willingness to have some sisters trained (in social science and in childcare), and a readiness to build a remand home at Gloucester Street, on the plot of land they had recently purchased, with his permission. The remand home would have a 'private clinic, where a doctor, by their own invitation, would attend'.[74] By 'clinic' was meant a centre for psychological assessment, the 'observation clinics' which the sisters in Dublin already knew something of from France and from the UK. McQuaid welcomed the proposal, but insisted that it operate as a 'clearing house', moving the girls on to more 'suitable' settings, namely what he termed the 'ordinary delinquents' to Gloucester Street, 'non-delinquents' to High Park, and 'sexual delinquents to St Anne's, 'at least, in general as scheme of operation, for all three types can on occasion be found in either High Park or Gloucester Street'.[75]

Lengthy, frequent, wide-ranging and well-documented consultations continued between the archbishop and government departments, with McQuaid citing the good work of the OLC sisters in Kilmacud in favour of their involvement with this new project.[76] Notes taken, in Irish, on the sequence and content of the meetings, indicate that the Taoiseach and his officials did not allow the archbishop to set the agenda nor dictate the pace of progress.[77] At the start of December 1959, Dr McQuaid received the welcome news that all was in order for the long-sought 'remand home for young offenders', 'an achievement of which you may be justly proud'.[78] However, it was not until April 1960 that the Bill by which the law could be amended 'so as to permit young girls charged with offences to be remanded to St Mary Magdalen's Asylum, Sean MacDermott Street, instead of to prison' was introduced to the Dáil.[79] The principle of consent was written into the Bill. Only with the consent of the girl could she be remanded to 'an institution approved by the Minister for Justice', such as Gloucester Street; the option of being remanded to prison instead was always open to her. There was also a clause ensuring that no person be committed to an institution conducted other than in accordance with his or her religion.[80] The financial implications of the Bill were minimal, as only capitation (not building) grants would be paid to any institution approved as a remand home, as was already done for juvenile remand

74    MS notes, in J.C. McQuaid's hand, headed '31st January 1957', 1 p. (DDA, McQuaid Papers, Department of Justice).
75    Ibid.
76    Máire Ní Cheallaigh, rúnaí pearsanta, to An Taoiseach, 25 Aibreán 1957, note also, 'The Taoiseach dictated above note on his return from the Archbishop on Saturday morning the 23rd March 1957' (NAI, Department of An Taoiseach, S13290 A/1).
77    MS note dated 24 Apr. 1957, 'Dúirt an Taoiseach go raibh an ní seo príobháideach agus go labharfadh sé leis an t-Aire ina taobh [?] ar maidin – roimh criunniú an rialtais dá m'fhéidir.' See also MS note dated 2 May 1957 (NAI, Department of An Taoiseach, S13290 A/1).
78    Sister M. Carmel Staunton to Dr McQuaid, 3 Dec. 1959 (DDA, McQuaid papers, OLCR, Kilmacud, no. 3).
79    Oscar Traynor, Office of the Minister for Justice, to Archbishop McQuaid, 7 Apr. 1960 (DDA, McQuaid Papers, Department of Justice).
80    Sections 9 to 11, Criminal Justice Bill 1960. An Act to amend criminal law and administration (Dublin: Stationery Office, 1960).

cases: 'Having regard to the small number of prisoners who are likely to be remanded, and to the short periods involved, it is unlikely that the annual cost would exceed £100'.[81] In the Seanad debate on the Bill there was some concern that the proposed remand home would carry the stigma of the magdalen laundry. Senator Margaret Pearse, a past-president of the Holy Faith Schools Past Pupils' Union, 'said she thought that the Holy Faith convent in Glasnevin might be willing to receive remand girls of a type not suitable for sending to St Mary Magdalen's Asylum', but nothing further came of that proposal.[82] The second named remand home, under the 1960 Act, was to be Our Lady's Home, Henrietta Street, which included a hostel or 'school for girls of a servant type'. It was already recognised under section 7 of the Criminal Justice Administration Act 1914 as a society devoted to 'the care and control of youthful offenders aged 16 to 21 years' which would receive girls sent by the courts on probation, and was in receipt of state grants towards their maintenance of (in 1960) 26s per girl per week.[83] It had never been a magdalen asylum and so, in the public mind, was free of that disability. The two convents, Our Lady's Home, Henrietta Street, and St Mary Magdalen's Asylum, Sean MacDermott Street, were approved as remand centres by signed instrument on 21 October 1960, two days after the new Act was passed.[84]

The more significant matters, but glossed over in the Department of Justice memo as headings that 'do not call for special comment', was the shift in responsibility from the prison authority to the superior of Gloucester Street convent, and the possible removal of a girl on remand from Gloucester Street to the women's prison. Under the new legislation, a young person on remand

> would be deemed to be in the lawful custody of the person for the time being in charge of the approved institution while being taken to or from the institution or while in the institution or while otherwise under the control of the person for the time being in the charge of the institution.[85]

Although the period of remand was often one or two days, and rarely longer than seven days, nevertheless, for that short time, it placed on the superior of Gloucester Street the task of acting as prison officer. 'At the request of the person so committed or at the request of the person in charge of the approved institution', the girl on remand could be moved from Gloucester Street into the prison under the direction of the minister who was in overall charge of the criminal justice system.[86]

81   Memorandum for the Government, Proposed Criminal Justice Bill, 9 Dec. 1958 (NAI, Department of An Taoiseach, S13290 A/1). Hereafter, Memorandum, 9 Dec. 1958.
82   Debate summarised in McAleese report, ch. 9, p. 217.
83   Department of Justice, internal note titled 'Our Lady's Home, Henrietta Street, and St Mary Magdalen's Asylum – proposed use of as remand institutions for girls', 20 Oct. 1960, quoted in McAleese report, ch. 9, p. 220.
84   Ibid.
85   Memorandum, 9 Dec. 1958.
86   Ibid.

## Sean MacDermott Street as a Place of Remand 1960–1981

The recognition of Sean MacDermott Street as a place of remand is marked in the community annals for 1960:

> This year [1960] we were asked by the authorities to accept remand cases in our class. This responsibility we willingly accepted, as we were aware that such was the wish of His Grace the archbishop – and we feel that it is, without doubt, the work of our Holy Order.[87]

It was a very new situation for the community, as spelled out in the instructions sent by the Department of Justice: these girls, aged 16 to 21, were 'prisoners on remand', not voluntary entrants, Should any girl absent herself without permission, the sister in charge was under an obligation to notify the local garda station and the clerk or registrar of the court concerned.[88] (There were no such obligations attaching to a girl on probation; if she left or was asked to leave before her probation was up, it was a matter for herself, the probation officer and the court to sort out). A girl on remand was assigned a probation officer, who was expected to visit her in Sean MacDermott Street, as was established practice with girls on probation.[89] The weekly rate for remand cases, first set at 25s, was increased to 35s in 1962 and to 45s in 1966, a sum that was (as the McAleese inquiry noted) considerably lower than the combined weekly payment for inmates of reformatory and industrial schools.[90]

The first girl to take up residence in Sean MacDermott Street under its new status was a 16-year-old who arrived first on remand and then was on probation for three years. She was given the house name Finbar, a continuation of the standard practice, and a reminder that girls on remand or on probation were not separated from the general intake. There was another 1960 remand case which, however, ended badly after two days ('taken to Mountjoy by guards after causing great trouble'). There were four further remand cases in 1961–63 inclusive and two in 1964. Thereafter much greater demands were placed on the refuge, with ten cases in 1965 and five in 1966, at which date the 'old' asylum of Sean MacDermott Street was superseded by two new developments.

The Ri Villa home, started in July 1964, was intended to remove younger girls from the adult refuge (chapter 9) and to educate them for an independent life. Of the 376 girls admitted between July 1964 and June 1976, there are 14 remand cases and no probation cases, according to the register. Thus, over the 12 years of its operation, only a small fraction – 4% – of the girls resident in Ri Villa were ever remand cases, but the recognition of Sean MacDermott Street convent as a remand centre in 1960 gave this flexibility.

87  Gloucester Street, book of the community [annals], 1960 (DARGS, OLC2/5/2 no. 6).
88  Department of Justice to the Sisters of Our Lady of Charity of Refuge, Lower Sean MacDermott Street, 24 Oct. 1960, quoted in McAleese report, ch. 9, p. 221.
89  Ibid.
90  Ibid., p. 224.

The opening in 1971 of the Casual Unit in Sean MacDermott Street provided more suitably for the large number of girls and women needing emergency accommodation, who had no intention of staying long-term. Girls and women on remand and on probation were provided for in this unit also. The numbers are relatively large. Between 1 January and 17 November 1973, a total of 172 women and girls went through the Casual Unit, of whom 31 'were on remand from the courts'; three of these were admitted to the Teenage Unit (Ri Villa).[91] Thus, in 1973, about 18% of all admissions came from the courts. There were also 'informal placements', broken down in a memo of 1973 as runaways, vagrants, stranded, deserting or deserted. The category 'stranded' might include: money stolen, unbalanced, over from England and no place to go, assaulted.[92] A draft memorandum prepared by the Department of Justice for the Department of Finance reveals that one government department at least recognised the value of this service to the state and to society:

> The fact that the convent is willing to accept these girls is of the greatest assistance to both the Gardaí and the Welfare Officers. It obviates the necessity of charging them with an offence and a subsequent appearance in Court. The convent authorities however receive no payment for the maintenance of the girls, as the approved capitation rate is payable only if the girls have been before the Courts.[93]

Of the 1,913 entries, from 1971 to the last remand case entered on 29 December 1981, there is a total of 163 remand and probation cases; 8.5%, therefore, of the women who went through the Casual Unit – by definition for short stays – were there in fulfilment of a condition attached to their probation, or were remanded there – rather than to Mountjoy Prison – while awaiting sentencing. In both Ri Villa and the Casual Unit, the way in which the remand and probation cases are lost in the larger body provided anonymity and the chance of a fresh start under these new OLC systems, as it had already under the old asylum model, though this time with a more outward-looking approach.

## Overall Assessment of Entrances and Exits, Gloucester Street (Sean MacDermott Street) Asylum, 1949–66

The total Gloucester Street household numbered 188 persons in April 1941, of whom 143 were women residents, 38 were sisters and seven were men (vanmen, engineers, labourers and gardeners).[94] On any given day in the 1940s and 1950s, the number of women residents was not likely to fall below 120 (figure 12.4). In August 1949, the oldest woman (Raphael), then

91    Report on Casual Unit, 1 Jan.–17 Nov. 1973 (DARGS, OLC5/5/7 no. 1).
92    McAleese report, ch. 9, p. 317.
93    Department of Justice, draft letter, Mar. 1973, quoted in McAleese report, p. 318.
94    Sister Stanislaus Masterson, superioress, to Fr Glennon, 17 Apr. 1941 (DDA, OLCR, Gloucester Street no. 1).

**Figure 12.4**  Total residents in Gloucester Street/Sean MacDermott Street
convent and refuge, 1890–1966

| Year | 1890 | 1892 | 1896 | 1901 | 1905 | 1910 | 1911 | 1937 | 1941 | 1967 |
|---|---|---|---|---|---|---|---|---|---|---|
| total household (nuns, women, workmen) | 70 | 74 | 91 | 107 | 131 | 145 | 106° | 163 | 188 | 166° |
| women only | 54 | 56 | 70* | 80 | 100 | 115 | 83 | 122 | 143 | 134 |

*average
°excludes workmen

*Sources:* circular letters from 1890 (DARGS, OLC1/3/2) and women's entrance
register (DARGS, OLC1/8/2 no. 2)

resident in the asylum died, aged 88 years; she had entered the Mercy asylum aged 26 or less, and stayed during its transfer to the sisters of Our Lady of Charity in 1887.[95] The woman longest resident in Gloucester Street/Sean MacDermott Street asylum in May 1967 (Brendan) had entered aged 16 in 1912; by then she had completed 55 years, broken by several very short breaks 'in a situation' which evidently did not work out. Of the 134 women residents present on 1 May 1967, 42 (just under one third) had entered the home before 1949, and another 48 between 1949 and 1959 (inclusive). There are many cases of residents dying aged 80 and upwards, having completed more than 60 years' residence in OLC care.

Two aspects of the admissions brought particular pressures on accommodation: one was the speedy throughput of a large proportion of the women, but the other was the fact that practically each year, one or more of the entrants decided to stay for life, and these were often very young. The incompleteness of some registry entries (where there is no date of departure but, from the evidence of another source, the woman may be presumed to have left), along with the possibility that some women had come and gone before there was ever a note made of their presence, make exact statistical analysis impossible. But these two general trends can be established with confidence.

Providing what could be termed emergency accommodation for a wide range of categories – former prisoners, women en route to or from Britain, girls found living rough brought by gardaí, social workers and members of the Legion of Mary – meant that the total numbers were in constant flux. Though not always spelled out in the register of entry, there were also unmarried women who had given birth in one of the mother-and-baby homes or in a city hospital who could not return home immediately and were without the resources to set up on their own. Whether their babies were fostered out informally or by the local authority, or were placed in industrial

95   Gloucester Street, annals, 1949.

schools, is the subject of the work by Moira Maguire; their position was especially precarious prior to the 1952 Adoption Act.[96] Gloucester Street/Sean MacDermott Street, like other OLC refuges, dealt only with the women who arrived at the door. Throughout the 1940s and 1950s, large numbers of girls came and left and came again, as had been the practice from its foundation as an OLC house in 1887. For the first 50 years of its existence, to its golden jubilee in 1937 (inclusive), 75 out of 1,505 first-time entrants (5%) have been identified through the register and other records as long-term residents (defined as staying two years or more). Of the 657 who entered in 1938 to 1966 inclusive (excluding Ri Villa), 15 can be identified from the register as staying long-term (2.3%), but the full number must be higher. The girls who 'came from the courts' can be identified in the register with more certainty. Though small in number – even after 1960 when it was formally approved as a place of remand for girls aged 17 to 21 – they brought their own particular energy and liveliness to the house. By definition, these girls were short-term – often overnight – residents who did not subscribe to the traditional asylum ethos. Girls who gave Gloucester Street to the judge as their home address for the duration of a term of probation were in a similar category, and likely to leave immediately their probation expired, if not before.

The fact that, most years up to the 1950s, one or more girls did stay – and stayed for the rest of their lives – and that others who had some previous contact with the asylum returned months or years later and settled down permanently up to their death, meant that the stable, core population was augmented steadily. The young age on entry, in most cases, of these permanent residents – and their longevity, again in most cases – meant that they were in the care of the asylum for many decades. It was this steady, unrelenting addition, year on year, to the core long-term population of mostly young people, who then went on to live for perhaps 50, 60 or more years in the asylum, that made for a large core population and a broad range of ages. As with the sisters, who entered mostly young and stayed for life, golden jubilees of women residents were landmark (but not infrequent) celebrations. The losses through deaths ran several decades behind the rate of admissions.

Of the 492 women who were first-time entrants to Gloucester Street between 1949 and 1966, only a handful can be identified for certain as long-term residents of two years or more. Three or four from each year's intake appears to be the average number staying long-term or permanently (to death). To this number might be added some Gloucester Street women who moved to High Park, either directly from Gloucester Street or some years later, having returned 'to the world' in the meantime. This would bring the long-term number up, though by exactly how much is merely speculation, as the register does not always note that the woman was previously resident in an OLC home. While only a very small percentage of those who entered Gloucester Street continued to reside there until their death (under 3%, according to this admittedly incomplete analysis – for reasons explained in respect of the High Park registers) but, for those who did die in the care of

96   Moira Maguire, *Precarious childhood in post-independence Ireland* (Manchester, 2009), pp 48–112, 133–142.

the order, there was usually a short obituary or account of their virtues written up in the circular letters, as was done for the sisters who had died over
the same period. The detail in those few obituaries that have been located is
scant; typical is the note made of Ethnea, died in 1951, 'a very holy simple
soul, got a very peaceful death'.[97] The length of stay was often noteworthy,
as with Clothilde, died in 1952, 'a remarkable penitent, spent a long exemplary life, first for many years in High Park then with us', and similarly with
Patricia, also died in 1952, whose 26 years in Gloucester Street was interrupted by a short, temporary stay in High Park which she evidently did not
like.[98] Also among the deaths in 1952 was Bernardine, 'a great sufferer being
afflicted with acute rheumatism. She passed long hours in the Infirmary
making countless pious objects with her poor, crippled hands'.[99] Her first
stay in Gloucester Street had been for seven months (entered January 1922,
aged 36 years); she left and returned three more times before settling down
long-term. The return of women in old age and debility to the asylum,
where they would stay until death, was interpreted as a consolation to the
community, as in the return of two residents in 1952 who had left many
years earlier, 'We were grateful to God for having brought back to us those
wandering sheep'.[100]

Up to the 1960s, the register of admissions records remarkably little in
each case, and family circumstances are limited to a perfunctory 'parents
alive'/'mother alive'/'father alive', and the county or town of origin. Not
much more can be added to the personal story from the obituary for that
small percentage of entrants who died in the care of OLC, even in the fullest
entry. However, in the mid-1960s, a little more is entered in the register for
at least some of the girls, usually a relative's address. There are tentative
movements towards the modern social work practice of compiling a 'case
history' on each entrant, though limited to a few instances and dependent
on what the girl was prepared to divulge, and what the sister interviewing
her decided to put in writing.

## Women Resident in Sean MacDermott Street Asylum on 1 May 1967

A list titled 'Girls resident on 1 May 1967' was drawn up by the sister-
in-charge for the purpose of recording the women's home addresses or the
addresses of family members. When analysed in conjunction with the register of admissions, it provides a valuable glimpse into the life of the old asylum
at the exact point when it was about to be dismantled and the 'group system'
introduced in earnest.[101] It also records which women had a relative whose
address was known to them, and those who had not even this minimum
knowledge of, or connection with, their families. Even when combined,
there are too many blanks in the entrance register and the 1967 list – such

---

97   Gloucester Street, annals, 1951.
98   Ibid., 1952.
99   Ibid.
100  Ibid.
101  This 1967 list is to be found in the women's entrance register, after the last entries dated
Nov. 1966.

as no age on admission, 'left' but no date of departure, present in 1967 but no date of entry – to allow for rigorous analysis. Nevertheless, there is sufficient information to allow commonalities among the women resident on 1 May 1967 to be identified, what brought them to Gloucester Street/Sean MacDermott Street and – perhaps –why they were still there. By that date, younger girls have been redirected to the separate teenage unit 'Ri Villa' opened July 1964 on the Sean MacDermott Street campus (chapter 9).

No dates of admission have been found in the register for 26 of the 134 women listed as resident on 1 May 1967, nor have dates been found outside this list. All of these incomplete entries appear to be short-term stays, but this cannot be relied on, so they are excluded from the calculation of years resident in Sean MacDermott Street on 1 May 1967 (figure 12.5). Age on admission had not been recorded for 27 of the 134 women in this sample, so they are also excluded from the calculations. Without an entry date and some indication of age on admission, it has not been possible to estimate the age of 28 of the 134 women resident in May 1967. Having to dispense with 20% of the cohort at the outset does somewhat undermine the exercise, but nevertheless it is clear that there was a wide mix of ages among the women present in May 1967 – from 17 to 71 years – and that more than half (73/134) had already lived in Sean MacDermott Street above a decade, with at least 21 women already with more than 30 years' residence. The explanation for the spectacularly long terms of residence is in the youth of most women on admission. When those whose ages are not known are excluded, 44% of the women present in May 1967 first entered the asylum aged 15 to 20 inclusive. A further 35% of that cohort had entered for the first time aged between 21 and 30 inclusive. Of those present in 1967 and whose dates of admission are known (108), breaking the entrances down decade by decade, there were five entrances between 1912 and 1918, another ten in the 1920s, 14 in the 1930s, 20 in the 1940s, and 39 in the 1950s. The remainder (20) were from the 1960s, including 13 from the previous two years.

Even where only one or two of the entrants who were admitted in any calendar year stayed permanently, if these were very young (aged 20 or less), the pattern of retention was consistent (averaging two or three per year) and the asylum was open for many years, then it was possible for a large permanent core of residents to build up, well outstripping by several decades the losses through death. Sean MacDermott Street fulfilled all these criteria: by 1967 it had been open under OLC management for 80 years, the large majority of those who sought shelter were young and, while there were cases of former residents returning in their later years to the asylum to retire (multiple entrances are noted for 17 of the 134 women resident in 1967), most of those for whom this became their permanent home lived all their adult lives within its walls.

For 63 of the 134 women resident in Sean MacDermott Street on 1 May 1967, there is nothing in the register to hint at why or how they were directed to this convent. The name, date of entry and of departure, county of origin, parents living (or not) and the house name given on admission is about all that is supplied (as illustrated in figure 2.2). In some cases, even this minimum is not quite complete. But for the other 71, just over half the

Total No. = 134

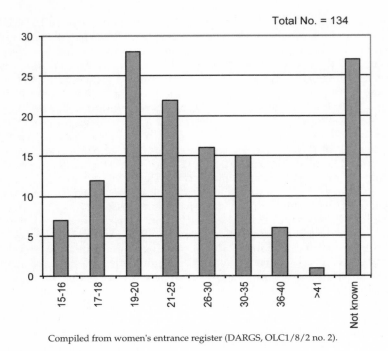

Compiled from women's entrance register (DARGS, OLC1/8/2 no. 2).

**Figure 12.5** Women resident in Sean MacDermott Street refuge on 1 May 1967: age on first entrance.

cohort, there is some extra information which, however scanty, reveals something of the personal story behind each admission.

The first striking factor is the number of entrants who were reared as children in industrial schools and arrived directly on discharge under that school's supervision certificate or – the more usual scenario – sought admission after the lapse of a few months or years, with a sad story over the intervening period. These include two former residents of Goldenbridge (entered Gloucester Street/Sean MacDermott Street aged 17, 22), of the Mercy industrial schools in Cork (entered aged 18 years), of Athlone (entered aged *c.*18), and of Navan (entered aged 36). There was also a former resident of the Poor Clare orphanage, Ballyjamesduff, who appears to have been found homeless in the city ('brought by garda', aged 17), and two past-pupils of the Sacred Heart Home, Drumcondra (aged 16, 18). A smaller group, but also with childhood experience of institutional care, arrived indirectly from special schools of various sorts, including one woman from Holy Angels Glenmaroon (aged 23 on admission, previously reared in St Vincent's home, Cabra), a young woman from St Philomena's, Stillorgan, Sisters of Charity ('born Navan Road'), and another from Kill of the Grange, the residential home opened by the sisters of Our Lady of Charity in 1956 (discussed in chapter 10). At least 12 women in this cohort – that is, resident in Sean MacDermott Street in 1967 – had been reared as children in institutional settings. None of these institutions could hold adults as residents, even if (for whatever reason) the girl was unequipped to make her way independently in the world and had no family or friends willing and able to provide her with a home.

But what the largest number of women resident in 1967 (and about whom something is known) had in common was that they had come from one of the mother-and-baby homes, having given birth within the previous two years. These homes were set up to keep unmarried girls, pregnant for the first time, separate from what were described as more 'hardened' cases in the county home, and also to ensure that 'respectable though poor' married women giving birth in the county home did not have to share wards with unmarried women.[102] The local authority paid towards the upkeep of the girls, and had the responsibility of finding homes for those infants that the mothers were not able to – or did not wish to – keep, though the homes themselves were run by religious orders. The institution which the largest number of women had in common was Sean Ross Abbey, Roscrea, County Tipperary. At least 17 of the women resident in Sean MacDermott Street in 1967 had come from Sean Ross (aged from 20 to 37, with an average age on entry of 23½ years). Next in rank order was St Patrick's Home, Pelletstown (Navan Road), County Dublin, an auxiliary local authority home run by the Daughters of Charity (nine women, age range of 22 to 30, average age on entrance 25 years). This was followed closely by Manor House, Castlepollard, County Westmeath (seven women aged 27 to 37, average age 26 years). The women who came from the county home in Galway (aged 20), from the county home in Mullingar (aged 18) and from St Kevin's Hospital, Dublin (aged 30), can be grouped with these others. In summary, 36 of the 71 women in Sean MacDermott Street in 1967 for whom something of the circumstances surrounding their admission is known from the OLC records (and where the total number of women was 134) came directly from one or other of the mother-and-baby homes. As Moira Maguire's research reveals, women in these homes who did not have the financial resources to rear their babies, or the necessary moral and family support, could leave after two years (though some did leave earlier). The two years was to allow the baby to be weaned, and arrangements to be made for the boarding-out or adoption overseas or in Ireland of their child (legal adoption came with the Adoption Act of 1952). There is no mention in the Gloucester Street/ Sean MacDermott Street register of what has happened to the infants of these mothers, and it is likely they were left in the hands of the local authority to find homes for them, whether in families or in an industrial school – the latter often preferred by the council as less time-consuming and troublesome.[103]

Another distinct group among the women resident in 1967, and for whom there is some further information, is those brought along by their father or another family member. Though not stated, it can be safely presumed that some were young women who had given birth outside wedlock and at least someone in the family wanted them out of sight (and out of mind). 'Sent by her father' (aged 18), 'brought from Baggot Street Mercy nuns by her father' (aged 25), 'brought in by her brother', a garda

102   Maguire, *Precarious childhood*, p. 88.
103   Ibid., p. 59.

sergeant (aged 36), 'brought in by her brother and Guard Gantley' (aged 19), and (aged 17½ years) 'brought by her step-sister'. The latter appears to be an outrageous case of domestic abuse, where a Munster girl had her first baby aged 13 years (the baby was adopted), and a second baby was now awaiting adoption. She lived with her parents, three step-siblings and two siblings, and the family home (the register implies) was not a safe place for her.

There were two cases of priests directing women to Sean MacDermott Street, and these may be further examples of being put 'out of sight' to protect the family's 'good name'. An 18-year-old was 'sent by' a priest in Ashford, a 19-year-old by a priest in Balbriggan, 'Mother went to High Park same day'. Former residents of psychiatric hospitals are represented by at least one case ('from St Brendan's', but had also been in Sean Ross), and there is one entrant simply classed as 'retarded' (aged 35 years). There was also one entrant directly from Crumlin children's hospital, aged 19 at the time she arrived, but whether this young woman had been a domestic worker or a former patient, there is no way of knowing.

Several of the 1967 cohort had previous experience of other hostels and asylums in the city. One woman came from the Legion of Mary's Sancta Maria Hostel when she was aged 40 (in 1934), and lived out the remainder of her days in OLC care, between Sean MacDermott Street and High Park. Another entrant from the Harcourt Street hostel had met Legion workers in England when resident in 'Scotts lodging house' before coming to Dublin and settling permanently in Sean MacDermott Street, aged 29 (1934). A Wexford woman resident in the hostel in Henrietta Street moved to Sean MacDermott Street in 1964 aged 27, where she stayed for three years. From the magdalen home in Donnybrook, three young girls came to Sean MacDermott Street: one aged 16 in 1965: 'sent from' Donnybrook, on probation from the courts, went out to hospital work from Sean MacDermott Street ('very troublesome', eventually left on the expiration of her probation in 1968); the other girls from Donnybrook, aged 16 years (1965, 'reared with Mercy nuns') and 19 years (1966) on admission to Sean MacDermott Street, subsequently moved out.

There are three cases, among the 1967 cohort, of women with previous experience of High Park, as well as Gloucester Street/Sean MacDermott Street asylums (entered 1931, 1942 and 1951). All of these women entered and left several times, and one also had experience of the Good Shepherd asylum in Edinburgh.

On the few occasions where the phrase 'Came herself' is encountered in the register, it is safe to classify the entry as self-referral, but it is likely that some of the entries that do not have 'sent by' or 'came from' or any other hint of third-party involvement are where women simply arrived on the doorstep seeking accommodation due to some unrecorded crisis (or ongoing crises), and left (the vast majority) some weeks or months later with just as little ceremony.

What is particularly moving in the 1967 list, which was compiled with the express purpose of listing family contacts, is that the address then current of a parent or sibling is entered for 102 of the 134 residents.

One resident has the name of a friend entered in place of family, for 13 women the only current address is that of the institution from which she came in the first place, and for a further 18, 'no address' is entered after their name. For about 76% of the women, home addresses and/or immediate family members were recorded. When these women are tracked back to the date of admission, most are entered as having one or both parents alive at the time; the note 'parents dead' is entered after 13 of 106 entries and, of these, three state that there are siblings alive (at the time of admission). At least 64 – or about 69% – of the women had one or both parents alive at the time of their admission. For a further 32 entries, there is no information at all on whether parents are alive or dead. Whatever way the blank entries are interpreted, one fact is unavoidable: few of the women on admission were without immediate family. Over the course of – what were for some – very long periods of residency, the majority of these women had parents, brothers and sisters, uncles and aunts, whose addresses they knew. It is not possible to judge from the institutional record what contact these outside family members maintained with their daughter, sister or niece in Sean MacDermott Street, or what – if any – efforts family members made to provide a home for them outside the asylum. Anecdotal evidence suggests that many had nothing at all to do with them, particularly in the period prior to the 1970s.

One further fragment of information to be gleaned from a trawl of the – admittedly minimal – case histories of the women resident in 1967 is the work experience that they had in common: only instances of domestic work are recorded, either in a family home ('a situation') or (more usually) in a hospital or other institution. No other field of paid employment prior to their arrival is mentioned, though that is not to say that no-one among the cohort had worked outside this realm. Those who came from their own homes had probably been engaged in the usual domestic duties, or had been, prior to their time in the mother-and-baby home or in the county home; there is no note of any other employment. Evidence was given to the McAleese inquiry by a priest chaplain and by a local hotel owner of how some women in Sean MacDermott Street from about 1966 got themselves weekend cleaning jobs in local hotels and hostels while living still at the convent, a move which was in tune with the more open regime that was taking hold. But it also shows how enterprising these women were, and that they had sufficient skills and experience in housework to be taken on, and kept, by an employer.[104] In the very few instances where it is known from another source that a girl was attempting to support herself by prostitution, this is never indicated in the register; a girl convicted for soliciting and placed on probation was entered only as 'on probation' or from the courts, and multiple entrances and exits, though grounds for suspicion, did not mean a girl was working 'on the streets'. The occasional obituary up to the 1950s made much of the penitence of a 'great sinner', but such mentions are too infrequent to be statistically useful. The mention of Legion of Mary workers and the Sancta Maria hostel in Harcourt Street may hint that a girl has been found to be in

---

104    McAleese report, ch. 9, p. 315.

the company of persons involved in prostitution or was frequenting an area well known for the sex trade, but that did not mean a girl had been working as a prostitute herself. As noted with reference to High Park (chapter 11), Legion members were among the 'voluntary probation officers' assisting the paid probation service from 1942.[105] From 1962, under a re-invigorated scheme, members of the two Dublin *praesidia* recognised for the purpose were assigned cases by the courts, and granted powers to supervise young people on probation in precisely the same manner as the state's probation officers.[106] The Legion of Mary therefore could become involved with a girl because she had been found guilty of the offence of soliciting and placed on probation. There is only one case in the 1967 list that can be read in that light; any others there may have been are well hidden by the OLC tradition of recording the barest facts in the register of admissions, while the use of house names screened each entrant's identity from her companions.

Of the 134 women resident in May 1967, 91 (68%) were already living in Sean MacDermott Street for six years and over, and – as confirmed by later evidence – very few of these women were likely to return to working life outside the asylum. A substantial number, 41 (30%) of the women were already resident more than 20 years. If the 134 residents in May 1967 are followed through to August 2011 (when this research was completed), 13 were to be found in the hostels and nursing home that had long replaced the Gloucester Street/Sean MacDermott Street home. Among this group, the resident with the longest unbroken period in the care of the sisters of Our Lady of Charity – 64 years – entered in 1947; four other women had more than 60 years' residence, six more between 50 and 60 years' residence, and a further two had 44 and 48 years' respectively. (Three of these 13 women had left Sean MacDermott Street for a period and returned; 'length of stay' is calculated from their first entrance). A further 76 women of the May 1967 cohort have died in the interim, all of whom can be classed as in the care of OLC Sean MacDermott Street, even where they died in hospital or in the nursing home at Beechlawn, High Park. Many of these women also lived into their 80s and even 90s, having spent 60 or more years in the convent. Forty-five of the 134 persons listed on 1 May 1967 left Sean MacDermott Street at some later date, exactly one third of the house population. Some went home, others to flats. Of the 34 girls who came from one of the mother-and-baby homes, or from the county home, and were resident in 1967, 25 continued to live in Sean MacDermott Street (or its successor houses) for the rest of their lives. One woman was transferred, at her own request, to a similar institution (the Good Shepherd convent) in Limerick, another left when her father died and it was possible for her to return home (according to the register), three others set up in their own flats and kept in contact, the other five left and nothing further is known about them.

## Modernisation of Sean MacDermott Street Asylum in the 1960s

The incremental modernisation that was undertaken in Gloucester Street/ Sean MacDermott Street in the 1950s and the 1960s paralleled what was

---

105    Ibid., ch. 9, p. 235.
106    Ibid., ch. 9, p. 246.

happening in St Mary's, High Park but, in the absence of local council or house minutes, the process cannot be reconstructed in the same detail. It was driven not just by changes in Irish society and in the Catholic Church but, by what the sisters learned of their order's work overseas, where some communities had embraced 'modern methods' with a freshness and courage that was admired (if not envied) in Dublin. The exchange of circular letters was the standard way of learning the news, but there were also a number of recruitment drives in Ireland which brought sisters to stay in the Dublin convents. The sisters of Our Lady of Charity in Dallas, Texas, received permission (from the archbishop of Dublin) to recruit Irish postulants for their foundation in 1949 and were hosted in Gloucester Street:

> We entered fully into their joy in producing so many young Irish girls, brave souls, ready to leave their own beloved Erin, to labour for the extension of God's kingdom in the land of the stranger, and to carry on the noble work of our holy Founder, St John Eudes. [107]

The following year there were visitors from Bitterne (Sister Dominic) and from Ormskirk (Sister Perpetua) in England:

> It gave us much joy to hear of the good work being done by our houses abroad, and by all the modern improvements these fervent daughters of St John Eudes are making for the continuation of his work.[108]

Visits from sisters in England continued throughout the 1950s, including 'questing for postulants' in 1958 and 1959.[109] The American mother general, Mother Mary of St John, accompanied by her secretary, Sister Mary of St Clement, visited in July 1960, when the annalist records, 'both endeared themselves to our hearts during their brief stay with us'.[110]

The Gloucester Street annals recall the opening up of study and training opportunities for the sisters. A start was made in July 1952 when 'the mistress of the class went with a sister from High Park and Kilmacud to Blackpool in England to follow a course on child welfare'.[111] The role of the superior of the federation in facilitating further studies – with the archbishop Dr McQuaid leaving her in no doubt as to her responsibilities in this – is also evident; the house council was assembled on 16 January 1957 to be told of the mother general's wishes 'that two sisters from the community were to be selected to attend lectures twice weekly at the University to study child psychology'.[112]

107   Gloucester Street, annals, 1949.
108   Ibid., 1950.
109   Visits from sisters of Redcote, Bitterne, and Waterlooville, Gloucester Street, annals, 1951; see also annals, 1958, 1959.
110   Ibid., July 1960.
111   Ibid., 1952.
112   Gloucester Street local council, minutes, 16 Jan. 1957.

The centralised novitiate in High Park and the facility to move sisters between houses (subject to their willingness, for those who made vows before federation) that came in 1949 prised open Sean MacDermott Street – at least a little – to what was happening in other OLC houses in Dublin, though real exchange and partnership would develop only in the wake of Vatican II. Despite the limited powers of the superior general and her council, minutes of meetings reveal how the modernisation process gathered pace as one house heard about what was happening elsewhere and (it appears) no house wanted to be seen as 'behind the times', at least when compared with the other OLC houses in the same diocese.[113] At the general chapter of 1960, when Sean MacDermott Street needed to report on what it had achieved since the last general chapter (in 1954), it listed the 'commodious and well-equipped refectory' and the new recreation ground having 'greatly added to the happiness of the girls there'.[114] Under the heading of post-asylum care, it was claimed that 'contacts by personal interview and by correspondence are kept up with the girls who have been re-habilitated, and in this way the beneficial influence of the Sisters continues to be exercised'.[115] Though no-one could find fault with any of these improvements, far more substantive changes were expected. Almost a decade had passed since the archbishop had overseen the addition to their constitutions of a commitment to 'a system of instruction and education in keeping with modern needs' that would fit young persons for their life in the world.[116] His blunt call for the dismantling of 'the present Penitentiary system' could not be misread.[117] At the visitation of 1962, the usual report on the sisters' fervour and regular attendance to their religious exercises is made, with the note, 'We hope to send them extra sisters as their work is heavy'.[118]

In November 1965, the superior general, Mother M. Eithne, reported that 'the laundry needs to be reorganised, which will leave the sisters more leisure to work for the girls with the modern methods'.[119] This is the first explicit statement that Sean MacDermott Street convent has consciously embraced – or been pushed into – adopting 'modern methods' towards the women in its charge. The circular letter of the following month opens the section on the refuge with the phrase 'Following the modern trend, our girls are revelling in their new found freedom and responsibility', and then lists what has been happening. While laundry work still takes up most of their work-day, there is more variety,

---

113    There are no Gloucester Street/Sean MacDermott Street local council minutes extant for 1969 to 1987.

114    Record of the third general chapter of the Irish Federation of the Order of Our Lady of Charity of Refuge, held 22–24 Nov. 1960 (DARGS, OLC5/1/3).

115    Ibid.

116    *Additions and amendments to the constitutions of the Order of Our Lady of Charity of Refuge, in accordance with the decree of the Sacred Congregation of Religious, dated 28 June 1948, and the rescript of the same Sacred Congregation dated 12 Feb. 1951* (Dublin, 1951), p. 43. Hereafter, *Constitutions, 1951 additions.*

117    John C. McQuaid to Revd Mother M. Carmel, 15 Oct. 1953, copy letter (DARGS, OLC3/2/2 no. 9).

118    Gloucester Street local council, minutes, 30 Mar. 1962; superior general, visitation report, Gloucester Street, Mar. 1962.

119    Gloucester Street local council, minutes, 26 Nov. 1965; superior general, visitation report, Gloucester Street, Nov. 1965.

'they turn out very fine Celtic embroidery, knit wear and other handcrafts'. The recreations are more varied, with indoor and outdoor games, dramatic and choral classes, 'together with TV and a monthly film show'. A group visit to a city cinema to see 'Mary Poppins', though a minor event in itself, takes on an added significance when the tradition of enclosure is recalled. Three of 'our girls' went on pilgrimage to Lourdes in 1965, by air, each with a different pilgrim group, 'all returned full of fervour and appreciation of the great privilege which was theirs', a trip made possible by the 'great generosity of good ladies who befriend our girls'.[120] Further 'opening up' can be read into the weekly visits by senior boarders in Holy Faith Convent Glasnevin, who invited their new Sean MacDermott Street friends to stage a performance of their 'variety concert' for the schoolchildren and community in Glasnevin: 'this was an unprecedented thrill, and undoubtedly for the girls concerned the highlight of the year'.[121]

The participation of the women and girls, as well as the sisters, in the ordinary life of the parish in the 1960s merits a note, as photographic, documentary and oral evidence taken together give a glimpse of Catholic culture in a very poor part of mid-20th century Dublin. In a photo that has been dated to May 1965 (figure 12.6), 'following the modern trend' the girls and women in Sean MacDermott Street, at the request of the local parish administrator Fr Murray, first participated 'in the public parochial procession in honour of Our Lady'.[122] Members of the sodality of the Children of Mary, wearing blue cloaks and white veils, carry the statue of Mary, which is bedecked with flowers. They are followed by other members of the sodality, each wearing her Child of Mary medal, and joined by young children in their First Communion dresses and veils, a mixture of parishioners of all classes and ages in what is a colourful, inclusive public procession. Gardaí on 'processional duty' provide a guard of honour. The devotional spirit was kept up by interspersing the recitation of the decades of the rosary and the litany to Our Lady with well-known hymns, starting at the new parish church of Our Lady of Lourdes (blessed in 1958), continuing along the public road past the wayside altars and window shrines put up by local people to mark the occasion, as illustrated, and concluding in the grounds of the convent with benediction of the Blessed Sacrament and the final hymn. One of the banners has an image of Our Lady and St Bernadette at the grotto of Lourdes, especially appropriate in the circumstances. The girls and women took part also in the procession in honour of the Blessed Sacrament on the feast of Corpus Christi held in June 1965, and continued to do so over the short period left to such processions (most were abandoned in the 1970s in the wake of the liturgical reforms introduced by Vatican II).[123]

The same Sean MacDermott Street photograph (figure 12.6) has been cropped and used in publications and online as evidence of police actively preventing women residents of this refuge from escaping by forming a cordon around them.[124] It is reproduced here in full (figure 12.6) to fill out the evidence gleaned from the registers of the asylum – and also that given

120    Sean MacDermott Street, circular letter, Dec. 1965 (NDC Caen, Archives Besançon).
121    Ibid.
122    Ibid.
123    Ibid.
124    James A. Smith, *Ireland's magdalen laundries and the nation's architecture of containment* (Notre Dame, Ind., 2007), pp 146–7.

**Figure 12.6** May procession, 1965, Sean MacDermott Street parish. (Garda
        Museum)

to the McAleese inquiry by retired gardaí – on the role played by An Garda
Síochána *vis à vis* the asylum.[125] Only where there was a court order compelling a girl to reside at the convent (on remand or on early release from prison) would the gardaí be contacted about a girl absconding.[126] They played
no role in 'guarding' against escapes, and the claim that girls were flanked
by police for that purpose at a May procession is a misreading of Irish Catholic culture on the threshold of Vatican II. Gardaí were sent on 'processional
duty' to countless such religious events throughout the 1950s and 1960s, as
borne out by photographs of other events, as well as documentary and oral
evidence.[127]

The 'easing' of the enclosure gathered pace in the 1960s, at least for
the women, with opportunities for more regular, outside engagement in
numerous small ways. Inside the asylum, the upgrading of living standards
continued, but with a recognition of the need for more privacy and respect
for the individual. There was a particular concern for the training of the
younger women. In February 1964, the local superior announced that 'she

125  'Girls or women returned to the magdalen laundries by the Gardaí', McAleese report,
     ch. 9, pp 306–16.
126  Ibid., ch. 9, p. 312.
127  Ibid., ch. 9, p. 313.

desired to improve the appearance of the Girls Cloister by having the existing cement floor replaced by tiles'; an architect was consulted, builders' estimates received and the project agreed.[128] The renovation of the dormitories in 1967–8 to give each girl or woman a personal space was a small but significant milestone in this ongoing process.[129] The first dedicated training course began in January 1966 when cookery classes for the girls in 'Gloucester Street monastery' commenced.[130] A proper classroom for this programme was built 'adjoining the refectory' later that year.[131]

The modernisation of services at Sean MacDermott Street, the Ri Villa training centre for teenagers, the girls' hostel and the Casual Unit were the principal new ventures of the late 1960s and early 1970s. That there were 834 admissions to the Casual Unit in under six years of operation can be taken as reading correctly the need to move from the enclosed, 'permanent' asylum to short-term, emergency accommodation for women in what had always been a well-placed, city-centre location.[132] The creation of the apostolate committee in 1969 (chapter 13) as a body to promote communication across the federation brought real collaboration in planning for the first time.[133] In-house entertainments continued throughout the 1960s – the fancy dress parades, with outside 'celebrity' judges are particularly well documented, organised by a detective garda Paddy Murray and the previously-mentioned accordion-player John Murray, but these came to a natural end in the 1970s when the women went out much more to the cinema and the shops.[134] In the main house, a complete break with the old magdalen asylum tradition was made – or at least attempted – in 1973 with a new name, 'Our Lady of Charity Home' (used 1973 to 1981). Once ajar, the door that was opened to new thinking about adolescent psychology and social work practices from about 1952 was not to be closed.[135] Nor did the sisters want it closed, according to their own internal records and despite the weight of tradition, which can be dated to the 1830s, well before Our Lady of Charity was even heard of in Dublin.

128   Gloucester Street local council, minutes, 22 Feb. 1964.
129   Ibid., 26 May 1967.
130   Irish federation general council, minutes, Jan. 1966 (n.d.)
131   Gloucester Street local council, minutes, 20 Jan. 1966.
132   'Gloucester Street Intake Unit (Casual Unit)', register of admissions, 28 June 1971–Feb. 1977 (DARGS, OLC2/8/3 no. 2).
133   Minutes, meeting of the apostolate committee, 14 Dec. 1970 (DARGS, OLC5/5/7 no. 1)
134   Bruton, 'On entertainment'.
135   The superior general visited Gloucester Street Monastery 'relative to the question of hostels', Irish federation general council, minutes, 9 Feb. 1953.

# Chapter 13

## Vatican II and the Renewal of Religious Life: The *Aggiornamento* General Chapter of Our Lady of Charity 1969 and the Irish Federal Chapter of 1973

The shift towards 'modern methods' in the magdalen asylums and certified schools of Our Lady of Charity in Ireland that took hold in the 1950s and early 1960s, and that drove the new initiatives of hostels, training centres, small units and 'family group homes', had to do specifically with the ministry of the sisters. These changes, though demanding in themselves, did little to upset their rule of life and how authority was exercised among them. Their own daily, weekly and annual routines carried on much as they had for decades. It was in the mid-1960s that real and irrevocable changes to religious life would come about, and with them, further far-reaching changes to ministry also.

Precedence must be given to the Second Vatican Council as the most important catalyst for change in the lives of the sisters of Our Lady of Charity in Ireland and those in their care in the 1960s. The overall orientation or spirit of the Council's teaching – namely a wholehearted engagement with 'the joy and hope, the sorrow and anxiety of the men of our time' – mandated the embracing of change under the headings of renewal and adaptation.[1] Its published documents, and the ferment of discussion and experimentation that resulted – that, indeed, the Council called for – would require the sisters to re-think the very purpose of their particular way of life and to articulate in 'modern' language what they were about in the 'modern' world. The women, girls and younger children for whom they already had responsibility would be caught up in the gathering pace of change. Things would, or could, never be the same again.

The Council was not however the only agency for change. As Diarmaid Ferriter explores in *The transformation of Ireland 1900–2000*, young economists, pioneering journalists, fearless priests, lawyers and female trade unionists were among those who dared challenge the status quo

---

1  *Gaudium et spes, Pastoral constitution on the Church in the modern world*, Rome, 7 Dec. 1965, preamble, para. 1, English trans., Catholic Truth Society (London, 1966). The Second Ecumenical Council of the Vatican was announced on 25 Jan. 1959, opened 11 Oct. 1962 (meeting over four separate autumn periods of roughly ten weeks each), and concluded 8 Dec. 1965; it is here abbreviated Vatican II or simply the Council.

with thoughtful, critical analyses. The 1960s brought television into Irish homes, foreign investment and international trade were opened up, involuntary emigration slowed, the opportunity of second-level education was greatly extended and married women began to form a significant segment of the paid labour force. There were new forums for discussion, and some serious analysis of sociological and economic information. The establishment in 1970 of the First Commission on the Status of Women was the result of more than a decade of discourse on women's rights. The introduction of the Unmarried Mothers Allowance in the Social Welfare Act 1973 was on the recommendation of the Council for the Status of Women. The journalism of Michael Viney has been singled out by Ferriter for its role in throwing light on dark and often shameful corners of Irish life during the 1960s, including the neglect of the Traveller population, the isolation of the elderly in county homes and the stigmatisation of adults with mental illness.[2] Louise Fuller, in her study of Irish Catholicism since 1950, highlights the power and immediacy of television, how it allowed all manner of views and opinions to be aired, especially through live shows with panel guests, stimulating further discussion and giving people more confidence in expressing their ideas.[3] The documentary-type programme *Radharc* from 1962 investigated social, as well as religious, topics in Ireland and overseas, contributing to a broadening social consciousness.[4] In summary, areas previously glossed over or hidden from view were opened up; there was more critical media coverage of Church affairs and Church control with priests – as well as lay Catholics – better informed and more free to speak their mind.

It must also be acknowledged that, in terms of religious life and the regulation of its many forms by the Church, there were already moves afoot to address some of the more pressing concerns well in advance of the surprise announcement of the Second Vatican Council in January 1959.[5] The apostolic constitution *Sponsa Christi*, issued 21 November 1950 by Pope Pius XII, marked another stage in Rome's long-running efforts to persuade religious institutes of the same founder to have some sort of centralised government, and to get different institutes involved in the same field of work to communicate with each other, for the purposes of better addressing the needs of the modern world.[6] It was delivered at the close of the first congress of orders and congregations of nuns held in Rome at the end of the 1950 Holy Year, and touched on issues that would get a much fuller, more rounded treatment in the conciliar and post-conciliar documents: the need to modify the law of enclosure; all nuns to share in the apostolic mission of the Church; the distinction between basic, principal

2   Diarmaid Ferriter, *The transformation of Ireland 1900–2000* (London, 2004), pp 536–622.
3   Louise Fuller, *Irish Catholicism since 1950: the undoing of a culture* (Dublin, 2002), pp 127–38.
4   Ibid., p. 134.
5   Maryanne Confoy, 'Religious life in the Vatican II era: "State of perfection" or living charism?', *Theological Studies*, 74 (2013), pp 323–4.
6   Pius XII, *Sponsa Christi*, 21 Nov. 1950, in *The states of perfection according to the teaching of the Church, papal documents from Leo XIII to Pius XII*, ed. Gaston Courtois, trans. John A. O'Flynn (Dublin, 1961), pp 158–9.

and necessary elements of religious life, and those which are extrinsic and accessory and may not need to be retained; and the obligation of labour. Leading by example, gatherings of religious to exchange ideas, to 'render more close their collaboration and more frequent their contacts', were welcomed by the Sacred Congregation for Religious. For example, that held in Liverpool 2–6 January 1956 when judicious adaptations 'to the needs of the present in the matter of formation, apostolate and organisation' were urged, and superiors reminded of their responsibility to assure to their subjects, 'a professional and technical training which will not be inferior to that of lay persons exercising the same function'.[7] It was the Sacred Congregation for Religious that called for a conference of major superiors of women's institutes in Ireland; the 1959 inaugural meeting set in train an important annual gathering, in which OLC always participated.[8] The exhortation of Pope Pius XII was much quoted at such assemblies: 'Adapt yourselves – and do what your holy Founders and Foundresses would do if they were living in the world today.'[9]

It was devotion to the founder that perhaps created the greatest difficulty for OLC sisters, as they wrestled with the problem of the relationship of past to present thrown up by the upheavals of the 1960s.[10] Statues, stained glass windows and holy pictures showed St John Eudes personally handing the rule to his spiritual daughters, whose training centred on the more perfect living out of this venerable rule (figure 1.1). The preamble to the customs book stated that the founder 'expressly enjoined us, with all possible exactitude, to put in practice the regulations contained in this Book, and never in the future to admit into it any change or innovation whatsoever'.[11] Right up to the renewal demanded by the Second Vatican Council, the OLC constitutions admitted only of the most minor and unavoidable revisions, generally prompted by some change in the law of the universal Church, such as a new canon or a revision to the Roman missal. Across all religious institutes, there was a certain permanence or inviolability to constitutions which, once recognised by Rome, could not be changed by the local bishop.[12] The memorandum circulated by sisters representing the French federation on a visit to Ireland in March 1964 'concerning different points of the customs, usages and observances' illustrates perfectly how little was up

---

7  Cardinal Valerio Valeri to William Godfrey, 21 Dec. 1955, *Religious life today, papers read at the Liverpool Congress of Religious, January 2nd to 6th, 1956* (Liverpool, 1956), opening address, xi–xii.
8  'Conference of Major Religious Superiors', Register of the Sisters of Our Lady of Charity of Refuge in Ireland, 1948–2005, pp 187–90 (DARGS, OLC1/6/1 no. 4).
9  Pius XII, quoted in Valeri, opening address.
10  John W. O'Malley, *What happened at Vatican II* (Cambridge, Mass., 2008), p. 9.
11  'Capitular Act of the first Mothers and Sisters of Our Lady of Charity', 1682, reprinted in *The book of customs for the religious of Our Lady of Charity ...* trans. Peter Lewis (Aberdeen, 1888), xiv–xv. Hereafter, *Customs, directory and ceremonial*.
12  *Conditae a Christo*, 8 Dec. 1900, reprinted in D. I. Lanslots, *Handbook of canon law for congregations of women under simple vows* (9th edn, New York, 1920), p. 253. Hereafter, Lanslots, *Handbook of canon law* (1917).

for discussion at that time.[13] The need for exact, unfailing conformity to an unchanging rule – however unsatisfactory or outdated portions of that rule might be – was written in to the very nature of religious life as understood by the sisters of Our Lady of Charity.

The obstacles which this devotion to the founding rule placed before renewal and reform has its parallels in the wider Catholic Church for which elaborations of Church teaching that went beyond – or contravened – previous teaching were problematic. The Council observer John O'Malley terms this 'the problem of change in an institution that draws its lifeblood from a belief in the transcendent validity of the message it received from the past, which it is duty-bound to proclaim unadulterated.'[14] In reflecting on how Vatican II dealt with this contentious issue, O'Malley identifies three approaches: change understood as development, inserted into an unfolding continuity ('evolution', 'progress'), and thus legitimate and necessary; *rassourcement*, skipping over what is currently in place to retrieve from the past something more appropriate or more authentic; and *aggiornamento*, bringing up-to-date, accepted as a broad principle, not a rare exception, at Vatican II.[15] All three approaches, separately and intertwined, were employed with respect to religious life, and would therefore become part of the new thinking that the sisters of Our Lady of Charity were to struggle with during the 1960s and 1970s.

From what is admittedly a large and complex topic in itself, it is nevertheless possible to isolate a number of themes in the teaching of the Second Vatican Council which had particular applicability to the OLC sisters according to the archival evidence. The common baptism of all the faithful, the Church in the modern world, religious life in the Church and its nature. The revisions of the liturgy, the new prominence given to sacred scripture and the concept of 'founding charism' are taken up in turn. Attention then shifts to the practical implementation in OLC of the Council's call for the renewal of religious life, first at general chapter level (encompassing the entire institute) and then at federation level (in Ireland), both of which generated a massive body of paperwork. What is striking is the earnestness with which these sisters tried to put into practice the central teachings of the Council and the decisions of the *aggiornamento* general chapter of 1969, despite the dense language of the documentation and their own limited training in theology. Not surprisingly, there are parallels in the Vatican II history of many other institutes – the Presentation Sisters make for a particularly apt comparison, as they too had both independent communities and federations in several countries loosely held together by adherence to a much-revered rule and constitution, honouring Nano Nagle as their common foundress.[16] But whatever

13   Decisions taken by the general chapter of 1964 [French federation] concerning the customs, usages and observances. Translated from French (DARGS, OLC1/5/2 no. 2). The delegation consisted of Mother M. of Jésus Le Levier, superior general of the French federation; Mother M. of Mercy, St Brieuc, and Sister M. of St Paul, Le Mesnil; 'Minutes of meetings of general council of the federation, Union of the three monasteries of the order of Our Lady of Charity of Refuge in the archdiocese of Dublin, amalgamated 5 Nov. 1948', 6 Mar., 3 July 1964 (DARGS, OLC5/5/1 no. 1). Hereafter, Irish federation general council, minutes.
14   O'Malley, *What happened at Vatican II*, p. 9.
15   Ibid., pp 300–301.
16   Louise O'Reilly, *The impact of Vatican II on women religious: case study of the Union of Irish Presentation Sisters* (Newcastle Upon Tyne, 2013).

difficulties the institutes had in common, each had to wrestle with what the Council called for within its own structures and with its own membership. In that sense, the sisters of Our Lady of Charity had to write their own story.

## Key Conciliar Teaching and the Renewal of Religious Life

The Constitution on the Church, *Lumen gentium* (21 November 1964) is regarded as one of the four key documents providing the orientation according to which the remaining documents of the Council were to be interpreted.[17] In its theology of the Church as the baptised people of God where 'one and the same holiness is cultivated by all' regardless of rank or station in life, religious sisters are lay people, theologically and sacramentally.[18] Rather than a 'higher calling', *Lumen gentium* presents religious life as a particular expression of a common baptism, characterised by an explicit profession of the evangelical counsels (the vows of chastity dedicated to God, poverty and obedience), positioned within the Church and devoted to the welfare of the whole Church.[19] It is this common baptism that constitutes the Church as a single people, brothers and sisters in the one Christ, each called to bear witness to Him 'especially by means of a life of faith and charity'.[20]

What was asked of the Church in *Lumen gentium* (and further developed in *Gaudium et spes* and other documents), was asked of religious life: deep reflection on its nature and limits, its functions, its meaning and mission in the world. The challenge posed by *Lumen gentium* was to see what religious life might look like when its countless small regulations, observances, mortifications, customs, devotions and rules on precedence – as exemplified in OLC in its four-part Book of Customs – were put to one side. The long-entrenched view of the Church as somehow a closed society, 'confronting' the world, was paralleled in religious life in its self-understanding as 'apart from' the world or 'flight from' the world, where (as in OLC), the enclosure was regarded as 'the very basis of the religious state' and its infraction a matter of punishment.[21] The new understandings of the Church – as a leaven in human society, the keeper of the gospel conscience of the world, a people on pilgrimage, all of whom, without exception, are called to holiness – would destabilise the old certainties in religious life. Far from being cut off from the world, *Lumen gentium* taught, 'Let no one think that religious have become strangers to their fellowmen or useless citizens of this earthly city by their consecration'.[22]

The world, as the theatre within which holiness is to be lived, is taken up in the final major constitution of the Council, *Gaudium et spes*, on the Church in the modern world (7 December 1965). It sets out the call to 'continually examine the signs of the times and interpret them in the light of the gospel' and to get to know and understand this world, 'its expectations, its aspirations, its often dramatic character'.[23] The High Park sisters employed the language of

---

17 O'Malley, *What happened at Vatican II*, p. 2.
18 *Lumen gentium, The Constitution on the Church of Vatican Council II*, English trans., Missionary Society of St Paul the Apostle/Darton, Longman and Todd (London, 1965), nos. 40, 41.
19 *Lumen gentium*, nos. 43, 44.
20 Ibid., nos. 10, 12.
21 *Customs, directory and ceremonial*, article xx, Enclosure, p. 234.
22 *Lumen gentium*, no. 46.
23 *Gaudium et spes*, no. 4.

*Gaudium et spes* as they extolled Pope Paul VI for his unremitting efforts 'to bring the Church to the world and the world to God' and pledged their best efforts 'to renew our spiritual life in compliance with the decrees of the Vatican Council II'.[24] For apostolic religious with a tradition of strict enclosure, who had long prided themselves on their self-sufficiency, 'apartness' and loyalty to an unbroken tradition, the new direction taken by the Church would require a new mind-set, not merely the shedding of outdated practices and customs.

The Vatican II document concerned expressly with religious life and the implementation of the Council's teaching is *Perfectae caritatis* (28 October 1965). The norms for the programme of *aggiornamento*, or renewal of religious life, were issued in *Ecclesiae Sanctae II* (6 August 1966), coming into effect on 11 October 1966. It placed the onus for renewal on the religious themselves, which was unprecedented for the sisters of Our Lady of Charity, as indeed it was for many other congregations. The making of the OLC Irish federation of 1948, their most recent experience of major change, had been masterminded from start to finish by the archbishop, Dr McQuaid, with only their *fiat* required. The pursuit of perfect love, *perfectae caritatis prosecutio*, following the teaching and example of Jesus Christ and by means of the evangelical counsels (chastity dedicated to God, poverty and obedience), is presented by the Council as a universal call, not at all the preserve of religious. As a distinctive way of life, the Church accepts religious life as a gift, but one which will become ever more fruitful insofar as religious join themselves to Christ and involve themselves in the life and mission of the Church.[25] The decree *Perfectae caritatis* places the following of Christ, *sequela Christi*, as put before mankind in the gospel, as the supreme rule of life for all institutes.[26] It allows for the special character and functions of each institute (its charism)[27] and relates religious life closely to the general pattern of the Church:

> All institutes should share in the life of the Church. They should make their own and should foster to the best of their ability, in a manner consonant with their own natures, her initiatives and plans in biblical, liturgical, dogmatic, pastoral, ecumenical, missionary and social matters.[28]

Institutes were called to ensure that their members had 'a proper understanding' of mankind, of present-day conditions and of the needs of the Church – a theme that was taken up even more forcefully in *Gaudium et spes*, and left no room for misreading.[29]

Not only 'the manner of life, prayer and of work' but also 'the manner of governing' in religious institutes were to be re-examined to bring them into line with the 'present-day physical and psychological circumstances

---

24    High Park, circular letter, 8 Dec. 1966 (DARGS, OLC1/3/1 no. 31).

25    *Perfectae caritatis, The decree on the renewal of religious life*, promulgated 28 Oct. 1965, Paulist Press edn, trans. Austin Flannery, commentary by Gregory Baum, New York, 1966), no. 1.

26    *Perfectae caritatis*, 'General principles of renewal', no. 2 (a).

27    Ibid., no. 2 (b).

28    Ibid., no. 2 (c).

29    Ibid., no. 2 (d).

of the members', the demands of culture and social and economic circumstances:

> For this reason, constitutions, directories, books of customs, of prayers, of ceremonies and suchlike should be properly revised, obsolete prescriptions being suppressed, and should be brought into line with conciliar documents.[30]

Key themes in *Perfectae caritatis* had been heralded some years earlier.[31] Cardinal Giovanni Battista Montini, archbishop of Milan (later Pope Paul VI), addressed an assembly of nuns on 11 February 1961, calling on them to take their place in the world today, to become active collaborators in the Church 'which seeks to sanctify and save the world', to live in small groups, in direct contact with 'modern humanity', and to prepare well, to become qualified so that you will be able to influence, to educate, to Christianise the world'.[32] His address to sisters in the diocese of Albano, delivered on 8 September 1964 and widely reprinted, set out in unequivocal terms what the new Pope thought of those religious who remained 'on the outskirts of the Church constructing for oneself a spirituality which is cut off from the circulation of word, of grace and charity in the Catholic community of brothers in Christ'.[33] Decades of agonising within OLC over the nature and obligation of enclosure[34] was cut short by Rome with the bald statement that 'minor enclosure is abolished', with papal enclosure reserved to those monasteries of nuns for whom withdrawal from the world was intrinsic to their vocation.[35] Even when Rome had ruled, it took time to come to terms with what exactly this meant for the institute.[36] And there were more surprises. Young American OLC sisters studying in Rome at the time of the Council wrote of their astonishment at discovering, for the first time, that encyclical letters were addressed 'to all the Clergy and Faithful of the Catholic world', not just to the bishops, and realising that

---

30   *Perfectae caritatis*, 'Criteria of renewal', no. 3.

31   George Andrew Beck, 'The schema on religious', *Doctrine and Life*, vol. 15, no. 8 (Aug. 1965), pp 419–29.

32   John Baptist Montini, 'Apostolic involvement', *Supplement to Doctrine and Life*, no. 8 (Winter 1964), pp 177, 179.

33   Paul VI, 'Nuns and the Church', trans. Austin Flannery, *Supplement to Doctrine and Life*, vol. 3, no. 3 (Autumn 1965), p. 146.

34   See general council, minutes, 11 May 1960; 'Synopsis [Rome meeting] delivered to general council on 5 July 1960', 'Explanations of enclosure to be observed to sisters in High Park' (10 July 1960), Gloucester Street (14 July 1960), St Anne's (15 July 1960), The Grange (18 July 1960), Irish federation general council, minutes, 26 Oct. 1953; Third general chapter of the Irish federation of the Order of Our Lady of Charity of Refuge, Nov. 1960 (DARGS, OLC5/1/3).

35   *Ecclesiae Sanctae II*, 6 Aug. 1966, 'Rules for the execution of the decree *Perfectae caritatis* of the Second Vatican Council' in *Vatican Council: applying the decrees*, trans. by J.G. McGarry, Catholic Truth Society of Ireland (Dublin, 1966), no. 3, pp 20–27.

36   'The Special Chapter of the Order of Our Lady of Charity convened October 5, 1969, under the presidency of Revd Fr Lacroix, superior general of the Congregation of Jesus and Mary, delegate of the Holy See for the aggiornamento of the Order, at the Institute of St John Eudes, Rome', detailed minutes, fourth session, 8 Oct. 1969 (DARGS, OLC5/3/1). Hereafter, general chapter, detailed minutes.

they personally had an obligation to be well-informed 'dynamic Catholics', not just 'static Catholics': 'the Church has no need of Holy Sleepers in our needs of today'.[37] In Ireland, as elsewhere, there was a dawning recognition of how the ground was shifting. As one sister worded it, the challenge was to stimulate within themselves the outward-looking spirit of the Council, *l'œcuménisme*.[38]

By stating as the first norm of religious life, and the supreme rule of all institutes, 'the following of Christ, as it is put before us in the Gospel', *Perfectae caritatis* overrode the constitution or rule created by an individual institute, no matter how sanctified by long usage it might be or how perfectly it embodied the founder's prescriptions.[39] Within Our Lady of Charity, the focus had long been on obedience to the rule as 'the means of perfecting and sanctifying' the sisters in their vocation.[40] Under canon law, superiors had (and have) the right to command subjects (*potestas dominative*), a right that extends 'solely to the observance of the lawfully-approved constitutions, and to all that concerns the proper direction of the congregation'. By her vow of obedience, freely made, the sister makes a promise to God to obey her lawful superior in all things which she has a right to command, according to the same constitutions.[41] While Vatican II did not sweep away the superior's right to command and the sister's obligation to obey – and the OLC rule placed great store on the superior acting in kindness, charity and gentleness, and the sister herself making known her needs – the pronouncements from the Council introduced a very different dynamic. Inclusion, dialogue, partnership, collaboration, persuasion and invitation recur so often and so forcefully that they could not be ignored. There was an emphasis on the individual, on the psychological maturity required for religious life and on the respect due to the sister by virtue of her uniqueness. There were new insights into the religious sister as a sexual being and how her femininity was an integral part of her identity, while spiritual writers and retreat directors reflected on how the vow of celibacy might be lived in an authentic way, based on acceptance, not fear, of what it is to be truly human, and sustained by close friendships within and outside the community.[42] A more holistic and human approach that attends to the relational aspect of celibacy was urged, while the greater awareness of the co-responsibility of all for the common life, a breaking down of autocratic approaches and the subordination of 'subjects' led to what Maryanne Confoy calls a new emphasis on 'the

---

37    Sister M. of St Francis (Rochester) and Sister M. of the Holy Spirit (Wheeling), Vatican City, circular letter, 14 Jan. 1962 (DARGS, OLC1/3/3 no. 45).
38    Sainte Anne, *circulaire*, janvier 1966 (DARGS, OLC3/3/1 no. 11).
39    *Perfectae caritatis*, 'General principles of renewal', no. 2 (a).
40    Dedicatory letter of St John Eudes, reprinted in the preamble to *Customs, directory and ceremonial*, xi.
41    Lanslots, *Handbook of canon law* (1917), p. 171 (referring to canon 501); p. 111 (referring to canon 572).
42    Among the very many texts available to sisters in High Park and marked up are Joseph H. Gallen, SJ, *Femininity and spirituality*, reprinted from *Review for Religious* (US), vol. 20, no. 4 (1961) pp 237–56; Fergal O'Connor OP, 'Sexuality, chastity and celibacy' in O'Connor, Auer and Egenter, *Celibacy and virginity* (Dublin and Sydney, 1968), pp 25–45; *Psychological realities and religious life*, Vita Evangelica 3, Canadian Religious Conference (Ottawa, 1969).

mutuality of responsibility for authentic communal relationships'.[43] The instruction to communities 'to arrive at having but one category of sister'[44] abolished the distinction between lay and choir sisters and was certainly in the spirit of the Council – though in many institutes, including OLC, steps had already been taken towards this end.[45]

An 'active and responsible obedience' was to be fostered among the sisters, and superiors were to listen willingly to their subjects and to promote co-operation.[46] The renewal and adaptation hoped for by the Council was presented as depending on the collaboration and real involvement of every member of the institute, a major change in orientation and requiring the sisters to read, to meet, to offer opinions and advice. Chapters and councils, formerly rather closed fora, were 'to give expression to the involvement and the concern of all the members of the community for the good of the whole'.[47] Active engagement was to take the place of passive acceptance and all, without exception, were to be drawn in to the process of renewal, with its questionnaire surveys, discussion groups and assigned reading. The Council advocated a new style of authority and new forms for the exercise of authority, which required conversion to a new style of thinking, speaking and behaving, a more 'reciprocal and responsive model'.[48] While hierarchy was not abolished, horizontal rather than vertical power structures were stressed and conscience was to be preferred over coercion. In the monasteries of Our Lady of Charity, offering the sisters a choice of retreat director and retreat venue, from 1965, for 'a more perfect renewal of mind and body', was one of many small changes that, cumulatively, led to a very different experience of religious life.[49] Numerous expert and sympathetic commentators (mostly male) tried to tease out how the Council's teaching might look in practice and to advise local communities, institutes and gatherings of religious superiors (mostly female) on how to handle the work of renewal. The series of lectures of Paul Molinari SJ to the Conference of Major Religious Superiors (Women's Section) at the annual general meeting of 1971, which were shaped by the question and answer sessions that followed each lecture, dealt with difficult and troubling aspects of the process, including experimenting with models of community

---

43   Confoy, 'Religious life in the Vatican II era', p. 328.

44   Beck, 'The schema on religious', pp 422, 425; see also *Perfectae caritatis*, no. 15.

45   The first vote taken by the general council of the new federation, 2 Feb. 1950, was unanimously 'in favour of giving white tunics and sleeves to lay sisters', also voted through at the 1960 meeting in Rome of the four superiors general or federation presidents. The 'unification of the habit', when all novices, choir and lay, received the black veil on profession, was finally achieved on 19 Aug. 1964, but without the suppression of the category of lay sister. The 'unification of the ranks', suppressing *tourière*, lay and choir, was announced in High Park on 10 Jan. 1967 and, the following day, 'the sisters took their place in the refectory according to seniority of first profession'. Irish federation general council, minutes, 2 Feb. 1950, 31 July 1960, 10 Jan. 1967; Sacra Congregatio Religiosis, protocol n.6003/64 (11 Aug. 1964); protocol n.10793/66 (10 Jan. 1967), copies in OLC post-federation register, pp 33, 108 (DARGS, OLC1/6/1 no. 4).

46   *Perfectae caritatis*, 'General principles of renewal', no. 14.

47   Ibid., no. 4.

48   O'Malley, *What happened at Vatican II*, p. 11.

49   Sean MacDermott Street, circular letter, Dec. 1965 (NDC Caen, Archives Besançon).

and the exodus of members.[50] Something of the upheaval involved for the traditional institute of Our Lady of Charity can be reconstructed from the wealth of records, including transcripts of the Molinari lectures, created at the time and in which the voices of the 'grassroots' feature strongly for the first time.

## Vatican II and the Renewal of the Liturgy

Liturgical renewal was one area of reform that was well under way before the Second Vatican Council was convened.[51] Within the Irish federation of OLC, study of the scriptural basis of the Divine Office and efforts to improve its recitation were under way from at least 1950.[52] In *Christus Dominus*, 1953, Rome had signalled its intentions for liturgical reform, but it was the promulgation on 4 December 1963 of *Sacrosanctum Concilium*,[53] the Constitution on the Sacred Liturgy, that set in train a progressive series of changes that would affect Catholics universally.[54] As approved translations of liturgical texts – the ordinary of the Mass, the readings, funeral rites, baptism rites – became available in the vernacular, the changes were gradually implemented. For the sisters of Our Lady of Charity, the obligation to attend daily Mass and to sing in choir the canonical hours, the public prayer of the Church, had long been seen as the 'sacred duty' that underpinned their vocation as religious and gave shape to daily life.[55] In addition, the new liturgy was presented as intrinsic to the renewal called for by the Council, helping to 'stir up that formation of the faithful and pastoral activity which has the sacred liturgy as summit and fount'.[56] Liturgy had always mattered in OLC but, with Vatican II, it took on an added significance; the efforts made to implement the new liturgy were interconnected with the efforts made to co-operate with the Council's call to *aggiornamento*. Under neither heading were things easy or predictable.

'Full, active and conscious participation' was presented by the Council as the touchstone of liturgical renewal, 'the aim to be considered before all else'.[57] The rites were to be distinguished by 'a noble simplicity', 'short, clear and unencumbered by any useless repetitions and within the powers of comprehension of the people'.[58] At Mass, the Church's desire was that the faithful should not be mere spectators, but 'conscious of what they are

---

50  'Lectures given by Rev. P. Molinari SJ at the Annual General Meeting, 1971, Conference of Major Religious Superiors, Women's Section' (DARGS, Library).
51  Austin Flannery, Foreword, *Doctrine and Life*, vol. 14, no. 2 (Feb. 1964), p. 61.
52  'Training of sisters and courses, lectures etc. attended', 1950–64, Register of the Sisters of Our Lady of Charity of Refuge in Ireland, 1948–2005 (DARGS, OLC1/6/1 no. 4).
53  *Sacrosanctum Concilium*, Constitution on the Sacred Liturgy, promulgated 4 Dec. 1963, came into force 16 Feb. 1964, trans. Clifford Howell, *Doctrine and Life*, vol. 14, no. 2 (Feb. 1964), pp 130–159.
54  'Liturgy renewal in Ireland: a report', in *The Furrow*, vol. 17, no. 5 (May 1966), p. 307; 'Liturgical news', Eucharistic fast', *Doctrine and* Life, vol. 15, no. 1, (Jan. 1965), p. 50.
55  The sisters were obliged to say 'the Little Office of Our Lady as reformed by the holy Council of Trent and by Pope Urban VIII'. *Customs, directory and ceremonial*, iv, p. 3.
56  Joseph Cunnane, 'Instructions on the liturgy', *The Furrow*, vol. 16, no. 1 (Jan. 1965), pp 24–9, quoting Constitution on the Sacred Liturgy, no. 10.
57  *Sacrosanctum Concilium*, no. 14.
58  Ibid., no. 34.

doing, with devotion and full collaboration'.[59] In teaching of liturgy as 'celebrations of the Church, which is the "sacrament of unity"',[60] there was no place for independent ceremonials or additional honours.[61] The feasts of the Lord were to be given preference over the feasts of the saints, 'so that the entire cycle of the mysteries of salvation may be suitable recalled'; to declutter the liturgical calendar, only those saints that were judged truly of universal importance would be kept on the universal calendar, with local saints to be celebrated by the particular Church, congregation or nation only.[62] The Council left little room for devotions or 'trimmings', unless they were in tune with the liturgical season and accord with the sacred liturgy, 'are in some fashion derived from it and lead the people to it'.[63] Novices were to be inducted into the spiritual life through the Divine Office and the liturgical year, 'the attuning of one's personal prayer and piety with the Church cannot fail to give a balanced and Christocentric quality to the former'.[64] The architecture and furnishing of church and chapel would undergo change to accommodate the priest facing the people, the new understandings of what the liturgy involved and the role of the faithful. The sanctuary and choir of the convent chapel at High Park would be reordered in due course (figure 13.1), with the main altar brought forward, the tabernacle placed on the back wall and the reredos re-created around it, the side chapels or wings opened up to the main body of the church, the carved oak stalls moved into two sets (not one) and the superior's ornate chair (the president's chair) removed.[65]

What was asked of the OLC sisters, in brief, was to abandon practices they cherished as peculiarly their own and to take on the new, simpler but as yet untried Roman liturgy. They had their own choir ceremonial, which the 'good father and founder' himself, John Eudes, had named, along with the constitutions, directory and book of customs, as 'the foundation, soul and heart' of the congregation. Though unfinished at his death, the later compilation carried the full weight of his authority.[66] It taught that 'the order, the uniformity and the majesty of external ceremonies' would aid interior recollection, detailing how exactly the Divine Office was to be recited, the roles to be played by each person, what prayer was to be intoned and who was to respond.[67] It specified the order of the procession, when to bow, when to incline and when to genuflect, when to sit, kneel or stand, when to make

59   Ibid., no. 48.
60   Ibid., no. 26.
61   Ibid., nos. 22, 32.
62   Ibid., nos. 108, 111.
63   Ibid., no. 13.
64   Vincent Ryan, 'Liturgical formation of religious', in *Doctrine and Life*, vol. 15, no. 6 (June 1965), p. 304.
65   William H. Byrne and Son, architectural drawing no. 37113, Convent of Our Lady of Charity of Refuge, High Park Convent, 1 Apr. 1970 (DARGS, OLC1/9/2 no. 54); High Park local council, minutes, 1, 15 June, 18 July, 6 Aug., 4 Sept., 31 Dec. 1970 (DARGS, OLC1/5/2 no. 1).
66   Dedicatory letter, n.d., of St John Eudes, d. 1680, reprinted in the preamble to *Customs, directory and ceremonial*, xi–xiii.
67   Ibid., iv.

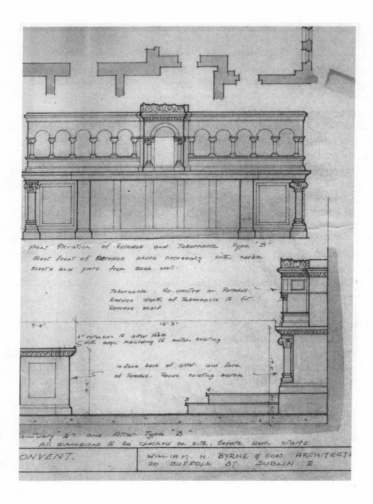

**Figure 13.1** Extract from architect's plan for the reordering of the convent chapel, High Park, March 1970 (DARGS, OLC1/9/2 no. 54).

the sign of the cross and who was to give the blessing.[68] The ceremonial around Mass, bringing Communion to the sick, assisting at the death bed of a sister or a woman or at their burial was also spelled out in elaborate detail. The Council also required the sisters to abandon their own crowded liturgical calendar in which OLC anniversaries and feasts had been given pride of place. On 8 February, the Holy Heart of Mary, for example, the calendar gave the ritual that was to be employed to solemnise this titular feast of the

68    *Customs, directory and ceremonial*, pp 2–158.

congregation, from the vigil the evening before to the end of the octave.[69] The intricate and lengthy rituals of the OLC ceremonial were out of step with much of the new thinking, though the Council did expect 'sincere piety and decorum',[70] in which the OLC sisters were certainly well practised.

Fuller participation in the Mass was enabled first by 'the practice of the Dialogue Mass' (in Latin).[71] The superior of St Anne's reported that it was 'very devotional and most encouraging to see these poor girls finding joy in being allowed to answer the priest and say the prayers with him' and was confident it would led them to 'a better understanding of the tremendous significance of the Holy Sacrifice'.[72] Mass in English in March 1965 in High Park, with congregational singing, was warmly welcomed in the very words of the constitution on the liturgy, as having successfully led 'to that conscious and active participation by all the people in liturgical celebration which is rightly theirs'.[73] In Sean MacDermott Street, the adoption of the vernacular for the Mass was also judged a great success: 'it has been inspiring to witness the attention and interest with which our girls participated therein, not once have they been caught off guard for the responses'.[74] So, too, the Sean MacDermott Street community began to say the Divine Office in English in 1965, a change 'accepted with satisfaction and fervour'.[75] High Park was a little slower to make the shift, having a far larger community to bring along, but from 1 March 1967 this community also began to recite lauds (morning prayer), vespers (evening prayer) and compline (night prayer) in English.[76] In the revision of the Divine Office[77] morning and evening prayer were prioritised over the other hours, making them become 'the two hinges, as it were, of the daily office'.[78] The teaching that the recitation of morning and evening prayer alone or in common was a full participation in the public prayer of the Church,[79] gave the sisters the leeway to dispense with 'lesser' devotions and the pressure to have everything said in common and in the chapel.[80]

The profession Mass at which the new rite was first used was that of Sister Mary of St Raphael Cooper, who was making her perpetual vows on 9 June 1967 in High Park. The officiating priest, Patrick Boylan, was chairman

69  The additional prayers were named as the *Beato Patri Augustino*, the litany of the Sacred [Holy] Heart of Mary and the *Te Deum, Customs, directory and ceremonial*, pp 11–14.
70  *Sacrosanctum Concilium*, no. 29.
71  St Anne's, circular letter, Christmas 1960 (DARGS, OLC3/3/1).
72  Ibid.
73  High Park, circular letter, 8 Dec. 1965 (DARGS, OLC1/3/1, no. 30).
74  Sean MacDermott Street, circular letter, Dec. 1965 (NDC Caen, Archives Besançon).
75  Ibid.
76  The rescript from Rome is dated 2 Feb. 1967. Irish federation general council, minutes, 3–25 Jan. 1967.
77  Paul VI, Apostolic constitution, *Laudis canticum*, 1 Nov. 1970, announcing the completion of the reform of the Divine Office and approving it; Sacred Congregation for Divine Worship, decree, *Horarum liturgia*, announcing the publication of the liturgy of the hours, and stating that it is the *editio typica*, publication 11 Apr. 1971.
78  Paul VI, *Apostolic constitution, the canticle of praise*, 1 Nov. 1970, reprinted in *The Divine Office* (Dublin, 1974), i, xi–xviii, no. 2.
79  The general instruction on the liturgy of the hours, *The Divine Office*, i, xix – xcii, nos. 9, 20–27, 32.
80  *Sacrosanctum Concilium*, nos. 91, 94; High Park local council, minutes, 6 Mar. 1964.

of the liturgical commission for the diocese and well placed to assure the superior (who had her doubts) that nothing had been done contrary to canon law. The novelty of the ceremony merited a lengthy entry in the general council minutes: the sister was handed a lighted candle as a reminder of her baptismal commitment, the new proper of the Mass for religious profession was used, the candidate was interrogated, pronounced her vows, signed them and received the crown of flowers – the latter an OLC custom, not part of the official ritual. 'At the Communion she entered the sanctuary, knelt on the predella, and received Holy Communion under both kinds', a first for High Park chapel. After Mass – in English – elements of the old ceremonial featured, with benediction of the Blessed Sacrament, the singing of a *Te Deum* and the kiss of peace, 'after which the community went in processional order to the novitiate'.[81] It was thus that the liturgical changes were introduced; there was no special permission required and no recourse to Caen.

## Conciliar Teaching on Sacred Scripture and the Charism of the Religious Founders

While great store was placed by the sisters of Our Lady of Charity on having the revised liturgy carried out with correctness and reverence – albeit with fewer candles, less processing and little plainchant – it was the conciliar teaching on the special place to be given to the scriptures that had the greatest impact. *Sacrosanctum Concilium* taught that the public worship of the liturgy was at the core of the Church's life, manifesting 'the mystery of Christ and the real nature of the true Church'.[82] In the Mass above all, Christ is present in the priest, in the bread and wine, in the word, in the assembled people. But to truly nourish the faithful, for men and women to discover God in the liturgy and to open themselves to him, they needed to understand what they were about, the connections between the rites or actions and the prayers, what was the nature and purpose of the different parts and how they were connected.[83] Above all, Catholics needed to know the scriptures:

> For it is from holy scripture that lessons are read and explained in the homily, and psalms are sung; the prayers, collects and liturgical songs are scriptural in their inspiration; and it is from the scriptures that actions and signs derive their meaning. Thus to achieve the restoration, progress and adaptation of the sacred liturgy, it is essential to promote that warm and living love for scripture to which the venerable traditions of both eastern and western rites give testimony.[84]

In the revised liturgy, the treasures of the bible were to be opened up 'more lavishly', and a more representative, varied and suitable portion of the holy

81    Irish federation general council, minutes, 9 June 1967.
82    *Sacrosanctum Concilium*, no. 2.
83    Ibid., nos. 7, 35, 50.
84    Ibid., no. 24.

scriptures was to be read.[85] In the Dublin diocese, a lead was given by the Dublin Institute of Catholic Sociology which used the school hall of the Dominican College, 62 Eccles Street, from October 1964 onwards to host courses on theology and scripture, advertising them in the supplement to *Doctrine and Life*.[86] Among the earliest and most faithful attendees were sisters from the nearby OLC convents of High Park and Sean MacDermott Street.[87] An assembly of major religious superiors was called by the archbishop Dr McQuaid in August 1966 – as the norms for the renewal of religious life were issued – to announce the start-up of a programme for the young religious of the diocese to be held in Clonliffe College, the diocesan seminary. This was relaunched in 1969 as the Mater Dei formation programme, 'a course of basic instruction in Doctrine, Liturgy, Sacred Scripture and Spiritual Life such that juniors and novices could attend on several mornings in the week'.[88] This programme, too, was availed of by OLC sisters, along with young religious, male and female, from other congregations. The development of courses at Clonliffe/the Mater Dei Institute of Education may have been prompted by a survey published in 1964 pointing out that there was no course of studies available in Ireland leading to a diploma in theology for sisters, brothers and lay people 'who may for one reason or another feel the need for such a training', and then describing very attractive programmes on offer in Britain, the US, Rome, Paris and Brussels.[89] Apart from formal outside programmes, the OLC rank and file pressed for talks on scripture and on the Council's teaching, for the replacement of topics for meditation by scripture extracts, for 'bible study', for 'weekly reading and discussion among the sisters' and for access to a suitable library, demonstrating a heartfelt desire to go along with the renewal called for by the Council, however clumsy and imperfect their efforts.[90]

The Council's teaching that up-to-date renewal involved 'a constant return to the sources of the whole of the Christian life and to the primitive inspiration of the institutes' also sparked new interest in the founder, John Eudes, and in his 'spirit and aims'.[91] While the first of the general principles of renewal was to keep sights set on Christ and on his gospel (hence the concern with knowing the scriptures), the second principle stated:

> It is to the benefit of the Church herself that institutes should have their own proper characters and functions. Therefore, the spirit and aims of each founder should be clearly recognised and faithfully preserved, as indeed should each institute's own traditions, for all of these constitute the patrimony of an institute.[92]

85  Ibid., nos. 35.1, 51.
86  'Chronicle', *Supplement to Doctrine and Life*, vol. 2, no. 3 (1964), p. 157.
87  'Training of sisters and courses, lectures etc. attended', 1950–64.
88  Irish federation general council, minutes, 18 Aug. 1966, 6 June 1969.
89  'Chronicle', *Supplement to Doctrine and Life*, vol. 2, no. 3 (Autumn 1964), p. 158.
90  'Compilation of the results of the discussions held by the Sisters of the Irish Federation on the response to the questionnaire which was sent out in January 1967', nos. 124, 135, 137, 219 (DARGS, OLC5/3/1). Hereafter, Questionnaire.
91  *Perfectae caritatis*, 'General principles of renewal', no. 2.
92  Ibid., no. 2 (b).

For the sisters of Our Lady of Charity, an anxiety to conform ever more perfectly with the wishes of the founder, St John Eudes, was long engrained in the congregation. Alongside veneration of the rule as coming directly from John Eudes, they had been unswerving in their efforts to spread knowledge of and devotion to the saint, utilising in particular the beatification in 1909 and the canonisation in 1925 to promote his cult. He was honoured in the Church art and devotional life of each monastery. The salutations he had composed were recited faithfully in common each day: Hail heart most holy, Hail Mary, daughter of God the Father, Hail Joseph, image of God the Father.[93] The library shelves at High Park held English translations of some at least of the many biographies of John Eudes; most publication dates can be matched to the occasion of his being declared venerable (1874), blessed (1909) and saint (1925).[94]

But what the average Sister of Our Lady of Charity in Dublin knew of John Eudes was what she learned of him through the constitutions and customs, prayers, house devotions, sermons – sometimes from visiting Eudist priests – and stories on his goodness and zeal for souls, culled from the biographies and passed down over the years. John Eudes had left behind a body of writing, but few OLC sisters in Ireland had ever had the opportunity of engaging directly with this for themselves. Even if any sister felt so called – and had excellent French – she was unlikely to make much progress without the kind of training in theology and doctrine enjoyed by priests of the Eudist congregation.[95] Although High Park did hold copies of some early abridgements and compilations of John Eudes' writings, and an English edition of his *Selected works* was published in the 1940s and held in the High Park library, it was only in the mid-1960s that this heritage was made accessible to the sisters.[96] Significantly, it was the call of Vatican II, 'to strive to achieve a true understanding of the spirit of their foundation', that led the sisters to think about the founder and the founding period in terms

93　The recitation in common of these salutations continued after the liturgical reforms of Vatican II, but the time was to be decided by the local community, Federal chapter, Irish federation of the Order of Our Lady of Charity, minutes, 8 Oct. 1973, fourth session, p. 27 (DARGS, OLC5/1/7). (Hereafter, Federal chapter, minutes).

94　The English publications listed here are largely based on French sources; Ch. De Montzey, *Life of the Venerable John Eudes, with a sketch of the history of his foundations from A.D. 1601–1874*, first published 1879 (2nd edn, London, 1883); Matthew Russell, *The life of Blessed John Eudes* (London, n.d. but between 1909 and 1925); P. A. Bray, *Saint John Eudes* (Halifax, 1925); Henri Joly, *A life of Saint John Eudes*, trans. Joseph Leonard (London, 1932); Peter Herambourg, *Saint John Eudes, a spiritual portrait*, trans. Ruth Hauser (Westminster, Maryland, 1960). The Herambourg text is from a 1926 edition (by Denis Boulay) of a manuscript completed in the late 1600s and preserves its 17th-century flavour.

95　*Oeuvres complètes du Vénérable Jean Eudes*, ed. Charles Lebrun and Joseph Dauphin, 12 vols (Vannes, 1905–11); 2nd edn published as *Oeuvres choisies du Saint Jean Eudes* (1935).

96　To mark the tercentenary of the foundation of the Eudist fathers in 1943, an English trans. was commissioned, titled *Selected works of St John Eudes* (6 vols, 1945–48). The volumes held in the DARGS Library, Beechlawn, are: *The life and kingdom of Jesus in Christian souls, a treatise on Christian perfection for use by clergy or laity*, by St John Eudes, trans. Trappist father (New York, 1945); *The Sacred Heart of Jesus by St John Eudes*, trans. Richard Flower (New York, 1945); *The priest, his dignity and obligations by John Eudes*, trans. W. Leo Murphy (New York, 1947); *Letters and shorter works by St John Eudes*, trans. Ruth Hauser (New York, 1948).

other than as a rule of life to be preserved intact, come what may.[97] Study of the community's founding spirit or special charism was to ensure it was preserved in the many and necessary adaptations about to be made, that 'their religious life may be purified from elements alien to it and freed from matters that have become obsolete'.[98] Probably the most practical tool in this task was the new scholarship of Paul Milcent, whose *Saint John Eudes: Presentation and selected texts* (Paris & Glasgow, n.d. but *c.* 1965) was accessible, relevant, short (132pp) and in modern language, the commentary tightly tied to selected texts. Milcent himself was an important contributor to the 1969 general chapter. By moving the heritage of John Eudes beyond the four-part book of customs (with directories, ceremonials, rituals), the wishes he had for his spiritual children and some of the prayers he had left them, new interest in his teaching was generated and new insights were possible, not least an understanding of how his response to need was circumscribed by time and place.

## Practical Implementation among the Sisters of Our Lady of Charity of the Second Vatican Council's Call for the Renewal of Religious Life

It was the promulgation on 11 October 1966 of the norms for implementing the decree on the renewal of religious life that put the business of adaptation and renewal into action; *Ecclesiae Sanctae II* forced an immediate engagement through its ruling that, 'to promote adaptation and renewal', each institute must convoke a special general chapter within two – or, at most, three – years.[99] The International Union of Superioresses General (UISG) teased out the norms with its own summaries and studies, most usefully in *Revision of the constitutions* (August 1967).[100] The rewriting of constitutions was the principal and obligatory task, to introduce into the constitutive laws of each religious community the *aggiornamento* that the Council applied to the whole Church, that sees religious life as gift to the Church and for the mission of the Church.[101] The preparatory work that would be required, Rome hoped, would help 'to bring about an opening of the mind, an evolution of opinion on vital points of religious life in general and in the congregation'. This hope was bolstered by the expectation that *aggiornamento* would be undertaken in dialogue with associated houses and institutes.[102] The journey was to be undertaken with others, a direct challenge to the self-contained, autonomous character of houses such as the monasteries of

---

97   *Ecclesiae Sanctae II*, no. 16.3.
98   Ibid.
99   *Ecclesiae Sanctae II*, no. 3.
100   International Union of Superioresses General (UISG), *Revision of the constitutions*, bulletin no. 5 (Rome, Aug. 1967), 24 pp. This body is also abbreviated, in English, as IUSG.
101   *Lumen gentium*, no. 43.
102   International Union of Superioresses General (UISG), 'Methods of work', *Revision of the constitutions*, bulletin no. 5 (Rome, Aug. 1967), pp 7–19. The UISG was required under article 42 of *Ecclesiae Sanctae II* to offer opinions and views to a Consilium established at the Congregation for Religious, and the various issues of its bulletin may be seen as fulfilling this mandate, in part at least.

the Irish federation of OLC. High Park was quick to endorse the principle of co-operation, rightly recognising it as 'so essential for the good of our holy Order and the difficult apostolate in the modern world'.[103] Responsibility for renewal lay with the institutes and would require the co-operation of every superior and of every member at each stage of the process; this was not a task that could be subcontracted or 'bought in' from another institute and there were no short cuts.

In the absence of a supreme, over-arching government (such as a generalate), Rome could appoint a delegate to act in its name to oversee the process of renewal. Fr Fernand Lacroix (1919–94), a French-Canadian newly-elected as superior general of the Eudist fathers, circulated all the OLC monasteries and federations proposing himself for the post, and explaining that he had already been approached by a number of sisters.[104] He was well known to the leadership of all four federations – American, English, French and Irish – from a meeting held 21 to 31 May 1960 at the Eudist house in Rome.[105] Irish sisters who attended this or subsequent meetings state that he was greatly liked, skilled in moving matters along and possessed infinite patience.[106] He had an unrivalled knowledge of the rules and customs across all federations, what renewal was already under way and, as he stated himself, he knew the need for a 'quickening pace to canalize all efforts' lest the deviations become too great and a final synthesis near impossible.[107] His role as superior general of the Congregation of Jesus and Mary made him the 17th successor of St John Eudes, and his knowledge of the 'spirit and aims' of the founder and the 'sound traditions' of the order were beyond question.[108] However, these unassailable Eudist credentials would not have moved the Irish OLC sisters, nor those in other countries, to have him officially appointed 'to gather the observations and desires of the nuns themselves' unless they also had trust and confidence in him. Any of the monasteries could have opted to go it alone. He received his decree of appointment on 30 November 1966.[109] It was thus that the sisters of Our Lady of Charity of Refuge in Ireland were inducted into *aggiornamento* by Père Lacroix, so that their local experience cannot be considered without reference to the other houses and federations. The processes he proposed to OLC were, in all respects, the match of the 'methods of work' set out by the UISG in its interpretation of *Ecclesiae Sanctae II* with the explicit aim of 'exchanging experiences' across institutes.[110] The steps taken in OLC from preparatory discussion meetings through to the 1969 general chapter in Rome and the local chapters to implement the reforms were thus fairly standard, though that did not lessen their novelty to those involved.

103    High Park, circular letter, 20 Dec. 1963 (DARGS, OLC1/3/1 no. 28).
104    Fernand Lacroix, Rome, to All the Sisters of Our Lady of Charity of the Refuge, 7 Oct. 1966, copy letter, 2pp (DARGS, OLC5/3/1).
105    Irish federation general council, minutes, 4 Dec. 1959, 11 May 1960.
106    Personal communication, Sister Lucy Bruton OLC, member of the secretariat at the 1969 *aggiornamento* general chapter, Rome. 14 July 2012.
107    Lacroix to OLC, 7 Oct. 1966.
108    *Perfectae caritatis*, 'General principles of renewal', no. 2 (a).
109    Irish federation general council, minutes, 30 Nov. 1966.
110    UISG, *Revision of the constitutions*, p. 11.

The first step in the process of renewal, a questionnaire survey, translated from what the French federation had already implemented a year earlier, was distributed in November 1966. It asked sisters to suggest the problems that arose under various headings: the practice of obedience, poverty and the apostolate among the girls; exercises of piety; community life; work together (team-work); enclosure and relations with one's family; maintaining unity between contemplative and active life; the opinions of outsiders on religious life as it was lived in their monastery; and an open 'suggestions and views' question.[111] No indication of their name or monastery was to be given. Written responses were forwarded to the federation leadership, who followed this up with the novelty of discussion groups in each monastery, where there was a further sharing of opinions.[112] The responses were duly collated, numbered and indexed under the questionnaire headings, but with chastity and government given their own sections. These 231 propositions – though unscientific in that opinions were generally returned without weighting (said by one person? By 20?) – nevertheless allowed the concerns of the ordinary OLC sisters in Dublin to be heard, and revealed what in the conciliar teaching most immediately caught their imagination.

Not surprisingly, the 1967 survey results brought to notice a large number of domestic arrangements around which there was dissatisfaction, most of which were tackled – if not over the next few months, at least within the next decade – and which would not be the business of a post-conciliar general chapter: the lack of hot water, the bulk purchase of shoes and the false economy of over-repairing, the asking of 'petty permissions' within the house to lend or borrow small items, the barrack-like community room, which 'ought to have the appearance of a home, even to have arm chairs is recommended'.[113] The day's timetable left little, if any, choice to the individual, with repeated appeals to lift the obligation to sew during recreation time, to be 'allowed to go out walking in groups and not in procession', even perhaps to walk in the locality 'with choice of companion or perhaps with some of the girls'.[114] Norm 26 was quoted verbatim and underscored by one respondent: 'In all cases the order of the day must be arranged in such a way as to provide for the religious, besides the time given to spiritual exercises and apostolic activities, *a little time for themselves* and sufficient time also for legitimate recreation.'[115]

There are demands for further updating in all that related to the work with the girls (chapters 11 and 12), and a concern about equity, justice and greater respect for the individual girl or woman resident: 'Opportunities, equipment and time for developing gifts of intellect and nature should be available to all, according to their capabilities; at present, only a select few are benefiting by such openings'.[116]

---

111  Irish federation general council, minutes, 19 Nov. 1966.
112  Ibid., 26 Apr. 1967.
113  Questionnaire, nos. 8, 10, 13, 34, 47, 49, 160.
114  Questionnaire, nos. 155, 159, 162, 174, 180, 184.
115  *Ecclesiae Sanctae II*, no. 26 as quoted in Questionnaire, 162. Emphasis as in the original.
116  Questionnaire no. 66, see also nos. 6, 56, 114.

Most strongly-expressed in the survey returns was a desire for more autonomy, with entreaties from the sisters to be allowed decide on and purchase what they judged necessary for their own department.[117] The Council's teaching on obedience, traditionally at the heart of religious life, had a strong appeal: 'we agree that the sisters be treated as mature, responsible adult women, like our sisters in the world and be given scope to use our initiative in our employments'.[118] The superior's right to decide finally was not at issue, but the right to submit views and to be heard, to have 'regular discussions and staff meetings where opinions could be freely given and problems sorted out' was pressed, also that letters might come and go without being opened by the superior.[119] The traditional 'obedience', a short daily assembly for the exchange of information, was surrounded in ceremony and rather one-sided as, on most occasions, only the superior spoke.[120] It was not the kind of setting that promoted the open exchange of views that was now being urged.

Just before the questionnaire survey was activated, the council of the Irish federation went ahead and adopted the decisions of the French federation to suppress certain customs that were self-evidently archaic – kissing the ground, mortifications in the refectory – and which one could safely bet would be extinguished in the new constitutions, whatever their shape.[121] But until the process of *aggiornamento* had at least reached the point of experimental constitutions, federation and local leadership in Ireland played it safe, awaiting developments.

The guidelines that accompanied the setting-up of the discussion groups in 1967 – 'to follow the procedure of our other federations' – make it clear how unfamiliar the process was to the sisters: chairs to be arranged in a circle, a group leader to be chosen from the group, each sister assured that she had something to contribute, try to stay on the point, avoid exclusive arguments between two or three group members, encourage the silent to participate and those who 'have all the answers' to exercise restraint.[122] Co-responsibility was urged, as was patience and perseverance: 'Do not be tempted to give up trying because the discussion appears at time to be going badly; a session in which there is difficulty, tension and even a violent disagreement may be [of] more value than one in which there is only an exchange of platitudes'.[123] The suggested reading fits in exactly with the 'principal documents' listed in the UISG bulletin: the New Testament, conciliar documents (*Perfectae caritatis* and the published norms, also *Lumen gentium*), the current *Supplement to Doctrine and Life*, the OLC constitutions with amendments and the spiritual teaching of St John Eudes ('Charles Lebrun or any other').[124]

117   Ibid., nos. 21, 33, 42, 50, 58, 60.
118   Ibid., no. 81.
119   Ibid., nos. 2, 76, 83, 85, 81, 145, 165, 188.
120   Personal communication, Sister Teresa Coughlan OLC, 24 July 2012.
121   Irish federation general council, minutes, 26 Oct. 1966; copy letter, Superior General to My very dear Mother, 26 Oct. 1966 (DARGS, OLC5/3/1).
122   Sister M. of Blessed Oliver and Sister M. of St Aloysius to Dear Mother and Dear Sisters, 'Renewal and adaptation of our religious life', Apr. 1967 (DARGS, OLC5/3/1).
123   Typed memos, 'Formation of discussion groups', 'Group discussion', n.d. but from Apr. 1967 (DARGS, OLC5/3/1).
124   UISG, *Revision of the constitutions*, p. 5.

The move into discussion groups marked a transition: 'Our consider-ations have begun with surface problems and let us get these sorted out so that as time goes on our readings, discussion and serious thinking will result in contributions of more depth'.[125] The subjects for discussion had been drawn up by Fernand Lacroix for all houses, with the end view of in-forming a consultative meeting he planned for September 1967 in Rome.[126] This was to be purely a 'first contact' of representatives of the federations and non-federated houses, to agree the plan of work in preparation for the general chapter of the whole order and the revision of the constitutions, as requested by the Vatican Council.[127] The fruits of the Rome discussion, in terms of general principles, guidelines and suggestions, and the full min-utes of the meeting, were returned to the sisters for study and discussion, in line with the new *modus operandi*.[128]

There was a third purpose to the 1967 preparatory meeting, 'to study the possibilities of the unification of the whole Order, the necessity of which is felt more and more each day'.[129] This additional purpose was to create some sort of centralised authority superior to the federations and the non-federated monasteries, not strictly demanded by the Council, though in the general spirit of the reforms.[130] Fr Lacroix had raised it at the first American federation meeting of 1958 and it was on the agenda for the 1960 and 1967 meetings in Rome.[131] Centralisation, Lacroix urged, was 'absolutely neces-sary' to safeguard the unity of the order, 'to co-ordinate and direct the work of the *aggiornamento* and the evolutions which follow'.[132] There were already practical differences between the houses and, with the reforms now called, for more were certain. The four federations that existed by the time of the 1969 general chapter differed from each other in terms of governance struc-tures and powers. Even within geographical areas, there were houses that kept aloof from federation, as in North America and Mexico. Any sort of confederation, union or supra-council was viewed with apprehension – if not outright horror – by certain monasteries. The first federation, the French federation, expanded in August 1967 to become the more centralised Latin Union, with houses whose sisters were of Latin origin, in Spain, Italy and Portugal and, of course, France. That the American houses (federation com-menced 1954) feared a French takeover under the cloak of confederation was no secret. The Irish sisters gave full assent to Lacroix's 1967 address on

125   'Some reflexions (*sic*) in preparation for discussion', memo circulated by Sister M. of Blessed Oliver and Sister M. of St Aloysius, Apr. 1967 (DARGS, OLC5/3/1).

126   Of the seven sisters elected on 8 Jan. 1967 to the 'commission for the updating of our order', the general council elected Sister M. Aloysius (High Park) and Sister M. Blessed Oliver (Gloucester Street) to work together on the questionnaires and feedback from discussion groups in advance of the Rome meeting, Irish federation general council, minutes, 3 Jan. 1967.

127   Order of Our Lady of Charity, Rome meeting, minutes, 10–20 Sept. 1967, no. 1 (DARGS, OLC5/3/1).

128   'Summary of discussions on the minutes of the Roman meeting' – response of the Irish federation, Sept. 1967 (DARGS, OLC5/3/1).

129   OLC, Rome meeting, minutes, Sept. 10–20, 1967, no. 1.

130   *Perfectae caritatis*, no. 22.

131   General chapter, detailed minutes, 22nd session, 28 Oct. 1969.

132   OLC, Rome meeting, minutes, Sept. 10–20, 1967, nos. 3, 17.

the need for a central authority, despite being well aware of the disdain that their archbishop, Dr McQuaid (retired 1972, died 1973), had for the concept. They specified only that they would like it to be in Rome 'where it would be more neutral and international'.[133] Some of the Irish grassroots favoured a confederation or union over what they regarded as the pointless federation structure they had so far.[134] Although Lacroix delivered several tightly-argued papers in favour of centralisation, offered different versions of what it might look like, and patiently answered the many objections raised at a succession of meetings leading up to the general chapter of October/November 1969 at which it was a highly contentious issue, there was to be no agreement, so this matter may be left aside for the present.[135]

What the 1967 Rome meeting did manage to agree on was the creation of a 'Commission for the *aggiornamento* of the Order' made up of 16 members, with Sister Mary of St Bernard Scanlon (England) its chairman. She was to reside in Rome – 'in order to be impartial to the federations' – assisted by three of the commissioners, who together would form the 'central bureau'; one was the English-speaking Sister Bernadette Garritty from Buffalo, US. Though having no authority over the order, merely over the commission which would itself cease on the opening of the general chapter, Scanlon nevertheless was expected to acquire a 'concrete knowledge of the different parts of the order', and to work closely with the delegate, Fr Lacroix, to co-ordinate the work of preparation. The central bureau was funded by all the houses, equitably shared, federated and non-federated.[136] It therefore became a central OLC authority, albeit temporary and with few powers. Once the general chapter was formally convoked – to open on 5 October 1969 – and the election of delegates was completed, real plans took shape.[137] It was the central bureau in Rome that planned all the logistics of the chapter – formed the commissions, set the budget, organised a secretariat (a team of translators and secretaries, with all the necessary technology, such as translation booths, tape-recorders and 'spirit-duplicators'), sourced electronic voting machines, assigned bedrooms, arranged for daily Mass. From among the elected delegates, a smaller number of sisters was assigned to be part of a commission working on the texts for a particular area, such as community, prayer life and liturgy.[138] It was the central bureau that sent out to all chapter members syntheses of the material collated to date, what amounted to a 'preliminary draft' of the text of constitutions,

133   'Summary of discussions on the minutes of the Roman meeting' – response of the Irish federation, Sept. 1967 (DARGS, OLC5/3/1).

134   Questionnaire, nos. 89, 205.

135   Sister Lucy Bruton to Dear Mother and Sisters, 9 Oct. 1969 (DARGS, OLC5/3/1).

136   OLC, Rome meeting, minutes, Sept. 10–20, 1967, no. 18.

137   The general chapter was formally convoked on 25 Nov. 1968 to open on 5 Oct. 1969; for a lengthy discussion on why there was need for an indult of the Holy See to hold it and the structure of the electoral colleges, see Fernand Lacroix to Dear Revd Mothers and very dear Sisters, 25 Nov. 1968, copy letter (DARGS, OLC5/3/1).

138   Seven delegates were elected for Ireland, of whom four were chosen to be commission members: Carmel Staunton, Aloysius Pilkington, Columba Cunningham, and Divine Child (Anne) Kerrane. Mother M. Eithne O'Neill to My dear sisters, 24 Feb. 1969 (DARGS, OLC5/3/1).

but 'as a basis only for discussion'.[139] The work was conducted in four languages.

The January 1969 central bureau meeting in Rome was expanded to a 'consultative meeting' of all the federation presidents, chaired by Fernand Lacroix, in advance of the general chapter to open in October of that year. Another pre-chapter meeting important to the Irish federation was held in Bitterne in April at which three of the Irish sisters already elected as chapter delegates were present, along with Lacroix, the superior of the Latin Union and a number of others from outside the English federation.[140] The French houses and those associated with them in the Latin Union (including the houses in Mexico) held their pre-chapter meeting at Le Mesnil in February 1969, while the American federation also had pre-chapter meetings. No sister or house could say they did not know what was happening, except perhaps the OLC sisters of Carrollton, Ohio, which was not part of the American federation and which did not participate at all in the preparations for the general chapter or send a representative. Lacroix did all possible to persuade the superior to become involved, and suspicions were entertained that she simply ignored all his entreaties and told her subjects nothing at all.[141]

## The 1969 *Aggiornamento* General Chapter, Rome

The *aggiornamento* general chapter of the Order of Our Lady of Charity opened on 5 October 1969 at the Institute of St John Eudes in Rome (figure 13.2). The 45 capitulants or chapter members, representing all four federations and practically all non-federated monasteries, were drawn from houses in France, Ireland, US, England, Portugal, Italy, Canada, Spain, Mexico and Kenya.[142] The president was the special delegate of the Holy See, Fr Fernand Lacroix, CJM, who had been directing preparations, assisted by the central bureau, for three years. For the next few weeks, the general chapter itself became the supreme governing authority of the order, with its own internal dynamic. In a sense, all that had gone before was now suspended: the chapter would vote its own rules and procedures, agree its own programme and order of day, appoint its own six-member central committee (taking over from the central bureau) and other committees (liturgy, finance, 'other services'), approve the secretaries and translators, elect scrutineers (for the voting) and decide on the moderator for each session. It was the chapter that would decide the composition of the various commissions, the subject matter of each, and the ways in which this group

---

139  Central bureau, Rome, 'Preliminary project of a text of constitutions to form a basis for discussion now and the general chapter in October', 16 June 1969 (DARGS, OLC5/3/1).

140  The meeting was scheduled for 13 to 20 Apr. 1969 and the sisters were Carmel Staunton, Aloysius Pilkington and Columba Cunningham, Irish federation general council, minutes, 12 Apr. 1969.

141  General chapter, detailed minutes, seventh session, 10 Oct. 1969 and 26th session, 31 Oct. 1969.

142  The chapter sent a formal letter to Mother M. Clare Huriek, superior, Carrollton, Ohio, insisting on the necessity of her presence or that of a delegate. She replied, giving as the reason for non-involvement that no sister could be spared from their 'exceptionally busy' work. General chapter, detailed minutes, seventh session, 10 Oct. 1969 and 26th session, 31 Oct. 1969.

**Figure 13.2** Group photo of delegates at the 1969 OLC general chapter meeting in Rome along with committee members, secretarial assistants, Fr Fernand Lacroix CJM, president, and Fr Paul Milcent CJM, theologian. Mother Eithne O'Neill, superior general of the Irish federation (1964–71), seated, front row, is in the old version of the habit; Sister Lucy Bruton, Sean MacDermott Street and one of the secretaries at the chapter, is standing to the far left. (DARGS, OLC5/3/1).

work would be carried out and brought back to the full assembly.[143] Only the chapter could declare itself closed. In his opening address, Lacroix set out the goal of the chapter, the renewal of the order demanded by Vatican II, and made more explicit in the *motu proprio* (in the Pope's own words) of 1966, *Ecclesiae Sanctae II*:

> The revisions of the constitutions is really the technical part, *aggiornamento* is much larger, it concerns the spirit, a change of mentality. But this must be put into concrete texts, the basic texts of the Institute. The directories also have to be renewed, but the constitutions are the prime concern.[144]

143    'The Special Chapter of the Order of Our Lady of Charity convened October 5, 1969, under the presidency of Rev Fr Lacroix … at the Institute of St John Eudes, Rome', general minutes of sessions 1–3, held 7–8 Oct. 1969 (DARGS, OLC5/3/1). Hereafter General chapter, general minutes.
144    General chapter, general minutes, first session, 7 Oct. 1969.

The sisters were not free to ignore the requirement to update the consti-tutions, nor could each house or group work alone to produce their own version, 'the entire Order must be represented – For only as a decision of the entire order – federations, union and autonomous houses – can they be presented to the Holy See for approval'.[145]

The second goal, establishing a confederation of the entire order, was added by Lacroix; this he appreciated was 'contested by some' (as indeed it was) and, though not as important as the first goal, was flagged by him at the opening session.[146]

Lacroix dealt at length with the difficulties that the sisters would face in chapter. They had little experience of such meetings and few traditions or routines to draw on – since its foundation in 1641 there had been only three OLC chapters, 1734, 1909 and 1931, all held in Caen, compared to the 57 chapters held over a shorter life-span by the Eudist fathers. The challenge of conducting proceedings in the four languages of the chapter, English, French, Spanish and Italian, was first technological, but it was more than that: words 'even when translated' do not mean the same thing. There was the difficulty of 'the various mentalities of the sisters' and the nationalistic, even antagonistic, feelings brought to the meeting: 'we religious try to re-main above these human difficulties and weaknesses but we are human and the products of our own countries and mentalities and therefore find it hard to understand one another. We consciously or unconsciously prejudices (*sic*) against one another'.[147] He urged at length what he termed the 'means of a moral and psychological order' that would ensure the success of the chapter:

> Liberty taken means that we must feel completely free to say what we think that the order should be, with respect for other opinions, but still to be sincere and frank in what we think and feel. Liberty recognised and accepted by others. If this is not recognised we will go astray. So we must have a great respect for other's opinions, whether they are of the same country or not. We must control our sensibilities and listen to the opin-ions expressed by other countries. When a point comes when we are in opposition, we should not just express opposition, but try to come closer to understand why the sister feels this way. In this way we have liberty taken and recognised.[148]

From his involvement in numerous federation, inter-federation and individual house meetings in North America and in Europe over at least a decade, including the meetings in Rome in 1960 and 1967, and from his knowledge of the discussion feedback that came from every federation and from every house in the two years of intensive preparation for this very meeting, Lacroix may be credited with knowing his audience well. He

145   Ibid.
146   Ibid.
147   Ibid.
148   Ibid.

urged great objectivity among the chapter delegates, 'which means in practice great elasticity and suppleness', warning against giving what happened
in any country 'an absolute value': 'if you feel you cannot accept another
country's views and values as being of use, it is better that you leave immediately as otherwise we will do no good'. The sisters were assembled, not
merely to represent their own monastery or federation, but to consider the
good of the order as a whole. In the face of radical opposition,

> We must find a formula to take both points of view into ac-
> count. This is elasticity. We must have courage to find solu-
> tions to problems, but above all, we must have imagination.
> It is this which is often lacking. At the end of the chapter, we
> must find ourselves not three or four congregations but one
> unique order.[149]

In urging the sisters to have confidence in each other, to believe that each
sister loved the order, the final necessity for a successful conference was an
atmosphere of prayer and union with God:

> He has told us that He is the way, the truth and the life. He
> will show us the way if we put ourselves in His light, and He
> will give us the grace to arrive at the right decisions. He is
> the motor, the animator. We must come close to the Lord and
> we will meet each other in Him. He will be the guarantee of
> Union that we wish to create and preserve.[150]

Of all the matters that were to concern the delegates over the seven weeks of
the chapter (it was declared closed on 29 November 1969), the need to identify the end or purpose of the order, to be clear about what it was, and what
it was not, was paramount. This was exactly in accord with what Rome
had prescribed in the general principles of renewal enunciated in *Perfectae
caritatis*.[151]

The 'free exchange of views' set out for the first few days of the chapter
and undertaken initially in language groups centred on the theme: 'Our
Lady of Charity in the Church and in the world of today; what it was, what
it is and what it should become'. This resulted in a storm of requests for
clarification, no doubt the intention of its skilled facilitator. 'The end of the
Order is important, we must have a very precise idea of it, and the best
opportunity to do this is when all the countries are meeting here together'.[152]
There were also some timely contributions from outside experts, such as
Bishop Le Bourgeois of Autun, a former superior general of the Eudists,
who in question-and-answer session cut straight to the core: 'the good of the

149   Ibid.
150   Ibid.
151   *Perfectae caritatis*, 'General principles of renewal', no. 2 (b).
152   General chapter, general minutes, fourth session, 8 Oct. 1969.

work must command the institute, not the other way round'.[153] But it was the work of the commissions that moved the programme along. Each commission had to produce a text on the subject assigned to it. 'These texts will be studied, criticised and pulled apart in all the other commissions, then brought to chapter and as a whole and voted upon.' What enabled progress, not just *non placet*, was the rule that the reports from the groups must give both the majority and minority criticisms, 'and Fr Lacroix has been very dogmatic on the fact that if they criticise a text they must be able not only to say why they criticise, but they must be able to give an alternative text'.[154]

The work of Commission 1 is a good example of how the entire chapter membership, across all languages and countries, was active in shaping successive versions of what would appear finally under the heading, 'Constitution 1: Our Lady of Charity in the Church'. The ponderous and jargon-filled language of committee-speak gave way, at least in part, to short, direct statements. Commission number 1, titled 'The apostolate' had as its secretary Sister Emmanuel O'Connor of Green Bay, Wisconsin, USA. Its subject matter was listed as 'the end of the order – the fourth vow – zeal for the salvation of souls – the missions'.[155] A prodigious amount of preparatory work had been completed by the central bureau and passed on to the pre-chapter commissions, including syntheses of questionnaire returns and discussion feedback. The sisters who formed each of the five commissions had themselves undertaken close study of the relevant conciliar and post-conciliar documents, the scriptures, the OLC constitutions and customs and the writings of John Eudes, in whatever editions or languages they had access to, knowing that they would be required to tie whatever articles they proposed to these primary sources. But, notwithstanding all this advance work, the first schema of Commission 1, Apostolate, as presented to the chapter was garbled and lengthy, trespassing into areas to be handled by other commissions, mixing the second person and the first person, and still not clear on what was, and was not, matter for constitutions. But in her oral presentation to the chapter, Sister Emmanuel O'Connor made clear the deep engagement there had been with the Council's teaching, and the real effort that was being made to take on civic responsibility, to become 'knowledgeable and involved' on matters such as welfare legislation, to participate in public debate and even – where it might arise – to campaign.[156] The other five commissions subjected this first draft to a very critical reading; they were not yet happy with the content, and the language still fell short of the 'simple, clear, unadorned' style advised by the UISG.[157] Among the points queried was the need to ensure that the apostolate was no longer perceived as tied to residential care but allowed family outreach, and that the inclination to brand women and girls as 'guilty' was extinguished. The fact that many of the girls admitted to the various houses had no idea of God or of sin, and certainly did not want to hear anything of religion, made carrying

153   Sister Lucy Bruton to Dear Mother and Sisters, 14 Oct. 1969 (DARGS, OLC5/3/1).
154   Ibid.
155   General chapter, general minutes, third session, 8 Oct. 1969.
156   General chapter, detailed minutes, 18th session, 24 Oct. 1969.
157   UISG, *Revision of the constitutions*, p. 11.

out the mission of John Eudes problematic. An assurance was given that, by treating the girl with great respect, 'though you cannot go as far as speaking to her of her Christian dignity, because she does not stay long enough in your house to be able to come to that point. Yet you give her a sense of human dignity and behaviour, and that for you is modified by Christian principles', a point that would be developed in the next version of the text.[158]

Pre-chapter submissions from Ireland were clear on the vocation of the order: 'we have been founded for the fallen and delinquent girl, we should not depart from our vocation in this important matter'. Underlying this was a concern that the institute in Ireland was being used as a home for 'mentally retarded girls', for whom the sisters could do very little in terms of training and for whom the concept of rehabilitation had no relevance. This was a concern for OLC communities elsewhere also.[159] Another concern that was raised at the chapter was of elderly women remaining in the house, 'because in the past, it was more our policy to protect them than to rehabilitate the younger ones into society. We believe now that we must keep those with us, but that it is not the aim of our Order to accept or receive any others'. Fr Lacroix gave a sharp rejoinder to the lengthening lists of all those whom OLC houses 'continue to receive': 'It is not a question of whether it was necessary to continue or not, but to know if there were other institutions in the country which would be able to take care of them'.[160]

Fr Lacroix insisted that the commission members draw up a list of exactly the types of persons who could, or could not, be beneficiaries of OLC work, so that they could find a formula for the constitutions which covered that point exactly, across all federations and all houses: 'As soon as you leave the field of social work for which you have been founded, if you are not careful in describing how far you can go you will be very easily brought into all kinds of social work which would bring you outside your specific service'.[161] Group discussion revealed an alarmingly wide range of activities across all countries. It was already evident that, unless the institute knew what its work was, and was not, it could not refuse anything at all that might be asked of it by bishop or state authority.

The first draft of article 1, on the apostolate, made reference to 'the charism of John Eudes' by which each sister was dedicated totally 'to the special service of those who suffer from spiritual, social and moral difficulties'; the judgemental language of 'fallen' or 'penitent' had been completely excised. There were also several references to the need to help women and girls to recover their dignity as children of God. The second (even lengthier) draft developed another line of thought, the sisters witnessing to the human dignity of the individual and more generally advancing respect for human dignity, justice and charity; it enlarged on the natural means (developing professional competences, co-operation and co-ordination with other agencies, and periodic evaluation of the community's mission) with

---

158  General chapter, detailed minutes, 21st session, 28 Oct. 1969.
159  Questionnaire nos. 99, 116, 117. See also General chapter 1969, general minutes, fourth session, 8 Oct. 1969.
160  General chapter, general minutes, fourth session, 8 Oct. 1969.
161  General chapter, detailed minutes, 21st session, 28 Oct. 1969.

the 'supernatural means' by which the goals would be pursued: the work of 'human readjustment' was one of spiritual collaboration with God's grace, already active. Far from insisting on religious conformity, the stance was one of sensitivity to real human values and real human goodness, 'to remain confident in God's action in them without forcing grace'. This respect for the 'personal liberty and the rhythms of grace' followed the headline set by *Gaudium et spes*.[162] There was an opening up of the institute to work among 'young Churches' and in the developing world, according to its own possibilities, and 'conscious of the missionary duty imposed on all Christians', a direct tie-in with the decree on the Church's missionary activity, *Ad gentes* (7 December 1965).[163]

In the third schema, very close to what was eventually ratified, the teaching of John Eudes was expounded: 'It is in the heart of Jesus and Mary that we discover those who are confided to us', and learned 'to see them with the eyes of Christ, and to love them with the heart of Christ'. In the revised version, there was a succinct rephrasing of the institute's traditional devotion that left less room for misinterpretation: the following of Christ was dealt with in one article, and devotion to Mary placed in another, worded to be more in accord with the teaching on Mary in *Lumen Gentium*, where her close connection to the history of salvation is emphasised, along with the unassailable centrality of Christ to the Church's faith.[164]

The wording of the first constitution as finally approved by the 1969 chapter was as follows:

> Art. 1. The Order of Our Lady of Charity, founded by St John Eudes in 1641, is an apostolic religious institute of pontifical right.
>
> Art. 2. It is especially for the service of socially and morally maladjusted girls and women who voluntarily ask for their help or who are confided to their care.
>
> Art. 3. As religious of Our Lady of Charity we ought to help those persons to recover confidence in life, to acquire or regain the sense of their human dignity and their personal value as children of God.
>
> Art. 4. We perform our work where the Lord has already called us, but in addition, conscious of the missionary duty imposed on all Christians, and sensitive to the urgent calls of the Church, we desire to work according to our own possibilities and among the young Churches and in developing countries.

---

162   *Gaudium et spes*, nos. 21–22.
163   *Ad gentes*, 'Decree on the missionary activity of the Church', *The documents of Vatican II*, Walter M. Abbott ed., trans. Joseph Gallagher (London and Dublin, 1966), p. 584, art. 2.
164   *Lumen gentium*, chapter VIII, pp 177–90.

Art. 5. Our special apostolate and the charity which animates it move us to be courageous witnesses in the Church and in the world regarding the human dignity of the individual.

Art. 6. It is in the Heart of Jesus that we discover those who are confided to us. We learn to see them through His eyes, to love them with His heart. We wish Christ to continue through us and by us His work of mercy and love.

Art. 7. God has associated Mary in the salvation of the world: the Holy Spirit has formed Jesus in her, and wishes her to co-operate also in the formation of Christ in the hearts of men. That is why, in our apostolic effort, we ask Mary to obtain for us the grace that, united with her, we may better co-operate in the action of the Holy Spirit whose humble instruments we wish to be.

The unanimous decision of the commission working on these articles, and endorsed by the chapter, to place the 'special wishes' of St John Eudes and his 'fundamental constitution' together as a preamble to the revised constitutions, turned what could have been an obstacle to the work of revision into an inspiration: the traditional, core teaching was given pride of place and without being dismembered.[165] It allowed the institute to move forward with the task as spelled out by the UISG, to 'spiritualise and personify the norms of life, re-discovering the primitive evangelical spirit and inspiring them with a new dynamism in the spirit of the Council'.[166] Scholarly input also helped in the discernment of what John Eudes had been about and how the 'primitive evangelical spirit' of the founding days might speak to the present. Four weeks into the chapter, Fr Paul Milcent delivered a long talk on the spirit of St John Eudes (he was later to publish the authoritative modern study of the founder).[167] The young Irish secretary, Sister Lucy Bruton, wrote back to Dublin that 'Everyone had been talking about the spirit of St John Eudes, but no one really knew what it meant, so it was decided that it was about time that someone defined it.'[168]

Progress was also furthered by Lacroix's close adherence to the advice that the constitutions should be a short book and hold 'only what is common to the whole Institute, what is essential and should not normally change'; into a separate book would go 'disciplinary prescriptions, particular and transitory'. The general chapter quietly shelved the customs book and made a fresh start with what came to be called the General Practical Directory (GPD).[169] This can also be seen as in part fulfillment of the instruction to free the institute from what had become obsolete:[170]

165   General chapter, detailed minutes, 29th session, 3 Nov. 1969.
166   UISG, *Revision of the constitutions*, p. 11.
167   Paul Milcent, *Un artisan du renouveau Chrétien au XVIIe siècle, Saint Jean Eudes* (Paris, 1985).
168   [Sister Lucy Bruton] to Dear Mother and Sisters, 7 Nov. 1969 (DARGS, OLC5/3/1).
169   UISG, *Revision of the constitutions*, p. 11.
170   *Ecclesiae Sanctae II*, no. 16.3.

By obsolete are meant those matters which do not constitute
the nature and objectives of the institute, and which, having
lost their significance and value, are no longer of real help in
the religious life, account being taken of the witness which the
religious life must provide.[171]

As noted already, the issue of confederation dominated the latter part of the
1969 general chapter. It took up many hours of meetings, variously constituted, and all of which were minuted in detail, testifying to the immense
efforts invested and the frustration felt by advocates of union when an agreement could not be reached. A compromise solution, which would avoid a
split (with some communities 'inside' and others 'temporarily outside') was
eventually voted through.[172] The 'council of the order' was modelled along
the lines of an episcopal conference, which a bishop did not need to join:
'by the very fact of being a member of the Order, you belong'.[173] It had few
powers and fell far short of what Lacroix had hoped for. Composed of the
federation presidents and an elected delegate from each federation, with
arrangements for the non-federated houses to have a representative, it was
to meet annually, and was to take responsibility for organising a general
chapter at six-yearly intervals. It elected from among its members a moderator for two years, whose powers were not at all those of a superior general.
Its role was primarily one of animation:

It seeks to keep the Institute faithful to the spirit of its founder, and the end for which it was founded; to work over its
spiritual and temporal interests, to work to strengthen unity
between the different federations, unions and autonomous
houses which compose it, and finally to encourage the sisters
to lead a spiritual and apostolic life, both personal and community, on all points conforming to the spirit of the Gospel
and the intention of St John Eudes.[174]

The first meeting of the provisional council of the order was held before
the chapter ended, on Friday 28 November 1969, though the fact that Fr
Lacroix would continue as the delegate of the Holy See for the *aggiornamento* of the order until the constitutions received the final approval of
Rome probably took somewhat from its sense of purpose. Under Sister
Bernard Scanlon of the English federation as its first moderator, its immediate and most practical task was to nominate a secretary and to appoint
competent sisters to do the final editing on the *ad experimentem* text of the
constitutions in the four languages, carrying forward the work of the general chapter.

171  Ibid., no. 17.
172  General chapter, detailed minutes, 43rd session, 17 Nov. 1969.
173  Sister Lucy Bruton to Dear Mother and Sisters, 21 Nov. 1969 (DARGS, OLC5/3/1).
174  Constitutions as approved by 1969 chapter, article 205.

## Implementing the 1969 *Aggiornamento* Chapter:
## The Federal Chapter of the Sisters of Our Lady of Charity,
## October 1973, Dublin

Only eight sisters – seven capitulants and one secretary – from the Irish federation were present at the *aggiornamento* general chapter in Rome 5 October
to 29 November 1969. The long letters composed each week on behalf of the
'Irish contingent' by Sister Lucy Bruton brought to those left at home some
sense of the unfolding drama of the chapter, as well as more homely matters – there were outings on Sundays, new foods and mad motorists. The
chapter itself was a 'veritable tower of Babel at the outset', with Mass (in the
vernacular) 'a polyglot affair'.[175] Rome itself was a wonder; there were tours
of the catacombs of St Callixtus, a visit to San Clemente thanks to the Irish
Dominicans, and an audience with Pope Paul VI, at which he extended his
apostolic blessing.[176] In St Peter's, 'the statue of St John [Eudes] is looking
down as you come in to the basilica and you would think he was peeping
out to see us'.[177] The principal work, the revision of the constitutions, had
been accomplished, and nobody could accuse the capitulants of rushing
them through. A compromise had been reached on centralised government
which did not threaten the existing structures. But the close of the general
chapter marked merely the first stage in the real business of *aggiornamento*.
Bringing the story home to Ireland, making it real in Dublin – with the sisters who made up the federation, in the works they had responsibility for,
in the convents and homes they owned – would be the test.

A short federal chapter was held in March 1970 at which the outcomes
of the general chapter in Rome were certainly discussed and typescripts of
the new constitutions were available, but much was left on hold until these
were formally presented to Rome.[178] The next federal chapter was held,
as scheduled, in January 1971, at which a new federal superior, Mother
Nativity Kennedy, was elected. The matter of simplifying the habit and veil
of the sisters, the dress of future novices, and when lay dress might be worn,
were among the matters aired.[179] But the chapter that mattered was the federal chapter of October 1973, held at Our Lady's Retreat House, Finglas, a
northside Dublin suburb. By this date, the revised English translation of
the constitutions, still *ad experimentem*, were in force. The local discussion
groups had been studying them 'in varying depth' and, 'in so far as they
are understood', the new constitutions were being practised.[180] The act of
promulgating the new constitutions on 4 January 1973 formally suspended
the constitutions of 1931; Fr Fernand Lacroix, who continued as the delegate

175   Sister Lucy Bruton to Dear Mother and Sisters, 9 Oct. 1969.
176   Same to same, 20 Oct., 7 Nov., 14 Nov. 1969.
177   Same to same, 20 Oct. 1969. This marble statue – funded jointly by the Eudist fathers,
OLC sisters and Good Shepherd sisters – was unveiled on 18 Feb. 1932; *Dans la charité du
Christ: Vie de la Très Honorée Mère Marie de Saint Ambroise Desaunais* (Caen, 1939), p. 229.
178   This was a continuation of the Aug. 1969 federal chapter which had been adjourned,
not closed.
179   Memo, Chapter 1971, Matters to be decided by the superior general and her council
(DARGS, OLC5/1/1 no. 6).
180   Federal chapter, minutes, 5 Oct. 1973, preliminary session, p. 7.

of the Holy See to the order (though by then also bishop of Edmundston, New Brunswick), declared the new constitutions 'the special legislation of your order' until the date of the next general chapter of the order, at which they would be reviewed.[181]

The Irish federal chapter of October 1973 followed much the same pattern as the *aggiornamento* general chapter of 1969: composed of *ex officio* and elected delegates (22 sisters in all), at the preliminary session it voted its own rules and procedures, appointed secretaries and scrutineers and elected four moderators to chair the sessions. With the chapter secretary and one other nominee, these would form the central co-ordinating committee.[182] The group that had overseen the preparations thus dissolved on the opening of the chapter. It voted to allow observers from the different communities to attend the plenary sessions, an invitation that was taken up most days, and there was also one outside observer, Sister Mary Coyne of the English federation, present on behalf of the council of the order in a symbolic or supportive role only. The preliminary commissions were constituted by the federal chapter to be chapter commissions; each had prepared a draft document to be presented, discussed and voted on in plenary session. The report of the apostolate committee (figure 13.3) would be especially far-reaching. Before the voting stage was reached, there was ample time for the responsible commission to study the document in the light of interventions and to make amendments – it could be returned for discussion as many times as required – but it was the chapter – as the highest authority in the federation – that made decisions: 'all capitulants must expect differences of opinions and realise that ultimately it is the vote which decides issues'.[183] The headings dealt with by the commissions, as they featured in the final agreed 'Statutes, regulations and recommendations of the Federal Chapter', were religious apostolic life (prayer, community life, community regulation), apostolate, missions, formation, government, temporal administration. Given the task of producing a local directory, the challenge was to be faithful to the spirit of *aggiornamento* as articulated in the conciliar documents and in the order's new constitutions, in a way that could be embraced by four essentially autonomous communities. The challenge was nowhere on the scale of what was faced in Rome in 1969, but it was not to be discounted either.

The federal superior's summary report covering 1970–73 details how much the move to small group care had advanced, including the reconstruction of houses into self-contained units (see chapters 9–12). There were residential units for teenagers (High Park, Sean MacDermott Street), for children (two units in High Park, one in the Grange), an after-care unit (The Grange) and groups for older women (three in High Park, three in Sean MacDermott Street). But there were also 'new works', involving the reconstruction or reallocation of existing buildings: a project with women working in prostitution (bungalow at High Park), a transition hostel (Sean MacDermott Street) and casual unit (Sean MacDermott Street), also the 'Girlsville' transition unit at

181 Letter of promulgation, 4 Jan. 1973, Constitutions of Our Lady of Charity, 1973, p. 3 (DARGS, OLC5/3/1).
182 Federal chapter, minutes, 5 Oct. 1973, preliminary session, p. 2.
183 Ibid.

"WE WISH CHRIST TO CONTINUE THROUGH US AND BY US HIS WORK OF MERCY AND LOVE"

*Apostolate Report* 1972

*Irish Federation of Our Lady of Charity*

**Figure 13.3** Cover sheet of apostolate report, 1972, Irish federation of Our Lady of Charity. (DARGS, OLC 5/5/7 no. 2).

St Anne's, Kilmacud, and two new 'family group homes', accommodating 12 each, at The Grange.[184] Martanna House Hostel, in the grounds of High Park, for girls in transition, was supplemented by 124 Grace Park Road (seven girls). A very small number of girls on remand, no more than four in total at any given time, could be received in Grianán (High Park), the Casual Unit (Sean Mac-Dermott Street) and St Anne's (Kilmacud) 'for a temporary period pending the building of a new state prison for women'.[185] Residential care for 'persons of low intellectual ability, likely to be exploited and for whom no other provision is made' would continue for those already in OLC care, but the chapter resolved that no other persons in this class were to be admitted, even for short-term care, without careful prior investigation and with full consultation with the health board and with organisations 'directly involved with mentally handicapped'.[186] Accommodation for 'lady boarders', the guest houses at

184   For young people, 'small group' meant 10 to 15 maximum; for the women, the groups were 35 to 40 maximum.
185   Report on the state of the Irish federation 1970–73, federal chapter, minutes, 5 Oct. 1973, preliminary session, pp 1–8a.
186   Statutes, regulations and recommendations of the federal chapter, minutes, 7–13 Oct. 1973, no. 15. Hereafter, Statutes, regulations and recommendations.

High Park (St Michael's) and Kilmacud (Kilmacud House) would be 'retained but not developed', with a note that, in the long term, this work might be entrusted to another body.[187] These changes were to realign with what the new constitutions specified as the purpose of the order, 'for the service of socially and morally maladjusted girls and women who voluntarily ask for their help or are confided to their care'.[188] Emphasis was to be placed on rehabilitation in 'open settings', each unit to make explicit provision 'with regard to visits, holidays, training in use of leisure time, giving help when out of work, etc.'[189] In what was traditionally called the field of 'preventive work', those children 'deprived of a normal home life' (in addition to 'young persons endangered by the irregularities or immorality of their families') could be cared for, but 'we aim at giving them a home in keeping with today's standard of living and at preparing them to meet life according to their ability and background'.[190]

The 1973 federal chapter reported on non-residential care, still a very new field for OLC in Ireland, and made possible further experiments through clubs 'or any other acceptable forms of rehabilitation that may present themselves'.[191] There was co-operation with the Legion of Mary in its 'picket work', and in its future plans to provide an emergency service for women working in prostitution. The involvement of legionaries with the sisters of Our Lady of Charity dates from the very foundation of the Legion in the 1920s, but for the sisters in Ireland to get personally involved in street rescue work was unprecedented.[192] Of broader appeal was the 'foyer project' or 'Contact' set up at federation level as an experimental project in October 1972.[193] This advertised itself as a free, confidential and non-denominational advisory service that aimed 'to offer to young people a preventative and supportive service that will help short-term wanderers avoid becoming long-term drifters, and to inform them of existing services'.[194] It had drop-in offices in the centre of the city, 13 Westmoreland Street, and involved three qualified social workers (two sisters and a young lay woman). It offered a six-day service with a telephone number for further out-of-hours contact and, in its first nine months of operation, it reported 416 persons assisted with 1,129 visits.[195] Another development was the presence of two sisters teaching catechetics part-time in local schools.[196]

The efforts of the sisters to become better informed about contemporary problems, as the general chapter had urged, is evident from a scrapbook titled '1973: news cuttings re the Apostolate'.[197] This collection reflects how lively and informed public debate had become across a wide range of social

---

187   Statutes, regulations and recommendations, no. 17.
188   Constitutions of Our Lady of Charity, 1973, art. 2.
189   Statutes, regulations and recommendations, nos. 18, 21.
190   Ibid., no. 16.
191   Ibid., no. 18.
192   Report on the state of the Irish federation 1970–73, p. 6; High Park local council, minutes [2 May 1972–21 Nov. 1978], 8 Jan., 25 June, 9 July, 8 Aug., 16 Aug., 20 Aug., 3 Sept., 1 Oct., 22 Oct. 1973 (DARGS, OLC1/5/2 no. 4).
193   High Park local council, minutes, 13, 19 June, 12 Sept. 1972, 29 May 1973.
194   'Youth advisory service', *Irish Press*, 6 Feb. 1973. See also 'Contact for the needy', *Irish Independent*, 8 Feb. 1973; 'Helping the young who are at risk', *Sunday Press*, 11 Feb. 1973.
195   Report on the state of the Irish federation 1970–73, p. 6.
196   Ibid.
197   Scrapbook of news cuttings (DARGS, OLC1/12/4).

issues and how many different groups and individuals contributed to the discourse, with the Catholic Church a very active participant. Student research papers, undertaken by a number of OLC sisters with other classmates both lay and religious, show that some at least of the community were keeping abreast of the new thinking. One research paper, on adolescent girls 'in need of care and protection in Dublin', had as preamble an extract from the Constitution on the Church in the modern world (*Gaudium et spes*), which warns against being content with an 'individualistic morality' in this time of 'profound and rapid change':

> It grows increasingly true that the obligations of justice and love are fulfilled only if each person, contributing to the common good, according to his own abilities and the needs of others, also promotes and assists the public and private institutions dedicated to bettering the conditions of human life.[198]

The willingness to at least try to read 'the signs of the time', to collaborate with others and to experiment with new ways of assisting what had always been the target group – women and girls on the margins of society – was grounded in the new Church teaching. There was data collection, reflection and much discussion, but there was some action also.

The desire expressed by the federal superior at the opening of the chapter in 1973 is a succinct summary of the challenge of *aggiornamento*: she hopes that, with prayer and dialogue, they might continue the attempt 'to reconcile the best of the old and the new as we search for a community life that is truly based on the spirit of the Gospel and the charism of St John Eudes'.[199] This recalls the teaching of *Perfectae caritatis*, that the gospel be taken as the supreme rule of all religious institutes, and that the spirit and aims of the founder be faithfully accepted and retained.[200] How the founding charism might be understood was central to the deliberations of the general chapter in Rome, but the federal *aggiornamento* chapter was, rightly, more concerned with its interpretation in concrete, local circumstances, with all their inherited limitations and real potential, than with reflection on it academically or historically.

## Girls on Remand

In the reflections on religious life and the apostolate proper to Our Lady of Charity called for from 1966 onwards, one area of work features in the records as contentious, namely the admission of girls on remand from the courts to certain of the homes operated by the sisters. The 'inappropriateness of religious sisters managing high security centres' was minuted at meetings in the

---

198   *Constitution on the Church in the modern world*, chapter II, no. 30, as quoted in preamble to 'Report on adolescent girls between the ages of 14 to 18 years in need of care and protection in Dublin', working team Sister Mary Wall OLC, Colette Murphy, Bernadette Ryan, Francis Barrington, Brendan Jackson, Mark Mulvin, Dublin Institute of Adult Education, 62 Eccles Street, Dublin 7, Apr. 1973 (DARGS, Library).
199   Report on the state of the Irish federation 1970–73, p. 7.
200   *Perfectae caritatis*, nos. 2 (a–b).

late 1960s, and continued to be a matter of contention in the 1970s.[201] The sisters had no problem facilitating 'probation with condition of residence', because this always involved the consent of the girl given before the judge. How real and informed the consent was is another matter, but at least the principle of consent was there and the girl had her own probation officer, appointed by the court, to see to her welfare and to speak up on her behalf.[202] The remand girls were simply there as short-term prisoners and unlikely to derive much benefit from their stay. Where 'involuntary admission' might fit into the charism of the order was a serious matter for reflection among the sisters. After all, their mandate, to look out for those on the edges of society, included those 'who lack the desire to profit from good example'.[203] Extricating themselves from involvement in remand would be one of the priorities of the Irish federation's apostolate committee, despite the fact that it was the express wish of Archbishop McQuaid that they facilitate the Department of Justice.

The use of religious institutes as remand centres was symptomatic of the failure of the state to provide its own remand home in which young females or first-time offenders could be kept separate from convicted prisoners. Various proposals for a stand-alone remand home, accessible to the city yet 'removed from its less favourable atmosphere', had been advanced – and abandoned – in the early 1940s, including the conversion of the Mercy working girls' holiday house at Ballyroan, County Dublin, and of St Michael's ladies' guest house at High Park.[204] Use of the OLC convent at Sean MacDermott Street as a remand home from 1960 was seen by the sisters as something to reverse as soon as possible.

In their unease with remand centres, the sisters had the support of their colleagues overseas. The superior of the French union spoke of how, in line with current trends, they had moved their work of education and re-education into 'more open settings', using 'more liberal methods that place the young people in as much contact as possible with real life', so that they might 'give those in our care the sense of their dignity, the opportunity of exercising their freedom and the possibility of developing their autonomy'. The OLC sisters in France were speaking from long and, at times, bitter experience, and their advice was unequivocal: 'resist the advances of the state authorities who would, for their own peace, wish us to continue to care for difficult young persons far from the society they disturb.'[205] The agreement in 1972,[206] to keep places for a very small number of teenage girls on remand – no

---

201   For example, 'Report on the work of the Apostolate Committee, appointed August 1969', 1972 (DARGS, OLC5/5/7 no. 1).
202   J. Boland, private secretary to Minister for Justice, to private secretary to Roinn an Taoisigh (*sic*), 6 May 1957 (NAI, Department of An Taoiseach, S13290 A/1). Minutes, meeting of the Apostolate Committee, 11 Sept. 1969 (DARGS, OLC5/5/7 no. 1).
203   'Some passages from the Annals relevant to the Apostolate' (DARGS, OLC 5/5/7 no. 1).
204   See correspondence involving J. C. McQuaid; J.F.R. MacDonnell, chief probation officer; Mr J. Boland, Minister for Justice; S. A. Roche, Secretary, Department of Justice; Justice M. J. Hannan, various dates between 1 Jan.–7 Apr. 1942 (DDA, McQuaid Papers, Department of Justice).
205   Soeur Monique Marie Peron, French Union to Sisters of Our Lady of Charity, 30 Aug. 1973 (DARGS, OLC5/5/7 no. 2).
206   An Grianán, Sean Mac Dermott Street and St Anne's were registered on 9 June 1972, 'as places of detention for the purposes of Part V of the Children's Act, 1908'. General correspondence (unlisted), (DARGS, OLC1/3/8 no. 1).

more than four in total at a given time – between Grianán (High Park), the Casual Unit (Sean McDermott Street) and St Anne's (Kilmacud) was written up explicitly as a short-term expedient only, 'for a temporary period pending the building of a new state prison for women'.[207] The dilemma the sisters faced across all houses receiving girls and women committed by the courts was exemplified in the case of St Anne's in 1973, which they proposed to turn into a modern 'junior training centre' with built-in flexibility, 'to begin with a clean slate, freed from shackles of rigid departmental control as in reformatory'. But they were held back by the need for it to stay officially as a reformatory school, the only one for girls in the country, pending the setting up of a substitute by the Department of Education. But by doing so, they were once more letting the department off the hook and allowing it to do nothing:

> In fact, it looks like we are falling over backwards to preserve what we know to be an inadequate system. In the long term, the best service we can give delinquents would be to have the law – under which both we and they have suffered – changed.[208]

In the re-assessment of apostolate that was intrinsic to the renewal of religious life called for by Vatican II, why they had found themselves acting as prison warders, albeit occasionally and for a very small number of young women, with state funding, was something they wanted resolved.

## Governance Structures, the Apostolate Team, Formation and Overseas Collaboration

The creation of a new federal structure which would oversee both the ongoing modernisation of residential care and the new initiatives was perhaps the most significant post-Vatican II structural change to the institute in Ireland. What was named the 'apostolate team' was appointed by the federal leadership to operate across all houses and works, 'to be a co-ordinating centre for information and communication on matters relating to the apostolate within the Federation'.[209] It had its origins in the apostolate committee created in February 1971, and reconstituted by the federal chapter of 1973 as the apostolate team of four members, each with her area of special responsibility: older women, adolescents, children, special projects (Contact, Bungalow and others).[210] For near-autonomous houses, where the other communities barely knew their business and certainly did not proffer advice on how they might better conduct it, this was a departure that would have real, long-term effects: 'At stated intervals each member will hold meetings with the sisters

---

207   Federal superior's report, 'Report on the state of the Irish federation 1970–73, Federal chapter, Irish Federation of the Order of Our Lady of Charity minutes, 5 Oct. 1973, preliminary session, pp 1–8a (DARGS, OLC5/1/7).

208   Special meeting of the apostolate team, minutes, 28 Dec. 1973 (DARGS, OLC5/5/7 no. 1).

209   Statutes, regulations and recommendations, no. 22.

210   Irish federation general council, minutes, 17 Feb. 1971 also a local apostolate committee established in High Park, see High Park local council, minutes, 16 Oct. 1972, 13 Nov. 1972; Statutes, regulations and recommendations, no. 22, p. 9.

working in the field she represents, and at least once a year a general meeting of all involved in all fields.'[211] There was also a gesture towards collaboration with outside diocesan projects 'in work pertaining to our apostolate', though in the form of a recommendation not a regulation.[212]

In the area of formation or training to be offered to new entrants, measurable progress was made between the general chapter of 1969 and the federal chapter of 1973. An enthusiastic five-strong formation team, appointed early in 1971, took on as its first task the organising of 'live in' weekends and open days for girls interested in the OLC apostolate and also drew up an advertising brochure. Members of the team attended lectures and workshops on the topic held in Bellinter, County Meath, with formation personnel from other congregations, both men and women.[213] Given due credit for their efforts at studying and trying to implement 'the recommendations of recent decrees, documents etc. on novitiate formation', there were calls at the chapter to give the new formation programme and personnel a chance to develop.[214]

What the formation team proposed was derived largely from *Renovationis causam*, on the renewal of religious formation, issued by the Sacred Congregation for Religious and for Secular Institutes (6 January 1969). This instruction broadened the canons or regulations governing formation, to allow each congregation 'to make a better adaptation of the entire formation cycle to the mentality of younger generations and modern living conditions, as also to the present demands of the apostolate, while remaining faithful to the nature and special aim of each institute'.[215] The innovative OLC programme included apostolic formation periods outside the novitiate and a scholasticate after first vows, which would include 12 months 'complete integration in the community and apostolate of a house of the federation'.[216] The two-month programme of preparation before final vows was to be tailor-made to suit the individual candidate.[217] At the time of the federal chapter, the two novices with the congregation had just enrolled on the formation programme in Mater Dei Institute of Education in Dublin.[218] The concept of 'ongoing renewal', promoted in *Ecclesiae sanctae II*, was built into the remit of the formation team, and a period of renewal, every ten years or so, was legislated for in the federal statutes.[219]

The issue that dominated the later stages of the 1969 general chapter in Rome, namely centralised government, was barely mentioned at the Irish federal chapter of 1973. Governance issues that did arise were much more local: the powers of the federal leadership, the role of the federal chapter and

---

211  Statutes, regulations and recommendations, no. 22, p. 9.

212  Ibid., no. 22, p. 10.

213  Irish federation general council, minutes, 17 Feb. 1971; High Park local council, minutes, 15 June, 4 Sept., 9 Oct. 1970, 20 Apr. 1971.

214  Federal chapter, minutes, 9 Oct. 1973, eighth session, p. 38.

215  Introduction, Sacred Congregation for Religious and for Secular Institutes, *Renovationis causam*, Instruction on the renewal of religious formation, 6 Jan. 1969, English trans. from *L'Osservatore Romano*, CTS edn (London, 1969), p. 7.

216  Statutes, regulations and recommendations, nos. 32, 33.

217  Irish federation general council, minutes, 17 Feb. 1971.

218  Report on the state of the Irish federation 1970–73, p. 8.

219  *Ecclesiae Sanctae II*, no. 19; federal chapter, minutes, 11 Oct. 1973, 14th session, p. 56; Statutes, regulations and recommendations, no. 4.

the idea of having a separate federal house or headquarters, so that the federal leadership might be disentangled from the daily life of High Park.[220] The Irish federation was playing its part in the council of the order. It had returned comments and suggestions, the fruit of the small group discussions, to the secretary in Rome when the final editing of the new constitutions, in English, was under way.[221] It had sent two delegates to the council of the order meeting held in Wisconsin in October 1970,[222] and welcomed Sister Mary Coyne as the council's observer at the Irish federal chapter in October 1973, at which she shared with the Irish sisters lessons learned in England on the usefulness of an apostolate survey, and the setting up of commissions.[223] The formation statutes gave a glimpse of future possibilities of collaboration, with the note that, for sisters in temporary commitment, 'one year may be spent in a community of another federation, union or autonomous house of the order'.[224]

But, in terms of collaborating with OLC federations, unions and houses overseas, it was the precarious position of the foundation in Nairobi, Kenya, where there were already two Irish sisters 'on loan', that was taken up by the Irish federation. This was a follow-up of the Council's teaching that the Church is by definition missionary and, as articulated in the new OLC constitutions: 'Sensitive therefore to the urgent calls of the Church, we desire to work as far as we are able among young Churches and in developing countries'.[225] A report on the needs of Edelvale, the Nairobi house, was delivered to the federal chapter; founded in 1959 from the English federation at the request of Bishop McCarthy CSSp. It had become autonomous in 1967 to enable the setting up of a novitiate and because of the political situation at the time. It was now seriously overstretched, with low morale: 'The next three to five years will be crucial for this community and could mean survival or extinction'.[226] The chapter declared itself 'anxious to co-operate', despite the sacrifices it would entail, and drew up contract terms to cover the possible temporary transfer of a sister to Kenya.[227] It also voted to write into the statutes on formation an explicit invitation to new recruits: 'The Irish federation is anxious to promote our apostolate in missionary countries. Candidates who wish to devote some time in missionary service and whose qualities fit them for this work shall be encouraged and given appropriate training'.[228]

## Enclosure, Obedience and Life in Community

An engagement with 'the world' and an anxiety to keep abreast of developments was evident from the reports submitted to the federal chapter of 1973 and in the statutes, regulations and recommendations that came from the

220   Federal chapter, minutes, 7 Oct. 1973, third session, pp 16, 21.
221   High Park local council, minutes, 28 Apr. 1970.
222   Sister Columba Cunningham and Mother Mary Carmel Staunton were the delegates,
Irish federation general council, minutes, 4 Oct. 1970.
223   Federal chapter, minutes, 12 Oct. 1973, 16th session, pp 60–1.
224   The one year could also be spent in a house of another congregation. Statutes, regulations
and recommendations, no. 32.
225   *Ad gentes*, art. 2; Constitutions of Our Lady of Charity, 1973, art. 4.
226   Irish federation general council, minutes, 20, 31 Mar. 1958; 1 May 1959; Federal chapter,
minutes, 9 Oct. 1973, eighth session, p. 40.
227   Federal chapter, minutes, 9 Oct. 1973, ninth session, pp 40–2.
228   Statutes, regulations and recommendations, no. 29.

chapter. The ending of the obligation to maintain enclosure had been fully grasped by then, at least, if the number of sisters holding driving licences is taken as an indicator. About 12 sisters passed the driving test between 1970 and 1973 (there were 87 sisters in the federation).[229] An impressive amount of recent and ongoing training of the sisters could be reported in 1973: in arts, nursing, childcare, religious education, commercial subjects, at courses both full-time (11 sisters) and part-time (25 sisters). At the time of reporting, there were four sisters in full-time training: two in residential childcare, one preparing for her master's degree in psychology and one in career guidance.[230] Training for the apostolate required OLC sisters to travel outside the enclosure to lectures and workshops, widening their circle of contacts and their understanding of religious life as they saw – or heard about – other ways of doing things and the thinking that underpinned these different approaches.

On obedience, the Council's teaching on the relationship that ought to subsist between superior and subjects, and the right of each sister to have a voice in what pertains to the life of the community and to her own life and work, was taking concrete form. The small discussion groups created in preparation for the general chapter of 1969 sowed the seeds for a more inclusive local government at the largest monastery of High Park, where the sisters numbered 46 in October 1973.[231] The leaders of the four discussion groups became the first 'councillors' for High Park, each bringing her group's suggestions and findings to a larger 'council meeting', which included the superior and her assistant. In due course, the federal chapter decreed that 'the community as a whole is the local council' but, if a need was felt for a more restricted council, 'the community shall decide on the number of councillors and their method of election'.[232] The new statutes legislated for two kinds of community meetings: a meeting at which spiritual matters were discussed, and an administrative meeting, the form to be left to a local decision, but always to be with agenda, advance notification and minutes taken.[233]

In the midst of all the upheavals, it was the sharing in the Church's liturgical life through daily Mass and Office, as well as the opportunities for personal prayer, spiritual reading, retreats and recollection, that was credited with supporting and strengthening the life of the federation.[234] The chapel timetable had been simplified, with morning and evening prayer said in common, and compline (night prayer) to be said in groups or in private.[235] One of the challenges was to protect the Divine Office from having trimmings added, a balancing act between being true to the new teaching on the

229  Report on the state of the Irish federation 1970–73, p. 7; High Park local council, minutes, 30 May, 6 June 1972.
230  Report on the state of the Irish federation 1970–73, p. 7.
231  Ibid.
232  High Park local council, minutes, 28 Apr. 1970; Statutes, regulations and recommendations, no. 111.
233  Statutes, regulations and recommendations, no. 12.
234  Report on the state of the Irish federation 1970–73, p. 6.
235  Statutes, regulations and recommendations, no. 7.

liturgy and yet faithful to the much-loved prayer tradition of the order.[236] To manage this aspect of *aggiornamento*, a liturgical committee was to be set up in each house.[237] There had been some interesting input by speakers from other congregations on the subject of renewal and community life, with two workshops held before the chapter,[238] but the federal superior's report hints at the struggle to manage so much upheaval over such a short span: 'Many questions in the areas of unity, diversity, communal prayer, pluralism of lifestyle, interior renewal, emphasis on the person, mutual trust and under-standing, etc. remain to be answered'.[239]

In terms of community regulation, it was through numerous small changes, rather than a single upheaval, that daily life was brought more into accord with the spirit of *Perfectae caritatis* and with the new OLC consti-tutions. The 1973 statutes set out that 'the order of the day shall be arranged in such a way that each sister has time also for relaxation', and formalised one half day free per week, either morning or afternoon. The new statutes allowed each sister to 'assume personal responsibility for correspondence and phone calls' and also made provision for an annual holiday. The con-stitutions and statutes were to be studied and discussed in small group set-tings, no longer read aloud in the refectory.[240]

## Religious Dress

The group photo of delegates at the 1969 chapter meeting in Rome shows most of the sisters in a more modern version of the veil – showing some hair – and a mid-length cream habit, with scapular or pleats. Mother Eithne O'Neill, the superior general 1965–71 of the Irish federation, appears to be the only sister (among about 50 OLC sisters) still dressed in the old 'Sister Perpetua' version of the habit that had been set down by Caen (figure 13.1). As superior of High Park, there is evidence of Mother Eithne taking a hard line on any creativity with the habit – such as sisters 'tying on their ban-deurs in a new way' – so she was unlikely to be at the forefront of change to the dress.[241] The requirement by *Perfectae caritatis* that the religious habit, as a symbol of consecration, 'be at once simple and modest, poor and be-coming', in keeping with the requirements of health, suited to the times and place and to the needs of the apostolate, demanded some simplifica-tion at least of the OLC dress.[242] This was put in train in the High Park community in the early summer of 1970, when arrangements for remodel-ling the habits were made: 'Miss Pat Coyle is being employed part-time for measuring and cutting-out and Charlotte will come from the work-room to do machining'.[243] A month later, another machinist, Miss White, is also employed on the dresses, but the new veils and collars were the charge of

236   Federal chapter, minutes, 12 Oct. 1973, 15th session, p. 58.
237   Statutes, regulations and recommendations, no. 1.
238   Fr Cassidy CP, on community and prayer; Sister Sheila Noonan, Holy Rosary sisters, on community life. Federal chapter, minutes, 7 Oct. 1973, third session, p. 12.
239   Report on the state of the Irish federation 1970–73, p. 7.
240   Statutes, regulations and recommendations, no. 14, pp 4, 6.
241   High Park local council, minutes, 9 Aug. 1964.
242   *Perfectae caritatis*, no. 16.
243   High Park local council, minutes, 13 May 1970.

Sister M. Paschal, and the caps (for under the veils) the handiwork of Sister M. Rose.[244] At the 1973 chapter, there was heated opposition to legislating on the length of the dress: 'a sister's innate sense of modesty would tell her the proper length for her habit and how to comport herself as becoming a religious', and the approved statute simply states that the habit shall be cream with a scapular and the veil shall be black.[245]

The change in religious habit and the greater visibility of the sisters in the diocese were probably the aspects of *aggiornamento* that most caught the attention of outsiders in the mid-1970s. The teenage groups and training centres, the hostels and 'family group homes', with their comings and goings and more 'ordinary' style of life, also merited comment, at least among those with a genuine interest in the welfare of girls and women on the margins of Irish society. The 'old' refuges or asylums were still in existence in High Park and Sean MacDermott Street, but anyone who took the trouble to call would see how much more open and homely they had become, with small numbers and an older, settled clientele. Behind these identifiable changes was a much larger, complex and unfinished story. For each of the sisters, without exception, Vatican II would usher in a momentous personal upheaval. Hardly any aspect of life would be left untouched, and there was no standing back, unmoved by the flow.

Margaret Mac Curtain stops her study of Catholic sisterhoods on the threshold of the post-Vatican II era, recognising that the narrative commenced in the mid-19th century, for very many religious institutes in Ireland, is complete by the 1970s.[246] The present study of Our Lady of Charity in Ireland stops here for the same reasons. What happened next belongs to a new Ireland and a Catholicism that is very different nationally and internationally to that of the period 1853 to 1973. Post-Vatican II will be a separate historical study, but this work may help in understanding something of what went before.

---

244   Ibid., 15 June 1970, 16 Oct. 1972, 16 Apr. 1973.
245   Federal chapter, minutes, 12 Oct. 1973, 15th session, pp 58–9; Statutes, regulations and recommendations, p. 7.
246   Margaret Mac Curtain, 'Godly burden: Catholic sisterhoods in twentieth-century Ireland', reprinted in Margaret Mac Curtain, *Ariadne's thread, writing women into Irish history* (Galway, 2008), p. 323.

# Appendix A

Monasteries of Our Lady of Charity of Refuge, foundation dates and statistics 1909

| Name of monastery | Date of foundation | Address | Sisters | | Women and Girls | | | | Total household 1909 |
| | | | professed (choir, lay, tourier) | novices & postulants | penitents | preservation class | preservants | boarders / pensionaires | |
|---|---|---|---|---|---|---|---|---|---|
| Caen | 8 Feb. 1641 | 12 Quai Vendeuvre, Caen, Calvados | 69 | 14 | 150 | 102 | 91 | 36 | 462 |
| Rennes | 11 Nov. 1673 | Maison St Cyr, Rennes, Île-et-Vilaine | 79 | 5 | 139 | 169 | 68 | | 460 |
| St Brieuc | Jan. 1783 | Montbareil, St Brieuc, Côtes-du-Nord | 51 | 10 | 56 | 69 | 56 | 40 | 282 |
| La Rochelle | 21 Nov. 1715 | 23 Quai Maubec, La Rochelle, Charente-Inférieure | 41 | 2 | 36 | 29 | 28 | | 136 |
| Chevilly-Paris | 29 Sept. 1724 | Chevilly, par L'Hay, près Paris Seine | 70 | 5 | 217 | 45 | | | 337 |
| Versailles | 2 July 1804 | 18 rue du Refuge, Versailles, Seine-et-Oise | 57 | 6 | 166 | 24 | | | 253 |
| Nantes | 18 Dec. 1809 | 41 rue de Gigant, Nantes, Loire-Inférieure | 88 | 7 | 170 | 110 | 85 | | 460 |
| Lyon | 24 June 1811 | 69 rue des Machabées, Lyon, Rhône | 46 | 7 | 61 | 43 | 40 | | 197 |
| Valence | 19 Mar. 1819 | Près la Gare, Valence, Drôme | 38 | | 30 | 21 | 8 | | 97 |

*(Continued)*

*Appendix A continued*

| Name of monastery | Date of foundation | Address | Sisters | | Women and Girls | | | | Total household 1909 |
|---|---|---|---|---|---|---|---|---|---|
| | | | professed (choir, lay, tourier) | novices & postulants | penitents | preservation class | preserverants | boarders / pensionnaires | |
| Toulouse | 18 Oct. 1822 | 61 rue des Récollets, Faubourg St Michel, Toulouse, Haute-Garonne | 47 | 3 | 80 | 31 | 39 | | 20 |
| Le Mans | 3 May 1833 | Paroisse du Pré, Le Mans, Sarthe | 65 | 5 | 88 | 115 | | | 273 |
| Blois | 10 Aug 1836 | 9 rue de la Paix, Blois, Loir-et-Cher | 32 | 5 | 20 | 22 | 20 | | 99 |
| Montauban | 19 Aug 1836 | 105 Côte de Sapiac, Mountauban, Tarn-et-Garonne | 42 | 1 | 64 | 44 | | | 151 |
| Marseilles 1st monastery | 11 Jan. 1838 | 145 Boulevard Baille, Marseilles, Bouches-du-Rhône | 55 | | 89 | 32 | 16 | 40 | 232 |
| Besançon | 22 July 1839 | 10 rue de la Vieille Monnaie, Besançon, Doubs | 45 | 2 | 42 | 40 | 29 | | 158 |
| Dublin, 1st monastery | 14 Sept. 1853 | St Mary's Asylum, High Park, Drumcondra, Dublin, Ireland | 62 | 1 | 193 | 45 | 22 | 9 | 332 |
| Buffalo, 1st monastery | 8 July 1855 | 485 Best Street, Buffalo, USA | 55 | 4 | 45 | 52 | 75 | | 231 |
| Lorette | 19 Nov. 1856 | Refuge of St Joseph, Monte Reale, Loreto-Marches, Italy | 29 | 8 | 18 | 24 | 12 | | 91 |

| Name of monastery | Date of foundation | Address | Sisters | | Women and Girls | | | | Total household 1909 |
|---|---|---|---|---|---|---|---|---|---|
| | | | professed (choir, lay, tourier) | novices & postulants | penitents | preservation class | perseverants | boarders / pensionnaires | |
| Bilbao | 19 April 1857 | Refugio de la Caridad, Bilbao, par Begona, Spain | 37 | 3 | 80 | | 30 | | 150 |
| Bartestree | 23 Aug. 1863 | Refuge of St Anne, Bartestree, near Hereford, England | 41 | 5 | 62 | 39 | 45 | | 192 |
| Marseilles, 2nd monastery | 25 Jan. 1864 | St Coeur de Marie, près le Cabot, Quartier Ste Marguerite, Marseilles, Bouches-du-Rhône | 35 | 2 | 25 | 33 | 15 | | 110 |
| Ottawa | 19 Aug 1866 | 411 rue St Andrew, Ottawa, Canada | 58 | 9 | 96 | 60 | 42 | 2 | 267 |
| Valognes | 15 June 1868 | Rue de la Gare, Valognes, Manche | 52 | 3 | 72 | 74 | 61 | | 262 |
| Allegheny, Pittsburgh | 1 Nov 1872 | Troy Hill, N.S. Pittsburgh, Pa., Allegheny, USA | 32 | 14 | 84 | 80 | 56 | | 266 |
| Toronto | 15 Oct. 1875 | 14 West Lodge, Toronto, Ontario, Canada | 43 | 7 | 46 | 45 | 58 | | 199 |
| Green Bay | 14 June 1882 | Top Polier and Webster Avenue, Green Bay, Wisconsin, USA | 24 | 10 | 16 | 70 | 39 | 32 | 191 |

*(Continued)*

*Appendix A continued*

| Name of monastery | Date of foundation | Address | Sisters | | Women and Girls | | | | Total household 1909 |
|---|---|---|---|---|---|---|---|---|---|
| | | | professed (choir, lay, tourier) | novices & postulants | penitents | preservation class | perseverants | boarders / pensionnaires | |
| Waterlooville | 5 Oct. 1885 (re-established 1900 from High Park) | Refuge and St Michael, Cosham, Waterlooville, Portsmouth, England | 22 | 2 | 75 | | | | 99 |
| Dublin, 2nd monastery | 17 Feb. 1887 | 104 Gloucester Street, Dublin, Ireland | 21 | 1 | 110 | | | | 132 |
| Salzburg | 2 July 1888 | Monastère St Josef, Salzburg, Hellbrunner, Allée 14, Austria | 44 | 13 | 56 | 24 | 11 | | 148 |
| Vancouver | 8 Dec. 1890 | 14th Avenue Fairview, Vancouver, British Columbia, Canada | 18 | 5 | 18 | 30 | 11 | | 82 |
| San Antonio | 27 April 1897 | Corner of Rio Grande and Montana Avenue, San Antonio, Texas, USA | 13 | 0 | 74 | 38 | | | 125 |
| Saltillo | 16 Feb. 1900 | House of the Good Shepherd, 13 Calle Ramon Corona, Saltillo–Coah, Mexico | 6 | 9 | 38 | 32 | 4 | | 89 |
| Wheeling | 1 Mar. 1900 | Edginton-Wheeling, West Virginia, USA | 10 | 6 | 124 | 32 | 18 | | 190 |

| Name of monastery | Date of foundation | Address | Sisters | | Women and Girls | | | | Total household 1909 |
|---|---|---|---|---|---|---|---|---|---|
| | | | professed (choir, lay, tourier) | novices & postulants | penitents | preservation class | perseverants | boarders / pensionnaires | |
| Monterrey | 17 April 1905 | Senorita Directora, Casa del Buen Pastor, San Lusito, 123 Calle de Matamoros, Monterrey, N. L. Mexico | 6 | 3 | 40 | 23 | | | 72 |
| Northfield | 28 May 1906 | Bristol Road near Birmingham, Northfield, England | 7 | 3 | 24 | | | | 34 |
| Pittsburg | 31 May 1906 | Lincoln Avenue, E. E., Pittsburg, Pa., USA | 10 | 3 | 57 | 103 | | | 173 |
| Monmouth-Troy | 23 July 1906 | Troy House, Monmouth, Wales | 8 | 4 | 20 | | | | 32 |
| Buffalo, 2nd monastery | 26 Dec. 1907 | 3233 Main Street, Buffalo, New York, USA | 10 | 0 | 15 | | | | 25 |
| Hot Springs | 29 Sept. 1908 | Good Shepherd Convent, 118 Olive Street, Arkansas; Hot Springs, Texas, USA | 8 | 1 | 4 | 16 | | | 29 |
| Dallas | 1 Jan. 1909 | Convent of the Good Shepherd, Oak Cliff, Dallas, Texas, USA | 3 | 2 | 12 | | | | 17 |

*Source:* 'Liste des Monastères de l'Ordre de Notre Dame de Charité, dates de fondation et adresses'; 'État actuel des Monastères de l'Ordre de Notre Dame de Charité, 1909' (CIVSCVA B79/2)

# Appendix B

Federal superiors and local superiors, Federation of the Irish monasteries of Our Lady of Charity, created 5 November 1948, to 1977

| Date of election (by federal chapter) | Federal superior (superior general) | Died | Date of election (by general council) | Local superior, High Park | Died | Date of election (by general council) | Local superior, Sean MacDermott Street | Died | Date of election (by general council) | Local superior, St Anne's, Kilmacud | Died | Date of election (by general council) | Local superior, Kill of the Grange | Died |
|---|---|---|---|---|---|---|---|---|---|---|---|---|---|---|
| 24 Nov. 1948 | Mother M. of St Eithne O'Neill | | 24 Nov. 1948 | Mother M. of Blessed Imelda Jennings | 1 May 1960 | 2 June 1949 | Sister M. of the Sacred Heart Conroy | | 1944 sister in charge | Sister M. of St Carmel Staunton | | 6 May 1956 | Sister M. of St Francis Assisi Smyth | |
| 23 Nov. 1954 | Mother M. of St Eithne O'Neill | | 24 Nov. 1951 | Mother M. of St Eithne O'Neill | | 2 June 1952 | Sister M. of the Sacred Heart Conroy | 20 Mar. 1955 | 2 Feb. 1950 | Sister M. of St Carmel Staunton | | 6 May 1959 | Sister M. of St Francis Assisi Smyth | 30 Jan. 2000 |
| | | | | | | | | | 2 Feb. 1953 | Sister M. of St Carmel Staunton | | | | |

(Continued)

*Appendix B continued*

| Date of election (by federal chapter) | Federal superior (superior general) | Died | Date of election (by general council) | Local superior, High Park | Died | Date of election (by general council) | Local superior, Sean MacDermott Street | Died | Date of election (by general council) | Local superior, St Anne's, Kilmacud | Died | Date of election (by general council) | Local superior, Kill of the Grange | Died |
|---|---|---|---|---|---|---|---|---|---|---|---|---|---|---|
| 24 Nov. 1960 | Mother M. of St Rita Cutler | 22 Sept. 1964 | 29 Nov. 1957 | Mother M. of St Rita Cutler | | 18 April 1955 | Sister M. Immaculate Heart Walshe | | 2 Feb. 1956, elected superior | Sister M. of St Carmel Staunton | 19 July 1986 | 7 June 1962 | Sister M. de Montfort Goss | |
| | | | 29 Nov. 1960 | Sister M. of St Aloysius Pilkington | | 18 April 1958 | Sister M. Immaculate Heart Walshe | 7 Jan. 1963 | 2 Feb. 1959 | Sister M. Agnes Carlin | 30 Aug. 1983 | 3 June 1965 | Sister M. de Montfort Goss | |
| | | | 14 May 1964 | Mother M. of St Eithne O'Neill | | 18 April 1961 | Sister M. of St Joseph Dunne | | 2 Feb. 1962 | Sister M. of St Carmel Staunton | | 30 May 1968 | Sister M. de Montfort Goss | |
| 26 Jan. 1965 | Mother M. of St Eithne O'Neill | 2 Sept. 1993 | 3 Feb. 1965 | Mother M. of the Nativity Kennedy | | 14 May 1964 | Sister M. of St Joseph Dunne | 12 Feb. 1971 | 3 June 1965 | Sister M. of St Carmel Staunton | | | | |

| Date of election (by federal chapter) | Federal superior (superior general) | Died | Date of election (by general council) | Local superior, High Park | Died | Date of election (by general council) | Local superior, Sean MacDermott Street | Died | Date of election (by general council) | Local superior, St Anne's, Kilmacud | Died | Date of election (by general council) | Local superior, Kill of the Grange | Died |
|---|---|---|---|---|---|---|---|---|---|---|---|---|---|---|
| 26 Jan. 1971 | Mother M. of the Nativity Kennedy | 30 Nov. 1979 | 30 May 1968 | Mother M. of the Nativity Kennedy | | 11 May 1967 | Sister Blessed Oliver Murray | 22 April 1976 | 30 June 1968 | Sister M. of St Carmel Staunton | 30 Aug. 1983 | 8 Feb. 1970 | Sister M. de Montfort Goss | 12 Jan. 2012 |
| | | | 3 Feb. 1971 | Sister M. Aloysius Pilkington | | 14 May 1970 | Sister M. Kevin Smythe | | 27 May 1971 | Sister Veronica McCarthy | | 2 June 1973 | Sister M. de Montfort Goss | |
| 14 Feb. 1977 | Sister Teresa Coughlan | | 30 May 1974 | Sister M. Aloysius Pilkington | 28 Dec. 1999 | 2 June 1973 | Sister M. Kevin Smythe | 14 Aug. 2013 | 30 May 1974 | Sister Veronica McCarthy | 19 Jan. 2008 | 4 June 1976 | Sister Frances Thérèse Walsh | 19 July 2013 |
| | | | 19 April 1977 | Sister M. Genevieve Tobin | | 4 June 1976 | Sister Thomas Griffin | 21 Oct. 2000 | 10 June 1977 | Sister Alphonsus Lehane | | | | |

# Bibliography

**Primary Sources: Manuscript**

**Congregation of Our Lady of Charity of the Good Shepherd, Maison Mère du Bon Pasteur, Rue Euphrasie Pelletier, Angers**

### Archives historiques

Entrées et sorties des postulantes et novices depuis l'année 1829 commencement de cette fondation d'Angers, 1829–1872, Z-20.

Register of receptions and professions, EB1.01

Prises d'Habit, 1855–1935, Z-15

Obituaries, Irlande: Limerick, Belfast, Cork, New Ross, Waterford, DJ-6-01b

Statistiques de la Congrégation de N.D. de Charité du Bon Pasteur d'Angers, 1900–1921, bound volume, R-24

*Bulletin du Bon Pasteur*/Bulletin of the Congregation of the Good Shepherd of Angers, French and English versions, 1893–1939

'Recensement du personnel', Reports on the monasteries of Hammersmith, Limerick, Glasgow, Bristol, Waterford, Liverpool, New Ross, juillet 1861; other correspondence and memoranda 1840–89 relating to Good Shepherd foundations in Britain, EB-1.01

Community letters, notes on foundation and correspondence from 1840, Good Shepherd houses in Britain, HC-35

Community letters, notes on foundation and correspondence 1848–90, Good Shepherd houses in Ireland, HC-444 (b-f)

Letters, Mary Euphrasia Pelletier, foundress of Our Lady of Charity of the Good Shepherd; English trans. made in 1996 of French originals, vols I (1825–34), II (1835–36), III (1837–38), IV (1839–1840–1841 (Jan.–June)); V (July 1841–1844), VI (1845–48), VI (1849–55); VIII (1856–68)

**Union Notre Dame de Charité, Archives générales et provinciales de France, Cormelles-le-Royal, Caen**

Archives Besançon

Archives Caen

Archives Paris-Chevilly

Archives Rennes

Archives Tours

Archives Versailles

Archives NDC Chevilly Larue

Féderation Française (1945–67)

Paul Milcent, 'Notre-Dame de Charité, relations entre maisons', unpublished typescript, novembre 1998.

Delphine Le Crom, 'A la découverte des archives: la correspondance
entre les monastères', typescript notes, 27 août 2010

Delphine Le Crom, 'Coutumier: livres du couvent', typescript notes,
n.d.

## Dublin Archives, Religious of the Good Shepherd (Our Lady of Charity of the Good Shepherd), Beechlawn, Grace Park Road, Dublin 9

High Park, from 1829, OLC1

Gloucester Street / Sean MacDermott Street, founded 1887, OLC2

St Anne's, Kilmacud, founded 1944, OLC3

The Grange, Kill of the Grange, founded 1956, OLC4

Central Administration, Ireland, post-1948, OLC5

St Joseph's School, founded 1858, SJ

St Anne's School, founded 1944, SA (re-catalogued OLC3/8)

Lectures given by Rev. Paul Molinari SJ at the Annual General Meeting, 1971,
Conference of Major Religious Superiors, Women's Section, typescript
of four lectures.

OLC Beechlawn community, regional and congregational correspondence
2007–14

Memorandum titled 'On entertainment' by Sister Lucy Bruton, 8 Aug. 2011

## National Archives of Ireland, Bishop Street, Dublin

Census of population (Ireland), 1901, Household census returns for 1901

Census of population (Ireland), 1911, Household census returns for 1911

Department of An Taoiseach, Correspondence and memoranda 1943–58,
including 'Children: General; Kennedy Report and "Care" Proposals',
S13290 A/1

## Dublin Diocesan Archives, Clonliffe College, Dublin 3

Murray papers

    1847    32/3
    1848    32/4
    1849    32/5
    1850    32/6
    1851    33/1 (Laity, undated)

Cullen papers

    1852    325/4 priests
    1853    325/1 foreign bishops; 325/8 nuns
    1854    332/2 priests regular and secular; 332/3 laity; 332/4 nuns

1855   332/3 laity (Jan.–June); 332/7 file I, secular priests

1856   339/3, file II, nuns

1857   339/6, file II, nuns

1858   319/4 file II, nuns

1859   319/7 file III, nuns

1860   333/1 bishops

1860   333/2, secular clergy

1863   340/9, nuns

1866   327/5, bishops

1869   321/2, laity

1871   328/7, file V, nuns

1872   335/1, file III, nuns

1874   342/4, male religious

1876   322/6, file V, nuns

1877   329/4, file VI, nuns

## McCabe Papers

1878   337/3 file I, nuns

1879   337/3 file I, nuns; 337/5 file II, nuns; 337/4 file IV, secular priests

1880   346/3 file II, nuns

## Walsh Papers (uncatalogued)

Laity, 1884/5, 350/8

Religious, 1893–1920

## McQuaid Papers

Department of Justice, 1940–61

Government box, 545, Eamon de Valera, xviii/4/6/491–498: 1940–1947; 1952–1954; 1957–1959

Our Lady of Charity of Refuge, Sisters of, File 1, 22 Jan. 1942–26 June 1952; High Park no. 2, 1953–10 Dec. 1959; High Park no. 3, 20 Mar. 1962–28 Aug. 1963; High Park no. 4, 1 April 1964–7 Oct. 1969; High Park no. 5, 15 Aug. 1969–11 Nov. 1971

Our Lady of Charity of Refuge, Sisters of, Gloucester Street no. 1, 17 April 1941–22 Nov. 1948; Gloucester Street no. 2, 3 Aug. 1949–19 May 1970

Our Lady of Charity of Refuge, Sisters of, Kilmacud, no. 1, 11 Feb. 1944–29 July 1949; Kilmacud no. 2, 31 Jan. 1950–21 Dec. 1955; Kilmacud, no. 3, 5 Jan. 1956–15 Nov. 1971

Our Lady of Charity of Refuge, Sisters of, Amalgamation no. 1, 18 July 1945–10 July 1948

Our Lady of Charity of Refuge, Sisters of, Kill of the Grange, 29 Nov. 1954–29 Jan. 1971

## Daughters of Charity of St Vincent de Paul, Provincial Archives, Dunardagh, Blackrock, County Dublin

Henrietta Street, legal papers 1895–1898, undated MS history, file 1

'Règles des Filles de la Charité, servants des pauvres maladies, Paris, 5 Aug. 1672', translated as 'Common rules of the Daughters of Charity', trans. approved Paris, 14 May 1892

## Holy Faith Sisters, Generalate Archives, Glasnevin, Dublin 11

Register of St Brigid's Orphanage, 1857–75, vols 1–4.

## General Register Office, Abbey Life Centre, Dublin

Registration of deaths, quarterly compilations, from 1864, Dublin North City

## Valuation Office, Abbey Life Centre, Dublin 1

Cancelled book, Dublin, North Dock, 1855–1869

Cancelled book, Dublin, North Dock, 1887–95

## Mercy Archives, Western Province, Forster Street, Galway

Deed of Conveyance of a house and premises in Gibralter Lane (sic), Galway. 23 Oct. 1824, GY6/1/69a

## Archives of the Sacred Congregation for Religious and Secular Institutes, Rome (CIVCSVA)

Notre Dame de Charité du Refuge

Les actes ou procès verbaux des sessions de l'Assemblée Générale des Soeurs de Notre Dame de Charité du Refuge, tenne au Monas-tère de Caen, première session. 27 mai 1909. Also associated cor-respondence. B79/1

Marie du Cours, bishop of Marseilles to La Puma, 21 April 1933. B79/2

Gabriel Mallet aux Monastères de N.D. de Charité dite du Refuge, à Buffalo, Ottawa, Allegheny, Toronto, Green Bay, Vancouver, San Antonio, Salthill, Wheeling, Monterrey, Pittsburg, Hot Springs, Dallas et autres villes d'Amérique, 29 sept. 1918, B79/3

Bon Pasteur

Suore del Buon Pastore – Soeurs Madeleines Angers, Francia; Suore di Nostra Signora della Caritata del Buon Pastore Roma, Italia, manuscript and typed (*stampati*) documents, in French, Italian, Latin, 1854–1980, carella A.7-1, plichi 1-4

Documents concerning approval of the institute and internal situation, 1834–1941, carella A.7-1, plico 1, documents 1-39

Documents including statistics and transfer of houses to Angers, 1891–1966, carella A.7-2, plichi 1-5

'Congrégation de Notre Dame de Charité du Bon Pasteur d'Angers, Œuvres – Statistique, appréciation de nos Seigneurs les Evêques de France et de l'Étranger sur les divers Établissement du Bon Pasteur dans leurs diocèses respectifs', bound volume, 1903, carella A.7-2, plico n. 2, document 5

Copies (bound) of series of *règles*/constitutions, 12 items, carella A.7-4, plico 1

## Primary Sources: Printed
## Our Lady of Charity of Refuge

*Additions and amendments to the constitutions of the Order of Our Lady of Charity of Refuge, in accordance with the decree of the Sacred Congregation of Religious, dated 28 June 1948, and the rescript of the same Sacred Congregation dated 12 Feb. 1951* (Dublin, 1951).

*Dans la charité du Christ: Vie de la Très Honorée Mère Marie de Saint Ambroise Desaunais* (Caen, 1939).

Dubosq, René. *Le nouveau 'berceau' de Notre-Dame de Charité du Refuge de Caen* (Caen, n.d. but 1948).

Molloy, T. J., '1887–1937, Monastery of Our Lady of Charity of Refuge, Gloucester Street Dublin, Golden Jubilee Celebrations', *Father Matthew Record and Franciscan Mission Advocate*, vol. 30, no. 5 (May, 1937), pp 279–82.

*Order of Our Lady of Charity of Refuge, spirit, aim and work* (Dublin, 1954).

Ory, Joseph-Marie, *Les origines de Notre-Dame de Charité ou son histoire depuis sa fondation jusqu'à la Révolution* (Abbeville, 1891).

Ory, Joseph-Marie. *The origin of the order of Our Lady of Charity or its history from its foundation until the Revolution, translated from the French of Father Joseph Mary Ory by one of the Religious of Our Lady of Charity of Buffalo, New York* (Buffalo, 1918).

'Règles et constitutions pour les religieuses de Notre-Dame de Charité, édition entièrement conforme au texte original [1682] avec des introductions et des notes', *Oeuvres complètes de Bienheureux Jean Eudes*, x (Vannes, 1909).

*Report and statistical sketch of the magdalen asylum, High Park, Drumcondra, June 1881* (Dublin, 1881).

*Souvenir of golden jubilee of Monastery of Our Lady of Charity of Refuge, Gloucester Street, Dublin* (Dublin, 1937).

*The book of customs for the religious of Our Lady of Charity of the Order of St Augustine, containing the directory and the ceremonial of the Divine Office, the ritual for administering the last sacraments and for burying the dead, according to the Roman rite; together with the customs and usages of their congregation, and the directories of the offices of the house*, trans. Peter Lewis (Aberdeen, 1888).

*The Order of Our Lady of Charity of Refuge, 1853–1953, a centenary record of High Park Convent, Drumcondra, Dublin* (Dublin, 1953).

*The Religious of Our Lady of Charity in Buffalo, 1855–1955, 485 Best Street* (Buffalo, 1955).

## St John Eudes (and associated studies in Eudist spirituality)

*Letters and shorter works by Saint John Eudes*, trans. Ruth Hauser (New York, 1948).

*Oeuvres complètes du Vénérable Jean Eudes*, 12 vols, ed. Charles Lebrun and Joseph Dauphin (Vannes, 1905–11).

*The life and kingdom of Jesus in Christian souls, a treatise on Christian perfection for use by clergy or laity, by St John Eudes* (New York, 1945).

*The priest, his dignity and obligations by John Eudes*, trans. Leo W. Murphy (New York, 1947).

*The Sacred Heart of Jesus by St John Eudes*, trans. Richard Flower (New York, 1945)

Bray, P.A., *Saint John Eudes* (Halifax, 1925).

Herambourg, Peter, *Saint John Eudes, a spiritual portrait*, trans. Ruth Hauser (Westminster, Maryland, 1960).

Joly, Henri, *A life of Saint John Eudes*, trans. Joseph Leonard (London, 1932).

Milcent, Paul, *Un artisan du renouveau Chrétien au XVIIe siècle, Saint Jean Eudes* (Paris, 1985).

Milcent, Paul, *Saint John Eudes: Presentation and selected texts* (Paris & Glasgow, n.d. but *c.* 1965).

de Montzey, M. Ch, *Life of the venerable John Eudes, with a sketch of the history of his foundations from A.D. 1601 to 1874* (London, 1883).

Pinas, P.A., *Venerable Père Eudes and his works 1601–1901*, trans. (Edinburgh, 1903).

Russell, Matthew, *The life of Blessed John Eudes* (London, n.d.).

*St John Eudes* (Dublin, 1927).

## Religious of the Good Shepherd

Bernoville, Gaëtan, *Saint Mary Euphrasia Pelletier, foundress of the Good Shepherd sisters* (Dublin, 1959), trans. *Une apôtre de l'enfance delaissée* (Paris, 1950).

O'Shea, Noreen, *Brief sketch of the life of Mary Euphrasia* (Waterford, n.d.).

## Pamphlet and Other Literature, to 1900

Alcom, James, 'Discharged Prisoners' Aid Societies', *Irish Quarterly Review* (Dec. 1881), vol. viii, part lviii, pp 217–23.

*A letter to the public on an important subject* (Dublin, 1767).

Barrett, Rosa M., *Guide to Dublin charities* (Dublin, 1884).

Carpenter, Mary, 'Reformatory schools for girls', *The Reformatory and Refuge Journal*, xxxiv – xlv (1867–9), pp 273–9.

Carpenter, Mary, *Juvenile delinquents, their condition and treatment* (London, 1853).

Déchy, Edouard, *Voyage, Irlande en 1846 et 1847* (Paris, 1847).

Dodd, William, *An account of the rise, progress, and present state of the Magdalen Hospital, for the reception of penitent prostitutes, together with Dr Dodd's sermons, to which are added, the advice to the Magdalens, with the psalms, hymns, prayers, rules, and list of subscribers* (London, 1776).

Dodd, William, *An account of the rise, progress, and present state of the Magdalen Hospital, for the reception of penitent prostitutes* (5th edn, London, 1776).

Duchâtelet, Alexandre Parent, *De la prostitution dans la ville de Paris, considerée sous le rapport de l'hygiène publique, de la morale et de l'administration, ouvrage appuyé de documents statistiques puisés dans les archives de la Préfecture de police* 2 vols (Paris, 1836).

Durnford, Richard, *A sermon preached in St Paul's church, Knightsbridge, for the Church Penitentiary Association, on Thursday, May 4, 1871* (London, 1871).

'Extracts from Proceedings of the Council', *The Reformatory and Refuge Journal*, no. xxvi – xxxiii (1865–6), p. 82.

Fielding, John, *A plan for a preservatory and reformatory, for the benefit of deserted girls, and penitent prostitutes* (London, 1758).

Greg, William Rathborne, *The great sin of great cities, being a reprint, by request, of an article entitle 'Prostitution' from the Westminster and Foreign Quarterly Review for July 1851* (London, 1853).

Leduc, St Germain, *L'Angleterre, l'Ecosse, l'Irlande, relation d'un voyage dans les trois royaumes* (Strasbourg, 1838).

Lentaigne, John, 'The treatment and punishment of young offenders', *Journal of the Statistical and Social Inquiry Society of Ireland*, vol. viii, part lxiii (1881), appendix 3.

Logan, William, *An exposure from personal observation of female prostitution in London, Leeds and Rochdale, and especially in the city of Glasgow, with remarks on the cause, extent, results and remedy of the evil* (3rd edn, Glasgow, 1845).

Logan, William, *The great social evil, its causes, extent, results and remedies* (London, 1871).

Massie, Joseph, *A plan for the establishment of charity-houses for exposed or deserted women and girls and for penitent prostitutes: observations concerning the Foundling-hospital shewing the ill consequences of giving public support thereto. Considerations relating to the poor and the poor-laws of England* (London, 1758).

Murray, Patrick Joseph, *An Act to promote and regulate Reformatory Schools for Juvenile Offenders in Ireland, 21st & 22nd Vic. Cap. 103, with commentary and forms of procedure, and hints on the formation and management of reformatory institutions* (Dublin, 1858).

O'Brien, Dr, *Sermon preached by the Reverend Dr O'Brien of Limerick on behalf of the Female Penitents' Retreat, Mecklenburgh Street, on Sunday 15th October 1848* (Dublin, 1849).

Potton, A., *De la prostitution et de la syphilis dans les grandes villes: dans la ville de Lyon en particulier, de leurs causes, de leur influence sur la santé* (Paris, 1843).

'Reformatory and industrial schools', *Dublin University Magazine* (Nov. 1858), vol. lii, pp 554–8.

'Reformatory and Ragged schools, article v, *Irish Quarterly Review*, iv (June 1854), pp 361–429.

Roussel, Napoleon, *Trois mois en Irlande* (Paris, 1853).

Taylor, Fanny, *Irish homes and Irish hearts* (London, 1867).

'The Magdalene, a fragment, by a Catholic priest' ('Patritius'), *Catholic Penny Magazine*, 21:1 (1834), pp 237–40.

*The Reformatory and Refuge Journal*, no. xxxiv – xlv (1867–9), pp 273–4.

Woodlock, Mrs, 'The relief of pauper children', to the Social Science Association, printed in the *Times*, 22 Aug. 1861.

## Books of Reference

*Acta Apostolica Sedis.*

*A concise dictionary of the French and English languages*, compiled by F.E.A. Gasc (5th edn, London, 1892).

*Concise Oxford dictionary of the Christian Church*, ed. E.A. Livingstone (3rd edn, Oxford, 2013), online edn 2015.

*Dictionnaire Cambridge Klett concise* (Cambridge, 2002).

*Dictionary of Irish biography, from the earliest times to the year 2002*, 9 vols, edited by James McGuire and James Quinn (Dublin and Cambridge, 2009).

*Electronic pocket Oxford Latin dictionary* (Oxford, 2002).

*The Oxford companion to the mind*, ed. Richard L. Gregory (Oxford, 1987).

*The concise Oxford French-English dictionary*, compiled by Abel Chevalley and Marguerite Chevalley (Oxford, 1974).

## Newspapers and Directories:

*Catholic Penny Magazine*

*Catholic Weekly*

*Dublin Gazette*

*Dublin Almanack*

*Freeman's Journal*

*Irish Catholic*

*Irish Independent*

*Irish Press*

*Irish Times*

*Sunday Press*

*Thom's Irish Almanac and Official Directory*

*The Standard*

*The Times*

## Acts of Parliament, United Kingdom & Ireland

Youthful Offenders Act 1854

An Act to promote and regulate Reformatory Schools for Juvenile Offenders in Ireland. 21 and 22 Vic. 1858

Industrial Schools (Ireland) Act 1868

General Prisons Act (Ireland) 1877, 40 & 41 Vic., c. 49, sec. 44

Public Health (Ireland) Acts 1878–1907

Local Government (Ireland) Act 1898

Probation of Offenders Act 1907

An Act to diminish the number of cases committed to prison, to amend the Law with respect to the treatment and punishment of young offenders, and otherwise to improve the Administration of Criminal Justice, 4 & 5 Geo. 5, ch. 58. 1908 (Children Act 1908)

Criminal Justice Administration Act 1914

## Acts of Dáil Éireann (available online at Irish Statute Book, www.oireachtas.ie)

National Health Insurance Act 1924

School Attendance Act 1926

Children Act 1929

Widows and Orphans Pensions Act 1935

Conditions of Employment Act 1936

Public Assistance Act 1939

Emergency Powers Act 1939

Children Act 1941

Children (Amendment) Act 1949

Adoption Act 1952

Criminal Justice Act 1960

Social Welfare Act 1973

Residential Institutions Redress Act 2002

## Reports, Inquiries, Parliamentary Papers to 1922 (in chronological order)

*Report from the select committee appointed to inquire into the expediency of making provision for the relief of the lunatic poor in Ireland*, 1817, H.C. 1817 (430) viii.

Census of population (Ireland), 1841, City of Dublin, vi, Table of Occupations of persons above and under 15 years of age; General report.

*Report of select committee on criminal and destitute juveniles*, H.C. 1852 (515) vii.

*Report of select committee on criminal and destitute juveniles*, H.C.1852–3 (674) xxiii.

*General and first annual report of St Joseph's Reformatory School for Catholic girls, High Park, Drumcondra, established under the Act 2st and 22nd Vic. cap 103* (Dublin, 1862).

*Sparks Lake Reformatory, Monaghan, report for 1861* (Dublin, 1862).

*Thirteenth Annual Report of the Reformatory and Refuge Union* (London, 1869).

*Fifteenth annual report of the Reformatory and Refuge Union* (1871).

'Rules and regulations of industrial schools', appendix to *Ninth Report of the Inspector appointed to visit the reformatory and industrial schools of Ireland* ... (H.C. 1871 [c.461], xxviii.927), pp 81–8.

*Third Annual Report of the Dublin Discharged Female Roman Catholic Prisoners' Aid Society* (Dublin, 1884).

Reports of inspectors of factories as to hours of work, etc. [C. 7418], HC 1894, XXI, 709.

*Thirty-sixth report of the inspector appointed to visit the reformatory and industrial schools of Ireland, 1898* [C.9042], HC 1898.

List of religious and charitable institutions in which laundries are carried on [Cd. 2741], HC 1905, XCVIII, 85.

*Fifty-seventh report of the Inspector appointed to visit the reformatory and industrial schools of Ireland* (Dublin, 1920).

## Government and Other Reports, 1922 to Present (in chronological order)

*Commission on relief of the sick and destitute poor* (Dublin, 1927).

Duff, Frank, *The Morning Star; the theory and practice of a great experiment,* Commission on the Relief of the Poor, statement of Mr Frank Duff (Dublin, 1928).

*Report of the Commission of Inquiry into the Reformatory and Industrial School System* (Dublin, 1936).

Fahy, E., 'Reformatory schools in Ireland', in *Hermathena*, lx, (Nov. 1942), pp 54–73.

*Commission on Youth Unemployment* (Dublin, 1951).

Sister Veronica, 'Social work in the light of the Curtis report', *Religious life today: papers read at the Liverpool Congress of Religious, January 2nd to 6th 1956* (Liverpool, 1956), pp 140–52.

*Report of the Commission of Inquiry on Mental Handicap* (Dublin, 1965).

*The report of the Commission of Inquiry on Mental Illness* (Dublin, 1966).

*Annual report on prisons for the year 1958, Department of Justice* (Dublin, 1959).

Tuairim, London Branch Study Group. 'Some of our children, a report on the residential care of the deprived child in Ireland' *Tuairim Pamphlet*, no. 13 (London, 1966); reprinted in Eoin O'Sullivan and Ian O'Donnell (eds), *Coercive confinement in Ireland, patients, prisoners and penitents* (Manchester, 2012), pp 212–21.

*Reformatory and industrial schools systems report, 1970* (Dublin, 1970).

CARE, Campaign for the care of deprived children, chairman Séamus Ó Cinnéide, *Children deprived, the CARE memorandum on deprived children and children's services in Ireland* (June 1972).

*Focus on residential care in Ireland, 25 years since the Kennedy report,* Patricia McCarthy, Stanislaus Kennedy, Caroline Matthews (Dublin, 1996).

McNally, Gerry, 'Probation in Ireland, a brief history of the early years', *Irish Probation Journal*, vol. 4 no. 1 (2007), pp 5–24.

*Final Report of the Commission to Inquire into Child Abuse dated 20th May 2009*, 5 vols (Dublin, 2009). [Ryan report] Online at www.childabusecommission.ie.

First interim progress report of the Inter-Departmental Committee set up to establish the facts of State involvement with the Magdalen Laundries, October 2011, independent chair Senator Martin McAleese. Online at www.justice.ie.

*Final report of the Inter-Departmental Committee set up to establish the facts of State involvement with the Magdalen Laundries* (Dublin, 2013), independent chair Senator Martin McAleese. Online at www.justice.ie.

*Report of Mr Justice John Quirke on the establishment of an ex gratia scheme and related matters for those women who were admitted to and worked in the Magdalen Laundries*, May 2013. Online at www.justice.ie.

*Report of the Inter-Departmental Group on Mother and Baby Homes*, Department of Children and Youth Affairs, 16 July 2014. Online at www.dcya.gov.ie.

## Church Documents (in chronological order)

*Testem benevolentiae*, On the dangers of activism, Leo XIII, 22 January 1899, trans. John O'Flynn, in Gaston Courtois (ed.), *The states of perfection according to the teaching of the Church, papal documents from Leo XIII to Pius XII* (Dublin, 1961), pp 1–4.

*Canonical legislation concerning religious*, authorised English trans., Vatican Press (Vatican City, 1919).

*Conditae a Christo*, trans. D. I. Lanslots, reprinted in, *Handbook of canon law for congregations of women under simple vows* (9th edn, New York, 1920).

*Sponsa Christi*, Pius XII, 21 November 1950, in Lincoln T. Bouscaren, James O'Connor (eds), *The canon law digest for religious*, i (1917–1963), (Milwaukee, 1964).

*Sacrosanctum Concilium*, trans. Clifford Howell, in *Doctrine and Life* vol. 14 no. 2 (Feb. 1964), pp 130–59.

'Nuns and the Church', Paul VI, trans. Austin Flannery, in *Supplement to Doctrine and Life*, vol. 3 no. 3 (Autumn 1965), pp 145–7.

*Lumen gentium*, The constitution on the Church of Vatican Council II, English trans. Missionary Society of St Paul the Apostle / Darton, Longman and Todd (London, 1965).

*Ad gentes*, Decree on the missionary activity of the Church, *The documents of Vatican II*, Walter M. Abbott ed., trans. Joseph Gallagher (London and Dublin, 1966), pp 584–633.

*Ecclesiae Sanctae II*, 6 August 1966, 'Rules for the execution of the decree *Perfectae caritatis* of the Second Vatican Council', trans. J.G. McGarry, in *Vatican Council: applying the decrees*. Catholic Truth Society of Ireland (Dublin, 1966).

*Perfectae caritatis*, The decree on the renewal of religious life, trans. Austin Flannery (New York, 1966).

*Gaudium et spes*, Pastoral constitution on the Church in the modern world, 7 December 1965, English trans. Catholic Truth Society (London, 1966).

*Revision of the constitutions*, International Union of Superioresses General (UISG), bulletin no. 5 (Rome, 1967).

*Renovationis causam*. Instruction on the renewal of religious formation, 6 January 1969, English trans. from *L'Osservatore Romano*, CTS edn (London, 1969).

*Horarum liturgia*, Sacred Congregation for Divine Worship, 11 April 1971, reprinted in *The Divine Office, i*, (Dublin, 1974), ix.

*Laudis canticum*, Apostolic constitution, the canticle of praise, Paul VI, 1 November 1970, reprinted in *The Divine Office* i (Dublin, 1974), xi–xviii.

'The general instruction on the liturgy of the hours', Paul VI, in *The Divine Office* i (Dublin, 1974), xix–xcii.

*Catechism of the Catholic Church* (Dublin, 1994).

## Other Printed Primary Sources:

*Rule and constitution of the religious called Sisters of Mercy* (Dublin, 1863); extract reprinted in Luddy, *Women in Ireland 1800–1918, a documentary history*, pp 57–60.

*The rule and constitutions of the religious called Sisters of Mercy in Italian and English* (Dublin, 1863).

Viney, Michael, '*No birthright, a study of the Irish unmarried mother and her children, the Irish Times articles*', September 1964.

Viney, Michael, 'The young offenders', *Irish Times*, 4 May 1966.

## Secondary Reading

Beck, George Andrew. 'The schema on religious', *Doctrine and Life*, vol. 15, no. 8 (Aug. 1965), pp 419–29.

Barnes, Jane, *Irish industrial schools 1868–1908* (Dublin, 1989).

Caron, Jean-Claude, Review of Marie-Sylvie Dupont-Bouchat and Eric Pierre (eds), *Enfance et justice au XIXe siècle* (Paris, 2001) in *Revue d'Histoire Moderne et Contemporaine*, no. 1 (2003), pp 185–7.

Cholvy, Gérard, *Christianisme et société en France au XIXe siècle*, 1790–1914 (Paris, 2001),

'Chronicle', *Supplement to Doctrine and Life*, vol. 2, no. 3 (Autumn 1964), p. 157.

Clear, Caitríona, *Social change and everyday life in Ireland, 1850–1922* (Manchester, 2007).

Confoy, Maryanne, 'Religious life in the Vatican II era: "State of perfection" or living charism?', *Theological Studies*, 74 (2013), pp 321–45.

Cousins, Mel, *The birth of social welfare in Ireland, 1922–1952* (Dublin, 2003).

Cox, Catherine, 'Institutionalisation in Irish history and society, 1650–2000', in Leeann Lane, Katherine O'Donnell & Mary McAuliffe (eds), *Palgrave advances in Irish history* (Hampshire, 2009), pp 169–90.

Crowe, Catriona, *Dublin 1911* (Dublin, 2011).

Cunnane, Joseph, 'Instructions on the liturgy', *The Furrow*, vol. 16 no. 1 (Jan. 1965), pp 24–29.

Department of Defence (Ireland). *Air raid precautions, memorandum no. 17* (Dublin, 1941).

Department of Defence/British Home Office, *The protection of your home against air raids* (Dublin, n.d.).

Donohue, Bill, *Myths of the Magdalene laundries*, Catholic League for Religious and Civil Rights (New York, 2013).

Dupont-Bouchat, Marie-Sylvie and Pierre, Eric (eds), *Enfance et justice au XIXe siècle, essai d'histoire comparée de la protection de l'enfance, 1820–1914, France, Belgique, Pays-Bas, Canada* (Paris, 2001).

Earner-Byrne, Lindsey, 'Child sexual abuse: history and the pursuit of blame in modern Ireland' in Katie Holmes and Stuart Ward (eds*)*, *Exhuming passions, the pressure of the past in Ireland and Australia* (Dublin, 2011), pp 51–70.

Earner-Byrne, Lindsey, *Mother and child, maternity and child welfare in Dublin, 1922–60* (Manchester, 2013).

Facteau, Jean-Marie, 'Note sur les enjeux de la prise en charge de l'enfance délinquante et en danger au XIXe siècle', *Lien Social et Politiques*, no. 40 (1998), pp 129–38.

Farrell, Elaine (ed.), *"She said she was in the family way": Pregnancy and infancy in modern Ireland* (London, 2012).

Ferriter, Diarmuid, 'Report by Dr Diarmaid Ferriter, St Patrick's College, DCU, June 2006', *Ryan report*, v, pp 1–37 after p. 353.

Ferriter, Diarmaid, *The transformation of Ireland 1900–1970* (London, 2004).

Ferriter, Diarmaid, *Occasions of sin: sex and society in modern Ireland* (London, 2009).

Flannery, Tony (ed.), *Responding to the Ryan report* (Dublin, 2009).

Fuller, Louise, *Irish Catholicism since 1950: the undoing of a culture* (Dublin, 2002).

Gallen, Joseph H., 'Femininity and spirituality', *Review for Religious* (US), vol. 20, no. 4 (1961) pp 237–56.

*Good Housekeeping's laundry book* (London, 1955).

Goodbody, Rob, *Dublin part III, 1756–1847*, Irish Historic Towns Atlas no. 26, edited Anngret Simms, H.B. Clarke, Raymond Gillespie, Jacinta Prunty (Dublin, 2014).

Gwynn Morgan, David, 'Society and the schools', in Ryan report, iv, pp 201–44.

Hill, Myrtle *Women in Ireland, a century of change* (Belfast, 2003).

Hostie, Raymond, *The life and death of religious orders, a psycho-sociological approach* (English trans. and revision of *Vie et mort des ordres religieux*, 1972), Center for Applied Research in the Apostolate (CARA), (Washington, 2013).

Howell, Philip, 'Venereal disease and the politics of prostitution in the Irish Free State', *Irish Historical Studies*, 33:131 (2003), pp 320–41.

Jenkins, Keith, *Rethinking history* (London, 2008).

Kearney, Noreen and Skehill, Caroline (eds), *Social work in Ireland: historical perspectives* (Dublin, 2005).

Kearney, Noreen, 'The historical background', in *Social work and social work training in Ireland, yesterday and tomorrow,* Trinity College Dublin, Occasional Papers in Social Work, 1 (Dublin, 1987), pp 5–15.

Kenny, Ann, 'The deprived child', *Christus Rex*, x, no. 2 (1956), pp 99–114.

Keogh, Dáire, 'Peter Tyrrell, Letterfrack and the Ryan Report' in Tony Flannery (ed.), *Responding to the Ryan report* (Dublin, 2009), pp 56–81.

Kilroy, Phil, *The Society of the Sacred Heart in nineteenth-century France, 1800–1865* (Cork, 2012).

Kingston, John, 'Rev. John Smyth, C.C., 1791–1858', *Reportorium Novum, Dublin Diocesan Historical Record*, 4:1 (1971), 17–32.

Kirkus, Sister Gregory, *Mary Ward* (Strasbourg, 2007).

Lane, Leeann, O'Donnell, Katherine and McAuliffe, Mary (eds), *Palgrave advances in Irish history* (Hampshire, 2009).

Larkin, Maurice, 'Religion, anticlericalism, and secularization', in James McMillan (ed.), *Modern France 1880–2002* (Oxford, 2003), pp 203–27.

'Liturgical news: Eucharistic fast', *Doctrine and Life*, vol. 15, no. 1, (Jan. 1965), pp 49–52.

'Liturgy renewal in Ireland: a report', in *The Furrow*, vol. 17, no. 5 (May 1966), p. 307.

Luddy, Maria, 'Convent archives as sources for Irish history' in Rosemary Raughter (ed.), *Religious women and their history, breaking the silence* (Dublin, 2005), pp 98–115.

Luddy, Maria, 'Magdalen asylums in Ireland, 1880–1930: welfare, reform, incarceration?' in Inga Brandes and Katrin Marx-Jaskulski (eds), *Armenfürsoge und Wohltätigkeit, Ländliche Gesellschaften in Europa, 1850–1930* (Franfurt am Main, 2008), pp 283–305.

Luddy, Maria, *Women, philanthropy and the emergence of social work in Ireland*, pamphlet, Trinity College Dublin (2005).

Luddy, Maria, *Prostitution and Irish society, 1800–1940* (Cambridge, 2007).

Luddy, Maria, *Women in Ireland 1800–1918, a documentary history* (Cork, 1995).

Lysaght, C.E. 'Report on industrial schools and Reformatories, submitted to the Minister for Education, 11 Nov. 1966', *Ryan report*, iv, p. 290.

MacCurtain, Margaret, 'Fullness of life: defining female spirituality in twentieth-century Ireland', reprinted in Mac Curtain, *Ariadne's thread*, pp 175–210.

MacCurtain, Margaret, 'Late in the field: Catholic sisters in twentieth-century Ireland and the new religious history', reprinted in MacCurtain, *Ariadne's thread*, pp 275–97.

MacCurtain, Margaret, 'Godly burden: Catholic sisterhoods in twentieth-century Ireland, reprinted in MacCurtain, *Ariadne's thread, writing*, pp 309–24.

MacCurtain, Margaret, *Ariadne's thread, writing women into Irish history* (Galway, 2008).

Macauley, Mrs M., 'Our children', *Christus Rex*, ix, no. 2 (1955), pp 126–33

McGuire, Agnes, 'Some careers in social work', *Christus Rex*, ii, no. 3 (1948), pp 33–45.

McGuire, Agnes, 'Why almoners?', *Christus Rex*, vi, no. 3 (1952), pp 243–9.

Maguire, Moira, *Precarious childhood in post-independence Ireland* (Manchester, 2010).

de Maeyer, Jan, Sophie Leplae & Joachim Schmiedl (eds), *Religious institutes in Western Europe in the 19th and 20th centuries, historiography, research and legal position* (Leuven, 2004).

McCarthy, Justice H.A., 'The Children's Court', *Christus Rex*, ii, no. 4 (1948), pp 3–12.

McMillan, James F. 'Catholic Christianity in France, 1815–1905', in *The Cambridge History of Christianity: world Christianities c. 1815–c.1914*, viii (Cambridge, 2006), pp 217–32.

McNicholl, Ambrose, 'Why the Council was needed', *Doctrine and Life*, vol. 16, no. 2 (Feb. 1966), pp 87–102.

Montini, John Baptist, 'Apostolic involvement', *Supplement to Doctrine and Life*, no. 8 (Winter 1964), pp 171–80.

O'Brien, Susan, 'A survey of research and writing about Roman Catholic women's congregations in Great Britain and Ireland (1800–1950)' in de Maeyer, Leplae & Schmiedl (eds), *Religious institutes in Western Europe* (Leuven, 2004), pp 91–115.

O'Connor, Fergal, 'Sexuality, chastity and celibacy' in O'Connor, Auer and Egenter, *Celibacy and virginity* (Dublin and Sydney, 1968), pp 25–45

O'Flaherty, Eamon, *Limerick*, Irish Historic Towns Atlas no. 21, edited Anngret Simms, H.B. Clarke, Raymond Gillespie, Jacinta Prunty (Dublin, 2010).

O'Keeffe, Tadhg, & Patrick Ryan, 'At the world's end: the lost landscape of Monto, Dublin's notorious red-light district', *Landscapes*, 10 (1) (2009), pp 21–38.

O'Malley, John W. *What happened at Vatican II* (Cambridge, Mass., 2008),

O'Reilly, Louise, *The impact of Vatican II on religious women: case study of the Union of Irish Presentation Sisters* (Newcastle-upon-Tyne, 2013).

O'Shea, Noreen, *Brief sketch of the life of Mary Euphrasia* (Waterford, n.d.).

O'Sullivan, Eoin, 'Residential child welfare in Ireland, 1965–2008: an outline of policy, legislation and practice, a paper prepared for the Commission to Inquire into Child Abuse', Ryan report, iv, pp 245–423.

Parkes, Susan and Rafferty, Deirdre, *Female education in Ireland, 1700 – 1900, Minerva or Madonna* (Dublin, 2002).

Prunty, Jacinta, *Dublin slums 1800–1925, a study in urban geography* (Dublin, 1998).

Prunty, Jacinta, 'Military barracks and mapping in the nineteenth century: sources and issues for Irish urban history', in Jacinta Prunty, Howard Clarke and Mark Hennessy (eds), *Surveying Ireland's past* (Dublin, 2003), pp 420–578.

Prunty, Jacinta, *Margaret Aylward 1810–1889, lady of charity, sister of faith* (Dublin, 1998, 2011).

Prunty, Jacinta, 'Where compassion went awry', *The Tablet*, 15 Mar. 2013, p. 20.

Prunty, Jacinta, 'Religion' in H. B. Clarke and Sarah Gearty (eds), *Maps and texts, exploring the Irish Historic Towns Atlas* (Dublin, 2013), pp 119–39.

Prunty, Jacinta, O'Neill, Bríd, and Devlin, Eileen, 'Our Lady's, Henrietta Street, accommodation for discharged female prisoners', in Jacinta Prunty and Louise Sullivan (eds), *The Daughters of Charity of St Vincent de Paul in Ireland, the early years* (Dublin, 2014), pp 181–99.

Prunty, Jacinta, 'Reception of the call of Vatican II for renewal of religious life: case study of the Irish Federation of the Sisters of Our Lady of Charity' in Dermot Lane (ed.), Vatican II in Ireland, fifty years on, essays in honour of Pádraic Conway (Bern, 2015), pp 121–50.

Prunty, Jacinta and Walsh, Paul, *Galway*, Irish Historic Towns Atlas no. 28, Royal Irish Academy, edited by H.B. Clarke, Anngret Simms, Raymond Gillespie, Jacinta Prunty (Dublin, 2016).

*Psychological realities and religious life*, Vita Evangelica 3, Canadian Religious Conference (Ottawa, 1969).

Raftery, Deirdre, 'Rebels with a cause: obedience, resistance and convent life, 1800–1940', *History of Education*, vol. 42, no. 6 (2013), pp 729–44.

Redmond, Jennifer, 'In the family way and away from the family: examining the evidence for Irish unmarried mothers in Britain' in Elaine Farrell (ed.), *"She said she was in the family way"* (London, 2012), pp 163–85.

Rhattigan, Clíona, *"What else could I do?" Single mothers and infanticide in Ireland 1900–1950* (Dublin, 2012).

Robins, Joseph, *The lost children, a survey of charity children in Ireland 1700–1900* (Dublin 1980).

Ryan, Vincent, 'Liturgical formation of religious', in *Doctrine and Life*, vol. 15, no. 6 (June 1965), pp 299–312.

Scott, John *A matter of record, documentary sources in social research* (Cambridge, 1990).

Sister Mary Pauline, *God wills it! Centenary story* [of the Sisters of St Louis, Monaghan] (Dublin, 1959).

Smith, James A., *Ireland's magdalen laundries and the nation's architecture of containment* (Notre Dame, Ind., 2007).

Strimelle, Véronique, 'La gestion de la deviance des filles a Montréal au XIXe siècle. Les institutions du bon Pasteur d'Angers (1869–1912)', *Revue d'histoire de l'enfance irrégulière*, 5 (2003), pp 61–83.

Tyrrell, Peter, *Founded on fear: Letterfrack Industrial School, war and exile*, ed. Diarmuid Whelan (Dublin, 2006).

Valeri, Cardinal Valerio to William Godfrey, archbishop of Liverpool, 21 Dec. 1955, in *Religious life today, papers read at the Liverpool Congress of Religious, January 2nd to 6th, 1956* (Liverpool, 1956), opening address, xi–xii.

Wright, Mary, *Mary Ward's Institute, the struggle for identity* (Sydney, 1997).

## Electronic Sources

www.childabusecommission.ie

www.justice.ie

www.logainm.ie

www.magdalenelaundries.com

www.rirb.ie

www.ruhama.ie

Oireachtas debates, Houses of the Oireachtas, www.oireachtasdebates.oireachtas.ie

# Index